TOP TEN GLOBAL JUSTICE LAW REVIEW ARTICLES 2007

TOP TEN GLOBAL JUSTICE LAW REVIEW ARTICLES 2007

Edited and Selected by
Amos N. Guiora

Oceana®
NEW YORK

OXFORD
UNIVERSITY PRESS

Oxford University Press, Inc., publishes works that further Oxford University's objective of excellence in research, scholarship, and education.

Published by Oxford University Press, Inc.
198 Madison Avenue, New York, New York 10016

Cataloging-in-Publication information is available from the Library of Congress.

ISBN 978-0-19-537658-6

Printed in the United States of America on acid-free paper.

Note to Readers:

This publication is designed to provide accurate and authoritative information in regard to the subject matter covered. It is based upon sources believed to be accurate and reliable and is intended to be current as of the time it was written. It is sold with the understanding that the publisher is not engaged in rendering legal, accounting, or other professional services. If legal advice or other expert assistance is required, the services of a competent professional person should be sought. Also, to confirm that the information has not been affected or changed by recent developments, traditional legal research techniques should be used, including checking primary sources where appropriate.

(Based on the Declaration of Principles jointly adopted by a Committee of the American Bar Association and a Committee of Publishers and Associations.)

TABLE OF CONTENTS

To a truly extraordinary, dedicated group of students at the S.J. Quinney College of Law, The University of Utah: Christian Bjarnson, Sandra Hartman, Matthew Holmes, Pete Lattin, Emily Pettit, Josh Rupp, Virginia Tomova, Linh Tran, Guy Tshiteya, Artemis Vanianakis, Tasha Williams, Brooke Wilkinson, Ben Whisenant, Clark Whisenant and Phil Wormdahl whose work was invaluable to this project and in particular to Rich Roberts, the true soul and spirit behind this project.

PREFACE

Professor Amos N. Guiora

By proposing an annual anthology of the "top ten" published law review articles of the calendar year addressing Global Justice, Oxford University Press raised important, obvious questions. What is Global Justice? What is the desired impact of such a project? What are the best articles in this field? What are the criteria by which to measure them? What importance is attached to the reputation of an author, his or her institutional affiliation, and which journal or law review published the article? Why not look at the top ten law reviews (e.g., Harvard, Yale, or others) and simply cherry-pick ten articles tangentially related to Global Justice written by the most well-known and respected legal academics? Would not a top ten that automatically republishes the great names currently in the academy be sufficient?

In framing this anthology and, indeed, the public debate, I define Global Justice (through the security prism) as the merger of the following topics: national security, human rights law, civil liberties, the law of war, and public policy. These topics must be addressed from an inter-disciplinary perspective that includes law, policy, ethics, operations, sociology, anthropology and psychology.

In undertaking this project, I established the following criteria: the ten articles individually and collectively must have an impact on, if not shape, the public debate on the most important issues of the day. To that end, the articles selected had to be well-written, reflect both theoretical analysis and practical application, and address an issue of public importance. The author's name and institutional affiliation, as well as the journal that originally published the article, were not considered relevant criteria. Of critical importance was whether the article could assist scholars, policy and decision makers, the media, and the public to better understand the issues.

The criteria by which law reviews accept or reject articles are a matter of much conjecture amongst academics; however, the fundamental premise of this annual anthology is clear: the chosen articles are the "best of the best" in a rapidly developing, highly integrative field. The anthology combines previously existing and relatively new areas of the law. Leading academics in this yet to be fully defined field come from varying areas of expertise including constitutional law, comparative law, criminal law, criminal procedure, international law, national security law, and others. Some of those writing in this area are relatively new to academia. Others are established academics with sterling accomplishments in other areas of the law who are crossing-over in an effort to bring their expertise to this field. Moreover, some were practitioners in the field before joining the ranks of academia.

In sum, the articles in this anthology demonstrate that the field of Global Justice is unquestionably attracting the best legal minds of our generation. The reasons are clear. Global Justice is a hot topic that will be with us for years, if not generations, one that incorporates some of the most troubling legal questions confronting the public, government, the Courts, and the international community.

The essence central issue of this field is the limit of government power; in particular, how government balances legitimate civil and political rights of the individual with the equally legitimate national security rights of the state. Executive excess endangers the individual; the slippery slope is just around the corner. No one—including Superman—can get off the slope once on it. Conversely, a government that fails to adequately protect the public can be accused of dereliction of duty, for the preventable death of innocent civilians is unacceptable. When force is to be used and who is to authorize its implementation are issues critical to this discussion.

The field of Global Justice addresses many of the issues mentioned above. It is, however, broader and more complex than that. It requires us to compare how different nations and differing judicial and legal regimes address similar issues, subject to local pressures and restraints. Comparative analysis is not merely a phrase; it must be an active academic pursuit. Global Justice also suggests developing mechanisms for governments to engage in education and investment in order to address the roots of the conflicting interests with respect to freedom and security. Global Justice also requires us to articulate guidelines for when the nation-state may operationally engage those determined to bring harm upon innocent civilians.

To address these issues requires an understanding of the inter-play between law, policy, morality and security. Without analyzing and understanding the issue from interdisciplinary points of view, improving the quality of debate and outcomes will be difficult. The articles chosen in this initial anthology meet this most challenging of requirements.

In deciding the "top ten", I was the beneficiary of extraordinary assistance from law students at the S.J. Quinney College of Law, University of Utah. When my editor, Kevin Pendergast, suggested the project, I immediately said "of course." Then sobriety struck, and the inevitable questions of how to approach—much less accomplish–the proposal hit, for I had just accepted an offer from the S.J. Quinney College of Law to join the faculty. I immediately contacted my new Dean, Hiram Chodosh, and updated him regarding the project. I intimated that I would welcome his suggestions regarding implementation .

I knew whom I was asking, for Hiram is a visionary, enthusiastic, and innovative legal scholar and leader. In other words, he is a Dean who can make such a project happen. This is a wonderful quality which provides extraordinary experiential learning opportunities for students. This method of learning should be the desired direction of legal education. Hiram, and my former Dean at Case Western Reserve Law School, Prof. Gerald Korngold, are nationally recognized leaders in this approach.

Their vision and impact have proven extraordinarily effective and will, no doubt, positively impact the future of legal education.

At the S.J. Quinney College of Law, students enrolled in an innovative, non-traditional course called a think-tank in "Global Justice through Research" worked with me in choosing the articles to be included. The project leader, Rich Roberts (JD '08), was as good as Hiram promised. Rich developed and implemented an infrastructure that enabled a systematic and methodical approach to the complex selection process. Each of the nearly 200 articles considered were read multiple times by numerous readers to ensure a fair and objective process, but, more importantly, to ensure that the best articles would ultimately be chosen for the anthology. While we initially determined that only articles (as compared to Notes) would be included, I have chosen to include one Note because of the importance of the issue and the insight of the writer.

The team of law students that Rich organized—Christian Bjarnson, Sandra Hartman, Matthew Holmes, Pete Lattin, Emily Pettit, Josh Rupp, Virginia Tomova, Linh Tran, Guy Tshiteya, Artemis Vanianakis, Tasha Williams, Brooke Wilkinson, Ben Whisenant, Clark Whisenant and Phil Wormdahl—was most impressive. Their dedication, professionalism and willingness to contribute to the project's success were crucial. To those students, under Rich's guidance, this project owes enormous thanks.

A project such as this requires an initiator; the sole credit for that goes to my editor Kevin Pendergast, who suggested that I undertake such an endeavor. It is a pleasure to work with an editor who thinks outside-the-box, is engaged with the project, and yet provided the freedom for me to formulate the ideas as I saw fit. For that combination, I am grateful to Kevin.

INTRODUCTION

Professor Amos N. Guiora

The term Global Justice was not chosen by chance or happenstance; it is an attempt to think outside the box in defining the post 9-11 world. Admittedly, the term has different meanings for different people in different disciplines. It may well be that the ten authors whose works have been included in this inaugural volume—of what promises to be a very exciting and important series—would not agree with the term nor its proposed definition. They may have even scratched their heads and asked themselves what this term means and what this Series is about.

I define Global Justice (through the security prism) as the merger of the following topics: national security, human rights law, civil liberties, the law of war, and public policy. These topics must be addressed from an inter-disciplinary perspective that includes law, policy, ethics, operations, sociology, anthropology and psychology. The ten articles address a wide range of issues that fall under the umbrella of Global Justice. They address broad themes and specific issues alike. Both tactical and strategic considerations are reflected in the ten articles. International and domestic issues are discussed and analyzed.

The writers reflect an important and relevant cross-current of thinkers, scholars, and practioners. The field of Global Justice is clearly not a classical subject studied in law school—it is neither contracts nor criminal law. There is no casebook called "Global Justice". Precisely because of its inherent interdisciplinary nature, a series addressing this topic requires a broad range of articles written by an eclectic group of contributors.

To choose ten law review articles written only by academics would not have provided the reader with a broad view regarding Global Justice. Similarly, to include only articles that examine the issue from an American perspective would require calling the volume, "Global Justice—An American Perspective". As global justice is just that—global—the volume includes articles that address the issue from a global perspective.

The articles are presented in a manner reflecting how I suggest the issue of Global Justice be viewed—from broad thematic, theoretical reflections addressing critical strategic considerations to concrete, practical application of concrete issues. The broader thematic strokes are the frame; the practical application represents the more detailed nuance captured within the frame.

The two are clearly intertwined; strategic concepts divorced from tactical considerations are devoid of meaning. Similarly, practical, tactical issues without a strategic back-drop are, at best, *ad-hoc* recommendations that do not stand the course of time.

Global justice must be examined from both strategic and tactical perspectives. Simply put, strategic considerations are the essence of the issue, be it law or policy. However, a policy or law to be effective *must* include both strategic and tactical considerations. In the context of this discussion, an effective policy reflects a balanced approach to civil rights, and national security considerations predicated on the rule of law. This facilitates protection of innocent civilians thereby minimizing collateral damage.

The proposed definitions are just that—proposed definitions. What is important is that they be subjected to serious dialogue and debate. Society is defined by how it defines these terms. A society steeped in the traditions of the rule of law inherently understands the principles of separation of power, and checks and balances. Otherwise, an "unfettered executive" (quoting Justice Jackson in *Youngstown Sheet and Tube*) and the slippery slope of lawlessness and immorality are the inevitable consequences. Global justice without limits of power is devoid of justice

In confronting various threats, the democratic nation-state must conduct operational counter-terrorism in a manner that does not violate international law principles of collateral damage, military necessity, proportionality, and alternatives. Similarly, relevant domestic law must be respected so as to avoid trampling on the rights of protected, innocent individuals. Perhaps *the* question in the post 9/11 world is: what are the limits of government power? In that context, Global Justice addresses the limits of power while seeking to protect the public.

Any discussion regarding the limits of power and protecting innocent civilians requires addressing whether security defined as "*by all means necessary*" is justifiable and acceptable. This phrase—based on my professional experience in the legal and policy realms of operational counter-terrorism—is of particular concern. Other scholars, however, compellingly argue that certain circumstances justify extreme measures. Those advocating such a position suggest protecting the nation-state in the face of attack requires measures otherwise illegal, perhaps immoral.

There is no one right answer. There are, however, extraordinarily important questions that require candid debate and discussion. To summarily dismiss a point of view we may disagree with is easy; it is also irresponsible. The ten articles included in this volume represent different perspectives intended to encourage and facilitate debate. Some readers will agree with arguments advocated by particular authors, while others will find the same articles highly objectionable. That diversity of response is to be expected and is, frankly, healthy.

In the post 9/11 world, the philosophical and existential essence of societies has been challenged. Whether the attacks take place in Bali or New York, London or Madrid, Tel Aviv or Beslan, Mumbai or Nairobi, Mosul or Kabul, Rawalpindi or Sinai, the issues and dilemmas are strikingly similar. The modern nation-state is under attack. Traditional warfare as articulated by the fathers of international law is a thing of the past. Tanks attacking tanks, planes attacking planes and large infantry units engaged in combat are largely relegated to the pages of history. War between nation states has been replaced by the nation-state protecting itself from the dark shadows of an unseen enemy.

The unseen enemy attacks boldly and largely without limits. The limits—if any—are based on tactical considerations, devoid of obligation to international law. The essence of lawful operational counter-terrorism is targeting specific terrorists while minimizing collateral damage. In other words, the exact opposite of terrorism. Terrorism is the killing or injuring of innocent civilians (or their property) or intimidating the civilian population from conducting its regular daily lives for the purpose of advancing a political, religious, economic, or social cause. To achieve their goals, terrorists are committed to killing the maximum number of innocent civilians. The personal identity of the innocent civilian is as irrelevant as his ethnic or national identity.

However, we are obligated to address issues regarding what motivates terrorism. In that context, it is insufficient and inappropriate to lump terrorists together and say "they are all the same". Because different terrorist organizations have different goals, the State is obligated to develop counter-terrorism policies reflecting these differences. Counter-terrorism policies must include operational measures ranging from targeted killing to education to re-financing. Multiple approaches are not mutually exclusive; rather, nation-states should seek to implement them simultaneously. Such an integrated policy would enable the operational targeting of a specific terrorist who poses a threat while enabling outreach to segments in the population, not necessarily in the terrorist camp.

Global Justice, then, is the articulation of the above mentioned considerations. It has a price. It requires sensitivity to the demands of affected population groups. It also requires vigilance and steadfastness in the face of attacks against innocent civilians. That vigilance requires leaders to make difficult decisions regarding operational counter-terrorism subject to stringent demands regarding the rule of law and morality in armed conflict.

To help us better understand these issues and the dilemmas they address, we turn now to the Top Ten Global Justice Law Review Articles.

Professor Martha Minow's article "Tolerance in the Age of Terrorism" articulates the broad themes critical for a discussion regarding Global Justice. In describing and analyzing the dilemmas of tolerance, Prof. Minow asks whether tolerance or intolerance leads to terrorism. Tolerance implies equality, freedom, and justice; intolerance is an over-reaction to attacks on the nation state resulting in minimizing racial and religious equality. Accordingly, the question is how does society strike a balance in protecting itself?

Herein lies the critical question that Prof. Minow poses: what are the limits of democracy and what are the limits of protecting democracy? In the context of multicultural sensitivities, what are the limits of tolerance and intolerance?

Do over-response and under-response *equally* endanger democracy? In seeking to determine the relationship between security and tolerance, one of the important questions Prof. Minow ponders is whether tolerance should be replaced with equality and mutual respect. Needless to say, in a world were dangers to democracy are palpable (these lines are written in the immediate aftermath of Benazir Bhutto's assassination and on the morning of Ben Laden's promise to bring jihad to Palestine, not to mention Iraq), there are—necessarily—limits to democracy and tolerance.

The extent of tolerance (both in prevention and response) is at the heart of how the nation state develops, implements, and articulates counter-terrorism policy. If the nation-state's policy is intolerant, then civil rights abuses are inevitable. However, intolerance does not guarantee successful prevention or response on an operational level. Understanding the essence of global justice requires examining the limits of power regarding terrorism and counter-terrorism alike.

Conversely, tolerance can be equally problematic for it suggests acceptance of conduct and behavior that may threaten the stability of the nation state. Put another way, Prof. Minow asks whether misdirected policies constrain liberties and target minorities without increasing the safety for the civilians of the nation state.

Professor Jules Lobel's article, "The Preventive Paradigm and the Perils of Ad Hoc Balancing" addresses the discussion regarding the limits of democracy. It is an issue of enormous significance and naturally follows Prof. Minow's article. Prof. Lobel asks whether the nation state's appropriate response to attacks should be open-ended—*ad hoc* in essence—rather than predicated on clear rules. Should the nation state's response to attacks be premised on principles outlined in advance of attacks or should the response be a reflection of the attack, devoid of principles?

In seeking to limit—or at least advocate limits to—when the nation state can act, Prof. Lobel's article makes a most important contribution to the discussion. Global Justice explicitly recognizes that the state is obligated to protect its citizens; the question is when, under what circumstances, and subject to what criteria. Prof. Lobel asks how the nation-state can truly balance civil rights and national security considerations if the applicable standard is *ad hoc*-based rather than bright-line predicated. Without clearly articulated standards and criteria, the preventive paradigm will result in significant violations of civil rights.

A preventive paradigm, according to Prof. Lobel, is open-ended, devoid of objectively verifiable standards. Such a paradigm is based on vagueness rather than bright-line rules where, as an example, suspicion is treated as evidence. Standard-less, *ad hoc* definitions directly contribute to the establishment of a paradigm invariably involving violations of civil and political rights. Rather than articulating the limits of power, respecting separation of powers and checks and balances, a preventive paradigm predicated on *ad hoc* principles results in excess. Restraint requires articulated (as compared to *ad hoc*) core principles, developed in advance rather than in response to a particular act of terrorism.

In analyzing Global Justice, it is paramount that justice be at the centerpiece of the discussion. Prof. Lobel's concern regarding the lack of bright-line rules is the essence of this debate. In clearly and eloquently expressing concern regarding "inherent executive power", Prof. Lobel suggests that the preventive paradigm devoid of clear standards. This will result in the unilateral initiation of warfare predicated on hunches and fears, reflecting an abandonment of legal rules.

The danger to civil society is significant. Much as Prof. Minow argues for tolerance in an age of terror (but not at all costs), Prof. Lobel advocates articulating bright line rules. In essence, both Prof. Minow and Prof. Lobel emphasize the importance of limits. Otherwise, excess is not only around the proverbial corner its inevitable fall-out is but a stone's throw away.

If excess is problematic and an unrestrained executive may choose *ad hoc* responses to terrorism, where may an Administration seeking bright-line rules turn for direction? That is one of the themes offered by Professor Cuellar in his article, "The Untold Story of Al-Qaeda's Administrative Law Dilemmas". In his article, Prof. Cuellar proposes a creative and exciting approach to operational counter-terrorism: by analyzing how terrorist networks confront problems akin to entities facing administrative law challenges and dilemmas.

By studying the organizational behavior of terrorist networks from the perspective of administrative law dilemmas, the nation-state would be positioned to develop operational counter-terrorism measures. An effective strategy would not be based on "groping in the dark" but on the balanced rule of law. In the context of a balanced, rule-of-law predicated counter-terrorism policy, Prof. Cuellar's recommendation would significantly contribute to the reduction of human rights violations. Rather than developing policies based on guessing—with the inherent pitfalls involved—Prof. Cueller's model proposes a rational approach to counter-terrorism.

Much as Prof. Lobel's article raises profound concerns regarding the dangers of *ad hoc* measures, Prof. Cueller's thesis could immeasurably contribute to the development of bright-line rules predicated on an empirical understanding of terrorist organizations. That is, Prof. Cueller's theory could immeasurably contribute to the development of bright-line rules predicated on an empirical understanding of terrorist organizations.

From the perch of strategic thinking and analysis, Prof. Cueller's article addresses the over-arching theme of this volume—how the nation-state protects itself while simultaneously protecting both its core values and innocent civilians. Prof. Cueller's proposed paradigm would significantly enhance the balancing of competing dilemmas while protecting *both* national security and human rights.

Prof. Cuellar's thesis is akin to "know your enemy" with one significant difference—know your enemy in order to better know yourself. That is, were government leaders to engage in a sophisticated analysis of terrorist networks by examining strategic dilemmas and organizational challenges, they would be able to better understand *both* terrorism and counter-terrorism. Such an analysis, according to Prof. Cuellar, would give decision-makers greater insight into terrorist networks. This approach would significantly contribute to knowledge-based, rather than hunch-predicated, operational counter-terrorism

By examining a broad range of issues including hierarchy, grievance procedures, recruiting methods, financing mechanisms, institutional goals, and services provided, the nation state would better understand terrorist networks from an organizational perspective. Given certain organizational similarities—administrative dilemmas, hierarchy issues, goals—the comparative analysis would assist decision makers in assessing how to more effectively respond to threats. In other words, Prof. Cueller's model proposes a rational approach to counter-terrorism.

By examining terrorist organizational dynamics, assessment of terrorism and consequently of counter-terrorism would be significantly enhanced. Such an enhancement, in the context of global justice, would enable the nation state to develop more cautious, temperate measures predicated on keener insight into terrorism, from an organizational perspective.

The dilemma of balancing civil liberties with legitimate national security considerations requires careful analysis of the "limits of power". Simply stated: what are the limits of executive power? What are the limits of judicial review and Congressional oversight? These questions are the core of a Constitutional debate regarding issues such as "inherent powers", the "unitary executive", enumerated powers, and an unfettered executive. Those issues are relevant to the core discussion regarding what Global Justice is. In the post-9/11 world, these issues take on added importance, precisely because of their heightened relevance.

Professors Minow, Lobel and Cueller have raised critical issues regarding the broad themes relevant to Global Justice. Their articles "set the table" for the discussions to follow. Those broad themes are brilliantly complemented by discussion regarding the limits of power. Global justice without limits of power is devoid of justice. How to define, articulate, and implement those required limits is critical to the discussion. Some scholars and policy makers argue that, given the contemporary threat facing the nation state, broad executive powers are an absolute must.

In his article, "Terrorist Surveillance Program and the Constitution", Professor Yoo makes the argument that President Bush's Terrorist Surveillance Program (TSP) is a valid exercise of the President's Commander-in-Chief authority to gather intelligence during war-time. The question is whether the wire-tapping program initiated by the White House in the aftermath of 9/11 is an unconstitutional expansion of Presidential power. While CIA Director Michael Hayden has stated that TSP is "successful in preventing attacks", the larger issue is whether the President can begin military hostilities without Congressional approval.

According to Prof. Yoo, the President, as Commander-in-Chief, has both the constitutional authority and responsibility to wage war in response to a direct attack on the US. In the context of the "unitary executive" theory he proposes Prof. Yoo advocates a shift in power to the executive during wartime. To that end, the ability to gather intelligence is critical to operational counter-terrorism.

Otherwise, counter-terrorism will be nothing more than "groping in the dark". Violations of human and civil rights are the tragic results of operational counter-terrorism not based on reliable, viable, and valid intelligence information. That being said, the question is whether Prof. Yoo's argument regarding "inherent power" and the "unitary executive" meet Constitutional muster. As Prof. Lobel argues, "bright-line" rules are critical in avoiding an *ad hoc* preventive paradigm.

The Authorization to Use Military Force (AUMF, passed by the Congress in 9/11's immediate aftermath) granted the President implicit authorization to carry out electronic surveillance. The AUMF did not explicitly mention wiretapping or surveillance. In the same breath, it is important to note that Congress (1978) legislated the Foreign Intelligence Surveillance Act, intended to establish a mechanism whereby courts would issue judicial warrants authorizing wiretapping of foreign intelligence agents working for hostile nations. Prof. Yoo observes that "FISA was written with Soviet spies in DC in mind" rather than for counter-terrorism.

While Prof. Yoo advocates the principle of inherent powers and unitary executive, one of the principle questions in the context of Global Justice is whether wiretapping powers should not be explicitly granted to the President by the Congress, rather than an approach relying on implicit powers arising from the AUMF. There are, of course, no "right answers" in this debate. Some scholars argue that unless Congress explicitly grants powers, the President cannot act.

Other scholars, such as Prof. Yoo, make compelling arguments for a broad expansion of Presidential powers in the face of an attack on America. What is important—and hence the vitality of the discussion in these pages—is articulating the contours of global justice. In that discussion, the question whether executive power should be limited in the face of an attack demands our full attention.

Captain Ford's article, "Intelligence Demands in a Democratic State", addresses the question of intelligence gathering from the perspective of congressional oversight. Capt. Ford examines the limits of "inherent powers" in the context of intelligence operations during war time. In this analysis, Capt. Ford asks the critical, practical question: how does Congress monitor, direct, approve or disapprove of intelligence operations and activities? Unlike Prof. Yoo, whose argument is predicated on "inherent powers", Capt. Ford argues that enumerated powers (declaration of war, raising and supporting armies, calling forth the militia) grant Congress authorization to maintain an important role in intelligence operations.

In recalling the work of the Church Committee, Capt. Ford reminds us that Senator Frank Church inquired into the functions and activities of the intelligence community. In doing so, the Committee uncovered significant misdeeds committed by the CIA with respect to both domestic and foreign intelligence gathering.

According to Capt. Ford, the Congress, until recently, has not effectively asserted its oversight responsibilities. That fact leads Capt. Ford to the conclusion that there is an immediate need for oversight reform in the Congress.

In the context of checks and balances and separation of powers, this article is of enormous importance. Capt. Ford clearly delineates how Congressional oversight of the intelligence community should be implemented. Ford's recommendations include the need to combine the appropriations and authorization processes, improve internal information-sharing mechanisms and minimize over-classification of information. Perhaps most importantly, Capt. Ford recommends developing a uniform framework for intelligence oversight that would lead to increased aggressiveness on the part of Congress.

Much as Prof. Lobel recommends the development of bright-line rules, Capt. Ford advocates the development of effective oversight mechanisms for Congress. The implication is clear: an unfettered executive, freed of oversight how it gathers intelligence information, is doomed to repeat the mistakes of previous Administrations. However, oversight in and of itself, without proper skills, is insufficient and ineffective. Precisely because of those profound concerns, Capt. Ford articulates a clear recipe for the development of those much-needed skills.

In the context of Global Justice, Capt. Ford's recommendations are clear: the executive *must* be restrained by a Congress trained with respect to intelligence gathering. Unlike Prof. Yoo, who advocates a unitary executive, Capt. Ford argues for Congress to engage in close and sophisticated oversight. Prof. Yoo and Capt. Ford's articles propose radically different approaches to a similar issue. Much like other issues discussed in this volume, the over-arching principles addressed in these two articles are the limits of power and the balancing of competing principles. The eloquence of the writers speaks for itself, as does the power of their argument. Readers will decide which philosophical approach to the same issue resonates with them.

Any discussion regarding global justice *must* address just that—global and justice issues. While the term "global" is clear; the word "justice" is less so. Global suggests international or comparative; justice -in the context of this volume—includes addressing how nations address the detention of individuals suspected of involvement in terrorist activity. How a nation treats such an individual is a critical criterion in determining whether it conducts operational counter-terrorism within the rule of law. The relationship between justice and detainee treatment is of supreme importance.

After all, the detained individual is no more than a suspect and has not committed a crime, unless proven otherwise in a court of law. The question, naturally, in the "post 9/11 world" is what exceptions to that principle are either legislatively or unilaterally (by the executive) created. In addition to "what", the question of "when" is equally relevant. That is, "when" -if ever—are exceptions are justified.

The discussion regarding detentions will be addressed by examining the US, the United Kingdom, Canada, Australia, New Zealand, and France. Our guide for all but France is Prof. John Ip; Ms. Calliope Sudborough analyzes France, which we discuss first.

In a short but highly succinct manner, Ms. Sudborough's analyzes French counter-terrorism measures in "The War Against Fundamental Rights". The title is telling, for according to Ms. Sudborough, French policy is best articulated as "one must terrorize the terrorists". In recognizing the threat emanating from radical Islamic terrorism in France, the implications to civil liberties must be addressed. The inherent complexity of the question is compounded in the context of modern French society, which faces the crucial dilemma of "multiculturalism v. assimilation". Simply put, how does France respond to potential internal threats while preserving democratic values and principles?

According to Ms. Sudborough, the concept of vigilantly protecting civil liberties from government infringement is not as fervent in France as elsewhere. In examining detention policy, Ms. Sudborough suggests that French counter-terrorism policy reflects a basic failure to protect human rights obligations essential to a democratic society. How does that policy translate into practical, rule of law based operational counter-terrorism? The legislative response speaks volumes: the enacting of law enabling the arrest of hundreds, without a need to present evidence that a particular individual has contributed to a terrorist plot. In addition, according to French legislation, an individual may be held in preventive detention for up to four days without seeing an attorney.

The issue of human rights—and protecting the rights of suspects—is further magnified when the definition of terrorism is scrutinized. The overwhelming impression, as clearly articulated by Ms. Sudborough, is that the definition is vague, devoid of specificity, to the extent that there is no intent element required distinguishing terrorism from a lesser crime. Furthermore, French legislation criminalizes association with people "involved in terrorist enterprises". The implication, according to Ms. Sudborough's compelling analysis, is that French law does not distinguish criminal from innocent association.

How does that lack of distinction affect detention policy? Simply put, French authorities may arrest an individual for *mere contact* with an individual suspected of terrorist involvement. In other words, French law criminalizes association without requiring some form of culpable intent or strategic participation in terrorism. Furthermore, an individual may be detained until police can locate more persuasive evidence required for conviction. Ms. Sudborough's conclusion is clear: fundamental rights are sacrificed for security in France. The key question is: can Global Justice be served, much less enhanced, if fundamental rights are so easily disregarded? How does the tolerance-intolerance debate respond to the French detention policy as articulated by Ms. Sudborough? Furthermore, does the restriction of basic human rights serve French interests with respect to operational counter-terrorism? Does the apparent over-response to terrorism contribute to effective counter-terrorism? While there are no clear answers to these queries, the importance of Ms. Sudborough's analysis is that the it clearly addresses an issue of enormous significance—the significant minimizing of rights with respect to who—and when—the state may detain individuals on the basis of mere suspicion.

Prof. Ip eloquently and effectively brings to light one of the most important issues with regard to detainee rights: what is the role of Courts during war-time? His article, "Comparative Perspectives on Detention of Terrorist Suspects", highlights alternative detention paradigms in the aftermath of 9/11. The US has adopted a "law of war" paradigm that includes discretionary executive decisions, whereas the UK, Canada, and New Zealand have adopted a detention model based on immigration law legislatively driven. According to Prof. Ip, the difference between the two paradigms is critical: the American model excludes human rights norms whereas the UK, Canadian and New Zealand paradigms respect human rights. In other words: one paradigm is "war"-based; the other, predicated on "criminal justice".

In analyzing whether the respective paradigms protect the civil rights of the detainee, Prof. Ip recommends that the following questions be addressed: what the standards of proof required for detention are; whether secret evidence can be used; what the standard and depth of review by independent duties are, and what procedural protections are provided the detainee.

Put another way, do (or should) courts "bow to the exigencies of the situation"? Re-articulated, the question is what should be the level of judicial review in the post 9/11 world, and do courts genuinely affect change? The question Prof. Ip compellingly poses is critical to any discussion regarding global justice: *who* can be legitimately detained as a terror suspect *and* under what circumstances? If the American "war" paradigm is applied, the answer is clear: the Bush Administration denies application of any body of law to the detainees and has, in essence, created a "legal vacuum". The establishment of the military commissions has created a legal regime free of judicial review, enabling indefinite detention premised on complete executive discretion. Prof. Ip's analysis resonates with Prof. Yoo's defense of President Bush's Terrorism Surveillance Program.

In direct contrast to the American post 9/11 model, Prof. Ip suggests that the paradigm adopted by Canada, the UK, and New Zealand grants detainees greater rights, with certain, important caveats. In both the UK and Canada, indefinite detention is permissible, with a critical distinction from the American model. The American war paradigm is predicated on the decision of a "unitary executive" acting in accordance with a very liberal interpretation of the Authorization to Use Military Force. The indefinite detention in the UK and Canada is the result of specific legislation enacted by the parliaments of both countries.

While indefinite detention is extraordinarily problematic—legally and morally—the distinction Prof. Ip draws is critical. By engaging in an important comparative analysis, Prof. Ip highlights an important difference between the two regimes: legislative as compared to executive-based deprivations of individual rights. The distinction is critical; will the executive unilaterally deprive detainees of rights, devoid of legislative oversight and judicial review, or will the legislature act (either on its own initiative or at the executive's request), subject to a process including hearings, oversight, and judicial review.

This question—the answer to which necessarily depends on the reader's political, philosophical, and jurisprudential perspectives—is one of the most important issues facing jurists, the public and policy makers. The significance of Ms. Sudborough and Prof. Ip's articles is their analysis of how different nation states articulate the limits imposed on individual freedom.

Ultimately, any discussion regarding global justice must be concrete; analysis must include concrete threats to the nation state. The discussion in the preceding pages has largely focused on critical legal and policy issues that define the essence of the nation-state. Whether and how separation of powers and checks and balances are implemented is critical. The extent of tolerance and whether bright line rules are adopted or the preventive paradigm is *ad hoc* premised is central to the debate. However, unless specific threats are addressed, the discussion regarding global justice is academic, theoretical, and devoid of concreteness and ultimately of importance.

Therefore, the final three articles included in this volume address three different threats facing the nation state: cyber-terrorism, weapons of mass destruction, and terror financing. These three threats, while seemingly very different, bear significant similarities. All three represent "new" threats quantifiably different from the traditional threat nation states perched on the eve of battle with another nation state faced. In the classical military paradigm, the "rules of the game" were largely known to those involved, as were the weapons available—tanks, planes, missiles, infantry soldiers, and war-ships.

The traditional laws of war addressed the use of those weapons and provided for the protection of the captured soldier. As a brigadier general in the IDF recently commented, "the position of the company commander today is *immeasurably* more complicated than twenty years ago." If traditional war has been replaced by new threats, then the nation state must develop the military, policy, and legal means to respond. In these pages, we have addressed the legal and policy tools required to respond to the new threat. In the following pages, we shall discuss these extraordinarily complicated, complex and amorphous new threats and the measures available to the nation state seeking to protect its citizenry.

Mr. Gary Sharp addresses the Proliferation Security Initiative ("PSI"), whereby the international community has the authority to seize weapons of mass destruction (WMD's) and their components in transit as a means to pro-actively combat WMD proliferation. In his article, "Proliferation Security Initiative: The Legacy of Operation Socotra", Mr. Sharp convincingly argues for the development of effective mechanisms for combating global WMD in a world dominated by global trade and commerce.

The seizure is primarily, if not exclusively, dependent on intelligence information. The reality of high sea interdiction is that the decision to board a ship requires reliable, valid, and viable intelligence information. Not only is the nation-state interfering with the passage of a ship, *but*, if the intelligence is incorrect, the possibility for significant financial loss cannot be ignored.

In advocating the adoption of the PSI, Mr. Sharp's argument addresses one of the critical aspects of operational counter-terrorism: the right to self-defense. However, in the context of Prof. Lobel's argument regarding the requirement to establish bright-line rules, self-defense is not a "blanket approach" devoid of standards and limitations. Global Justice—as defined in this volume—requires that self-defense be applied rigorously, in a measured manner, not blindly and at all costs.

Mr. Sharp's compelling advocacy for interdiction on the high seas is tempered by an articulate call for the development and standards *when* the nation-state can board a ship. That is, similar to Prof. Lobel's call for the development of bright-line rules, Mr. Sharp advocates standards. Those standards would be based on the right to interdict (premised on self-defense), the adoption of streamlined procedures for information-sharing between nation states, and a review of relevant national authorities. The ultimate question Mr. Sharp poses is how the nation-state responds to the proliferation challenge. His answer is an explicit grant of broad legal authority rather than a fluid, *ad hoc* regime.

In the aftermath of 9/11, the issue of self-defense, particularly pre-emptive, is a matter of much debate amongst legal scholars. Mr. Sharp's article makes an enormously important contribution to the debate with respect to WMD's.

Cyber-terrorism presents an equally dangerous threat to the nation-state, for it directly impacts critical national infrastructure. Major Condron's article, "Getting it Right", asks the following question: is cyber-terrorism a criminal or national security activity? The importance of this article and the issue it addresses is enormous. The answer dictates what legal measures may be brought to play with respect to what is largely a "new threat". Cyber-terrorism perhaps more than any other threat (with the possible exception of WMD's) illustrates the significant difference between traditional warfare and contemporary conflict.

In advocating that the appropriate response is to view cyber-terrorism as a national security activity, Major Condron articulates a self-defense model. To that extent, balancing between civil liberties and self-defense from cyber-terrorism requires examining the potential damage to the nation's critical infrastructure. According to Major Condron, existing US policy is to favor civil liberties at the expense of national security with respect to cyber-terrorism. In clear, concise, and convincing language, Major Condron recommends adopting a new presumption: that any cyber attack on a nation's critical infrastructure is a national security threat *rather* than criminal activity.

The essence of Major Condron's article is his call for a cyber-defense strategy that enables the state to more effectively protect itself against a new threat that poses enormous dangers. Viewed in the context of global justice, the issue is of significant importance, for it raises the question of *how* the state most effectively protects itself and what is the appropriate legal regime.

The question that Major Condron poses—criminal or national security—dictates the rights and status of those involved in cyber-terrorism. If the paradigm is criminal law, then the suspect (potentially a defendant) is subject to criminal law protections as articulated in the relevant jurisdiction. However, if the national security paradigm is adopted, that requires development of a new legal regime or at least adapting existing, alternative legal regimes, such as the military tribunals established by President Bush in November 2001. Developing new legal regimes in response to new threats needs to be carefully weighed against the possibility of over-reach with respect to violating civil rights. In other words, caution would be the recommended approach.

Nevertheless, the state must respond. The debate *how* to respond to this new threat is an issue of major importance that deserves our fullest attention. Major Condron's article has made an enormous contribution by proposing a model that would more effectively protects the nation's infrastructure while simultaneously protecting civil rights. Whether the model, if adopted, would result in an imbalance must be subject to further inquiry and discussion as cyber-threat's severity will increase in the coming years.

If intelligence gathering is the heart and soul of counter-terrorism, then money is the heart and soul of terrorism. Terrorist organizations are dependent on enormous financial resources in order to conduct effective attacks. Whether the terrorist organization is financially solvent, such as Al-Qaeda, or dependent on state support (Hezbollah's dependency on Iran is a prime example), the requirement for significant financial resources is an absolute.

Where do those much-needed funds come from? In the aftermath of 9-11, there was overwhelming evidence that Islamic charities were important sources of funding. In many cases, the question was whether the charities were "legitimate" or "front" organizations. If a front, then attention turned to the giver: did the individual believe the charity was legitimate; was the donor a fraud victim or did the individual knowingly give to a front that served as an important conduit for financing terrorism?

The upshot of the discussion is a significant clamping down on charities in an effort to hamper the financing of terrorism. However, as Professor Jenkins in his article "Soft Power, Strategic Security" cogently argues, there is a significant price to be paid for such a policy. According to Prof. Jenkins, international philanthropy advances US security interests for three different reasons: it is a powerful tool of public diplomacy, America's international image is enhanced, and it enables partnering to solve particular problems. It is, in essence, a matter of enlightened self-interest.

That enlightened self-interest has been put to a severe test. According to Prof. Jenkins, the policies developed by the Bush Administration in response to 9/11 have had *unintended* consequences, as guidelines have significantly constrained international giving. In an effort to ensure that charitable assets are not delivered to terrorists, government policy has—possibly—"over-reached". Prof. Jenkins argues that the US views international philanthropy as a threat requiring containment *rather* than as a source of legitimate power-generating credibility.

Responding to the identified and documented threats of money laundering for terrorist purposes by significantly limiting funds made available for international aid purposes, the government has missed an opportunity. That is the essence of Prof. Jenkins' thoughtful and important article, which addresses this issue. If international aid is an essential element of US national security policies, why would the government respond as it has? Are not image, values, and international cooperation important for a successful foreign policy? What are the limits of reaction to a threat?

The policy implications are clear—according to Prof. Jenkins, vital American interests are negatively affected because of an over-reaction. However, the nation-state's primary obligation is to protect its citizens. In the context of global security, the question is "what price protection". If previously the issue was phrased as "what price freedom", the additional question of "what price protection?" is similarly valid.

Prof. Jenkins argues—compellingly and convincingly—that limits on protection are valid when larger interests are at stake. Much like other articles in this volume that have analyzed the balancing dilemma, ultimately this article also suggests a balancing discussion. While international aid is undoubtedly an important aspect of foreign policy, ensuring that charities are not used as conduits for terror financing is similarly critical. Balancing—between encouraging charitable giving and money laundering—is the essence of Prof. Jenkins' article. The argument Prof. Jenkins presents requires addressing the issue from a long-term policy perspective. Decision must determine to what extent international aid is a priority, particularly when documented examples of misuse of charities are abundant.

FINAL WORD:

The ten articles included in this initial volume of what promises to be an exciting series address an extraordinarily broad range of issues that are the essence of the contemporary debate. Their importance is that they serve as a basis for determining how civil, democratic societies balance powerful competing tensions and dilemmas. One of the primary purposes of the series, and of the articles chosen, is to enable multiple audiences to better understand the dilemmas faced by decision and policy makers. It is hoped that the inclusion of these ten articles in one volume will contribute to that understanding.

TOLERANCE IN AN AGE OF TERROR

Martha Minow†

Should the government forbid school girls in France or female college students in Turkey from coming to school with their hair covered according to an Islamic tradition? Were one hundred members of Congress right to call for the resignation of Columbia University assistant professor Nicholas de Genova, who, during a teach-in on the Iraq war, publicly wished for "a million Mogadishus," a reference to the violent assault of U.S. troops in Somalia, depicted in the film Black Hawk Down?[1] Should the U.S. government refrain from law enforcement and surveillance tactics targeting people because they share the race, ethnicity, or religion of others identified as terrorists? Should the media be forbidden from revealing how the food supply, electricity, chemical production, transportation, and border security could be vulnerable to terrorist attack?[2] Should the government screen curricula of private religious schools to guard against political extremism and terrorism?[3]

---

† Jeremiah Smith, Jr. Professor, Harvard Law School. Thanks to Larry Blum, Stephen Holmes, Elena Kagan, Leila Ahmed, Martha Nussbaum, Phil Heymann, Seth Klarman, Gerald Neuman, Avi Soifer, Adrian Vermeule, and Joe Singer, as well as the participants at the Law, History, and Cultural session, the Gann Academy, and the Jewish Theological Seminar for comments and insights, and Jude Volek, Scott Lemon, and Kristin Flower for research assistance.

1 *See* Robert M. O'Neil, *Academic Freedom in the Post-September 11 Era: An Old Game with New Rules*, *in* ACADEMIC FREEDOM AT THE DAWN OF A NEW CENTURY: HOW TERRORISM, GOVERNMENTS, AND CULTURE WARS IMPACT FREE SPEECH at 43, 45 (Evan Gertsmann & Matthew J. Streb eds., 2006).

2 *See* Dennis Pluchinsky, *They Heard It All Here, and That's the Trouble*, WASH. POST, June 16, 2002, at B03.

3 *See* Avigael N. Cymrot, *Reading, Writing, and Radicalism: the Limits on Government Control Over Private Schooling in an Age of Terrorism*, 37 ST. MARY'S L.J. 607 (2006). "Terrorism" should be understood as a means, not an ends, and as a complex collection of many types of threats, perpetrated by many different kinds of actors. *See* Arthur Paecht, *Opening Speech: Europe Faces Terrorism*, INSTITUTE DE RELATIONS INTERNATIONALES ET STRATEGIQUES, EUROPE FACE TO FACE WITH TERRORISM (Mar. 8, 2005) (speeches from conference in Paris sponsored by IRIS, European Commission and NATO). The head of the French National Antiterrorist Division commented in 2005 that Europe faces four different forms of terrorism: "Islamic terrorism, separatist-inspired terrorism, politically extremist terrorism, and others—including extortion threats." Frederic Veaux, *Fighting Terrorism Efficiently* 95, 95–96, *in* INSTITUTE DE RELATIONS INTERNATIONALES ET STRATEGIQUES, EUROPE FACE TO FACE WITH TERRORISM (Mar. 8, 2005) (speeches from conference in Paris sponsored by IRIS, European Commission and NATO).

Should a democracy forbid the participation in electoral politics of parties dedicated to dismantling secular democracy?[4]

Questions such as these have circulated in legal and political circles for decades but 9/11 pushed them to the forefront. Although terrorism has a long history, and despite the fact that dilemmas of tolerance may be traced to the first human societies, new urgency and new levels of difficulty seem apparent now as governments and private individuals navigate between perceptions of increasing threats of terrorism and commitments to free speech, free exercise of religion, and equal treatment and respect for all.[5] "Tolerance" has surfaced often in public discourse since 9/11. For example, on September 30, 2001, the Anti-defamation League took out a large ad in the *New York Times* with the headline: *Empowering Children in the Aftermath of Hate: A Guide for Educators and Parents*.[6] Discussing the damage done by stereotypes, prejudice and discrimination, the ad continued, "intolerance of difference is at the root of most violence," and explained that adults therefore should give children tools to confront hate effectively." Yet, policies confronting terrorism can also express intolerance: intolerance of terrorism, but also at times intolerance toward people who look like terrorists, people who criticize counter-terrorism tactics or the leaders who pursue them.

Indeed, a review of contemporary scholarship and of news coverage reveals two narratives linking tolerance and terrorism. The first see overreaction and intolerance as responses to terror; and the second sees under-reaction and too much tolerance. Law review articles and public interest advocates charge the United States since 9/11 with overreaction that jeopardizes legal and cultural commitments to tolerance. Recent books and articles allege under-reaction on the part of several European nations, citing an ideal of multicultural tolerance that offers space for intolerant and even murderous individuals and groups to plan and carry out violent acts.[7] I will suggest, however, that a single nation may seem to or actually produce

---

4 For a recent thoughtful treatment of this topic, *see* Samuel Issacharoff, *Fragile Democracies*, Harv. L. Rev. (forthcoming 2007).

5 Many people in other parts of the world suggest that 9/11 simply taught Americans about the threats of terrorism that other nations have already seen and experienced. Yet the scale of the 9/11 assault and the attack on the U.S. superpower stands out even to people in countries with deeper experiences with terrorism. *See* Elisabeth Young-Bruehl, Why Arendt Matters, 64 (2006) (describing world reactions to 9/11).

6 *Educational Programs to Teach Tolerance Grew After 9/11*, N.Y. Times, Sept. 30, 2001,. *See, e.g.*, Mike Rose, *Teaching Tolerance After Terrorism*, Educ. Dig., Feb. 2002, at *2–4*. But some objected and called instead for more instruction in patriotism. *See* Chester E. Finn, Jr., *Teachers, Terrorist and Tolerance*, Commentary, Dec. 2001, at 54.

7 Talking of "Europe" risks neglecting the significant national and cultural differences within particular European nations, and yet the commonalities—and the shared practices of an increasingly unified Europe—help to explain the frequent invocation of "Europe" as the comparison with the United States. The greater American propensity to use military force in international contexts, in comparison with European nations, may reflect similar tendencies toward coercive action in response to terrorism. *See* Robert Kagan, Of Paradise and Power: American and

both intolerance and too much tolerance, generating both overreactions and under-reactions to terrorism. Because the United States and European nations each have pursued policies that threaten civil liberties and indicate intolerance of immigrants and dissenters, a detailed assessment is necessary—and so is analysis of the rhetorical arguments about overreaction and under-reaction. Moreover, tolerance can be a feature of personal ethics, or national character, or public policy, and the connections between tolerance and anti-terrorism can take complex forms at each of these levels.

"Overreaction" and "under-reaction" each presuppose that there is a proper reaction in relation to two dimensions: the scope of the harm triggering the response and the departure from a baseline set of values or commitments. Assuming the baseline commitments to civil rights and civil liberties, overreaction could involve policies that depart from commitments to racial and religious equality by pursuing a discriminatory purpose, through a means such a racial profiling, without clearly advancing security, while underreaction would mark a failure to adopt policies that address specific known treats from a specific group, such as adherents to radical Islam. Similarly, surveillance, intelligence, and detention policies that significantly and disproportionately affect members of racial and religious minorities could be an overreaction in the absence of a demonstration that security requires that degree of unfairness. Further, policies fomenting increased prejudices toward or unfounded fears of members of religious and ethnic minorities signal overreaction, while as failures to restrict recruitment by violent terrorist groups mark underreaction.

It is common to describe these dangers as an inevitable trade-off between liberty and security, with the reminder that our constitution is not a suicide pact.[8] But I have joined others in arguing that the security we seek includes the liberty

---

EUROPE IN THE NEW WORLD 23, 31 (2003). Or this foreign affairs contrast may instead affect public perceptions of American overreaction to threat.

8 The classic statement is Justice Robert Jackson's in *Terminiello v. Chicago*, 337 U.S. 1, 37 (1949) (Jackson, J., dissenting) (judges should not "convert the constitutional Bill of Rights into a suicide pact"). *See e.g.*, Fareed Zakaria, *Freedom vs. Security*, NEWSWEEK, July 8, 2002, at 26; Robert M. Chensey, *Civil Liberties and the Terrorism Prevention Paradigm: The Guilty by Association Critique*, 101 MICH. L. REV. 1408, 1413 (2003); Oren Gross, *Chaos and Rules: Should Responses to Violent Crises Always be Constitutional?*, 112 YALE L.J. 1011 (2003). For a contemporary elaboration of the argument, see ERIC A. POSNER & ADRIAN VERMEULE, TERROR IN THE BALANCE: SECURITY, LIBERTY, AND THE COURTS (2007); RICHARD POSNER, NOT A SUICIDE PACT: THE CONSTITUTION IN A TIME OF NATIONAL EMERGENCY (2006). *See also* William H. Renhquist, ALL THE LAWS BUT ONE: CIVIL LIBERTIES IN WARTIME (1998) (arguing that civil liberty should not occupy the same favored position in wartime as it does in peacetime); Zakaria, *supra*, at 26; Chensey, *supra*, at 1413; *Civil Liberties and the Terrorism Prevention Paradigm: The Guilty by Association Critique*, 101 MICH. L. REV. 1408, 1413 (2003); Oren Gross, *supra*, at 1011. Many of these authors argue that the trade-off of liberty to achieve security is inevitable. Some also argue that the executive branch is likely to make accurate judgments about the trade-off. *See e.g.*, POSNER & VERMEULE, *supra*.

we cherish.[9] In a liberal democracy, our security encompasses the guarantees of our freedom as well as our physical safety, and in a global struggle that includes ideological as well as military conflict, we lose a key advantage if we sacrifice the ideals that we hope attract hearts and minds around the world. Fear and hatred are the underlying issues: understandable fear of terrorism and the sadly familiar hatred of people identified as threatening circulate among longstanding residents while fear of government abuse and hatred of those associated with it can grow among immigrants and people outside the country. Overreaction in the form of systematic mistreatment of minorities can stoke fires of alienation, jeopardizing support for the nation and potentially increasing the numbers of people who support terrorists. Overreaction can undermine tolerance and the freedoms it advances. Underreaction tolerates behavior by enemies and haters and jeopardizes our existence and our ways of life.

The two dangers represent in fact a genuine dilemma, with trade-offs and catch-22s, whether measured in terms of effects on rights (of speech, assembly, due process, privacy, and equal protection) or sheer social welfare. I first consider the dilemmas of tolerance emerging now, and then turn to the narratives of overreaction and underreaction and what they further reveal. Because some of the issues along the way can be traced to the project of liberal tolerance and role ideas can play in this difficult time, these dimensions figure in the analysis.

I. THE DILEMMA OF TOLERANCE

Tolerance, at minimum, means forbearance: the restraint against expressing or enacting disapproval of another.[10] It is not tolerance if you do not disapprove of the

---

9 Emanuel Gross, The Struggle of Democracy Against Terrorism 9, 157–93 (2006); Anthony Lester, *Counter-Terrorist Measures, Human Rights and Multiculturalism in the United Kingdom*, Madrid Conference Paper, Sep. 2006 (unpublished paper); Ally Hack, Note, *Forfeiting Liberty: A Collective Sense of Vulnerability and the Need for Proactive Protection After 9/11, 2* Cardozo Pub. L. Pol'y & Ethics J. 469, 471–72 (2004); Martha Minow, *The Constitution as Black Box During Times of National Emergencies: Comment on Bruce Ackerman's Before the Next Attack: Preserving Civil Liberties in an Age of Terrorism*, 75 Fordham L. Rev. 693 (2006); David Pannick, *Human Rights in an Age of Terrorism*, 36 Isr. L. Rev. 1, 3–4, 6 (2002); Paul Rosenzweig, *On Liberty and Terror in the Post 9/11 World: A Response to Professor Chemerinsky*, 45 Washburn L.J. 29, 45 (2005); Jeremy Waldron, *Security and Liberty, and the Image of Balance*, 11 J. Pol. Phil. 191 (2003). *See also* Cass R. Sunstein, *National Security, Liberty, and the D.C. Circuit*, 73 Geo. Wash. L. Rev. 694 (2005–06) (arguing against extremes of national security fundamentalism and liberty perfectionists and in favor of judicial minimalism to advance both goals). There remain potential tradeoffs between immediate security and long-run security, but it is helpful to locate the policy choices within the security framework rather than between security and liberty. For then it would be clear that there is not a zero-sum game between liberty and security.

10 *See* Webster 7th Collegiate Dictionary 930 (1977) (". . . sympathy or indulgence for beliefs or practices differing from or conflicting with one's own b: the act of allowing something;" toleration is defined as: "a: the act or practice of tolerating something . . ." Tolerance as a concept is associated with overlapping notions; I take here a pragmatic approach and look to

other person or view.[11] Philosopher Thomas Scanlon explains that tolerance "involves an attitude that is intermediate between wholehearted acceptance and unrestrained opposition."[12] Tolerance demands a kind of humility and self-critique to guard against acting on absolute judgments; it also requires a commitment to create and preserve the conditions of peaceful co-existence among people with clashing religious, culture, or political beliefs.[13] One established political structure solution to such clashes granted relative autonomy to groups with practices that diverged from those in control. The millet system devised in the Ottoman Empire grouped people by religious communities and granted them some degree of self-governance, permitting peaceful co-existence among Muslims, Christians, and Jews as well as maintaining avenues for minority communities to persist.[14]

A different political solution emerged in the form of liberal tolerance when Europeans pursued of peaceful co-existence after the Seventeenth Century's Thirty Years War between Protestants and Catholics. The Treaty of Westphalia in 1648 registered agreement of competing states to respect one another, and acknowledged the power of each local ruler to dictate his state's religion. Accordingly, respect for national borders became the mutual condition of peaceful coexistence across different sovereign states. Over time, political leaders drew on Protestant ideas of individual conscience in crafting constitutional democracy norms of free speech and equality, with religious freedom left largely to individuals. In contemporary form, liberal tolerance has come to include practices of multiculturalism, assuring room for the expressive activities of members of different religious and cultural groups. At times, this multiculturalism has been attacked for being a kind of ethical relativism, suspending any collective judgment about the good or the right.[15]

---

the debates and positions in which the concept is often invoked. *See* ANNA ELISABETTA GALEOTTI, TOLERATION AS RECOGNITION 225 (2002) (explaining pragmatic approach).

11 *See* Joshua Halberstam, *The Paradox of Tolerance*, 14 PHIL'ICAL FORUM. 190–206 (1982–83); Geoffrey Harrison, *Relativism and Tolerance*, 86 ETHICS 122–35 (1976).

12 T.M. SCANLON, *The Difficulty of Tolerance*, THE DIFFICULTY OF TOLERANCE: ESSAYS IN POLITICAL PHILOSOPHY 187(2003); See AVIAM SOIFER, LAW AND THE COMPANY WE KEEP (1998).

13 *See, e.g.*, Marc Gopin, *Counter Religious Extremism with Religious Compassion*, CHRISTIAN SCI. MONITOR, Sept. 7, 2006, *available at* http://www.csmonitor.com/2006/0907/p09s02-coop.html; David Little, Senior Scholar, Special Initiative on Religion, Ethics, and Human Rights, United States Institute of Peace, Remarks at a Presentation at the University of Texas entitled Moral Values in a Free Society, *Tolerance, Equal Freedom, and Peace: A Human Rights Approach*, (Nov. 11, 1996) *(transcript available at* http://www.usip.org/religionpeace/rehr/equalfree.html); W. Paul Voigt, TOLERANCE & EDUCATION: LEARNING TO LIVE WITH DIVERSITY AND DIFFERENCE (1997); RECONCILIATION, JUSTICE, AND COEXISTENCE: THEORY AND PRACTICE (Mohammed Abu-Nimer ed., 2001); IMAGINE COEXISTENCE: RESTORING HUMANITY AFTER VIOLENT ETHNIC CONFLICT (Antonia Chayes & Martha Minow eds., 2003).

14 *See generally*, AYELET SHACHAR, MULTICULTURAL JURISDICTIONS: CULTURAL DIFFERENCES AND WOMEN'S RIGHTS (2001). *See also* MARIA ROSA MENOCAL, THE ORNAMENT OF THE WORLD: HOW MUSLIMS, JEWS, AND CHRISTIANS CREATED A CULTURE OF TOLERANCE IN MEDIEVAL SPAIN (2002).

15 See JOHN BOWEN, WHY THE FRENCH DON'T LIKE HEADSCARVES 83 (2006).

It remains difficult to distinguish the suspension of disagreement required for co-existence from the suspension of all judgments about right and wrong.

This ambiguity about values is hardly the only problem with tolerance. Liberal tolerance has always struck me as a second-best, a kind of "putting up with" difference that falls short of genuine respect. Tolerance implies an imbalance of power: some have the power to grant—or withhold—tolerance toward others. As Amalie Taubels wrote in 1839: "Even the word tolerance is intolerable. No one has a right to tolerate another."[16]

Yet tolerance seems so much better than it's opposite. Intolerance, the dictionary tells us, entails the "unwillingness or refusal to tolerate or respect contrary opinions or beliefs, persons of different races or backgrounds."[17] To be intolerant is to be bigoted, which, in one of those unhelpfully circular dictionary definitions, means being "so obstinately attached to a creed, opinion or practice as to be illiberal or intolerant."[18] Intolerance is scolding and degrading; it plants seeds for harassment and even violence. In this difficult first decade of a new century, intolerance of immigrants, headscarves, and political dissenters is palpable in politics, in the media, and even in classrooms. Abortion clinics are sites of intolerance and, at times, violent protest; right-to-life protesters can also name their own ample encounters with intolerance.[19] Growing rights for gays, lesbians, and other sexual minorities meet with overt expressions of hatred and intolerance.

Some theorists place tolerance as the precondition for equality, freedom and justice. Then intolerance deserves the most serious response.[20] But we soon hit the dilemma: the most serious response to intolerance is to stop it, to refuse to endure it, to object, scorn, to become intolerant. Tolerance was supposed to endure the objectionable and establish peaceful co-existence with disagreeable others. How can the tolerant be intolerant of intolerance? But how can the tolerant tolerate intolerance?

---

16 Rosalie Maggio, The New Beacon Book of Quotations by Women 699 (1996) (quoting a letter dated 1839).

17 Random House Unabridged Dictionary (2006), *available at* http://dictionary.reference.com/browse/intolerance.

18 Webster 7th Collegiate Dictionary, *supra* note 10, at 83 (bigotry), 444 (intolerant). *See also* Random House Unabridged Dictionary, *supra* note 17, (defining bigoted as "utterly intolerant of any creed, belief, or opinion that differs from one's own"), *available at* http://dictionary.reference.com/search?r=2&q=bigoted.

19 *See* James Barron, *Abortion Issue Takes a Violent Turn*, N.Y. Times, Nov. 25, 1984, at A2; Dudley Clendinen, U.S. *Sends Warning of Potential Threat to Abortion Clinics*, N.Y. Times, Jan. 11, 1985, at A1; Dudley Clendinen, *The Abortion Conflict: What it Does to One Doctor*, N.Y. Times, Aug. 11, 1985, at F18.

20 *See* Chandran Kukathas, The Liberal Archipelago: A Theory of Diversity and Freedom 119 (2003); Wendy Brown, Regulating Aversion: Tolerance in the Age of Identity and Empire 19 (2006) (discussing the ambiguity surrounding tolerance and the tendency to conflate isses of religion, ethnicity, race, and culture).

Discerning precisely what tolerance demands and what its limits are has always been a conundrum.[21] This question of limits becomes especially vexing when symbols stand in for tolerance or for intolerance—or even for both. Take the dispute over whether the Turkish government could ban the wearing of headscarves in its public university.[22] The Supreme Administrative Court upheld the ban because "wearing the headscarf is in the process of becoming the symbol of a vision that is contrary to the freedoms of women and the fundamental principles of the Republic."[23]

Leyla Sahin enrolled at the medical school at Istanbul University prior to the issuance of a university order excluding students from lectures, courses or tutorials if they wore clothes "symboli[zing] any religion, faith, race or political or ideological persuasion."[24] Denied the ability to pursue her studies, she filed a challenge to the circular, pursued judicial review in Turkey without success, and then she pursued an action in the European Court of Human Rights.

That Court in 2005 agreed that the ban interfered with Sahin's right to manifest her religion but the Court nonetheless affirmed the ban—in the name of pluralism, broadmindedness, and tolerance. The European Court reasoned that to advance those values, the government of Turkey needed to act as an impartial arbiter, protecting democracy, and it could adopt the ban as a proportional means to advance such legitimate aims.[25] British, German, French, and Dutch universities would not adopt such a ban, and would instead construe pluralism, broadmindedness and tolerance to require accommodating the religious dress of its students.

21 Karl Popper presented the paradox of tolerance this way: "If we extend unlimited tolerance even to those who are intolerant, if we are not prepared to defend a tolerant society against the onslaught of the intolerant, then the tolerant will be destroyed, and tolerance with them." KARL POPPER, THE OPEN SOCIETY AND ITS ENEMIES, 1 PLATO 265 n.4 (1971). For recent examinations of these and related difficulties with tolerance, see Milner Ball, *Beyond Tolerance*, 24 CARDOZO L. REV. 1621 (2003); Lasse Thomassen, *The Inclusion of the Other?: Habermas and the Paradox of Tolerance*, 34 POLITICAL THEORY 439–62 (2006); Michel Rosenfeld, *Extremist Speech and the Paradox of Tolerance, 100* HARV. LAW REV. 1457 (1987) (reviewing LEE C. BOLLINGER, THE TOLERANT SOCIETY: FREEDOM OF SPEECH AND EXTREMIST SPEECH IN AMERICA (1986)).

22 *See* Christopher D. Beleliu, Comment, *The Headscarf as a Symbolic Enemy of the European Court of Human Rights'* Democratic Jurisprudence: Viewing Islam through a European Legal Prism in Light of the Sahin Judgment, 12 COLUM. J. EUR. L. 573, 584–85 (2006) (recounting 1981 regulations by Turkish Cabinet requiring ordinary modern dress for staff and female students in public institutions, 1982 ban of headscarves in lecture rooms by the Council of Higher Education, 1984 endorsement by Supreme Administrative Court of the headscarf ban, and 1988 judicial rejection of Act permitting headscarf wearing).

23 *Id.* at 584 (citing Sahin v. Turkey, App. No, 44774/98. Nov. 10, 2005, at ¶ 37.)

24 *Id.* at 606 (citing Sahin v. Turkey, at ¶ 47).

25 *Id.* at 607 (citing Sahin v. Turkey, at ¶¶ 78, 98–99, 108, 113–14, 117–21).

But, reasoned the European Court of Human Rights, the Turkish government would know better how to advance these goals in its national context.[26]

That context includes the fact that Turkey, alone with Senegal among all Islamic nations, elevates secularism as part of its constitution.[27] But because ninety-nine percent of the population is Muslim, religious tension takes the form of conflicts over degree of orthodoxy. A woman who goes uncovered is at risk of derision or worse by fellow citizens who are more Orthodox, unless the government creates a space where she is not allowed to cover her hair. The state is deeply engaged in the project of secularism but this does not mean that it separates itself from religion; indeed, the Turkish government pays the salaries of 60,000 imams and dictates the contents of their sermons.[28] After a military coup in 1980, the political party regained democratic control in 1983 and relaxed restrictions on religious expression[29] and subsequent leaders have pressed for greater room for religious expression while trying to contain religious fundamentalism.[30] As Turkey struggles to find a path between Islamic fundamentalism and secular fundamentalism,[31] its prime minister at the time of the Sahin decision had two daughters attending school in the United States in order to avoid the headscarf restrictions in Turkish universities.[32]

The headscarf, worn in a university setting, is at once the symbol of intolerance and the symbol of tolerance. To some, it represents patriarchal domination, and the intransigent demands for individual conformity by a group willing to use intimidation. To others it represents space enabling for individual expression and produces the diversity and mutual encounters of multicultural respect.[33] To many in the West,

---

26 *Id.* at 589–92, 607–09 (citing Sahin v. Turkey, at ¶¶ 78, 98–99, 108, 113–14, 117–22, and discussing the Court's reliance on Turkey's case law, and the concept of "the margin of appreciation" used by the Court to allow latitude for member states in their decision-making and adherence to the Convention on Human Rights).

27 *Id.* at 577 (on Turkish history).

28 *Id.* at 581 (quoting Nicole Pope & Hugh Pope, Turkey Unveiled: A History of Modern Turkey 317 (2004)).

29 *Id.*

30 *Id.* at 582.

31 Marvine Howe, Turkey Today: A Nation Divided over Islam's Revival 248 (2000).

32 Beleliu, *supra* note 22, at 583.

33 The debate over the headscarf in public schools in France has a specific inflection due to the traditional French conception of republican citizenship. After several girls in one school were suspended for wearing headscarves, a national debate ensued, and ultimately a nation-wide policy was adopted; the government forbids students from wearing conspicuous religious apparel, including Muslim headscarves. *See France Bans Head Scarves in School, Senate Adopts Controversial Law Forbidding Religious Apparel*, CBSNews.com, (Mar. 3, 2004), *available at* http://www.cbsnews.com/stories/2004/02/02/world/main597565.shtml; Bowen, *supra* note 15. For a comment on an earlier stage of the issue in France, *see* Martha Minow, *Identities*, 3 Yale J.L. & Human. 97, 122 (Winter 1991). From afar, the policy may look intolerant and biased. It allows a Christian student to wear a small cross but does not allow a Muslim girl

the headscarf ban seems like an act of intolerance. But at least as defended, it instead represents intolerance of the intolerant: it marks an effort to prevent male students and others from disciplining women who prefer not to wear a head covering. Here is the paradox of tolerance: either the tolerant must tolerate intolerance or instead turn to intolerance—of the intolerant.[34]

---

to cover her hair or a Sikh boy to wear a turban. It could however be defended as a long-term effort to promote integration and unity around a shared, secular, French identity. Certainly the government defends it in terms of the historic vigor with which the country has both pursued a separation between religion and government and also worked to tie education to a shared national identity.

Especially given the timing of its adoption, the ban can be viewed as an expression of anxiety about the growing Muslim presence in France. *See* BOWEN, *supra* note 15, at 242. And it can also be understood as a political effort by moderates to hold the line against more reactionary regulation of immigrants. *See* BOWEN, *supra* note 15, at 242; Helen Harden Chenut, *Translator's Introduction* to FADELA AMARA, BREAKING THE SILENCE: FRENCH WOMEN'S VOICES FROM THE GHETTO 1, 20–21 (2006). Some of its supporters claim that it offers special protection for Muslim girls who do not want to wear the scarf and yet are pressured by family members and neighbors to do so. *See* BOWEN, *supra* note 15, at 209, 231–33, 244. As political scientist Seyla Benhabib comments, "Ironically, it was the very egalitarian norms of the French public education system that brought these girls out of the patriarchal structures of the home and into the French public sphere, and gave them the confidence and the ability to *resignify the wearing of the scarf.*" SEYLA BENHABIB, THE CLAIMS OF CULTURE: EQUALITY AND DIVERSITY IN THE GLOBAL ERA 191 (2002). The ban may have counterproductive effects if it leads some girls to depart from the state's school or school altogether. *See* Chenut, *supra*, at 20 (summarizing Le Foulard et la Republique (1995), reporting on interviews indicating some young women between the ages of 16–25 wore the headscarf to please parents or older brothers, while others chose to wear it to affirm their identities as both French and Muslim); Anthony Giddens, *French Headscarf Ban Against Interests of Women*, 23 NEW PERSP. Q., (Jan. 5, 2004), *available at* http://www.digitalnpq.org/global_services/global%20viewpoint/01-05-04.html. On the complex arguments among women about these and other human rights issues, see Martha Minow, *About Women, About Culture: About Them, About Us*, 4 Daedalus: J. AM. ACAD. ARTS & SCI. 125, 125–45 (2000).

Informed and engaged participants in the debate over the headscarf in France themselves change their views as events unfold. Fadela Amara is the founder of a movement of human rights for Muslim women in France called Ni Putes Ni Soumises (Neither Whore Nor Submissive). Chenut, *supra*, at 20. Amara launched the movement after a gang set an eighteen-year-old Muslim woman on fire apparently because she had resisted Islamic codes of behavior. Chenut, *supra* at 16. Initially, she believed the ban would be ineffective and stigmatizing; later she saw how girls reappropriated the headscarf and found it empowering, but she grew to favor the ban. AMARA, *supra* at 154, 159.

34 Meanwhile, an elementary school teacher in Germany wanted to cover her hair while teaching contrary to the dictates of the school authorities. Fershta Ludin is a German citizen with roots in Afghanistan. The German Constitutional Court recognized her rights of conscience and access to public office under the Basic Law, but reserved the question to state legislative response. BENHABIB, *supra* note 33, at 198–99. Four German states have legislated laws forbidding teachers from wearing an Islamic headscarf to school. *The Islamic Veil Across Europe*, BBCNews.com, (Nov. 17, 2006), *available at* http://news.bbc.co.uk/2/hi/europe/5414098.stm. British Home Secretary Jack Straw who represents a district that is 25–30% Muslim, controversially urged Muslim women to take off the veil when meeting with him, which some Muslims read as an insult. *See* Mark Simpson, *Straw Met by Applause—and Boos*, BBCNews.com,

Either choice undermines tolerance, but at least showing intolerance to the intolerant preserves a domain of tolerance. It seems absurd to tolerate the intolerant for that undermines tolerance itself. But intolerance of tolerance of course terminates tolerance, too. To mute such a dilemma, we may try to anticipate how one person's actions could so insult another as to trigger their intolerance and attempt to create conditions of mutual respect to minimize such insults; this is one multiculturalist view. But a fair response is, no, we should not bend ourselves out of shape to accommodate the intolerant.[35]

This pattern recurs in clashes between efforts those who urge multicultural sensitivity and those who stress instead commitments to individual equality, freedom, and mutual respect. After a Danish journal published cartoons ridiculing intolerance by radical Muslims, the depictions of Mohammed offended many and triggered violent protests around the world. Other media outlets then faced the choice over whether to follow multicultural sensitivities and refrain from republishing the cartoons or instead pursue full coverage of the news and to exercise free speech rights. Similar issues recur in other settings. Should local police punish an assault by an immigrant against a local gay couple or instead excuse it based on recognition of his culture's disapproval of homosexuality?

Sorting out the collisions between tolerance and intolerance is especially arduous when the fights produce physical violence or bloodshed. With massive riots causing several deaths after publication of the Danish cartoons,[36] republication raised risks of sheer physical danger, not simply charges of intolerance. In the midst of a multicultural street far in Berlin in 2002, for example, a group of immigrant teens beat up a gay couple. According to journalist Bruce Bawer, "That day, [the couple] lost their belief in the ideal of a multicultural society in which minorities act together in solidarity."[37] Political theorist Wendy Brown argues that Israel and the United States have engaged in violence in the name of "tolerance" and "democratic" ideals.[38]

Thus, tolerance presents the dilemma of its own limits. Even if we rule out the self-contradicting position that the tolerant must refrain from enforcing tolerance itself,

---

(Oct. 13, 2006), *available at* http://news.bbc.co.uk/2/hi/uk_news/politics/6048896.stm; Jo Coburn, *Straw Gets the Debate He Wanted*, BBCNews.com, (Oct. 6, 2006), *available at* http://news.bbc.co.uk/2/hi/uk_news/politics/5413012.stm; Nasreen Suleaman, *How Veil Remarks Reinforced Its Support*, BBCNews.com, (Nov. 5, 2006), *available at* http://news.bbc.co.uk/2/hi/uk_news/6117480.stm.

35 Yet even as tolerance is not the correct response to the intolerant, something surpassing tolerance—something more like efforts to understand—may be necessary and appropriate as a response to people who commit intolerable acts. *See* Ball, *supra* note 21, at 1623–24.

36 *Muslim Cartoon Fury Claims Lives*, BBCNews.com, (Feb. 6, 2006), *available at* http://news.bbc.co.uk/2/hi/south_asia/4684652.stm.

37 Bruce Bawer, While Europe Slept: How Radical Islam is Destroying the West from Within 39 (2006).

38 *See* Brown, *supra* note 20, at 104–05.

tolerance defends the persecuted.[39] Tolerance is not a substantive position, not a retreat to neutrality. But if tolerance can authorize a live-and-let-live, simplistic version of multiculturalism, it undermines vigilance against intolerance. It may help us to distinguish tolerance of the *people* who hold intolerant views from tolerance of those *views* themselves.[40] Also it may help to distinguish a personal attitude of tolerance—as in restraint against getting into a fist-fight over undeniable disagreement—from institutional arrangements of law and politics that are designed for those most in disagreement with one another to accept.[41]

Yet another version of the dilemma of tolerance resurfaces here. Consider what happened in England when Iranian Ayatollah Khomeini issued a fatwa, calling for a ban of Salman Rushdie's novel, *The Satanic Verses*. The fatwa represented high religious authority not only to ban the novel but also to offer a bounty for Rushdie's death even in England, where Rushdie lived.[42] Beyond the police protection that Britain then offered as Rushdie went into hiding, what could the British government or anyone do to protect him from the physical danger he faced? One rule that we can identify as unhelpful was Britain's own blasphemy law, which was intolerant of religious heresy but only if the heresy targeted Christianity.[43] To be fair—and to have any fighting chance of winning respect by Rushdie's critics—England would either need to extend the blasphemy law to Islam or eliminate it altogether. The choice itself extends the dilemma of tolerance. Once the system of tolerance includes some explicit statements of what cannot be tolerated, there will also be disagreements over what should or should not be on that list. Perhaps it would be better not to use secular law to punish religious blasphemy at all. For those whose religion—or whose secularism—is not on the forbidden list, religious blasphemy laws invite charges of bias, hypocrisy, and disrespect. But how can a tolerant society

39 *See* SCANLON, *supra* note 12, at 197.

40 *See* SCANLON, *supra* note 12, at 197 (discussing Voltaire's statement, "I disapprove of what you say, but I will defend to the death your right to say it.").

41 *See* SCANLON, *supra* note 12, at 198.

42 GARAN HOLCOMBE, *Salman Rushdie*, CONTEMPORARY WRITERS IN THE UK (2004), *available at* http://www.contemporarywriters.com/authors/?p=auth87 ("The publication in 1988 of his fourth novel, *The Satanic Verses*, led to accusations of blasphemy against Islam and demonstrations by Islamist groups in India and Pakistan. The orthodox Iranian leadership issued a *fatwa* against Rushdie on 14 February 1989—effectively a sentence of death—and he was forced into hiding under the protection of the British government and police. The book itself centers on the adventures of two Indian actors, Gibreel and Saladin, who fall to earth in Britain when their Air India jet explodes. It won the Whitbread Novel Award in 1988.") *Id.*

43 *See* R. v. Chief Metropolitan Stipendiary Magistrate, ex parte Choudhury 3 W.L.R. 986 (1991) (ruling that the blasphemy law did not encompass Islam). *See also* LEONARD W. LEVY, BLASPHEMY: VERBAL OFFENSE AGAINST THE SACRED FROM MOSES TO SALMAN RUSHDIE (1995); DAVID NASH, BLASPHEMY IN MODERN BRITAIN 1789-PRESENT (1999); *Q & A: Blasphemy law*, BBCNews.com (Oct. 18, 2004), *available at* http://news.bbc.co.uk/3753408.stm).

allow religious authorities to punish what the secular world permits? Using law, politics, and social sanctions to establish the limits of tolerance creates the dilemma of intolerance toward intolerance, or tolerance of intolerance. This dilemma affords a useful window in to assessing contemporary responses to terrorism, and the narratives of over- and under-reaction to which I will now turn.

II. RISKS OF OVERREACTION

Books and articles, as well as lawsuits filed since 9/11, tell a narrative of intolerant overreaction to terror in the United States. Academic and popular writings, watchdog reports, and test case litigation describe and criticize post-9/11 domestic restrictions on speech and assembly targeting protesters;[44] increased government surveillance;[45] diminished administrative and judicial oversight;[46] new registration requirements and ongoing monitoring of non-citizens in the United States that subject individuals to arrest, detainment, loss of legal immigrant status, criminal charges, and deportation for failures to register;[47] attempts to deport or hold indefinitely

---

44 *See* Mary M. Cheh, *The Treatment of Demonstrators: Demonstrations, Security Zones, and the First Amendment Protection of Special Places*, 8 D.C. L. Rev. 53 (2004); Nick Suplina, Note, *Crowd Control: The Troubling Mix of First Amendment Law, Political Demonstrations, and Terrorism*, 73 Geo. Wash. L. Rev. 395 (2005). The central decision upholding the restriction is United For Peace & Justice v. City of New York, 243 F. Supp. 2d 219 (S.D.N.Y. 2003).

45 Mark Sidel, More Secure, Less Free?: Antiterrorism Policy & Civil Liberties After September 11 (2004); Tony Loci, *Report Outlines Rights Violations in Sept. 11 Act*, USA Today, July 22, 2003, at 2A (describing thirty-four "credible" allegations of civil rights violations by the Justice Department in executing the Patriot Act). *See also* USA Patriot Act, Pub. L. No. 107-56, 115 Stat. 272 (2001) (codified as amended by 18 U.S.C. §§ 2510–22, 18U. S.C. §§ 3121–27, 18 U.S.C. §§ 2701–12, 50 U.S.C. §§ 1801–11, and in eleven other sections (2006)) [hereinafter "USA Patriot Act"]. The Patriot Act was renewed on March 9, 2006, with only minor changes. *See* USA Patriot Improvement and Reauthorization Act of 2005, Pub. L. No. 109-177, 120 Stat. 192 (2006).

46 The Bush Administration established a system of military tribunals for Guantanamo detainees, bypassing Article III courts; the Supreme Court struck down that system as a violation of the Uniform Code of Military Justice ("UCMJ"). *See* Hamdan v. Rumsfeld, 126 S.Ct. 2749 (2006). Congress quickly overturned that decision, thereby reestablishing the military tribunal system. *See* Military Commissions Act of 2006, Pub. L. No. 109-366, 120 Stat. 2600 (2006).

47 *See* 8 U.S.C.A. § 1201(b) (establishing general registration requirements for all entering aliens). Congress also created a "special registration" system for aliens from certain countries, requiring regular reports to the Department of Homeland Security from 2002–03. *See* Registration and Monitoring of Certain Nonimmigrants, 8 C.F.R. § 264 (2002) (suspended 2003). *See also* Nina Bernstein, *In Search of Asylum After Reprieve Proves Temporary*, N.Y. Times, Sept. 21, 2006, at B2 (describing effects of special registration system); U.S. Immigration and Customs Enforcement, Public Information: Special Registration 1 (2006), *available at* http://www.ice.gov/pi/specialregistration/index.htm (describing special registration requirements).

non-citizens for minor or nonexistent immigration violations;[48] secrecy about the names of people detained;[49] and use of asset forfeiture[50] and other expanded governmental powers to obtain information, arrest, detain, and indict individuals, including citizens, for broadly defined terrorism-related activities.[51]

Turning to the international scene, overreaching by the U.S. government is the focus of journalism, scholarship, and lawsuits challenging the detention and interrogation techniques used for people captured in Afghanistan, Pakistan, and Iraq. These detentions by the United States almost always proceed without charges, and only recently has the government started a process of planning for hearings of any sort. Even so, the hearings are sharply confined in subject matter and proceed outside the traditional rules of evidence and the military code. The Administration has sharply fought independent judicial review while also limiting detainee access to counsel and subjecting detainee consultations with counsel to government monitoring.[52] Most explosive are the exposures of secret detention centers abroad and rendition of detainees to countries known to engage in torture, coupled with revelations of shockingly abusive interrogation and detention techniques in the Abu Ghraib prison in Iraq and in Guantanamo, Cuba, which the government specifically chose as a detention center in an effort to evade both domestic and international legal constraints.

Taken together, recent steps taken by the U.S. government create an extraordinary challenge to traditional civil liberties and civil rights. Particular jeopardy falls on dissenters to U.S. policies and on Muslims, Arabs, and Arab-Americans, as well as people who may be mistaken for them. Alongside the broad story of a power grab

---

48 *See* Ty S. Wahab Twibell, *The Road to Internment: Special Registration and Other Human Rights Violations of Arabs and Muslims in the United States*, 29 Vt. L. Rev. 407, 431 (2005).

49 Stanley Mark et al., *Have We Learned the Lessons of History? World War II Japanese Internment and Today's Secret Detentions*, Immig. Pol'y Focus, Oct. 2002, *available at* http://www.ailf.org/ipc/ipfl1002.pdf, cited in Twibell, *supra* note 48, n.130; American Immigration Lawyer's Ass'n, *Boiling the Frog Slowly: Executive Branch Actions Since September 11, 2001*, 7 Benders Immig. Bull. 1237 (2002).

50 Susan M. Akram & Maritza Karmely, *Immigration and Constitutional Consequences of Post-9/11 Policies Involving Arabs and Muslims in the United States: Is Alienage a Distinction without a Difference?*, 38 U.C. Davis L. Rev. 609, 632–640, 694–698 (2005) (citing provisions of the Patriot Act and related regulations).

51 A court rejected as impermissibly vague the prohibition of providing material support or resources in the form of "expert advice or assistance." Humanitarian Law Project v. Ashcroft, 309 F. Supp. 2d 1185 (C.D. Cal. 2004).

52 Akram & Karmely, *supra* note 50, at 654–657 (citing the Bureau of Prisons's post 9/11 power to monitor and review communications between detainees or inmates and their lawyers).

by the executive branch,[53] three specific narratives of government overreaching recur among the commentaries:

- Intolerance of protests
- Surveillance without checks
- Intimidating treatment of non-citizens and "targeting" of Muslims and Arabs

By calling them "narratives," I do not suggest that claims of government overreaction to terrorist threats are untrue.[54] Critical accounts contain many points of undeniable truth, and justify deeper analyses that these narratives only partially suggest. By discussing "narratives," I do mean to estrange ourselves from the debate, to establish critical distance, and to see the frames used to make sense of often overwhelming experiences.

A. On Intolerance of Protests

The federal government has denied all permits for large demonstrations in Lafayette Park, the open space directly across from the White House that has historically hosted assemblies and protests.[55] Police have denied parade permits and confined assembly and protests after 9/11 to "free speech zones" removed from government officials and the broader community. In a leading example in 2003, the New York City police denied a permit for the anti-war parade proposed by protestors of the anticipated U.S. military action in Iraq. The police confined the protesters to a location bounded by metal pens.[56] A federal district court upheld the

53 *See, e.g.*, Erwin Chemerinsky, *Civil Liberties and the War on Terrorism*, 45 WASHBURN L. REV. 1 (2005). Observers note that President Bush has announced intentions to ignore more than 750 laws, keep without charges nearly 500 "enemy combatants" in detention in Guantanamo, authorize warrantless wiretapping of domestic telephone calls, and to report only to a handful of leaders rather than full Congressional oversight committees, relying on assertions of the inherent powers of the commander in chief and the unitary executive and elevating the President's control over the other branches. Elizabeth Drew, *Power Grab*, The NEW YORK REVIEW OF BOOKS, June 22, 2006, *available at* http://www.nybooks.com/articles/19092. The White House lawyers maintain there is precedent for the administration's activities. For the administration's argument in favor of its authority with regard to domestic surveillance, *see, e.g.*, U.S. DEP'T. OF JUSTICE, LEGAL AUTHORITIES SUPPORTING THE ACTIVITIES OF THE NATIONAL SECURITY AGENCY DESCRIBED BY THE PRESIDENT (2006), *available at* http://www.usdoj.gov/opa/whitepaperonnsalegalauthorities.pdf. But some commentators characterize the administration's activities as a power grab. *E.g.*, Alan Bock, *Breathtaking Power Grab*, Jan. 29, 2006, http://www.antiwar.com/bock/?articleid=8452).

54 Decisionmakers reflecting on decisions made in the wake of 9/11 have commented on the context of fear and ignorance while debating about the appropriateness of the response. *See, e.g.*, John J. Farmer, Jr., *The Rule of Law in an Age of Terror*, 57 RUTGERS L. REV. 747, 753, 755 (2005) (reflections of former New Jersey Attorney General current Senior Counsel of the National Commission on Terrorist Attacks upon the United States (9/11 Commission)).

55 Cheh, *supra* note 44, at 55 n.7. Mahoney v. Norton, No. 02-1715 (D.D.C. 2001) (upholding ban imposed after 9/11 on protests in Lafayette Park).

56 *See* Ian Urbina, *Police Face Lawsuits over Tactics at Big Protests*, N.Y. TIMES, Nov 19, 2003, at B 4.

restrictions in part because the police had too limited a time frame to plan for the event after advance negotiations with protestors stalled. Critics claim that the government caused the stall, and used the permissible time, place, and manner restrictions on free speech and assembly to alter the expressive content of the demonstration. Affirming the decision, the federal court of appeals warned against talismanic justifications for denying parade permits.[57] During the same incident, police arrested an estimated 250 people, most of whom had tried without success to reach the permitted protest site.[58] Law enforcement officials similarly restricted protestors to "free speech zones" during the 2004 Democratic National Convention in Boston and the 2004 Republican National Convention in New York. In other public events, supporters of President Bush have been allowed in public settings to hear him speak, while protesters have been confined to zones where they cannot see or hear or be seen or heard by the President, federal officials, or other members of the public.[59]

B. Surveillance Without Checks

If we are lucky, we will learn more about the surveillance pursued by the federal government since 9/11. Because the usual checks and limitations increasingly do not apply, we may not. Nevertheless, the media has begun to expose practices that the government hoped to keep secret. Recently, the *New York Times* reported on the new use of security letters by the Central Intelligence Agency to obtain domestic financial records while following leads about terrorist threats—including sudden increases in assets held by particular individuals.[60] Although presented as noncompulsory letters to the financial institutions, the requests nonetheless involve the military in the domestic law enforcement domain without clear authority or specified checks on the scope of power and quite coercion they exercise.[61]

---

57 United for Peace & Justice v. City of New York, 323 F.3d 175, 178 (2d Cir. 2003). *See also* Suplina, *supra* note 44, at 418 n.169.

58 Shaila K. Dewan, *War Protesters Say They Were Bound to Rally, but Ended up in a Human Traffic Jam*, N.Y. TIMES, Feb. 17, 2003, at B4.

59 *See* Amended Complaint, Acrod v. City of Philadelphia 2004 U.S. Dist. LEXIS 8446 (E.D. 2004) (No 03-412); Jonathan Janiszewski, Comment, *Silence Enforced Through Speech: Philadelphia and the 2000 Republican Convention*, 12 TEMP. POL. & CIV. RTS. L. REV. 121 (2002); Coalition to Protest the Democratic Nat'l Convention v. City of Boston, 327 F. Supp. 2d 61 (D. Mass 2004), *aff'd sub nom.* Bl(a)ck Tea Soc'y v. City of Boston, 378 F.3d 8 (1st Cir. 2004); Diane Cardwell, *Police Offer Protesters a Site Far From Garden*, N.Y. TIMES, July 15, 2004, at B1; Jay Weaver, *Groups to File Lawsuits over Actions by Police*, MIAMI HERALD, Dec. 8, 2003, at B1.

60 Eric Lichtblau & Mark Mazzetti, *Military Expands Intelligence Role in U.S.*, N.Y. TIMES, Jan. 14, 2007, at A1.

61 *Id. See also* Bob Bauman, Letter from the Editor, *Overreaction*, SOVEREIGN SOCIETY OFFSHORE A-LETTER, Aug. 4, 2005, *available at* http://www.sovereignsociety.com/offshore1368.html. ("Referring to the London bombings and the death of an innocent man who was mistaken for a terrorist, Rep. Barr noted that while such a tragedy has not occurred in the US,

Like the increased surveillance of domestic telephones, mail, and email brought to light by investigative journalists, this investigation of financial records depends on aggressive interpretations of federal authority and government secrecy about its own assertions of authority. It thereby undermines legal and democratic accountability in

---

"our government continues to overreact to terrorist incidents, real and perceived, in ways that threaten to erase our liberties if not our lives."). The report continues:

> Barr also touched upon a topic we often address—financial privacy.
>
> Echoing our sentiments, he notes: "It was not so many years ago that Americans could open a bank account and rest assured its contents would be free from prying government eyes unless federal agents could establish to the satisfaction of a federal judge that the bank customer had violated the law. While the Internal Revenue Service was exempted from this prohibition on routine disclosure of a law abiding citizens' financial records, even that agency was severely limited in how it could use the tax related data and with whom it could share the information. In other words, as a man's home was his castle, so too his finances were his secret. No more.
>
> Under the USA Patriot Act, versions of which were reauthorized recently by both houses of the US Congress, and the ease with which "sneak and peek" warrants may now be issued to the government, a man's home is the government's play ground. And, also thanks to the Patriot Act, a person's bank accounts are now routinely analyzed and reported to government agencies for little or no reason whatsoever.
>
> Barr also notes the futility of all the unnecessary bureaucratic paperwork: Banks are under increasing pressure to file more and more "Suspicious Activity Reports" or "SARs" with the feds; at the current rate of some 800,000 per year (nearly triple the rate of just three years ago). Until recently SARs were limited to instances in which truly unusual banking activity triggered a legitimate suspicion the customer was engaged in money laundering or some other illegal financial activity. Now, thanks to both the Patriot Act, which greatly expanded the category of suspicious activities that would trigger an SAR filing, and as a result of "defensive filings" by banks, the types of transactions that are coming under scrutiny are often routine and not indicative of any unlawful activity.
>
> This kind of mindless reporting is little more than plain snooping by bank officials eager to gain favor with federal regulators, and reflects the federal government's increasing desire to gather data on all of us for no reason or any reason.
>
> It has gotten so bad that one US banker told Barr his bank has set quotas for increased numbers of SARs to be filed each reporting period.
>
> While you might sympathize with the banks, since the federal government is now prosecuting banks for not filing enough SARs, filing a report with the feds on a customer simply because he or she engages in heavy use of an ATM seems an overreaction but it is happening.
>
> What happens to all this information the government is gathering from banks filing more SARs? Not much, beyond gathering data in its massive computers. Of the nearly 700,000 SARs filed in 2004, fewer than 900 were actually passed on to a law enforcement agency for follow-up. Lost in all this is financial privacy, something that used to be important in America but which now appears to have been discarded as 'quaint' and outdated.
>
> We reiterate what we have said before—real financial privacy does exists in many offshore havens where banking secrecy is the law; where privacy is not waived on a routine basis, but only after judicial review, notice to account holders and determination of probable cause.
>
> It is still legal to have, use and enjoy offshore bank and investments accounts. We can and will assist you in opening these accounts where you get far better asset protection, increased investment opportunities and the kind of peace of mind no longer available in America. That's the way it looks from here.

BOB BAUMAN, Editor

the course of pursuing what many understand as a campaign to restore executive powers curbed after abuses under the Nixon administration.[62] For example, President Bush recently announced that he believes that federal law enforcement has authority to read materials sent through the U.S. mail. Some new surveillance techniques are no doubt appropriate in light of terrorist threats, but the pattern of concealing the techniques and forestalling demands for authorization has become a series of disturbingly familiar end-runs around democratic checks. These measures are striking especially given the ongoing willingness of Congress to give broad authorization for new surveillance techniques, including techniques that loosen traditional checks on governmental searches and investigations.

Thus, the USA PATRIOT Act increases government power to wiretap and obtain electronic communications.[63] It permits law enforcement to demand libraries, bookstores, and businesses to produce tangible items, such as papers, books, and records,[64] while also forbidding disclosure to any person of such a demand.[65] It further authorizes searches conducted without giving contemporaneous notice of the search or a warrant for the search.[66] Civil libertarians objected but secured only

62 *See* ANDREW RUDALEVIGE, THE NEW IMPERIAL PRESIDENCY: RENEWING PRESIDENTIAL POWER AFTER WATERGATE (2005).

63 USA PATRIOT Act, *supra* note 45, at § 204 (2006).

64 USA PATRIOT Act, *supra* note 45, at § 215 (2006).

65 USA PATRIOT Act, *supra* note 45, at § 215(d) ("No person shall disclose to any other person (other than those persons necessary to produce the tangible things under this section) that the Federal Bureau of Investigation has sought or obtained tangible things under this section.") *See* STEPHEN J. SCHULHOFER, THE ENEMY WITHIN: INTELLIGENCE GATHERING, LAW ENFORCEMENT AND CIVIL LIBERTIES IN THE WAKE OF SEPTEMBER 11 2 (2002).

66 USA PATRIOT Act, *supra* note 45, at § 215; USA PATRIOT Improvement and Reauthorization Act of 2005, *supra* note 45. On signing the renewal of the Act into law, President Bush indicated, as he has on other occasions, his intention to construe the law's obligations according to his own view of what the Constitution permits:

> The executive branch shall construe the provisions of H.R. 3199 that call for furnishing information to entities outside the executive branch, such as sections 106A and 119, in a manner consistent with the President's constitutional authority to supervise the unitary executive branch and to withhold information the disclosure of which could impair foreign relations, national security, the deliberative processes of the Executive, or the performance of the Executive's constitutional duties.
>
> The executive branch shall construe section 756(e)(2) of H.R. 3199, which calls for an executive branch official to submit to the Congress recommendations for legislative action, in a manner consistent with the President's constitutional authority to supervise the unitary executive branch and to recommend for the consideration of the Congress such measures as he judges necessary and expedient.

George W. Bush, President's Statement on H.R. 199, the "USA PATRIOT Improvement and Reauthorization Act of 2005," *available at* http://www.whitehouse.gov/news/releases/2006/03/20060309-8.html (Mar. 9, 2006). Thus, although Congress inserted a provision to guard against executive abuses of the power to search private homes and seize papers, the President responded by announcing he did not feel bound to report to Congress if, in his view,such disclosure would impair national security or the performance of the Executive's duties.

small changes as the Act was reauthorized in 2006. Now libraries can consult a lawyer and try to challenge whether the government acts in bad faith in demanding the records.[67] The Act gives police and other government agents authority to use "sneak-and-peek warrants," obtained with no advance notice to the subject, to search homes and possessions, and to conduct surveillance on the Internet or email without notice. Electronic surveillance bypasses prior approval previously required by a secret panel of judges on the Foreign Intelligence Surveillance Act ("FISA") court; after 9/11, the government claimed this process of seeking warrants was too burdensome.[68] Actually, since 1978, Congress has given the government authority to proceed for seventy-two hours in an emergency case without a warrant. Nonetheless, the Bush administration argued that this broad authority actually contained too onerous a limit.[69] With challenges to the administration's practices pending, the President recently agreed to submit electronic surveillance to review by the secret Foreign Intelligence Surveillance Court ("FISC"). Some observers treated this as a victory for the rule of law and checks on excessive governmental power, yet in 2005, FISC approved all 2072 requests that it received.[70] The government has not

---

See Charlie Savage, *Bush Shuns Patriot Act Requirement*, Boston Globe, Mar. 24, 2006, *available at* http://www.boston.com/news/nation/articles/2006/03/24/bush_shuns_patriot_act_requirement/.

67 As the Department of Justice summarized:

> Amendments to section 215 orders. The reauthorizing legislation's amendments provide significant additional safeguards of Americans' civil liberties and privacy while continuing to allow investigators to use so-called "section 215 orders"—court orders requiring production of business records—in all phases of authorized national security investigations. The reauthorizing legislation clarifies that a section 215 order cannot be issued unless the information sought is relevant to an authorized national security investigation (other than a threat assessment).
>
> With respect to certain categories of documents that are viewed as more sensitive—such as library, bookstore, medical, tax return, and gun sale records—the reauthorization legislation still allows the FISA court to issue a section 215 order for those documents but requires that the application be signed by either the Director or Deputy Director of the FBI. As another safeguard, the Attorney General must develop and apply so-called "minimization procedures" limiting the retention and dissemination of information concerning U.S. persons that is obtained through section 215 orders. Recipients may explicitly seek judicial review and disclose receipt of a 215 order to attorneys to obtain legal advice or assistance and to other people necessary to comply with the request.

Office of Public Affairs, U.S. Dep't of Justice, Publ'n No. 06-113, Fact Sheet: USA PATRIOT Act Improvement and Reauthorization Act of 2005, (2006), *available at* http://www.usdoj.gov/opa/pr/2006/March/06_opa_113.html. *See also* Charles Doyle, Congressional Research Service, USA PATRIOT Act Reauthorization in Brief (2005), *available at* http://fpc.state.gov/documents/organization/51133.pdf (summarizing changes in the Act).

68 USA PATRIOT Act, *supra* note 45. *See also* U.S. Department of Justice Fact Sheet, *supra* note 67; Elaine Cassell, The War on Civil Liberties: How Bush and Ashcroft have Dismantled the Bill of Rights 13–14(2004).

69 *See* Responses from the Dep't of Justice to Questions from Chairman Sensenbrenner (Mar. 24, 2006), *available at* http://www.fas.org/irp/agency/doj/fisa/doj032406.pdf.

70 Donna Leinword, *Court to Oversee Wiretap Program*, USA Today, Jan. 18, 2007, at 1A.

disclosed whether its new willingness to submit requests for warrants to FISA court review—in a secret, nonadversarial, and unreported session—pertains to specific requests or to the program as a whole.[71]

Ashton Carter, a former U.S. Assistant Secretary of Defense who is now a professor of international affairs, argues that a government should have more latitude to conduct surveillance of things—including means and channels—than it has for surveillance of persons.[72] Yet surveillance since 9/11 in the United States seems—or is—more intensive on Muslims, Arabs, and people thought to be Muslim or Arab than anyone else. Restrictions on Muslims figure prominently in the narratives of government overreaching, including anecdotes of discriminatory treatment in ordinary government activities. One account describes how a Catholic nun "covered from head to toe" passed through an airport security checkpoint without a body search, while Enaas Sansour, a seventeen-year-old Muslim girl wearing a headscarf, was forced to remove her scarf in front of men, contrary to her religious views.[73] In another incident, Florida revoked the driver's license of a Muslim woman who refused to comply with an order issued after 9/11 to retake her driver's license photo with her veil removed.[74] Because courts have found the photo requirement unconstitutional as applied to objecting Christian plaintiffs,[75] one critic charged that revoking the Muslim woman's driver's license showed religious bias. This objection is not fully persuasive, as the other decisions occurred before the general tightening of security measures after 9/11 and the development of face recognition technology, which increases the usefulness of digitalized drivers' licenses in law enforcement.[76] Even so, discrimination in surveillance is only the tip of the iceberg in the third narrative.

---

71 Eric Lichtblau & David Johnston, *Court to Oversee U.S. Wiretapping in Terror Cases*, N.Y. Times, Jan. 18, 2007, at A1, A16. *See also* Editorial, *Bush's Change of Heart (or Not)*, Boston Globe, Jan. 21, 2007, at F8.

72 Ashton B. Carter, *The Architecture of Government in the Face of Terrorism, in* Countering Terrorism: Dimensions of Preparedness 12 (Arnold M. Howitt & Robyn L. Pangi eds., 2003).

73 Ally Hack, Note, *Forfeiting Liberty: A Collective Sense of Vulnerability and the Need for Proactive Protection After 9/11*, 2 Cardozo Pub. L. Pol'y & Ethics J. 469 (2004) (citing Katherine Shaver, *Freedom of Expression: BWI Screening Prompts Complaint from Virginia Muslim*, Wash. Post, Jan. 9, 2002, *available at* http://loper.org/george/trends/2002/Jan/87.html).

74 Freeman v. State of Florida, No. 2002-CA-2828, 2004 WL 21338619 (Fla. Cir. Ct. 2003). For critique, see Patrick T. Currier, Note, *Freeman v. State of Florida: Compelling State Interests and the Free Exercise of Religion in Post-September 11th Courts*, 53 Cath. U. L. Rev. 913 (2004) (arguing that the Freeman decision reflected post 9/11 biases and will deteriorate strict scrutiny analysis and constitutionally protected rights).

75 Quaring v. Peterson, 728 F.2d 1121 (8th Cir. 1984), *aff'd*, Jensen v. Quaring, 72 U.S. 478 (1985); Bureau of Motor Vehicles v. Pentecostal House of Prayer, Inc., 380 N.E.2d 1225 (Ind. 1978).

76 *See* Freeman v. State of Florida, *supra* note 74.

C. The Intimidating Treatment of Noncitizens and "Targeting" of Muslims and Arabs

These narratives encompass government practices within the United States and in the wars in Afghanistan and Iraq.

Immigration lawyers have been in the front tier of critics exposing government practices following 9/11, including the immediate round-up and detention of thousands of Arabs and Arab Americans,[77] detentions of non-citizens even after they posted bond, and detentions of people who came forward with information to assist investigations of terrorist activities.[78] Due to government assertions of emergency, people have been held without bond for unlimited durations of time. Threatened and actual deportations for technical immigration law violations or criminal offenses are coupled with enforcement of the new National Security Entry-Exit Registration System. It required male visitors to the United States from twenty-four Arab and/or Muslim countries (and North Korea) to register with law enforcement officials. The government defended this approach as based on nationality rather than ethnic or religious profiles. But the resulting surveillance and detentions produce real fear among many Arabs and Muslims in the country.[79] The government is also working to implement a program to deport all immigrants lacking proper papers—a plan that could expel twelve million people.[80] Some even warn that the government is laying the ground for internment of Arabs and Muslims, in the mode of the Japanese-American internment during World War II.[81]

---

77 *E.g.*, Dan Eggen, *Delays Cited in Charging Detainees*, Wash. Post, Jan. 15, 2002, at A1.

78 Twibell, *supra* note 48; Akram & Karmely, *supra* note 50.

79 Citizens of Iran, Iraq, Libya, Sudan and Syria were the first group called to register, followed by a second wave that included citizens of Afghanistan, Algeria, Bahrain, Eritrea, Lebanon, Morocco, North Korea, Oman, Qatar, Somalia, Tunisia, United Arab Emirates, and Yemen. United States Immigration and Customs Enforcement, Special Registration, *available at* http://www.ice.gov/pi/specialregistration/index.htm. *See* Registration of Certain Nonimmigrant Aliens from Designated Countries, 67 Fed. Reg. 77,642 (Dec. 18, 2002). *See also* Deborah Ramirez & Stephanie Woldenberg, *Balancing Security and Liberty in a Post-September 11th World: The Search for Common Sense in Domestic Counterterrorism Policy*, 14 Temp. Pol. & Civ. Rts. L. Rev. 495, 497 (2005).

80 Carol Rose & Christopher Ott, *Inhumane Raid Was Just One of Many*, Boston Globe, Mar. 26, 2007, at A9 (describing the Department of Homeland Security plan named Endgame). *See also* Bureau of Immigration and Customs Enforcement, U.S. Dep't of Homeland Security, ENDGAME: Office of Detention and Removal Strategic Plan, 2003-12, *available at* www.aclum.org/endgame.pdf.

81 Twibell, *supra* note 48; Jim Buchanan, *Detention Centers For Who, Exactly?*, Asheville Citizen-Times, Feb. 26, 2006, at 13A (questioning the motives behind a $385 million contingency contract awarded to a Halliburton subsidiary for the construction of detention centers on U.S. soil). *See also* Simon Romero, *Halliburton Says Unit Will Offer Shares*, N.Y. Times, Jan. 28, 2006, at C3 (describing the detention center contract briefly).

Others find this implausible.[82] But the post 9/11 registration system was preceded by a 1986 U.S. contingency plan for interning Arabs.[83] Shortly after 9/11, the Department of Justice launched an interviewing program based on the list it compiled of 8,000 men, aged eighteen to thirty-three, who entered the United States on nonimmigrant visas from Muslim or Arab countries. The current administration piloted data-mining law enforcement strategies with this group.[84] The General Accounting Office review of the interviewing project cast substantial doubt on the value of the project, which generated fewer than 20 arrests—all on immigration or criminal charges, with no link to terrorism.[85]

The registration system and visa restrictions also have made it more difficult for academic institutions to bring in foreign students and visiting scholars from abroad to study, teach, or attend conferences—and they deter communication more broadly by generating suspicion about such individuals.[86] Chiefly affecting people from Muslim and Arab countries, these policies also hamper the ability of colleges and universities to increase understanding about precisely those regions of enormous American ignorance, misunderstanding, and intolerance. Yet when the University of North Carolina tried to address some of this lack of understanding by requiring incoming students to read portions of the Qu'ran, state legislators sought to attach to an appropriations bill the requirement that if any religion is studied at the state university, equal time would have to be given to others.[87]

The narratives of oppressive treatment of Arabs and Muslims reach a crescendo with the unprecedented exercise of executive authority in detaining individuals in Guantanamo Bay, the Iraq prison at Abu Ghraib, and other prison facilities abroad,

---

82 Twibell, *supra* note 48, at 420 (citing David Cole's view that internment would not be practical due to the geographic dispersal of Arabs in the U.S.).

83 Susan M. Akram, *Scheherezade Meets Kafka: Two Dozen Sordid Tales of Ideological Exclusion*, 14 Geo. Immigr. L.J. 51, 94 (1999); David Cole, Enemy Aliens 102 (2003).

84 Nancy Murray, *in* Civil Rights in Peril: The Targeting of Arabs and Muslims 39 (Elaine C. Hagopian ed., 2004).

85 U.S. Gen. Accounting Office, Report to Congressional Committees GAO-03-459, Homeland Security: Justice Department's Project to Interview Aliens after September 11, 2001, 5 (2003), *available at* http://www.gao.gov/cgi-bin/getrpt?GAO-03-459.

86 American Association of University Professors, *Academic Freedom and National Security in a Time of Crisis, in* Gertsmann & Streb, *supra* note 1, at 15. *See* O'Neil, *supra* note 1, at 43–59; John Akker, *in* Gerstmann & Streb, *supra* note 1, at 114.

87 *See* Gerstmann & Streb, *supra* note 1, at 10–11. For further discussion of rethinking academic freedom in the wake of 9/11, *see* Lynn V. Cheney, *Defending Civilization: How Our Universities are Failing America and What can be done About it*, TOTSE.COM, Nov. 2001, http://www.totse.com/en/politics/political_spew/162419.html (last visited Apr. 10, 2007); Gerstmann & Streb, *supra* note 1, at 7. Attracting considerable public attention, Ward Churchill compared victims of Sept. 11 attacks to the victims of Nazi Adolf Eichmann. *See id.* at 11. Overall, observers conclude that after 9/11, in American universities, free speech was successfully defended by administrators or outside advocates. *See generally* O'Neil, *supra* note 1, at 44–59.

including secret sites.[88] As most of those held as terrorists in the United States and taken into custody from Afghanistan and Iraq are Arabs and Muslims, critics charge ethnic and religious discrimination in the treatment of non-citizens in the United States and of detainees in Guantanamo, Afghanistan, and Iraq.[89] This narrative is summarized in the book, *Civil Rights in Peril: The Targeting of Arabs and Muslims*.[90] The essays within the book examine negative media portrayals of Arabs and Muslim Americans as well as U.S. immigration and surveillance policies and what it calls "the criminalization of Arab and Muslim communities" in the United States and in the Middle East.[91]

Many observers link the U.S. treatment of Arab and Muslim countries with policies and attitudes affecting Arab and Muslim Americans, and anyone—a Sikh, a Mexican—who can be mistaken for one. The narratives of government overreaction thus combine critiques of American foreign policies, criminal law enforcement, immigration policy and practice, and private harassment and stereotyping.

Critics argue that general law enforcement and anti-terrorism policies can be deployed disproportionately against Muslims and Arabs, and this very risk especially frightens members of those communities. Under the International Economic Emergency Powers Act of 1977,[92] and other legislation, the U.S. Department of Treasury investigates and blocks contributions to charities for activities suspected of jeopardizing national security. Furthermore, Executive orders signed by President Clinton before 9/11 and President Bush afterwards allow the government to identify an organization or an individual as a terrorist organization and subsequently prevent them from receiving funds, goods, or services.[93] After 9/11, the government rigorously reviewed Muslim charities, listing at least twenty-seven Islamic charities as terrorist and chilling donations to many others.[94] The Treasury Department offered guidelines to assist charities in avoiding suspicion of terrorist ties but has not produced a list of charities that comply with the guidelines.[95]

---

88 David Cole, *How to Skip the Constitution*, New York Review of Books, Nov. 16, 2006, at 22 (reviewing Posner, Not a Suicide Pact: The Constitution in a Time of National Emergency, (2006)).

89 Akram & Karmely, *supra* note 50, at 611, 658–56, 691–99, and n. 428.

90 *See generally* Elaine C. Hagopian, Civil Rights in Peril: The Targeting of Arabs and Muslims (2004) [hereinafter Civil Rights in Peril].

91 *See* Robert Morlino, *"Our Enemies Among Us!": The Portrayal of Arab and Muslim Americans in Post-9/11 American Media,* in Civil Rights in Peril, *supra* note 90, at 71–103.

92 International Emergency Economic Powers Act of 1977, 50 U.S.C. §§ 1701–07 (2000).

93 *See* Exec. Order No. 12,947, 60 Fed. Reg. 5,079 (Jan. 23, 1995); Exec. Order No. 13,224, 66 Fed. Reg. 49,079 (Sept. 23, 2001).

94 Kathryn A. Ruff, Note, *Scared to Donate: An Examination of the Effects of Designating Muslim Charities as Terrorist Organizations on the First Amendment Rights of Muslim Donors,* 9 NY.U. J. Legis. & Pub. Pol'y 447, 472–77 (2005/2006).

95 *Id.* at 499.

These government activities and perceptions of their unfairness occur against a backdrop of harassment and degradation reported or unreported by Muslim citizens and residents.[96] Intense negative responses to Muslims and Arabs appeared in the United States shortly after 9/11,[97] and negative stereotypes of Muslims persist in the broader American population five years later. Some argue that expert commentators contribute to faulty images of fanatical Muslim fundamentalists.[98] Surveys of American Muslims—and people perceived to be Muslims—indicate persistent feelings of stigma and experiences of discrimination.[99] After 9/11, public opinion shifted from opposition to the use of racial profiles for law enforcement investigations to majority support of more intensive security checks of Arabs before they could board airplanes in the United States.[100] Such profiling is conceivable only with prior social construction of the racial, religious, or national identities as salient to be mobilized for law enforcement or security measures.[101] Extensive academic debate surrounds the use of profiling after 9/11, whether based on race, ethnicity, or national origin.[102] Even the metaphor of war rather than criminal justice produces a group stereotype as enemy rather than individualized suspect.[103]

96 Karen Engle, *Constructing Good Aliens and Good Citizens: Legitimizing the War on Terror(ism)*, 75 U. Colo. L. Rev. 59, 75 (2004); Kathryn A. Ruff, *supra* note 94, at 448–49 (describing graffiti and street harassment).

97 *See* James Curry Woods, Commentary, *The Third Tower: The Effect of the September 11th Terrorist Attacks on the American Jury System*, 55 Ala. L. Rev. 209, 210 (2003) (citing a survey showing 44% of Americans surveyed believed that the terrorist attacks represented the feelings of Muslim Americans toward the United States and 84% favored tighter restrictions on immigrants form Muslim or Arab countries; 55% of those surveyed between the ages of eighteen and twenty-nine had heard negative comments about Arabs in America); Mohamed Nimer, *Muslims in America After 9–11*, 7 J. Islamic L. & Culture 1, 15–22 (2002/2003) (citing examples of anti-Muslim rhetoric and increased reports of hate crimes against Muslims after 9/11).

98 Liaquat Ali Khan, *The Essentialist Terrorist*, 45 Washburn L.J. 47, 47 (2005).

99 *See* Stephen J. Ellmann, *Racial Profiling and Terrorism*, 19 N.Y.L.Sch.J. Hum. Rts. 305, n. 43 (2003) (reporting tabulated complaints of discrimination against Arab-American and Sikhs); *id.* at n. 85 (reporting polls with 3/5 of Arabs and Muslims polled reporting discrimination or harassment and individual accounts indicating perceived stigma and discrimination).

100 David A. Harris, New Risks, New Tactics: An Assessment of the Re-Assessment of Racial Profiling in the Wake of September 11, 2001, 2004 Utah L. Rev. 913, 913–16 (2004) (citing surveys).

101 On stereotyping and socially constructed identities and their relationship to security and criminal justice, *see* Bernard Harcourt, Anne Schneider & Helen Ingram, *Social Construction of Target Populations: Implications for Politics and Policy*, 87 Am. Pol. Sci. Rev. 334, 334–17; Samuel L. Gaertner, Frances Aboud, Maria Pia Amato, Birgit Aufderheide & Rupert Brown, Blackwell Handbook of Social Psychology: Intergroup Processes (2002).

102 *See* Harcourt, Schneider & Ingram, *supra* note 101; Samuel R Gross & Debra Livingston, *Racial Profiling Under Attack*, 102 Colum. L. Rev. 1413 (2002) (would allow it); Stuntz (would allow it sometimes); Ellmann, *supra* note 99, at 305 (costs and benefits of racial profiling); Deborah Ramirez & Stephanie Woldenberg, *Balancing Security and Liberty in a Post-September 11th World: The Search for Common Sense in Domestic Counterterrorism Policy*, 14 Temp. Pol. & Civ. Rts. L. Rev. 495 (2005) (would disallow it).

103 Thanks to Stephen Holmes for this point.

In December 2006, conservative commentator and radio show host Dennis Prager condemned the first Muslim elected to Congress "for planning to use a Koran during the private part of his swearing-in ceremony."[104] Prager said that Keith Ellison should give up his post if he could not take his oath on a Bible.[105] A spokeswoman for President George W. Bush responded to questions about Prager's remarks by indicating that the President "respects religious freedom and the right to free speech." Others, including Prager's fellow Holocaust Museum board members, explicitly criticized Prager's comment.[106] It is important not to blow this one extreme remark by a radio personality out of perspective, as his statement was not a public expression of anxiety about the election of a Muslim congressman. By way of contrast, Representative Virgil H. Goode, Jr. announced that Ellison's election posed a threat to traditional American values.[107] Perhaps showing that his comment really was a pretext for anti-immigration views, Congressman Goode said he wanted to restrict legal immigration to avoid a majority of Muslims being elected to the U.S. House of Representatives, although in fact Ellison himself was born a U.S. citizen. These, let us hope, are not widespread views, but the comments support the narrative of suspicion toward Muslims—and the view that they are outsiders. Two commentators point out that societies scapegoat minorities even when there is no emergency, so the problem is not new during anti-terrorist periods.[108]

Thus, governmental restrictions on protests, surveillance without checks, intimidating treatment of non-citizens, and "targeting" of Muslims and Arabs domestically and internationally figure prominently in critiques of the U.S. government's behavior since 9/11, along with skepticism about the manipulation of public fears to serve electoral ends. An implicit punchline in narratives describing overreaction to terrorism is the actual or hoped-for pushback from the courts. Until the 2006 election, the only official check on the federal government's anti-terrorism policies and practices has come from courts, even though they are largely populated by Republican appointees. The Supreme Court rejected the Administration's efforts to avoid judicial review of detentions in Guantanamo and to avoid application of

104 Rachel L. Swarns, *Holocaust Museum Rebukes Member for Koran Comment*, N.Y. Times, Dec. 22, 2006, at A26.

105 *Id.*

106 *Id.*

107 *Id.*

108 Posner & Vermeule, *supra* note 8, at 110. They also doubt the dominant view—expressed by Congressional reparations and judicial correction of war-time judgments—that Supreme Court improperly deferred to the U.S. government's internment of Japanese-Americans during World War II. *Compare id.* at 112–14 *with* Civil Liberties Act of 1988: Restitution for World War II Internment of Japanese-Americans and Aleuts, 50 U.S.C. app. § 1989 (1988) *and* Richard C. Rueben, *Justices Declare Wrong Court Ruled in Internment Case: No Decision on Merits*, L.A. Daily J., June 2, 1987, at 1 (discussing U.S. v. Hohri). For further discussion of the history of the Japanese-American internment during World War II, *see generally* Peter Irons, Justice at War (1983); Eric K. Yamamoto, et al., Race, Rights and Reparation: Law and the Japanese American Internment (2001).

the Geneva conventions to those detentions.[109] The Court expressly reserved to Congress the power to authorize the federal detention practices with minimal judicial review, and Congress did so this past fall, despite objections from legal experts.[110] Challenges to that legislation are pending now.[111] Courts of appeal have also rejected some of the incursions on individual rights, as illustrated by the 11th Circuit's requirement of more than an asserted amorphous interest in preventing terrorism as a justification for random searches and metal detector screenings.[112]

The legal narratives emphasize excessive executive actions, and often call for legislation and judicial checks. Moderately chastened by the Supreme Court, officials in the executive branch claim their actions have protected the nation from renewed attacks.[113] After the Supreme Court declared that the executive did not have authority, the Republican-dominated Congress granted the authority that the Executive had already seized without initial permission.[114] Nowhere on the new Democratic Congress's one-hundred-hour agenda did there appear any effort to roll back the broad executive authority to restrict speech, association, privacy, and

---

109 *See* Hamdi v. Rumsfeld, 542 U.S. 507 (2004); Rasul v. Bush, 542 U.S. 466 (2004), Hamdan v. Rumsfeld, 126 S. Ct. 2749 (2006); Louise Richardson, What Terrorists Want 236 (2006): "Where the U.S. government did violate fundamental principles and behave in a manner wholly unworthy of the country's traditions was in the decision that the Geneva Conventions do not apply to the war on terror and the indefinite detention and mistreatment of suspects that resulted." Richardson suggests that the PATRIOT Act, in contrast, included appropriate efforts to promote information sharing between law enforcement and intelligence agencies, and ineffective provisions, such as requiring libraries to disclose information on their patrons. *Id.*

110 *See* United States Military Commissions Act (MCA) of 2006, Pub. L. No. 109-366, 120 Stat. 2600 (Oct. 17, 2006) (codified 10 U.S.C. § 47(A)).

111 Salim Ahmed Hamdan included a challenge to the MCA's declination of habeas corpus to "alien unlawful enemy combatants" but Judge James Robertson refused to rule in favor of Hamdan in this case regarding habeas corpus because:

> The Constitution does not provide alien enemy combatants detained at Guantanamo Bay with the constitutional right to file a petition for habeas corpus in our civilian courts, and thus Congress may regulate those combatants' access to the courts.

Robert Barnes, *Judge Rejects Detention Challenge of Bin Laden's Driver*, Wash. Post, Dec. 14, 2006, at A09. Further challenges are underway. Warren Richey, *New Lawsuits Challenge Congress's Detainee Act*, Christian Science Monitor, Oct. 6, 2006, *available at* http://www.csmonitor.com/2006/1006/p01s03-uspo.html (last visited Apr. 8, 2007).

112 *See* Bourgeois v. Peters, 387 F.3d 1303, 1311 (11th Cir. 2004).

113 Dick Cheney implied that this was true in the 2004 election campaign, saying that the Bush team was the "right choice." "If we make the wrong choice, then the danger is that we'll get hit again—that we'll be hit in a way that will be devastating from the standpoint of the United States," Cheney said. Dana Milbank & Spencer S. Hsu, *Cheney: Kerry Victory Is Risky; Democrats Decry Talk as Scare Tactic*, Wash. Post, Sept. 8, 2004, at A1.

114 *See* Saskia Sassen, *Beyond Flawed Elections: Toward a Privatized Presidency*, 9(4) Theory & Event para. 14 (2006) (discussing USA PATRIOT and Military Commission Act).

equal treatment that Congress approved after 9/11.[115] Public fears, both warranted or manipulated by descriptions of terrorism risks, motivate repeated and increasing sacrifices of liberties and the scapegoating practices of the discriminatory treatment of minority groups.[116] Radio talk show commentators and callers, bloggers, and government officials mutually reinforce intolerance toward political critics of Bush administration policies. Narratives of overreaction emphasize the incursion on rights and values in the United States, most often affecting immigrants, Muslims, and political dissenters.[117]

III. RISKS OF UNDER-REACTION

Dramatically different narratives of under reaction—and too much tolerance—are emerging in Europe. These are narratives of inaction and negligence, warning that European freedoms and decency are exploited by those who would constrict or attack the very systems that support them.[118] These narratives also reflect scapegoating or intolerance of minority groups in a different key, but the contrast between these and the stories of U.S. overreaction is striking.

A good example of the narratives of underreaction in Europe is Ian Buruma's book, *Murder in Amsterdam: The Death ofTheo van Gogh and the Limits of Tolerance*.[119] Buruma returned to the Netherlands, the country of his birth, to try to understand the murder of a public intellectual by Mohammed Bouyeri, a twenty-six-year-old Morrocan-Dutchman who wielded a curved machete on the street in Amsterdam in what seemed a religious ritual, and left a long letter in Dutch, calling for a holy war against unbelievers.[120] The letter also urged death for three others: Ayaan Hirsi Ali,

---

115 Although some members of Congress have indicated that they plan to revisit the Military Commissions Act and other recent legislation authorizing executive counterterrorism action, other priorities appear more pressing. *See* Ari Melber, *Blink Tanks Fight to Restore Habeas Corpus*, The Nation, Jan. 16, 2007, http://www.thenation.com/doc/20070129/melber; *MCA to be Revisited*, Dec. 29, 2006, http://www.thecarpetbaggerreport.com/archives/9476.html.

116 *See* Peter Galison & Martha Minow, *Our Privacy, Ourselves in the Age of Technological Intrusions*, *in* Human Rights in the "War on Terror" 258–89 (Richard Ashby Wilson ed., 2005) (discussing magical thinking); Michael McClintock, Everyday Fears: A Survey of Violent Hate Crimes in Europe and North America 13–21 (2005); R. Wistrich, Demonizing the Other: Antisemitism, Racism and Xenophobia (Studies in Antisemitism) (1999).

117 The war in Iraq represents, at least in hind-sight, another disproportionate response. Discerning a proportional response is difficult, but becomes easier in hind-sight; thus, Louise Richardson writes: "three thousand casualties, in a country long accustomed to more than five times that many homicides a year, might have elicited a more focused and more moderate reaction." Richardson, *supra* note 109, at 150.

118 Some narratives approve of European tolerance compared with American intolerance after 9/11. *See* Michel Rosenfeld, *Derrida's Ethical Turn and America: Looking Back from the Crossroads of Global Terrorism and the Enlightenment*, 27 Cardozo L. Rev. 815, 843 (2005).

119 Ian Buruma, Murder in Amsterdam: The Death of Theo van Gogh and the Limits of Tolerance (2006).

120 *Id.* at 2–3.

a Somalian-born woman who had renounced Islam, become a politician, and made a film with Van Gogh criticizing abuse of women under Islam;[121] Jozua van Aarsten, leader of the conservative party to which Ali belonged; and Job Cohen, Mayor of Amsterdam and a proponent of multicultural harmony.[122]

Buruma describes how he remembered the Europe he left as awash in cultural relativism, letting immigrants have their own identities and communities. But intervening events changed the mood and the politics. The murder of Van Gogh, the earlier fatwa issued by Islamic clerics against Salman Rushdie after he published a novel deemed blasphemous to Islam, and the terrorist bomb attacks in Madrid and London, [123]combined with world-wide Muslim protests against the Danish cartoons of Mohammed, created reasons for Europeans to fight for multiculturalist tolerance. In this narrative, Europeans need to push for enlightenment values of secularism, science, equality between men and women, and free speech—and to push against male domination, tribal honor, and divine laws.[124]

Conservatives had long been arguing that tolerance had gone too far and that multiculturalism was a mistake. Secularism, in this view, had gone too far to bring back authority of churches, so conservatives turned to Enlightenment traditions to reassert order.[125] Accordingly,

> Islamist revolution, like any violent creed, needs to be resisted, and a nation-state, to be viable, must stand for something. . . . But an essential part of Enlightenment thinking is that everything, especially claims to "nonnegotiable" or 'fundamental" values, should be open to criticism. The whole point of liberal democracy, its greatest strength, especially in the Netherlands, is that conflicting faiths, interest, and views can be resolved only through negotiation. The only thing that cannot be negotiated is the use of violence.[126]

---

121 *Id.* at 4–5. Ayann Hirsi Ali, born in Somalia, went with her family as a refugee to Saudi Arabia, the Sudan, Ethiopia, and Kenya. While young, she became a Muslim fundamentalist, wore the hijab, and went along with the planned marriage arranged by her parents to a cousin, but on her journey to the cousin in Canada, she escaped to Germany, then sought asylum in Holland. She was advised to seek political asylum from the civil war in Somalia rather than asylum from the forced marriage, so she lied on her application. Ultimately this came to haunt her when an immigration official decided to make an issue of it precisely when Ali was evicted from her home for drawing too much controversy and making her neighbors feel unsafe. So she moved to the United States and currently lives in New York. *Id.* at 151–58. She tells her story and offers her critiques of Islam in Ayaan Hirsi Ali, Infidel (2007) and The Caged Victim: An Emancipation Proclamation for Women and Islam (2006).

122 Buruma, *supra* note 119, at 5–6.

123 On European views of terrorism by Muslims prior to 9/11, *see* Antonio Brown, *Academic Freedom in Western Europe: Right or Privilege, supra* note 1, at 127.

124 Buruma, *supra* note 119, at 34.

125 Buruma, *supra* note 119, at 34–35.

126 Buruma, *supra* note 119, at 35.

Due to immigration patterns and birthrates, Buruma argues that "Islam may soon become the majority religion in countries whose churches have been turned more and more into tourist sites, apartment houses, theaters, and places of entertainment."[127] This very recognition fuels the claim that multicultural accommodation has gone too far.

Accommodation has not halted segregation. Muslim immigrants still live in enclaves in European cities or in dreary suburbs remote from central city jobs and activities. Tuned in to al-Jezerra and other Arab-language satellite television, immigrants can and do live as much in a transnational world as in the host country. Satellite dishes give these communities the nickname "dish cities."[128] Through global media, it is the children of immigrants who often develop a sense of diasporic identity, tied less to the territory where they live than the imagined territories of Muslim countries that they have not even visited. Buruma quotes Pim Fortuyn, a successful, conservative, gay populist who said, "successive Dutch governments had been far too tolerant of intolerance. They should never have allowed those dish cities to grow into hotbeds of religious bigotry."[129]

The cosmopolitan, multicultural cities of Europe afford the freedom for Muslim immigrants and their children and grandchildren to make new lives, replete with their own preferred cultural practices. That same freedom has enabled women, gays, lesbians, prostitutes, and other immigrants from around the world to circulate with the Muslim immigrants on city streets, in internet cafes, cinemas, and within commercial life. The collisions are not all happy ones. Buruma interviewed Jolande Withuis, a leftwing feminist historian, who said, "I find it terrible that we should be offering social welfare or subsidies to people who refuse to shake hands with a woman."[130] Hence, the critique emerging from Buruma's informants is that the Netherlands—and other parts of Europe—failed to set sufficient limits on tolerance in order to protect tolerance.

---

127 Buruma, *supra* note 119, at 35.

128 Buruma, *supra* note 119, at 35.

129 Buruma, *supra* note 119, at 54–55. Fortuyn was himself murdered. Buruma comments, "To almost universal relief, Fortuyn was not killed by a Muslim jihadi of foreign descent but by an earnest Dutch animal rights activist on a bicycle." Buruma, *supra* note 119, at 40.

130 Buruma, *supra* note 119, at 128. Buruma elaborates:

> Tolerance, then, has its limits even for Dutch progressives. It is easy to be tolerant of those who are much like ourselves, whom we feel we can trust instinctively, whose jokes we understand, who share our sense of irony and might even have heard of Michael Ignatieff. It is much harder to extend the same principle to strangers in our midst, who find our ways as disturbing as we do theirs, who watch fearfully as their own children, caught in between, slip from the paternal grasp into a new and bewildering world. Jolande Withuis and Paul Scheffer, like Theo van Gogh, are quite ready to extend their hands to those children, so long as they renounce the same things that the Dutch progressives renounced not so very long ago. But this will not help those who go the other way and seek salvation, or at least a degree of comfort, in the reinvention of tradition.

Buruma, *supra* note 119, at 128–29.0

The central jeopardy, in this account, targets the social ethos within European nations rather than the physical safety of its inhabitants. But physical jeopardy to residents would come from networks that recruit people to join terrorist causes from communities of immigrants and their children living in Europe. Individuals could be recruited to join local groups or to travel to training camps in Afghanistan. Narratives of these risks link European tolerance to its vulnerability to global terrorism.[131] In a speech at a North Atlantic Treaty Organization conference, one consultant engaged in antiterrorism work explained that Muslim communities in Europe provide camouflage for terrorist combatants.[132] He cites a survey conducted by *The Guardian* in May 2004, which found that thirteen percent of British Muslims responded that "'further attacks on the United States by Al Qaeda would be justified.'"[133]

Melanie Phillips' book, *Londonistan*[134] and Bruce Bawer's book, *While Europe Slept: How Radical Islam is Destroying the West from Within*[135] make the case even more strongly. Phillips argues that due to neglect by police and intelligence agencies, London has become the European hub for promoting, recruiting, and financing Islamic terror and extremism.[136] She attributes this development to a loss of confidence in the traditional British identity and to accommodation of a particularly virulent form of multiculturalism.[137] The politically correct policies allow manipulation by those who plan terrorist activities.

Phillips argues that public accommodation of immigrants who do not want to assimilate is mirrored by the government's benign neglect of terrorist cells, extremist groups, fundraising that supports recruitment efforts by Islamic jihad organizations, and other networks drawing people to radical Islam.[138]

Bawer similarly criticizes the Dutch and others in Western Europe for treating Islam as a kind of ethnic identity, and failing to condemn Islamic fundamentalism.[139] He recounts multiple instances like the case of Pela Atroshi, whose family emigrated from Iraq to Sweden. One night when she was 19, she stayed out all

---

131 *See* Piero Luigi Gigna, *Islamic Terrorism in Italy* (Paris, March 8, 2005), *in* Institute De Relations Internationales et Strategiques, Europe Face to Face with Terrorism 23, 24–25 (speeches from conference sponsored by IRIS, European Commission, and NATO); Mladen Vulinec, *Fighting Terrorism World-Wide* (Paris, March 8, 2005), *in id.* at 29, 30–31).

132 Mark Baillie, *Terrorism: A Social Phenomenon* (Paris, March 8, 2005), *in id.* at 51–52.

133 *Id.* at 53.

134 Melanie Phillips, Londonistan: How Britain is Creating a Terror State Within (2006).

135 Bruce Bawer, While Europe Slept: How Radical Islam is Destroying the West from Within (2006).

136 *See* Phillips, *supra* note 134, at xi.

137 Phillips, *supra* note 134, at xi.

138 Phillips, *supra* note 134, at xi.

139 Bawer, *supra* note 135, at 34.

night and returned home where she met her parents' fury; several male family members insisted that she be murdered. Her parents forgave her and she agreed to an arranged marriage. Bawer explained, "When she traveled with her father to Iraq for the ceremony, however, it turned out that her family had arranged not for a marriage but a murder. An Iraqi court sentenced Atroshi's father and uncle to five months' probation for the crime. The reason for the lenient sentence was that their 'motive was honorable.'"[140]

Relying on a European Union report, Bawer also summarizes a series of anti-Semitic incidents between 2002 and 2003, some moving beyond vandalism to violence, and points to the pattern of tepid responses in Britain, France, and Scandinavia, which he attributes to efforts "'not to upset the Muslim community.'"[141] He also emphasizes that many of the incidents occur in schools where young people enact what they have heard at home, in the mosque, and through Arab-language media.[142]

Bawer turns to the March 11, 2004 bombings in the Madrid train stations that killed 200 and wounded thousands more, and the subsequent election of a Socialist government that vowed to loosen its ties with the United States and to withdraw troops from Iraq.[143] Protesters then blamed the Spanish government and its prior support for U.S. policy in Iraq for the terrorist attack.[144] Bawer argues that Western Europeans in general have the delusion that they have no enemies, and instead live in a multicultural political community of tolerance and collegiality.[145] He concludes that even after the Madrid bombings, "most of the Western European establishment continued to embrace the pretense of Islamist terrorism as too complex, too ambiguous, and too nuanced a problem to make possible a direct, forceful response."[146] He warns that Western Europe may succumb to radical Islam through appeasement of Islamic militants and deference to new immigrants.[147] His evidence includes reports of an Italian trial of writer Oriana Fallaci for "vilification of Islam," another trial of Ayann Hirsi Ali for making derogatory comments about Islam, and a new Norwegian law passed in 2005 that prohibits discriminatory

140 BAWER, *supra* note 135, at 24.

141 BAWER, *supra* note 35, at 145. He describes an initial report, *Manifestations of an Anti-Semitism in the European Union*, commissioned by the European Monitoring Center on Racism and Xenophobia, and prepared by the Center for Research on Anti-Semitism, that was not released apparently due to desires to avoid naming Muslims as the offenders, and a later report making clear that most of the perpetrators were young Muslim males—and a press release suppressing that conclusion. BAWER, *supra* note 135, at 143–44.

142 BAWER, *supra* note 135, at 143–44.

143 BAWER, *supra* note 135, at 153–57.

144 BAWER, *supra* note 135, at 158.

145 BAWER, *supra* note 135, at 158–82.

146 BAWER, *supra* note 135, at 158.

147 BAWER, *supra* note 135, at 158–72.

comments on the basis of skin color, ethnicity, religion, or sexual orientation and presuming guilt until the accused can disprove it.[148] Bawer concludes that Europe's enemy is not radical Islam but Europe's own passivity and appeasement.[149]

These are obviously polemical views, affected by Bawer's own shock to encounter anti-gay insults and harassment in Europe at the hands of Moslem residents, though his account is echoed by other authors without that experience who write similar warnings about the new Europe.[150] These narratives each portray neighborhoods in and outside of European cities in which young men of Arab backgrounds become targets for recruitment to radical Islam, as both local and distant religious leaders convey their messages through schools, mosques, private gatherings, satellite dishes, and the internet.

The narratives charging "too much tolerance" propose or imply concrete policy measures in response. To guard against the specters of illiberalism within liberal societies—and to end hospitality for hatred and terrorism, Europe must root out recruitment to radical Islam, and lift the handcuffs from governments so that they can protect the citizens of democracies from dangers in their midst.

Legal authors in particular often propose steps Europeans have failed to take that could guard against too much tolerance and might check forces of illiberal recruitment:

- *Permit punishment for any who preach hatred* Against Israel and Jews, coalition forces in Iraq, or against Americans?[151] Speeches and sermons encouraging young people to join the "global jihad" may be protected by laws protecting speech and religious expression. Britain's Terrorism Act of 2000 does permit charges against individuals for incitement of terrorist acts abroad,[152] and Scotland Yard investigated a Muslim cleric Sheikh Omar Bakri Muhammad for allegedly

148 Bawer, *supra* note 135, at 216–17.

149 Bawer, *supra* note 135, at 233.

150 Mark Steyn, America Alone: The End of the World as We Know It (2006); Bat Ye'Or, Eurabia: The Euro-Arab Axis (2002).

151 In the United States, a Muslim preacher named Ali Al-timimi was prosecuted and convicted in federal district court for urging eight followers to join the fight against Americans before the expected invasion of in Afghanistan. Jerry Markon, *Jurors Convict Muslim Leader in Terrorism Case*, Wash. Post, Apr. 27, 2005, at A1. For a complex view of the case, *see* Milton Viorst, *The Education of Ali Al-timimi*, The Atlantic Monthly, June 2006, at 68.

152 Terrorism Act of 2000, Part IV, § 59: (1) A person commits an offence if—

(a) he incites another person to commit an act of terrorism wholly or partly outside the United Kingdom, and

(b) the act would, if committed in England and Wales, constitute one of the offences listed in subsection (2).

available at http://www.opsi.gov.uk/Acts/acts2000/0001 1--g.htm#56.

inciting terrorism and hatred.[153] Great Britain banned him from the country,[154] but some critics charge that the government has been slow and insufficient in pursuing incitement to hatred and terrorism. Prosecutors took three years to indict the former lead preacher in Finsbury Park Mosque of London for urging people to kill non-Muslims, especially Jews.[155] The bombing of the London subway in July 2005 galvanized Parliament to adopt the Terrorism Act of 2006, which criminalizes publication of statements that directly or indirectly encourage or induce others to commit or prepare acts of terrorism.[156] It also allows prosecutions of such acts even when they are committed outside of Britain.

- Shut or tightly regulate religious schools—and notably, Muslim schools—to prevent instruction in hatred and recruitment to terrorism.[157] Critics warn that there may be special perils when the schools are funded by groups outside the country, if the curriculum is supplied by another country, or if the teachers' training and loyalty tie them to another country, and if the schools teach hatred or incite people to join Islamic jihad militant groups. Muted but still genuine warnings persist about the religious schools that manifest and pass on views about women and homosexuals that conflict with the equality, liberty, and privacy commitments of the liberal democracy that permits the schools to exist. The English Chief Inspector of Schools urged Muslim schools to make sure that their students "acquire an appreciation of and respect for other cultures in

153 *Islamic Cleric 'Incitement' Probe*, BBC News, Jan. 18, 2005, *available at* http://news.bbc.co.uk/1/hi/uk/4185085.stm; Don vanNatta Jr. & Lowell Berman, *Militant Imams Under Scrutiny Across Europe;* N.Y. Times, Jan. 25, 2005, at A1.

154 Andrew Alderson, *Ex-UK Cleric 'Inspired Plot to Kidnap Soldier,'* Telegraph, May 2, 2007, http://www.telegraph.co.uk/news/main.jhtml?xml=/news/2007/02/04/nterr104.xml.

155 Kenneth Lasson, *Incitement in the Mosques: Testing the Limits of Free Speech and Religious Liberty*, 27 Whittier L. Rev. 3, 15–16 (2005).

156 The Act places criminal sanctions on one who publishes "a statement that is likely to be understood by some or all of the members of the public to whom it is published as a direct or indirect encouragement or other inducement to them to the commission, preparation or instigation of acts of terrorism or Convention offences." Indirect encouragement statements include every statement which "glorifies the commission or preparation (whether in the past, in the future or generally) of such acts or offences; and is a statement from which those members of the public could reasonably be expected to infer that what is being glorified is being glorified as conduct that should be emulated by them in existing circumstances." Terrorism Act of 2006, *available at* http://www.opsi.gov.uk/acts/acts2006/ukpga_20060011_en.pdf (last visited Apr. 20, 2007).

157 *See* Cymrot, *supra* note 3. *See also* Kumquat Ali Kahn, *The Essentialist Terrorist*, 45 Washburn L.J. 47, 84 (2005). Short of closing or tightly regulating Muslim schools, a government could create a rival Muslim school that teaches the Qu'ran and Arabic but compatibly with secular Western norms; similarly, government or other actors could try to compete with Al-jezera by producing compelling Arabic-language mass media that does not espouse hatred of the West, Jews, or secularism. Competing for attention in these ways, however, would be viewed by some as giving up on the ideal of assimilation. Yet assimilation to the secular world may be too unattractive—and private choice may be too hands-off—if the shape of the entire polity is shifting through the practices of newcomers.

a way that promotes tolerance and harmony," ensure encouragement of higher education for girls and guard against demeaning people in same-sex relationships, and recommended government monitoring of faith schools to ensure instruction in the common heritage of Britain.[158] Muslim leaders reacted with hurt and anger over what they perceived to be biased and unfair concerns about Muslim schools.[159] Similarly, in pursuit of the greater social integration of Muslims, the British government proposed and then, in the face of opposition, withdrew a requirement that state-sponsored, faith-based schools admit twenty-five percent of students from another religion.[160]

- *Prohibit political parties that seek to undermine liberal democracy.* Precautionary steps to prevent the subversion of democracy through its own liberal processes represent another set of policies to remedy what some charge as Europe's insufficient response to the terrorist threat. Memories of the Nazi rise to power initially through elections during the Weimar Republic make this a concrete concern for many in Europe. Germany specifically forbids political parties that threaten the free basic democratic order,[161] and has banned both the neo-Nazi party and the Communist party on that basis.

To prevent threats to democracy and individual rights, the Turkish Constitutional Court banned the Refah party in 1998. That political party planned to introduce Islamic law into the country's governance scheme—proposing to divide the society into religious orders which in turn would govern each individual, contrary to the separation of religion and government in Turkey's constitution.[162] The Refah party defended its proposal as a kind of voluntary private law, but others viewed it as the end of the secular state. When the country's high court dissolved the party, the party had already gained twenty-two percent of the popular vote and Turkey's own prime minister was a member of the party.[163] The European Court of Human Rights affirmed the dissolution of the party, despite alleged violations of the freedom of association protected by Article 11 of the European Convention on Human Rights.

---

158 Polly Curtis, *Faith Schools 'Failing to Teach Obligation to Society,'* GUARDIAN UNLIMITED, Jan. 17, 2005, *available at* http://education.guardian.co.uk/ofsted/story/0,,1392274,00.html.

159 Sean Coughlan, *Muslim Schools 'Deeply Upset,'* BBC, Jan. 18, 2005, *available at* http://news.bbc.co.uk/2/hi/uk_news/education/4184319.stm.

160 Mike Baker, *Why the U-Turn on Faith Schools?*, BBC, Nov. 4, 2006, *available at* http://news.bbc.co.uk/2/hi/uk_news/education/6114938.stm. For debates over Saudi funding for Muslim schools in Germany, and over whether German Muslims as well as children of diplomats can attend religious schools that are not subject to a state-approved curriculum, *see* Cymrot, *supra* note 153, at 612–13.

161 Art. 21, German Basic Law. For similar bans, *see* Patrick Macklem, Militant Democracy, Legal Pluralism, and the Paradox of Self-Determination, at 8–9, (U. Toronto, Legal Studies Research Paper No. 05–03, April 2005), *available at* http://ssrn.com/abstract=702465.

162 Rafeh Partisi (the Welfare Party), and Others v. Turkey, application nos. 413040.87, 41342/98, 41343/98 and 41344/98 (2001). *See also* Macklem, *supra* note 157.

163 Macklem, *supra* note 157, at 28.

The court found the dissolution of the party a fair means to protect state institutions from an association that itself jeopardizes democracy by threatening to impose religious law and undermines the state's ability to ensure individual rights and liberties. The Court also specifically found Islamic law incompatible with fundamental democratic principles.[164]

Other democratic nations, committed to free speech and elections, may face potential electoral victory of parties that would dismantle national liberal commitments.[165] If so, these countries would need, in advance of any crisis, to establish a constitutional basis for banning such a party that would itself undo liberal democratic norms—a formal intolerance for intolerance.[166]

Stand back and consider the two narratives of reactions to terrorism—both under-response and over-response, too much tolerance and not enough. The overreaction threatens freedom, privacy, and equality. But the under-reaction could do so as well. To fix the under-reaction, to awaken to the dangers, Europe could regulate preaching, teaching, and religious and political associations;[167] it could extend detentions without charges—and then government methods would contradict the ends of a liberal democracy.[168] Once again, the dilemma of tolerance returns, but now with stark programmatic choices. Should a liberal democracy try to prevent terrorism through measures that themselves vitiate liberal democratic values?

IV. RECONSIDERING THE PROBLEM

The narratives of U.S. overreaction to terrorism and European under-reaction reflect not only differences in the policies taken but also in the constellation of internal political pressures affecting each. Certainly, important differences in history, demography, economics, and politics can explain diverging patterns in responses to terror by the United States and European nations. With the first major external terrorist attack within the United States in decades—and the largest in the world—post-9/11 responses reflect both the shock of vulnerability and the scale that may distinguish recent U.S. experience from the experiences of European nations.[169]

164 *See* Rafeh Partisi, *supra* note 162, at para. 123.

165 *See* Issacharoff, *supra* note 4.

166 Careful analysis should also attend to the success of Islamic groups in mobilizing youth in the context of apparently secular authoritarian states. *See* Carrie Rosefy Wickham, Mobilizing Islam: Religion, Activism, and Political Change in Egypt (2002).

167 Should governments have authority, as in the United States, to use law enforcement against individuals who raise funds for groups with terrorist ties even without evidence of specific intention to pursue the illegal goals? *See* Laura K. Donahue, *Terrorist Speech and the Future of Free Expression*, 27 Cardozo L. Rev. 233, 318–19 (2005).

168 *See* Andrew Tully, *Can West Fight Terror and Still Maintain Civil Liberties* (part 3), Radio Free Europe Radio Liberty, Oct. 7, 2005, *available at* http://www.rferl.org/featuresarticle/2005/10/a6fbd4c9-808d-4fe6-81d9-f79b908f08b5.html.

169 Richardson, *supra* note 109.

Responses to Muslims reflect the different national histories and ideologies in the United States and in European countries such as Germany, France, and the Netherlands. The self-conception as a nation of immigrants, the route to becoming American by being an outsider,[170] the patterns of economic and social mobility, and the availability of jobs and entrepreneurial opportunities affect the reception of Muslims in America—as does the persistence of a racialized underclass, filling the social position of the societal bottom. The contrasting conceptions of nationality linked to ethnicity and blood, the unemployment rates, and new encounters with racialized differences precisely when the European Union destabilizes what it means to be "Dutch" or "French" or "German" contribute to uneasy attitudes by old-time residents toward Muslims in Amsterdam, Paris, and Frankfurt. The relatively small percentage of Muslim immigrants hovering at one percent in the United States contrasts with five percent across Western Europe,[171] heavier concentrations rising to ten percent in France,[172] and far greater percentages in specific regions of Paris, Amsterdam, and London.[173] When connected with the low birthrate among longstanding European residents and the high birthrate among immigrants, some predict that 1 in 5 Europeans will be Muslim in the next decades,[174] and some Western observers predict that Europe will become Islamic over time.[175] And the secularization of Europe—perhaps abetted by a lack of formal state support of religion—contrasts sharply with the religiosity of new immigrants, while immigrants can match many Americans with their religiosity.[176]

But in fact the stories of under-reaction resonate within the United States and the narrative of overreaction may have its echo in Europe. Thus, Thomas Carothers of

---

170 *See* R. LAURENCE MOORE, THE RELIGIOUS OUTSIDER AND THE MAKING OF AMERICANS (1987).

171 RICHARDSON, *supra* note 109, at 237.

172 Muslim Population Worldwide, http://www.islamicpopulation.com/europe_islam.html.

173 "Muslims made up 8 per cent [*sic*] of London's population overall but 36 per cent [*sic*] of the Tower Hamlets and 24 per cent [*sic*] of the Newham populations." National Statistics Online, http://www.statistics.gov.uk/cci/nugget.asp?id=956 (last visited Apr. 20, 1007).

174 Evan Osnos, *Islam Shaping a New Europe: Staking Out Their Place in Europe,* CHI. TRIB., Dec. 19, 2004, at C01.

175 *See* Daniel Pipes, *Muslim Europe*, N.Y. SUN, May 11, 2004, at 9; *Muslims in Europe: Country Guide*, http:/news.bbc.co.uk/2/hi/europe/4385768.stm. For commentary perspectives, *see* ORIANA FALLACI, THE FORCE OF REASON; Omer Taspinar, *Europe's Muslim Street*, FOREIGN POLICY, March 2003, *available at* http://www.brook.edu/views/op-ed/fellows/taspinar20030301.htm; Osnos, *supra* note 174; Robert S. Leiken, *Europe's Angry Muslims*, FOREIGN AFFAIRS, July /Aug. 2005, at 120.

176 Hume advised governments to create secular society by establishing a state church and undermining the entrepreneurship of religious groups. DAVID HUME, AN ENQUIRY CONCERNING HUMAN UNDERSTANDING; DIALOGUES AND NATURAL HISTORY OF RELIGION (1748). *See also* CHARLES GLENN, THE AMBIGUOUS EMBRACE (2000) (documenting decline in religiosity in Europe alongside state support for religious institutions). In contrast, work on religious entrepreneurship in the United States, past and present—with mega churches; R. LAWRENCE MOORE, RELIGIOUS OUTSIDERS AND THE MAKING (1987).

the Democracy and Rule of Law Program at the Carnegie Endowment for International Peace argues that Europe has overreacted to terrorism by curbing civil liberties, while the United States, with its traditional suspicion of government, has remained measured, except—and it's a big exception—in its victimization of immigrants.[177]

Others warn of American under-reaction when it comes to speech and expression.[178] Dennis Pluchinsky, Senior Intelligence Analyst in the U.S. Department of State, has called for censorship in the United States because media accounts could reveal vulnerabilities in food supply, electricity, chemical production, transportation, and border security.[179]

It is possible to view the United States as under-regulating hate speech and political activity that aims to overthrow democracy, when compared with the French and Germany hate speech bans and the German prohibition of political parties that would challenge liberal democracy. That such steps might well violate the U.S. Constitution is taken simply to be further evidence of U.S. failures to address terrorist risks seriously.[180] Note how this set of constitutional restraints is not up for debate, even though the executive branch strains other constitutional limits. If the constitution is not a suicide pact, and the danger is severe enough, some argue that this country should regulate hate speech,[181] religious school messages,[182] political parties opposed to liberal democracy,[183] and some forms of privacy. Moreover, the United States looks like it is under-responding when compared with Britain's

---

177 Quoted in Tully, *supra* note 168, at Part 3. *See also* Thomas Carothers, *Promoting Democracy and Fighting Terror*, Foreign Affairs, Jan.–Feb. 2003, at 84; Paula J. Dobriansky & Thomas Carothers, *Democracy Promotion*, Foreign Affairs, May/June 2003, at 141.

178 The closest discussion comes with historical arguments. For example, Yale Professor Paul Kennedy compares the situation currently faced by the United States with Britain's in the nineteenth century, and concludes that the United States is in a more difficult predicament mainly because of the openness of today's world. Strobe Talbott, The Age of Terror: America and the World after September 11 (2002).

179 Dennis Pluchinsky, *They Heard It all Here, and That's the Trouble*, Wash. Post, June 15, 2002, at B03.

180 See Frederick Schauer, *Freedom of Expression Adjudication in Europe and the United States: A Case Study in Comparative Constitutional Architecture, in* European and U.S. Constitutionalism 47–74 (GeorgNolteed., 2005).

181 *See* John C. Knechtle, *When to Regulate Hate Speech*, 100 Penn. St. L.R. 539 (2006) (describing the differences between hate speech restrictions in Europe and the United States). *See also* Keith B. Richburg & Alan Cooperman, *Swede's Sermon on Gays: Bigotry or Free Speech?; Pastor Challenges Hate-Law Restrictions*, Wash. Post, Jan. 29, 2005, at A01.

182 There could even be problems with requiring public or private schools to teach tolerance if private schools framed challenges to such a requirement as content-based compelled speech, burdens on religious freedom, or unconstitutional conditions on public funding. *See* Cymrot, *supra* note 3.

183 See Shawn Boyne, *The Future of Liberal Democracies in a Time* of *Terror: A Comparison of the Impact on Civil Liberties in the Federal Republic of Germany and the United States, 11*

extensive use of face recognition cameras and national I.D. cards with biometrics. Failures to devise increased security for chemical plants, water works, cargo shipments, and nuclear material that could end up in terrorist hands also look like underreaction, given security analyses and expert recommendations.[184] And, undoing even the categories of over- and under-reaction are the critics of the war in Iraq for its effect in escalating international recruitment of young disaffected Muslims by jihadists opposed to the United States, globalization, and secularism.[185]

Great Britain in fact is criticized for both over- and underreacting. When Prime Minister Tony Blair proposed extending government power to detain people without charges for 90 days, he and his party suffered defeat not only of the proposal but general diminution of his authority.[186] Critics claimed that the detention proposal was an overreaction, but Blair's proposal and related initiatives grew from concerns that Britain generally has failed to take sufficient actions to anticipate and quell terrorist risks.[187] Others charge Great Britain with underreacting to terrorist threats by indulging Muslim fundamentalists' hate speech and failing to cooperate with other nations seeking to extradite a terrorist suspect.[188] With heightened scrutiny

---

TULSA J. COMP. & INT'L L. 111 (2003); Yigal Mersel, *The Dissolution of Political Parties: The Problem of Internal Democracy*, 4 INT'L J. CONST. L. 84 (2006).

184 *See* GRAHAM ALLISON, NUCLEAR TERRORISM: THE ULTIMATE PREVENTABLE CATASTROPHE 104 (2004) (explaining the weaknesses in port, cargo, and facility security); Dan Eggen & Spence S. Hsu, *Democrats Still Face Hurdles in Enacting 9/11 Panel's Ideas*, WASH. POST, Nov. 11, 2006, at A03 (describing the proposals of the 9/11 Commission and the difficulties of enacting them); Sally Goldenberg, *Mayor Faults Way Anti-Terror Funds are Allocated*, STATEN ISLAND ADVANCE, Jan. 10, 2007, at A08 (detailing Mayor Bloomberg's assessment that the federal government should provide more funding for port and cargo security).

185 *See* Jessica Stern, *How America Created a Terrorist Haven*, THINKING PEACE, Aug. 20, 2003, http://www.thinkingpeace.com/pages/Articles/Archive 1/arts021.html.

186 *Blair Defeated Over Terror Laws*, BBC NEWS, Nov. 9, 2005, *available at* http://news.bbc.co.uk/1/hi/uk_politics/4422086.stm; *A Failure of Political Judgment*, GUARDIAN, Nov. 11, 2005, *available at* http://www.guardian.co.uk/leaders/story/0,3604,1639795,00.html. *See also*, Souad Mekhennet & Dexter Filkins, *British Law Against Glorifying Terrorism Has Not Silenced Calls to Kill for Islam*, N.Y. TIMES, Aug. 21, 2006, at A8 (Parliament did approve detentions for twenty eight days).

187 *See also* Virginia Mantouvalou, *Council of Europe: UK Anti-Terrorism Measures Fall Short of European Standards*, EUROPEAN CIVIL LIBERTIES NETWORK, Apr. 10, 2007, http://www.ecln.org/essays/essay-5.pdf (summarizing criticisms of the European Committee for the Prevention of Torture about conditions of detention under Anti-Terrorism, Crime and Security Act of 2001 and criticism of Prevention of Terrorism Act of 2005).

188 *See* John Kampfner, *It is Easier to Diminish Our Freedoms Than to Root Out The Terrorist*, THE INDEPENDENT, Aug. 7, 2005, www.findarticles.com/p/articles/mi_qn4159/is_20050807/ai_n14862538 (discussing criticisms of Britain for harboring terrorists and giving them freedom to act, for blocking extradition of Rashid Rama, a person accused of bombing the Paris Metro, and allowing fundamentalists to incite violence). *See also* RANDALL L. SCHWELLER, UNANSWERED THREATS: POLITICAL CONSTRAINTS ON THE BALANCE OF POWER (2006); Randall L. Schweller, *Unanswered Threats: A Neoclassical Realist Theory of Underbalancing*, 29 INT'L SECURITY 159 (2004) (devising a theory to explain why nations fail to respond to threats).

of immigrants since the London and Madrid bombings, anti-immigrant politics also increased in Europe. Moderate Muslims argue that British foreign policy is radicalizing residents with immigrant roots, just as photographs of abusive treatment at the Abu Ghraib prison probably promoted recruitment by racial Islamic terrorist networks.[189]

What might we learn by reading the narratives or over- and under-reaction together? We could learn that any liberal democracy can be criticized both for over- and under-reacting to terror. Perhaps this simply reflects diverging views about the right balance. But alternatively it could reveal how misdirected policies can constrain liberties and target minorities without increasing safety for resident populations. The reversibility and simultaneity of narratives of over- and under-reaction might well be a clue to a defect in the analysis that links security and tolerance. Policies invading civil rights and civil liberties can in fact distract from security measures that would not impair rights. Looking at the narratives of under- and over-reaction together, we could come to the following: (1) to focus on measures to increase security without increasing intolerance, and (2) to address unsatisfactory reception of minorities and treatment of immigrants without confusing these with security issues.

A. Improving Security

A crucial difficulty comes in measuring government responses to terrorism. Terrorism, well defined by Louise Richardson as "deliberately and violently targeting civilians for political purposes," is a means, advocated and used by a variety of individuals and groups, with quite a range of techniques. Assessing growth or reduction in the threats of terrorism is not only complex but elusive as a target.[190] Confining the focus to al-Qaeda, given its role in 9/11 in 2001, the 2005 bombings of the London underground, the 2004 Madrid commuter train bombings, and the 1998 and 2000 bombings of U.S. embassies in Kenya and Tanzania helps little. What are the measures to tell if terror risks are reduced when the risks come from a set of secret self-replenishing global networks of potential terrorists? A repressive government can defend its repression by pointing to the absence of new attacks without beginning to demonstrate that the repression itself was responsible. A government can announce that it has "foiled" terrorist plots when in fact the suspects had no serious plan or only plans developed with government enticement.[191] But "sleeper cells" of

189 Richardson, *supra* note 109.

190 *See* Richardson, *supra* note 109, at 4. "To declare war on what is, after all, a tactic does not appear to make a great deal of sense.... There were, of course, alternatives available to declaring war on terrorism, terror, and evil. The administration might, for example, have declared war on al-Qaeda or on Afghanistan, the state that harbored it. Had it done so, there would have been some clear matrices of success or failure by which progress could have been measured." Richardson, *supra* note 109, at 175.

191 Rudolph Bush & Jeff Coen, *Man Held in Terror Plot Near Rockford*, Chi. Tri., Dec. 10, 2006, at C3 (describing the arrest of Derrick Shareef for discussing an attack and acquiring grenades

terrorists can in fact persist anywhere in the world, and plans can be decades in the making. Geopolitical changes and economic opportunities affect the prospects of al-Qaeda. The "war on terror" waged in Afghanistan and Iraq and economic stagnation in parts of Europe seem to have increased the recruitment activities and yield for al-Qaeda.[192]

The quandary compounds as the risk of home-grown terrorists grows. Terrorists can hide out within a free society and that very freedom constrains efforts to locate them. Those nations that have defeated terrorism, like Argentina and Brazil, did so through domestic deployment of military death squads, torture, surveillance, and internal repression—all forbidden within and contrary to the norms of a democratic society.[193] With the mounting concern of homegrown terrorists, any disaffected teen or any disillusioned twenty-something could answer the call of the satellite dish. Thus large swathes of that generation and those that follow become suspect. If you are skeptical of such speculations, then steps such as national ID cards, street-corner face recognition technology, and airport screenings are overreactions. Indeed, absent evidence that diminishing civil liberties and targeting Muslims and immigrants actually reduce risks of terrorism, there seems to be a kind of magical thinking in policies that link the two. It is as if we imagine that by sacrificing our values, we will make ourselves safer.[194] If it hurts us (or hurts others), we ward off danger. Perhaps it would improve analyses to de-link security policies from the preoccupations with tolerance; policies in each area are difficult enough to design and assess, and the link between them difficult to diffuse.

There remain many policies to promote security that have nothing to do with immigration or civil liberties. These include safeguarding nuclear materials and materials that could be turned into biological weapons, protecting vulnerable targets like water supplies and chemical plans, monitoring all cargo through shipping ports, creating surveillance cameras with face recognition software read only by computers until there is a sufficient match with terror suspects to satisfy legal search requirements, and building and improving intelligence services including

---

from undercover FBI agents); *7 Suspects Allegedly Plotting to Attack Sears Tower Arrested in Miami*, Chic. Tri., June 23, 2006, at 8 (describing the arrest of seven Miami men after they held "criminal discussions"); Jerry Seper, *FBI Foils New York Terror Plot; Lebanese Arrest One in Tunnels-Attack Plan*, Wash. Times, July 8, 2006, at A01 (describing a thwarted terrorist attack as "aspirational, rather than operational").

192 National Intelligence Estimate, Trends in Global Terrorism: Implications for the United States (2006), *available at* http://www/dni.gov/press_releases/Declassified_NIE_Key_Judgments.pdf (last visited Apr. 20, 2007); *Stating the Obvious: Terrorism and Iraq*, The Economist, Sept. 30, 2006 (describing al-Qaeda's increasing strength since the Iraq invasion). Richardson suggests that, "To be elevated to the status of public enemy number one is just what a terrorist group wants. It gives the group stature among its potential recruits, which in turn wins it more followers. Declaring war on terrorists, in effect, hands it the renown it seeks." Richardson, *supra* note 109, at 177.

193 Richardson, *supra* note 109, at 183–84.

194 *See* Galison & Minow, *supra* note 116, at 258–94.

the language capacity of agents. Each of these steps not yet taken in the United States would make us more secure without jeopardizing freedoms or tolerance.[195] Specifying goals keyed to enhancing security would have the benefits of measurable targets and also would put to the side confused and easily manipulable ideas about how treatment of immigrants, Muslims, and other minority members affects national security.

One vital connection with immigrant communities and terrorism worth further exploration involves the resources those communities offer to assist law enforcement and intelligence activities. Louise Richardson, an expert on terrorism, reports that "[e]very government that has faced a threat from terrorism has found that good intelligence has been the most crucial weapon in its armory." She reviewed evidence from Venezuela, France, Peru, Israel, and Great Britain that underscored her point.[196] One approach would be to replace ethnic and religious profiling with behavioral profiling.[197] Another would be to develop deep partnerships between government officials and members of American Muslim, Arab, and Sikh communities to develop domestic intelligence.[198] Experts in terrorism emphasize the central role of intelligence resources and criticize the failures in coordinating intelligence and law enforcement activities in the United States.[199] Besides generating potentially critical information about the presence—and absence—of risks, such efforts could communicate as little else could that individuals in these groups are trusted and valued members of the larger society.

If risks of homegrown terrorism are massive, the only precedents for success in defeating it require degrees of repression and authoritarian rule that no liberal democracy has taken or could pursue while remaining a liberal democracy.[200] This very prospect raises a new dilemma of tolerance: how can the society communicate tolerance when it also summons suspicion of everyone, and especially of those who already feel marginal?

195 *See* Minow, *The Constitution as Black Box During National Emergencies: Comment on Bruce Ackerman's Before the Next Attack: Preserving Civil Liberties in an Age of Terrorism*, 75 Fordham L. Rev. 593, 601–02 (2006); Daniel Benjamin & Steven Simon, The Next Attack: the Failure of the War on Terror and a Strategy for Getting It Right (2005).

196 Richardson, *supra* note 109, at 210.

197 *See* Harris, *supra* note 100.

198 Ramirez & Woldenberg, *supra* note 79, at 501–11.

199 Richardson, *supra* note 109; Eben Kaplan, *Examining Counterterrorism Culture*, Council on Foreign Relations, Apr. 10, 2007, http://www.cfr.org/publication/11922/#2; DoD USS Cole Commission Report (2001), http://www.defenselink.mil/pubs/cole20010109.html; Philip B. Heymann & Juliette Kayyem, Protecting Liberty in an Age of Terror (2005) (based upon the published report "Long-Term Legal Strategy Project for Preserving Security and Democratic Freedoms in the War on Terror"); Philip B. Heymann, Terrorism, Freedom, and Security: Winning Without War (2003).

200 *Id.*

B. Improving Treatment of Minority Groups and Their Members

Improving the treatment of minority groups and their members should be a priority for the United States and Europe quite separate from security concerns. Thinking about this topic distinctly clarifies what the dimensions are that are relevant to enhancing security. Adhering to national values of equal and fair treatment and restricting government intrusions strengthen the nation's legitimacy among its residents and outside observers. Fair and equal treatment has, of course, intrinsic value. Moreover, reducing reasons for alienation is a practical, indeed a vital, step in preventing recruitment by radical terrorists or the ranks of those who sympathize with them.[201]

By contrast, a government that tries to justify intolerant measures in the name of tolerance risks alienating both the targets and the observers of such measures. British journalist Mick Hume commented, "Some of us are finding it increasingly hard to tolerate the way that appeals to British tolerance are being used to justify intolerant censorship and repression."[202] He then contrasted calls for freedom, tolerance, and respect for others by Prime Minister Tony Blair with plans to criminalize direct and indirect incitement to religious hatred following the bombing of the London subway in July 2005.[203] Hume suggests that new laws punishing incitement are unnecessary, given existing criminal laws and the minute threat posed by "a few crank preachers."[204]

If used, would such new laws be counterproductive? Yes, Hume argues, because such prosecutions would create martyrs to inspire disaffected Muslim youth.[205] Further, a law punishing people for ridiculing Islam in the name of cultural sensitivity is, according to Hume, "far more likely to intensify a sense of grievance on all sides: among Muslims who might feel that the continual calls for tolerance and condemnations of 'Islamophobia' confirm their special victim status in society; and among white people who might feel aggrieved at being lectured and policed as if they were a mob of bigots straining at the leash to burn down a mosque or beat up a Muslim."[206] Hume makes just a guess, however, just as it is a guess that those who cited free speech commitments when printing and reprinting cartoons that most Muslims found offensive also enjoyed offending the newcomers in their midst. Even principles of freedom can be pushed in ways that betray nationalist or intolerant motives or become instruments for resentment.

---

201 Richardson, *supra* note 109, at 215–17.

202 Mick Hume, *The Age of Intolerant Tolerance*, Spiked, Aug. 19, 2005, http://www.spiked-online.com/index.php?/site/article/815/. (Hume identifies himself as an "[a]ngry middle-aged libertarian Marxist;" he is also a journalist for The Times).

203 *Id.*

204 *Id.*

205 *Id.*

206 *Id.*

The empirical record is simply too confusing for us to know whether any of these predictions is right—and whether suppressing speech to enhance tolerance in any particular context is elusive. Does tolerance advance by publishing the Danish cartoons of Mohammed or by refraining from doing so because of the insult many Muslims read into them? Is tolerance aided by authorizing and subsidizing Muslim schools, or by directing Muslims to secular public schools, or by regulating all public and private schools to ensure that they teach tolerance and respect across different religious, ethnic, and racial groups?

A commitment to curb speech and equality protections—to increase intolerance—only when there is strong evidence that security requires such measures would provide a useful guide. Another useful rule would universalize security restrictions—to minimize real and perceived targeting of minority groups. For security purposes, the Muslim woman might well have to remove her veil for an identification photo—if all others must also show their faces for such photos. The curriculum and hiring practices of Islamic private schools should be regulated in the same degree that other private schools face government review. Profiling by race and nationality for criminal and terrorist suspects could be avoided both by more specific details in the profiles or via more general searches.[207] If universalizing security measures prompts the objection that civil liberties would be too much invaded, then the issue would be properly presented as one affecting everyone. There is a risk that some would use even this development as a pretext for curbing civil liberties and expanding law enforcement power, but broad coalitions would more likely respond to universal restrictions than to ones that fall largely on minority groups.

It would help to unwind the paradox of tolerance—and to identify good policies—if we acknowledge that "tolerance" signals a particular, substantive vision, not a neutral or nonjudgmental stance. Tolerance strives to be inclusive in terms of respecting all persons, yet tolerance also means to differ with and even rebuke intolerant views. Those who pursue tolerance should not be embarrassed about the substance of their commitments: to open-mindedness, criticisms, and self-criticisms. If this is not what tolerance means, then we probably should forget "tolerance" and embrace these values of open inquiry alongside cultural literacy, inclusion, and respect for all members of society.

Switching the framework from tolerance to equality offers more promise for improving Western treatment of minority groups and viewpoints—and of recent immigrants and their families. It is preferable to focus on anti-subordination, rather than tolerance, a concept that embeds its own advice in hierarchical power relationships. Political theorist Herbert Marcuse launched this kind of analysis in his *Critique of Pure Tolerance*

207 *See* Ramirez & Woldenberg, *supra* note 79. Technology and intelligence information can work together to produce refined techniques, avoiding crude profiling by race or nationality. *See New Israeli System IDs Terrorists Without Profiling*, http://www.worldtribune.com/worldtribune/05/front2453545.904861111.html (last visited Apr. 10, 2007).

in 1970,[208] and Wendy Brown's 2006 book, *Regulating Aversion: Tolerance in the Age of Identity and Empire*, brings such an approach up to date by encompassing not only political dissenters but identity politics.[209] Brown criticizes invocations of tolerance for presuming and maintaining a hierarchical power structure;[210] she argues that tolerance poses as universal and neutral when it is instead particular and culturally tied to Western Europe and the United States.[211] Brown claims that people may invoke "tolerance" to try to legitimate violent war and imperialist aspirations.[212] Tolerance discussion these days reduces people to their groups' memberships or identities rather than engaging with their beliefs.[213] In addition, Brown states that talk of tolerance obscures politics by treating issues in terms of interpersonal ethics rather than power struggles.[214]

To Brown, tolerance as a concept may simply cover the arrogance of personal and national power, disguising such power from those smug enough to offer it but not from those insulted enough to know it is less than real respect. Brown may well be right, although her account neglects the multiple power relationships in contemporary societies. Occupants of different economic and social statuses—rich and poor, longtime residents and new immigrants—can offer or withhold forbearance, or direct scorn toward one another. A Muslim resident of Norway who spits on a gay couple may occupy a lower economic class and more tenuous political status, but he still has the power to wound a member of a different minority group by disapproval . . . or by fists.

Addressing mutual respect and civility in a multi-ethnic society is hard enough without imagining that this is a key beachhead in the war against terrorism. Concerns about security permeate the mutual distrust between longstanding residents and Muslim immigrants in Europe, even in nations that extend money and rights to newcomers. The newcomers—and their children and grandchildren—may

208 *See* Robert Paul, Barrington Moore & Herbert Marcuse, Critique of Pure Tolerance (1970); Herbert Marcuse, One Dimensional Man: Studies in the Ideology of Advanced Industrial Society (1964).

209 Brown, *supra* note 20.

210 By invoking tolerance the powerful are able to grant or withhold tolerance, and offer not equality, but at best protection for the less powerful. *See* Brown, *supra* note 20, at 12, 36, 39, 87, 178. Hence, the language of tolerance displaces "articulations of inequality, abjection, subordination, and colonial and postcolonial violence." Brown, *supra* note 20, at 205. This implies that equality rhetoric would work better—but others stress failures of equality rhetoric to acknowledge or remedy social hierarchies. *See, e.g.*, Galeotti, *supra* note 10, at 226–28; Martha Minow, Making all the Difference: Inclusion, Exclusion and American Law (1990).

211 Brown, *supra* note 20, at 7, 21, 31–33, 78, 86.

212 Brown, *supra* note at 37, 99, 103.

213 Brown, *supra* note 20, at 19, 45, 70, 78 (arguing that contemporary tolerance rhetoric, in educational and political settings, equates religion with race, culture, and gender and assumes the tribalism it supposedly rejects).

214 Brown, *supra* note 20, at 13–16, 129.

perceive continual slights and exclusions.[215] Mutual distrust is likely to be exacerbated by public discussions linking policies toward immigrants—whether coercive or supportive—to anti-terrorism.

Finding ways to truly integrate more recent immigrants seems to elude much of Europe. Economic and physical segregation produce parallel lives, but not a common society joining long-standing residents and immigrants—even when the immigrants (and their children and grandchildren)—have spent decades in France, or Germany, or the Netherlands. Ian Buruma urged contemporary Dutch people to discern "how to stop future Mohammed Bouyeris [the murderer of Theo van Gogh] from becoming violent enemies of the country in which they grew up—how to make those boys pissing on the seventeenth-century door feel that this is their home too"[216]—rather than finding ritualized murders or dreams of death as their only way home.

"Home" in this sense need not be a sentimentalized or fictive identification with an alien past, nor need it require the suspension or repression of affinities that draw an individual to identify with traditions, nations, or hopes lying outside the territory in which he or she resides. Feeling entirely "at home" may be elusive to everyone in periods of mass migration and globalization. The very unease that long-time residents have due to the shifting composition of their neighborhoods demonstrates how evanescent the sense of being "at home" can become. But the disproportionate sense of displacement experienced by so many immigrants and their children often gives rise to alienation.[217] And alienation is a crucial element of the toxic cocktail that inspires terrorism.[218]

---

215 The ex-Moslem politician, Ayann Hirsi Ali, and an Eastern European immigrant writer, Dubravka Ugresic, described the public generosity and private conformity of the Dutch. Buruma summarized:

> The generosity of the state toward refugees and other newcomers can lead to a peculiar resentment. The Dutch feel, in Ayaan's words, that since they 'have been so kind' to the foreigners, the foreigners should behave as the Dutch do. Then there is the other kind of resentment, of the recipients of Dutch government largesse, who feel that it is never enough.

Dubravka went on to explain that people from Balkans "develop a criminal mentality in Holland. . . . They think this country is a soft touch." BURUMA, *supra* note 119, at 203. *See also* Sabine Mannitz & Werner Schiffauer, *Taxonomies of Cultural Difference: Constructions of Otherness, in* CIVIL ENCULTURATION: NATION-STATE, SCHOOLS AND ETHNIC DIFFERENCE IN FOUR EUROPEAN COUNTRIES 60, at Epilogue (2004).

216 BURUMA, *supra* note 119, at 240 (Buruma criticized the Dutch for using World War II as their template, and returning to guilt over their behavior during the Holocaust, when the Dutch failed to resist the Germans and turned over their Jewish neighbors).

217 *See* Rose-Anne Clermont, *Integration in Theory, Alienation in Practice*, SPIEGEL ONLINE INTERNATIONAL, Aug. 23, 2006, http://www.spiegel.de/international/0,1518,433006,00.html; CHERIF RIFAAT, IMMIGRANTS ADAPT, COUNTRIES ADOPT . . . OR NOT: FITTING INTO THE CULTURAL MOSAIC (Inc. 2004) (an account based in Canada); ZEEV BEN-SIRA, IMMIGRATION, STRESS, AND READJUSTMENT (1997) (an account based in Israel).

218 *See* RICHARDSON, *supra* note 109; JESSICA STERN, TERROR IN THE NAME OF GOD: WHY RELIGIOUS MILITANTS KILL (2003); JESSICA STERN, THE ULTIMATE TERRORISTS (1999).

Offering a way for newcomers and their children to feel at home is especially challenging when modern technologies of communication and travel allow them to maintain stronger ties outside the new country than they have inside it. Such a challenge, even if grasped and accepted, will require perceptive readings of subtle daily exchanges to unearth and alter the cues of exclusion woven into everyday interactions. Prevailing approaches have not worked, and proceeding with business as usual is not likely to meet either the challenges of terrorist threats or a key test: do the heirs of the immigrants feel at home?

Consider this example. Social scientists observing a German school described a history class addressing Kristallnacht and the attacks on Jewish shops and synagogues during the night of November 9, 1938.[219] A Turkish student asked why the Jews had not fled Germany. The teacher replied by asking why Turks do not flee Germany today, following murders, assaults, and arson attacks against them. The student answered, "Things won't get that bad." The teacher replied, that is what many Jews believed as well and thereby found it difficult to leave, just as a Turk who owns a shop or an apartment in Germany today would find it difficult to leave without his or her possessions.[220] This effort to build on the student's own experience and position in this context may make empathy an ingredient of education—but it also communicates: you, like the Jews, are vulnerable here, there is no long-term future for you here.[221] French schools direct students to put aside their differences and absorb the abstract model of French civilization, including the ideal of equality, but the schools convey hidden codes of exclusion in individual classrooms and in sorting students at young ages between academic tracks with promising jobs and technical schools with much lower economic prospects.[222]

If virtually every day includes episodes such as this exchange between the German teacher and the Turkish student, the sources of alienation for immigrants and their children are not hard to find. To understand what it would mean for non-natives to feel more at home requires subtle readings of cultural, psychological, generational, and sexual symbolism, shifting through time and differing across national contexts.[223]

---

219 Mannitz & Schiffauer, *supra* note 215, at 80–81.

220 Mannitz & Schiffauer, *supra* note 215, at 80.

221 The same observer comments that the Germans use the term Mittburger, "fellow citizen," for foreign residents rather than simply the word for citizen, and perpetuate a boundary between Germans and foreigners, based on ethic identity. Mannitz & Schiffauer, *supra* note 215, at 81.

222 Mannitz & Schiffauer, *supra* note 215; Bowen, *supra* note 15.

223 Fershta Ludin, a German citizen with roots in Afghanistan who taught elementary school in Germany, wanted to cover her hair while teaching contrary to the dictates of the school authorities.. The German Constitutional Court recognized her rights of conscience and access to public office under the Basic Law, but reserved the question to state legislative response. Benhabib, *supra* note 33, at 198–99. Four German states have legislated laws forbidding teachers from wearing an Islamic headscarf to school. *The Islamic Veil Across Europe*, BBC News, Nov. 17, 2006, *available at* http://news.bbc.co.uk/2/hi/europe/5414098.stm. British Home Secretary Jack Straw who represents a district that is twenty-five to thirty percent

The motivation to revise interactions with newcomers is tested or depleted for many natives who themselves feel threatened and less at home as their communities change. When newcomers appear to reject the Western norms of gender and sexual equality, secularism, and individual rights, they may be tempted to announce, "Why should we tolerate those who do not tolerate us?" Religious fundamentalists living in the West may be disturbed or disoriented by commercial, secular, or hedonistic values. Politicians and public figures in the West struggle over how to express respect for viewpoints quite critical of their countries and cultures. Longtime residents, even without realizing it, are degraded by living next to people who are not accepted as or invited to be equal citizens in their own society. Competitive intolerance could be the new motor for dehumanization, accelerated by the larger fears of terrorism and uncontrollable change.

Perhaps, instead, people from each of these walks of life will come increasingly to live in more than one discourse, taking each other's perspectives, and even developing multiple identities.[224] Even such a hopeful vision must foresee that instability will emerge and some tragic choices will be inevitable components of global change.[225] More than bland tolerance is required for encounters with hatred, and at times, understanding is crucial. This calls for the extraordinary dexterity to avoid demonizing those who demonize you—without, however, relenting on the insistence against demonization by anyone.[226] Perhaps only an idea of "home" as a destiny rather than the target of nostalgia can be large enough to house the competing hopes of newcomers and longtime residents as each struggle with the shock of the new—amid the intensified insecurities of an age of terrorism.

The clashes between old and new, natives and newcomers, East and West, are frightening when intolerance seems to be a tool of anti-terrorism. Instead of assuming this to be the case, let us pay attention to the competing narratives of European and American responses to terrorism, and actually debate anti-terrorism policies without assuming a core trade-off between tolerance and security. We might less ambivalently address how to navigate these challenging times by both whole-heartedly pursuing security and emphatically resisting the subordination of "others." Ideas about tolerance, security, equality, and terror matter here. So does thinking hard about what is done in our name.

Muslim, controversially urged Muslim women to take off the veil when meeting with him, which some Muslims read as an insult. Mark Simpson, *Straw Met by Applause—and Boos*, BBC News, Oct. 13, 2006, *available at* http://news.bbc.co.uk/2/hi/uk_news/politics/6048896.stm; Jo Coburn, *Straw Gets the Debate He Wanted*, BBC News, Oct. 6, 2006, http://news.bbc.co.uk/2/hi/uk_news/politics/5413012.stm; Nasreen Suleaman, *How Veil Remarks Reinforced its Support*, BBC News, Nov. 5,2006, http://news.bbc.co.uk/2/hi/uk_news/6117480.stm.

224 Richard Ned Lebow, The Tragic Vision of Politics: Ethics, Interests and Orders (2003).

225 *Id.* at 378 (Lebow discusses the sense of flux and instability produced by the combination of economic globalization and the world-wide international political system, bringing different political cultures into closer contact).

226 "Tolerance, practiced as 'you believe what you like and so will I,' makes no effort and has no reason to make an effort at understanding—it is self-absorbed and oddly lacking in curiosity." Ball, *supra* note 21, at 1625.

THE PREVENTIVE PARADIGM AND THE PERILS OF AD HOC BALANCING

Jules Lobel†

Originally published in Minnesota Law Review, Volume 91, No.5 (2007)

The Bush administration's response to the September 11 attacks has been characterized by a paradigm shift in fighting terrorism: from a defensive to offensive strategy, from reliance on deterrence to a new emphasis on preemption, from backward to forward-looking measures, and from prosecution to prevention.[1] At the heart of this shift is what Attorney General John Ashcroft termed the "new . . . paradigm of prevention."[2] The Bush administration has invoked this sweeping new preventive paradigm to justify the coercive use of state power to preventively detain suspected terrorists, to engage in extraordinary rendition of suspects to foreign states, to interrogate detainees, and to go to war against Iraq.[3] While the traditional rules of both international and domestic law prevent a state from using physical force against an individual or another nation except in response to some demonstrable wrongdoing, the new preventive paradigm allows the state to use such coercive power to prevent possible wrongdoing in the future.[4]

The shift to prevention has shaped the administration's response to terrorism in a wide variety of domestic and international contexts. Domestically, the Justice Department now views the prevention of future terrorist acts as "even 'more important

---

† Professor of Law, University of Pittsburgh Law School. This Article draws upon a larger book project, co-authored with Professor David Cole, entitled *Less Safe, Less Free: The Failure of Preemption in the War on Terror* (forthcoming New Press 2007). Any mistakes or errors are, of course, my own, as are any views expressed in this Article. I wish to thank my research assistant Sarah Vuong for her research help with this Article and the staff of the Document Technology Center at the University of Pittsburgh for their invaluable assistance in preparing this Article.

1 David Cole & Jules Lobel, Less Safe, Less Free: The Failure of Preemption in the War on Terror (forthcoming New Press 2007) (manuscript at 1, on file with authors).

2 John Ashcroft, U.S. Attorney Gen., Prepared Remarks Before the Council on Foreign Relations (Feb. 10, 2003), *available at* http://www.usdoj.gov/archive/ag/speeches/2003/021003 agcouncilonforeignrelation.htm ("In order to fight and to defeat terrorism, the Department of Justice has added a new paradigm to that of prosecution—a paradigm of *prevention*.").

3 *See infra* Part I.

4 Cole & Lobel, *supra* note 1 (manuscript at 5).

than prosecution' [of] past crimes."[5] Similarly, in foreign policy, the *National Security Strategy* announced a "new doctrine called preemption,"[6] which states that we are living in a "new world"[7] where the U.S. "can no longer solely rely on a reactive posture as ... in the past."[8] The *National Security Strategy* maintained that in order to prevent a future attack, the United States could initiate warfare unilaterally even when it neither had been attacked nor faced a threat of imminent attack.[9] In the name of preventing future attacks, the administration detained thousands of individuals without trial, the vast majority of whom were never even charged with committing a terrorist crime.[10] The administration has justified its use of coercive interrogation tactics against detainees and its establishment of secret CIA prisons, which house allegedly high-value al Qaeda suspects, by asserting the necessity of preventing future terrorist attacks.[11] The administration has transformed the practice of extraordinary rendition from a mechanism used to transfer accused criminals to a country where they would face trial to a preventive technique whereby suspects are sent to third countries not to try them for crimes they allegedly committed, but to torture and preventively detain them without charge in order to obtain information to prevent future crimes.[12]

The adoption of this preventive model in both domestic and foreign affairs is closely linked to the President's assertion of inherent executive power and to the executive branch's reliance on military force and war powers to fight its war on terror. Critics of the Bush administration have argued that the administration has asserted unprecedented views of unchecked, inherent executive authority to fight terrorism, and these critics have claimed that the expansion of executive power underlies the war on terror.[13] Few, however, have noted the close relationship between the administration's expansive view of executive power and its adoption of a coercive preventive paradigm. Yet, the Bush administration justifies its assertion of sweeping executive authority by claiming the need to use coercive preventive strategies.

5 Alan M. Dershowitz, Preemption: A Knife That Cuts Both Ways 3 (2006) (quoting Curt Anderson, *Ashcroft Cites "Monumental Progress" in U.S. War on Terrorism,* Associated Press, Feb. 13, 2003).

6 Remarks at a Reception for Governor Rick Perry of Texas in Houston, 1 Pub. Papers 990, 994 (June 14, 2002).

7 George W. Bush, *Introduction* to White House, the National Security Strategy of the United States of America (2002) [hereinafter National Security Strategy].

8 *Id.* at 15.

9 *Id.*

10 David Cole, *Are We Safer?,* N.Y. Rev. Books, Mar. 9, 2006, at 15, 17.

11 *Id.*

12 *See* Douglas Jehl & David Johnston, *Rule Change Lets C.I.A. Freely Send Suspects Abroad,* N.Y. Times, Mar. 6, 2005, § 1, at 1 ("[Rendition is the] Bush administration's secret program to transfer suspected terrorists to foreign countries for interrogation. . . .").

13 *See, e.g.,* Geoffrey R. Stone, Perilous Times: Free Speech in Wartime 554 (2004).

Indeed, immediately after September 11, top White House lawyers agreed "'that [the administration] had to move from retribution and punishment to preemption and prevention. Only a warfare model allows that approach.'"[14]

The turn toward prevention is not surprising. When faced with potential terrorist threats, it makes sense to focus efforts on preventing future attacks, as opposed to merely punishing those who have attacked the United States. Preventive diplomatic, law enforcement, and security measures are crucial to U.S. security, just as preventive medicine is important to one's physical wellbeing. What is problematic about the administration's preventive paradigm is not its preventive focus, but the state's reliance on the preventive use of physical force against individuals or nations in circumstances where traditional law normally prohibits such use. Instead of focusing on preventive measures like increased port security or monitoring terrorist funding, both of which have been underfunded by this administration,[15] the executive has emphasized coercive prevention. In pursuit of this aim, the administration has deployed physical and military force to detain suspected terrorists, to kidnap and send individuals to nations that will detain and likely torture them, to engage in coercive interrogations, and to go to war against nations that it believes pose a future threat.[16] Of course, a state may use force against individuals or other nations in circumstances narrowly prescribed by the rule of law.[17] A function of the preventive paradigm is to nullify those prescriptions in the name of prevention.

The preventive paradigm was making disturbing inroads into traditional notions of preventing harmful conduct even prior to September 11. Some scholars have argued that democratic societies are experiencing a basic shift in their approach to controlling harmful behavior, moving from a traditional reliance on deterrence and backward-looking reactions toward a more preventive and forward-looking approach.[18] Professor Paul Robinson has observed that over the past few decades, the criminal justice system's focus has shifted from punishing past violations to preventing future crimes by means of a system of preventive detention.[19] Americans' increased fear of crime has made the criminal justice system more receptive to the preventive rationale.[20] September 11 dramatically escalated Americans' fears and

14 Jane Mayer, *The Hidden Power*, New Yorker, July 3, 2006, at 44, 51 (quoting Associate White House Counsel Bradford Berenson).

15 Mathew Brzezinski, *Red Alert*, Mother Jones, Sept.–Oct. 2004, at 39, 94.

16 *See infra* Part I.

17 U.N. Charter arts. 39, 41, 42, 51.

18 Dershowitz, *supra* note 5, at 2.

19 Paul Robinson, Commentary, *Punishing Dangerousness: Cloaking Preventive Detentions as Criminal Justice*, 114 Harv. L. Rev. 1429, 1429 (2001).

20 *See id.* at 1433–34 ("[P]olitical forces inevitably will press for protective measures if a perception of public vulnerability exists. . . . [I]t is understandable that today's citizens are demanding greater protection and that legislators are seeking new ways to provide it.").

insecurities, leading to greater acceptance of the preventive rationale in the war on terror.

The Bush administration's argument for the adoption of a new preventive paradigm is based on the threat of a potentially catastrophic attack.[21] In a variety of settings, the administration and its supporters pose worst-case hypotheticals to justify highly coercive preventive measures. For example, they often invoke the ticking bomb scenario to justify preventive torture; they argue that if a suspect is known to have planted a bomb in a building, the only way to prevent thousands of people being killed is to torture the suspect. So too, in the run up to the preventive war against Iraq, President Bush invoked the specter of nuclear attack: "America must not ignore the threat gathering against us. Facing clear evidence of peril, we cannot wait for the final proof, the smoking gun, that could come in the form of a mushroom cloud."[22] And when administration supporters argue in favor of preventive detention, they ask what the government should do when it captures a person known to be planning a terrorist attack when that knowledge is based on solid, reliable evidence that cannot be disclosed.

The preventive paradigm is thus premised on an emergency situation which purportedly requires modifying or discarding the normal rules of law. These preventive measures are grounded in a claim that when the potential risks are catastrophic the normal cost-benefit calculations of law do not apply.[23] Hence, while in ordinary times society generally accepts that it is preferable to let ten guilty persons go free than to convict one innocent person, some suggest that we cannot sustain that balance when the risk is that one of the ten who go free will get his hands on a weapon of mass destruction.[24]

Preventive paradigm advocates therefore suggest replacing the clear rules of law applicable in normal times with a more ad hoc balancing approach attuned to the exigencies of emergencies, in which officials may undertake preventive action when such action is deemed the "lesser evil" because it is necessary to avoid catastrophic harm.[25] As Professor Ruth Wedgwood stated:

> We tolerate multiple acts of individual and social violence as the cost of safeguarding our privacy and liberty, demanding that the government meet an extraordinary standard of proof before it can claim any power over our person, acting with a retrospective rather than anticipatory glance. But now the stakes seem different. . . . The deliberate temperance and incompleteness of criminal law enforcement seem

---

21 National Security Strategy, *supra* note 7, at 13.

22 Address to the Nation on Iraq from Cincinnati, Ohio, 2 Pub. Papers 1751, 1754, (Oct. 7, 2002).

23 *See infra* text accompanying notes 25–34.

24 *See infra* text accompanying notes 25–26.

25 *See, e.g.*, Richard A. Posner, Not a Suicide Pact: The Constitution in a Time of National Emergency 34 (2006); John Yoo, *Using Force*, 71 U. Chi. L. Rev. 729, 751–61 (2004).

> inadequate to the emergency, when the threat to innocent life was multiplied by orders of magnitude.[26]

Resorting to coercive preventive measures when threatened with an emergency of potentially catastrophic proportion is not, of course, confined to the current Bush administration. The United States has often turned to preventive measures in times of war or national emergency. The post-World War I Palmer raids and the World War II internment of over 100,000 Japanese Americans are two of the more infamous twentieth century examples of governmental deployment of coercive preventive measures in perceived times of crisis.[27] The country's first war with a European power after the Constitution's ratification, the undeclared war with France in the late 1790s, led Congress to enact the Alien and Sedition Acts of 1798 authorizing the President to deport aliens who had not committed any crime but were judged to be "dangerous to the peace and safety of the United States."[28] Some historians have characterized southern secession and the attack on Fort Sumter, which brought on the Civil War, as forceful preventive measures taken to forestall the Northern Republicans gathering threat to the system of slavery.[29] Other nations such as Great Britain,[30] Israel,[31] and India[32] have a long history of using preventive detention in response to a perceived crisis. Preventive war in response to a looming crisis has a long and generally sordid history in Europe.[33]

Perceived emergencies are thus likely to provoke coercive preventive responses. Because preventive measures are so closely linked to emergencies, there is an inherent tension between such measures and the rule of law. Countries undertake these preventive measures because of perceived necessity, and as Oliver Cromwell once

---

26 Ruth Wedgwood, *The Law's Response to September 11,* 16 Ethics & Int'l Aff. J. 8, 9 (2002).

27 David Cole, *Enemy Aliens,* 54 Stan. L. Rev. 953, 989–97 (2002).

28 Alien Friends Act, ch. 58, § 1, 1 Stat. 570, 570–71 (1798) (expired 1800) ("[I]t shall be lawful for the President of the United States at any time during the continuance of this act, to *order* all such *aliens* as he shall judge dangerous to the peace and safety of the United States . . . to depart out of the territory of the United States. . . ."); *see also* Alien Enemies Act, ch. 66, 1 Stat. 577 (1798) (current version at 50 U.S.C. §§ 21–24 (2000)); Sedition Act, ch. 74, 1 Stat. 596 (1798) (expired 1801).

29 James M. McPherson, *The Fruits of Preventive War,* Perspectives, May 2003, at 5, 5.

30 Cornelius P. Cotter, *Emergency Detention in Wartime: The British Experience,* 6 Stan. L. Rev. 238, 238 (1954).

31 Amnesty Int'l, Israel and the Occupied Territories: Administrative Detention: Despair, Uncertainty And Lack of Due Process 2 (1997), *available at* http://web.amnesty.org/library/pdf/MDE150031997ENGLISH/$File/MDE 1500397.pdf; Alan Dershowitz, *Preventive Detention of Citizens During a National Emergency—A Comparison Between Israel and the United States,* 1 Isr. Y.B. Hum. Rts. 295, 309 (1971).

32 Benjamin N. Schoenfeld, *Emergency Rule in India,* 36 Pac. Aff. 221, 225 (1963).

33 *See* Cole & Lobel, *supra* note 1 (manuscript at 189).

pithily put it, "Necessity hath no law."[34] The coercive preventive paradigm substitutes ad hoc balancing for the relatively clear rules designed to limit executive discretion.

This Article will address the claim that times of crisis require jettisoning legal rules in favor of ad hoc balancing. Part I will demonstrate that the coercive preventive measures adopted by the Bush administration discard clear legal rules in favor of ad hoc balancing and rely on suspicions rather than objective evidence. Part II will examine the claims of prevention paradigm supporters that ad hoc balancing is necessary in the new post-9/11 era in order to reach decisions that correctly weigh the values of liberty and peace versus national security. This Article will argue that discarding the legal rules that prevent or limit the application of coercive preventive measures in favor of an ad hoc balancing test not only undermines law and liberty, but fails to protect our security.

I. COERCIVE PREVENTIVE MEASURES, THE RULE OF LAW, AND AD HOC BALANCING

The constellation of tactics that form a core of the administration's new preventive paradigm—detaining individuals who are believed to pose dangerous threats, rendering suspects to third countries where they are likely to be indefinitely detained and tortured, engaging in "preventive" torture or inhumane treatment in order to obtain information to prevent future terrorist actions, and initiating war to prevent a nation from eventually either attacking us or transferring weapons to terrorists who will use them against us—all have common elements. Each substitutes ad hoc balancing for clear rules, makes judgments based on suspicions and not hard evidence, and discards legal checks on unilateral decision making. These elements sacrifice integral components of what democratic nations have come to accept as the rule of law in the name of national security.

A. Substituting Open-Ended Standards for Clear Rules

Democratic societies have sought to restrain the use of state violence against fundamental human interests by means of clear, bright-line rules. The government may not incarcerate a person for violating vague rules, nor can it deny her freedom of speech based on an open-ended ad hoc balancing test. The prohibition on torture and cruel and inhumane treatment is absolute.[35] International law has also sought to protect international peace and national self-determination by setting forth a bright-line rule against non-defensive use of force.[36]

---

34 Max Radin, *Martial Law and the State of Siege*, 30 CAL. L. REV. 634, 640 (1942) (quoting Oliver Cromwell, Speech to Parliament (Sept. 12, 1654), *in* 5 THOMAS CARLYLE, OLIVER CROMWELL'S LETTERS AND SPEECHES WITH ELUCIDATIONS 74 (1870)).

35 *See infra* notes 42, 65 and accompanying text.

36 U.N. Charter arts. 39, 41, 42, 51.

The preventive paradigm favors open-ended standards and ad hoc balancing over clear rules. When the government acts preventively it requires flexibility and discretion, and it seeks to avoid being hemmed in by clear strictures. Moreover, government actions that are based on predictions or suspicions about future conduct are inherently less subject to clear rules than those based on evidence of what has already occurred.[37] Since the government asserts that coercive preventive action is required by necessity, the typical formula weighs the magnitude of the harm the government seeks to avoid versus the probability that the government's action will avoid such harm—both of which are imponderables undefined by any clear rule.[38]

For some, the essence of law is rules. To Justice Scalia, "a government of laws means a government of rules," and a decision "ungoverned by rule" is "hence ungoverned by law."[39] To be sure, despite Scalia's formulation, the law frequently employs open-ended balancing tests and speculative cost-benefit assessments. Courts or governmental agencies frequently utilize cost-benefit analyses to determine which acts constitute negligence or how stringent environmental and occupational safety regulations should be.[40] And the Supreme Court has often relied on balancing tests to resolve issues such as the validity of state laws that impinge on interstate commerce.[41] But such decisions are fundamentally different from decisions to attack another nation, to incarcerate an individual indefinitely, or to employ coercive interrogation. Domestic and international law recognize that the more fundamental the human interests at stake, the less appropriate are flexible, open-ended balancing tests. The prohibitions on torture, cruel and inhumane treatment, genocide, and summary executions are absolute.[42] Similarly, because of the importance of the interests protected by the First Amendment, the Supreme Court has rejected a balancing approach for the regulation of subversive speech. In the 1950s, the Court had employed such a test, holding that the gravity of the threat of communist revolution was sufficiently great that even a small probability that it might come to fruition was sufficient to justify the punishment of speech advocating communism.[43] Ensuing abuse under that standard, however, ultimately led the Court to articulate a bright-line rule prohibiting the suppression of speech that advocates

37 *See* Cole & Lobel, *supra* note 1 (manuscript at 5–6).

38 Yoo, *supra* note 25, at 751–61.

39 Morrison v. Olson, 487 U.S. 654, 733 (1988) (Scalia, J., dissenting).

40 Balt. Gas & Elec. Co. v. Natural Res. Def. Council, Inc., 462 U.S. 87, 107 (1983); Thompson v. Hirano Tecseed Co., 456 F.3d 805, 809 (8th Cir. 2006); Pennington v. Holiday Ret. Corp., 100 F. App'x 301, 302 (5th Cir. 2004).

41 Am. Trucking Ass'ns, Inc. v. Mich. Pub. Serv. Comm'n, 545 U.S. 429, 434 (2005); Pike v. Bruce Church, Inc., 397 U.S. 137, 142 (1970).

42 *See* International Covenant on Civil and Political Rights art. 7, Dec. 16, 1966, S. Treaty Doc. No. 95–20, 999 U.N.T.S. 171; Convention for the Protection of Human Rights and Fundamental Freedoms art. 3, Nov. 4, 1950, 213 U.N.T.S. 221; Convention on the Prevention and Punishment of the Crime of Genocide art. 1, Dec. 9, 1948, S. Treaty Doc. No. 81-15, 78 U.N.T.S. 277.

43 Dennis v. United States, 341 U.S. 494, 501–11 (1951).

crime unless the state can demonstrate that the speaker intends to cause violence and that such violence is in fact likely and imminent.[44]

The government's use of non-coercive preventive measures is typically a discretionary policy decision ungoverned by a clear rule. Whether to deploy new detection equipment at airports or seaports, how many visas to issue to foreign students, or whether to undertake diplomatic initiatives designed to make it more difficult for terrorists to obtain chemical or nuclear weapons are all determinations best left to political discretion. But when the state employs force against individuals or other nations, clear rules are an important legal mechanism to prevent abuses that inevitably arise from the exercise of discretion.

The tension between clear rules and coercive preventive strategies is illustrated by the preventive war doctrine articulated by the administration in its *National Security Strategy* and applied to justify the invasion of Iraq.[45] The terrible destructiveness of modern warfare led the world's leaders to conclude that individual nations' use of force should not be left to the political discretion of national leaders using vague balancing tests.[46] These leaders concluded that they needed a clear rule to restrain the resort to war—a rule that prohibited nations' use of force except in narrowly defined circumstances.[47] Just as legal protection for speech calls for bright-line rules limiting political discretion, the UN Charter articulates a clear rule that individual nations may not unilaterally decide to use force except in self-defense in response to an armed attack.[48] Customary international law broadens that self-defense exception somewhat to allow the use of force in response to imminent attacks.[49]

The principle that individual nations may unilaterally use military force against other nations only in self-defense is designed to discourage resort to war by creating a bright-line legal rule. An armed attack is an objective fact; an imminent attack involves some amount of prediction, but generally requires objective evidence that the attack is indeed imminent, such as the massing of troops at the border. As Secretary of State Daniel Webster stated in 1842, self-defense is permitted under customary international law only where the threat is "'instant, overwhelming, and leaving no choice of means, and no moment of deliberation.'"[50]

---

44 Brandenburg v. Ohio, 395 U.S. 444, 447–49 (1969).

45 *See* National Security Strategy, *supra* note 7, at 5–6.

46 Louis Henkin, How Nations Behave 136–37 (2d ed. 1979).

47 *See id.*

48 U.N. Charter art. 51.

49 Michael N. Schmitt, *Preemptive Strategies in International Law,* 24 Mich. J. Int'l L. 513, 518, 535 (2003).

50 Letter from Daniel Webster, U.S. Sec'y of State, to Alexander Baring, Lord Ashburton, British Plenipotentiary (Aug. 6, 1842), *in* 2 John Bassett Moore, A Digest of International Law 412, 412 (1906) (quoting Letter from Daniel Webster, U.S. Sec'y of State, to Henry Fox, British Minister in Wash. (Apr. 24, 1841)).

The Pentagon's definition of a permissible "preemptive attack" undertaken in self-defense echoed Webster's: "an attack initiated on the basis of incontrovertible evidence that an enemy attack is *imminent*."[51]

The new preventive war doctrine departs from this bright-line rule and substitutes a much more open-ended and less objectively verifiable standard. Not a single administration official argued that Iraq had plans of an imminent attack against the United States or anybody else. Rather, the administration's claims were based on a calculation of inevitability or probability. For example, Deputy Secretary of State Richard Armitage asserted that rogue states' "'unrelenting drive to possess weapons of mass destruction brings about the inevitability that they will be used against [the United States] or [United States] interests.'"[52]

The decision to launch a preventive war invariably involves speculation about future events and intentions, which is a judgment that defies clear rules. Thus, the *National Security Strategy* replaces the clear legal rule of self-defense with a vague and necessarily speculative balancing test in which the greater the threat, the less certainty there needs to be about the probability of the risk eventuating.[53] The administration makes no attempt to define when a threat is sufficient to justify the use of force.[54] As former administration official John Yoo recognized, the preventive war doctrine is based upon a flexible cost-benefit standard rather than the clear rule contained in the UN Charter.[55]

The open-ended standard of the preventive war doctrine eviscerates the notion of legal rules controlling warfare, a point perhaps best described by Abram Chayes, the legal advisor to the State Department during the Cuban missile crisis.[56] In explaining why the Kennedy administration refused to rely on preventive self-defense to justify its actions, Chayes accepted that the notion of self-defense included an anticipatory response to an *imminent* attack.[57] But to permit preventive self-defense where there is no threatened imminent attack, he maintained, would mean that "[t]here is simply no standard against which this decision could be judged. Whenever a nation believed that interests, which in the heat and pressure of a crisis it is prepared to characterize as vital, were threatened, its use of force in response would become permissible."[58] Because such a doctrine would destroy any

---

51 Department of Defense Dictionary of Military and Associated Terms 418 (2007), *available at* http://www.dtic.mil/doctrine/jel/doddict/data/p/04196.html. (emphasis added).

52 Jeffrey Record, Dark Victory: America's Second War Against Iraq 32 (2004) (quoting Richard Armitage).

53 National Security Strategy, *supra* note 7, at 13–16.

54 Yoo, *supra* note 25, at 735.

55 *Id.* at 730, 758–62, 787.

56 Abram Chayes, The Cuban Missile Crisis 6 (1974).

57 *Id.* at 65.

58 *Id.*

clear limits on the use of force, Chayes argued that it would amount to a concession that "'law simply does not deal with such questions of ultimate power.'"[59]

This imminent attack requirement has prompted the Bush administration to claim that it has merely "adapt[ed] the concept of imminent threat to the capabilities and objectives of today's adversaries."[60] Yoo and other administration officials have attempted to redefine imminence to shift the inquiry from timing to probability of harm. Yoo argues that the post-9/11 world "renders the imminence standard virtually meaningless, because there is no ready means to detect whether a terrorist attack is about to occur."[61] Therefore, the imminence standard applied literally to a world of modern weaponry, rogue states, and terrorists "would be a suicide pact."[62] Instead of defining imminence as the moment when a blow is just about to land, Yoo would define imminence in terms of the likelihood of the attack occurring. Where the magnitude of the harm is great, as in a potential terrorist nuclear attack on the United States, Yoo would require a lesser probability.[63] In short, the preventive war doctrine substitutes ad hoc balancing for clear rules.

The problem with substituting "probable" or even "inevitable" for "imminent" is that odds-making is an inherently speculative enterprise. We simply cannot know whether the odds were five percent, fifty percent, or ninety percent that Saddam Hussein eventually would have obtained and used weapons of mass destruction against the United States or given them to terrorists to use against the United States. As former German Chancellor Otto van Bismarck once remarked in rejecting similar arguments for preventive war, "'one can never anticipate the ways of divine providence securely enough for that.'"[64] A test that requires decision makers to divine the possibility of a probable attack in the future contains no meaningful standard at all.

The other coercive preventive tactics employed as part of this new paradigm also substitute vague balancing tests for clear rules. Few rules are clearer than domestic and international law's absolute ban on torture and cruel and inhumane treatment.[65]

---

59 *Id.* (quoting Dean Acheson, Remarks at the Proceedings of the American Society of International Law, 57th Annual Meeting 14 (Apr. 25–27, 1963), *in* INTERNATIONAL RULES: APPROACHES FROM INTERNATIONAL LAW AND INTERNATIONAL RELATIONS 107, 108 (Robert J. Beck et al. eds., 1996)).

60 NATIONAL SECURITY STRATEGY, *supra* note 7, at 15. "[N]ew technology requires new thinking about when a threat actually becomes 'imminent.'" Condoleezza Rice, Remarks on the President's National Security Strategy at the Waldorf Astoria Hotel in New York City (Oct. 1, 2002), *available at* http://www.whitehouse.gov/news/releases/2002/10/20021001-6.html.

61 Yoo, *supra* note 25, at 750.

62 *Id.* at 756.

63 *Id.* at 753–55.

64 GORDON A. CRAIG, THE POLITICS OF THE PRUSSIAN ARMY 1640–1945, at 255 (1955) (quoting Otto van Bismarck).

65 18 U.S.C. §§ 2340–2340A (2000); Convention Against Torture and Other Cruel, Inhuman or Degrading Treatment or Punishment art. 2, Dec. 10, 1984, S. TREATY DOC. No. 100-20, 1465 U.N.T.S. 85; International Covenant on Civil and Political Rights, *supra* note 42, art. 4.

Yet, driven by the need to obtain information believed essential to preventing future terrorist attacks, the administration effectively abandoned the law's clear rule and embraced a totality of circumstances, ad hoc balancing test. In the Office of Legal Counsel's August 1, 2002 memorandum on torture, Assistant Attorney General Jay Bybee not only set forth an extremely narrow view of what constitutes torture, but also argued that government employees who engage in torture would have a defense of necessity, based on a vague balancing of the likelihood that a suspect had information needed to prevent a future attack and the magnitude of the potential harm.[66]

The Bybee memo was consistent with the administration's amorphous, ill-defined pledge to treat detainees humanely where "consistent with military necessity."[67] Administration officials provided an ambiguous definition for "inhumane treatment," claiming that techniques such as waterboarding, mock executions, physical beatings, and painful stress positions could be lawful "depend[ing] on the facts and circumstances" of each particular case.[68] That approach led soldiers to complain that there were no clear rules for interrogations.[69]

Similarly, when Attorney General Ashcroft oversaw the round-up of more than one thousand foreign nationals in the weeks after 9/11, he substituted a vague standard for a clear rule in order to justify holding them without charges for extended periods of time.[70] Had those nationals been arrested under criminal law, prosecutors would have faced a constitutional mandate to charge them immediately and to demonstrate, within forty-eight hours before a federal judge, the existence of probable cause that they had committed a crime.[71] Before 9/11, immigration regulations contained a similar bright-line rule, requiring that charges be filed within twenty-four hours of any arrest.[72] Even the USA PATRIOT Act

---

66 Memorandum from Jay S. Bybee, U.S. Assistant Attorney Gen., to Alberto R. Gonzales, Counsel to the President, and William J. Haynes, Gen. Counsel to the Dep't of Def. (Jan. 22, 2002), *reprinted in* The Torture Papers 81, 108 (Karen J. Greenberg & Joshua L. Dratel eds., 2005).

67 Memorandum from George W. Bush, U.S. President, to Richard Cheney, U.S. Vice President, et al., on the Humane Treatment of Taliban and al Qaeda Detainees (Feb. 7, 2002), *reprinted in* The Torture Papers, *supra* note 66, at 134, 135.

68 Editorial, *Mr. Flanigan's Answers*, Wash. Post, Sept. 28, 2005, at A20 (quoting Timothy Flanigan, Nominee to be Deputy Attorney General, in response to written questions from Senator Richard Durbin).

69 Charles Babington & Shailagh Murray, *Senate Supports Interrogation Limits*, Wash. Post, Oct. 6, 2005, at A1.

70 *See infra* text accompanying note 75.

71 County of Riverside v. McLaughlin, 500 U.S. 44, 56 (1991).

72 Administrative Comment, *Indefinite Detention Without Probable Cause: A Comment on INS Interim Rule 8 C.F.R. § 287.3*, 26 N.Y.U. Rev. L. & Soc. Change 397, 399 (2001).

(Patriot Act),[73] while significantly expanding executive power to detain persons without charging them, still maintained a clear rule. That Act provided the Attorney General with the authority to detain a non-citizen for as long as seven days without charging them with a crime, upon certification that the authority has "reasonable grounds to believe" that the non-citizen is engaged in terrorist activities or other activities that threaten national security.[74] Yet Ashcroft chose not to rely on the Patriot Act, but rather on a newly enacted regulation replacing the bright-line rule with a provision allowing the government in times of emergency to detain aliens for a "reasonable period of time" while it investigates the detainee.[75] What was "reasonable" turned out to be measured in weeks and months.

The administration discarded the clear rules relating to the detention of prisoners of war and instead claimed the authority to indefinitely detain "unlawful enemy combatants," a term which remains ill-defined. Until 2001, this term appeared nowhere in U.S. criminal law, international law, or the law of war.[76] It was appropriated from the U.S. Supreme Court's opinion in *Ex parte Quirin*.[77] At first, the government provided virtually no criteria at all for defining enemy combatants. A plurality of the Supreme Court in *Hamdi v. Rumsfeld* upheld the government's authority to detain an individual as an enemy combatant, but for the purpose of that case defined the term "enemy combatant" narrowly as an individual who was "part of or supporting forces hostile to the United States or its coalition partners" in Afghanistan *and* "who engaged in an armed conflict against the United States there."[78] After *Hamdi*, the government did not adopt the Court's definition, but instead drafted vague regulations that would include as an enemy combatant persons who had never committed a belligerent act and who never directly supported hostilities against the United States.[79] The government conceded that its definition of an enemy combatant would cover a "'little old lady in Switzerland who writes checks to what she thinks is a charity that helps orphans in Afghanistan but [what] really is a front to finance al-Qaeda activities,' [or] a person who teaches English to

---

73 Uniting and Strengthening America by Providing Appropriate Tools Required to Intercept and Obstruct Terrorism (USA PATRIOT Act) Act of 2001, Pub. L. No. 107-56, 115 Stat. 272 (codified in scattered sections of the U.S.C.).

74 *Id.* § 412, 115 Stat. at 350–52 (codified at 8 U.S.C. § 1226a).

75 8 C.F.R. § 287.3(d) (2001).

76 Gary Solis, *Even a Bad Man Has Rights*, Wash. Post, June 25, 2002, at A19; *see also* ABA Task Force on Treatment of Enemy Combatants, Report to the House of Delegates 4 (2003) [hereinafter ABA Report], *available at* http://www.abanet.org/leadership/recommendations03/109.pdf (describing the various forms of the term "combatants" in domestic and international law).

77 317 U.S. 1, 31 (1942); *accord* ABA Report, *supra* note 76, at 4; Solis, *supra* note 76.

78 542 U.S. 507, 516 (2004) (quoting Brief for the Respondents at 3, *Hamdi*, 542 U.S. 507 (2004) (No. 03-6696)).

79 *In re* Guantanamo Detainee Cases, 355 F. Supp. 2d 443, 475 (D.D.C. 2005).

the son of an al-Qaeda member."[80] Similarly, William Haynes II, General Counsel of the Department of Defense, defined the term enemy combatant in December 2002 as a member, agent, *or associate* of al Qaeda or the Taliban.[81] The use of the term associate harkens back to the McCarthy era's attacks on those who associated in any way with the Communist Party.[82]

The Military Commissions Act of 2006, enacted by Congress in response to the Court's *Hamdan v. Rumsfeld* decision,[83] also includes a definition with no clear standard as to who can be indefinitely detained as a preventive matter without charge in the war on terror.[84] The Act defines an unlawful enemy combatant as "a person who has engaged in hostilities *or* who has purposefully and materially supported hostilities against the United States or its co-belligerents who is not a lawful enemy combatant."[85] The Act, however, leaves unclear who exactly is covered by the ambiguous phrase "purposefully and materially supported hostilities against the United States or its co-belligerents."[86] The government could claim that any civilian who knowingly teaches English to the son of an al Qaeda member is covered under the definition, despite the absence of any belligerent act or any direct support of hostilities. Even more standardless than that definition, the statute also provides that persons can be considered enemy combatants so long as they have been so deemed "by a Combatant Status Review Tribunal or another competent tribunal established under the authority of the President or the Secretary of Defense."[87] This circular reasoning establishing that a person is an enemy combatant if the government says so provides no standard whatsoever.

The preventive paradigm's substitution of amorphous balancing tests for clear rules in all these areas invites abuse. Indeed, the history of governmental use of physical coercion for pretextual reasons against disfavored minorities, dissenters, aliens, and weaker nations is one important reason for the law's insistence on reasonably clear rules limiting the state's coercive power.[88] The preventive war doctrine is particularly

80 *Id.* (citation omitted).

81 Memorandum from William J. Haynes, Gen. Counsel of the Dep't of Def. to Members of the Am. Soc'y of Int'l Law Council of Foreign Relations (Dec. 12, 2002), *available at* http://www.cfr.org/publications/5312/enemy_combatants.html.

82 *See* David Cole, Enemy Aliens 129–53 (2003).

83 126 S. Ct. 2749 (2006).

84 Military Commissions Act of 2006 § 3, Pub. L. No. 109-366, 120 Stat. 2600, 2601–02 (codified at 10 U.S.C. § 948a).

85 *Id.* (emphasis added).

86 *See id.*

87 *Id.*

88 *Cf.* Trinkler v. Alabama, 414 U.S. 955, 957 (1973) (Douglas, J., dissenting) ("A vague law impermissibly delegates basic policy matters to policemen, judges, and juries for resolution on an *ad hoc* and subjective basis, with the attendant dangers of arbitrary and discriminatory application.").

susceptible to pretextual justifications. Some suspect, for example, that the administration's emphasis on illicit weapons and on the connection between Iraq and al Qaeda were pretexts to justify a war that the administration actually launched for other reasons: increasing American influence in the Middle East, spreading democracy, or simply demonstrating United States resolve to its enemies.[89] That suspicion is furthered by the fact that for years prior to the September 11 attacks key administration officials, most notably Paul Wolfowitz, had advocated war to get rid of Saddam Hussein.[90] Indeed, after the war Wolfowitz admitted that the administration chose the weapons of mass destruction rationale for "bureaucratic reasons," as it was "the one reason everyone could agree on."[91]

Paul Pillar, the intelligence community's senior analyst for the Middle East from 2000 to 2005,[92] concluded that the administration's invasion of Iraq was not based on its concern about Iraqi weapon programs. In a recent article in *Foreign Affairs,* Pillar stated that the administration's "decision to topple Saddam was driven by other factors—namely, the desire to shake up the sclerotic power structures of the Middle East and hasten the spread of more liberal politics and economics in the region."[93] For Pillar, what was most remarkable about prewar U.S. intelligence on Iraq was not how wrong it was, but that it played so small a role in the decision to go to war.[94] Pillar, in charge of coordinating all of the intelligence community's assessments regarding Iraq, did not receive a single request from any administration policymaker for any such assessment prior to the war.[95]

Even where a government is not acting pretextually, but honestly believes coercive preventive measures are necessary to prevent a terrorist attack, the absence of clear rules creates a strong danger of abuse. For example, the government's vague instructions governing interrogations allowed some soldiers to engage in inhumane tactics not simply for sadistic reasons but also in the course of honestly attempting to obtain information, as apparently happened frequently at Guantánamo and in detention centers in Iraq.[96] Ad hoc balancing thus provides little or no restraint on wrongful executive conduct, whether such conduct is undertaken pretextually or for sincere reasons.

---

89 *E.g.,* Thomas L. Friedman, Editorial, *A War for Oil?,* N.Y. Times, Jan. 5, 2003, § 4, at 11; Paul R. Pillar, *Intelligence, Policy, and the War in Iraq,* Foreign Aff., Mar.–Apr. 2006, at 15, 15–16; James P. Rubin, *Stumbling into War,* Foreign Aff., Sept.–Oct. 2003, at 46, 48.

90 *United States Policy Toward Iraq: Hearing Before the H. Comm. on National Security,* 105th Cong. 74–78 (1998) (statement of Paul Wolfowitz).

91 Joseph Cirincione et al., WMD in Iraq: Evidence and Implications 13 (2004).

92 Pillar, *supra* note 89, at 15.

93 *Id.* at 16.

94 *Id.* at 17–18.

95 *Id.*

96 *E.g.,* Kevin Bohn et al., *FBI Reports Guantanamo "Abuse,"* CNN.com, Dec. 8, 2004, http://www.cnn.com/2004/US/12/08/guantanamo.abuse/.

B. Substituting Suspicion for Objective Evidence

Closely linked to the law's requirement that clear rules, not vague standards, limit a government's ability to use coercive measures against individuals or other states, is the requirement that such measures be based on objectively determinable proof and not mere suspicion. Yet predicting future threats inevitably relies on suspicion, inference, probabilities, circumstantial evidence, and hunches rather than on solid, objective, and visible evidence. Professor George Fletcher at Columbia University aptly articulated the reason that democratic law generally forbids the preventive use of force against both other states as well as individuals:

> Preemptive strikes are illegal in international law as they are illegal internally in every legal system of the world. They are illegal because they are not based on a visible manifestation of aggression; they are grounded in a prediction of how the feared enemy is likely to behave in the future.[97]

There are, of course, occasions when the state can use force to prevent a wrong that has not yet occurred: to thwart conspiracies or attempted attacks, or to respond to imminent attacks from another nation.[98] Conspiracies or attempts, however, generate some objective evidence of an agreement to commit wrongdoing, and the law requires some overt act in furtherance of the plan or some evidence of a substantial step to commit wrongdoing.[99] In contrast, in times of emergency the state often claims that its preventive response cannot be limited by a rule requiring objective evidence that a crime is being planned and that concrete steps have been taken in furtherance of the crime; rather, the government claims that a coercive response may be based on suspicion.[100]

The substitution of suspicion for objective evidence can be seen in the administration's coercive preventive measures: preventive war, preventive detention, and extraordinary rendition. To justify each of these tactics, the administration has presented suspicions and hunches masquerading as objective certainty. As journalist Ron Suskind reported, the war on terror has been guided by little more than "the principle of actionable suspicion," as one former intelligence chief called it.[101] "We were operating, frantically, in a largely evidence-free environment. But the whole

97 George P. Fletcher, Basic Concepts of Criminal Law 134 (1998); *see also* Jane Campbell Moriarty, *"While Dangers Gather": The Bush Preemption Doctrine, Battered Women, Imminence, and Anticipatory Self-Defense,* 30 N.Y.U. Rev. L. & Soc. Change 1, 21–22 (2005). While the *Model Penal Code* attempted to introduce some flexibility into the concept of imminence, *id. at 21* n. 112, most states have adhered to the traditional notion of imminence as temporally imminent, and even the states that have interpreted the language liberally still require that the defendant have a reasonable "perception of imminent harm," *id.* at 21 n.111.

98 *See supra* text accompanying notes 48–51.

99 *See* Model Penal Code §§ 5.01(1), 5.03(5) (1985).

100 *See* Ron Suskind, The One Percent Doctrine: Deep Inside America's Pursuit of Its Enemies Since 9/11, at 166 (2006).

101 *Id.*

concept was that not having hard evidence shouldn't hold you back."[102] As Vice President Dick Cheney argued, if there is just a one percent chance of the unimaginable happening, we have to treat that chance as a certainty.[103]

The preventive paradigm's treatment of suspicion as objective fact was most evident in the administration's headlong drive toward war against Iraq from 2002 to 2003.[104] The administration's suspicions that Iraq was hiding stocks of chemical and biological weapons were shared by many observers, including Hans Blix, the director of the UN Monitoring, Verification and Inspection Commission for Iraq (known as UNMOVIC), whose task was to determine Iraqi compliance with the UN's mandate that it destroy its dangerous weapons and dismantle its prohibited weapons programs.[105] But as a lawyer and long-time diplomat, Blix viewed his mandate as most lawyers would: to find solid, reliable evidence to determine whether Iraq still had or was producing weapons of mass destruction.[106] Despite his "gut feeling" that Iraq was hiding stocks of chemical and biological weapons, Blix had not been "asked by the Security Council to submit suspicions or simply to convey testimony from defectors."[107] "Assessments and judgments in our reports," Blix felt, "had to be based on evidence that would remain convincing even under critical international examination."[108]

Blix's focus on solid evidence—evidence that would withstand critical international scrutiny—of whether Iraq actually had outlawed weapons increasingly collided with the preventive paradigm's inevitable reliance on suspicion, inferences, probabilities, circumstantial evidence, and hunches. As National Security Advisor Condoleezza Rice and President Bush argued, waiting for conclusive proof of Saddam Hussein's determination to obtain nuclear weapons was simply too risky, because "we don't want the smoking gun to become a mushroom cloud."[109]

U.S. officials repeatedly treated suspicions as if they were fact. Administration officials continuously asserted that they were not merely suspicious of Iraq, but rather that they "knew," were "absolutely certain," or had "no doubt" that Saddam Hussein had a reconstituted nuclear weapons program, had hundreds of tons of chemical

102 *Id.*

103 *Id.* at 62.

104 *See id.* at 166–68.

105 Hans Blix, Disarming Iraq 3, 264 (2004).

106 *Id.* at 264.

107 *Id.*

108 *Id.*

109 Record, *supra* note 52, at 33 (citing Scott Peterson, *Can Hussein Be Deterred?*, Christian Sci. Monitor, Sept. 10, 2002, at A1). President Bush also said in an October 7, 2002 speech in Cincinnati, Ohio that "[f]acing clear evidence of peril, we cannot wait for the final proof, the smoking gun, that could come in the form of a mushroom cloud." Address to the Nation on Iraq from Cincinnati, Ohio, *supra* note 22, at 1754.

and biological weapons, and was producing more of such weapons. On September 8, 2002, for example, Vice President Cheney stated on *Meet the Press* that we "know, with *absolute certainty* that [Saddam Hussein] is using his procurement system to acquire the equipment he needs in order to enrich uranium to build a nuclear weapon."[110] On *Fox News*, Secretary of State Colin Powell claimed that "[t]here's *no doubt* that [Saddam Hussein] has chemical weapon stocks."[111] A month later, in a speech in Cincinnati, Ohio, President Bush again exuded certainty: "If we know Saddam Hussein has dangerous weapons today—*and we do*—does it make any sense for the world to wait to confront him as he grows even stronger and develops even more dangerous weapons?"[112] In March 2003, Secretary of Defense Donald Rumsfeld made the astounding claim that U.S. officials not only knew that Iraq had weapons of mass destruction, but knew their location. "We know where they are," he told *ABC News*.[113]

Hans Blix and his inspection team sought to find objective evidence to verify these claims.[114] The inspectors searched almost seven hundred sites for potential evidence of prohibited chemical, biological, or nuclear weapons, including many sites identified by U.S. and other nations' intelligence services.[115] Blix reported that "at none of the many sites we actually inspected had we found any prohibited activity."[116]

Similarly, the International Atomic Energy Agency (IAEA), after three months of intrusive inspections, including the inspections of all sites identified in overhead satellite imaging as having suspicious activity, found no evidence or plausible indication of the revival of a nuclear weapons program in Iraq.[117] The IAEA concluded after extensive investigation that the much publicized aluminum tubes that Iraq had attempted to import were not likely to have been connected to the manufacture of centrifuges for the enrichment of uranium.[118] And, the IAEA and outside experts also determined that the reported uranium contracts between Iraq and Niger, cited by President Bush in his 2003 State of the Union address, were forgeries.[119]

Administration officials' claims that Iraq had a collaborative relationship with al Qaeda were also based on suspicions, surmise, possibilities, and speculative, secret

110 *Meet the Press* (NBC television broadcast Sept. 8, 2002) (emphasis added).

111 *Fox News Sunday* (Fox News Network television broadcast Sept. 8, 2002) (emphasis added).

112 Address to the Nation on Iraq from Cincinnati, Ohio, *supra* note 22, at 1752 (emphasis added).

113 *This Week with George Stephanopoulos* (ABC television broadcast Mar. 30, 2003).

114 Blix, *supra* note 105, at 264.

115 *Id.* at 156.

116 *Id.*

117 U.N. SCOR, 58th Sess., 4714th mtg. at 8, U.N. Doc. S/PV.4714 (Mar. 7, 2003).

118 *Id.* at 7.

119 *Id.* at 8.

intelligence masquerading as reliable fact. After the September 11 attacks, Wolfowitz estimated that there was a ten to fifty percent chance that Iraq was behind the attacks—a probability analysis based on no reliable intelligence data.[120] Immediately after September 11, Wolfowitz and Rumsfeld urged the President to confront Iraq.[121] President Bush had the same gut feeling, telling his advisors that "I believe Iraq was involved."[122]

While the U.S. intelligence community generally correctly concluded that Iraq and al Qaeda had no collaborative relationship,[123] President Bush repeatedly claimed that Saddam Hussein was "dealing with Al Qa[e]da,"[124] had "provided al Qa[e]da with chemical and biological weapons training,"[125] and that "you can't distinguish between al Qa[e]da and Saddam when you talk about the war on terror."[126] In addition, Colin Powell warned the Security Council of the "sinister nexus between Iraq and the al Qaeda terrorist network."[127]

Administration officials afterwards admitted that they had lacked concrete facts, but argued that they needed to act based on possibilities, not objective evidence. Powell later admitted that he indeed had no "smoking gun, *concrete evidence* about the connection" between Iraq and al Qaeda.[128] "But," he continued, "I think *the possibility* of such connections did exist."[129] General Richard B. Myers, Chairman of the Joint Chiefs of Staff, recognized the limitations of intelligence. "Intelligence doesn't necessarily mean something is true," he said at a Pentagon news briefing after major combat ended in Iraq.[130] He further remarked that "You know it's your

120 Daniel Benjamin & Steven Simon, The Next Attack: The Failure of the War on Terror and a Strategy for Getting It Right 147 (2005).

121 *Id.*

122 *Id.*

123 *Staff Statement No. 15 "Overview of the Enemy," in* 4 The 9/11 Commission Proceedings and Analysis 441, 445 (2005) (concluding that there was no "collaborative relationship" between Saddam Hussein and al Qaeda); see *also* S. Rep. No. 108-301, at 346 (2004) ("The Central Intelligence Agency reasonably assessed that there were likely several instances of contacts between Iraq and al-Qaida throughout the 1990s, but that these contacts did not add up to an established formal relationship."); Douglas Jehl, *Questioning Nearly Every Aspect of the Responses to Sept. 11 and Terrorism,* N.Y. Times, June 18, 2004, at A18.

124 The President's News Conference, 2 Pub. Papers 2039, 2049 (Nov. 7, 2002).

125 The President's Weekly Radio Address, 1 Pub. Papers 140, 140 (Feb. 8, 2003).

126 Remarks Prior to Discussions with President Alvaro Uribe of Columbia and an Exchange with Reporters, 2 Pub. Papers 1656, 1657 (Sept. 25, 2002).

127 *Powell's Address, Presenting 'Deeply Troubling' Evidence on Iraq,* N.Y. Times, Feb. 6, 2003, at A18 (transcript of Secretary of State Colin Powell's address to the United Nations Security Council).

128 Christopher Marquis, *Powell Admits No Hard Proof in Linking Iraq to Al Qaeda,* N.Y. Times, Jan. 9, 2004, at A10 (emphasis added).

129 *Id.*

130 James Risen et al., *In Sketchy Data, Trying to Gauge Iraq Threat,* N.Y. Times, July 20, 2003, at A1.

best estimate of the situation. It doesn't mean it's a fact. I mean, that's not what intelligence is."[131] In the absence of hard evidence on Iraqi programs, officials developed a "mosaic," or a "threat picture," and "connected a lot of dots from multiple sources" to form a "judgment."[132] Or as Donald Rumsfeld later conceded, we "did not act in Iraq because we had discovered dramatic new evidence of Iraq's pursuit of weapons of mass destruction. We acted because we saw the existing evidence in a new light through the prism of our experience on 9/11."[133]

Therefore, even if the administration was not using the preventive rationale as a pretext to achieve other goals, the administration's substitution of suspicion for observable, verifiable evidence allowed real fears to distort, shade, or color the actual evidence so as to, in Cheney's words, treat a very small possibility as if it were a certainty.[134] To Blix, the administration in effect adopted a "faith-based" approach to war: the administration "knew," as if on faith, that Hussein was evil, had dangerous weapons, and was associated with evildoers like Osama bin Laden.[135] All it needed to do was to find the evidence to confirm that view. Blix analogized the administration's approach to the Salem Witch Trials: "The witches exist; you are appointed to deal with these witches; testing whether there are witches is only a dilution of the witch hunt."[136] As in the Middle Ages, because people were convinced there were witches, "'they certainly found them.'"[137]

The substitution of suspicion for objective evidence is endemic to the preventive paradigm, for predictions about the future are inherently speculative. This same substitution characterizes the administration's coercive prevention programs that it has used to fight the war on terror since September 11. As with Iraq, suspicion often masquerades as certainty.

The extraordinary rendition of Maher Arar to Syria illustrates the preventive paradigm's reliance on suspicion, often with draconian results. Arar, a Canadian citizen born in Syria, was on his way home to Canada from a family vacation in Tunisia in September 2002 when he stopped to change planes at Kennedy Airport in New York.[138] He was detained by the U.S. government at the airport based on

---

131 *Id.*

132 Cirincione et al., *supra* note 91, at 17 (quoting *This Week with George Stephanopoulos* (ABC television broadcast June 8, 2003) (Condoleeza Rice); *Meet the Press* (NBC television broadcast Sept. 8, 2002) (Dick Cheney)).

133 Record, *supra* note 52, at 112.

134 Suskind, *supra* note 100, at 62.

135 Blix, *supra* note 105, at 263.

136 *Id.* at 202.

137 *Blix Attacks Iraq Weapons 'Spin,'* CNN.com, Sept. 18, 2003, http://www.cnn.com/2003/WORLD/meast/09/18sprj.irq.blix.bush/index.html (quoting Hans Blix).

138 *60 Minutes II: His Year in Hell* (CBS television broadcast July 15, 2005).

information supplied by the Canadian Royal Mounted Police.[139] The Canadian Police had sent a report to the United States which, based on Arar's mere acquaintances with other men under suspicion of being terrorists, listed Arar and his wife as "Islamic Extremist individuals suspected of being linked to the al Qaeda terrorist movement."[140] The Canadian suspicions turned out to be completely false. After an exhaustive two-year investigation, in September 2006, a Canadian Commission chaired by appellate judge Dennis R. O'Connor concluded that Arar was never a member of al Qaeda or associated with any terrorist group.[141] Judge O'Connor stated "categorically that there is no evidence to indicate that Mr. Arar has committed any offense or that his activities constitute a threat to the security of Canada."[142]

Nonetheless, the U.S. Justice Department detained Arar in New York for two weeks, harshly interrogated him, and then secretly flew him to Jordan, where he was then taken to Syria.[143] The Syrians held him in a tiny cell termed the grave cell, and in the initial weeks of detention tortured him.[144] Over a year later, after concluding that Arar had no connection to terrorism, the Syrian government released him.[145]

At the time the U.S. government rendered Arar to Syria it knew that it had no objective evidence that Arar was a terrorist or al Qaeda member.[146] Nonetheless, INS officials operated as if they were certain that Arar was a terrorist. In deciding to deport Arar, the INS Regional Director determined that the evidence "clearly and unequivocally reflects that Mr. Arar is a member of a foreign terrorist organization, to wit, Al Qaeda."[147] Yet, according to the Canadian Commission's Report, only three days earlier, Canadian counter-terrorism officials sent a fax to the FBI which stated that while Arar "had contact with" suspicious individuals, the officials were "unable to indicate links to al-Qaeda," and had "yet to complete . . . a detailed investigation of Mr. Arar."[148] The Commission also reported that the next day a Canadian official and an FBI officer spoke by phone and both concluded that there was insufficient evidence to charge Arar with a crime either in Canada or in the

---

139 *Ottawa Must Act Now on RCMP Watchdog: Arar,* CBC News, Dec. 12, 2006, http://www.cbc.ca/canada/story/2006/12/12/oconnor-report.html?ref=rss.

140 Comm'n of Inquiry into the Actions of Can. Officials in Relation to Maher Arar, Report of the Events Relating to Maher Arar: Analysis and Recommendations 20–21 (2006) [hereinafter Can. Comm'n Report].

141 *See id.*

142 *Id.* at 59.

143 60 Minutes II, *supra* note 138.

144 *Id.*

145 *Id.*

146 Can. Comm'n Report, *supra* note 140, at 154.

147 Scott Shane, *Torture Victim Had No Terror Link, Canada Told U.S.,* N.Y. Times, Sept. 25, 2006, at A10.

148 Can. Comm'n Report, *supra* note 140, at 148.

United States—a conclusion that would not have been true if they had clear and unequivocal information that Arar was an al Qaeda member.[149]

Not only did U.S. officials inflate the information they received from Canada, treating suspicion as if it were clear and unequivocal evidence, but they also kept Canadian officials in the dark about their plans for Arar. The Canadian foreign ministry was not initially informed of Arar's detention, and American officials denied Mr. Arar's requests to talk to the Canadian Consulate in New York, a violation of U.S. treaty obligations with Canada.[150] The Canadian Commission concluded that the American officials kept Canadian officials in the dark about the plans with respect to Arar because they "believed—quite correctly—that, if informed, the Canadians would have serious concerns about the plan to remove Mr. Arar to Syria."[151] Even after Arar's deportation to Syria, the U.S. government did not inform Canada of Arar's whereabouts, and the Canadians only learned two weeks later from the Syrians that he was there.[152] Once the Canadians learned that Arar was in Syria, his torture and interrogations stopped.[153]

The Arar case raises the question of why the U.S. government would send a detained Canadian citizen whom it suspects may be a terrorist to Syria, a country which the State Department accuses of practicing torture and being a state sponsor of terrorism, and not to Canada, the United States' friend and ally. The answer lies in the preventive paradigm: U.S. government officials must have believed that Syria would detain and use coercive interrogation methods on Arar to obtain information needed to prevent future terrorist acts—information that could not be obtained by normal police methods used by Canada or the United States. The Canadian Commission Report found that, unlike Syria, Canada would not have detained Arar.[154] Canadian officials told their American counterparts that they would place Arar under surveillance.[155] But that measure obviously did not suffice for the United States; relying on suspicions, the U.S. government wanted to detain Arar and coerce him into disclosing what U.S. officials believed he knew.

Similarly, the more than one thousand mainly Muslim immigrants rounded up after September 11 were detained based on mere suspicions, often with no objective evidence, and sometimes held for months before the government released them or deported them for immigration violations unrelated to terrorism.[156] As one example, a Yemeni man was arrested after accompanying his American wife to her

149 *Id.* at 152.

150 *Id.* at 172.

151 *Id.* at 158.

152 *Id.* at 154, 184.

153 *Id.* at 188–89.

154 *Id.* at 154.

155 *Id.*

156 Cole, *supra* note 82, at 25–26.

military base in Kentucky because his wife was wearing a hijab (the head scarf that many Muslim women wear).[157] The FBI investigators noticed the couple speaking a foreign language—French—and in their suitcase they carried box cutters which they had both used in their work.[158] He was held for almost two months without any evidence ever being presented against him.[159] His wife, who had also been detained, accepted an honorable discharge from the Army.[160] Indeed, of the more than five thousand aliens who have been preventively detained in the United States since September 11, not one has been convicted of any terrorist crime.[161]

An inherent problem with the preventive paradigm's reliance on suspicions and hunches about future conduct is what psychologists and scientists have long recognized to be a deeply rooted human tendency to interpret evidence in a manner that confirms one's preexisting theories or beliefs.[162] As early as 1620, Sir Francis Bacon explained this phenomenon:

> The human understanding when it has once adopted an opinion draws all things else to support and agree with it. And though there be a greater number and weight of instances to be found on the other side, yet these it either neglects and despises, or else by some distinction sets aside and rejects, in order that by this great and pernicious predetermination the authority of its former conclusion may remain inviolate.[163]

Such "confirmation bias" was certainly operative in the run up to the Iraq war, as U.S. officials cherry-picked and manipulated the facts, exaggerating evidence supporting their position and disregarding contrary indications.[164] As the Senate Commission investigating the intelligence failure leading to the Iraq war observed, there was "a tendency of analysts to believe that which fits their theories," and that

---

157 *Department of Justice Oversight: Preserving Our Freedom While Defending Against Terrorism Hearing Before the S. Comm. on the Judiciary*, 107th Cong. 215–17 (2001) (statement of Ali Al-Maqtari).

158 *Id.* at 216.

159 *Id.* at 217.

160 *Id.*

161 *See* COLE, *supra* note 82, at 26; Alex Gourevitch, *Detention Disorder: Ashcroft's Clumsy Round-up of Foreigners Lurches Forward,* AM. PROSPECT ONLINE, Jan. 31, 2003, http://www.prospect.org/webfeatures/2003/01/gourevitch-a-01-31.html.

162 *See, e.g.*, Raymond S. Nickerson, *Confirmation Bias: A Ubiquitous Phenomenon in Many Guises,* 2 REV. GEN. PSYCHOL. 175, 175–77 (1998).

163 Charles G. Lord et al., *Biased Assimilation and Attitude Polarization: The Effects of Prior Theories on Subsequently Considered Evidence*, 37 J. PERSONALITY & SOC. PSYCHOL. 2098, 2098 (1979) (quoting Sir Francis Bacon).

164 *See* Pillar, *supra* note 89, at 19.

analysts had "tunnel vision," meaning that they "simply *disregarded* evidence that did not support their hypotheses."[165]

Senior intelligence official Paul Pillar suggests that intelligence analysts and policymakers seeking to tie an individual or government to terrorism face other common biases and difficulties.[166] Finding a tie between a particular government or individual and a terrorist organization is particularly subject to bias because

> [i]n the shadowy world of international terrorism, almost anyone can be "linked" to almost anyone else if enough effort is made to find evidence of casual contacts, the mentioning of names in the same breath, or indications of common travels or experiences. Even the most minimal and circumstantial data can be adduced as evidence of a "relationship". . . .[167]

Law cannot rid us of the predisposition to perceive evidence through the lens of our preconceptions, nor can it eliminate the other biases that affect policymakers and intelligence analysts. But one function of law is to create institutional and normative safeguards to counteract these biases. One means of offsetting bias is to require objectively verifiable evidence of wrongdoing, rather than relying on suspicions or hunches masquerading as fact. Because it substitutes open-ended prediction for hard evidence, the preventive paradigm opens the door to biases, preconceptions, and conscious or unconscious manipulation of the evidence.

C. The Absence of Institutional Checks

The inherent tension between the rule of law and the preventive paradigm is heightened by the government's insistence that executive discretion requires discarding institutional checks on its power—checks that are ordinarily provided by independent review. The government thus claims that its authority to launch a preventive war is not subject to the UN Charter's requirement that the Security Council approve of such wars.[168] The government has engaged in extraordinary renditions of over one hundred individuals, yet when it is challenged in court by Arar, or by the German citizen El-Masri, who was kidnapped by mistake, the administration has argued, thus far successfully, that its actions are shielded from judicial review by the state secrets doctrine, the political question doctrine, and other principles which counsel against judicial scrutiny.[169] In order to prevent

165 The Comm'n on the Intelligence Capabilities of the U.S. Regarding Weapons of Mass Destruction, Report to the President of the United States 87, 162, 169 (2005).

166 Pillar, *supra* note 89, at 20–21.

167 *Id.*

168 *See* The President's News Conference, 1 Pub. Papers 255, 251 (Mar. 6, 2003) ("I'm confident the American people understand that when it comes to our security, if we need to act, we will act, and we really don't need United Nations approval to do so.").

169 Arar v. Ashcroft, 414 F. Supp. 2d 250, 287 (E.D.N.Y. 2006), *appeal docketed*, No. 1:04CV00249 (2d Cir. Sept. 12, 2006); El-Masri v. Tenet, 437 F. Supp. 2d 530, 539 (E.D. Va. 2006), *aff'd*, No. 06-1667, 2007 WL 625130 (4th Cir. Nov. 28, 2006).

judicial scrutiny of the detention of aliens after September 11, the administration promulgated another emergency regulation that provided for an automatic stay of bond pending appeal, de facto allowing the government to detain aliens for more than a year before courts could order their release.[170] And, the administration argued that any alien detained abroad as an enemy combatant was not entitled to a hearing to determine if he was in fact a combatant, and the judiciary could not scrutinize any such detention.[171] According to the government, even U.S. citizens detained as enemy combatants were entitled to only limited judicial review to determine whether the government facially set forth some evidentiary basis for the detention.[172] After the Supreme Court rejected both of these propositions, the administration nonetheless succeeded in pressing Congress to remove the judiciary's habeas jurisdiction over aliens detained as enemy combatants.[173]

The administration's short-circuiting of independent checks on executive power is related to the administration's acceptance of vague standards and suspicions in place of objective evidence of clearly defined wrongdoing. For an independent entity to allow the United States to take preventive coercive action, the entity would require the government to proffer some objective evidence. For example, a majority of nations on the Security Council refused to authorize the United States-led preventive war against Iraq, in part because inspectors had not uncovered any objective evidence that Iraq was hiding prohibited weapons.[174] Hence, the United States had to circumvent the Security Council.[175] In addition, it is hard to believe that any U.S. court would have authorized Arar's deportation to Syria; therefore, the administration misled Arar's lawyer and the Canadians, thereby denying Arar the opportunity to challenge his pending deportation in court.[176] And when the government was forced by the Supreme Court to provide alleged enemy combatant Hamdi a due process hearing, the government released him to Saudi Arabia rather than conduct such a hearing.[177]

II. BALANCING LIBERTY, PEACE AND SECURITY

The argument for coercive preventive measures is based on a purported trade-off between liberty and security. Proponents of the preventive paradigm contend that the normal rules of law are too heavily weighted in favor of liberty to be useful in a

170 Jules Lobel, *The War on Terrorism and Civil Liberties,* 63 U. Pitt. L. Rev. 767, 780 (2002).

171 Brief of Respondents at 21, Rasul v. Bush, 542 U.S. 466 (2004) (Nos. 03-334, 03-345).

172 Brief of Respondents at 19–21, Hamdi v. Rumsfeld, 542 U.S. 507 (2004) (No. 03-6696).

173 Military Commissions Act of 2006 Pub. L. No. 109-366, § 7, 120 Stat. 2600, 2635–36 (codified at 28 U.S.C. § 2241(e)).

174 *Nations Take Sides After Powell's Speech,* CNN.Com, Feb. 6, 2003, http://www.cnn.com/2003/WORLD/meast/02/06/sprj.irq.powell.world.reax/index.html.

175 *See Bush Sends Iraq War Letter to Congress,* CNN.Com, Mar. 19, 2003, http://www.cnn.com/2003/ALLPOLITICS/03/19/sprj.irq.bush/index.html.

176 Can. Comm'n Report, *supra* note 140, at 154, 184.

177 Jerry Markon, *Hamdi Returned to Saudi Arabia,* Wash. Post, Oct. 12, 2004, at A2.

national emergency or crisis. Supporters of supplanting those rules, such as Richard Posner, argue that when an emergency arises, "cases involving a clash between liberty and safety cannot yet be governed by rules."[178] The new terrain created by the September 11 attacks, they argue, makes it more sensible for both the executive and the courts "to govern by standard," allowing decision makers to employ ad hoc balancing to reach a more optimal, flexible balance between the protection of liberty and the requirements of security—at least until they gain more experience dealing with the new terrorist threat.[179] Accurate balancing requires decision makers to accept less certainty in this new situation than the legal rules require and to pay more attention to an evaluation of the competing risks involved.[180]

The argument that the post-9/11 threat requires us to jettison the legal principles that have hitherto been deemed essential to constitutional and international law inevitably starts with the claim that we now face a novel situation which represents a dramatic departure from the context of past emergencies or crisis. President Bush has argued that we have entered a "new world,"[181] that "we face a threat with no precedent,"[182] and that the war against terrorism has ushered in a new paradigm which requires "new thinking."[183] In the aftermath of the September 11 attacks, government officials, judges, the media, and academics emphasized this "new paradigm" confronting the United States.[184]

The mentality that we have entered a "new era," and must adopt a "new paradigm," because "everything has changed" may hinder reasonable balancing of liberty and security. First, the perception of a new, unprecedented situation leads to the belief that historical experience and lessons—often encapsulated in legal rules—now can be safely ignored. Posner argues that the civil libertarians are fundamentally misguided "in their assumption that the past is a good guide to the future. . . . The past does not include attacks on the United States by terrorists wielding nuclear bombs [or] dirty bombs . . . [T]he future may well include such attacks."[185] Posner also

178 Posner, *supra* note 25, at 34.

179 *Id.*

180 *Id.*

181 National Security Strategy, *supra* note 7, at 4.

182 West Point, New York, 1 Pub. Papers 917, 919 (June 1, 2002).

183 Memorandum from George W. Bush, *supra* note 67, at 134.

184 *See, e.g.*, Hamdan v. Rumsfeld, 126 S. Ct. 2749, 2830 n.6 (Thomas, J., dissenting); Memorandum from Alberto R. Gonzalez to the President (Jan. 25, 2002), *reprinted in* The Torture Papers, *supra* note 66, at 118, 119 ("In my judgment, this new paradigm renders obsolete Geneva's strict limitations on questioning of enemy prisoners. . . ."); *see also* Memorandum from George W. Bush, *supra* note 67, at 134 ("[The] new paradigm . . . requires new thinking in the law of war. . . .").

185 Posner, *supra* note 25, at 47.

surmises that civil libertarians "are looking backward rather than forward."[186] History, according to Posner, is irrelevant.[187]

Likewise, the administration's argument for preventive war asserts that past experience, as encapsulated in the norms of international law, is not a relevant guide for balancing the interests of world peace and national security in the post-9/11 world.[188] The administration believes that this new threat "without precedent" makes our historical rejection of preventive war doctrine irrelevant to the present situation.[189]

The legal rules that preclude preventive war, "preventive" torture, and indefinite and prolonged preventive detention all encapsulate the bitter lessons of historical experience. The sordid American experience with preventive detention in the twentieth century suggests that generally such detentions neither safeguard security nor ensure our liberty.[190] It is obvious in hindsight that these disastrous experiences with preventive detention were unnecessary to protect security; and even at the time, some informed observers argued that the policies were flawed and unnecessary. None other than FBI Director J. Edgar Hoover, a man not generally known as a civil libertarian,[191] argued against the Japanese internment camps, claiming that the FBI had sufficient capacity using traditional law enforcement surveillance to ferret out and charge any potential Japanese American saboteurs and spies.[192]

Just as the domestic use of preventive detention to preempt perceived threats has a troubled history, the use of preventive war to preempt new dangers before they occur has often had calamitous consequences. The history of western civilization is filled with major wars commenced for preventive reasons: Sparta's declaration of war against Athens commencing the Peloponnesian War,[193] Carthage's preemptive attack on Rome,[194] the preventive war Germany declared against Russia that initiated World War I,[195] and Japan's surprise attack on the American fleet at Pearl Harbor,[196] to name just a few of the more notable examples. As political scientist

186 *Id.*

187 *Cf. id.* at 51 (rejecting the tendency of civil libertarians to "narrate a history of civil liberties violations").

188 *See* Yoo, *supra* note 25, at 734–36 (describing how the administration's preemptive actions violate international law).

189 *See supra* text accompanying notes 181–84.

190 *See* Cole, *supra* note 27, at 990–97.

191 *See* Arthur M. Schlesinger, Jr., The Imperial Presidency 274 (1973).

192 *See* 117 Cong. Rec. H31551–52 (daily ed. Sept. 13, 1971) (statement of Rep. Railsback), *quoted in* Padilla v. Rumsfeld, 352 F.3d 695, 719–20 (2d Cir. 2003), *rev'd,* 542 U.S. 426 (2004).

193 Dale C. Copeland, The Origins of Major War 210–11 (2000).

194 *See id.* at 211–13.

195 *See id.* at 82–85.

196 *See* Nobutaka Ike, *Introduction* to Japan's Decision for War, at xiii, xxiv (Nobutaka Ike ed., 1967) ("By the fall of 1941, the Japanese leaders . . . had come to believe that they were being

David Hendrickson observes, "Repugnance for preventive war became deeply embedded in the world community because the use of that doctrine in the twentieth century led to results nearly fatal to civilization."[197]

The generally disastrous history of preventive war is not confined to the twentieth century. According to one study, virtually all of the major wars in Europe between the sixteenth and twentieth centuries were motivated by prevention; typically a powerful but declining state "engaged in a desperate race against time"[198] to defeat a growing new danger which, it perceived, would inevitably overwhelm it.[199] Another study concludes that between 1848 and 1918, "[e]very war between Great Powers . . . started as a preventive war, not as a war of conquest."[200] All but one "brought disaster on their originators."[201] Yet another analysis of centuries of European warfare finds that "[p]reventive logic . . . is a ubiquitous motive for war."[202] In 1760, Edmund Burke concluded that the military policy of preventing emerging new threats to the balance of power had been the source "of innumerable and fruitless wars" in Europe.[203] One prominent scholar of the history of warfare concluded after an exhaustive study that the "chief source of insecurity in Europe since medieval times . . . lies in [nations'] own tendency to exaggerate the dangers they face, and to respond with counterproductive belligerence."[204] Another scholar of warfare, Columbia Professor Robert Jervis, surveyed the historical record and concluded that, "[o]n balance, it seems that states are more likely to overestimate the hostility of others than to underestimate it."[205]

The argument that we should abandon the rules restricting the use of coercive preventive measures because we are now facing a new world with terrorists capable of possessing and using weapons of mass destruction ignores the fact that these rules emerged, at least in part, from our experience addressing perceived new and dangerous threats. States have often argued that the threat they faced was new or unprecedented to justify uses of coercive preventive measures.[206] These arguments date back to

---

pushed into a corner by the United States and her allies. . . . [N]o course but war seemed possible to the Japanese.").

197 David C. Hendrickson, *Imperialism Versus Internationalism: The United States and World Order*, Gaiko Forum, Fall 2002, at 35, 36.

198 Copeland, *supra* note 193, at 220.

199 *See id.* at 214–34.

200 A.J.P. Taylor, The Struggle for Mastery of Europe 1848–1918, at 166 (1954).

201 *Id.*

202 Stephen Van Evera, Causes of War: Power and the Roots of Conflict 76 (1999).

203 Michael Walzer, Just and Unjust Wars 76 (1977).

204 Van Evera, *supra* note 202, at 192.

205 Robert Jervis, *War & Misperception,* 18 J. Interdisc. Hist. 675, 688 (1988).

206 *See, e.g.*, Copeland, *supra* note 193, at 71; James Joll, The Origins of the First World War 87 (1984).

ancient times, when Spartans debated whether to launch the disastrous Peloponnesian War because of the "completely different" threat from Athens.[207]

Similarly, the development of atomic weapons created a new, unprecedented threat after World War II that led many Americans to advocate preventive war, arguing that the Soviet nuclear threat created a fundamentally new international environment in which the normal rules could no longer apply.[208] Fortunately, American leaders from Truman to Kennedy rejected these arguments.[209] So too the experience with the World War II roundup of Japanese Americans was justified as a response to a very real, brand new, and qualitatively different threat: the first significant attack by a foreign power on U.S. soil in over a century, and the first to use the new technology of air power capable of striking the United States in a fraction of the time foreseen by the framers.[210] Congress enacted the Non-Detention Act of 1971 to ensure that such preventive detentions of U.S. citizens would not occur in response to any future real or imagined new threat.[211] In short, new threats, a changed world, and new paradigms are nothing new, and the rules of law reflect the lessons of our experience in responding to such new threats.

While this history cannot definitively prove that preventive war and preventive detention are always counterproductive, it certainly suggests that we ought to be cautious about replacing the relatively clear rules of law with the ad hoc balancing test of the coercive preventive paradigm. Modern social science research also demonstrates the need for skepticism about assertions that the threat of a catastrophic attack requires that we abandon rules limiting government discretion and adopt a pure cost-benefit balancing test.[212] If as a rule, people rationally calculate the risk of catastrophic harm and counterbalance the risk of using coercive preventive measures mistakenly, we might be able to discard the bright-line rules that guard against emotional and irrational decision making.[213] But it makes little sense to do so if emotion typically prompts people to exaggerate the risk of catastrophic harm, and therefore to tolerate many more false positives than any rational calculation

207 Thucydides, History of the Peloponnesian War 75 (1972).

208 *See* Copeland, *supra* note 193, at 171; Marc Trachtenberg, *A "Wasting Asset": American Strategy and the Shifting Nuclear Balance,* Int'l Security, Winter 1988–99, at 5, 8–11.

209 *See* Copeland, *supra* note 193, at 173–74.

210 *See* Dershowitz, *supra* note 5, at 111–14.

211 Pub. L. No. 92-128, 85 Stat. 347 (codified as amended at 18 U.S.C. § 4001(a) (2000)); *see also* H.R. Rep. No. 92-116, at 2 (1971).

212 *See* Cass R. Sunstein, Laws of Fear 105 (2005) ("[W]orst-case scenarios have a distorting effect on human judgment, often producing excessive fear about unlikely events. . . . The result is a situation in which people often show baseless fear. . . .").

213 *Cf.* Richard A. Posner, Catastrophe: Risk and Response 139–40 (2004) (arguing that cost-benefit analysis is an important step in assessing catastrophic risk).

would permit.[214] In addition, engaging in ad hoc balancing in emotionally laden crisis situations is likely to undervalue the potential costs of coercive preventive action, because people tend to consider only the short term, highly vivid and accessible costs, while ignoring the dangers that are more abstract.[215] Widespread preventive detention without adequate safeguards, for example, creates numerous risks generally: some detainees will be radicalized by their treatment and will become terrorist sympathizers, the Arab and Muslim communities in the United States will grow distrustful and be less likely to cooperate in tracking down terrorists, and al Qaeda will use our actions to recruit more terrorists.[216] If one could rationally calculate the total costs, one might find out that such preventive detention may very well increase the risk of a terrorist attack instead of reducing it.

Psychological studies highlight the difficulties in rationally balancing these costs and benefits. Decision making is often based on emotive, affect-based mental processes, which tend to diverge from rational cognitive assessments of risk.[217] When faced with a potential catastrophe that has a small chance of eventuating, people tend either to ignore the risk or to exaggerate it.[218] At times, to be sure, we may discount risks that would warrant more forceful action.[219] Particularly where worst case scenarios evoke vivid, emotion-laden images of recent events, however, people are much more likely to overreact.[220] As University of Chicago Professor Cass Sunstein has noted, "worst-case scenarios have a distorting effect on human judgment, often producing excessive fear about unlikely events."[221]

---

214 *Cf.* Jules Lobel & George Loewenstein, *Emote Control: The Substitution of Symbol for Substance in Foreign Policy and International Law,* 80 Chi.-Kent L. Rev. 1045, 1082 (2005) ("[C]ontrary to the intuitive perspective reached by many academics and policymakers, careful deliberative process is most important in deciding to go to war or responding to international threats precisely at those times when it is most likely to be discarded.").

215 *See id.* at 1073 ("[E]mote control typically produces an overreaction to . . . problems . . . that are vividly described and easy to visualize."); *cf.* Jeffrey Rosen, The Naked Crowd: Reclaiming Security and Freedom in an Anxious Age 74 (2004) ("People believe that they are most likely to be victimized by the threats of which they are most afraid."); Cass R. Sunstein, *Terrorism and Probability Neglect,* 26 J. Risk & Uncertainty 121, 127–28 (2003) ("[T]he word 'terrorism' evokes vivid images of a disaster. . . .").

216 Cole, *supra* note 82, at 183–87.

217 *See* George F. Loewenstein et al., *Risk as Feelings,* 127 Psychol. Bull. 267, 269 (2001) (describing the "divergence of emotional responses from cognitive evaluation of risks").

218 Posner, *supra* note 213, at 248.

219 *See, e.g., id.* at 249 ("There is no historical memory of asteroids colliding with the earth and so we find it hard to take the threat of such collisions seriously even if we accept that it exists.").

220 *See* Lobel & Loewenstein, *supra* note 214, at 1070 ("The problem of vivid, emotional miscalculation of risk is particularly acute in the antiterrorism context, since fear is a particularly strong emotion. . . .").

221 Sunstein, *supra* note 212, at 105.

Three phenomena particularly distort the rational cost-balancing equation proposed by the preventive paradigm. The first is that humans react more emotionally to perceived new situations than to things they have already experienced.[222] Our affective systems are much more sensitive to situations that appear to be new, but they adapt readily to ongoing or repeated stimuli.[223] In contrast, the deliberative system is much more aligned to "ongoing, stable situations."[224] As a result, when we face what is widely perceived to be a new, qualitatively different terrorist threat—as occurred after September 11—we are much more likely to emotionally overreact rather than rationally balance costs and benefits.

Second, emotions are highly attuned to visual imagery; such images skew cost-benefit balancing.[225] Terrorist incidents are likely to prompt what Sunstein terms "probability neglect," the tendency to overreact to small risks of catastrophic harms.[226] The aftermath of the September 11 attacks demonstrated the propensity of emotions that are activated by an immediate, vivid, and potentially catastrophic situation to exaggerate risks. A study conducted a few weeks after 9/11 found that the average person believed that he or she faced a twenty percent chance of being personally hurt in a terrorist attack within the next year.[227] This risk perception was seriously exaggerated. Indeed, individuals would not have faced that high a risk even if a terrorist attack of the same magnitude as the 9/11 attacks took place every day for an entire year.[228]

Similarly, when people were asked how much they would pay for flight insurance to cover losses resulting from terrorism, they agreed to pay more than when asked what they would pay for flight insurance to cover losses from all causes.[229] This patently irrational result can be explained by the fact that asking about terrorism evokes vivid images of disaster, leading people to overestimate the risk.[230] Canadians, cognizant of recent vivid examples of persons afflicted with the Severe Acute Respiratory Syndrome virus in their country, evaluated their risk of contracting the disease as much higher than did Americans, despite the fact that citizens of both

222 *See* Lobel & Loewenstein, *supra* note 214, at 1056–57.

223 *See id.*

224 *Id.*

225 *See* Sunstein, *supra* note 212, at 81 ("[V]isualization or imagery matters a great deal to people's reactions to risks.").

226 *See id.* at 64–65.

227 Rosen, *supra* note 215, at 73.

228 *Id.* at 74.

229 Eric J. Johnson et al., *Framing, Probability Distortions and Insurance Decisions,* 7 J. Risk & Uncertainty 35, 39–42 (1993).

230 Sunstein, *supra* note 212, at 40.

nations faced statistically similar risks.[231] In short, when vivid visual images trigger strong emotions, people tend to overestimate the danger of small, disastrous risks.[232] As Sunstein argues,

> In the context of terrorism, the implication is clear. The risks associated with terrorist attacks are highly likely to trigger strong emotions, in part because of the sheer vividness of the bad outcome and the associated levels of outrage and fear. It follows that even if the likelihood of an attack is extremely low, people will be willing to pay a great deal to avoid it.[233]

Studies confirm that people will overestimate the risk of danger when their emotions are triggered. In one study, people were informed that radon and nuclear waste in the foundation of their homes presented similar risks of cancer, but they reported an exaggerated risk with respect to the nuclear waste because they were angry about the source of the threat.[234] In another study, people repeatedly judged the risks of an activity based on whether they had positive or negative feelings about it, irrespective of its actual risk.[235] When they felt positive about an activity, they interpreted its risks as low and its benefits as high.[236] If they felt negative about the activity, they judged its risks as high and its benefits as low.[237] In fact, risk and benefit are often positively correlated.[238] Many risky activities have substantial benefits and many activities that are not risky at all have virtually no benefit, but people routinely substitute their feelings about an activity for a rational calculation of its risks and benefits.[239]

These studies suggest that emotional issues such as terrorism will inevitably skew policymakers' application of ad hoc analysis based on worst-case scenarios. Individuals and political leaders will be unable to rationally assess the dangers and benefits of coercive preventive policies. Moreover, to the extent that the costs of these policies tend to be borne in the future, and are intangible and abstract—such as the costs associated with undermining the rule of law—those costs will be undervalued.[240]

---

231 *See* Neal Feigenson et al., *Perceptions of Terrorism and Disease Risks: A Cross-National Comparison*, 69 Mo. L. Rev. 991, 995, 999 (2004).

232 *See* Sunstein, *supra* note 212, at 81; Loewenstein et al., *supra* note 217, at 275–76.

233 Sunstein, *supra* note 215, at 124.

234 Peter M. Sandman et al., *Communications to Reduce Risk Underestimation and Overestimation*, 3 Risk Decision & Pol'y 93, 106–07 (1998).

235 Paul Slovic, *What's Fear Got to Do with It? It's Affect We Need to Worry About*, 69 Mo. L. Rev. 971, 977 (2004).

236 *Id.*

237 *Id.*

238 *Id.* at 976–77.

239 *See id. See generally* Paul Slovic et al., *The Affect Heuristic, in* Heuristics & Biases 397, 400–01 (Thomas Gilovich et al. eds., 2002) (describing studies that demonstrated the impact of affect over costs and benefits in behavior).

240 *See* Lobel & Loewenstein, *supra* note 214, at 1082.

The resulting cost-benefit analysis will inevitably be distorted in favor of taking coercive preventive action, even when rational consideration demonstrates that the costs outweigh the benefits.

Of course, government officials do not always overestimate threats and risks in times of crisis. Indeed, social science posits that where a threat has no new vivid, visual example, people tend to ignore it.[241] Global warming and the rise of fascism in Germany are historical examples of that tendency.[242] However, where there is a visually vivid, outrageous, and immediate threat, decision makers generally overreact to the detriment of both liberty and security.[243]

Third, and potentially even more problematic, the risks posed by terrorist threats are often not quantifiable at all. Insurance experts and psychologists distinguish between "risk," a probability that is capable of being estimated, and "uncertainty," a probability that is unquantifiable.[244] Terrorist threats generally fall in the latter category.[245] Because of the difficulty of estimating risk of catastrophic harm, the private insurance market would not provide insurance against terrorism at reasonable rates.[246] Consequently, Congress enacted the Terrorism Risk Insurance Act of 2002, which in effect requires the public to insure the insurers against calamitous losses from a terrorist attack.[247]

Cost-benefit advocates such as Posner and Yoo recognize that cost-benefit analysis in this context is purely subjective. Posner admits that in the present setting "risks and harms cannot be measured,"[248] and that assessing the relevant needs and dangers of preventive detention is a subjective process that "requires a weighing of imponderables."[249] Ironically, Yoo admits the difficulties of balancing costs and benefits in his critique of the *Hamdi* plurality's reliance on the *Mathews v. Eldridge* balancing test[250] to weigh the citizen's interest to be free from involuntary confinement against the government's national security interest.[251] Yoo argues that "[i]t is

241 *See* Posner, *supra* note 213, at 247–49 (describing how familiar threats like nuclear weapons are feared, while risks of unknown calamities like asteroid collisions are ignored).

242 *See id.;* Record, *supra* note 52, at 80.

243 *See* Sunstein, *supra* note 212, at 81.

244 Michelle E. Boardman, *Knowing Unknowns: The Illusion of Terrorism Insurance,* 93 Geo. L.J. 783, 784 (2005).

245 *Id.* (describing the risk of terrorism as "fundamentally incalculable," and discouraging insurers from issuing terrorism insurance).

246 *See A Safety Solution: Terrorism Insurance Program Spreads Risk Around,* Pittsburgh Post-Gazette, Sept. 13, 2005, at E8.

247 Pub. L. No. 107-297, 116 Stat. 2322 (2002) (codified in scattered sections of 15 U.S.C.).

248 Posner, *supra* note 25, at 41.

249 *Id.* at 66.

250 424 U.S. 319, 335 (1976).

251 *See* John Yoo, *Courts at War,* 91 Cornell L. Rev. 573, 587–89 (2006).

difficult to understand how the *Mathews* test can be applied with any serious coherence."[252]

> Should a court gauge the government's interest in protecting the national security by multiplying the number of lives potentially saved by the reduction in the probability of an attack—factoring in the uniform value of a life as measured by the Environmental Protection Agency? And how should the government measure the individual liberty interest in not being detained—as the average price that an average citizen would pay per hour to avoid detention? If these efforts to monetize the prongs of the *Mathews* test seem silly, it may be because there is no systematic, rational way to quantify these competing values.[253]

But if judges cannot rationally weigh these competing interests, why should executive officials be able to do so? Yoo's argument proves too much: it suggests that the elaborate balancing facade of the preventive paradigm really masks emotional decision making based on fears, hunches, and intuitions, rather than costs and benefits.

This critique of the use of ad hoc balancing to decide whether coercive preventive measures are warranted prompts several objections. First, virtually all legal rules involve some sort of balancing, and therefore one cannot escape the problem of attempting to balance competing values and costs simply by relying on purportedly clear rules. There are almost always exceptions to the supposed clear rules, and whether the exceptions should apply in any particular case requires the decision maker to balance competing interests and costs.

While it is true that legal decision making generally involves some sort of balancing, the existence of fairly clear rules and the need to present objective evidence provide checks, restraints, and presumptions to guide our decisions. Law cannot rid us of our predispositions, emotional biases, or our exaggerated fears, but adopting and attempting to follow clear rules can provide a counterbalance to these emotional reactions. In that sense, legal rules help us balance correctly, by imposing a test which reflects a balance articulated by our deliberative processes before a crisis hits for one more likely to be influenced by emotional reactions in the immediate aftermath of a crisis.[254] Ironically, the need for clear legal rules is greatest precisely when the crisis seems to demand discarding them.[255]

For example, the rule that only the Security Council, and not individual or ad hoc groups of nations, can launch or authorize preventive wars does not absolutely remove the need for balancing a particular threat against the dangers of warfare. The rule does, however, reflect a strong substantive presumption that such wars are undesirable, and it imposes the procedural check that the decision be made by an international body composed of countries which may have a less emotional stake in

252 *Id.* at 588.

253 *Id.* at 588–89.

254 *See* Sunstein, *supra* note 212, at 105–106.

255 *See id.*

going to war.[256] Similarly, the absolute prohibition against torture may not prevent a military officer from disobeying the law and torturing a prisoner if he strongly believes that thousands of lives are imminently threatened by a ticking bomb and can be saved by coercive interrogation. This type of balancing, however, must be informed by the fact that the officer is acting unlawfully and is subject to criminal prosecution for his actions. That the criminal law imposes a serious penalty for faulty balancing will presumably act as a substantial restraint on the officer. In contrast, ad hoc balancing under vague standards imposes virtually no legal restraints on decision makers.

Another objection to maintaining clear rules during crisis concedes that exaggerated fears during a crisis may skew decision making, but argues that nonetheless the elevated risk of harm warrants a modification of the legal rules that apply in non-emergency periods. That people may have an exaggerated, emotional response to a new threat does not necessarily mean that the new threat does not create new risks which justify changing the status quo.

I do not argue that emergencies never require reevaluating or modifying legal rules to meet new situations; I merely contend that we should not abandon legal rules for ad hoc decision making whenever a new crisis hits. Of course we should always evaluate the legal rules in the context of a complex and changing environment. For example, prior to September 11, international law did not clearly define non-state terrorist attacks as armed attacks that would accord the victim state a right of self-defense.[257] After September 11, NATO unequivocally, and the UN Security Council more ambiguously recognized such a right of self-defense.[258] A new threat may require some modification of the legal rules, but policymakers should avoid discarding the relevant legal rules in favor of ambiguous standards and ad hoc balancing tests simply because we face a new crisis.

Second, despite the increased risk of harm in times of emergency, we should be skeptical about proposals made in the heat of crisis to significantly modify the rules developed prior to the crisis. Many of the existing rules were not developed simply for "normal" times but were explicitly based on experience with past crises and with prior arguments that new conditions required coercive measures. For example, Congress enacted the Non-Detention Act of 1971 prohibiting preventive detention of U.S. citizens unless explicitly authorized by congressional statute because it wanted to ensure that what happened to Japanese American citizens

256 *See* U.N. Charter art. 51 (permitting individual nations to act in self-defense in response to an armed attack); Mark A. Drumbl, *Victimhood in Our Neighborhood: Terrorist Crime, Taliban Guilt, and the Asymmetries of the International Legal Order*, 81 N.C. L. Rev. 1, 16 (2002) (describing the UN prohibition on the use of force).

257 *See* Drumbl, *supra* note 256, at 26–33.

258 *See* S.C. Res. 1368, ¶ 4, U.N. Doc. S/RES/1368 (Sept. 12, 2001); Press Release, North Atlantic Treaty Organisation, Statement by the North Atlantic Council (Sept. 12, 2001), *available at* http://www.nato.int/docu/pr/2001/p01-124e.htm.

during World War II would not occur in any future war.[259] Congress enacted the law to deal with wartime and other national emergency conditions because it concluded—based on historical experience—that despite the increased dangers of wartime, executive preventive detention was not warranted unless explicitly authorized by Congress.[260] We should not discard that calculation simply because we are now experiencing dangers that differ from those we have faced in the past. Shouldn't we trust the balance that Congress thought should apply in wartime when it studied the problem in a non-crisis situation, rather than the balance which seems to make sense in the immediate and emotional aftermath of the crisis? At a minimum, we should be skeptical of claims to modify protections intended to apply in wartime, simply because there is a new wartime crisis. So too, the international community and U.S. Senate concluded that torture and cruel and inhumane treatment could never be justified—even during wartime and emergencies.[261] We should not discard or modify that legal principle, even if the risk of harm is now greater because of the September 11 attacks, because countries dispassionately and explicitly considered the elevated risk of harm during war and emergency when they drafted and ratified the Geneva Conventions, the International Covenant on Civil and Political Rights, and the Convention against Torture. None of those treaties permit torture in times of war or emergency, even though their drafters undoubtedly recognized that in such situations, the necessity to obtain information would be much greater than in peacetime or non-emergency periods. We should not modify that rule because decision makers might reach a different judgment in the immediate emotional aftermath of a crisis; both history and social science ought to make us suspicious of judgments reached in crisis situations that are so fundamentally at odds with the rules people thought ought apply to wartime situations before the crisis eventuated.

There are, of course, occasions when it is appropriate for the government to take strong, coercive measures. But in almost all of these situations the law permits the government to take forceful action. For example, Condoleezza Rice and Donald Rumsfeld maintain that "millions are dead because Britain and France failed to take preventive military action to thwart the gathering Nazi threat in the 1930s."[262] But at that time, legal rules permitted those countries to take military action that would have stopped Hitler before he could have obtained the military power he did. When Hitler attacked the Rhineland, Austria, or Czechoslovakia, Britain and France could have responded in collective self-defense to those attacks without the need to resort to any doctrine of preventive war. What prevented them from doing so was not international law, but rather the lack of political will to prepare militarily

259 *See* H.R. Rep. No. 92-116, at 2 (1971).

260 *Id.* at 3–5.

261 Convention Against Torture and Other Cruel, Inhuman or Degrading Treatment or Punishment, *supra* note 65, art. 2.

262 Record, *supra* note 52, at 79–80.

and forge a strong alliance with the Soviet Union to counter Hitler's attacks.[263] Indeed, Winston Churchill unsuccessfully advocated the formation of a strong defensive alliance with the Soviet Union and military preparation, and not the initiation of preventive war with Germany.[264]

Of course, there are hypothetical situations where policymakers may deem coercive preventive measures necessary to prevent catastrophic harm—as in torture and the ticking bomb scenario—but the legal rules simply prohibit executive officials from taking such action. However, real cases that present these dilemmas are likely to be rare, and as I and other scholars have written, it is better to force the executive official to violate the law openly and seek either indemnification or ratification, or accept punishment for his actions, than to permit officials to have the legal authority to engage in torture, preventive detention, and preventive war whenever they deem these measures necessary.[265] To provide officials with the legal authority to take such measures when, in their opinion, emergency so requires is to take us down the path to normalizing those measures.

CONCLUSION

It is not surprising that governments often respond to an emergency or crisis by resorting to coercive preventive measures. When a danger becomes potentially catastrophic, it seems to make sense to take strong, aggressive preventive measures to avoid the danger from eventuating. Similarly, the tendency of governments to substitute ad hoc balancing for clear rules in determining which actions to take to resolve a crisis is not irrational. Discarding the clear rules affords government officials more discretion to take the preventive measures they deem necessary to meet the crisis.

Yet ironically, the turn toward coercive preventive measures may heighten instead of diminish the risk of the catastrophic danger occurring. In the heat of the crisis, the government will often fail to accurately consider the risks of the preventive action—risks that not only will imprison innocent people unnecessarily, but that these preventive measures will induce a reaction that will threaten the very security interests the government seeks to protect.

The Iraq war presents a vivid illustration of these dangers. A war that was waged ostensibly to prevent terrorists from obtaining access to weapons of mass destruction has created a terrorist haven in Iraq where none existed before the war.[266] The war

263 *See id.* at 79.

264 Tuvia Ben-Moshe, Churchill: Strategy and History 108–09 (1992); A.J.P. Taylor, Churchill, Four Faces and the Man 28–31 (1969); Alfred Vagts, Defense and Diplomacy 311 (1956).

265 *See, e.g.*, Oren Gross, *Chaos and Rules: Should Responses to Violent Crises Always Be Constitutional?*, 112 Yale L.J. 1011, 1022–23 (2003); Jules Lobel, Emergency Power and the Decline of Liberalism, 98 Yale L.J. 1385, 1396–97 (1989).

266 Jessica Stern, *How America Created a Terrorist Haven*, N.Y. Times, Aug. 20, 2003, at A21.

has spawned a breeding ground for terrorists in Iraq, inspired more terrorists throughout the world, embroiled the U.S. Armed Forces in a seemingly unwinnable conflict, and emboldened other nations such as North Korea and Iran to accelerate their efforts to produce nuclear weapons.[267] An April 2006 classified National Intelligence Estimate concluded that the Iraq war "has made the overall terrorism problem worse."[268] Similarly a report by Britain's top intelligence and law enforcement officials concluded that "[e]vents in Iraq are continuing to act as motivation and a focus of a range of terrorist related activity in the U.K."[269]

The Iraq war as well as the other coercive preventive measures the Bush administration has employed in its war on terrorism thus stand as a cautionary note to those who seek to rely on ad hoc balancing of competing interests instead of clear rules to decide to preventively detain individuals, to preventively use coercive interrogation methods to gain information, or to wage preventive war against other nations. Such preventive actions are often justly condemned by civil libertarians as undermining our liberty and other values such as peace. Unfortunately, their use can often undermine our security as well.

267 Cole & Lobel, *supra* note 1 (manuscript at 175–84).

268 Mark Mazzetti, *Spy Agencies Say Iraq War Worsens Terrorism Threat,* N.Y. Times, Sept. 24, 2006, at A1.

269 Elaine Sciolino & Don Van Natta Jr., *June Report Led Britain to Lower Its Terror Alert,* N.Y. Times, July 19, 2005, at A1.

THE UNTOLD STORY OF AL QAEDA'S ADMINISTRATIVE LAW DILEMMAS

Mariano-Florentino Cuéllar†

Originally Published in *Minnesota Law Review*, Volume 91, No.5 (2007)

In the months and years following September 11, senior al Qaeda strategists and sympathizers disseminated a series of manuscripts revealing the terrorist network's aims and its internal management dilemmas. This Article elucidates how we can better evaluate changes in our counter-terrorism laws and policies—from warrantless NSA surveillance to massive military operations abroad—by scrutinizing the goals and internal organizational problems of our adversaries. Conventional wisdom paints terrorist networks such as al Qaeda and state bureaucracies in advanced industrialized countries as starkly different. Al Qaeda and its allies are assumed to pose particularly severe dangers because they are flexible, adaptable, decentralized, and staffed by committed supporters with a common goal. By contrast, state bureaucracies in advanced industrialized nations are often described as suffering from plodding, rule-bound decision-making structures that hobble their response to our nimble adversary. But a closer look at al Qaeda's own strategic studies—read in light of social scientists' emerging analyses of terrorist organizations—reveals a more complex picture. In it, the distinction between terrorist networks and bureaucratic agencies is less pronounced than commonly supposed. Both entities face pervasive problems involving the harnessing of expertise, the resolution of conflict among politically important players, reconciliation of competing goals, restraints on over-zealous action, building public legitimacy, and monitoring subordinate activity. By scrutinizing terrorist networks as collective entities with conflicting goals facing evasive administrative problems, we can better understand three things: (1) that, in fact, terrorist networks have repeatedly sought to develop administrative procedures and law-like hierarchical arrangements to manage their problems; (2) that the efficacy of counter-terrorism strategies depends crucially on the extent to which such strategies exacerbate (at a reasonable cost) these networks' administrative problems; and (3) that legal arrangements characteristic of U.S. public

† Associate Professor and Deane F. Johnson Faculty Scholar, Stanford Law School; Faculty Affiliate, Stanford Center for International Security and Cooperation. I would like to thank Jake Shapiro, Barry Weingast, William McCants, Jarret Brachman, Robert Weisberg, Alan Morrison, and participants in the 2006 Minnesota Law Review Symposium, "9/11 Five Years On: A Look at the Global Response to Terrorism." I also appreciate excellent research assistance from Niki Carelli. Errors are mine.

law—particularly those governing the administrative decisions of bureaucratic institutions—are valuable in part because they assuage the very problems that our terrorist adversaries are so desperately trying to solve.

* * *

"By the grace of God, the organized Islamic work is beginning to be managed on the highest administrative level . . . especially the jihadi organizations. However there still needs to be more mastery, general training, and advancement in order to encompass the greatest amount of the sectors of the Islamic movement, especially since we are approaching (by the permission of God) a stage in which our administrative needs will be expanded in what we have called the stage of the administration of savagery, where we will mix with hundreds of thousands of people and they will require the administration of regions from us as diminished governments. If we are not prepared to deal with that, we will face dangerous problems, to say nothing of the harm (that results from) random behavior or (from) a rigid management organization which stops action by its inflexibility and prevents development and advancement."[1]

"Bureaucracies rationalize the problems and processes with which they work, allowing them to develop systems. . . . That system does not consist simply of rules and regulations. Rather, the rules are accompanied by standards, practices, guidelines, prototypes, models, and informal procedures, all shaped to some extent by a general goal. . . ."[2]

Americans lived through such a raft of changes in the half-decade after the September 11 attacks that evaluating those changes became a cottage industry in legal scholarship. Lawmakers entrusted the executive to manage sweeping new surveillance and war-fighting powers.[3] When the executive doubted whether Congress would convey even more powers for surveillance, it implemented some tactics without congressional authorization.[4] The American military engaged in complex missions in Afghanistan and Iraq.[5] It deposed brutal regimes, but thousands of American

---

1 Abu Bakr Naji, The Management of Savagery 23 (William McCants trans., Combating Terrorism Center, U.S. Mil. Acad., 2006) (discussing al Qaeda leadership).

2 Stephen Breyer, Breaking the Vicious Circle 61–62 (1993).

3 *See* Authorization for Use of Military Force, Pub. L. No. 107-40, 115 Stat. 224 (2001); Authorization for Use of Military Force Against Iraq Resolution of 2002, Pub. L. No. 107-243, 116 Stat. 1498 (2002); Uniting and Strengthening America by Providing Appropriate Tools Required to Intercept and Obstruct Terrorism Act (Patriot Act) of 2001, Pub. L. No. 107-56, 115 Stat. 272.

4 *See infra* Part III (discussing the administration's policy of using the National Security Agency for warrantless surveillance precluded by the Foreign Intelligence Surveillance Act (FISA) of 1978, Pub. L. No. 95-511, §§ 101–111, 92 Stat. 1783 (codified as amended in scattered sections of 50 U.S.C.)).

5 *See generally* Martin Ewans, Conflict In Afghanistan: Studies in Asymmetric Warfare 164–68 (2005) (discussing the U.S. invasion of Afghanistan); David L. Phillips, Losing Iraq: Inside the Postwar Recon-Struction Fiasco 7–11 (2005) (discussing U.S. difficulties associated with the invasion of and reconstruction of Iraq).

soldiers—and many tens of thousands of foreign civilians—died in the process.[6] U.S. intelligence organizations redoubled their efforts to track wire transfers and enemy operatives, and became embroiled in a now infamous tug-of-war with the White House about the justifications for war in Iraq.[7] Some of the nation's most distinguished diplomats staked their reputation on the strength of that intelligence.[8] U.S. personnel detained thousands,[9] abusing and killing some of them in the course of interrogations,[10] and rendering others to regimes with established track records of torture and human rights abuses.[11] Courts began sorting through fundamental questions—raised perhaps once in a generation—about the scope of executive power,[12] the role of international law in our legal system,[13] and the constitutional guarantees afforded to detained individuals.[14] Predictably, most of these developments inspired considerable public debate.

But they were far from the only changes. A bit further from the limelight, criminal justice bureaucracies achieved long-sought changes in criminal statutes and deployed their immense breadth against alleged supporters of terrorism[15] and

---

6 *See, e.g.*, Erik Mink, *Grasping for Answers as Iraq Unravels*, St. Louis Post-Dispatch, Oct. 24, 2006, at D11 (discussing estimates of civilian and military deaths and casualties).

7 *See generally* Comm'n on the Intelligence Capabilities of the U.S. Regarding Weapons of Mass Destruction, Report to the President of the United States 154–56 (2005) (criticizing the intelligence community's assessment of Iraqi programs allegedly involving weapons of mass destruction).

8 *See, e.g.*, Thomas E. Ricks, Fiasco: The American Military Adventure in Iraq 90–94 (2006) (discussing the weaknesses in the case then-Secretary of State Colin Powell presented to the United Nations regarding the administration's case for attacking Iraq).

9 *See generally* Diane Marie Amann, *Abu Ghraib*, 153 U. Penn. L. Rev. 2085, 2088–89 (2005) (indicating there were almost 700 detainees at Guantánamo and hundreds elsewhere).

10 *See id.* at 2092–93 (describing detainee abuse); Deaths of Detainees in the Custody of U.S. Forces in Iraq and Afghanistan from 2002 to 2005, http://www.medscape.com/viewarticle/547787 (last visited Apr. 9, 2007) (accounting for detainee deaths while in custody and describing causes of death).

11 *See* David Weissbrodt & Amy Bergquist, *Extraordinary Rendition: A Human Rights Analysis*, 19 Harv. Hum. Rts. J. 123, 129 (2006).

12 *See* Hamdan v. Rumsfeld, 126 S. Ct. 2749, 2773–74 (2006) (balancing executive and congressional power over the armed forces).

13 *Id.* at 2786.

14 *See* Hamdi v. Rumsfeld, 542 U.S. 507, 524–25 (2004).

15 *See* Patriot Act, Pub. L. No. 107-56, 115 Stat. 272 (2001) (containing numerous substantive criminal law provisions); Muneer I. Ahmad, *A Rage Shared by Law: Post-September 11 Racial Violence as Crimes of Passion*, 92 Cal. L. Rev. 1261, 1329 (2004) ("Although trumpeted as anti-terrorism legislation, it vastly expands police powers in terrorism and non-terrorism cases alike. As some members of Congress have admitted, they voted for the legislation without having read it entirely."). For the Department of Justice's perspective on terrorism-related prosecutions and investigations associated with the new Patriot Act passed in the wake of the attacks, see U.S. Dep't Of Justice, Report from the Field: The USA Patriot Act at Work 2–5 (2004).

other targets.[16] Executive branch officials prioritized secrecy in response to Freedom of Information Act requests,[17] environmental regulation,[18] and immigration proceedings.[19] Congress gave regulators complex new authority to control cross-border financial flows to disrupt money laundering and terrorist financing.[20] And working in tandem, legislators and the President undertook the most significant transformation of the federal bureaucracy in a half-century, forging a sprawling new Department of Homeland Security,[21] a new intelligence oversight bureaucracy,[22] and a new set of budget priorities reshaping the allocation of federal resources.[23] Together, these developments paint a startling picture, in which nearly a half-century of legal changes has been crammed into sixty months.

My purpose here is not to dwell directly on these developments.[24] Instead, this Article raises questions about how best to assess legal change by mining an under-appreciated vein of knowledge about the organization of terrorist activity. In the process, the Article contributes to an applied scholarly literature on national security law in the administrative state, and to a more theoretical one concerned with the legal implications of social science research on complex organizations.

The argument begins by engaging a familiar trope. Conventional wisdom suggests that terrorist networks such as al Qaeda are quintessentially different from the complex national security and regulatory bureaucracies charged with countering

16 *See* Eric Lictblau, *U.S. Uses Terror Law to Pursue Crimes from Drugs to Swindling*, N.Y. TIMES, Sept. 28, 2003, at 1.

17 *See* Keith Anderson, Note, *Is There Still a "Sound Legal Basis?": The Freedom of Information Act in the Post-9/11 World*, 64 OHIO ST. L.J. 1605, 1620–24 (2003).

18 *See* Rena Steinzor, *Democracies Die Behind Closed Doors: The Homeland Security Act and Corporate Accountability*, 12 KAN. J.L. & PUB. POL'Y 641, 660 (2003).

19 *See* David Cole, *Enemy Aliens*, 54 STAN. L. REV. 953, 961 (2002); Stephen H. Legomsky, *Deportation and the War on Independence*, 91 CORNELL L. REV. 369, 373 (2006).

20 *See* Patriot Act, tit. III (outlining regulatory provisions governing money laundering and terrorist financing). For a discussion of the significance of these changes, see Mariano-Florentino Cuéllar, *The Mismatch Between State Power and State Capacity in Transnational Law Enforcement*, 22 BERKELEY J. INT'L L. 15, 37–39 (2004).

21 *See* Dara Cohen et al., *Crisis Bureaucracy: Homeland Security and the Political Design of Legal Mandates*, 59 STAN. L. Rev. 673, 696–700 (2006).

22 For an insightful analysis of this development, see Anne Joseph O'Connell, *The Architecture of Smart Intelligence: Structuring and Overseeing Agencies in the Post-9/11 World*, 94 CAL. L. REV. 1655, 1673–75 (2006).

23 *See id.* at 1667.

24 Although it is tempting to do so, most of those developments have been the subject of substantial and often quite thoughtful commentary (including in some well-reasoned pieces appearing in this Symposium). On the other hand, certain occurrences—particularly the significance of bureaucratic changes, budget reforms, and criminal justice policies—have plainly received less reflection than they merit. *But see id.*; Cass R. Sunstein, *Administrative Law Goes to War*, 118 HARV. L. REV. 2663, 2669 (2005); David Zaring & Elena Baylis, *Sending the Bureaucracy to War*, 92 IOWA L. REV. (forthcoming May 2007) (manuscript at 11, on file with author).

the threat that terrorists pose.[25] Discussions of the aforementioned changes are often clouded by seductive assumptions derived from that conventional wisdom: that our terrorist adversaries can be understood as nimble, endlessly adaptable actors simultaneously able to capture the advantages of decentralization while functioning as a unitary actor motivated by a single coherent goal.[26] This Article

---

25 *See, e.g.*, Scott Canon, *West Will Win War on Terror, Rumsfeld Assures University*, BOSTON GLOBE, Nov. 10, 2006, at A15.

> [Rumsfeld, focusing on terrorism] described an effort that has battled against an elusive enemy and labored to overcome bureaucratic and political hurdles at home. . . . He said the military needs to transform to a more agile force capable of changing tactics to deal with terrorists. . . . "The enemy has a brain," he said. "They do things, and they adjust."

Id. Similar views are voiced by policy analysts outside government, as evidenced by the following statement from a well-placed observer of national security at a leading Washington, D.C. think-tank:

> The threat we face from al Qaeda and other terrorist groups is one of agile, non-bureaucratic adversaries who have the great advantage of being on the offense—knowing where, when and how they will attack. . . . [T]errorist groups have always been nimble opponents that were difficult to stop . . . No security threat to the United States matches this one. To fight this nontraditional threat, we must think outside [the] box and try to be as nimble as the opponent (a difficult task).

Protecting the Homeland: The President's Proposal for Reorganizing Our Homeland Defense Infrastructure, Before the Subcomm. on Technology, Terrorism, and Government Information of the S. Comm. on the Judiciary, *available at* http://judiciary.senate.gov/print_testimony.cfm?id=294&wit_id=667 (2002) (statement of Ivan Eland, Director, Defense Policy Studies, Cato Institute). As will emerge, reality is far more complicated. Although terrorists are adaptable, they face considerable organizational problems in adapting. And while they have partially decentralized (and some strategists would prefer even greater decentralization), terrorist networks such as al Qaeda also find crucial benefits from hierarchy. *See infra* Part I.B.4. This has kept such organizations partially hierarchical even in the midst of protracted crises. In addition, both before and during such crises, some theorists believe the most crucial characteristics terrorist networks should develop are essentially those sometimes considered to be outdated in some superficial observations of national bureaucracies, including law-like procedures, trained managers working as part of a hierarchy, and monitoring mechanisms to mitigate agency problems. *See* NAJI, *supra* note 1, at 23, 73–74; *infra* Part II.C. As used in this Article, the term "terrorist network" refers to organized nonstate entities whose leaders both desire and find it feasible to use a range of tactics including terrorist attacks.

26 For a sampling of presidential statements treating the terrorist threat as one posed by a unitary actor with a single, coherent ideology, see The President's News Conference, 42 WEEKLY COMP. PRES. DOC. 1877, 1880 (Oct. 25, 2006) ("Afghanistan was a front in this war against the terrorists. Iraq is now the central front in the war against the terrorists. This war is more than just finding people and bringing them to justice; this war is an ideological conflict between a radical ideology that can't stand freedom, and moderate, reasonable people that hope to live in a peaceful society."). For an example of a scholarly paper modeling a terrorist organization as a unitary actor, see Paul R. Pillar, *Counterterrorism after al Qaeda*, 27 WASH. Q. 101, 102 (2004); Robert Powell, Defending Against Terrorist Attacks with Limited Resources (Aug. 2005) (unpublished manuscript), *available at* http://www.wcfia.harvard.edu/seminars/pegroup/Powelldefendaug05.pdf (providing an example of a scholarly paper modeling a terrorist group as a unitary actor). Pillar eloquently emphasizes the "threat of decentralization" trope:

> The small, secretive nature of terrorist plots and the indeterminate nature of the target—likely to become an even greater problem as the Islamic terrorist threat further decentralizes—have

shows this assumption to be profoundly misleading. Terrorist organizations are complex entities. They are enveloped in a multitude of organizational problems that necessarily make principled discussions of legal responses to terrorism far more intricate than conventional wisdom might suggest.

The alternative is not to forswear the instrumental analysis of counter-terrorism tactics. Instead, the key to any reasonable policy response lies in systematically examining the strategic dilemmas and organizational challenges confronting terrorist networks such as al Qaeda. Terrorists, like drug cartels and legislatures, are a "they," not an "it," best understood as organized entities facing some of the same institutional problems that conventional state bureaucracies face.[27] Though animated by different strategic imperatives, leaders of terrorist networks and managers of public agencies shoulder common burdens. Their power depends on mitigating principal-agent problems.[28] They must harness expert knowledge, and they yearn for a beguiling yet endlessly elusive synthesis of technocracy and political vision.[29] Their power depends in part on fostering favorable public perceptions[30] and

---

> always made terrorism a particularly difficult target subject.... The danger now lies in the fact that the looser the operational connections become and the less Islamist terrorism is instigated by a single figure, the harder it will be to uncover exploitable links and the more likely that the instigators of future terrorist attacks will escape the notice of U.S. intelligence. In a more decentralized network, these individuals will go unnoticed not because data on analysts' screens are misinterpreted but because they will never appear on those screens in the first place.

Pillar, *supra*, at 102–04.

27 *See infra* Parts I, II. A. Although the focus of this case study is primarily on al Qaeda and its affiliates, other illicit nonstate actors (particularly those interested in using terrorist tactics) are likely to face substantially similar organizational problems. The analysis therefore holds broader implications.

28 For a discussion of principal-agent problems, see Mathew McCubbins & Thomas Schwartz, *Congressional Oversight Overlooked: Police Patrols Versus Fire Alarms,* 28 AM. J. POL. SCI. 165, 171–73 (1984). For an insightful analysis of how principal-agent problems distort the operations of terrorist networks, see Jacob Shapiro, *The Greedy Terrorist: A Rational-Choice Perspective on Terrorist Organizations' Inefficiencies and Vulnerabilities,* 4 STRATEGIC INSIGHTS 1, 2 (2005); *infra* notes 156–57 and accompanying text (providing examples of how al Qaeda strategists face principal-agent problems).

29 *See* NAJI, *supra* note 1, at 23 ("The mastery of the art of administration saves a lot of time and blesses the effort exerted (to acquire it), especially since we are in a race against time and we need to undertake any effort in such a way that we get the best results."). For a similarly effusive exaltation of technocratic ideals in the context of the American administrative state, see BREYER, *supra* note 2, at 61–62. For critiques discussing the simultaneous allure of technocracy along with the impossibility of using technocracy to resolve normative problems of administration, see generally Gerald E. Frug, *The Ideology of Bureaucracy in American Law,* 97 HARV. L. REV. 1276 (1984) (discussing the tension between administrative models founded on expertise and suggesting limits to agency actions); Richard B. Stewart, *The Reformation of American Administrative Law,* 88 HARV. L. REV. 1669 (1975) (comparing administrative discretion with judicial controls on discretion).

30 *See* PETER BERGEN, THE OSAMA BIN LADEN I KNOW 392 (2006). Referring to top al Qaeda strategist Ayman al Zawahiri, Bergen notes, "Zawahiri complained in his 2001 biography,

adjudicating disputes.[31] In short, both terrorist networks and conventional public agencies are burdened by some of the challenges routinely managed by U.S. administrative law. While scrutinizing the administrative problems of al Qaeda and analogous organizations is manifestly more challenging than merely restating common assumptions about nonstate actors,[32] this scrutiny will reward scholars and policymakers with a host of valuable insights crucial to any defensible evaluation of post-September 11 legal changes.

My argument focuses on three insights in particular. First, although circumstances have forced terrorist networks to adopt a measure of decentralization, those networks have often sought to build administrative procedures and law-like hierarchical arrangements to strike a balance between flexibility and control and to mitigate the recurring organizational problems associated with managing painfully scarce resources. Second, policymakers should evaluate counter-terrorism policies on the basis of whether they exacerbate terrorist networks' ongoing organizational challenges—challenges such as fostering public approval and mitigating agency problems—at a reasonable cost. Third, administrative arrangements characteristic of how advanced industrialized democracies manage organizational problems are valuable in part because they tend to manage pervasive organizational problems more effectively than non-state terrorist actors manage such problems. In contrast, a less organization-focused evaluation of terrorist networks is likely to emphasize simple but misleading assumptions over complexity,[33] shorter-term tactical gains

---

Knights Under the Prophet's Banner, that the masses have not embraced al-Qaeda . . . 'The jihad movement must come closer to the masses. We must win the people's confidence, respect, and affection.'" *Id.* For discussions of the value of favorable public perceptions to administrative bureaucracies in advanced industrialized countries, see Mariano-Florentino Cuéllar, *Rethinking Regulatory Democracy*, 57 Admin. L. Rev. 411, 495–97 (2005); *infra* note 134.

31 *See* Lawrence Wright, The Looming Tower 134 (2006) (discussing the problems faced by al Qaeda at its early stages of development as a result of internal squabbles).

32 *Compare* The President's News Conference, *supra* note 26, at 1880 ("[T]his war is an ideological conflict between a radical ideology that can't stand freedom. . . ."), *with* Martha Crenshaw, *The Causes of Terrorism*, 13 Comp. Pol. 379, 385 (1981) ("As purposeful activity, terrorism is the result of an organization's decision that it is a politically useful means to oppose a government. . . . Terrorism serves a variety of goals, both revolutionary and subrevolutionary. Terrorists may be revolutionaries[,] . . . minority separatists combating indigenous regimes[,] . . . reformists[,] . . . anarchists or millenarians . . . or reactionaries acting to prevent change from the top.").

33 *See, e.g.*, Eric A. Posner & Adrian Vermeule, *Emergencies and Democratic Failure*, 92 Va. L. Rev. 1091, 1099 (2006). Posner and Vermeule assume that terrorist threats are best modeled as unexpected, exogenous shocks. *Id.* A focus on the internal dynamics of terrorist organizations, however, reveals the extent to which recruits and funding flow to such networks as a result of government policies. Hence, the assumption that terrorist shocks are entirely unpredictable and unrelated to domestic government policy, rather than endogenous to the settings where governments choose policies and terrorists solve organizational problems may be unwarranted. Depending on the nature of the security policy, it may actually help solve terrorists' problems (e.g., if the costs fall disproportionately on minorities from among which terrorist groups seek to recruit, or if the alleged security policy—such as the invasion of Iraq—makes it dramatically easier for the terrorist network to gain attention and resources).

over gradual strategic progress,[34] and worst-case scenarios about the threats posed by terrorist networks rather than the considerable organizational difficulties and trade-offs our terrorist adversaries face in carrying out their most lethal attacks.[35]

Peering inside a terrorist network may seem like a nearly impossible task. After all, both experience (with the failures of our own intelligence bureaucracies) and intuition (about terrorist networks' incentives for secrecy) suggest that we can do little more than speculate about questions such as what al Qaeda's ultimate strategic objectives are and what organizational challenges it faces in achieving those objectives. Surprisingly, this turns out not to be the case. In the months and years following September 11, senior al Qaeda strategists and sympathizers disseminated documents divulging the terrorist network's aims and its internal management dilemmas.[36] Some of these documents have been posted on the Internet; others have been recently declassified.[37] When we examine these documents in the context of emerging political science literature on the organizational dilemmas associated with terrorist activity, these jihadi strategic studies (as some observers have christened them) provide a revealing portrait of al Qaeda's goals. Al Qaeda emerges as an organization that delegates power and money to regional affiliates who carry out recruiting, terrorist attacks, and political organizing.[38] Though it is decentralized, it appears still to have a coherent leadership structure and a cadre of strategic thinkers to chart its future course.[39] Both the leadership and the strategists are bent on turning the organization into a social movement with broad appeal in the

---

34 *See id.* (stating that "[a]s the benefits of security increase due to exogenous threats such as terrorism, a well-functioning government will supply more security and less liberty, because the value gained from the increase in security will exceed the value lost from the decrease in liberty," without considering whether governments have the knowledge or motivation to provide the right kind of "security" given the complexities of terrorist organizations).

35 *See* Jide Nzelibe & John Yoo, *Rational War and Constitutional Design,* 115 YALE L.J. 2512, 2533 n.56 (2006). The authors assume that "terrorist groups like al Qaeda seek to acquire weapons of mass destruction, are more likely to use them, and—because they have no population or territory to defend—may be immune to 'traditional concepts of deterrence' that permeate the crisis bargaining model." *Id.* Although the authors have reason to question whether bargaining dynamics would play out the same way with ordinary nation-states and terrorist networks, the discussion elides organizational complexities that force terrorist networks to contend with calibrating the intensity of their attacks, cultivating public support (and avoiding backlash), and trading off the investment of scarce resources in procuring or developing such a destructive weapon compared to other imperatives. *See generally* BERGEN, *supra* note 30 (describing factors important to the development of al Qaeda); *infra* note 109 (providing additional discussion of how the mass public tends to affect the incentives of terrorist networks).

36 *See infra* Part I.A.

37 *See infra* Part I.A.

38 *See* LAWRENCE WRIGHT, *The Master Plan,* NEW YORKER, Sept. 11, 2006, at 48, 50–51 (discussing the jihadists' alleged decision to decentralize after the September 11 attacks).

39 *See* NAJI, *supra* note 1, at 25 (discussing al Qaeda leadership); *Al Qaeda's No. 2 Criticizes Bush and Pope in Video,* CHI. TRIB., Sept. 30, 2006, at 12, *available at* 2006 WLNR 16955181 (describing a recent video by al Qaeda leader Ayman al Zawahiri).

Muslim world.[40] In this quest they are aided by U.S. policies that provoke outrage among rank and file Muslims,[41] and they are frustrated by the fact that some supporters have competing goals, like getting rich.[42]

These realities play out in illicit terrorist organizations that are unquestionably unique. Plainly, al Qaeda and its imitators differ in a host of ways from a bureaucratized nation-state, and even to some extent from previous insurgencies and other illicit organizations.[43] The irony is that scholars and policymakers can only fully grasp those distinctions, and their potentially subtle policy implications, after recognizing the extent to which terrorist networks face a class of dilemmas that reflect—and sometimes even mirror—those of the Defense Department, the Food and Drug Administration, the National Intelligence Director, and United Nations Peacekeeping Operations. Indeed, when the jihadi strategic studies are read in the context of political scientists' work on terrorist organizations, they reveal the extent to which terrorist networks confront problems that are analogous to those of our own administrative law.[44] Common predicaments include delegating executive and quasi-legislative powers to subordinate entities, harnessing expertise, solving problems associated with participation and legitimacy, and adjudicating disputes. Although al Qaeda strategists have been forced to manage their myriad of internal administrative dilemmas without the precise equivalent of administrative law, some

---

40 *See* Combating Terrorism Ctr., U.S. Military Acad., Harmony and Disharmony: Exploiting Al-Qa'ida's Organizational Vulnerabilities 52–54 (2006) [hereinafter Harmony and Disharmony], *available at* http://www.ctc.usma.edu/aq/Harmony%20and%20Disharmony%20--20CTC.pdf (discussing al Qaeda's continuing attempts to become a "social movement"); Wright, *supra* note 38, at 51 (quoting Suri as declaring that "[a]l Qaeda is not an organization, it is not a group, nor do we want it to be . . . it is a call, a reference, a methodology").

41 *See infra* Part II.B.

42 *See* Harmony and Disharmony, *supra* note 40, at 11, 13 ("Preferences aren't always aligned. When they are not, the covert nature of terrorist groups necessarily implies that agents can take advantage of delegation to act as they prefer, not as their principals would like.").

43 *See infra* Part I.B.4 (describing the administrative law analogy). Al Qaeda's cavalier willingness to kill civilians is its most readily discernable distinction. Organizational polymorphism is a fact of life, affecting both the public agencies that enforce laws as well as the licit and illicit entities subject to such enforcement. The point here is not to deny that fact, but to focus on common organizational problems that can provide a more realistic picture of terrorist networks as well as the public bureaucracies with which they interact. *Id.; see also infra* Part II.B (discussing differences between al Qaeda and other insurgencies).

44 For present purposes, the term "administrative law" is used both in the literal sense of a law-like system to solve administrative problems, which substantially overlaps with (though is obviously different from) using the term to describe the duties and functions of administrative law in the American system. Administrative law is used in a manner that encompasses procedural mechanisms not ordinarily considered part of administrative law but reflecting substantially similar goals of mitigating arbitrary action by organizations. FISA's judicial review provisions are an example of the latter category. *See* Exec. Order No. 12,866, 58 Fed. Reg. 51735 (1993) (discussing the effect of convergence between law and social, economic, and political norms on the implementation of legal rules); *infra* Part III.

strategists have occasionally identified the need to build the functional equivalent of bureaucratized, hierarchical, and even law-like structures to manage their administrative problems.[45] They have recognized the devilish trade-offs between the flexible, decentralized structure that allegedly makes the organization so dangerous and regularized procedures and more centralized hierarchy which offer substantial benefits.

It may be tempting to ignore these parallels, but it is also risky. In a world where conventional wisdom stresses the allegedly unique flexibility and post-modern structure of al Qaeda-type terrorist organizations,[46] citizens and policymakers would do well to recognize some of the parallels between our own established institutions and these nascent ones. The more we begin to see al Qaeda and its counterparts as entities struggling to solve their internal administrative law-related dilemmas, the better we can understand how to disrupt their efforts.

And there may be a subtler, but no less important, implication. In the process of adopting a more nuanced perspective on the organization of terrorist networks, citizens and policymakers may also better appreciate how administrative arrangements help advanced industrialized nations forge reasoned responses to a wide variety of threats, whether they arise from food adulteration, environmental degradation, or terrorist attacks. Inasmuch as organizational success depends on managing agency problems, generating information, securing legitimacy and participation, and adjudicating disputes, citizens and policymakers should understand strategic conflicts in part as a contest between dueling systems of administrative law. The United States should evaluate counter-terrorism policies in part based on how they affect those systems. Hence, when Americans evaluate the implications of presidential decisions to sidestep the literal terms of the Foreign Intelligence Surveillance Act,[47] they would do well to focus on more than just the short-term tactical implications of the President's decision. They should also weigh the price of interfering with an institutional arrangement designed to mitigate the same type of internal management problem that terrorist networks are themselves struggling to overcome.

The argument unfolds in three parts. Part I seeks to peer inside a terrorist network by examining jihadi strategic studies, al Qaeda documents captured and recently declassified, and political science research on the organization of terrorist activity. It also identifies four recurring themes that emerge from these sources and that

---

45 In some cases, al Qaeda's leaders have actually implemented law-like arrangements to legitimize internal control decisions. *See* BERGEN, *supra* note 30, at 124–25 (discussing al Qaeda's use of Sharian courts to legitimize the decision to execute the son of one of the organization's leaders after the son was discovered spying on the group).

46 *See* NAT'L COMM'N ON TERRORIST ATTACKS UPON THE U.S., THE 9/11 COMMISSION REPORT 71 (2004) [hereinafter 9/11 COMMISSION REPORT] (describing a "new kind of terrorist organization"). *But see* Martha Crenshaw, *Counterterrorism in Retrospect: Chronicle of a War Foretold*, 84 FOREIGN AFFAIRS 187, 189, 193 (2005) (criticizing the idea that al Qaeda represents a "new" kind of terrorism).

47 FISA of 1978, Pub. L. No. 95-511, §§ 101-111, 92 Stat. 1783, 1801 (codified as amended in scattered sections of 50 U.S.C.).

appear to epitomize the behavior of insurgent networks committed to using terrorist tactics. Part II explores the implications of the preceding analyses and the potential relevance of these implications for evaluating legal and policy responses to terrorism. Part III demonstrates that this exercise enables us to understand the extent to which strategic conflict is partly a contest among competing systems of administrative law (broadly defined), each seeking to solve internal agency, information, participation, and adjudication problems endemic to both complex nonstate actors and state bureaucracies.

I. PEERING INSIDE A TERRORIST NETWORK

No event in recent history so vigorously forced the machinery of the federal government into overdrive as the September 11 attacks. Within hours of the terrorist strikes, Washington was a flurry of activity.[48] Executive branch officials held countless emergency meetings, made spirited public statements, executed complex diplomatic maneuvers, and took part in urgent internal discussions about how to respond.[49] The same was true thousands of miles away in Afghanistan, where the Taliban regime had been sheltering al Qaeda for years. At the same time that congressional leaders and the Bush administration were gearing up for legal and policy changes in the United States, al Qaeda's Kabul storefront office was brimming with activity.[50] Operatives, recruits, and organizers braced for the American response. Anticipating the imminent reprisal attack, the organization put together a propaganda video entitled "The Big Job."[51] Meanwhile, Osama bin Laden wrote a long email to Mullah Omar, the leader of the Taliban government hosting al Qaeda, seeking simultaneously to reassure the Taliban about what would come next and to strengthen their decision to tolerate it:

> I would like to emphasize the major impact of your statements on the Islamic world. Nothing harms America more than receiving your strong response to its positions and statements. Thus it is very important that the Emirate respond to every threat or demand from America . . . with demands that America put an end to its support of Israel, and that U.S. forces withdraw from Saudi Arabia. Such responses nullify the effect of the American media on people's morale. . . . Their threat to invade Afghanistan should be countered by a threat on your part that America will not be able to dream of security until Muslims experience it as a reality in Palestine and Afghanistan. . . . Keep in mind that America is currently facing two contradictory problems: a) If it refrains from responding to *jihad* operations, its prestige will collapse, thus forcing it to withdraw its troops abroad and restrict itself to U.S. internal affairs. This will transform it from a major power to a third-rate power, similar to Russia. b) On the other hand, a campaign against Afghanistan will impose great long-term

48 *See* 9/11 COMMISSION REPORT, *supra* note 46, at 35–36.

49 *Id.*

50 *See* Alan Cullison, *Inside Al-Qaeda's Hard Drive,* ATLANTIC MONTHLY, Sept. 2004, at 55, 58, *available at* http://www.theatlantic.com/doc/print/200409/cullison.

51 *See id.* at 68.

> economic burdens, leading to further economic collapse, which will force America, God willing, to resort to the former Soviet Union's only option: withdrawal from Afghanistan. . . .[52]

Mullah Omar was not the only one needing reassurance. Within al Qaeda, the response to the attack's success was mixed. Some al Qaeda members expressed deep concern for how the U.S. response would affect the jihadi movement. Abu Musab al Suri, a member of the terrorist organization's inner leadership and a theorist of jihad, had sparred with bin Laden before about the potential risks of high-profile operations. "I think our brother has caught the disease of screens, flashes, fans, and applause," he wrote in an email to bin Laden in 1999, complaining about the al Qaeda leader's penchant for prioritizing attacks generating high-profile publicity over the difficult work of running the training camps and smoothing over relations with the Taliban.[53] Now, Suri had reason to fear that the September 11 attacks would imperil the rule of the Taliban, and the Taliban's control of Afghanistan was central to the movement's future because it provided a place to organize and train new recruits.[54] By June 2002, even bin Laden's son Hamzah had posted messages on an al Qaeda website lamenting al Qaeda's post-September 11 situation.[55] In response to these challenges—furtively exchanging messages online and occasionally meeting in secluded corners of Central Asia—the organization's strategic thinkers set about recapturing the group's momentum and renewing its institution-building project.[56]

A. Context and Methods

The arguments unleashed within al Qaeda after the September 11 attacks richly emphasize the dangers of treating a terrorist network as a monolithic entity, impervious to organizational challenges, and enjoying a bountiful supply of members guided by a single purpose. With a more textured image of terrorist networks, key players shaping national security policy would find it harder to ignore the value of peering inside a terrorist network. Scholars and analysts would find it more difficult to dismiss the insights to be gleaned from closely observing al Qaeda's goals,

---

52 *Id.* at 70.

53 Wright, *supra* note 38, at 48, 50.

54 *Id.* at 48.

55 *Id.* Bin Laden's son exclaimed: "Oh, Father! Where is the escape and when will we have a home? Oh, Father! I see spheres of danger everywhere I look. . . . Tell me, Father, something useful about what I see." *Id.* Bin Laden apparently replied: "Oh, son! Suffice to say that I am full of grief and sighs. . . . I can only see a very steep path ahead." *Id.* Then, trying to dissipate the link between the September 11 attacks and the organization's present challenges, Bin Laden laments that "[a] decade has gone by in vagrancy and travel, and here we are in our tragedy. Security has gone, but danger remains." *Id.*

56 *See* Jarret M. Brachman & William F. McCants, *Stealing Al-Qaeda's Playbook,* 29 Studies Conflict & Terrorism 309, 309–11 (2006); Cullison, *supra* note 50, at 64; Wright, *supra* note 38, at 50–51.

its approach to weighing the costs and benefits of choosing between truck bombs or time bombs, its canonical texts and political debates, its internal compromises, and its plans for appealing to the public. Domestic political realities playing out within advanced industrialized countries sometimes discourage legislators and executive branch officials from fully appreciating the complexities of their terrorist adversaries.[57] But facing a complex adversary with competing goals and a range of subtle weaknesses and strengths, politicians are almost foolish to ignore what leaders and strategists of terrorist networks actually say, what social scientists have gradually come to understand about the internal strategies of nonstate actors, and what these statements and conclusions reveal about our adversary's internal organizational challenges and its strategies to address these challenges.[58]

This is precisely the strategy that the nation's terrorist adversary has pursued. Its thinkers are hard at work scrutinizing Western management texts and Paul Kennedy's *The Rise and Fall of the Great Powers.*[59] Regarding the importance of understanding Western administrative practices and political behavior, one strategist said this:

> We urge that most of the leaders of the Islamic movement be military leaders or have the ability to fight in the ranks, at the very least. Likewise, we also urge that those leaders work to master political science just as they would work to master military science.[60] We can say that bargaining is a characteristic of the politics of the enemy because the substitute for successful bargains between them—even if they achieve some partial gains—is continuous war which might crush all of (their) interests.[61]

And while an important goal in studying Western practices closely is to understand the weaknesses of those practices, the terrorist networks' strategists also emphasize the value of leveraging technocratic Western ideas about how to solve administrative challenges—challenges that are likely to prove increasingly critical to al Qaeda.[62]

---

57 *See* Ethan Bueno de Mesquita, *Politics and the Suboptimal Provision of Counterterror*, 61 Int'l Org. 9, 9–11 (2007) (discussing the potentially suboptimal provision of counter-terrorist policy); Cuéllar, *supra* note 20, at 44–48 (discussing the potentially diverging incentives of politicians and the public in the context of transnational security and law enforcement policy); Mark Schlesinger & Richard R. Lau, *The Meaning and Measure of Policy Metaphors*, 94 Am. Pol. Sci. Rev. 611, 611–14 (2000) (indicating ho4w politicians have an incentive to simplify the discussion of complicated issues).

58 *See* Bergen, *supra* note 30, at 392 ("One of the lessons of September 11 is that we should pay careful attention to what the jihadists are actually saying.").

59 *See* Brachman & McCants, *supra* note 56, at 310.

60 Naji, *supra* note 1, at 37–38.

61 *Id.* at 38.

62 *Id.* at 23 ("We must make use of books on the subject of administration, especially the management studies and theories which have been recently published, since they are consonant with the nature of modern societies. There is more than one site on the Internet in which one can obtain management books."). The strategists betray little awareness of the complexities associated with how larger political, economic, legal, and social circumstances combine to both shape the production of the Western management practices they lionize, as well as shape the conditions potentially allowing such practices to be instrumentally effective. For an interesting

Al Qaeda's thinkers have good reason to focus on understanding their adversaries. Al Qaeda's goals are ambitious and its resources are scarce. Its adversaries are complex and capable at times of tremendously nimble feats; yet, they also face substantial practical and political obstacles.[63] Some of the terrorist network's recurring internal challenges—involving agency problems, filling gaps in information, and adjudicating disputes—have analogues in advanced industrialized countries, and even turn out to be the province of an elaborate body of administrative law imposing non-arbitrariness requirements and managing public participation.[64] Policymakers in advanced industrial democracies would be ill-advised to neglect a symmetrical opportunity to scrutinize terrorist networks' organizational life. Such neglect would almost certainly diminish policymakers' capacity to mitigate the dangers that some terrorist networks pose, while also limiting society's capacity to evaluate the strategies justified in the name of disrupting terrorism.

To counter the existing dearth of attention to organizational problems in prevailing evaluations of counter-terrorism strategies, the sections that follow scrutinize strategic documents and studies produced by al Qaeda strategists and sympathizers. This scrutiny sheds light on the organization's goals and its internal administrative dynamics. I focus particularly on Abu Bakr Naji's book-length study, entitled *The Management of Savagery,* because of the unparalleled volume of details it provides about jihadi terrorist networks' goals and challenges, and because it was published through *Sat al-Jihad,* the main organ of al Qaeda in Saudi Arabia.[65] I also draw from accounts of three other works described by some leading al Qaeda observers as authentic and influential jihadi strategic studies describing the thinking of al Qaeda affiliates. These include a long tract by Abu Musab al-Suri entitled *Call for Worldwide Islamic Resistance;*[66] Ayman al Zawahiri's *Knights Under the Prophet's Banner;*[67] and a book entitled *Al Zarqawi: The Second Generation of al Qaeda,*

---

discussion of how macro-level social forces and legal practices shape the administration of organizations in the Middle East, see Timur Kuran, *Why the Middle East is Economically Underdeveloped: The Historical Mechanisms of Institutional Stagnation,* 18 J. Econ. Persp. 71, 82–83 (2004).

63 *See infra* Part I.B.

64 *See, e.g.,* Administrative Procedure Act § 4, 5 U.S.C. §§ 551–59 (2006) (providing, among other things, for notice and comment in the context of most regulatory rulemaking proceedings, and subjecting administrative action to review against arbitrariness).

65 *See* Wright, *supra* note 38, at 52, 56; Combating Terrorism Ctr., Abu Bakr Naji's The Management Of Savagery (2005) (unpublished document on file with author).

66 *See id.* at 50.

67 The translation of al Zawahiri's book-length analysis of al Qaeda's goals and strategies consulted here is included in Laura Mansfield, His Own Words: Translation and Analysis of the Writings of Dr. Ayman Al Zawahiri (Includes Knights Under the Prophet's Banner and Selected Post September 11, 2001 Communiqués and Messages) (2006). Al Zawahiri is "widely credited with being the brains behind the terror infrastructure of Al Qaeda." *Id.* at 13. Al Zawahiri's analysis was initially serialized in a Middle Eastern newspaper in December 2001. *Id.* at 13–14.

by radical Jordanian journalist Fouad Hussein, which is based on sympathetic interviews with individuals such as the late Abu Musab al Zarqawi (the former leader of al Qaeda in Mesopotamia) and al Qaeda security chief Saif al Adl.[68] To place these sources in context, I have also drawn from a growing cache of declassified al Qaeda documents translated and analyzed by the Combating Terrorism Center at the United States Military Academy,[69] and from political scientists' studies (which in turn reflect qualitative, game-theoretic, or quantitative analyses) of the organization of terrorist networks.[70]

It is natural to question whether such studies genuinely reflect al Qaeda's position. Given the reality that al Qaeda is an organization subject to internal disagreement and political competition, it is more accurate to say that these sources are likely to reflect what some of the organization's key strategists are thinking.[71] Al Qaeda factions jockey for support within the organization and for recruits outside it. In doing so, they are almost certainly drawn to articulating visions in written documents—much like political parties or government agencies in advanced industrial democracies develop written justifications for their own policies.[72] In some cases, the materials have been posted in known al Qaeda websites by individuals long known to have authored previous works published by the terrorist network.[73] In other cases (as with some of the declassified sources), documents have been captured directly from al Qaeda operatives.[74] Sometimes the sources provide insight into internal disagreements within al Qaeda in particular, and among supporters of the jihadi movement more generally. Some favor more regionally focused goals culminating in the control of territory in the Middle East, while others (particularly some of Hussein's sources)

68 *See* WRIGHT, *supra* note 38, at 56–57; Souad Mekhennet & Michael Moss, *In Lebanon Camp, A New Face of Jihad Vows Attacks on U.S.*, N.Y. TIMES, Mar. 16, 2007, at A1.

69 *See* HARMONY AND DISHARMONY, *supra* note 40, at 2–3.

70 *See infra* notes 71–75 and accompanying text.

71 The claim is not that these studies are representative, in a statistical sense, of what a random member of al Qaeda's leadership would think. A large study of available al Qaeda-related documents could prove revealing in many ways, though making inferences from such an analysis might prove tricky given the selection problems affecting the documents presently available. Instead, my goal here is to focus on some of the works that experts consider to be indicative of the major strands of thinking among some of al Qaeda's key strategists, to place them in context by referring to a larger body of captured al Qaeda documents and political science research, and to use the process as an opportunity for gaining some insights (and generating theories) about the role of law-like administrative arrangements in strategic conflict.

72 *Cf.* Brachman & McCants, *supra* note 56, at 309 ("Jihadi leaders are surprisingly frank when discussing the vulnerabilities of their movement and their strategies for toppling local regimes and undermining the United States. Their candor is, in large part, a consequence of struggles for leadership within the movement. . . .").

73 *See* WRIGHT, *supra* note 38, at 53, 56 (discussing the provenance of Abu Bakr Naji and his likely role as a leading al Qaeda strategist).

74 *See* HARMONY AND DISHARMONY, *supra* note 40, at 2.

seek an eventual "clash of civilizations" with the West.[75] In other domains, however, there is considerable overlap—even remarkable agreement—among these sources, and the themes evident therein also prove remarkably consistent with the analyses in political scientists' accounts of the logic of terrorist organizations.[76]

B. Themes Evident in Jihadi Strategic Studies

1. Western Resolve and Imperial Overstretch

Organizations nearly always claim to have a purpose.[77] For example, some public bureaucracies ostensibly aim to protect the environment through regulatory policies, while some clandestine insurgent groups claim responsibility for casting off the yoke of a brutal colonial occupation. To understand any collective entity which claims for itself the mission to accomplish particular goals, one should know something about its alleged objectives.[78]

Jihadi strategists repeatedly place among their most important strategies to carefully manage public reactions in Western democracies. In particular, the strategists see opportunity in the risks to the United States and its Western allies of what could be termed imperial overstretch, where the burdens of commanding the affairs of distant lands begins to weaken the government and the economy. This trope bears some resemblance to the account Paul Kennedy provides in *The Rise and Fall of the Great Powers*, in which empires crumble because of the staggering financial, geostrategic, and logistical burdens of maintaining their imperial capabilities.[79] A second and related theme is the goal of making Western republics sufficiently sensitive to these burdens to provoke a political demand for disengagement from the Muslim world. They find historical support for this possibility in the U.S. experience with Vietnam and Somalia, and Soviet Russia's debacles in Afghanistan. In one jihadi strategic tract, Abu Bakr Naji makes these points by quoting Paul Kennedy himself:

> When a state submits—whatever the extent of its ability—to the illusion of the deceptive power and behaves on this basis, that is when its downfall begins. It is just as the American author Paul Kennedy says: "If America expands the use of its military power and strategically extends more than necessary, this will lead to its downfall." This overwhelming power is also assisted by the cohesion [tamasuk] of the society in the central country and the cohesion of that society's institutions and sectors.

---

75 *See* Wright, *supra* note 38, at 57–59 (discussing differences between the more nationalistic activists focused on securing control of Arab countries, and comparing their purpose to the dark utopian vision of conflict in Hussein's book).

76 *See supra* notes 71–75 and accompanying text.

77 *See* James G. March & Herbert A. Simon, Organizations 22 (2d ed. 1993) ("Roles in organizations, as contrasted with many of the other roles that individuals fill, tend to be highly elaborated, relatively stable, and defined to a considerable extent in explicit and even written terms.").

78 This is not the same as assuming those objectives fully explain what organizations actually seek to do. *See generally* Cohen et al., *supra* note 21, at 702–12.

79 *See* Paul Kennedy, The Rise and Fall of the Great Powers 100 (1987) (discussing the weaknesses of the French and Russian empires).

> The overwhelming military power (weapons, technology, fighters) has no value without the cohesion of society and the cohesion of (society's) institutions and sectors. But this overwhelming military power may become a curse to this great superpower if the cohesion of society [literally "the social entity"] collapses.[80]

Bin Laden's aforementioned email to Mullah Omar immediately after the September 11 attacks voices similar hopes to

> [a]ttempt to cause a rift between the American people and their government, by demonstrating the following to the Americans: That the U.S. government will lead them into further losses of money and lives. That the government is sacrificing the people to serve the interests of the rich. . . . That the government is leading them to the war front to protect Israel and its security. America should withdraw from the current battle between Muslims and Jews.[81]

While the strategists sometimes differ in the extent to which they believe imperial overstretch to be essentially inevitable, they often highlight the importance of undertaking violent resistance operations that will encourage Westerners to tire of involvement in the Middle East and the Muslim world.[82] They also highlight an additional benefit of the controlled use of violence: it helps to puncture the myth that Western forces generally, and the United States in particular, are invincible.[83] Thus, in an argument that echoes game theorists' identification of prisoners' dilemma problems facing those who might resist authorities that have greater power,[84] Naji notes:

> There is no doubt that the power which God gave to the two superpowers (America and Russia) was overwhelming in the estimation of humans. However, in reality and after careful reflection using pure, human reason, one comes to understand this power is not able to impose its authority from the country of the center—from America, for example, or Russia—upon lands in Egypt and Yemen, for example, unless these (latter) countries submit to those powers entirely of their own accord. It is correct that this power is overwhelming and that it seeks help from the power of local regimes controlled by proxies who rule the Islamic world. Yet all of that is not enough (to completely control the satellite states). Therefore, the two superpowers must resort to using a deceptive media halo which portrays these powers as non-coercive and

---

80 Naji, *supra* note 1, at 7.

81 Cullison, *supra* note 50, at 70.

82 Naji, *supra* note 1, at 38 ("As for [the Americans'] persistence in continuing war, that is only when they think that their opponent is weak and it is possible to crush his will. When there is violent resistance which leads to invasions that cost a great deal and are of little use, the factions of the coalition began to withdraw one after another preferring (their own) security or delaying the conflict until more suitable circumstances.").

83 *Id.* at 9.

84 *Cf.* Barry R. Weingast, *The Political Foundations of Democracy and the Rule of Law*, 91 Am. Pol. Sci. Rev. 245, 245 (1997) (modeling a "game theory approach to . . . political officials' respect for political and economic rights of citizens").

> world-encompassing, able to reach into every earth and heaven as if they possess the power of the Creator of creation.[85]

Al Zawahiri sounds a similar theme in *Knights Under the Prophet's Banner*, noting the extent to which Western powers work through local allies inveigled by the appearance of power:

> We need to admit that successful attempts have been made to infiltrate our ranks, that these attempts have attracted some of our prominent names, and our enemies have added them to the crowds that serve their purposes, including the writers of falsehoods, those who exploit principles for personal gain, and those who sell their fat-was (religious rulings) as commodities.[86]

Because the Afghan experience punctured the myth of superpower invincibility, it was incredibly valuable to the jihadi movement.[87] Imperial overstretch, characterized by crumbling Western resolve and diminished perceptions of invincibility resulting from attacks in the Middle East, yields a toxic brew that strategists can use to undermine Western objectives and to acquire converts and territory. The organization must garner sufficient resources, supporters, and administrative capacities to calibrate its tactics and to survive long enough to reap the reward of the West's imperial overstretch, which brings us to the next theme.

2. Protecting Organizational Survival

Save in the rarest of circumstances, conflict over means, ends, or decision-rules is an inevitable byproduct of collective decision making.[88] Just as members of the Securities and Exchange Commission or the Federal Election Commission often disagree about the proper content of a regulatory rule, al Qaeda strategists do not agree on everything. For example, Suri differs from other writers because he believes the organization should largely eschew high-profile attacks against Western targets.[89] His concern is borne largely from a desire for the survival of the movement to which he is so profoundly devoted and from experiences where that movement faced collapse because of meager financial resources, captured leaders, relentless pressure at

85 Naji, *supra* note 1, at 7.

86 Mansfield, *supra* note 67, at 20.

87 *Id.* at 38 ("A further significant point was that the jihad battles in Afghanistan destroyed the myth of a superpower in the minds of the Muslim mujahideen young men. The USSR, a superpower with the largest land army in the world, was destroyed and the remnants of its troops fled Afghanistan before the eyes of the Muslim youths and as a result of their actions.").

88 *See* March & Simon, *supra* note 77, at 132–56; Terry M. Moe, *The New Economics of Organization*, 28 Am. J. Pol. Sci. 739, 758–65 (1984).

89 *See* Wright, *supra* note 38, at 51 ("Unlike most jihadi theorists, Suri acknowledges the setback caused by September 11. He laments the demise of the Taliban, which he and other Salafi jihadists considered the modern world's only true Islamic government.").

the hands of intelligence agencies, and the lack of territory from which to organize and recruit.[90]

On the other hand, the disagreements are only partial. Although other strategists are somewhat more willing to contemplate attacks against Western targets (particularly if they have the appealing quality of fomenting exhaustion rather than outrage among the Western public), they tend to share Suri's concern for organizational survival. Despite Naji's relatively greater willingness to sacrifice secrecy for some of the benefits of a more hierarchical bureaucracy,[91] he shares Suri's view about the need to focus on organizational survival by learning from the past:

> In the beginning of the Afghani war in the [19]70s . . . the jihad went through critical periods in which a number of strikes were directed against the mujahids, until—according to some accounts—only thirty men remained. However, . . . after . . . a decade of confrontation with the regime . . . the jihad offered up one and a half million martyrs . . . Where did these numbers of people come from? The response is that it happened by means of leading the masses to the battle and turning them into an army, especially when we established regions that were secure from the chaos and savagery that resulted from fighting and the people emigrated to these regions. We can make these regions theaters for proselytizing, training, and education.[92]

Naji's exhortation to turn adversity into opportunity is similarly reflected in the efforts made by al Zarqawi's organization in Iraq to learn from the mistakes of the al Tali'a movement in Syria.[93] Al Tali'a's experience in Syria, for example, taught the brash entrepreneur of terrorism that organizational survival depended in part on the existence of a media and political arm to complement war-fighting.[94]

Suri, al Zarqawi, and Naji were not alone in seeking to protect the organizational viability of the jihadi movement by extracting lessons from previous failures. Zawahiri also dwells on the critical imperative of learning from past mistakes in order to protect organizational survival, focusing particularly on ostensible allies of the jihadi movement that instead "stabbed . . . [it] . . . in the back."[95] And echoing recent

90 *See* Mansfield, *supra* note 67, at 201 ("Victory by the armies cannot be achieved unless the infantry occupies the territory. Likewise, victory for the Islamic movements against the world alliance cannot be attained unless these movements possess an Islamic base in the heart of the Arab region."); Naji, *supra* note 1, at 61 (discussing the value of territory); Wright, *supra* note 38, at 50 (discussing how poorly the movement was doing in the early to mid 1990s).

91 *See* Naji, *supra* note 1, at 63.

92 *Id.* at 62.

93 *See* Harmony And Disharmony, *supra* note 40, at 37.

94 *See id.* Other jihadi strategists, including Naji, agree about the importance of political activity as being central to organizational survival. *See* Naji, *supra* note 1, at 37 ("If we meditate on the factor common to the movements which have remained, we find that there is political action in addition to military action.").

95 Mansfield, *supra* note 67, at 46 ("The Islamic movement in Egypt, even though it made an effort against the enemies of Islam in the past, its general line was not against the ruling regime but against the external enemy. The movement's ideology and media continued

empirical work in political science emphasizing the importance of geography to the success of insurgencies, Zawahiri notes that:

> The problem of finding a secure base for jihad activity in Egypt used to occupy me a lot, in view of the pursuits to which we were subjected by the security forces and because of Egypt's flat terrain which made government control easy, for the River Nile runs in its narrow valley between two deserts that have no vegetation or water. Such a terrain made guerrilla warfare in Egypt impossible and, as a result, forced the inhabitants of this valley to submit to the central government and be exploited as workers and compelled them to be recruited in its army.[96]

The September 11 attacks did nothing to diminish the imperative of organizational survival. The survival imperative was intensely apparent in the hectic days following the September 11 attacks, as operatives and leaders responded to American pressure and eventually decided to further decentralize the organization.[97] One should expect concerns about organizational survival to be both profound and stable. While al Qaeda has produced its share of suicidal violence, the conclusion that it is a suicidal *organization* is profoundly deceiving. Indeed, the organizations involved in recruiting, preparing, and fielding suicide bombers tend to exhibit a long-term, even quasi-rational, regard for their own survival which is essential to creating the elaborate infrastructure which supports suicide bombing campaigns.[98] More generally, players within organizations such as al Qaeda have both politically instrumental and more self-regarding reasons for their movement—and indeed, for their particular faction or organization—to survive. Whether they crave some measure of political power or whether they seek the satisfaction of seeing like-minded individuals affect the larger political environment, they are unlikely to want their investment in a particular organization to dissipate.[99] Moreover, their own well-being, including access to the necessities of life and support in eluding capture, depends to some extent on the organization in which they have invested.[100] Finally, as Bruce Hoffman observes, terrorist organizations are subject to a process of natural selection, which

---

to try to get close to the head of the ruling regime (the king) and to recognize him as the legitimate authority in the country. This arbitrary separation between the external enemies and their internal agents led to many disasters and setbacks because the movement's members faced their enemy with their chests but left their backs exposed to his ally. Thus, they were stabbed in the back on the orders of those whom they faced with their chests.").

96 *Id.* at 28.

97 *See* Bergen, *supra* note 30, at 392 (discussing the pressures placed on the organization as a result of "the loss of Afghanistan as a base, and the U.S.-led campaign to detain members of jihadist movements around the world").

98 *See* Robert Pape, Dying to Win: the Strategic Logic of Suicide Terrorism 20–24 (2005) (describing the strategic, social and individual logic behind terrorist organizations).

99 *See infra* notes 129–35 and accompanying text.

100 *See supra* Part I.B (discussing the importance of public approval for the survival of al Qaeda).

constantly weakens or even decimates those that do not focus on the importance of their own survival.[101]

3. Crafting a Long-Term Plan to Achieve (Surprisingly Conventional) Strategic Goals

Terrorist organizations have reason to take the long view. Even by their own admission, they must surmount staggering difficulties to achieve their political goals, and their tactics sometimes require feats of extraordinary complexity. They are marginalized from political power yet crave the authority to govern.[102] Al Qaeda strategists are no exception: they too live for the future. They emphatically reject the notion that violent activity is a mere outlet for pent-up frustration.[103] Al Qaeda strategists envision a campaign that will take, at a minimum, decades.[104] Naji's vision, as summarized by WRIGHT, takes the following shape:

> [J]ihadis [should] continually attack the vital economic centers of [regimes in Muslim countries that cooperate with the West], such as tourist sites and oil refineries, in order to make the regimes concentrate their forces, leaving their peripheries unprotected. Sensing weakness, Naji predicts, the people will lose confidence in their governments, which will respond with increasingly ineffective acts of repression. Eventually, the governments will lose control. Savagery will naturally follow, offering Islamists the opportunity to capture the allegiance of a population that is desperate for order (Naji cites Afghanistan before the Taliban as an example.) Even though the jihadis will have caused the chaos, that fact will be forgotten as the fighters impose

---

101 *See* BRUCE HOFFMAN, INSIDE TERRORISM 157–84 (1998) (discussing organizational survival). Though it would be all but impossible to deny the importance of survival for his own organization, Abu Bakr Naji indulges his evident sense of moral superiority when discussing how Westerners think about survival:

> [W]hat fuels their action are material interests and the desire to *survive*. Thus, they strive to survive, but it is not just any survival; rather it is a survival which guarantees for them an unruffled life of comfort and luxury. As for their allies and those who support them, they continue and remain steadfast in their coalition with them as long as (their) interest is served by that alliance. Therefore, we must understand this very well.

NAJI, *supra* note 1, at 37 (emphasis added).

102 *See* NAJI, *supra* note 1, at 15–22 (discussing the goal of establishing a caliphate in the Middle East). As one observer notes:

> [A]ll terrorists exist and function in hopes of [acquiring the power to govern]. For them, the future rather than the present defines their reality. Indeed, they can console themselves that it was only a decade ago that the British prime minister, Margaret Thatcher, said of the African National Congress, "Anyone who thinks it is going to run the government in South Africa is living in cloud-cuckoo land." Exactly ten years after that remark was uttered, Queen Elizabeth II greeted President Nelson Mandela on his first official state visit to London.

HOFFMAN, *supra* note 101, at 184.

103 *See* NAJI, *supra* note 1, at 72 (discussing the problem of "idiots").

104 *See id.* at 38.

> security, provide food and medical treatment, and establish Islamic courts of justice.[105]

Surpassing even Naji's ambition (though overlapping with his account on key points), Hussein details a twenty-year plan for al Qaeda beginning with the September 11 attacks. The details of Hussein's plan bear at least some resemblance to what the United States has experienced in the succeeding years.[106] In a stage that is to last until 2006, Iraq will become the focus of recruiting for foot-soldiers eager to attack the United States.[107] Subsequently, al Qaeda will turn attention to Syria and Turkey, while ratcheting up direct confrontation with Israel.[108] The organization, gradually transforming itself into a decentralized social movement, will then be in a position to undermine Arab governments, to bolster its capabilities to deploy electronic warfare, and to more openly confront the United States.[109]

---

105 WRIGHT, *supra* note 38, at 56.

106 *Id.* at 56–58.

107 *Id.* at 57–58.

108 *Id.*

109 *See id.* Suri also celebrated the potential to transform jihadi organizations into the backbone of a more deeply-rooted but decentralized social movement. *See* BERGEN, *supra* note 30, at 245 (discussing Suri's vision of decentralization). In achieving such a goal, Suri seems to have sought not only a means of enlisting untold numbers into his cause but also of solving (however imperfectly) the hierarchy-operational security trade-off otherwise pervasively affecting his movement. *Id.* "If a Muslim is in Britain he doesn't need to leave his job or university and go and fight jihad at the front. What he can do is call the press agency and tell them I'm from the global Islamic resistance and claim responsibility for whatever action is being done in the world." *Id.* But achieving this goal is easier said than done. The problem lies in a paradox Suri and his like-minded pro-decentralization strategists apparently fail to acknowledge. Building a movement requires broad public support, which in turn requires coordinated operations (particularly violent ones), a task that is nearly impossible without hierarchy. In principle, it is perhaps not impossible for al Qaeda and similar entities to innovate in the creation of postmodern organizational forms that combine attributes of hierarchy along with some of the benefits of decentralization (as when a central leadership sets broad goals that leave lower-level operatives a measure of flexibility but also constrain their priorities, and when resources can be spent independently by decentralized members but allocated centrally). Nonetheless, two observations are in order about such efforts. First, they are likely to require time, energy, and learning through mistakes (because of the technical complexities inherent in developing signaling systems, using technology, and otherwise harnessing the benefits of hierarchy when decentralization is the norm), thereby introducing large risks that must be weighed alongside other goals. Second, compelling theoretical rationales (supported by empirical observation) suggest that, even when organizations innovate in an attempt to achieve benefits of both centralization and hierarchy, certain inherent limits are likely to interfere with this process. Hierarchy depends on formal organizational structures, division of responsibility, authority relationships, and predictable forms of interaction that are generally considered to be the antithesis of decentralization. It is more plausible to expect that terrorist networks will find a viable means for operational security to exist with somewhat hierarchical arrangements than to expect terrorist networks to discover some entirely unique means of having their cake and eating it too by simultaneously being centralized and decentralized.

While the jihadi strategists differ about when to confront their political adversaries and how hierarchical to make terrorist organizations, their overarching goals are surprisingly similar. In particular, the terrorist networks appear to harbor not abstract ideological objectives but rather concrete strategic political and military goals. In some cases, these turn out to be surprisingly conventional goals relating to the accumulation of territory and control over commodities such as oil. For example, Naji writes:

> [T]he military goals of our movement in the stage of "the power of vexation and exhaustion" [are] especially the goal of (making) the enemy withdraw its forces and the forces of its helpers among the apostates from specific targets and making them withdraw from places where they are present (especially the regions where the masses live so that we can begin in the stage of the management of savagery.) (Furthermore), in accordance with the principle of (self) interest which the enemy follows . . . we must crown that (effort) by targeting petroleum sectors since petroleum is the artery of life in the West. . . . America views [oil] as a primary and vital strategic commodity in war and a necessity in peace and a requisite for international influence. The success of targeting the economy of the enemy politically and militarily is historically well-established. . . .[110]

Naji makes similar observations regarding the value of territorial control,[111] echoing Suri's emphasis on the importance of territory as a place to recruit, organize, train, and strategize.[112]

Admittedly, actors within terrorist networks differ in the extent of their ultimate aspirations. Some burn with a rage that will only assuage with vengeance,[113] while other participants in the network are more readily motivated by money[114] or abstract political and religious convictions.[115] In the midst of these competing agendas, leaders with a strategic vision have articulated a range of goals that fit onto a continuum, from obtaining control of existing nation-states,[116] fomenting broad regime change in the Middle East and creating a caliphate throughout the region or the Muslim world,[117] to engagement in a long-term military and ideological struggle

---

110 NAJI, *supra* note 1, at 41.

111 *See id.* at 61 (discussing the value of territory).

112 *See* WRIGHT, *supra* note 38, at 50–51.

113 *See id.* at 52 ("One line of thinking proposes that America's tragedy on September 11 was born in the prisons of Egypt. Human rights advocates in Cairo argue that torture created an appetite for revenge, first in Sayyid Qutb and later in his acolytes, including Ayman al-Zawahiri.").

114 *See* BERGEN, *supra* note 30, at 154–55 (quoting one of bin Laden's most trusted lieutenants in the early al Qaeda organization in Sudan who stole $110,000 from him); Shapiro, *supra* note 28 (discussing "greedy" terrorists).

115 *See* BERGEN, *supra* note 30, at 98–99 (interviewing a Libyan recruit about his ideological motivations for joining al Qaeda).

116 *See supra* Part I.B.

117 *See* NAJI, *supra* note 1, at 15–22.

with the West.[118] The most sophisticated analyses repeatedly bring the focus back to the concrete indicators of political and military success that one might expect from a more conventional nation-state adversary.[119] Assumptions that terrorist networks seek as their primary objective to undermine Western values may distort our capacity to appreciate how they might respond to familiar costs and benefits relating to the achievement of conventional political and military goals.[120]

4. Subtle Parallels Between Terrorist Networks and State Bureaucracies

If there is any image that epitomizes modern national security discourse, it is that of a faceless, lawless terrorist cabal— endlessly adaptable and antithetical to conventional rule-bound bureaucracies. Yet Lawrence WRIGHT's exhaustive study of al Qaeda's origins again confounds such imagery. In its stead, WRIGHT traces an image of an entity almost desperate for Weberian, rule-bound bureaucratic structure:

> The leaders of al-Qaeda developed a constitution and by-laws, which described the utopian goals of the organization in clear terms: "To establish the truth, get rid of evil, and establish an Islamic nation." This would be accomplished through education and military training, as well as coordinating and supporting jihad movements around the world. The group would be led by a commander who was impartial, resolute, trustworthy, patient, and just; he should have at least seven years of jihad experience and preferably a college degree. Among his duties were appointing a council of advisors to meet each month, establishing a budget, and deciding on a yearly plan of action. One can appreciate the ambition of al-Qaeda by looking at its bureaucratic structure, which included committees devoted to military affairs, politics, information, administration, security, and surveillance.[121]

This picture of an embryonic al Qaeda, steeped in legalisms and bureaucratic procedures, showcases the importance terrorist networks assign to institution-building. Time and again, terrorist leaders ponder how to simultaneously solve their most pressing short-term management problems, while instilling a sense of shared mission among members and forging procedures achieve their organizations' longer-term goals. Indeed, perhaps the most common recurring theme in the jihadi strategic studies concerns the central importance of creating a structure to solve organizational challenges. How should camps be run? Who should decide what operations are undertaken? Who makes decisions about how best to resolve disputes? How should work be delegated? How should differing opinions be harmonized? While a terrorist network's specific operational challenges are distinctive, its larger organizational dilemmas are not.

---

118 *See* WRIGHT, *supra* note 38, at 56.

119 *See id.* at 57–58.

120 *See supra* note 32 (comparing the Bush administration's assertions about the motivations of terrorist networks with a more scholarly historical analysis of terrorist groups).

121 WRIGHT, *supra* note 31, at 142.

To see this, consider how the jihadi strategic studies emphasize the importance of service-delivery to the growing populations they expect to control.[122] Some strategists recognize the need for effective administrative cadres to manage oversight responsibilities and particularly to ensure the delivery of services to civilian populations that come under the organization's control.[123] Not surprisingly, al Qaeda's vision of eventually administering the security, sustenance, and economic needs of a population would encompass the same burdens that a conventional public agency would encounter in providing services, including the need to recruit competent staff and to respond to the needs of the population being served. And crucial among these burdens is the need for managers. As Naji notes:

> [We have a need for] a large number of elements who have administrative experience, especially in the first periods of the management of savagery. Of course, we have previous experience from managing our organized groups. However, when we settle in the regions, our administrative elements will not be sufficient with respect to numbers for managing these regions, whose large numbers of residents will take us by surprise. The regions of savagery should be managed by us and by the people who live in them.[124]

Notwithstanding al Qaeda's ultimate and radically anti-Western goals, the basic insight ought to be familiar to anyone involved in planning for post-conflict reconstruction in Iraq or similar settings on behalf of the U.S. government.

Of course, the administrative cadres to which Naji refers are just one type of expert. In order to manage the period of "savagery" that Naji foresees and effectively provide services to civilians, the strategist readily anticipates the need for al Qaeda to deploy even more specialized expertise:

> One of the brothers said to me.... "This [territorial expansion] is not the way that will take us to our goals. Assuming that we get rid of the apostate regimes today, who will take over the ministry of agriculture, trade, economics, etc.?".... [I]t is not a prerequisite that the mujahid movement has to be prepared especially for agriculture, trade, and industry. *One even sees that the movements and the parties which come to power in the world govern on the basis of their political constituents.* They appoint ministers from within the party or the movement for managing the different ministries and for taking charge of general policy for each ministry in accordance with the general policy of the state. As for the one who manages the techniques in each ministry,

122 *See* WRIGHT, *supra* note 38, at 56.

123 NAJI, *supra* note 1, at 63.

124 *Id.* Note that Naji offers a somewhat more elaborate vision than al Zawahiri's, which hints at the ability of a terrorist network to take over a state's administrative apparatus essentially intact. *See supra* Part I.B.; *cf.* Andrew Rathmell, *Planning Post-Conflict Reconstruction in Iraq: What Can We Learn?*, 81 INT'L AFF. 1013, 1022 (2005) (discussing the problems that followed from U.S. planners' apparent assumption that they could take over the Iraqi government's administrative apparatus essentially intact). In contrast, Naji appears more willing to recognize service delivery and governance as a staggering challenge. NAJI, *supra* note 1, at 63.

> he can be a paid employee who has no interest in policy and is not a member of the movement or the party. There are many examples of that. . . .[125]

Many examples, indeed: unfamiliar though his context may be to external observers, Naji might as well have been providing a theoretical account of representative politics and bureaucratic delegation that underlies the conventional administrative state.

Solving management problems is relevant not only when terrorist networks enter their hoped-for "management of savagery" phase. Taxing Western resolve, seeking organizational survival, and executing their long-term plan to create the preconditions for the management of savagery all require resources and recruits.[126] Achieving these objectives requires calibrating violence and navigating the devilishly difficult trade-offs between operational security and innovation on the one hand and centralized control on the other. From an instrumental perspective, jihadist leaders would therefore view some of the challenges faced by public organizations and their leaders with considerable familiarity before the "management of savagery" phase.

Intricate contextual details unquestionably affect how any collective entity fashions an instrumental response to its organizational problems. Yet the underlying internal organizational problems have a common root, even in staggeringly different contexts. Public bureaucracies routinely face agency problems involving the alignment of goals between principals (political actors or agency managers) and agents.[127] Jihadi strategists foresee similar challenges, given the ambitious nature of their goals and the frequently demonstrated temptation of lower-level operatives to skim financial resources.[128] Both types of organizations must adjudicate disputes and explicitly turn to legal procedures to do so.[129] Like public bureaucracies, al Qaeda and its analogues also face the problem of restraining overzealous action. The language of some jihadi strategic studies even eerily parallels words in American judicial opinions recognizing the importance of administrative mechanisms to mitigate such overzealous behavior.[130] Commonalities emerge as well in how terrorist networks and public bureaucracies in the U.S. public law system—faced

125 NAJI, *supra* note 1, at 63 (emphasis added). As for the time it would take to explain, a semester's worth of administrative law would probably do the trick.

126 *Id.*

127 *See* KAREN M. HULT & CHARLES WALCOTT, GOVERNING PUBLIC ORGANIZATIONS: POLITICS, STRUCTURES, AND INSTITUTIONAL DESIGN 15–24 (1990) (describing characteristics of the different models of the organization as a political system).

128 *See supra* note 114 and accompanying text (discussing examples of "greedy" terrorists).

129 *See, e.g.*, BERGEN, *supra* note 30, at 124–25 (discussing al Qaeda's use of Sharian courts to legitimize its decisions); HULT & WALCOTT, *supra* note 127, at 44–45 (discussing prominent adjudicative structures within public organizations). Although both types of entities deploy formal legal rules, it is unsurprising that an illicit nonstate entity does so less frequently given the lack of a larger social, political, and bureaucratic context that would enable it to more fully acquire the attributes of a conventional nation-state.

130 *See* NAJI, *supra* note 1, at 61 (discussing the need to restrain certain groups from being excessively aggressive); Mariano-Florentino Cuéllar, *Auditing Executive Discretion*, 82 NOTRE

with the need to restrain overzealous action while harnessing expertise[131]—view management through strict and hierarchically imposed rules. Terrorist networks face an even more difficult trade-off than public bureaucracies in contending with hierarchy. This is because formal bureaucratic hierarchies value carefully administering scarce resources, a practice which can lead to particularly pronounced security problems.[132] But more striking than the distinctions in the intensity of the dilemma is the reality that such profoundly different types of organizations as public bureaucracies and terrorist networks nonetheless view hierarchy and formal rules as both a blessing and a curse.

Finally, although some strands of conventional wisdom regard terrorist organizations as entirely unconstrained by public reactions,[133] a closer examination reveals that both public agencies and terrorist networks seek to build public approval and gain legitimacy.[134] Terrorist networks can be constrained by their audiences in two crucial ways. First, leaders' tactical and egotistic political objectives depend on the internal support of participants, and that dependence requires leaders to employ strategies that engage and reward these constituents.[135] Second, the appeal of a terrorist network to the public (particularly in Middle Eastern countries) is pivotal because it cultivates greater organizational support and assuages opposition to the group's objectives.[136] This connection between public support and the mitigation of internal

---

DAME L. REV. 227, 258–60 (2006) (discussing the role of judicial review in restraining overzealous action among public bureaucracies).

131 *See, e.g.*, Far E. Conference v. United States, 342 U.S. 570, 574 (1952) ("[I]n cases raising issues of fact not within the conventional experience of judges or cases requiring the exercise of administrative discretion, agencies created by Congress for regulating the subject matter should not be passed over."); NAJI, *supra* note 1, at 25 ("[I]n our plan we open the door of management wide to those who have mastered its art.").

132 *See* BERGEN, *supra* note 30, at 244–46 (discussing Suri's critique of hierarchy).

133 *See* NZELIBE & YOO, *supra* note 35, at 2533 (contending that "terrorist organizations face . . . no political accountability for their foreign policy failures," and that therefore "they can afford to ignore their domestic audiences and take more aggressive stances in initiating international conflict").

134 *Compare* Kallstrom v. Columbus, 136 F.3d 1055, 1065 (6th Cir. 1998) (discussing the value of transparency and public accountability for both the judicial and executive branches), *and* DANIEL P. CARPENTER, THE FORGING OF BUREAUCRATIC AUTONOMY 366 (2001) (stating that much of the FDA's present power is derived from the public legitimacy and prestige that it gained early in its history as it "acted to stem vast consumer crises in adulterated medicines"), *with* NAJI, *supra* note 1, at 21 ("[T]he masses . . . will be our support in the future, provided that there is transparency in this plan and even an acknowledgement of error sometimes.").

135 *See* BRACHMAN & MCCANTS, *supra* note 56, at 315 (discussing the internal power struggles within terrorist organizations).

136 *See* NAJI, *supra* note 1, at 63–64 (discussing the importance of popular support in establishing a successful Islamic revolution). Indeed, al Qaeda strategists recognize that the need for public support extends not only to what the jihadi movement would have to achieve during the "management of savagery" stage, but also to what the organization would need at a more embryonic stage in the development of a terrorist network. *See* BERGEN, *supra* note 30, at 392

management problems may explain why some of the most contentious disagreements among terrorist leaders involve the question of how to cultivate broader public support.[137] It also explains why leaders temper their authoritarian impulses for tight control and security with an approach that values the legitimacy created by law-like administrative procedures.

Ignoring the terrorist networks' public constraints may distort counter-terrorism policy by downplaying the value of and potential for driving a wedge between terrorist leaders and their actual or potential supporters. Juxtaposing conventional public bureaucracies from advanced industrialized nation-states with nonstate actors deploying terrorist tactics is counterintuitive. Yet both share a tangle of common organizational problems that provide insights into the nature of strategic conflict which transcend the more superficial ideas about terrorist networks that prevail in much of the current political discourse.

As with any analogy, certain limits govern the comparison between problems confronting modern terrorist networks and those that bedevil conventional, rule-bound state bureaucracies. Illicit nonstate actors must sometimes adopt more costly organizational strategies than legitimate governmental agencies. For example, the risk of detection may force a terrorist leader to confer greater independence to subordinates than would otherwise be desirable.[138] Furthermore, illicit organizations must do without a formal legal system. With few exceptions, they lack the depth of expertise and bureaucratic capacity of a nation-state.[139] Public bureaucracies in advanced industrialized countries rarely face the range of constraints that terrorist networks do, leaving agency leaders with a broader range of options to solve their bureaus' management problems.

In the end, a more nuanced analysis reveals critical commonalities that are at least as important as the differences. Both terrorist networks and our own bureaucratized nation-state must strike a balance between hierarchy and expertise, simultaneously drawing on the strengths of each while trying to minimize their dependence on them.[140] Both must reconcile the potential disconnect between

---

(quoting al Zawahiri's call to win over greater public support for al Qaeda); *supra* note 124 and accompanying text.

137 *See, e.g.*, Wright, *supra* note 38, at 53.

138 *See* Jacob N. Shapiro & David A. Siegel, Underfunding in Terrorist Organizations (Nov. 3, 2006) (unpublished manuscript at 7, on file with author).

139 Naji, *supra* note 1, at 63.

140 *Compare* Harmony and Disharmony, *supra* note 40, at 12–13 (noting that the balance between hierarchy and expertise must be struck as a consequence of security concerns), *with* Hult & Walcott, *supra* note 127, at 92–93 (explaining that bureaucracies exist to develop organizational expertise, but that hierarchy is often imposed as a means of enhancing accountability).

low-level players and their superiors.[141] Both must deal with problems involving bounded rationality and tunnel vision.[142] And both must encourage participation while maintaining critical operational attributes such as secrecy and restraint.[143] In light of these parallels, what makes terrorist strategists such as Naji particularly insightful is that they recognize that many of their movement's strategic goals—including the exploitation of imperial overstretch and the survival of organizational structures—all depend on the fate of the network's administrative capacity.[144]

If one casts aside the more superficial descriptions of terrorist organizations, certain tentative implications begin to emerge. Jihadi terrorist networks simultaneously seek to achieve ambitious goals, such as provoking Western overstretch or competing with established governments in delivering services to civilian populations while facing complicated organizational realities. This combination of environment and aspiration gives rise to recurrent administrative law-type problems—problems borne from the amount and complexity of coordinated effort that leaders must expend to achieve their objectives in a complicated world,[145] and similar to those concerns existing at the core of domestic administrative law in a nation such as the United States. The problems involve delegation and oversight, expertise, participation, restraint of overzealous action, and adjudication of disputes.[146] Much like the managers of state bureaucracies in advanced industrialized countries, the nominal leaders of terrorist networks cannot assume the existence of optimal institutional conditions such as the alignment of the goals of low-level operatives with those of strategic decision makers. They must instead forge that alignment from the imperfect materials available to organizational entrepreneurs: raw recruits, imperfect monitoring strategies to oversee the work of low-level operatives, limited financial resources, and the ability to devise rules and standards that embody organizational goals.[147] A more nuanced view of institutional dynamics reveals the

---

141 *Compare* Harmony and Disharmony, *supra* note 40, at 19–21 (discussing how terrorist groups deal with the problem of "preference divergence" within their membership), *with* March & Simon, *supra* note 77, at 13–14 (discussing the preference divergence problem more generally in the context of large legitimate organizations).

142 *Compare* Naji, *supra* note 1, at 71 (complaining of operatives who cannot conceive of undertaking small missions instead of larger ones), *with* March & Simon, *supra* note 77, at 173–74 (discussing how departmentalization can lead to the emergence of subgoals which limit the overall rationality of agency actions).

143 *See* Bergen, *supra* note 30, at 245–46 (outlining Suri's lecture on the importance of a decentralized cell structure as a mechanism for maintaining secrecy and security); Naji, *supra* note 1, at 71 ("[T]he desire for large actions, especially battle, overcomes the minds of some . . . enthusiastic people . . . However, one of its harmful effects is that it moves them to scorn actions that are not large.").

144 Naji, *supra* note 1, at 23.

145 Staff of S. Comm. on the Judiciary, 86th Cong., Report on Regulatory Agencies to the President-Elect 1 (Comm. Print 1960).

146 *See* March & Simon, *supra* note 77, at 2.

147 *See id.*

organizational complexity of illicit nonstate actors who aim simultaneously to exhaust Western resolve, to ensure organizational survival, and to execute an ambitious long-term plan for achieving territorial control. This complexity undermines the assumptions made by some scholarly observers of terrorism-related legal developments.[148] Just as it is dangerous to assume that public agencies routinely achieve their stated goals, policymakers should be wary of presumptions that terrorist networks have routinely solved their own organizational problems. We should instead turn our attention to learning from al Qaeda's administrative law dilemmas, so that we might better address our own.

II. LEARNING FROM AL QAEDA'S ADMINISTRATIVE LAW DILEMMAS

Having traced some of the themes that appear in the works of al Qaeda strategists, we can now use them to evaluate potential changes to our own law and policy. In particular, we can observe how the recurring themes emphasize certain features of terrorist networks that are sometimes overlooked when politicians shape public perceptions. Since politicians' craft their statements and policy pronouncements to appeal to the public's prevailing views,[149] conventional assumptions about the uniform zeal of terrorist organizations, their time horizon, their interest in using weapons of mass destruction, and their aptitude for working in secrecy may confound our collective ability to manage terrorist risks at a reasonable cost. As an alternative to the more common, truncated depiction of terrorist networks in discussions about appropriate legal and policy responses, this Part discusses some of the implications that arise from dissecting al Qaeda's administrative law-related problems.

A. Agency Problems and Information Gaps

One challenge permeating the administrative state involves gaps in information.[150] Political actors in the legislatures and the executive branches of such states face substantial uncertainty. How is the Food and Drug Administration using its regulatory powers? How reliable is the Department of Homeland Security's rationale for deciding not to process asylum applications from certain countries? What is the best way of changing the public's nutritional or highway safety practices? To manage these problems, the administrative state balances the benefits of discretion with those of review.[151] It provides for deferential judicial review of executive branch decisions, forces Congress to delimit the bureaucracy's powers so courts can monitor

---

148 *See, e.g., supra* notes 33–35 and accompanying text.

149 *Cf.* Mariano-Florentino Cuéllar, *The International Criminal Court and the Political Economy of Antitreaty Discourse,* 55 Stan. L. Rev. 1597, 1629 (2003) ("[P]oliticians' treaty-related rhetoric shapes public opinion, but that opinion in turn shapes what politicians choose to emphasize to please key constituencies.").

150 *See, e.g.,* 9/11 Commission Report, *supra* note 46, at 416–17.

151 *See* Frug, *supra* note 29, at 1301–02.

agency activities,[152] and grants private parties the limited right to learn about government policies through the Administrative Procedure Act and the Freedom of Information Act. These measures survive in the U.S. system because politicians think the measures can reduce agency problems and (to a lesser extent) because the public occasionally supports such policies.[153]

For the leaders of terrorist networks, the information predicament is exacerbated by the rudimentary nature of their internal procedures and by the constraints of their security environment.[154] Nowhere is this more apparent than in the recurring problem of managing people and money to ensure action in accordance with the network's overall goals. Time and again, the strategists of terrorist organizations recognize that some members are motivated in part by the possibility of personal gain. For example, in 1999, leaders asked for an accounting from a Yemeni cell leader who had been provided with funds. In response to the report provided, he received the following email from Ayman al Zawahiri, already one of al Qaeda's major figures:

> With all due respect, this is not an accounting. It's a summary accounting. For example, you didn't write any dates, and many of the items are vague. The analysis of the summary shows the following: 1-you received a total of $22,301. Of course, you didn't mention the period over which this sum was received. Our activities only benefited from a negligible portion of the money. This means that you received and distributed the money as you please . . . 2-Salaries amounted to $10,085—45 percent of the money. I had told you in my fax. . . . That we've been receiving only half salaries for five months. What is your reaction or response to this? 3-Loans amounted to $2,190. Why did you give out loans? Didn't I give clear orders to Muhammad Saleh to . . . refer any loan requests to me? We have already had long discussions on this topic. . . .[155]

Such bickering over financial resources belies the stereotypical image of terrorist networks that are uniformly populated by cadres of operatives desperately eager to die for their cause. Instead, the picture that emerges from such exchanges is one of a network capable of raising considerable sums of money but uncertain about how, by whom, and to what degree of efficacy that money will be used. If the Yemeni leader had actually portrayed the stereotypical perception of a religious zealot whose only purpose is to serve a dark organizational master, then Zawahiri's exasperated

152 *See* Whitman v. Am. Trucking Ass'ns, 531 U.S. 457, 468 (2001) (requiring Congress to make a clear textual commitment of authority to agencies whenever it "alter[s] the fundamental details of a regulatory scheme").

153 *See* McNollgast, *The Political Origins of the Administrative Procedure Act,* 15 J.L. Econ. & Org. 180, 215 (1999) (arguing that Congress enacted the APA in order to control the actions of agency administrators who might be appointed by presidents of the other political party).

154 *See* Harmony and Disharmony, *supra* note 40, at 11; Shapiro & Siegel, *supra* note 138, at 6.

155 Harmony and Disharmony, *supra* note 40, at 42; Cullison, *supra* note 50, at 62, 64.

email hinting at the misuse of funds would hardly have been necessary.[156] In other examples, strategists almost seem to take pains to excuse their less-than-perfect supporters (while suggesting that the transgressions of those supporters should be kept secret), reinforcing the stereotype of the monolithic terrorist organization.[157]

Ironically, even the early history of al Qaeda amply reveals its leadership's pragmatic bent. During the 1980s, when the organization's leadership was holed up near Khost, Afghanistan, bin Laden and his allies recognized that many potential recruits would seek something more than spiritual deliverance. In response they designed an employment program that provided for members' decidedly material needs:

> Al Qaeda held its first recruitment meeting in the Farouk camp near Khost, Afghanistan. . . . New recruits filled out forms in triplicate, signed their oath of loyalty to bin Laden, and swore themselves to secrecy. In return, single members earned about $1,000 a month in salary; married members received $1,500. Everyone got a round-trip ticket home each year and a month of vacation. There was a healthcare plan and—for those who changed their mind—a buyout option: They received $2,400 and went on their way. From the beginning, al-Qaeda presented itself as an attractive employment opportunity for men whose education and careers had been curtailed. . . .[158]

Al Qaeda's leadership certainly would welcome the opportunity to dispense with the monetary incentives. In the process, it could avoid depending on anyone other than individuals who are entirely committed to the organization's cause.[159] The terrorist leaders may even agree with James Landis's observation that "[t]he prime key to the improvement of the administrative process is the selection of qualified personnel. Good men can make poor laws workable; poor men will wreak havoc with good laws."[160]

But those improvements are easier said than done. Most individuals harbor mixed motives for engaging in political activity.[161] Once the religious rhetoric is privately put aside, some supporters of jihadi movements are especially happy if the organization provides them with an opportunity for financial gain, but may become

---

156 This is similar to a long-running federal case involving the financial mismanagement of Indian funds which features a federal judge displaying similar degrees of exasperation with federal officials. *Cf.* Richard J. Pierce, Jr., *Judge Lamberth's Reign of Terror at the Department of Interior*, 56 ADMIN. L. REV. 235, 241 (2004) (describing a judge's discontent with the Treasury and Interior Departments, leading to multiple contempt proceedings).

157 NAJI, *supra* note 1, at 35 (warning leaders not to criticize the imperfections of their volunteers, and telling them to avoid publicizing errors).

158 WRIGHT, *supra* note 31, at 141–42.

159 HARMONY AND DISHARMONY, *supra* note 40, at 42–43 (advising against the removal of less committed operatives and strengthening the network as a result).

160 STAFF OF S. COMM. ON THE JUDICIARY, 86TH CONG., REPORT ON REGULATORY AGENCIES TO THE PRESIDENT-ELECT 66 (Comm. Print 1960).

161 *See* MARCH & SIMON, *supra* note 77, at 83–85.

cautious or unreliable if they feel exposed to personal danger.[162] Even if the world were filled with a large number of individuals who would be fanatically loyal al Qaeda members, it would not obvious who they were. Almost any successful effort to identify them would require placing them in positions of intermediate responsibility and observing their performance.[163]

Moreover, al Qaeda not only needs adherents, but also requires expertise and resources. The network must sift through pools of potential recruits to find collaborators who can raise, transfer, and administer financial resources; who can forge a communications strategy; and who can procure commodities such as explosives or weapons. Thus, the organization expands its recruitment circle beyond those who are most intensely committed to the organization.[164] Weapons and explosives traffickers, money launderers, communications specialists, individuals with valid documents or the ability forge them, and those with experience living in Western countries are all likely to display a mix of loyalties, including those to their own material and personal well-being.[165] And the most radical and loyal adherents might be drawn into particularly sensitive or specialized roles, such as serving on suicide missions, that would preclude their generalized use through out the network. For all these reasons, the organization confronts repeated and pervasive problems arising from the divergence between the organization's goals and the goals of some of its operatives.[166]

The tensions that arise from this disconnect are merely an example of a more general problem. Incomplete information limits the ability of the leaders of a terrorist network to assess the network's current tactical position. Those leaders have difficulty acquiring precise information about the potential effects of the group's attacks on the political and military environment, the progress made by adversaries in the pursuit of major leaders, and the activities and whereabouts of subordinates.[167] Information gaps hinder the organization's efforts to set strategic goals and work

162 *See* Shapiro & Siegel, *supra* note 138, at 13 ("[T]he longer individuals remain in [a terrorist] organization, and the further they move up the management structure, the more likely they are to place a heavy weight on monetary rewards. . . . [T]he threshold level of risk acceptance and commitment required for participation in support activities is much lower than for participation in technical roles.").

163 *See* March & Simon, *supra* note 77, at 59–61. *But see* Harmony and Disharmony, *supra* note 40, at 15.

164 *See* Naji, *supra* note 1, at 63; Shapiro & Siegel, *supra* note 138, at 11–12.

165 These agency problems, moreover, make it easier to understand the jihadi strategic studies' frequent focus on the importance of ideological indoctrination. *E.g.*, Naji, *supra* note 1, at 59; Wright, *supra* note 38, at 48. However, even that strategy is unlikely to ensure organization-wide orthodoxy. *See* March & Simon, *supra* note 77, at 59–61 (noting that departmentalization leads to the creation of subgoals which may not further the overall organizational objectives).

166 *Cf.* Cuéllar, *supra* note 130, at 261 (observing that while there are times when the good conscious of administration officials will sometimes contribute to action which is in line with institutional objectives, "such desirable circumstances do not always arise").

167 *See* Harmony and Disharmony, *supra* note 40, at 47; Shapiro & Siegel, *supra* note 138, at 6.

toward them. These gaps also create obstacles to resolving basic management problems such as those arising from the operation of training camps or in the planning of responses to potential enforcement operations. From a more parochial perspective, factions within the organization need information to better manage political competition.[168] These information needs are analogous to our own system, which is why so much of modern administrative law deals with creating institutional mechanisms that produce information that justifies particular regulatory decisions, and why information can have such strategic value for both military and political adversaries.[169]

Much like agencies within the administrative state, a terrorist network seeks to counter its information problems in a variety of ways. It could seek to promote broader participation to obtain more information; however, this would create additional security problems. It could attempt to infiltrate its enemies.[170] But, given the scarcity of operatives able to live unobtrusively in the West,[171] finding those capable of infiltrating Western security agencies would be very difficult. It could target individuals with special analytical capacities for recruitment. Ultimately, however, none of these approaches would entirely solve the problem: the environment is too complicated and even the most sophisticated organizations can only respond imperfectly to such uncertainty.[172]

As a result, terrorist networks such as al Qaeda remain vulnerable to strategies designed to exploit their information gaps. Their burden is a consequence of simultaneous pressures to operate secretly while managing broader organizational problems that can be mitigated through hierarchy, expertise, and broader participation. In the course of walking this tightrope, leaders of terrorist organizations almost inevitably create networks of people with heterogeneous motivations.[173] The presence

168 *See* MARCH & SIMON, *supra* note 77, at 150 (noting that in intra-organizational conflicts, problem solving requires an exaggerated emphasis on information assembly).

169 STEPHEN PETER ROSEN, WINNING THE NEXT WAR 253–55 (1991) (highlighting how uncertainty about the military capabilities of rival nations prompted the U.S. military to develop information through simulations); Erik Lichtenberg & David Zilberman, *Efficient Regulation of Environmental Health Risks,* 103 Q.J. ECON. 167, 167 (1988) (discussing environmental regulators' uncertainty as to the extent of the risks associated with environmental contaminants); Thomas W. Gilligan & Keith Krehbiel, *Collective Decision Making and Standing Committees: An Informational Rationale for Restrictive Amendment Procedures,* 3 J.L. ECON. & ORG. 287, 287–88 (1987) (discussing the impact of information gaps on the incentives of politicians to organize the legislature into committees, and to defer to the judgments of those committees).

170 *See* NAJI, *supra* note 1, at 52 (calling on the movement to infiltrate all institutions associated with its enemies).

171 *See* CULLISON, *supra* note 50, at 61.

172 *See* SHAPIRO, *supra* note 28, at 2 (indicating a trade-off between solving information problems and promoting security).

173 *See* HARMONY AND DISHARMONY, *supra* note 40, at 43. To avoid creating a pool of new recruits with heterogeneous motivations, leaders would have to incur two sets of costs: exceedingly elevated expenses screening potential participants, and high opportunity costs borne from

of individuals who are motivated by greed or personal political ambition also belies the assumption that terrorist networks are monolithic institutions, driven uniformly by religion and ideology.[174] In fact, reality is more complicated. Terrorist leaders must shoulder the burdensome cost of identifying zealous recruits while dealing with the security problems associated with its dependence on essential, though less reliable, foot soldiers.

The prevalence of mixed motives among illicit organizations leaves policymakers with a chance to drive a wedge between participants in terrorist ventures. Policymakers should value counter-terrorism policies that leave less-reliable members of terrorist organization in place (particularly if the members can be monitored) instead of detaining them. Allowing such operatives to stay in the organization forces al Qaeda to contend with a rank-and-file membership that is not fanatically committed to the group.[175] Enforcement practices that fail to consider the implications of removing the less reliable elements in the al Qaeda network can unwittingly aid the organization by effectively assuming the burden of separating the wheat from the chaff. As long as less reliable operatives remain readily observable (and, if necessary, subject to interception), focused surveillance may be a better strategy than a policy of detention that alerts the organization to enforcement activity and helps it identify its most valuable members.[176] Another way to exploit terrorist networks' agency problems would be to credibly communicate to less devoted terrorists the rewards they might enjoy in exchange for betraying the group.[177]

B. Centrality of Public Approval and Disapproval

Like administrative bureaucracies, terrorist networks depend on public approval to achieve both near-term goals of surviving, and longer-term instrumental goals of undermining pro-Western Middle Eastern regimes. Accordingly, popular support in the Muslim world is a critical asset to al Qaeda, its affiliates, and the broad social movement the organization wishes to spawn. Indeed, the desire of some al Qaeda strategists to found such a movement echoes the desire of some regulatory officials

---

excluding from participation eager individuals with expert knowledge, skills, personal contacts, or material resources that can be valuable to the leaders' vision of the organization.

174 Address to the Nation on the War on Terror, 42 Weekly comp. Pres. Doc. 597, 1598 (Sept. 11, 2006) ("[T]hey form a global network of extremists who are driven by . . . totalitarian ideology. . . .").

175 *See* Shapiro & Siegel, *supra* note 138, at 32–33.

176 Harmony and Disharmony, *supra* note 40, at 42. *Cf.* Neal K. Katyal, *Conspiracy Theory*, 112 Yale L.J. 1307, 1381 (2003) (calling for higher sentences on co-conspirators playing a minor role in a scheme to perpetrate illegal activity, without considering the extent to which such penalties align the incentives of the minor players and the ringleaders).

177 *See id.* at 43 (advocating providing an easier out for lower tier operatives than "indefinite detention or death").

in advanced industrialized countries to achieve their policy goals by leveraging public support.[178]

It follows for some strategists that their plans are especially threatened by the prospect of successful U.S. government efforts to counter the network's plans to build public support. Suri notes that the American "war of ideas" has had at least limited success in spurring modification of textbooks in some Muslim countries.[179] This success greatly rankles him, and he emphatically calls on adherents to promote Salafi jihadism as a response.[180] More generally, public supporters provide nearly all resources on which the organization relies, from financial backing to foot soldiers to safe houses. At the same time, Western public opinion is also crucial. It may create pressure on Western governments to withdraw from the Muslim world, but is also a potentially vindictive force that strategists must not overly provoke.[181] This tension forces al Qaeda and its sympathizers to conduct operations that generate enough publicity to spur recruitment and financial support without alienating the Middle Eastern general public; likewise they must provoke exhaustion rather than outrage among the public in the West.

Al Qaeda's leadership is not ignorant of these parameters. For example, Naji emphasizes the centrality of a "media plan" to any successful operation. This plan should

> target[ ] and focus[ ] on two classes. The first class is the masses, in order to push a large number of them to join the jihad, offer positive support, and adopt a negative attitude toward those who do not join the ranks. The second class is the troops of the enemy who have lower salaries, in order to push them to join the ranks of the mujahids or at least to flee from the service of the enemy.[182]

---

178 *See* David Kessler, A Question of Intent 388–89 (2001) (providing an example of a regulatory official pursuing a strategy of fostering broad social support). Former FDA Commissioner David Kessler was considering potential policies for curbing tobacco use when he had the following insight:

> I also began to think about the importance of removing the vestiges of social acceptability from tobacco in order to prevent future generations of children from becoming addicted to nicotine. I knew that changing priorities and attitudes, and ultimately creating new norms, is a far more complex task than achieving legislative victories, but in the end that is probably what it takes to reduce rates of smoking.

Id. at 388. A generation earlier, the Federal Narcotics Bureau, "faced with a non-supportive environment and a decreasing budgetary appropriation that threatened its survival, generated a moral crusade against marihuana use which resulted in the passage of the Marihuana Tax Act and the alteration of a societal value." Donald T. Dickson, *Bureaucracy and Morality: An Organizational Perspective on a Moral Crusade,* 16 Soc. Probs. 143, 143 (1968).

179 Wright, *supra* note 38, at 51.

180 *Id.*

181 *See* Bergen, *supra* note 30, at 392 ("[W]hat [many jihadist strategists] are saying about September 11 is that the attacks may have been a tactical victory, but they were a strategic disaster because of the overwhelming response it provoked."); *supra* Part I.B.1 (discussing the strategy of provoking imperial overstretch).

182 Naji, *supra* note 1, at 21.

Avoiding wanton and excessive brutality is crucial to the success of this media strategy. Such brutality can provoke sympathy for al Qaeda's enemies or give rise to such intense outrage among Western audiences that "success" could imperil the organization.[183] Ayman al Zawahiri espouses this principle, evidenced by his warning to the late al Zarqawi to curtail his brutality.[184] In shaping American public opinion, their key goal is to promote fatigue among the population—to make the public question why the U.S. government is spending lives and money.[185]

Carefully calibrating the amount of brutality is also crucial because too much violence can alienate the terrorist network's most important pool of potential support. Among Muslims in the Middle East—al Qaeda's primary audience—the terrorist network's leaders seek desperately to evoke sympathy and support. They endeavor to increase the flow of donations and recruits. They seek allies and sympathizers to smooth the organization's work and to promote efficient administration.[186] The thorniest predicament for the leaders therefore emerges anew in nearly every strategic decision: how to achieve sufficient public notoriety without unleashing the sort of backlash that followed the two American embassy bombings in Africa, the organization's earliest attacks against high-profile targets. As Lawrence notes:

> Muslims all over the world greeted the bombings with horror and dismay. The deaths of so many people, most of them Africans, many of them Muslims, created a furor. Bin Laden said that the bombings gave the Americans a taste of the atrocities that Muslims had experienced. But to most of the world and even to some members of al-Qaeda, the attacks seemed pointless, a showy act of mass murder with no conceivable effect on American policy except to provoke a massive response.[187]

The public support enjoyed by a terrorist organization has a direct impact on its ability to solve the nettlesome management problems that interfere with its ability to accomplish its goals. Having greater public support facilitates building expertise within the network because a larger base of support is more likely to produce skilled and knowledgeable recruits who would otherwise have to be carefully trained or hired at rates calculated to ensure loyalty. Greater public support also fills the network's coffers, allowing it to fund new activities, to enlarge its circle of supporters by providing services and security, and to mitigate its internal management

183 Brachman & Mccants, *supra* note 56, at 312–13.

184 Wright, *supra* note 38, at 53 ("Zawahiri advised Zarqawi to moderate his attacks on Iraqi Shiites and to stop beheading hostages. 'We are in battle,' Zawahiri reminded him. 'And more than half of this battle is taking place in the battlefield of the media.'").

185 Moreover, note how concern for public perceptions should naturally translate into a desire to develop bureaucratic and administrative mechanisms that both control operations and restrain excesses. *See* Naji, *supra* note 1, at 9 ("If the number of Americans killed is one/tenth the number of Russians killed in Afghanistan and Chechnya, they will flee, heedless of all else [because] . . . [t]hey [have] reached a state of effeminacy which [makes] them unable to sustain battles for a long period of time. . . .").

186 *See supra* Part I.B.4.

187 Wright, *supra* note 31, at 272.

problems by occasionally using money to purchase valuable expertise or services.[188] Deeper and broader support can also mitigate internal dispute resolution problems by making individual members more fungible, particularly the low- and mid-level operatives on which any organization depends.[189] As the organization becomes less dependent on a smaller group of individuals, it no longer has to please members that would otherwise have been able to veto operations.[190]

Certain policy implications follow from terrorist networks' thirst for public support. To further their long-term goal of dislodging U.S. influence in the Middle East, al Qaeda and its allies gain in the short-term by drawing U.S. forces into the region. Insurgents and terrorist networks can lure U.S. forces into using tactics, such as those inflicting collateral damage, that draw the ire of Arab and Muslim communities.[191] Thus, U.S. policymakers should weigh the potential reaction of the Muslim public among other factors as they craft counter-terrorism strategies.

The opposite point is unlikely to be lost on strategists for al Qaeda and its allies, whose unquestionably ruthless zeal for destruction must uneasily coexist with a desire to tire rather than enrage Western publics.[192] Meanwhile, the concern with tiring rather than indefinitely infuriating American public opinion suggests greater nuance and complexity in potential terrorist motivations to use weapons of mass destruction.[193] Some strategists aim to engage in sufficient violence to attract public

188 *E.g.*, Mansfield, *supra* note 67, at 257–58, 313–14; *see also* Shapiro & Siegel, *supra* note 138, at 11–12.

189 *See* Harmony and Disharmony, *supra* note 40, at 15.

190 *Cf.* March & Simon, *supra* note 77, at 61 (observing how organizational leaders can manage some of their problems by recruiting members to whom work can be delegated).

191 *E.g.*, Kim Gamel, *Troops Kill 20 in Iraq Clash*, Chi. Trib., Dec. 9, 2006, at A5; Jason Straziuso, *U.S. Night Raid Harms Afghans' Trust*, L.A. Times, Jan. 21, 2007, at A5 (providing examples of how American military responses to actual or perceived terrorist tactics have yielded civilian casualties); Press Release, U.S. Cent. Command, Civilians Wounded by Anti-Iraqi Mortar Attacks (Dec. 21, 2006) (on file with author); *see also* Ricks, *supra* note 8, at 332–35 (noting how insurgents were able to provoke the First Battle of Falujah and the ensuing collateral damage).

192 *See* Hoffman, *supra* note 101, at 155 (noting the danger, from the perspective of terrorist groups, that adverse publicity of severe terrorist attacks "helps an outraged public to mobilize its vast resources and produces information that the public needs to pierce the veil of secrecy all terrorist groups require"); *supra* note 130 and accompanying text (discussing overzealous action and the need to restrain it among terrorist organizations).

193 These complexities are not routinely appreciated even by some commentators on national security. *See, e.g.*, John M. Burkhoff, *The Fourth Amendment and Terrorism*, 109 Penn. St. L. Rev. 911, 925 (2005) (claiming without support, not only that "terrorist individuals and organizations undoubtedly seek to obtain chemical, biological, and nuclear materials" but that they do so "to assist in their assaults"); *supra* note 35 and accompanying text (discussing the trade-offs terrorist organizations face in deciding whether to use nuclear, biological, or chemical weapons).

support among some sympathetic Muslim and Arab groups,[194] while avoiding the most punishing tactics that might risk creating sympathy for Westerners or even provoking a maximally brutal response imperiling the entire movement.[195] And just as leaders may be able to exploit divisions in the motives of individuals working within these organizations, policymakers may be able to confound terrorist drives for recruits and public support by choosing policies that contradict negative assumptions about the U.S. which are rampant in the Arab and Muslim world.[196]

U.S. policymakers must contend with public opinion not only in the Middle East, but also among their own constituents. In the process, they must consider the possibility that, by seeking to dilute public resolve, terrorist networks accurately perceive an important feature of the interaction between the costs of using force and the constraints associated democratic institutions. Democracies are more likely to force their leaders to equilibrate the costs of a policy of military intervention with its perceived benefits.[197]

Whether democracy can force policymakers to learn from terrorist networks' organizational vulnerabilities is a different question. Although policymakers have plenty of principled reasons to train attention on the organizational problems affecting terrorist networks' competition for public support, the last five years suggest that U.S. officials have not always taken these insights seriously.[198] It may take time, bureaucratic capacity, or additional political support to fully appreciate the implications of these insights. And political dynamics may distort even the most determined efforts to develop more effective counter-terrorist policies.[199]

Ultimately we must await history's judgment on whether U.S. policymakers have sufficiently mined the organizational complexities of al Qaeda and its analogues. But three facts suggest that U.S. policymakers and the sprawling bureaucracies they supervise have yet to advance far enough on this path. First, much of their public

194 *See* Naji, *supra* note 1, at 15 (discussing the importance of public support in the "path to the establishment of an Islamic state").

195 *See supra* note 130 and accompanying text (discussing overzealous action).

196 *See* Zachary Shore, Breeding Bin Ladens: America, Islam, and the Future of Europe 5 (2006) (citing polls and concluding that "America's appeal in the Muslim world has rarely been lower").

197 James D. Fearon, *Domestic Political Audiences and the Escalation of International Disputes*, 88 Am. Pol. Sci. Rev. 577, 577, 586–87 (1994).

198 *See* 9/11 Commission Report, *supra* note 46, at 365–83 (stating that the "U.S. government must build the capacities to prevent a 9/11-scale plot from succeeding" and making a series of recommendations with respect to several countries with perceived terrorist threats); Ron Suskind, The One Percent Doctrine 342 (2006) ("It's five years after 9/11 [and] the country still [is not able] to tell everybody what [it] know[s] about the strategic targeting doctrine of al Qaeda.").

199 *Cf.* Bueno de Mesquita, *supra* note 57, at 29–30 (discussing politicians' incentives to provide less stringent counter-terrorism policies that might be optimal under certain conditions); Cuéllar, *supra* note 20, at 44–48 (discussing politicians' potential incentives to signal competence by undertaking visible and aggressive actions while neglecting activities with longer-term payoffs).

rhetoric about al Qaeda in particular, and about terrorist groups in general, fits poorly with the insights arising from a close observation of al Qaeda's ongoing administrative law dilemmas.[200] Second, some of the strategies the U.S. government has pursued play into the terrorist network's hands by dovetailing almost precisely with its explicitly avowed strategies.[201] Third, in order to apply some of the insights that can be gained from studying al Qaeda's organizational problems, we must ensure that our own bureaucracies are capable of assimilating such information and evaluating policies using new metrics sensitive to those insights. In keeping with such a focus, the September 11 Commission report called for greater capacity to analyze open sources.[202] Yet building such capacity, and repairing what ails existing intelligence bureaucracies, is only the tip of the iceberg. Security bureaucracies would deliver greater social value if they eschewed their tendency to analyze the threat of terrorism in the abstract. Instead, analysts' focus should turn to the question of how specific legal and policy changes affect terrorists' organizational vulnerabilities, and whether the steps our society has taken reasonably advance its security or instead play precisely into the hands of terrorist networks. Such capacity seems, at best, embryonic.[203]

C. Al Qaeda's Drive to Solve Its Administrative Law Dilemmas

Even a brief observation of terrorist organizations demonstrates that these entities lack a fully functioning analogue to the familiar administrative law framework found in the United States and other advanced industrialized countries. As non-state actors, terrorist networks have a limited ability to fully appropriate the functional architecture of nation-states.[204] Nonetheless, aligning the incentives of lower-level operatives and organizational leaders, restraining overzealous action endangering the organization's standing with the public, and maintaining operational confidentiality are all examples of organizational challenges that have encouraged some al Qaeda strategists to aspire to imitate the administrative structures of state bureaucracies in advanced industrialized countries.[205]

---

200 *See supra* notes 32–35 and accompanying text (discussing distinctions between political and scholarly discussions of terrorist motivations).

201 *See* Wright, *supra* note 38, at 59.

202 *See* 9/11 Commission Report, *supra* note 46, at 407–19 (discussing the importance of developing analytical capabilities to analyze both open-source and covertly obtained information, and of integrating such information).

203 Witness, for example, the Justice Department's relative lack of detailed theoretical or empirical analysis when its officials made the case for renewal of portions of the Patriot Act that were subject to sunsets. *Cf.* Dep't of Justice, USA PATRIOT Act: Sunsets Report (2005) (identifying the expiring provisions of the Patriot Act and providing analysis and argument for their renewal).

204 It is worth noting, however, that their leaders repeatedly voice the aspiration to acquire such capacity. *See supra* Part I.B.4.

205 *See* Naji, *supra* note 1, at 73.

In some cases, strategists have begun to realize their ambition for law-like administrative procedures within the terrorist network. Al Qaeda's increasingly frenetic pace of operations displays evidence of occasional attempts not only to address internal administrative problems, but also to attempt to do so through the creation of a law-like system of adaptive procedures. Though embryonic as an administrative process, the components of these systems seem to rely on a flexible mix of hierarchy (whenever possible) and loose decentralization (whenever necessary),[206] audits of lower-level officers,[207] efforts to require specialization,[208] dispute resolution bodies to administer Islamic law,[209] and a decidedly Weberian effort to match individuals to tasks on the basis of skill.[210] Al Qaeda's leaders have embraced delegation—providing guidance and leaving logistical planning and financing to regional officials.[211] An employment contract for potential recruits explains how the organization has developed administrative procedures for handling grievances and disputes that arise under Islamic law.[212] Reviewing what al Qaeda has already accomplished, Naji emphasizes what the organization has learned regarding the value of sorting recruits by intellectual ability and competence,[213] the successful division of responsibilities within al Qaeda units,[214] and the creation of promotion systems to reward those who invest in acquiring administrative skills.[215] The organization's most exalted instrumental goals, he reiterates at every turn, depend on procedures that will build on these developments, providing the organization with the means to make the most effective and legitimate use of its scarce resources.

If administrative procedures are important for the internal management of terrorist networks, they are even more important for the provision of services to external constituencies. Perceptive strategists within terrorist networks recognize the value of bureaucratic administration and service delivery. They seek more than tentative steps toward a formal internal administrative process—particularly during or immediately following periods of intense violence—and recognize that these steps are among their most difficult, complex, and pressing challenges. In order to manage such challenges, al Qaeda's strategists seek to develop administrative cadres with

---

206 *See id.* at 23.

207 *See* SHAPIRO, *supra* note 28, at 2.

208 *See* NAJI, *supra* note 1, at 23.

209 *See* BERGEN, *supra* note 30, at 123–25 (discussing al Qaeda's use of Sharian courts).

210 *See* NAJI, *supra* note 1, at 23, 72.

211 *See* HARMONY AND DISHARMONY, *supra* note 40, at 8.

212 *Id.* at 69 (summarizing Harmony Document AFGP-2002-600045, an al Qaeda employment contract which, inter alia, lays out "[p]rocedures for handling grievances and disputes . . . in accordance with Islamic law").

213 *See* NAJI, *supra* note 1, at 72.

214 *See id.* at 23.

215 *See id.*

special competence to manage organizational units.[216] They also seek experts to run the equivalent of cabinet-type ministries, and in some cases they openly advocate the study of Western management texts.[217] In contrast to some U.S. military planners, these strategists worry not only about the proverbial *day of,* but also about the *day after.*[218]

Underlying this concern is the recognition that administrative capacity is essential both to overseeing the operations of the network itself (including, among other things, the planning of terrorist operations and the training of new recruits), as well as to providing services to civilians in order to maintain their allegiance. The process begins with brutality:

> When savagery happens in several regions—whether we administer them or they are neighboring regions or further away—a spontaneous kind of polarization begins to happen among the people who live in the region of chaos. The people, seeking security, rally around the great personages of the country or a party organization or a jihadi organization or a military organization composed of the remainders of the army or the police of the regimes of apostasy.[219]

But it culminates in al Qaeda's version of the administrative state, where success depends on

> management of... needs with regard to the provision of food and medical treatment, preservation of security and justice among the people who live in the regions of savagery, securing the boarders [sic] by means of groups that deter anyone who tries to assault the regions of savagery, as well as setting up defensive fortifications. (The stage of) managing the people's needs with regard to food and medical treatment may advance to (the stage of) being responsible for offering services like education and so forth.[220]

While Naji's is perhaps the most elaborate and organizationally sophisticated vision associated with those who support the burgeoning movement that al Qaeda represents, it is worth noting that not every jihadi strategist is equally sensitive to the centrality of service delivery and administrative challenges. Take al Zawahiri's *Knights Under the Prophet's Banner.* The senior al Qaeda leader stresses the value of recruiting new adherents, publicizing the movement, and mobilizing supporters, using these goals as a strategic justification for massive terrorist attacks directly against the West.[221] By contrast, he pays little attention to the challenge of administering security and service delivery in areas where existing state authority collapses.

216 *See id.* at 1, 63.

217 *See supra* note 62 and accompanying text (discussing the value of Western management texts to al Qaeda).

218 *Cf.* Ricks, *supra* note 8, at 184.

219 Naji, *supra* note 1, at 47.

220 *Id.* at 11.

221 *See* Mansfield, *supra* note 67, at 349–50.

He assumes, instead, that the state will simply fall into the jihadists' hands after allegedly unpopular, pro-Western regimes begin to fail:

> The jihad movement must adopt its plan on the basis of controlling a piece of land in the heart of the Islamic world on which it could establish and protect the state of Islam and launch its battle to restore the rational caliphate based on the traditions of the prophet.[222]

There is an uncanny similarity between this assumption and some U.S. war planners' assumptions about Iraq. Perhaps the canny aspiration of some al Qaeda strategists to forge greater internal administrative capacity, and particularly a greater capacity to provide services to civilians during and after violent conflict, should be cause for reflection among U.S. policymakers and citizens. Despite the importance of post-conflict reconstruction, the U.S. government and its allies have confronted major problems in forestalling civilians' descent into despair in Afghanistan and Iraq. To improve the nation's capacity to manage these challenges, U.S. policymakers may need to forge new bureaucratic structures and international coalitions better able to address the security and service delivery challenges that jihadi strategists have rightly underscored.

But despite the unquestionable need for some bureaucratic improvements in conventional nation-states' security and humanitarian capabilities, the most cogent implication to draw from terrorist networks' organizational problems may not be about the need to change our domestic administrative arrangements. The most important point may be a more subtle one; whatever their degree of apparent ideological commitment and political audacity, even terrorists must overcome vast organizational challenges to achieve their goals. As the next Part details, this ineluctable pervasiveness of organizational problems—problems that have motivated both advanced industrialized nation-states and terrorist networks to seek rule-like mechanisms for managing administrative burdens—suggests that the tactical game of counter-terrorist law and policy is embedded within a longer-term, strategic struggle among competing systems to manage administrative problems.

III. STRATEGIC CONFLICT AS A DUEL AMONG COMPETING SYSTEMS TO MANAGE ADMINISTRATIVE PROBLEMS

Return to the now-familiar debates about specific legal changes in the wake of the September 11 attacks. These debates are familiar not only because of the significance of the legal changes in question, but also because the discussions tend to rely on three familiar approaches. One focuses on the potential tactical advantages that a new statute or constitutional interpretation would yield in the battle to detect potential

222 *Id.* at 214. In contrast to Naji, al Zawahiri provides considerably less evidence when discussing the objective of territorial control of the complex service-delivery challenges that would confront the organization, particularly in the transitional period before security could be established. Nonetheless, al Zawahiri does recognize that the *organization* (as opposed to the state he hopes to create) faces administrative challenges.

terrorist activity,[223] another on the new policy's effect on civil liberties,[224] and a third on trying to weigh the tactical advantages against the intrusions.[225] Though each of these approaches has something to offer,[226] each also neglects a more institutionally sensitive approach to evaluating the appropriate legal response to national security risks—an approach that emerges more clearly from the following insight. Despite their staggering differences, state bureaucracies in advanced industrialized countries and terrorist networks such as al Qaeda have something in common. Administrative problems are endemic to both, and hierarchical, law-like arrangements have been appealing (in varying degrees) to both. Neither commonality should be surprising upon reflection—achieving ambitious goals is all but impossible except through organized action, and undertaking such action without a measure of hierarchy and process is profoundly difficult. It follows that strategic competition is partly about the performance of administrative systems, and in particular, about how well those systems manage organizational problems. Even when competition occurs between seemingly radically different adversaries, such as advanced industrialized countries and terrorist networks, in some respects the underlying conflict might resemble a duel among administrative systems designed to lift an entity closer to achieving its goals while managing internal organizational problems.

To see how this insight applies in the continuing struggle against al Qaeda and similar groups, recall how time and again, problems that fall under the purview of administrative law in the American system prove central to terrorist networks' capacity to manage strategic conflicts.[227] These problems include restraining overzealous action, managing disputes among political actors, harnessing expertise, and weighing the costs and benefits of organizational activity. These very problems also help determine our own government's ability to respond to the threats posed by terrorist networks. Managing them depends in part on the organization of military bureaucracies. Budgetary priorities also matter, as do specific regulatory strategies that can enhance the security of transportation infrastructures, chemical plants, and nuclear facilities.[228]

Legal arrangements are a critical ingredient allowing advanced industrialized countries to manage such administrative problems, and for good reason. Although adherence to legal procedures depends on a measure of symbiosis with political circumstances and social practices, the procedures themselves plainly aim to strike a

223 *See supra* notes 33–34 and accompanying text.

224 *See* David Cole, *The Priority of Morality: The Emergency Constitution's Blind Spot*, 113 Yale L.J. 1753, 1759–60 (2004).

225 *Cf.* Posner & Vermeule, *supra* note 33, at 1110–14.

226 In fact, some of the preceding discussion falls squarely within the first trope. *See supra* Part II.B.

227 *See supra* Part I.B.4.

228 *Cf.* Eric A. Posner, *Fear and the Regulatory Model of Counterterrorism*, 25 Harv. J.L. & Pub. Pol'y 681, 689–90 (2002).

balance between flexibility and hierarchy.[229] They provide a framework for resolving disputes. They create procedural mechanisms to promote enhanced bureaucratic performance and restrain overzealous action. These advantages are not lost on some al Qaeda strategists; even when they lack the elaborate social arrangements and ability to operate openly that facilitates the implementation of legal rules as such, al Qaeda leaders have at various times aspired to create quasi-legal arrangements to better manage their endemic administrative burdens. Ironically, some government policies undermining existing legal arrangements in advanced industrialized countries may seem attractive only because of excessively simplistic depictions of terrorist networks. Policymakers and observers sometimes describe a ruthlessly efficient, entirely decentralized yet centrally coordinated, technologically sophisticated terrorist entity staffed monolithically by equally committed, zealous operatives with a common vision.[230] Instead, the reality of al Qaeda and similar networks exposes this description as a mirage—terrorist operatives manage to pose a threat not *because of*, but *despite*, their inability to fully address their pervasive administrative problems with hierarchical legal arrangements reminiscent of our own.

No entity with ambitious policy goals can avoid the recurring problem of how best to organize administrative activity to deliver services to members or external constituents. In some cases, severe problems in these domains persist for both al Qaeda and the United States, such as Iraq-style challenges of bureaucratic management in post-conflict situations where violence continues while services must be delivered. But the U.S. legal-bureaucratic system the post-conflict management problem is an exceptional one. Typically, the most pressing administrative challenges are gradually resolved in our own nation-state—perhaps not to perfection, but to a significant degree. The familiar administrative arrangements characteristic of modern regulatory policy not only reflect, but epitomize the qualities associated with advanced industrialized democratic states. U.S. law, for instance, reflects a broader trend among advanced industrialized nation-states to manage agency problems through some degree of legislative and judicial monitoring.[231] The U.S. regulatory state leverages organized interests' capabilities through bureaucratized notice and comment arrangements that permit participation and reshape those groups' relationships to the resulting regulation.[232]

---

229 *See* Leather Indus. of Am. v. Envtl. Prot. Agency, 40 F.3d 392, 402 (D.C. Cir. 1994) ("An agency has discretion to design rules that can be broadly applied, sacrificing some measure of 'fit' for administerability."); BREYER, *supra* note 2, at 77–78.

230 *See supra* notes 33–35 and accompanying text.

231 *See* Cuéllar, *supra* note 130, at 249–50. For a discussion of the development of administrative arrangements in other advanced industrialized countries, *see, e.g.*, Jeeyang Rhee Baum, *Presidents Have Problems Too: The Logic of Intra-branch Delegation in East Asian Democracies*, 37 BRIT. J. POL. SCI. (forthcoming Oct. 2007) (on file with author).

232 *See* MCNOLLGAST, *supra* note 153, at 213–15.

Far from being orthogonal to the struggle against adversaries such as al Qaeda, these features of the bureaucratized nation-state can be critical ingredients for strategic success. Nation-states and terrorist networks face pervasive organizational dilemmas regarding how best to organize people, committees, and scarce resources to achieve complicated goals in an unpredictable world. In the American public law system, lawmakers facing political pressures and seeking to achieve their own goals have been largely responsible for creating the modern administrative law system. They have done so in response to organizational dilemmas making it difficult to monitor and restrain government agencies. Despite its occasional prescriptive limitations, the basic system of administrative law that politicians have forged (along with associated legal doctrines and bureaucratic practices) addresses some of the most nettle-some dilemmas a nation-state faces. These include resolving disputes that embroil political actors,[233] allowing political actors to anticipate the public's reaction to administrative decisions,[234] mitigating agency problems,[235] allowing the executive branch to credibly signal its competence to a skeptical public,[236] and administratively weighing the costs and benefits of particular actions.[237] Because these administrative arrangements are capable of serving such crucial functions, they constitute a strategic resource of sorts. Diluting or dismantling these arrangements in order to achieve tactical goals can exacerbate problems that interfere with responses to a nation's adversaries.

Despite its politicized origins, the modern administrative law system has become a framework for crafting legal and policy decisions in a manner that mitigates some of the pervasive bureaucratic problems affecting politically controversial and factually complex decisions.[238] Such complexity arises not only in traditional regulatory

---

233 *See, e.g.*, Raines v. Byrd, 521 U.S. 811, 812–13 (1997) (adjudicating a dispute involving legislators' standing to challenge an executive branch administrative action).

234 *See* McNollgast, *supra* note 153, at 186 ("The positive political analysis of administrative law generates some ideas about the policy effects of administrative procedures.").

235 *See id.*

236 Enhancing executive branch discretionary powers and limiting judicial review of national security actions may weaken the executive's ability to credibly signal competence and good faith. *Cf.* Matthew C. Stephenson, Bureaucratic Decision Costs and Endogenous Agency Expertise 3–5 (June 26, 2006) (unpublished manuscript), http://www.law.uchicago.edu/files/stephenson.pdf.

237 *See* Exec. Order No. 12,866, 58 Fed. Reg. 51735 (1993).

238 *See, e.g.*, Lawrence M. Friedman, American Law in the 20th Century 170–71 (2002) (discussing how "[t]he new administrative state created a multitude of problems," and explaining the procedural and legal reforms that mitigated the difficulties). It should be readily apparent that administrative law is neither entirely rational nor balanced. As a product of the political process, its tenets reflect the particular distribution of political strength and weakness channeled into the lawmaking process. And because they are enmeshed in that larger political process, legal provisions associated with administrative law do not operate in a vacuum by themselves; they are instead acted upon in large measure because the existing political equilibrium makes it costly for various players to ignore the doctrine. Nonetheless, although legal arrangements do not function by themselves in the absence of norms and enforcement mechanisms, part of

contexts,[239] but also in the field of national security.[240] Because of this complexity, Professor Cass Sunstein underscores the practical relevance of the administrative law model—with its proscriptions on arbitrary decision making, its flexible logic of delegation and deference, and its increasing emphasis on cost-benefit analysis—for problems traditionally involving national security.[241] This approach is eminently sensible given the difficulties public bureaucracies face in resolving national security problems in light of the need for a measure of discretion in this domain.[242] Moreover, in principle modern national security law is concerned with limiting arbitrariness. The arbitrary exercise of national security power has the potential to waste resources, provide a false sense of security, provoke a backlash, or engender unnecessary restrictions on individual autonomy. These problems are no less serious merely because potential restraints on the arbitrary use of executive power can interfere with tactical operations.[243]

---

what makes advanced industrialized countries distinctive is that administrative law arrangements survived political efforts to address organizational problems that afflict public bureaucracies. The intense litigation, legislative conflict, executive branch interpretive disagreements, and scholarly debate concerning the definition of different legal provisions integral to administrative law is a testament to its importance in our system. Though it is plain that rules, by themselves, would not have the same impact within loose networks of illicit activity, the key point is that terrorist leaders have reason to seek the creation of law-like procedures to govern organized activity, regardless of whether such organizations have the necessary social and political context to make such procedures easy to impose. Indeed, such organizations tend to face precisely the circumstances that make following procedures difficult, including the need to operate in secrecy, the inability to recur to a formal legal system to enforce contractual arrangements, and the risk that seemingly loyal operatives will tend to have competing motives.

239 *See* Mariano-Florentino Cuéllar, *Rethinking Regulatory Democracy,* 57 ADMIN. L. REV. 411, 412–18 (2005) (discussing the complexity of regulatory policymaking).

240 *See* Cass R. Sunstein, *Administrative Law Goes to War,* 118 HARV. L. REV. 2663, 2663–64 (2005) (concluding that the United States should evaluate the authorization to use military force under administrative law).

241 *Id.* at 2672.

242 One may sensibly disagree with Sunstein's willingness to use this "administrative law at war" approach as a justification for expansive deference. Quite likely, some differences of opinion on this issue might be rooted in the extent of deference considered appropriate even within more traditional confines of administrative law. *Compare* Cass R. Sunstein, *Beyond* Marbury: *The Executive's Power to Say What the Law Is,* 115 YALE L.J. 2580, 2582–84 (2006) (exalting deference), *with* Cohen et al., *supra* note 21, at 743–45 (questioning rationales for deference in conventional administrative law), *and* Mariano-Florentino Cuéllar, *Auditing Executive Discretion,* 82 NOTRE DAME L. REV. 227, 261–65 (2006) (detailing the risks associated with expansive discretion).

243 Even if one leaves aside the direct benefits of hierarchical bureaucracy and external promotion of bureaucratic capacity in the short-term, the question remains whether matching the relatively greater decentralization of terrorist networks would actually serve the advanced industrialized nations strategic goal of responding to terrorist attacks. Greater decentralization implies, by definition, less control over critical decisions such as the projection of coercive force. Given scarce resources, more decentralization runs the risk of excessively spreading those resources, which is precisely what some terrorist networks' strategic studies emphasize as a crucial objective.

The National Security Agency (NSA) wiretapping controversy further illustrates the argument. Late in December of 2005, a newspaper revealed that President Bush had signed an order in 2002 directing the NSA to "monitor [] the international telephone calls and international e-mail messages of hundreds, perhaps thousands, of people inside the United States without warrants," in an effort to gather intelligence on al Qaeda.[244] President Bush quickly expressed regret—not that he signed the order, but that news of it leaked.[245] The newspaper article constituted a "shameful act," he said, adding that "the fact that we're discussing this program is helping the enemy."[246] That same day, Attorney General Alberto Gonzales and General Michael Hayden, Principal Deputy Director for National Intelligence, held a press briefing concerning the wiretapping program.[247] Although refusing to confirm details of the story, Gonzales stressed the program complied with the Fourth Amendment reasonableness standard for warrants.[248] Hayden explained that the judgment to warrant "targets" was "made by the operational work force at the National Security Agency using the information available to them at the time, and the standard that they apply—and it's a two-person standard that must be signed off by a shift supervisor."[249] Hayden later clarified that the judgments had "intense oversight by the NSA Inspector General, by the NSA General Counsel, and by officials of the Justice Department who routinely look into this process and verify that the standards set out by the President are being followed."[250]

Critics have ardently questioned the administration's legal basis for ordering the NSA to engage in wiretapping activities in contravention of the Foreign Intelligence Surveillance Act of 1978 (FISA).[251] Indeed, the administration has tacitly acknowledged that the wiretapping program violates FISA on its face, conceding that the Act "requires a court order before engaging in this kind of surveillance . . . unless there is somehow—there is—unless otherwise authorized by statute or by Congress."[252]

See supra note 77 and accompanying text (discussing the goal of rendering Western powers less effective by spreading their resources).

244 James Risen & Eric Lichtblau, *Bush Lets U.S. Spy on Callers Without Courts,* N.Y. TIMES, Dec. 16, 2005, at A1.

245 Edward Epstein, *Bush Plays Hardball on Spying, Patriot Act,* S.F. CHRON., Dec. 20, 2005, at A1.

246 *Id.*

247 Press Release, White House, Briefing by Attorney General Alberto Gonzales and General Michael Hayden, Principal Deputy Director for National Intelligence (Dec. 19, 2005) [hereinafter Press Release], *available at* http://www.whitehouse.gov/news/releases/2005/12/20051219-1.html.

248 *Id.*

249 *Id.*

250 *Id.*

251 FISA of 1978, Pub. L. No. 95-511, 92 Stat. 1783 (codified as amended in scattered sections of 50 U.S.C.).

252 Press Release, *supra* note 247.

In FISA's own terms, the statute is, together with the criminal wiretap statute, "the exclusive means by which electronic surveillance . . . and the interception of domestic wire, oral, and electronic communications may be conducted."[253] The structure of FISA essentially creates an administrative review system for presidential decisions to use national security-related authorities to wiretap. To this end, FISA creates a Foreign Intelligence Surveillance Court (FISC) as the means for secretly reviewing and approving wiretap requests.[254] These requests must show probable cause that the wiretapping target is "a foreign power or an agent of a foreign power," and must be approved by the Attorney General and certified by a high-ranking defense official.[255] Critics have questioned the administration's asserted need to avoid FISC. FISA provides for retroactive warrant applications and FISC has rejected only a handful of applications since its inception.[256] Some observers sympathetic to the administration's rationale nonetheless emphasize how the court's "cumbersome submission requirements and insistence on strict adherence to the law" result in "the government regularly withdrawing or modifying applications when it appeared the judges might disapprove them."[257]

Administration representatives emphatically maintained, however, that the wiretapping was rendered legal by a combination of the 2001 Authorization for Use of Military Force and the President's inherent constitutional authority. "History," its declarations contend, "conclusively demonstrates that warrantless communications intelligence targeted at the enemy in time of armed conflict is a traditional and fundamental incident of the use of military force authorized by the AUMF."[258] The administration's preferred analogy is between detention and surveillance, emphasizing the Supreme Court's holding in *Hamdi* that detention was authorized under the AUMF because it is an "inherent part of warfare."[259] The administration argues that because "signals intelligence is even more a fundamental incident of war," surveillance is therefore implicitly authorized by the AUMF.[260] From this perspective, the AUMF "does not lend itself to a narrow reading," and represents an explicit

253 18 U.S.C. § 2511(2)(f) (2006).

254 *See* 50 U.S.C. § 1803(a) (Supp. III 2005).

255 Katherine Wong, Recent Development, *The NSA Terrorist Surveillance Program,* 43 Harv. J. on Legis. 517, 518 (2000).

256 David Johnston & Neil A. Lewis, *Defending Spy Program, Administration Cites Law,* N.Y. Times, Dec. 23, 2005, at A20 (noting that of the 10,617 warrant applications the court received from 1995 to 2004, the court rejected only four).

257 *Id.*

258 U.S. Dep't of Justice, Legal Authorities Supporting the Activities of the National Security Agency Described by the President 2 (2006) [hereinafter DOJ White Paper], *available at* http://news.findlaw.com/hdocs/docs/nsa/dojnsa11906wp.pdf.

259 Hamdi v. Rumsfeld, 542 U.S. 507, 515 (2004).

260 Press Release, *supra* note 247.

endorsement by Congress of "the President's use of his constitutional war powers."[261] Thus, the administration argues that the AUMF transferred the war on terror from a "zone of twilight" to a situation in which the President is at the "zenith" of his powers.[262]

Second, the administration has argued that "[t]he NSA activities are supported by the President's well-recognized inherent constitutional authority as Commander-in-Chief and sole organ for the Nation in foreign affairs to conduct warrantless surveillance of enemy forces for intelligence purposes to detect and disrupt armed attacks on the United States."[263] Under this view, the AUMF merely "confirm[s]" the President's constitutional authority, as "intelligence gathering is at the heart of executive functions."[264] Thus, authorization of the NSA wiretapping program is "primarily an exercise of the President's authority as commander in chief during an armed conflict that Congress expressly has authorized the President to pursue."[265]

Both of the administration's claims are speculative at best. To the extent the enacting congressional coalition intended anything specific, it did not likely intend the AUMF to supersede FISA. Critics have argued that FISA is designed to regulate all NSA efforts to intercept transnational communications, and that there is no clear basis for believing that the legislature viewed the AUMF trumping such an explicit and well-established program.[266] These critics have further noted that Congress amended FISA five times after 9/11, indicating congressional intent for the statute to continue to govern wiretaps.[267] Additionally, the Congressional Research Service has argued that "[w]hile the collection of intelligence is also an important facet of fighting a battle, it is not clear that the collection of intelligence constitutes a use of force," as authorized under the AUMF.[268]

Critics also dispute that the President has constitutional authority, under Article II, to permit warrantless wiretapping. They note that, given the number of Congress's enumerated powers that touch on foreign affairs, "Congress under Article I plainly enjoys the power to decide what measures the government should take against its

---

261 DOJ White Paper, *supra* note 258, at 11.

262 *Id.*

263 *Id.* at 1.

264 *Id.* at 2, 30.

265 *Id.* at 31.

266 John Cary Sims, *What NSA Is Doing . . . and Why It's Illegal,* 33 Hastings Const. L.Q. 105, 132 (2006).

267 *Id.*

268 Elizabeth B. Bazan & Jennifer K. Elsea, Cong. Research Serv., Presidential Authority to Conduct Warrantless Electronic Surveillance to Gather Foreign Intelligence Information 35 (2006), *available at* http://www.fas.org/sgp/crs/intel/m010506.pdf.

enemies within and abroad."[269] As the Congressional Research Service indicates, "The statutory language in FISA . . . and the legislative history of the bill that became FISA . . . reflect the Congress's stated intention to circumscribe any claim of inherent presidential authority to conduct electronic surveillance . . . so that FISA would be the exclusive mechanism for the conduct of such electronic surveillance."[270]

Three things stand out about the administration's justifications for the existing surveillance program. First, the administration's justifications focus relatively little on the marginal security benefit gained from circumventing FISA, rather than complying with its requirements. Second, it offers even less justification of how the strategy disrupts al Qaeda's strategic goals, internal structure, and budding administrative law.[271] Finally, it presents almost no discussion of how this action weakens a system that has been relatively successful at avoiding the profound organizational challenges now afflicting al Qaeda.[272] When the President authorized the program in 2002, he explicitly diluted the administrative review mechanisms that Congress had created, thereby exacerbating the risks of principal-agent problems, diminishing the extent to which the executive could signal its competence to citizens and other branches of government, and disregarding institutional solutions to disputes between the legislature and the executive branch. At first, these concerns may seem far removed from those that should animate a presidential response to a terrorist adversary. Perhaps an ordinary, short-term tactical justification could still be found for the President's actions. My point is simply this: allowing the debate to play out at that level is a mistake. Whatever else Americans are, they are also institutional architects. It is in the details of this architecture—how it deals with agency problems and information gaps, what participation means, and how disputes are resolved—that they might win their battles and reasonably manage their risks.

269 Harold J. Krent, *The Lamentable Notion of Indefeasible Presidential Powers: A Reply to Professor Prakash*, 91 Cornell L. Rev. 1383, 1394 (2006).

270 Bazan & Elsea, *supra* note 268, at 27.

271 Perhaps intelligence analysts are hard at work doing precisely such investigations and evaluations behind closed doors. For three accounts questioning the capacity of current intelligence bureaucracies to do so, see The Comm'n on the Intelligence Capabilities of the U.S. Regarding Weapons of Mass Destruction, Report to the President of the United States 3–37 (2005), *available at* http://www.wmd.gov/report/wmd_report.pdf; 9/11 Commission Report, *supra* note 46, at 254–77; Suskind, *supra* note 198, at 192–220. Moreover, if the President had more compelling rationales to support his particular policy, it is likely he could have made a more persuasive case. Finally, it is not obvious why making such a case about the marginal benefit of dispensing with the FISA courts would have revealed valuable intelligence to our adversaries.

272 These problems include, among others, the risk that expanding the scope of executive branch surveillance without some external review mechanism will dilute scarce resources, and that heightened political conflict arising from executive branch failure to follow statutorily prescribed procedures will damage the executive's subsequent credibility when requesting new counter-terrorism authority from lawmakers.

Addressing these risks also depends on recognizing that transparency and process have costs as well as benefits.[273] The technical soundness of some regulatory policies may benefit from a measure of discretion, or even secrecy. What makes modern administrative law potentially valuable as a strategic resource is not necessarily its level of transparency and procedural complexity. It is the fact that its precepts embody a political compromise that allows policy implementation in a system that mitigates some of the recurring organizational problems bedeviling both states and nonstate actors.[274]

Given FISA's politically complex heritage and organizational impacts, the NSA wiretapping illustrates the potentially complex and troubling consequences of diluting procedural constraints, particularly when the dilution is premised on a questionable interpretive strategy that ignores existing statutory enactments. Policymakers should evaluate the consequences of such a move not only with regard to the potential short-term tactical advantages it offers for pursuing terrorist networks, but also with regard to the broader strategic effect of undermining existing institutional solutions to administrative problems, particularly when similar problems repeatedly bedevil terrorist adversaries. If citizens and policymakers are capable of recognizing the extent to which organizational capacities play an important role in responding to external threats, then it is ironic indeed if they fail to consider the impact of counter-terrorism policies on the administrative arrangements that shape those capacities. Lawyers, judges, and policymakers should therefore evaluate the NSA wiretapping program not only in terms of the tactical needs it allegedly serves. They should also consider its laudable institutional effects on administrative arrangements, that (over time) might otherwise allow us to avoid the problems our adversary is constantly seeking to resolve. Legislators are entirely capable of making mistakes, but it is worth recalling that FISA was created for a reason—one that resonates with tones of administrative supervision in a complex, bureaucratic state. Insisting that the President follow the most plausible reading of FISA is therefore considerably more than an appeal to formalism, and more even than an appeal to a particular view of privacy or rights.

Instead, FISA is best understood to encompass a basic insight about the nature of strategic competition among entities facing organizational problems. Competition among strategic adversaries—even of those as different as al Qaeda and our own advanced industrialized state—depends on the soundness and success of an internal administrative law that matches immediate tactics with broader strategic goals.

---

273 *Cf.* William J. Stuntz, *Against Privacy and Transparency*, New Republic Online, Apr. 7, 2006, *available at* http://www.tnr.com/doc.mhtml?i=20060417&s=stuntz041706 (discussing the negative aspects of government transparency).

274 *Cf.* Matthew C. Stephenson, *The Strategic Substitution Effect: Textual Plausibility, Procedural Formality, and Judicial Review of Agency Statutory Interpretations*, 120 Harv. L. Rev. 528, 544–52 (2006) (discussing how more elaborate procedural arrangements governing regulatory action can mitigate interpretive disagreements about the meaning of a particular legal text in the administrative state).

Legislative bargaining produced FISA specifically to harness certain qualities associated with our admittedly imperfect but nonetheless valuable administrative mechanisms. Those qualities include provisions for a form of external review with considerable speed and secrecy and a means of signaling to the larger public executive competence in its use of surveillance powers.[275] Dismantling FISA review thus runs the risk of leaving Americans without a solution to the same type of organizational monitoring and control problem that their terrorist adversaries are trying to solve.

Though it is useful to highlight these common problems, the argument is not meant to collapse the critical distinctions between nonstate actors and bureaucratic agencies in advanced industrialized countries. Neither is it meant to suggest that every aspect of strategic battles comes down to an entity's development of its administrative law. Though terrorist networks and state bureaucracies face similar problems, they also tend to confront different constraints in solving them. The costs of screening personnel or the importance of absolute secrecy, for instance, may be lower for a conventional state bureaucracy than for an illicit network.[276]

Rather, the preceding analogy underscores the advantages of recasting strategic conflicts in part as duels between different administrative arrangements. In the United States, American lawmakers and organized interests have built legal arrangements to manage recurring organizational problems. Al Qaeda members have made their own moves to solve pervasive organizational problems, and in some cases, these moves have included drives to create hierarchical arrangements not unlike those instituted in advanced industrialized countries. To wit: not all organizations must solve their dilemmas the same way. Yet no organization can avoid its encounter with a world of mixed motives, information gaps, and agency problems.

The implication of this comparison is deceptively simple, but ironically hints at the importance of complexity in evaluating the legacy of the September 11 attacks. It underscores the importance of thinking carefully about how organizational problems are being managed among adversaries. It suggests that the correct way to evaluate the NSA's warrantless eavesdropping tactics and similar enforcement strategies rests only partly on the immediate tactical advantage achieved against the adversary. Instead the evaluation should also include how the policy affects competition between administrative arrangements—and in particular, whether warrantless surveillance erodes the legal conventions and administrative arrangements

275 *Cf.* Alistair Smith, *International Crises and Domestic Politics*, 92 Am. Pol. Sci. Rev. 623, 633–34 (1998) (displaying a model predicting the behavior and reactions of nations in crisis).

276 Indeed, conventional nation states are likely to hold over illicit non-state actors in developing hierarchical bureaucracies, operating with less-severe secrecy constraints, and building support among (and delivering services to) the mass public. In some sense, the structure of the modern, functioning nation-state has evolved to perform precisely such functions, and may therefore ultimately pose a greater threat than an illicit non-state actor struggling to solve the most basic organizational problems.

that Americans have built to solve the challenges that more frequently bedevil adversaries such as al Qaeda.

CONCLUSION

Legal change is in some measure a product of how actors who can shape the law discuss the problems they are allegedly trying to solve, and how they choose to frame a conversation about the relevant costs entailed in solving those problems. In the years following the 9/11 attacks, those discussions have taken place in five subtly interconnected arenas: courtrooms, legislatures, executive branch offices, scholarly communities, and the media.[277] Americans have witnessed fierce disagreements in those arenas about the methods and even the propriety of consequentialist analysis, and about the extent to which the danger posed by a nimble, secretive, and ruthlessly effective nonstate adversary justifies reshaping the legal architecture of surveillance or executive power. Yet participants in these debates seldom question the analytic value of the prevailing metaphor of terrorist organizations themselves, one that repeatedly plays up the allegedly radical distinctions between our familiar bureaucratic structures and their disaggregated postmodern entities. Given the stakes in choosing a metaphor to depict organization of nonstate actors, one should ask whether the prevailing depiction matches what al Qaeda's own strategists describe.

Al Qaeda's own jihadi strategic studies provide a revealing portrait of the organization, particularly when they are read against the backdrop of political scientists' emerging studies of terrorists' organizational dynamics. Although obvious differences arise when comparing an occasionally amorphous non-state actor to the bureaucratized government of an advanced industrialized country such as the United States, certain parallels exist between the internal management problems al Qaeda faces and the problems our own government addresses through an elaborate body of administrative law. Terrorist networks struggle to restrain overzealous action, to align the incentives of leaders and staff, and to promote a sense of public legitimacy about their goals and strategies. Belying conventional images of their unrestrained radicalism, al Qaeda and its analogues often enlist technocratic solutions to manage their money, to plan the delivery of services in territories they control, and to analyze public reactions. But in harnessing such technical knowledge they face considerable difficulties resulting from operational security and recruitment problems. In part because of these constraints, terrorist strategists often seek internal arrangements—analogous to our own domestic administrative law—to realize long-term strategic goals. These arrangements emerge from learning from Western management texts, solving bureaucratic agency problems, harnessing expertise, generating information and participation, and adjudicating internal disputes. An investigation of al Qaeda's continuing efforts to fix its strategic goals

277 *Cf.* Friedman, *supra* note 238, at 588–91 (discussing the role of social change, public perceptions, political developments, and diffusion of ideas through the media as sources of legal change).

and construct a law-like administrative framework to achieve them yields a number of tentative policy implications, including (for example) the conclusion that policymakers should evaluate counter-terrorism policies in part on the basis of whether these policies assist or hinder the organization's efforts to foment sympathy and participation among the Muslim and Arab public.

Ironically, key features of the legal system associated with the modern regulatory state both reflect and play an important role in mitigating the challenges that confront terrorist networks. Terrorists networks, like a conventional advanced industrialized nation-state, face fundamental dilemmas where an element of hierarchy, bureaucracy, and rule-based norms is imprescindible. Terrorists do not have formal administrative law, nor have they developed the social and political norms to conform to it. But, in contrast to conventional wisdom, their leaders are hard at work trying to fashion analogous versions. In effect, organizational success—for both terrorist networks and bureaucratized nation-states—depends on managing classic administrative law concerns: agency problems, the generation of expertise and information, legitimacy and participation, and the adjudication of disputes among actors who share power. By appreciating these parallels, Americans may garner a richer perspective on the value of their own internal arrangements. They should therefore understand strategic conflicts in part as a contest between dueling administrative arrangements managing risks that can never be entirely extinguished. And they would do well to evaluate counter-terrorism policies in part on the basis of how those policies affect administrative capacity. Viewed this way, the persistent strategic challenge of managing terrorism-related risks will more readily resemble a struggle to reasonably mitigate murders, traffic accidents, and occupational safety deaths, and will less resemble an unrelenting struggle to reduce any possible danger to zero.

THE TERRORIST SURVEILLANCE PROGRAM AND THE CONSTITUTION

John Yoo†

Originally Published in *George Mason Law Review*, Vol. 14 (Spring, 2007)

INTRODUCTION

In response to the September 11 attacks, President Bush created the Terrorist Surveillance Program ("TSP"), which authorized the National Security Agency ("NSA") to intercept phone calls and emails traveling into and out of the United States.[1] One of the parties to the communication had to be someone suspected of being a member of al Qaeda.[2] This surveillance took place outside the framework of the Foreign Intelligence Surveillance Act, or FISA, which since 1978 has regulated the interception of communications entering or leaving the United States.[3] FISA requires the Justice Department to seek a warrant from a special Article III court, the Foreign Intelligence Surveillance Court ("FISC"), to conduct electronic surveillance within the United States for national security purposes.[4]

The legality of the TSP has sparked great controversy. Academic and political critics claim that it violates FISA and represents an unconstitutional expansion of presidential power.[5] The Bush administration argues that the program is fully legal

---

† Professor of Law, University of California at Berkeley School of Law (Boalt Hall); Visiting Scholar, American Enterprise Institute. I thank Sean Callagy for his excellent research assistance. Jesse Choper, Eric Posner, Sai Prakash, and Adrian Vermeule provided comments on the manuscript. This essay is adapted from John Yoo, War By Other Means: An Insider's Account Of The War On Terrorism (2006).

1 *See* James Risen & Eric Lichtblau, *Bush Lets U.S. Spy on Callers Without Courts,* N.Y. Times, Dec. 16, 2005, at A1; *see also* Press Release, Press Briefing by Attorney General Gonzales and General Michael Hayden, Principal Deputy Director for National Intelligence (Dec. 19, 2005), http://www.whitehouse.gov/news/releases/2005/12/20051219-1.html [hereinafter "December 2005 Briefing"].

2 *See* Risen & Lichtblau, *supra* note 1; December 2005 Briefing, *supra* note 1.

3 Foreign Intelligence Surveillance Act of 1978 ("FISA"), Pub. L. No. 95-511, 92 Stat. 1783 (codified as amended in scattered sections of U.S.C.), *amended by* Uniting and Strengthening America by Providing Appropriate Tools Required to Intercept and Obstruct Terrorism Act of 2001 ("USA PATRIOT ACT"), Pub. L. No. 107-56, 115 Stat. 272 (codified as amended in scattered sections of the U.S.C.).

4 *See* FISA § 1822.

5 *See, e.g.*, Will, *infra* note 15; Epstein, *infra* note 26.

and has produced valuable information allowing the government to prevent terrorist attacks on the United States.[6] As of this writing, a federal district court in Michigan issued an opinion enjoining the program, but the U.S. Court of Appeals for the Sixth Circuit has stayed the order, allowing the TSP to continue operating for the time being.[7] Proposals in the past Congress would have consolidated legal challenges in the FISC—which would have issued an authoritative decision on the constitutionality of the program—or mandated review by the Supreme Court upon appeal.[8]

This Essay argues that the TSP represents a valid exercise of the President's Commander-in-Chief authority to gather intelligence during wartime. Part I argues that critics of the program misunderstand the separation of powers between the President and Congress in wartime. Part II traces the confusion to a failure to properly understand the differences between war and crime, and a difficulty in understanding the new challenges presented by a networked, dynamic enemy such as al Qaeda. Part III explains that because the United States is at war with al Qaeda, the President possesses the constitutional authority as Commander-in-Chief to engage in warrantless surveillance of enemy activity, even communications entering or leaving the United States, to successfully prosecute the war.

I. CRITICS OF THE TSP: A FUNDAMENTAL MISUNDERSTANDING OF CONSTITUTIONAL POWERS

When *The New York Times* revealed the existence of the NSA program in December 2005,[9] a firestorm of controversy broke out. Some Democratic Congressmen suggested impeaching President Bush for violating federal law and the Constitution, a view shared by several liberal commentators.[10] A group of law professors and the Congressional Research Service argued that the President had broken the law by acting outside the federal wiretapping statutes.[11] In March of 2006, Senator Russell

---

6 December 2005 Briefing, *supra* note 1.

7 Am. Civil Liberties Union v. Nat'l Sec. Agency/Cent. Sec. Serv., 438 F. Supp. 2d 754, 782 (E.D. Mich.), *stayed pending appeal,* 467 F.3d 590, 591 (6th Cir. 2006).

8 *Compare* National Security Surveillance Act of 2006, S. 3876, 109th Cong. (2006) (vesting adjudicatory power in the FISC, with possible grant to certiorari to the Supreme Court), *with* Foreign Intelligence Surveillance Oversight and Resource Enhancement Act of 2006, S. 4051, 109th Cong. (2006) (authorizing mandatory Supreme Court review upon appeal by a party).

9 *See* Risen & Lichtblau, *supra* note 1; *see also* December 2005 Briefing, *supra* note 1.

10 Jonathan Last, *Impeach Bush Now (!)(?): It's Not as Outlandish as it May Seem,* PHILADELPHIA INQUIRER, Mar. 19, 2006, at D1, *available at* http://www.philly.com/mld/inquirer/news/special_packages/sunday_review/14131676.htm.

11 A letter to Congress from law professors and former government officials, many of them longtime critics of the Bush administration's war on terrorism or opponents of presidential war powers, concluded that there is no "plausible legal defense" of the NSA program, and that President Bush should have sought an amendment to the Patriot Act to allow it. They argued that "the President simply cannot violate criminal laws behind closed doors because he deems them

Feingold even introduced a motion in the Senate to censure President Bush for approving an illegal program "to spy on Americans, on American soil."[12] Feingold claimed that the NSA program was "right in the strike zone of what the founding fathers thought about when they talked about high crimes and misdemeanors," referring to the standard for impeachment.[13] Feingold, it should be added, was the only Senator to vote against the Patriot Act in 2001.[14]

Fire rained down not only from the left, but also from the right. Well-known conservative columnist George Will wrote in the *Washington Post* that the Bush administration had created a new danger, arguing:

> [B]ecause the president [sic] is commander in chief, he is the 'sole organ for the nation in foreign affairs.' That non sequitur is refuted by the Constitution's plain language, which empowers Congress to ratify treaties, declare war, fund and regulate military forces, and make laws 'necessary and proper' for the execution of all presidential powers. Those powers do not include deciding that a law—FISA, for example—is somehow exempted from the presidential duty to 'take care that the laws be faithfully executed.'[15]

Will and other critics fail to understand the leading role in foreign affairs that the Constitution grants the President.

First, the statement that the President is the "sole organ for the nation in foreign affairs" was not manufactured by the Bush administration, but in fact derives from *United States v. Curtiss-Wright Export Corp.*, a well-known 1936 Supreme Court case that recognized the President's control over diplomacy and setting

---

obsolete or impracticable." Letter from Beth Nolan et al., to the Members of the United States Congress, (Feb. 9, 2006), http://www.nybooks.com/articles/18650. A similar conclusion is reached by the Congressional Research Service. *See* Memorandum from Elizabeth B. Bazan & Jennifer K. Elsea, Legislative Attorneys, Congressional Research Service, to various congressional clients (Jan. 5, 2006), *available at* http://www.fas.org/sgp/crs/intel/m010506.pdf.

12 Sen. Russ Feingold, United States Senator, Statement on the President's Warrantless Wiretapping Program (Feb. 7, 2006), http://feingold.senate.gov/~feingold/statements/06/02/20060207.html (discussing S. Res. 398, 109th Cong. (2006)) [hereinafter Wiretap Press Briefing].

13 Sen. Russ Feingold, United States Senator, Statement on His Resolution To Censure President Bush (Mar. 16, 2006), http://feingold.senate.gov/~feingold/statements/06/03/2006316.html; *cf.* U.S. CONST. art. II, § 4.

14 U.S. Senate Roll Call Votes 107th Congress—1st Session, Vote Summary On Passage of the Bill H.R. 3162, http://www.senate.gov/legislative/LIS/roll_call_lists/roll_call_vote_cfm.cfm?congress=107&session=1&vote=00313 (last visited Nov. 19, 2006); *see also* Shailagh Murray, *Senate Maverick's Motion Stirs Angry Debate,* WASH. POST, Mar. 15, 2006.

15 George F. Will, *No Checks, Many Imbalances,* WASH. POST, Feb. 16, 2006, at A27 (emphasis omitted) (citing U.S. CONST. art. I, §§ 8, 10; U.S. CONST. art. II, § 3; United States v. Curtiss-Wright Export Corp., 299 U.S. 304, 319 (1936)), *available at* http://www.washingtonpost.com/wp-dyn/content/article/2006/02/15/AR2006021502003.html.

foreign policy.[16] Congress as a whole does not ratify treaties.[17] Rather, the Senate participates in advising and consenting to treaties in its executive capacity (treaties are discussed in the Constitution's Article II, where the presidency is established), but only after the President has negotiated and signed the treaty.[18] The President can even choose not to send a negotiated treaty to the Senate, or may refuse to "make" a treaty after the Senate has approved it.[19] So the treaty power is not the Congress's but the President's.[20]

Next, the Constitution's Necessary and Proper Clause gives Congress the power to implement the other powers of the government.[21] It does not, however, allow Congress to change the separation of powers in its favor by reducing the powers of the President. Finally, the President has the duty to "take Care that the Laws be faithfully executed."[22] But because the Constitution is the highest form of federal law, the President cannot enforce acts of Congress which are unconstitutional.[23] Will seems to imagine the Commander-in-Chief Clause[24] as being substantively empty—implying that its sole function is to execute the war policies of Congress.[25] What Will and other critics neglect is the President's war power independent of Congress.

---

16 *Curtiss-Wright Export Corp.*, 299 U.S. at 320 (positing the "plenary and exclusive power of the President as the sole organ of the federal government in the field of international relations").

17 *See* U.S. CONST. art. II, § 2, cl. 2.

18 *Id.* (The President "shall have power, by and with the Advice and Consent of the Senate, to make Treaties, provided two thirds of the Senators present concur").

19 *See id;* CONG. RESEARCH SERV., 106TH CONG., TREATIES AND OTHER INTERNATIONAL AGREEMENTS: THE ROLE OF THE UNITED STATES SENATE 12 (Comm. Print 2001) ("After the Senate gives its advice and consent to a treaty, the Senate sends it to the President. He resumes control and decides whether to take further action to complete the treaty.") [hereinafter TREATIES AND OTHER INTERNATIONAL AGREEMENTS]; *see also* John K. Setear, *The President's Rational Choice of a Prerati-fication Pathway: Article II, Congressional-Executive Agreement, or Executive Agreement?*, 31 J. LEGAL STUD. 5 (2002) (examining the President's broad power, largely unchecked by Congress or the courts, to decide the procedure by which a treaty or congressional-executive agreement is ratified); John C. Yoo, *Laws as Treaties?: The Constitutionality of Congressional-Executive Agreements*, 99 MICH. L. REV. 757 (2001).

20 *See* TREATIES AND OTHER INTERNATIONAL AGREEMENTS, *supra* note 19, at 12 ("The executive branch has the primary responsibility for carrying out treaties and ascertaining that other parties fulfill their obligations after treaties and other international agreements enter into force. . . .").

21 U.S. CONST. art. I, § 8, cl. 18.

22 U.S. CONST. art. II, § 3.

23 *See* U.S. CONST. art. VI, cl. 2; Marbury v. Madison, 5 U.S. (1 Cranch) 137 (1803) (striking down an act of Congress as unconstitutional).

24 U.S. CONST. art. II, § 2 ("The President shall be Commander in Chief of the Army and Navy of the United States, and of the Militia of the several States, when called into the actual Service of the United States. . . .").

25 *See* WILL, *supra* note 15.

In the *Wall Street Journal,* Richard Epstein, perhaps the nation's leading libertarian legal scholar, also argued that Congress has the upper hand in setting war policy.[26] He believes that Congress's constitutional powers to declare war, to make rules regulating the armed forces, and to fund the military signify that it could even prohibit the military from using live ammunition in combat.[27] Even so, Epstein does have a broader view of the Commander-in-Chief Clause than Will. Epstein's suggestions guarantee civilian control over the military and prevent Congress from issuing orders or evading the chain of command.[28] "The precise detailed enumeration of powers and responsibilities in Article II just do not confer on the president [sic] a roving commission over foreign and military affairs. He is a coordinate player, not a dominant one."[29] At best, he would allow the President to interpret, but not override, Congress's decisions when confronting a new situation unanticipated by the rules.[30]

Epstein's arguments are both more nuanced and rooted more in the constitutional text than Will's, but they are no more convincing. Scholars historically have understood the Commander-in-Chief Clause to be more than just a designation of the President as the top of the military chain of command.[31] The framing generation would have understood a Commander-in-Chief as having authority to determine when to resort to military hostilities and how to conduct them.[32] Article II of the

26 Richard A. Epstein, *Executive Power on Steroids,* WALL ST. J., Feb. 13, 2006, at A16, *available at* http://www.cato.org/pub_display.php?pub_id=5557.

27 *Id.*

28 *Compare id.* (reasoning that the Constitution grants coordinate powers to the President and Congress), *with* Will, *supra* note 15 (arguing that the constitutional power to ratify treaties, declare war, and fund and regulate the armed forces generally gives Congress significant power to constrain the President's actions in matters of foreign affairs).

29 EPSTEIN, *supra* note 26.

30 *See id.*

31 *See* John Yoo, *The Continuation of Politics by Other Means: The Original Understanding of War Powers,* 84 CAL. L. REV. 167 (1996); John Yoo, *War and the Constitutional Text,* 69 U. CHI. L. REV. 1639 (2002).

32 As Hamilton wrote in *The Federalist,* "[e]nergy in the executive is a leading character in the definition of good government. It is essential to the protection of the community against foreign attacks. . . ." THE FEDERALIST No. 70, at 471 (Alexander Hamilton) (Jacob E. Cooke ed., 1961). This point applies to the war context directly. Hamilton wrote: "Of all the cares or concerns of government, the direction of war most peculiarly demands those qualities which distinguish the exercise of power by a single hand." THE FEDERALIST No. 74, at 500 (Alexander Hamilton) (Jacob E. Cooke ed., 1961). Future Supreme Court Justice James Iredell argued that "[f]rom the nature of the thing, the command of armies ought to be delegated to one person only. The secrecy, dispatch, and decision, which are necessary in military operations, can only be expected from one person." 4 THE DEBATES IN THE SEVERAL STATE CONVENTIONS ON THE ADOPTION OF THE FEDERAL CONSTITUTION 107 (Jonathan Elliot ed., 1836); *see also* 3 JOSEPH STORY, COMMENTARIES ON THE CONSTITUTION OF THE UNITED STATES § 1485 (1833) (in military matters, "[u]nity of plan, promptitude, activity, and decision, are indispensable

Constitution also vests the President with "the executive power,"[33] which, in Justice Scalia's words, "does not mean *some of* the executive power, but *all of* the executive power."[34] Political theorists at the time of the framing considered foreign affairs and national security as quintessentially executive in nature,[35] and our Constitution creates an executive branch that can act with unity, speed, and secrecy to carry out those functions effectively.[36] Congress no doubt has important powers, such as the power to issue rules to regulate and govern the military, which gives it the sole authority to set the rules of military discipline and order.[37] But the Constitution nowhere vests in Congress any explicit authority to initiate national security policy, nor gives it an outright veto over executive decisions in the area.[38]

More broadly, these critics misunderstand the Constitution's allocation of warmaking powers between the executive and legislative branches. The Constitution vests in the President the authority and the responsibility to prevent future attacks against the United States,[39] a power re-affirmed by Congress in the wake of the September 11 attacks in the Authorization for Use of Military Force ("AUMF").[40] For much of the nation's history, Presidents and Congresses have understood that the executive branch's constitutional authority includes the power to begin military

---

to success; and these can scarcely exist, except when a single magistrate is entrusted exclusively with the power").

33 U.S. Const. art. II, § 1.

34 Morrison v. Olson, 487 U.S. 654, 705 (1988) (Scalia, J., dissenting).

35 *See* John Yoo, The Powers of War and Peace 30–45 (2005).

36 *See id.* at 30–45, 141–42; *infra* text accompanying notes 216–219.

37 *See* U.S. Const. art. I, § 8, cl. 14.

38 Epstein argues that the Commander-in-Chief is not textually a "power," but just a position. Epstein, *supra* note 26. But the lack of the word "power" there does not seem significant. Other authorities enjoyed by the President, such as the power to nominate and then appoint federal officials with the advice and consent of the Congress, do not use the word "power" either. *See* U.S. Const. art. II, § 2, cl. 2. But the authority to appoint individuals is not a position, but indeed a right of the President, and an important one at that. The Treaty Clause, by contrast, does designate the President as having a "power," *id.*, but the role of the President in both appointments and treaties are virtually identical. It does not seem as if there is anything significant in the latter's grant of a "power" and the former's silence on the matter.

39 *See* U.S. Const. art. II, § 2, cl. 1 ("The President shall be Commander in Chief of the Army and Navy of the United States, and of the Militia of the several States, when called into the actual Service of the United States. . . ."); sources cited *supra* note 31 (interpreting the historical meaning of the Commander-in-Chief clause).

40 Authorization for Use of Military Force, Pub. L. 107-40, 115 Stat. 224 (2001) [hereinafter AUMF]. In the AUMF, Congress resolved: "[t]he President is authorized to use all necessary and appropriate force against those nations, organizations, or persons he determines planned, authorized, committed, or aided the terrorist attacks that occurred on September 11, 2001, or harbored such organizations or persons, in order to prevent any future acts of international terrorism against the United States by such nations, organizations or persons." *Id.* § 2.

hostilities abroad.[41] During the last two centuries, neither has acted under the belief that the Constitution requires a declaration of war before the United States can engage in military hostilities abroad. Although this nation has used force abroad more than 100 times, it has formally declared war in only five conflicts against a total of eleven countries: the War of 1812, the Mexican-American War, the Spanish-American War, and World Wars I and II.[42] Without declarations of war or any other congressional authorization, Presidents have sent troops to oppose the Russian Revolution, intervene in Mexico, fight Chinese Communists in Korea, remove Manuel Noriega from power in Panama, and prevent human rights disasters in the Balkans.[43] Other conflicts, such as both Persian Gulf Wars, received "authorization" from Congress but not declarations of war.[44]

Critics of this long-standing practice of presidential initiative in war appeal to an original understanding of the Constitution.[45] But the text and structure of the Constitution, as well as its application over the last two centuries, confirm that the President can begin military hostilities without the approval of Congress. The Constitution does not establish a strict war-making process because the framers understood that war would require the speed,[46] decisiveness and secrecy that only the presidency could bring. "Energy in the executive," Alexander Hamilton argued in the Federalist Papers, "is a leading character in the definition of good government. It is essential to the protection of the community against foreign attacks...."[47] Indeed, according to Hamilton, "[o]f all the cares or concerns of government, the direction of war most peculiarly demands those qualities which distinguish the exercise of power by a single hand."[48] The Constitution does not create a legalistic process of making war, but rather gives to the President and Congress different powers that they can use in the political process to either cooperate or compete for primacy in policy.[49] To exercise that power effectively, the President must have the ability to engage in electronic surveillance that gathers intelligence on the activities of the enemy.

---

41 Yoo, *supra* note 35, at 155–60.

42 Yoo, *supra* note 31, at 177. *See generally* John Yoo, *War, Responsibility, and the Age of Terrorism*, 57 Stan. L. Rev. 793 (2004) (arguing that Congressional preapproval of the use of force abroad is not mandatory and evaluating American uses of force with and without formal declarations of war).

43 Yoo, *supra* note 31, at 177.

44 Authorization for Use of Military Force Against Iraq Resolution, Pub. L. No. 102-1, 105 Stat. 3 (1991); Authorization for Use of Military Force Against Iraq Resolution of 2002, Pub. L. No. 107-243, 116 Stat. 1498.

45 *See infra* notes 204–207.

46 *See supra* notes 37–38 and accompanying text.

47 The Federalist No. 70, *supra* note 32.

48 The Federalist No. 74, *supra* note 32.

49 Yoo, *supra* note 35, at 152–55.

II. THE TRADITIONAL LEGAL FRAMEWORK FAILS TO ACCOUNT FOR A NETWORKED, DYNAMIC ENEMY LIKE AL QAEDA

No one—even the critics—seems to doubt that the information gained from the NSA program has led to the successful prevention of al Qaeda plots against the United States.[50] According to General Michael Hayden, President Bush's choice to head the CIA in 2006 and leader of the NSA during much of the program's existence, "[t]his program has been successful in detecting and preventing attacks inside the United States."[51] When pressed by reporters whether it had succeeded where no other method would have, he said, "I can say unequivocally, all right, that we have got information through this program that would not otherwise have been available."[52] Attorney General Alberto Gonzales informed the press that the NSA program was perhaps the most classified program in the U.S. government, and that it had helped obtain information that had prevented attacks within the United States.[53] The main criticism has not been that the program is ineffective, but that it violates the Constitution and cannot be undertaken, no matter how successful or necessary to protect the public.[54]

Any legal work on the surveillance program conducted by the Office of Legal Counsel remains classified, but after the leak of the program's existence, the Department of Justice released a white paper about it.[55] But the crucial question remains unanswered: Why, as a matter of policy, would the Bush administration operate outside FISA,[56] especially after going to great lengths to pass the Patriot Act?

The Patriot Act made valuable improvements in our intelligence laws, but its true purpose was to update the outmoded law enforcement approach to national security that prevailed before 9/11.[57] The Patriot Act does not create or regulate the war power itself. Just as in the criminal justice system, where the police must have probable cause to believe that someone is involved in criminal activity before a warrant will issue,[58] the Patriot Act assumes that the government already has enough information to believe that a target is the "agent of a foreign power" before it even asks

50 *See, e.g.*, Risen & Lichtblau, *supra* note 1 (describing use of information obtained via wiretap to arrest suspect who plotted to destroy the Brooklyn Bridge).

51 December 2005 Briefing, *supra* note 1.

52 *Id.*

53 *See id.*

54 *See supra* notes 11-13, 15 and accompanying text.

55 U.S. Dep't of Justice, Legal Authorities Supporting the Activities of the National Security Agency Described by the President (2006), *available at* http://www.usdoj.gov/opa/white paperonnsalegalauthorities.pdf [hereinafter NSA Supporting Authorities].

56 *See* sources cited *supra* notes 11–13, 15.

57 *See* John Yoo, War By Other Means 70-98 (2006) (describing the background and the significance of the USA Patriot Act).

58 U.S. Const. amend. IV.

for a warrant.[59] FISA operates from the assumption that foreign intelligence agents are working for a hostile nation-state, and that it is relatively simple to determine who those agents might be.[60] Historically, surveillance targets were usually foreign embassy officials who were thought to be intelligence officers; the goal was to build as large a file on their activities and contacts as possible.[61] FISA's drafters had in mind, as a typical case, a Soviet KGB agent posing as a diplomat, conducting espionage.[62]

A. Information is the Key, but Current Laws are Retrospective and Prospective Programs are Met with Criticism

Al Qaeda, our current enemy, poses a very different challenge.[63] We do not have a list of diplomats to work from or an embassy to watch, as was the dominant paradigm in the Cold War. An intelligence search conducted today, as Judge Richard Posner has described it, "is a search for a needle in a haystack."[64] Rather than focus on foreign agents who are already known, counter-terrorism agencies must search for clues among millions of potentially innocent connections, communications, and links. "The intelligence services," Posner writes, "must cast a wide net with a fine mesh to catch the clues that may enable the next attack to be prevented."[65] Our best information about al Qaeda will be scattered and tough to gather, and our agents must be able to follow many leads quickly and move fast on hunches and educated guesses.

Members of the al Qaeda network can be detected, with good intelligence work or luck, by examining phone and e-mail communications, as well as evidence of joint travel, shared assets, common histories or families, meetings, and so on.[66] As the

---

59 USA PATRIOT ACT § 207 (codified at 50 U.S.C. §§ 1805, 1824 (2000 & Supp. IV 2004)) (updating but not procedurally changing FISA's requirements).

60 *See* S. Rep. No. 95-604(I) (1977), at 20–22, *reprinted in* 1978 U.S.C.C.A.N. 3904, 3921–23.

61 *See* Americo R. Cinquegrana, *The Walls (and Wires) Have Ears: The Background and First Ten Years of the Foreign Intelligence Surveillance Act of 1978*, 137 U. Pa. L. Rev. 793, 808–12 (1989).

62 *See* S. Rep. No. 95-604(I), at 20–22, *reprinted in* 1978 U.S.C.C.A.N. at 3921–23.

63 For information on al Qaeda, the terrorist group behind the September 11, 2001 attacks led by Osama bin Laden, see Nat'l Comm'n On Terrorist Attacks Upon The U.S., the 9/11 Commission Report 47, 59–70 (2004) [hereinafter 9/11 Commission Report], *available* at www.9-11commission.gov/report/911Report.pdf; *see also* Yonah Alexander & Michael S. Swetnam, Usama bin Laden's *al Qaida:* Profile of a Terrorist Network (2001).

64 Richard A. Posner, *A New Surveillance Act*, Op-Ed., Wall St. J., Feb. 15, 2006, at A16 [hereinafter *A New Surveillance Act*]. *See generally* Richard A. Posner, Preventing Surprise Attacks (2005).

65 *A New Surveillance Act, supra* note 64.

66 *See* 9/11 Commission Report, *supra* note 63, at 227 n.68, 361–98 (noting that the United Arab Emirates was able to track Marwan al Shehhi, one of the future 9/11 hijackers, when he contacted his family).

time for an attack nears, "chatter" on this network will increase as al Qaeda operatives communicate to coordinate plans, move and position assets, and conduct target reconnaissance.[67] When our intelligence agents successfully locate or capture an al Qaeda member, they must be able to move quickly to connect new information to other operatives before news of the capture causes these operatives to disappear. It is more important to chase them down quickly inside the United States than outside. Incredibly, critics want to place bureaucratic impediments precisely at this juncture,[68] where the danger to America is greatest.

Take the example of the 9/11 hijackers. Since the attack, links suggested by commercially available data have shown ties between every single one of the al Qaeda plotters and Khalid al Mihdhar and Nawar al Hazmi, the two hijackers known to the CIA in the summer of 2001 to have been in the country.[69] Mihdhar and Hazmi had rented apartments in their own name and were listed in the San Diego phone book.[70] Both Mohammad Atta, the leader of the 9/11 al Qaeda cell, and Marwan al-Shehi, who piloted one of planes into the World Trade Center, had lived with them.[71] Hijacker Majed Moqed used the same frequent flier number as Hazmi. Five hijackers used the same phone number as Atta when booking their flights.[72] The remaining hijackers shared addresses or phone numbers with Ahmed Alghamdi, a hijacker who was in the United States in violation of his visa at the time.[73]

Our intelligence agents, in fact, had strong leads that could conceivably have led them to all the hijackers before 9/11 had they located some of the operatives through intercepted communications.[74] CIA agents identified Mihdhar as a likely al Qaeda operative because he was spotted at a meeting in Kuala Lumpur and was mentioned in Middle East intercepts as part of an al Qaeda "cadre."[75] Hazmi too was known as a likely al Qaeda member.[76] In each case there was potentially sufficient evidence for a criminal arrest on either immigration charges or because of links to the *U.S.S. Cole* bombing.[77] According to the 9/11 Commission Report, however, intelligence officials lacked the tools to find the men once they were inside

---

67 *See id.* at 263–65.

68 *See, e.g.*, sources cited *supra* notes 11–13, 15.

69 Heather Mac Donald, *What We Don't Know* Can *Hurt Us*, City J., Spring 2004, at 14, 18, *available* at http://www.city-journal.org/html/14_2_what_we_dont_know.html.

70 *Id.*

71 *Id.*

72 *Id.*

73 *Id.*

74 *See id.*

75 9/11 Commission Report, *supra* note 63, at 158, 181.

76 *See id.* at 158–59, 181–82.

77 *Id.* at 272.

the United States.[78] Had our intelligence services been able to immediately track the hijackers' cell phone calls and emails, it is possible that enough of the hijacking team could have been rounded up to avert 9/11, or at the very least, to prevent Mihdar and Hamzi from boarding American Airlines Flight 77, which they flew into the Pentagon.[79] Our task is much more difficult today, because we might not have even this slender information in hand when the next al Qaeda plot moves toward execution.

As we have waged the Afghanistan and Iraq wars, we have captured al Qaeda leaders as well as their laptops, cell phones, financial documents, and other signs of modern high-tech life. Subsequent interrogations and investigations have uncovered information on dozens or hundreds of e-mail addresses, telephones, bank and credit account numbers, and residential and office addresses used by their network.[80] To exploit this wealth of information, our intelligence services must follow leads as fast as possible, before the network of al Qaeda operatives can migrate to a new leader. An e-mail lead can disappear as fast as it takes someone to open a new e-mail account. Our agents need to move even faster.

1. The Probable Cause Limitations of FISA

FISA, and the law enforcement mentality it embodies, creates several problems. FISA requires "probable cause" to believe that someone is an agent of a foreign power before one can get a warrant to collect phone calls and e-mails.[81] Suppose an al Qaeda leader has a cell phone with 100 numbers in its memory, 10 of which are in the United States. Surveillance of those 10 would normally require a warrant issued pursuant to FISA. Would a FISA judge find probable cause to think the users of those 10 numbers are "agents of a foreign power," in other words that their listing in the cell phone memory reasonably suggested that they were members of al Qaeda too? Probably not, because it is unlikely that our intelligence agencies would immediately know who answered the phone when the captured al Qaeda leader called the number, and a FISA Court would probably require such evidence. The same is true of the leader's e-mail, except it would not be immediately obvious what addresses are held by U.S. residents, making probable cause even more difficult to establish.

In this world of rapidly shifting e-mail addresses, multiple cell phone numbers, and internet communications, FISA imposes slow and cumbersome procedures on our

---

78 *See id.*

79 *Id.* For an illustration of the shortcomings of this approach, which prevented the FBI from examining Zacarias Moussaoui's laptop in August 2001, see *id.* at 273–76.

80 *See, e.g.*, 9/11 Commission Report, *supra* note 63, at 382 (detailing how the capture or death of several al Qaeda financial facilitators has caused disruptions to the organization's ability to finance operations).

81 50 U.S.C. § 1805(a)(3) (2000).

intelligence and law enforcement officers.[82] These laborious checks are based on the assumption that we still remain within the criminal justice system, and are looking backward in order to conduct prosecutions of those who have perpetrated crimes or infiltrated the government, rather than operating within the national security system, which looks forward in order to prevent deadly surprise attacks on the American people.[83] FISA requires a lengthy review process, in which special FBI and DOJ lawyers prepare an extensive package of facts and law to present to the FISC.[84] The Attorney General must personally sign the application, and another high-ranking national security officer, such as the President's National Security Advisor or the Director of the FBI, must certify that the information sought is for foreign intelligence.[85] It takes time and a great deal of work to prepare the warrant applications, which can run 100 pages long. While there is an emergency procedure that allows the Attorney General to approve a wiretap for 72 hours without a court order, it can only be used if there is no time to obtain an order from the FISC, and the Attorney General determines that the wiretap satisfies FISA's other requirements.[86] Thus, the Attorney General could not use the emergency procedure if the probable cause standard was not met.[87]

2. The Potential Utility of Data Mining

Living within FISA's law enforcement framework will hamper efforts to take advantage of what is known as data mining. Data mining refers to the practice of using powerful supercomputers and advanced algorithms to analyze vast amounts of information for patterns of behavior.[88] In the United States, corporations employ data mining techniques to market products, like credit cards and magazine

---

82 *See* Cinquegrana, *supra* note 61, at 825, reasoning in 1989 that:

> FISA also must keep pace with the continuing explosion in communications technologies available both to law enforcement agencies and potential surveillance targets. FISA was drafted to take account of experience and technology developed between 1968 and 1978, but the decade since its passage has witnessed substantial technological changes that could require amendments to FISA in order to extend its privacy protections and to facilitate legitimate government interests that might otherwise be frustrated.

83 *See* Yoo, *supra* note 57, at 71–74, 79–80 (noting that an artificial "Wall" in place for decades between information gathered for intelligence and information gathered for law enforcement purposes hindered the government's ability to piece together intelligence which could have stopped the 9/11 attacks).

84 *See* 50 U.S.C. § 1804 (2000) (current version at 50 U.S.C.A. § 1804 (West 2006)).

85 50 U.S.C. § 1804(a).

86 50 U.S.C. § 1805(f) (2000) (current version at 50 U.S.C. § 1805(f) (Supp. IV 2004)).

87 *See id.*

88 Open Directory—Data Mining Definition, http://dmoz.org/Computers/Software/Databases/Data_Mining/desc.html (last visited Dec. 24, 2006). For more detailed information on data mining, see generally Open Directory Project—Data Mining Database, http://dmoz.org/Computers/Software/Databases/Data_Mining/ (last visited Dec. 24, 2006).

subscriptions, and to identify likely buyers based on their income level, geographic location, and purchasing and travel histories—as well as to detect fraud.[89] Similarly, financial companies analyze various patterns of behavior to discover suspicious activity that might suggest someone has stolen a credit card or account number.[90] Government data mining theoretically could compile information from government, public, and commercial databases to allow investigators to search for patterns of behavior that might correlate with terrorist activity. Airline security uses a simple variant of this approach when it identifies passengers for extra security screening—a foreign citizen buying a one-way, full-fare ticket, in cash, on the day of the flight would likely trigger a second look from airline security personnel.[91]

Data mining is the best hope for an innovative counter-terrorism strategy to detect and prevent future al Qaeda attacks. Rather than hope an agent will one day penetrate al Qaeda's inner circles—a dubious possibility—or that we will successfully seal our vast borders from terrorists, data mining would allow us to see patterns of activity that reveal the al Qaeda network's activity before it can attack.[92] Computerized pattern analysis could quickly reveal whether anyone linked to al Qaeda made large purchases of chemicals or equipment that could be used for explosives or chemical weapons. We could learn whether they traveled regularly to certain cities, and we could discover where they stayed and who they called in those cities.

As civil libertarians complain, almost all transactions of this nature—calling, emailing, spending money, traveling—are innocent.[93] We engage in them every day. That is exactly why al Qaeda has trained its operatives to use them as tools to conceal their plots.[94] Al Qaeda's leaders understand the difficulty in analyzing billions of transactions and interactions every day to detect their cells, and they realize that western societies impose legal obstacles on government access to such information.[95] Civil libertarian critics apparently fail to notice that our government already employs modest forms of data mining to track down criminals and terrorists. In response to drug cartels and organized crime, our government has used simple data mining to track and

---

89 *A Golden Vein*, ECONOMIST, June 10, 2004, at 23, *available at* 2004 WLNR 6533278.

90 *Id.*

91 *See* 9/11 COMMISSION REPORT, *supra* note 63, at 392.

92 Sealing our borders, even if it were possible, would not prevent all attacks because Al Qaeda does not merely target places within the United States, but also flights entering the United States, as in the case of the "shoe bomber" Richard Reid, as well as American and Western symbols abroad. *See, e.g.*, *Three Decades of Terror*, FIN. TIMES, Feb. 7, 2003, http://www.ft.com/cms/s/e5470480-d0d5-11d8-9597-0003ba5a9905.html. Al Qaeda's ability to mastermind operations from far away only underscores the need to track down al Qaeda wherever it may operate. *See* 9/11 COMISSION REPORT, *supra* note 63, at 365–67.

93 *See infra* note 104 and accompanying text.

94 *See* 9/11 COMMISSION REPORT, *supra* note 63, at 157–58, 167.

95 *Id.* at 169.

analyze money flows for years.[96] Banks and financial institutions provide records of financial transactions to the Department of the Treasury, which searches the patterns for money laundering activity.[97] While the great majority of the transactions are legal, the information can piece together proof of criminal links after a conspiracy has been stopped, or it can help indicate suspicious activity that demands further investigation.[98] Analyzing money flows has also proven to be an important tool in detecting and breaking up terrorist networks.[99] If civil libertarians are right, consumers would also have an absolute right to privacy over their banking transactions and our government would lose this valuable, commonsense tool to combat crime, as well as terrorism. Two examples illustrate this point: (1) the NSA's use of phone records and (2) the Total Information Awareness program.

The civil libertarian overreaction can be seen in the outcry in the wake of the May 2006 revelation that the NSA sought call information from phone companies without a warrant.[100] Apparently the NSA obtained billing information on millions of phone calls within the United States, the same information used by telephone companies for billing and marketing purposes.[101] According to USA Today, the data had been stripped of names and addresses, but still contained the calls' phone numbers.[102] President Bush addressed the country to say that he had ordered the government to do everything it could to prevent a future attack while also protecting Americans' privacy. "Al Qaeda is our enemy, and we want to know their plans," he said, without confirming the program's existence.[103] Senator Patrick Leahy expressed outrage, suggesting that the government was watching every American for terrorist ties. "Are you telling me tens of millions of Americans are involved with al Qaeda?" he railed at a hearing the day after the USA Today story.[104] Harold Koh, Dean of the Yale Law School, called the disclosure "quite shocking" and said the courts

---

96 Anita Ramasastry, *Lost in Translation? Data Mining, National Security, and the "Adverse Inference" Problem,* 22 Santa Clara Computer & High Tech L. J. 765, 768–69 & n.32 (2006).

97 *See* the Financial Crimes Enforcement Network, http://www.fincen.gov (last visited Dec. 24, 2006), which administers the Bank Secrecy Act, 31 U.S.C. §§ 5311-5330 (2000) (current version at 31 U.S.C. §§ 5311-5330 (2000 & Supp. IV 2004)).

98 *See* About the Financial Crimes Enforcement Network, http://www.fincen.gov/YEreport/about Fincen.html (last visited Dec. 24, 2006).

99 *See* Ramasastry, *supra* note 96, at 768–69; Eric Lichtblau & James Risen, *Bank Data Sifted in Secret by U.S. to Block Terror,* N.Y. Times, June 23, 2006, at A1.

100 *See* Leslie Cauley, *NSA has Massive Database of Americans' Phone Calls,* USA Today, May 11, 2006, at 1A, *available at* http://www.usatoday.com/news/washington/2006-05-10-nsa_x.htm.

101 *Id.*

102 *Id.*

103 President George W. Bush, President's Radio Address (May 13, 2006), http://www.whitehouse.gov/news/releases/2006/05/20060513.html.

104 Susan Page, *NSA Secret Database Report Triggers Fierce Debate in Washington,* USA Today, May 11, 2006, at 1A, *available at* http://www.usatoday.com/news/washington/2006-05-11-nsa-reax_x.htm.

would never have approved it.[105] House Democrats have repeatedly called for a special prosecutor to investigate.[106] Newspaper columnists predicted that "phone calls are just the start" of a massive government program to collect all data on all Americans for analysis.[107]

These privacy concerns are exaggerated. The Supreme Court has found that such information does not receive Fourth Amendment protection because the consumer has already voluntarily turned over the information to a third party.[108] It is not covered by FISA because no electronic interception or surveillance occurred.[109] Meanwhile, the data is potentially of enormous use in frustrating al Qaeda plots. If our agents are pointed to members of an al Qaeda sleeper cell by a U.S. phone number found in a captured al Qaeda leader's cell phone, call pattern analysis would allow the NSA to determine the extent of the network and its activities.[110] It could track the sleeper cell as it periodically changed phone numbers.[111] This could give a quick, initial database-generated glimpse of the possible size and activity level of the cell in an environment where time is of the essence.

Through all the outrage, the limited nature of the data provided was downplayed—only the billing data was provided, devoid of information that could identify an individual.[112] Critics ramped up feverishly to use the confirmation hearings for General Hayden, whom President Bush nominated to head the CIA in 2006, as a platform to accuse the government of invasion of privacy.[113] Members of the Senate Intelligence Committee, who had earlier been briefed on the program, asked Hayden some tough questions,[114] but recommended him to the Senate, which confirmed him before the month was out.[115] For once, common sense held out.

---

105 *Id.*

106 *See, e.g.*, Rep. Jerrold Nadler (D-NY), Letter to the Editor, *Oversight on Wiretapping*, N.Y. Times, Aug. 25, 2006, at A20, *available at* 2006 WLNR 14725599.

107 Simson L. Garfinkel, *Big Brother Alert: Phone Calls Are Just the Start*, Wash. Post, May 14, 2006, at B2, *available at* 2006 WLNR 8320400.

108 Smith v. Maryland, 442 U.S. 735, 743-46 (1979); United States v. Miller, 425 U.S. 435, 442–43 (1976), *superseded by statute*, Right to Financial Privacy Act of 1978, 12 U.S.C. §§ 3401-3422 (2000).

109 50 U.S.C. § 1801(f) (2000) (defining "electronic surveillance" as acquisition of information "by a surveillance device") (amended 2001).

110 *See* Cauley, *supra* note 100.

111 *See id.*

112 *Id.*

113 Bill Nichols & John Diamond, *Controversy Shadows Hayden Confirmation*, USA Today, May 12, 2006, at 10A, *available at* http://www.usatoday.com/news/washington/2006-05-11-hayden-confirmation_x.htm.

114 *See Confirmation Hearing of General Michael V. Hayden to be the Director of the Central Intelligence Agency Before the Senate Select Committee on Intelligence*, 109th Cong. (2006), http://www.washingtonpost.com/wp-yn/content/article/2006/05/18/AR2006051800823.html.

115 Charles Babington, *Hayden Confirmed as Spy Chief*, Wash. Post, May 27, 2006, at A2.

Another example of libertarian overreaction is to the ill-fated and ill-named Total Information Awareness ("TIA") program proposed in 2002 by the Defense Advanced Research Projects Agency ("DARPA") under Admiral John Poindexter.[116] TIA proposed the use of supercomputers to data mine both government and commercial databases to spot potential terrorist activity.[117] Civil libertarians, both of the left and the right, engaged in a scare campaign against TIA—representing it as a big brother attempt to spy on Americans without any checks.[118] William Safire in the *New York Times* raised the alarm with the claim that the Defense Department would create "computer dossiers on 300 million Americans" and that Poindexter wanted to "snoop on every public and private act of every American."[119] An outpouring of misinformed criticism led Poindexter to resign and Congress to cut off funding for TIA before any research, which would have included a full analysis of privacy concerns, had begun.[120]

It seems that critics are mostly interested in blindly limiting the powers of the government, even as it fights a tough war. They presume the American government to be acting in bad faith, and so all of its activities must be treated with the highest possible level of suspicion. Meanwhile, data mining technology and databases are exploding in the private sector.[121] It would be ironic if al Qaeda and private individuals were permitted greater legal access to new data technology than our own government, especially in wartime.

Overreaction and plain scare tactics killed TIA, a potentially valuable tool to counter al Qaeda's offensive within the United States.[122] It made little sense to cut off TIA at the research and development stage out of sheer anti-government paranoia. There was no chance to see what computer technology could even do, no discussion of whether adequate safeguards for privacy could be installed, and no opportunity to evaluate whether data mining would yield leads on terrorist activity that would be worth any costs to privacy. No analysis could be done on the legal issues.

Perhaps worst of all, we could never explore the ways that computers could be used to *protect* privacy. Data mining scans many perfectly innocent transactions and activities, but this in itself does not make the search illegal; even searches of homes

---

116 *See* Jonathan Levin, *Total Preparedness*, NAT'L REV., Feb. 13, 2003, http://www.nationalreview.com/comment/comment-levin021303.asp. Admiral Poindexter resigned from his job as national security advisor under President Reagan during the Iran-Contra affair. *See* Biography of Admiral John M. Poindexter, http://www.computerbytesman.com/tia/poindexterbio.htm (last visited Dec. 24, 2006).

117 *See* MAC DONALD, *supra* note 69.

118 *See, e.g.*, PAGE, *supra* note 104.

119 William Safire, *You Are a Suspect*, N.Y. TIMES, Nov. 14, 2002, at A35.

120 Drew Clark, *Privacy Advocates Turn Tide In Homeland Security Debate*, CONGRESS DAILY, Sept. 15, 2003, 2003 WLNR 13647856.

121 *See supra* notes 88–91 and accompanying text.

122 *See* CLARK, *supra* note 120.

and businesses or wiretaps with warrants will encounter many items or communications that are not linked to criminal activity.[123] The understandable concern is that much innocent activity will come under scrutiny by data mining, unless controlled in some way by a warrant requirement.[124] But if computers are doing the primary scanning, privacy might not be implicated because no human eyes will ever see the data.[125] Only when the computer programs highlight individuals who fit parameters that reasonably suggest further study for terrorist links—say a young man who has traveled from Ohio to Pakistan several times, has taken flight lessons in the United States, has received large deposits of cash wired into his account from abroad, and has purchased equipment that could be used for bomb-making—would a human intelligence officer view the records.[126]

At this point it is important to emphasize that no one is being declared guilty of anything—all that might be done at this point is to seek more information, deploy more resources, or seek a warrant. It would be foolhardy to prevent our intelligence and law enforcement officers from studying patterns of private behavior to stop future attacks. Police routinely rely on the study of patterns, analyzing the "m.o." of past crimes, or patterns of criminal activity in certain neighborhoods at different times, in order to try to predict future crimes.[127] Computerization, though no panacea, could reasonably protect privacy by preventing human eyes from ever seeing the irrelevant records of innocent activity.[128]

B. Pursuing Alternatives to FISA's Shortcomings is Both Sound and Constitutionally Proper

The previous discussion underscores the real problem with FISA, and even the Patriot Act. The laws depend on individualized suspicion—that searches and wiretaps must target a specific individual already believed to be involved in criminal activity.[129] But catching al Qaeda members who have no previous criminal record in the United States and who are undeterred by the possibility of criminal sanctions requires more than that. We have to devote surveillance resources where there is a reasonable chance that terrorists will appear, or communicate, even if we do not know their specific identities. What if we knew that there was a fifty percent chance that terrorists would use a certain communications pipeline, like e-mails using a popular Pakistani website, but that most of the communications on that

123 *Cf.* Richard A. Posner, Not A Suicide Pact 100-01 (2006) (discussing the need for an attenuated probable cause requirement in the national security context, because "intelligence officers will often not have a good idea . . . what they are looking for").

124 *See* Page, *supra* note 104.

125 *See* Posner, *supra* note 123, at 97–100.

126 *See id.* at 97.

127 Mac Donald, *supra* note 69, at 20.

128 Posner, *supra* note 123, at 97.

129 *See supra* notes 58–60 and accompanying text.

channel would not be linked to terrorism? A FISA-based approach would prevent computers from searching through that channel for the keywords or names that might suggest terrorist communications, because we would have no specific al Qaeda suspects, and thus no probable cause.[130] Rather than individualized suspicion, searching for terrorists will depend on playing the probabilities, just as with roadblocks or airport screenings. The private owner of a website has detailed access to that information every day to exploit for his own commercial purposes, such as selling lists of names to spammers, or gathering market data on individuals or groups. Is the government's effort to find violent terrorists a less legitimate use of such data?

Individualized suspicion dictates the focus of law enforcement, but war demands that our armed forces defend the country with a broader perspective. Armies do not meet a "probable cause" requirement when they attack a position or fire on enemy troops or intercept enemy communications on a frequency. The purpose of the criminal justice system is to hold a specific person responsible for a discrete crime that has already happened. By contrast, the purpose of intelligence is to guide actions, such as killing or capturing members of the enemy, that prevent future harm to the nation from a foreign threat.

1. FISA's Framework Speaks to Prosecuting Criminal Acts, Not Preventing Attacks

FISA should be regarded as a safe harbor that allows the fruits of an authorized search to be used for prosecution. Using FISA sacrifices speed and breadth of information in favor of individualized suspicion, but it provides a path for using evidence in a civilian criminal prosecution. If the President chooses to rely on his constitutional authority alone to conduct warrantless searches, then he should only use the information for military purposes. As General Hayden said in his press conference, the primary objective of the NSA program is to "detect and prevent" possible al Qaeda attacks on the United States, whether another attack like September 11, or a bomb in apartment buildings, bridges, or transportation hubs such as airports, or a nuclear, biological, or chemical attack.[131] These are not hypotheticals; they are all plots by al Qaeda and its followers, some of which our intelligence and law enforcement agencies have already stopped.[132] A President will want to use such information to deploy our military, intelligence, and law enforcement personnel to stop an attack. The price to pay for the speed and action necessary to prevent an attack (i.e., killing or detaining an operative) may be to lose the chance for a future criminal prosecution, leaving the government with only the option of holding an operative as an enemy combatant—a price well worth paying.

130 *See* 50 U.S.C. §§ 1805, 1824 (2000 & Supp. IV 2004).

131 December 2005 Briefing, *supra* note 1; *see also* Risen & Lichtblau, *supra* note 1.

132 *See* Risen & Lichtblau, *supra* note 1.

This framework gives the President the ability to choose the best method to protect the United States, whether through the military or by reliance on law enforcement. It also means that warrantless surveillance will not be introduced into the criminal justice system, so long as the judiciary enforces the legal versus military distinction. President Bush could go some way toward alleviating concern about the NSA program by publicly declaring that no evidence collected from the program would ever be used in any criminal case.

Gathering intelligence has long been understood as a legitimate aspect of conducting war; indeed, it is critical to the successful use of force.[133] Our military cannot attack or defend to good effect unless it knows where to aim. America has a long history of conducting intelligence operations to obtain information on the enemy. General Washington used spies extensively during the Revolutionary War, and as President he established a secret fund for spying that existed until the creation of the CIA.[134] President Lincoln personally hired spies during the Civil War, a practice which the Supreme Court upheld.[135] In both World Wars I and II, Presidents ordered the interception of electronic communications leaving the United States.[136] Some of America's greatest wartime intelligence successes have involved signals intelligence ("SIGINT"), most notably the breaking of Japanese diplomatic and naval codes during World War II, which allowed the U.S. Navy to anticipate the attack on Midway Island.[137] SIGINT is even more important in this war than in those of the last century. Al Qaeda continues to launch a variety of efforts to attack the United States, including acquiring and deploying weapons of mass destruction.[138] The primary way to stop those attacks is to locate and stop al Qaeda operatives who have infiltrated the United States. One way to find them is to intercept their electronic communications entering or leaving the country.

---

133 In the 1907 Hague Regulations, one of the first treaties on the laws of war, the leading military powers agreed that "the employment of measures necessary for obtaining information about the enemy and the country is considered permissible." The Laws and Customs of War on Land (Hague IV) art. 24, Oct. 18, 1907, 1 Bevans 247, *available at* http://www.yale.edu/lawweb/avalon/lawofwar/hague04.htm; MORRIS GREENSPAN, THE MODERN LAW OF LAND WARFARE 325 (1959). Interception of electronic communications is known as SIGINT, or signals intelligence, as opposed to HUMINT, or human intelligence. *See* National Security Agency, Signals Intelligence, http://www.nsa.gov/sigint (last visited Feb. 3, 2007). Writers on the laws of war have recognized that interception of an enemy's communications is a legitimate tool of war. According to one recognized authority, nations at war can gather intelligence using air and ground reconnaissance and observation, "interception of enemy messages, wireless and other," capturing documents, and interrogating prisoners. GREENSPAN, *supra* note 133, at 326.

134 *See* Halperin v. CIA, 629 F.2d 144, 157–58 (D.C. Cir. 1980).

135 Totten v. United States, 92 U.S. 105, 105–7 (1875).

136 Exec. Order No. 2604 (Apr. 28, 1917) (World War I order); Exec. Order No. 8985, 6 Fed. Reg. 6625 (Dec. 19, 1941) (World War II order).

137 CHRISTOPHER ANDREW, FOR THE PRESIDENT'S EYES ONLY 124–25 (1995).

138 *See* 9/11 COMMISSION REPORT, *supra* note 63, at 1–14, 190, 381.

2. Opting for Intelligence Gathering, Instead of Prosecutions, Comports with the Fourth Amendment's Reasonableness Requirement

In the hours and days after 9/11, members of the government thought that al Qaeda would try to crash other airliners or use a weapon of mass destruction in a major east coast city, probably Washington, D.C.[139] Combat air patrols began flying above New York and Washington.[140] While at first strange, it soon became routine to leave the Justice Department building for lunch and to see F-15s and F-16s circling above. Suppose a plane was hijacked and would not respond to air traffic controllers. It would be reasonable for our anti-terrorism personnel to intercept any radio or cell phone calls to or from the airliner, in order to discover the hijackers' intentions, what was happening on the plane, and ultimately whether it would be necessary for the fighters to shoot down the plane.

Under the civil libertarian approach to privacy, the government could not monitor the suspected hijackers' phone or radio calls unless they received a judicial warrant first—the calls, after all, are electronic communications within the United States.[141] A warrant would be difficult to obtain, however, because it is unlikely that we would know the identities of all the hijackers, who might be U.S. citizens or permanent resident aliens.[142] But because we would be in a state of war, our military could intercept the communications of the plane to ascertain if it posed a threat, and target the enemy if necessary—without a judicial warrant, because the purpose would not be for criminal prosecution, but rather to prevent an attack. This comports far better with the principle of *reasonableness* that sits at the heart of the Fourth Amendment.[143] Defense against an attack on the United States or investigation of an active plot certainly would fall within the important governmental interests, independent of law enforcement, which justify warrantless searches under the Fourth Amendment.

When law enforcement undertakes a search to discover evidence of criminal wrongdoing, reasonableness generally requires a judicial warrant.[144] But when the government's conduct is not focused wholly on law enforcement, a warrant may not be necessary. For instance, a warrantless search can be constitutional "'when

139 See *Jack Sullivan, Attack on America; Probe Fans Out Across U.S.; Investigators Fear New Means of Terror*, Boston Herald, Sept. 17, 2001, at 9, available at 2001 WLNR 647965.

140 Andrea Stone, *Military Now aPresence on Home Front,* USA Today, Sept. 17, 2001, at 5A.

141 *See* Nolan et al., *supra* note 11.

142 *See* U.S. Const. amend. IV ("The right of the people to be secure in their persons, houses, papers, and effects, against unreasonable searches and seizures, shall not be violated, and no Warrants shall issue, but upon probable cause, supported by Oath or affirmation, and particularly describing the place to be searched, and *the persons or things to be seized.*") (emphasis added).

143 *See id.* (upholding the right of the people against "*unreasonable* searches and seizures") (emphasis added); *see also* Vernonia Sch. Dist. 47J v. Acton, 515 U.S. 646, 652–53 (1995).

144 *See* 79 C.J.S. Searches § 56 (2006).

special needs, beyond the normal need for law enforcement, make the warrant and probable-cause requirement impracticable.'"[145] In this context, the Court asks whether, under the totality of the circumstances, the "'importance of the governmental interests'" outweighs the "'nature and quality of the intrusion on the individual's Fourth Amendment interests.'"[146] If so, the government's search is reasonable under the Fourth Amendment.[147]

III. THE PRESIDENT HAS CONSTITUTIONAL AUTHORITY TO COLLECT FOREIGN INTELLIGENCE WITHOUT A WARRANT

As Commander-in-Chief, the President has the constitutional authority and the responsibility to wage war in response to a direct attack against the United States.[148] During World War II, for instance, the Supreme Court recognized that once war has begun, the President's authority as Commander-in-Chief and Chief Executive affords him access to the tools necessary to effectively wage war.[149] The President has the power "to direct the performance of those functions which may constitutionally be performed by the military arm of the nation in time of war," and to issue military commands using the powers to conduct war "to repel and defeat the enemy."[150] In the wake of the September 11 attacks, even Congress agreed that "the President has authority under the Constitution to take action to deter and prevent acts of international terrorism against the United States. . . ."[151] This statement recognizes the President's authority to use force, and any powers necessary and proper to that end, to respond to al Qaeda. The shift of power to the executive branch in wartime is not just an inference from the constitutional text and structure, but a lesson of history. In the Civil War, for example, President Lincoln raised an army, withdrew money from the treasury, and launched a blockade on his own authority

145 *Vernonia School Dist.*, 515 U.S. at 653 (quoting Griffin v. Wisconsin, 483 U.S. 868, 873 (1987)). The Court has found warrantless searches such as random employee drug testing, drunk driving checkpoints, and temporary stops to search for weapons to be consistent with the Fourth Amendment. *See, e.g.*, Pennsylvania v. Labron, 518 U.S. 938 (1996) (per curiam) (automobile searches); *Vernonia Sch. Dist.*, 515 U.S. 646 (drug testing of athletes); Mich. Dep't of State Police v. Sitz, 496 U.S. 444 (1990) (drunk driver checkpoints); Skinner v. Ry. Labor Executives' Ass'n, 489 U.S. 602 (1989) (drug testing railroad personnel); Nat'l Treasury Employees Union v. Von Raab, 489 U.S. 656 (1989) (drug testing federal Customs employees); United States v. Place, 462 U.S. 696 (1983) (baggage "sniff test"); Terry v. Ohio, 392 U.S. 1 (1968) (temporary stop and search).

146 Tennessee v. Garner, 471 U.S. 1, 8 (1985) (quoting *Place*, 462 U.S. at 703).

147 *Id.*

148 *See supra* notes 39–49 and accompanying text.

149 *See* Ex Parte Quirin, 317 U.S. 1, 26–29 (1942).

150 *Id.* at 28.

151 AUMF, Pub. L. No. 107-40, 115 Stat. 224 (2001).

in response to the Confederate attack on Fort Sumter—moves that Congress and the Supreme Court later approved.[152]

Even legal scholars who argue against this historical practice concede that once the United States has been attacked, the President can respond with force on his own.[153] The ability to collect intelligence is intrinsic to the use of military force.[154] It is inconceivable that the Constitution would vest in the President the power of Commander-in-Chief and Chief Executive, give him the responsibility to protect the nation from attack,[155] but then disable him by preventing him from gathering the intelligence needed to use the military most effectively. Evidence of the Framers' original understanding of the Constitution is that the government would have every available tool to meet a foreign danger.[156] As the Supreme Court declared after World War II, this "grant of war power includes all that is necessary and proper for carrying these powers into execution."[157] Collecting covert intelligence is clearly part of this authority.

A. The Constitution and the Case Law Support the Power to Gather Intelligence

Some of the Framers of the Constitution believed that the President needed to manage intelligence because only he could keep secrets.[158] Several Supreme Court cases have recognized that the President's role as the sole organ of the nation in foreign relations and as Commander-in-Chief must include the power to collect intelligence.[159] These authorities agree that intelligence rests with the President because the office's structure allows the President to act with unity, secrecy, and speed.[160]

152 *See* The Prize Cases, 67 U.S. (2 Black) 635, 640–41, 669–70 (1863).

153 *See, e.g.*, Louis Fisher, Presidential War Power 11 (1995); Michael J. Glennon, Constitutional Diplomacy 81 (1990). *But see* Yoo, *supra* note 35, at 143–60.

154 *See supra* notes 133–1338 and accompanying text.

155 *See* discussion *supra* Part I.

156 As James Madison wrote in *The Federalist*, "security against foreign danger is one of the primitive objects of civil society." Therefore, the "powers requisite for attaining it must be effectually confided to the federal councils." Federalist No. 41, at 269 (James Madison) (Jacob E. Cooke ed. 1961).

157 Johnson v. Eisentrager, 339 U.S. 763, 788 (1950).

158 The Federalist No. 64, at 435 (John Jay) (Jacob E. Cooke ed. 1961).

159 *See, e.g.*, Chi. & S. Air Lines v. Waterman S.S. Corp., 333 U.S. 103, 111 (1948); United States v. Curtiss-Wright Exp. Corp., 299 U.S. 304, 319-21 (1936). In a post-Civil War case, recently reaffirmed, the Court ruled that President Lincoln had the constitutional authority to engage in espionage. Totten v. United States, 92 U.S. 105 (1876). The President "was undoubtedly authorized during the war, as commander-in-chief . . . to employ secret agents to enter the rebel lines and obtain information respecting the strength, resources, and movements of the enemy." *Id.* at 106. On *Totten's* continuing vitality, see Tenet v. Doe, 544 U.S. 1, 8–11 (2005).

160 *Curtiss-Wright*, 299 U.S. at 319.

Presidents have long ordered electronic surveillance without any judicial or congressional participation. More than a year before the Pearl Harbor attacks, but with war clearly looming with the Axis powers, President Franklin Roosevelt authorized the FBI to intercept any communications, whether wholly inside the country or international, of persons "suspected of subversive activities against the Government of the United States, including suspected spies."[161] FDR was concerned that "fifth columns"—those people believed to be loyalists who clandestinely undermine the nation—could wreak havoc on the war effort.[162] "It is too late to do anything about it after sabotage, assassinations and 'fifth column' activities are completed," FDR wrote in his order.[163] FDR ordered the surveillance even though a Supreme Court decision and a federal statute at the time prohibited electronic surveillance without a warrant.[164] FDR continued to authorize the interception of electronic communications even after Congress rejected proposals for wiretapping for national security reasons.[165]

Until FISA, Presidents continued to monitor the communications of national security threats on their own authority, even in peacetime.[166] If Presidents could order surveillance of spies and terrorists during peacetime, as President Roosevelt did in 1940, or as Presidents from Truman through Carter did during the Cold War, then executive authority is all the more certain now, after the events of September 11. This is a view held by the Justice Departments in several recent administrations. The Clinton Justice Department, for example, held a similar view of the executive branch's authority to conduct surveillance outside the FISA framework.[167]

---

161 Memorandum from Franklin D. Roosevelt, President of the United States, to Tom C. Clark, United States Attorney General (May 21, 1940), *reprinted in* United States v. U.S. Dist. Court for the E. Dist. of Mich., 444 F.2d 651 app. at 669–70 (6th Cir. 1971).

162 *Id.*

163 *Id.* at 670.

164 *See* Nardone v. United States, 302 U.S. 379 (1937) (interpreting Section 605 of the Federal Communications Act of 1934 to prohibit the interception of telephone calls).

165 *See* ROBERT H. JACKSON, THAT MAN: AN INSIDER'S PORTRAIT OF FRANKLIN D. ROOSEVELT 68–69 (2003).

166 *Foreign Intelligence Electronic Surveillance: Hearings on H.R. 5794, H.R. 9745, H.R. 7308, and H.R. 5632 Before the Subcomm. on Legis. of the Permanent Select Comm. on Intelligence*, 95th Cong., 2d Sess. 15 (1978) (Statement of Griffin Bell, Att'y Gen. of the United States).

167 Most notably, Clinton Deputy Attorney General Jamie Gorelick testified before Congress that the Justice Department could carry out physical searches for foreign intelligence purposes, even though FISA at the time did not provide for them. *Amending the Foreign Intelligence Surveillance Act: Hearings Before the H. Permanent Select Comm. on Intelligence*, 103rd Cong. 56-73 (1994). Clinton's OLC issued a legal opinion that the President could order the sharing of electronic surveillance gathered through criminal wiretaps between the Justice Department and intelligence agencies, even though this was prohibited by statute. Sharing Title III Electronic Surveillance Material with the Intelligence Community (Oct. 17, 2000), http://www.usdoj.gov/olc/titleIIIfinal.htm.

Courts have never opposed a President's authority to engage in warrantless electronic surveillance to protect national security. When the Supreme Court first considered this question in 1972, it held that the Fourth Amendment required a judicial warrant if a President wanted to conduct surveillance of a purely domestic group, but it refused to address surveillance of foreign threats to national security.[168] In the years since, every federal appeals court to address the question, including the FISA Appeals Court, has "held that the President did have inherent authority to conduct warrantless searches to obtain foreign intelligence information."[169] The FISA Appeals Court did not even feel that it was worth much discussion. It took the President's power to do so "for granted," and observed that "FISA could not encroach on the President's constitutional power."[170]

In *United States v. Truong Dinh Hung*, for example, the Fourth Circuit observed that "the needs of the Executive are so compelling in the area of foreign intelligence, unlike the area of domestic security, that a uniform warrant requirement would, following *Keith*, 'unduly frustrate,' the President in carrying out his foreign affairs responsibilities."[171] Several reasons led the Fourth Circuit to find that the warrant requirement did not apply to searches for foreign intelligence information:

> (1) A warrant requirement . . . would reduce the flexibility of executive foreign intelligence initiatives, in some cases delay executive response to foreign intelligence threats, and increase the chance of leaks regarding sensitive executive operations [;] (2) the executive possesses unparalleled expertise to make the decision whether to conduct foreign intelligence surveillance, whereas the judiciary is largely inexperienced in making the delicate and complex decisions that lie behind foreign intelligence surveillance . . . [f]ew, if any, district courts would be truly competent to judge the importance of particular information to the security of the United States or the 'probable cause' to demonstrate that the government in fact needs to recover that information from one particular source[;] and (3) the executive branch . . . is also constitutionally designated as the pre-eminent authority in foreign affairs.[172]

To summarize, the Fourth Circuit held that the government was relieved of the warrant requirement when the surveillance involves both a foreign power and a foreign intelligence motive.[173] First, warrants are not required when the object of the search or surveillance is a foreign power, its agents, or its collaborators since such cases are "most likely to call into play difficult and subtle judgments about

168 United States v. U.S. Dist. Court for the E. Dist. of Mich., 407 U.S. 297, 320–22 (1972).

169 *In re* Sealed Case, 310 F.3d 717, 742 (FISA Ct. Rev. 2002) (footnote omitted).

170 *Id.*

171 629 F.2d 908, 913 (4th Cir. 1980).

172 *Id.* at 913–14.

173 *Id.* at 914–15.

foreign and military affairs."[174] Second, "when the surveillance is conducted 'primarily' for foreign intelligence reasons," warrants are unnecessary for two reasons: (1) "once surveillance becomes primarily a criminal investigation, the courts are entirely competent to make the usual probable cause determination [;]" and (2) "individual privacy interests come to the fore and government foreign policy concerns recede when the government is primarily attempting to form the basis for a criminal prosecution."[175] Several other circuits have employed a similar logic, and no federal appeals court has taken a different view.[176] The factors favoring warrantless searches for national security reasons are compelling under the current circumstances created by the war on terrorism. After the attacks on September 11, 2001, the government interest in conducting searches related to fighting terrorism is perhaps of the highest order—to defend the nation from direct attack. "It is 'obvious and unarguable' that no governmental interest is more compelling than the security of the Nation."[177]

Congress also implicitly authorized the President to carry out electronic surveillance to prevent further attacks on the United States.[178] Congress's September 18, 2001 Authorization for Use of Military Force ("AUMF") is sweeping; it has no limitation on time or place—the only directive is that the President pursues terrorists, such as al Qaeda.[179] Although the President did not need, as a constitutional matter, Congress's permission to pursue and attack al Qaeda after the attacks on New York City and the Pentagon,[180] AUMF's passage shows that the President and Congress fully agreed that military action would be appropriate. Congress's support for the President cannot just be limited to the right to use force, but to all the necessary subcomponents that permit effective military action.[181] Congress's approval of the killing and capture of al Qaeda must obviously include the tools to locate them in the first place.

B. A Policy Analysis Affirms the Need for the NSA Surveillance Program

Critics have argued that the NSA's electronic surveillance is illegal because the AUMF did not explicitly mention wiretapping or surveillance.[182] Of course it does

174 *Id.* at 915.

175 *Id.*

176 *See* United States v. Buck, 548 F.2d 871, 875 (9th Cir. 1977); United States v. Brown, 484 F.2d 418, 425-26 (5th Cir. 1973); United States v. Clay, 430 F.2d 165, 171-72 (5th Cir. 1970), *rev'don other grounds*, 403 U.S. 698 (1971).

177 Haig v. Agee, 453 U.S. 280, 307 (1981) (quoting Aptheker v. Sec'y of State, 378 U.S. 500, 509 (1964)).

178 *See* AUMF, Pub. L. No. 107-40, 115 Stat. 224 (2001).

179 *See id.* § 2.

180 *See supra* Part I.

181 *See* Curtis A. Bradley & Jack L. Goldsmith, *Congressional Authorization and the War on Terrorism*, 118 Harv. L. Rev. 2048, 2092 (2005).

182 *See* Nolan et al., *supra* note 11 and sources cited therein.

not mention detentions, either, which the Supreme Court later upheld as authorized by Congress, in spite of a law on the books known as the Anti-Detention Act.[183] Critics essentially argue that Congress must enact a grocery list of specific powers and otherwise the President cannot fight a war. For instance, FISA prohibits electronic surveillance within the United States without congressional permission.[184] However, in the AUMF, Congress authorized the President "to use all necessary and appropriate force . . . [against those] he determines" were involved with the 9/11 attacks, or those who aid, support, or harbor those involved.[185] Individuals who are communicating with suspected al Qaeda operatives after 9/11 are likely to fall within the scope of the AUMF. The power to use force impliedly *includes* the power to use surveillance and intelligence to find the targets.[186] According to the critics, Congress authorized the President to pull the trigger, but also ordered him to wear a blindfold.

Obviously, Congress cannot legislate in anticipation of every circumstance that may arise in the future. That is one of the reasons, along with the executive branch's advantages in expertise and structural organization, why Congress delegates authority. Those who consider themselves legal progressives generally support the administrative state and vigorously defend broad grants of authority from Congress to the agencies of the executive branch.[187] Agencies such as the Federal Communications Commission or the Environmental Protection Agency exercise powers over broad sectors of the economy under the incredibly vague and broad congressional mandate that they regulate in the "public interest."[188] These agencies make decisions with enormous

---

183 Hamdi v. Rumsfeld, 542 U.S. 507, 518 (2004) (plurality opinion). Although a plurality opinion, five Justices agreed on this point because Justice Thomas, in dissent, also concluded that the President had the constitutional authority to detain enemy combatants, based on Congress' authorization in the AUMF. *Id.* at 587 (Thomas, J., dissenting). The Anti-Detention Act, c. 645, 62 Stat. 847 (1948) (codified as amended at 18 U.S.C. § 4001 (2000)), was passed in response to the detention of Japanese-Americans in World War II and prohibits the detention of American citizens without authorization by Congress. The Center for Constitutional Rights, Docket: Hamdi v. Rumsfeld, http://www.ccr-ny.org/v2/gac/legal_article.asp?ObjID=SFG3oUP6Vx&Content=93 (last visited Dec. 26, 2006). The Supreme Court thus acknowledged in *Hamdi* that the AUMF suffices for this authorization. *Hamdi,* 542 U.S. at 518.

184 50 U.S.C. § 1809(a) (2000).

185 AUMF, Pub. L. No. 107-40, § 2, 115 Stat. 224 (2001).

186 *See supra* notes 153–157 and accompanying text.

187 *See generally* Richard A. Epstein, How Progressives Rewrote the Constituion (2006).

188 *See* Communications Act of 1934, Pub. L. No. 73-416, § 1, 48 Stat. 1064 (1934) (codified at 47 U.S.C. § 151 (2000)) (establishing the FCC); National Environmental Policy Act, Pub. L. No. 91-190, § 2, 83 Stat. 852 (1970) (codified at 42 U.S.C. § 4321 (2000)) (establishing the Council on Environmental Quality, the precursor to the EPA); *see also* Federal Communications Commission, About the FCC, http://www.fcc.gov/aboutus.html (last visited Dec. 26, 2006); U.S. Environmental Protection Agency: About EPA, http://www.epa.gov/epahome/aboutepa.htm (last visited Dec. 26, 2006). Such broad delegations were recently upheld in *Whitman v. Am. Trucking Ass'ns,* 531 U.S. 457, 475–76 (2001).

effects, such as which parts of the radio spectrum to sell,[189] or how much pollution to allow into the air,[190] all with little explicit guidance or thought from Congress.

> Yet, when Congress delegates broad authority to the President to defend the nation from attack, critics demand that Congress list every power it wishes to authorize.[191] While the threats to individual liberty may be greater in this setting, it makes little sense to place Congress under a heavier burden to describe every conceivable future contingency that might arise when we are fighting a war, perhaps the most unpredictable and certainly the most dangerous of human endeavors. Rather, we would expect and want Congress to delegate power to that branch, the Executive, which is best able to act with speed to combat threats to our national security.[192] War is too difficult to plan for with fixed, antecedent legislative rules, and war also is better run by the executive, which is structurally designed to take quick, decisive action. If the AUMF authorized the President to detain and kill the enemy,[193] the ability to search for them is necessarily included.

C. History Confirms the Appropriateness of a Swift Wartime Executive

Prominent Senators, including Patrick Leahy, Edward Kennedy, and Harry Reid, as well as organizations such as the ACLU, not only claim the NSA surveillance program violates FISA, but they charge that it shows that President Bush believes he is "above the law."[194] FISA, it might be argued, differs from the Anti-Detention Act because it is more comprehensive and also covers wartime. Even accepting, for the moment, the claim that the NSA program and FISA are in conflict, this does not make the program unconstitutional. Everyone would prefer that the President and Congress agree on war policy; it was one of the reasons the Bush administration sought the AUMF in the first place.[195] Our nation will wage war more effectively if the Executive and Legislature are unified in their purpose.

---

189 *See* Federal Communications Commission, Radio Spectrum Chart FAQ's, http://www.fcc.gov/oet/faqs/freqchart.html (last visited Dec. 26, 2006).

190 *See* U.S. Environmental Protection Agency, Air Topic Bank, http://www.epa.gov/ebtpages/air.html (last visited Dec. 26, 2006).

191 *See, e.g.*, Louis Fisher, *Lost Constitutional Moorings*, 81 Ind. L. J. 1199 (2006); *see also* Will, *supra* note 15 ("Congress, remembering what is happening today, might stipulate all the statutes and constitutional understandings that it does not intend the act to repeal or supersede.").

192 *See* sources cited *supra* note 32.

193 *See supra* note 185 and accompanying text.

194 Charlie Savage, *Three Democrats Slam President Over Defying Statutes*, Boston Globe, May 2, 2006, at A2; American Civil Liberties Union, ACLU Sues to Stop Illegal Spying on Americans, Saying President is not Above the Law (Jan. 17, 2006), http://www.aclu.org/safefree/nsaspying/23486prs20060117.html.

195 *See* Press Release, The White House, President Signs Authorization for Use of Military Force Bill (Sept. 18, 2001), http://www.whitehouse.gov/news/releases/2001/09/20010918-10.html ("[The AUMF] recognizes the seriousness of the terrorist threat to our Nation and the authority of the President under the Constitution to take action to deter and prevent acts of terrorism against the United States.").

Conflict between the branches of government, however, is commonplace in our history. The President and Congress have pursued conflicting war policies in many, indeed most, wars. Congress passed the Neutrality Acts, before World War II, in a largely futile effort to restrain FDR from assisting the allies.[196] Vietnam, the Iran-contra affair, and Kosovo are just the most recent examples of wars in which Congress tried to frustrate or micromanage executive war policy.[197]

The Constitution not only anticipated this struggle—it was written to ensure it. Our Framers did not give the President or the Congress complete control over war, foreign policy, or national security, but instead designed each branch differently, and gave them different powers that could be used to cooperate or fight. The President is the Commander-in-Chief and Chief Executive,[198] while Congress has the power over funding,[199] legislation,[200] the creation and discipline of the military,[201] and the power to "declare war."[202] National security is dramatically unlike other government powers, such as passing a statute, appointing a judge, or making a treaty, where the Constitution sets out a precise, step-by-step process for the roles of the different branches of government.[203] Thus, we should not find surprising the ongoing partisan conflict over terrorism policy after 9/11: it is the Framer's design made manifest.

---

196 *See* Neutrality Act of 1935, ch. 837, 49 Stat. 1081; Neutrality Act of 1937, ch. 146, 50 Stat. 121; Neutrality Act of 1939, ch. 2, 54 Stat. 4 (codified at 22 U.S.C. §§ 441, 444–45, 447–51, 453–57 (2000)).

197 *See generally* John Yoo, *Kosovo, War Powers, and the Multilateral Future*, 148 U. Pa. L. Rev. 1673 (2000).

198 U.S. Const. art. II, § 2, cl. 1.

199 U.S. Const. art. I, § 8, cl. 1, 12.

200 U.S. Const. art. I, § 1.

201 U.S. Const. art. I, § 8, cl. 11–15.

202 U.S. Const. art. I, § 8, cl. 11. The power to "declare" war is not the same as the power to "make" war. When defining Congress's war powers, the Framers deliberately struck the word "make" from a draft of the Constitution in favor of "declare." 2 The Records of the Federal Convention of 1787, at 318-19 (Max Farrand ed., 1911). Madison and Elbridge Gerry of Massachusetts moved for this alteration so as to "leav[e] to the Executive the power to repel sudden attacks." *Id.* at 318. While subsequent debate does not reveal a uniform understanding of the Declare War Clause, the alteration reflects an intention to prohibit Congress from encroaching on the executive power to conduct war. James Madison, pressed during the Virginia ratifying convention with the charge that the President's powers could lead to a military dictatorship, argued that Congress's control over funding would provide a sufficient check to the executive's powers, declaring: "The sword is in the hands of the British king. The purse in the hands of the Parliament. It is so in America as far as any analogy can exist." 10 The Documentary History of the Ratification of the Constitution 1282 (John P. Kaminski & Gaspare J. Saladino eds., 1986) (Madison speech of June 14, 1788) [hereinafter Madison Speech of 1788].

203 *Cf.* U.S. Const. art. I, § 7 (passing a statute); U.S. Const. art. II, § 2, cl. 2 (making a treaty and appointing judges).

1. The Framer's Vision of the Executive Wartime Power

Critics of the NSA program appeal to the Constitution as it works in peacetime, when Congress authorizes a policy and the President carries it out.[204] Critics imagine that the Constitution requires the President to check back with Congress on every strategy and tactic in the war on terrorism.[205] The NSA program is thus illegal, they say, because President Bush neglected to obtain yet another amendment to FISA approving it.[206] It is true that Congress offers more transparency and perhaps greater accountability to the public.[207] But it should also be clear that, over time, the Presidency has gained the leading role in war and national security because of its superior ability to take the initiative in response to emergencies.[208]

War's unpredictability makes unique demands for decisive and often secret action. John Locke first observed that a constitution ought to give the foreign affairs power to the executive because foreign threats are "much less capable to be directed by antecedent, standing, positive [l]aws" and the executive can act to protect the "security and interest of the public. . . ."[209] Legislatures are too slow and its members too numerous to respond effectively to unforeseen situations.[210] "Many things there are, which the [l]aw can by no means provide for; and those must necessarily be left to the discretion of him that has the [e]xecutive power in his hands, to be ordered by him as the public good and advantage shall require."[211]

The Framers well understood this principle. They rejected extreme republicanism, which concentrated power in the legislature, and created an executive with its own independent powers to manage foreign affairs and address emergencies which, almost by definition, cannot be addressed by existing laws.[212] The power to protect the nation, Hamilton wrote in the *Federalist Papers,* "ought to exist without limitation," because "it is impossible to foresee or define the extent and variety of national exigencies, or the correspondent extent and variety of the means which may be necessary to satisfy them."[213] It would be foolhardy to limit the constitutional power

---

204 *See* Nolan et al., *supra* note 11.

205 *See id.*

206 *Id.; see also* Wiretap Press Briefing, *supra* note 12.

207 *See,* e.g., Neal Kinkopf, *The Statutory Commander in Chief,* 81 Ind. L. J. 1169, 1195 (2006) ("Congress is constitutionally designed to introduce openness to governmental decision making. This openness, along with other aspects of Congress's structure, enhances public accountability and participation in the process of government decision making.") (footnotes omitted).

208 *See supra* notes 49–49, 158–160 and accompanying text.

209 John Locke, two Treatises of Government 365–66 (Peter Laslett ed., Cambridge University Press 1988).

210 *See id.* at 374–75.

211 *Id.*

212 *See* discussion *supra* Part I.

213 The Federalist No. 23, at 147 (Alexander Hamilton) (J. Cooke ed., 1961).

to protect the nation from foreign threats: "[t]he circumstances that endanger the safety of nations are infinite, and for this reason no constitutional shackles can wisely be imposed on the power to which the care of it is committed."[214]

The Framers located the responsibility to respond to emergency and war in the Presidency because of its ability to act with unity, speed, and secrecy.[215] In the *Federalist Papers,* Hamilton observed that "[d]ecision, activity, secrecy, and dispatch will generally characterise [sic] the proceedings of one man, in a much more eminent degree, than the proceedings of any greater number."[216] "Energy in the executive," said Hamilton, "is essential to the protection of the community against foreign attacks."[217] Wartime, that most unpredictable and dangerous of human endeavors, therefore ought to be managed by the President.[218] "Of all the cares or concerns of government, the direction of war most peculiarly demands those qualities which distinguish the exercise of power by a single hand."[219]

2. Executive Wartime Power in Practice

If ever there were an emergency that Congress could not prepare for, it was the war brought upon the United States on 9/11. FISA was a law written with Soviet spies working out of their embassy in Washington, D.C. in mind.[220] No one then anticipated war with an international terrorist organization wielding the destructive power of a nation. The Presidency was the institution of government best able to respond quickly to the 9/11 attacks and to take measures to defeat al Qaeda's further efforts. While the certainty and openness of a congressional act would certainly be desirable, the success of the NSA surveillance program depends on secrecy and agility, two characteristics Congress as an institution lacks.

But, critics respond, Congress foresaw that war might increase demands for domestic wiretapping, and still prohibited the President from using electronic surveillance

214 *Id.*

215 *See supra* notes 49–49, 158–160 and accompanying text.

216 *Id.*

217 The Federalist No. 70, *supra* note 32, at 472.

218 The Federalist No. 74, *supra* note 32, at 500.

219 *Id.* at 471. James Iredell (later an Associate Justice of the Supreme Court) argued in the North Carolina Ratifying Convention that "[f]rom the nature of the thing, the command of armies ought to be delegated to one person only. The secrecy, despatch, and decision, which are necessary in military operations, can only be expected from one person." Debate in the North Carolina Ratifying Convention, *in* 4 Jonathan Elliot, The Debates in the Several State Conventions on the Adoption of the Federal Constitution 107 (2d ed. Ayer Company, Publishers, Inc. 1987); *see also* 3 Joseph Story, Commentaries on the Constitution § 1485, at 341 (1833) (arguing that in military matters, "[u]nity of plan, promptitude, activity, and decision, are indispensable to success; and these can scarcely exist, except when a single magistrate is entrusted exclusively with the power.").

220 Cinquegrana, *supra* note 61, at 793–94 (1989) (describing the role of spying from the Soviet embassy in the origins of FISA).

without its permission.[221] Why should Congress's view not prevail here, as it would prevail in any other domestic question? It is simply not the case that the President must carry out every law enacted by Congress.[222] The Constitution is the supreme law of the land, and neither an act of Congress nor an act of the President can supersede it.[223] If Congress passes an unconstitutional act, such as a law ordering the imprisonment of those who criticize the government, the President must give force to the higher law, that of the Constitution.[224] Jefferson did just that as President when faced with the Alien and Sedition Acts.[225] He took the position that he, "believing the law to be unconstitutional, was bound to remit the execution of it, because that power has been confided to him by the Constitution."[226] That does not mean that the President is "above the law,"[227] it only means that the Constitution is above the Congress, and the President. FISA might be unconstitutional if it were read to forbid the President from gathering information necessary to prevent attacks on the United States in wartime.[228]

If the critics were right, and Presidents are duty bound to obey any and all acts of Congress, even those involving the Commander-in-Chief power, Congress could have ordered FDR not to attempt an amphibious landing in France in World War II, Truman to attack China during the Korean War, or JFK to invade Cuba in 1962.

---

221 *See supra* notes 11–13 and accompanying text.

222 *See, e.g.*, Michael D. Ramsey, *Torturing Executive Power*, 93 Geo. L.J. 1213, 1239 (2005) ("The President is not bound by unconstitutional laws, and it is routine constitutional doctrine that laws purporting to take away the constitutional powers of the President are themselves unconstitutional.").

223 *See supra* note 23.

224 *See supra* note 23.

225 *See* Letter from Thomas Jefferson, President of the United States, to Mrs. John Adams (Sept. 11, 1804), *available at* http://yamaguchy.netfirms.com/jefferson/1804.html.

226 *Id.* President Andrew Jackson expressed the same view in 1832, vetoing a bill that he regarded as unconstitutional even though the Supreme Court had upheld it as constitutional. "It is as much the duty of the House of Representatives, of the Senate, and of the President to decide upon the constitutionality of any bill or resolution which may be presented to them for passage or approval as it is of the supreme judges when it may be brought before them for judicial decision," he wrote. Andrew Jackson, Veto Message (July 10, 1832), *in* 2 A Compilation of the Messages and Papers of the Presidents 1789–1897, at 582 (James D. Richardson ed., 1897). Abraham Lincoln, in the aftermath of the *Dred Scott* case, famously announced in his first inaugural that thenceforth, he would not follow the rule that a slave would not be free once in northern territory, though he chose to obey the Supreme Court's order in the *Dred Scott* case itself. *See* First Inaugural Address of Abraham Lincoln (Mar. 4, 1861), http://www.yale.edu/lawweb/avalon/presiden/inaug/lincoln1.htm. Additionally, President Franklin Roosevelt evaded Congress's Neutrality Acts and provided aid and comfort to the allies before Pearl Harbor. *See* Franklin D. Roosevelt Presidential Museum and Library, Franklin D. Roosevelt: 32nd President of the United States, http://www.fdrlibrary.marist.edu/fdrbio.html (last visited Dec. 1, 2006).

227 *Cf.* sources cited *supra* note 194.

228 NSA Supporting Authorities, *supra* note 55, at 3.

But Presidents such as Jefferson, Jackson, Lincoln, and FDR believed that they had the right to take action, following their interpretation of the Constitution rather than the views of Congress or the Supreme Court, especially in their role as Commander-in-Chief.[229]

Decades of American constitutional practice reject the notion of an omnipotent Congress. While Congress has the sole power to declare war, neither Presidents nor Congresses have acted under the belief that a declaration of war must come before military hostilities abroad.[230] Without declarations of war or any other congressional authorization, Presidents have sent troops into hostilities abroad many times.[231] Other conflicts, such as both Persian Gulf Wars, received "authorization" from Congress but not declarations of war.[232]

Both the President and Congress generally agree that the legislature should not interfere in the executive branch's strategic and tactical decisions.[233] Congress's powers ought to be at their height at the decision to start a war, before troops have been committed and treasure or blood spent. Congress attempted to prevent Presidents from using force abroad, in the Nixon-era War Powers Resolution (yet another "reform" gone awry), by prohibiting the insertion of troops into hostile environments abroad for more than 60 days without legislative approval.[234] The Resolution has been a dead letter that has not prevented Presidents from using force abroad.[235] Presidents and Congresses alike have realized that the War Powers Resolution made little practical sense, and instead represented congressional overreaching into presidential expertise and constitutional authority in foreign affairs.[236]

---

229 *See supra* notes 41–44 and accompanying text.

230 *See supra* note 202.

231 *See supra* notes 41-44 and accompanying text.

232 *See* sources cited *supra* note 44. For representative works arguing that Congress has sole control over when to begin wars, see JOHN HART ELY, WAR AND RESPONSIBILITY: CONSTITUTIONAL LESSONS OF VIETNAM AND ITS AFTERMATH 3-11 (1993); LOUIS FISHER, PRESIDENTIAL WAR POWER 203 (1995); MICHAEL J. GLENNON, CONSTITUTIONAL DIPLOMACY 80-84 (1990); LOUIS HENKIN, CONSTITUTIONALISM, DEMOCRACY, AND FOREIGN AFFAIRS 29 (1990); HAROLD HONGJU KOH, THE NATIONAL SECURITY CONSTITUTION: SHARING POWER AFTER THE IRAN-CONTRA AFFAIR 158-61 (1990). My argument in response can be found in Yoo, *supra* note 35, at 143–81.

233 *Cf.* Saikrishna Prakash, *Regulating the Commander in Chief: Some Theories*, 81 IND. L.J. 1319, 1321 (2006) ("Many scholars clearly believe that the President has some exclusive CINC power because they admit that Congress cannot regulate tactical decisions involving the retreat and advance of soldiers.").

234 *See* War Powers Resolution of 1973, 50 U.S.C. §§ 1541–48 (2000).

235 *See, e.g.*, John Hart Ely, *Suppose Congress Wanted a War Powers Act That Worked*, 88 COLUM. L. REV. 1379, 1381 (1988).

236 *See id.* at 1380–81.

Presidential leadership has always included control over the goals and means of military campaigns.[237] As the Supreme Court has observed, the President has the authority "to employ [the armed forces] in the manner he may deem most effectual to harass and conquer and subdue the enemy."[238] President Lincoln did not seek a law from Congress over whether to defend Washington, D.C.; President Roosevelt did not ask Congress whether he should make the war in Europe a priority over the war in the Pacific; President Truman did not seek legislative permission to drop nuclear bombs on Japan. Many of the wars fought since World War II, ranging from Korea to Panama to Kosovo, never received congressional authorization.[239] Obviously Presidents should not ignore congressional leaders. A wise President will consult with Congress at the right time. But the Constitution does not force the President to get a letter from Congress every time he makes an important decision about wartime strategy or tactics.[240]

Nor is the Congress defenseless. It has ample powers to block wartime initiatives.[241] It has total control over funding and the size and equipment of the military.[242] If it does not like a war or a strategy, it can cut off funds, reduce the size of units, or refuse to provide material for it. War would be impossible without Congress's cooperation, or at least its acquiescence. This is increasingly true in the age of modern warfare, which requires material, high-technology weapons systems, and massive armed forces dependent upon constant congressional budgetary support.

Critics claim that Congress ought to have the upper hand in war to prevent military adventurism, to check war fever, and to guarantee political consensus.[243] This sounds plausible, but it neglects the benefits of executive action during time of foreign threat, and downplays Congress's faults, such as delay, inflexibility, and lack of secrecy. World War II clearly demonstrated that presidential initiative has been critical to the protection of American national security. When Europe plunged into war, Congress enacted a series of Neutrality Acts designed to keep the United States

237 *Cf.* Bradley & Goldsmith, *supra* note 181, at 2092 ("[I]n various nineteenth- and twentieth-century decisions upholding the validity of presidential actions during war, various members of the Supreme Court suggested, usually in dicta or dissents, that in the absence of express congressional restriction, the only limitations on presidential power during wartime were the laws of war.").

238 Fleming v. Page, 50 U.S. (9 How.) 603, 615 (1850).

239 *See supra* notes 41–44 and accompanying text.

240 *See* United States v. Smith, 27 F. Cas. 1192, 1199 (C.C.D.N.Y. 1806) ("Congress have [sic] the power of declaring war; and when that is done, the president is to act under it, and may authorize any military or hostile measure against the enemy.").

241 *See* U.S. CONST. art. I, § 8, cl. 11.

242 *See* U.S. CONST. art. I, § 8, cl. 12–13.

243 *See supra* notes 11-13 and accompanying text.

out of the conflict.[244] In 1940 and 1941, FDR recognized that America's security would be threatened by German control of Europe, and he and his advisers gradually attempted to bring the United States to the assistance of Great Britain and the Soviet Union.[245] FDR stretched his authority to cooperate closely with Great Britain in protecting convoys in the North Atlantic, and providing the British with 50 "obsolete" destroyers, among other things. American pressure on Japan to withdraw from China helped trigger the Pacific War, without which American entry into World War II might have been delayed by at least another year, if not longer.[246] Knowing what we now know, most would agree that America's earlier entry into World War II would have greatly benefited the United States and the world.

The Cold War is another example where consistent presidential leadership proved better for our national security than relying on Congress for leadership. Through their proxies, and often in secret, the United States and the communist bloc fought throughout the world. Congress only authorized the Vietnam War.[247] America and its allies fought Soviet proxies in Korea, Vietnam, and Nicaragua, the Soviet Union fought against American-backed forces in Afghanistan, and the two very nearly came into direct conflict during the Cuban Missile Crisis (notably JFK did not ask Congress for permission to throw a blockade around Cuba).[248] After Vietnam, Congress tried to prevent presidential action by passing the War Powers Resolution.[249] Presidents have ignored the resolution and never acknowledged its legality. Congress has never tried to enforce it.[250] Generally, we prevailed in the Cold War through the steady presidential application of the strategy of containment, supported by congressional funding of the necessary military forces, but not through congressional decisions on when and where to wage war.[251]

---

244 Neutrality Act of 1935, ch. 837, 49 Stat. 1081; Neutrality Act of 1937, ch. 146, 50 Stat. 121; Neutrality Act of 1939, ch. 2, 54 Stat. 4 (codified at 22 U.S.C. §§ 441, 444–45, 447–51, 453–57 (2000)).

245 For a standard historical source on the period see generally ROBERT DALLEK, FRANKLIN D. ROOSEVELT AND AMERICAN FOREIGN POLICY, 1932–1945 (1979); ROBERT DIVINE, ROOSEVELT AND WORLD WAR II (1969); WARREN F. KIMBALL, THE JUGGLER: FRANKLIN ROOSEVELT AS WARTIME STATESMAN (1991); FREDERICK W. MARKS III, WIND OVER SAND: THE DIPLOMACY OF FRANKLIN ROOSEVELT (1988); GADDIS SMITH, AMERICAN DIPLOMACY DURING THE SECOND WORLD WAR (1965).

246 Marc Trachtenberg, *The Bush Strategy in Historical Perspective*, *in* NUCLEAR TRANSFORMATION: THE NEW U.S. NUCLEAR DOCTRINE (James Wirtz & Jeffrey Larsen eds., 2005).

247 *See* Joint Resolution to Promote the Maintenance of International Peace and Security in Southeast Asia, Pub. L. No. 88-408, 78 Stat. 384 (1964).

248 *See* Yoo, *supra* note 42, at 803–04; Radio and Television Report to the American People on the Soviet Arms Buildup in Cuba 485 Pub. Papers 806 (Oct. 22, 1962).

249 War Powers Resolution of 1973, 50 U.S.C. §§ 1541–48 (2000).

250 *See supra* notes 234–236 and accompanying text.

251 This history is recounted in JOHN LEWIS GADDIS, STRATEGIES OF CONTAINMENT: A CRITICAL REAPPRAISAL OF AMERICAN NATIONAL SECURITY POLICY DURING THE COLD WAR (rev. ed. 2005); JOHN LEWIS GADDIS, WE NOW KNOW: RETHINKING COLD WAR HISTORY (1997).

D. The Executive, Not Congress, is Best Structured to Respond to al Qaeda

Critics also ignore how poor Congress's independent judgment can be on national security matters. Congress led us into two "bad" wars, the 1798 quasi-war with France and the War of 1812. And Congressional approval does not always bring consensus. The Vietnam War, one of the wars initially supported by Congress, did not meet with a consensus over the long term but instead provoked some of the most divisive politics in American history.[252] It is also difficult to claim that the congressional authorizations to use force in Iraq, either in 1991 or 2002,[253] reflected a deep consensus over the merits of the wars there. Indeed, the 1991 authorization barely survived the Senate, and the 2002 authorization received significant negative votes and has become a deeply divisive issue in national politics.[254]

Legislative deliberation can breed consensus in the best of cases, but it also can stand in the way of speed and decisiveness. Terrorist attacks are more difficult to detect and prevent than those posed by conventional armed forces and nations, and WMDs allow terrorists to inflict devastation that once only could have been achievable by a nation-state.[255] To defend itself from this threat, the United States will have to use force earlier and more often than at the time when nations generated the primary threats. In order to forestall a WMD attack, or to take advantage of a window of opportunity to strike at a terrorist cell, the President needs the flexibility to act quickly. By acting earlier, perhaps before WMD components have been fully assembled or before an al Qaeda operative has left for the United States, the executive branch might also be able to engage in a more limited, more precisely targeted, use of force.

Critics of the NSA program want to overturn American historical practice in favor of a new and untested theory about the wartime powers of the President and Congress.[256] We should encourage innovation and creativity in our intelligence and military—and the NSA program is precisely that—to confront the unprecedented challenges of al Qaeda. For too long, our system retarded aggressive measures to pre-empt terrorist attacks.[257] But seeking to give Congress the dominant hand in setting wartime policy would render our tactics against al Qaeda less, rather than more, effective. It would slow down decisions, make sensitive policies and intelligence public, and encourage risk aversion rather than risk taking. Requiring the President

---

252 *Cf.* Robin Toner & Jim Rutenberg, *Partisan Divide on Iraq Exceeds Split on Vietnam*, N.Y. Times, July 30, 2006, http://www.nytimes.com/2006/07/30/washington/30war.html?ex=1311912000&en=c6a6066ff004210e&ei=5088&partner=rssnyt&emc=rss.

253 *See* sources cited *supra* note 44.

254 *See* Senate Approves Iraq War Resolution, http://archives.cnn.com/2002/ALLPOLITICS/10/11/iraq.us (last visited Dec. 27, 2006).

255 9/11 Commission Report, *supra* note 63, at 361–62.

256 *See supra* notes 11–13 and accompanying text.

257 *See* 9/11 Commission Report, *supra* note 63, at 399–419.

to obtain Congressional approval prior to every important policy change ignores the reality the al Qaeda challenge presents.

1. Congress and the Courts Have Checks to Balance Presidential Power

Claims that the NSA program violates the Constitution appeal not to a concern about law, but rather to a concern about politics. They express the worry that if the President is waging a war, and war has slipped into the United States itself, we will centralize too much power in the President over our domestic affairs.[258] The NSA program, however, does not signal that we live under a dictator, or that the separation of powers has failed, the exaggerated claims of civil libertarians notwithstanding.

Instead, the other branches of government have powerful and important tools to limit the President should his efforts to defeat terrorism slip into domestic oppression. Congress has total control over funding and significant powers of oversight.[259] It could do away with the NSA as a whole. The Constitution does not require that Congress create an NSA or any intelligence agency. It need not engage in anything as drastic as doing away with the NSA, of course. Congress could easily eliminate the surveillance program simply by cutting off all funds for it. It could also link approval of administration policies in related areas to agreement on changes to the NSA program. Congress could refuse to confirm cabinet members, subcabinet members, or military intelligence officers unless it prevails over the NSA. It could hold extensive hearings that bring to light the NSA's past operations, backed up by the power of subpoena, and require NSA officials to appear and be held to account. It could even enact a civil cause of action that would allow those who have been wiretapped by the NSA to sue for damages, with the funds coming out of the NSA's budget. So far, Congress has not taken any of these steps, and in fact passed up an obvious chance when it confirmed General Hayden to head the CIA.[260] We should not mistake congressional silence for opposition to the President's terrorism policies.[261]

Courts can exercise their own check on presidential power, although one that is not as comprehensive as Congress's. Any effort to prosecute an al Qaeda member or

---

258 *See, e.g.*, Wiretap Press Briefing, *supra* note 12.

259 U.S. Const. art. I, § 8. The Framers clearly intended to replicate the British model of the executive which was in both theory and practice hemmed in by the Parliamentary power of the purse. Pressed during the Virginia ratifying convention with the charge that the President's powers could lead to a military dictatorship, James Madison argued that Congress's control over funding would be enough of a check to control the executive. Madison Speech of 1788, *supra* note 202.

260 *See supra* text accompanying notes 113–115.

261 "Congress cannot anticipate and legislate with regard to every possible action the President may find it necessary to take or every possible situation in which he might act," the Supreme Court has said. "Such failure of Congress . . . does not, 'especially . . . in the areas of foreign policy and national security,' imply 'congressional disapproval' of action taken by the Executive." Dames & Moore v. Regan, 453 U.S. 654, 678 (1981) (quoting Haig v. Agee, 453 U.S., 280, 291 (1981)).

a terrorism suspect within the United States will require the cooperation of the federal courts.[262] If federal judges believe that the NSA's activities are unconstitutional, they can refuse to admit into evidence any information discovered by warrantless surveillance.[263] The NSA's activities should remain in the field of war, in order to prevent a direct attack, rather than to promote the objects of the law enforcement system. Federal courts can police this distinction simply by refusing to admit any NSA-related evidence at criminal trials.

2. The Executive Can Operate These Programs in a Way that Reassures the Other Branches of Government and the Public

The President can structure the NSA program to enhance public confidence that its fruits will not be used for political or law enforcement goals. While he has the constitutional authority to carry out searches in secret,[264] it may be to the nation's advantage for the President to create a consultation process among the relevant cabinet officials, and then between the executive and legislative branches. This would give the public more confidence that the NSA was not being used to carry out political vendettas. By his own account, President Bush had already put into place a primitive version of this before December 2005: each time he approved the NSA program, he asked the cabinet officers responsible for defense and intelligence whether they believed it was necessary or not, and he submitted the operation to review by White House and Justice Department lawyers.[265] An expanded version of this could mirror, or simply adopt, the National Security Council structure, but without the legions of staff. The NSC already includes the Vice President, the National Security Adviser, the Secretaries of State and Defense, and the head of the intelligence community, among others, and it is responsible for approving all covert actions before they are sent to the President for approval.[266] Operation of the NSA program could come under the NSC's purview, although perhaps with restrictions on staff involvement to prevent leaks of sensitive information.

Presidents could also reach out to Congress along the lines of the current system for covert action. Under the National Security Act, the executive branch notifies the House and Senate Intelligence committees of presidentially-approved

262 On the difficulties of pursuing a criminal prosecution in a federal court against Zacarias Moussaoui, an admitted member of al Qaeda intent on making a mockery of the justice system, see Yoo, *supra* note 57, at 210–27.

263 *Cf.* Akhil Reed Amar, The Constitution and Criminal Procedure: First Principles 1-45 (1997).

264 *See* discussion *supra* Part III. A.

265 President George W. Bush, President's Radio Address (Dec. 17, 2005), http://www.whitehouse.gov/news/releases/2005/12/20051217.html.

266 National Security Act of 1947, ch. 343, 61 Stat. 496 (establishing the National Security Council), *amended by* National Security Act Amendments of 1949, ch. 412, 63 Stat. 578 (codified at 50 U.S.C. §§ 401-42 (2000 & Supp. IV 2004)); *see also* http://www.whitehouse.gov/nsc/ (last visited Dec. 27, 2006).

covert actions.[267] These committees have strong relationships with the intelligence community and hold extensive, classified oversight hearings over the nation's covert action programs and other classified intelligence systems.[268] Again, the Bush administration made initial steps toward such a system with the NSA program by briefing what is known as the "Gang of Eight"—the Senate majority and minority leader, the House speaker and minority leader, and the chair and ranking minority member of the Senate and House intelligence committees.[269] To improve public confidence in electronic surveillance of al Qaeda communications with individuals in the United States, intelligence officials could provide routine briefings to an expanded group of House and Senate leaders on the extent of NSA surveillance, its particular targets, and what intelligence of value it has produced. The group should be kept small, and probably would have to exclude staff, to prevent crucial secrets from leaking, an endemic problem in Washington and one that is especially dangerous in war.

CONCLUSION

The Constitution creates a presidency whose function is to act forcefully and independently to repel serious threats to the nation. Instead of specifying a legalistic process to begin war, the framers wisely created a fluid political process in which legislators would use their funding, legislative, and political power to balance presidential initiative.[270] As we confront terrorism, potentially armed with weapons of mass destruction, we should look skeptically at claims that radical changes in the way we make war would solve our problems, even those stemming from poor judgment, unforeseen circumstances, and bad luck. The worst thing we could do when confronted by a capable, shadowy enemy like al Qaeda would be to change our government to make it harder to develop innovative policies like the NSA surveillance program.

267 50 U.S.C. § 413(a) (2000 & Supp. IV 2004).

268 *See* U.S. Senate Select Committee on Intelligence, http://intelligence.senate.gov/index.html (last visited Jan. 12, 2007); U.S. House of Representatives, Permanent Select Committee on Intelligence, http://intelligence.house.gov/ (last visited Jan. 12, 2007).

269 Scott Shane, *Report Questions Legality of Briefings on Surveillance*, N.Y. TIMES, Jan. 19, 2006, at A19 (noting that the "Gang of Eight" had received briefings about the NSA warrantless surveillance program).

270 *See* discussion *supra* Part I.

INTELLIGENCE DEMANDS IN A DEMOCRATIC STATE: CONGRESSIONAL INTELLIGENCE OVERSIGHT

Christopher M. Ford†

Originally published in Tulane Law Review, Vol. 81 (Feb. 2007)

"I expect a covert policy that, if Americans saw it on the front page of their newspaper, they'd say, 'That makes sense.'"

—President Ronald Reagan[1]

I. INTRODUCTION

On December 16, 2005, a lead headline in the *New York Times—Bush Tets U.S. Spy on Callers Without Courts*—seriously tested Reagan's maxim.[2] The article detailed an operation in which President Bush "authorized the National Security Agency [(NSA)] to eavesdrop on Americans and others inside the United States . . . without . . . court-approved warrants."[3] The full extent of this program is largely unclear as it remains classified; however, "perhaps thousands" of telephone calls and e-mail messages were monitored since the program's inception in 2002.[4] The program immediately implicates a myriad of federal limits on the conduct of domestic intelligence operations, specifically, the Fourth Amendment,[5] the Foreign Intelligence Surveillance Act of 1978 (FISA),[6] and Title III of the Omnibus Crime Control and Safe Streets Act of 1968,[7] and Executive Order 12,333.[8]

---

† Assistant Professor of Law, United States Military Academy. J.D. 2002, University of South Carolinie; B.A. 1999, Furman Univerity. The auther thanks Terrance M. Ford for his assistance and comments. The views expressed are the author's own and do not reflect those of the United States Army or United States Military Academy.

1 President Ronald Reagan, Address to the Nation on Iran Arms and Contra Aid Controversy (Mar. 4, 1987) (transcript available at http://http://www.reagan.utexas.edu/archives/speeches/1987/030487h.htm).

2 James Risen & Eric Lichtblau, *Bush Lets U.S. Spy on Callers Without Courts,* N.Y. TIMES, Dec. 16, 2005, at A1.

3 *Id.*

4 *See id.*

5 U.S. CONST, amend. IV.

6 Foreign Intelligence Surveillance Act of 1978, 50 U.S.C. §§ 1801–1811 (2000).

7 Omnibus Crime Control and Safe Streets Act of 1968 § 802, 18 U.S.C. §§ 2510–2520 (2000).

8 Exec. Order No. 12, 333, 3 C.F.R. 200 (1982), *reprinted as amended in* 50 U.S.C. § 401(2000).

Beyond the instant questions of legality and privacy, the NSA surveillance program raises more expansive issues of separation of power and executive power, as the program was executed absent congressional approval and without the knowledge of the vast majority of Congress.[9] Congressional reaction, once known, was instantaneous and uncharacteristically bipartisan. Within hours, Senator Arlen Specter, Republican Chairman of the Senate Judiciary Committee, declared the matter one of "very, very high priority" and pledged to hold hearings as soon as the Senate reconvened.[10] This call was joined by virtually every ranking member of Congress.[11] Referencing Article II of the Constitution of the United States and the Congressional Authorization for the Use of Military Force,[12] the President vigorously rejoined the criticisms, arguing that the program was "consistent with U.S. law and the Constitution"[13]

While dramatic, this tension can hardly be characterized as surprising. Recent history is replete with examples of bold Presidential exercises of power in national security affairs.[14] *In Dames & Moore v. Regan*, Chief Justice Rehnquist noted:

> As we now turn to the factual and legal issues in this case, we freely confess that we are obviously deciding only one more episode in the never-ending tension between the President exercising the executive authority in a world that presents each day some new challenge with which he must deal and the Constitution under which we all live and which no one disputes embodies some sort of system of checks and balances.[15]

This tension is perhaps particularly acute in the realm of intelligence operations and oversight where these powers are not expressly delegated by the Constitution

---

9 *Democrats Call for Investigation of NSA Wiretaps,* CNN.COM, Dec. 18, 2005, http://www.cnn.com/2005/POLITICS/12/18/bush.nsa. Notification was provided to the "gang of eight": the leadership of both Houses and the Intelligence Committee leadership. *See* Memorandum from Alfred Cumming, Specialist in Intelligence & Nat'l Sec., Foreign Affairs, Def., & Trade Div, Congressional Research Serv., to Senator Dianne Feinstein 1-2 (Dec. 14, 2005) (available at http://feinstein.senate.gov/crs-intel.pdf); *see also* Dan Eggen, *Congressional Agency Questions Legality of Wiretaps,* WASH. POST, Jan. 19, 2006, at A5.

10 William McQuillen, *Specter Says Senate To Probe Report U.S. Broke Law on Spying,* BLOOMBERG.COM, Dec. 16, 2005, http://www.bloomberg.com (search "Search News" for "McQuillen and Specter"; follow top link); *see Democrats Call for Investigation of NSA Wiretaps, supra* note 9 (stating that the Democratic House of Representatives' leaders want an investigation into the NSA surveillance program).

11 *See Democrats Call for Investigation of NSA Wiretaps, supra* note 9.

12 Authorization for Use of Military Force, Pub. L. No. 107-40, 115 Stat. 224 (2001) (codified as amended at 50 U.S.C. § 1541 note (Supp. 2005)).

13 *See* President George W. Bush, Press Conference of the President (Dec. 19, 2005) (transcript available at http://www.whitehouse.gov/news/releases/2005/12/20051219-2.html); *see also* U.S. DEP'T OF JUSTICE, LEGAL AUTHORITIES SUPPORTING THE ACTIVITIES OF THE NATIONAL SECURITY AGENCY DESCRIBED BY THE PRESIDENT 7 (2006), *available at* http://www.usdoj.gov/opa/whitepaperonnsalegalauthorities.pdf.

14 *See* Noah Feldman, *Who Can Check the President?,* N. Y. TIMES, Jan. 8, 2006, § 6 (Magazine), at 52.

15 Dames & Moore v. Regan, 453 U.S. 654, 662 (1981).

and each side believes their uninhibited participation is critical for national security.[16]

This Article does not, however, seek to trade in a discussion of the legality of recent practices, but rather examines this dynamic relationship and, specifically, Congress's role in facilitating both legal and aggressive intelligence operations. All too often it seems the Executive has viewed Congress as an unwanted partner—interfering with executive powers and meddling in affairs best left to the professionals in the various agencies within the United States Intelligence Community (Intelligence Community or Community). Congress has historically acquiesced, thus largely allowing the Executive to conduct intelligence operations without oversight.[17] Congress has rejected this historical generalization twice in the last fifty years: first, and most significantly, in response to the intelligence activities relating to Watergate[18] and the Vietnam War;[19] and then again, in the late 1980s, in response to the Iran-Contra Affair and other actions involving the Intelligence Community.[20]

These instances of congressional action followed a similar pattern: long periods of executive autonomy punctuated by short bursts of congressional oversight grounded in public revelations of impropriety or illegality in the Intelligence Community[21] The events of 9/11, the failure to find weapons of mass destruction in Iraq, and the revelations concerning the NSA have combined to create a situation that may place Congress at the cusp of a third congressional reassertion of control over intelligence operations. These events provide a unique opportunity for Congress to reassert its role in intelligence operations: not to hinder operations, but rather to facilitate them.

In Part II, this Article describes the constitutional allocation of power regarding the conducting of intelligence operations. That Part specifically addresses both congressional and presidential claims of authority and how both have exercised these powers. Part HI provides a general overview of the history and current structure of the Intelligence Community. That Part provides a critical foundation for understanding the Community as it exists today, its limitations and restrictions, and the historic conflict between executive action and congressional oversight. Part IV examines the impetus for increased congressional assertiveness during the

---

16 As a recent Congressional Research Service report noted, "A review of the history of intelligence collection and its regulation by Congress suggests that the two political branches have never quite achieved a meeting of the minds regarding their respective powers." ELIZABETH B. BAZAN & JENNIFER K. ELSEA, PRESIDENTIAL AUTHORITY TO CONDUCT WARRANTLESS ELECTRONIC SURVEILLANCE TO GATHER FOREIGN INTELLIGENCE INFORMATION (2006), *available at* http://www.fas.org/sgp/crs/intel/m010506.pdf.

17 *See* United States v. Curtiss-Wright Export Corp., 299 U.S. 304, 316–22 (1936) (describing the President's unfettered executive powers and their historic development).

18 *See infra* notes 126–137 and accompanying text.

19 *See infra* notes 117–121 and accompanying text.

20 *See infra* notes 258–270 and accompanying text.

21 *See infra* Part IV.

late 1970s and the late 1980s. That Part focuses in part on the role of the public in guaranteeing the conduct of intelligence operations in accordance with majority views on mores, civil liberties, and human rights. Part V describes the current oversight structure, established largely in response to the events described in Part IV. Finally, Part VI examines congressional intelligence oversight in the wake of 9/11 and the current proposals for intelligence oversight reform. Part VTI offers a summation of suggested reforms.

In conclusion, this Article demonstrates that Congress plays a fundamental role in the conduct of intelligence operations. Perhaps most obviously, Congress acts as a check on the power of the executive, reflecting the will of the people in ensuring the conduct of operations is in accordance with applicable laws. Less intuitive is Congress's role in ensuring the efficient and aggressive conduct of operations. Observed historically, Congress has periodically abandoned these roles out of disinterest and institutional disorganization. Congress's ability to competently and efficiently execute these duties is contingent on a combination of three factors: (1) continued interest in robust, yet operationally cognizant, oversight; (2) aggressive efforts to continue to unify the Intelligence Community; and (3) implementation of internal reforms within congressional intelligence committees.

II. AUTHORITY FOR THE CONDUCT OF INTELLIGENCE OPERATIONS

A. The Constitution

The United States is a democratic country founded upon ideals of individual rights and limited government,[22] and the U.S. citizenry demands a certain balance between the oft-times competing needs of national security (embodied in the Executive) and civil liberties (embodied in constitutional and statutory provisions).[23] This presents a unique paradox: intelligence is required to ensure national security to preserve the citizenry's rights, yet limits on these rights are necessary to provide the intelligence.[24]

The sensitivity of the citizenry to intelligence operations is critically heightened when conducted domestically against, or with unwitting help of, American citizens.[25]

---

22 U.S. Const, pmbl.

23 Steven Emerson, Secret Warriors: Inside the Covert Military Operations of the Reagan Era 238 (1988). In discussing U.S. intelligence and associated operations, Emerson notes that "[t]he United States today faces a real paradox: It desperately needs a special operations capacity, but has repeated difficulty in reconciling that fact with representative government and bureaucratic accountability." *Id.* President Woodrow Wilson was quoted when signing the Espionage Act of 1917: "'I shall not permit . . . any part of this law to apply to me . . . as a shield against criticism.'" The Tree of Liberty: A Documentary History of Rebellion and Political Crime in America 297 (Nicholas N. Kittrie & Eldon D. Wedlock, Jr., eds., 1986).

24 *See* Emerson, *supra* note 23, at 238.

25 *See, e.g.*, Jason A. Gonzalez, *Constitutional Aspects of Foreign Affairs: How the War on Terror Has Changed the Intelligence Gathering Paradigm,* 51 Naval. L. Rev. 289, 290 (2005) ("[T]here has long been a debate on the scope of the President's power to collect foreign intelligence on

Such operations are further complicated, and come under increased public and political scrutiny, when elements of the United States Department of Defense (i.e., the NSA) become involved.[26] Chief Justice Warren eloquently noted the necessity of the military while warning against its potentially awesome force:

> The military establishment is, of course, a necessary organ of government; but the reach of its power must be carefully limited lest the delicate balance between freedom and order be upset. The maintenance of the balance is made more difficult by the fact that while the military serves the vital function of preserving the existence of the nation, it is, at the same time, the one element of government that exercises a type of authority not easily assimilated in a free society.[27]

Chief Justice Burger later noted that in the United States there is "a traditional and strong resistance of Americans to any military intrusion into civilian affairs. That tradition has deep roots in our history. . . ."[28]

Thus, in examining the division of responsibility and authority in the conduct of intelligence operations, it is important to first address the constitutional treatment of this question. From the outset, it is clear the Constitution does not expressly contemplate intelligence operations; rather, the powers claimed and exercised by both branches are implied from a collection of enumerated powers.

The most fundamental claim on executive power is the President's duty to "take Care that the Laws be faithfully executed."[29] The Constitution further establishes the President as the "Commander in Chief of the Army and Navy of the United States,"[30] a role that encompasses "something more than an empty title."[31] Further, the President's constitutional oath demands that the President do his best to "preserve, protect and defend the Constitution of the United States."[32] Taken collectively, these clauses establish the executive's primacy in foreign affairs and national defense.[33]

---

domestic targets during wartime, specifically U.S. persons, without having to obtain a judicially sanctioned warrant.").

26 *See, e.g.*, Bush, *supra* note 13 (responding to the public and press turmoil and concern after the disclosure of the NSA surveillance program).

27 Earl Warren, *The Bill of Rights and the Military*, 37 N.Y.U. L. Rev. 181, 182 (1962).

28 Laird v. Tatum, 408 U.S. 1, 15 (1972).

29 U.S. Const, art. II, § 3.

30 *Id.* art. II, § 2, cl. 1.

31 Youngstown Sheet & Tube Co. v. Sawyer, 343 U.S. 579, 641 (1952) (Jackson, I, concurring).

32 U.S. Const, art. II, § 1, cl. 8.

33 *See* United States v. Curtiss-Wright Exp. Corp., 299 U.S. 304, 319 (1936) ("'The President is the sole organ of the nation in its external relations, and its sole representative with foreign nations.'"); *see also* Hamdi v. Rumsfeld, 542 U.S. 507, 581–82 (2004) (Thomas, J., dissenting) ("The Court has acknowledged that the President has the authority to 'employ [the Nation's Armed Forces] in the manner he may deem most effectual to harass and conquer and subdue the enemy.'" (quoting Fleming v. Page, 50 U.S. (9 How.) 603, 615 (1850))).

The breadth of the President's powers under these provisions "ha[s] given rise to some of the most persistent controversies in our constitutional history."[34] The United States Department of Justice (DOJ) has recently taken the position that these provisions "grant[] the President inherent power to protect the Nation from foreign attack."[35] This proposition, however, is far from settled.[36] Indeed, Justice Jackson warned against such broad assumptions—particularly when the President is acting domestically:

> I should indulge the widest latitude of interpretation to sustain his exclusive function to command the instruments of national force, at least when turned against the outside world for the security of our society. But, when it is turned inward, not because of rebellion but because of a lawful economic struggle between industry and labor, it should have no such indulgence. His command power is not such an absolute as might be implied from that office in a militaristic system but is subject to limitations consistent with a constitutional Republic whose law and policy-making branch is a representative Congress.[37]

During the course of Senate Judiciary Committee hearings regarding the NSA program, several Senators expressed doubts as to the breadth of the President's inherent wartime powers in the realm of intelligence operations. In his opening statement, Committee Chairman Arlen Specter noted: "There is . . . a constitutional issue as to whether the President has inherent powers under Article II of the Constitution to undertake a program of this sort."[38] Senator Lindsey Graham expressed similar concerns: "[T]he inherent authority argument . . . [t]aken to its logical conclusion, it concerns me that it could basically neuter the Congress and weaken the courts."[39] It is, however, virtually undisputed that the President does possess very broad powers when acting in the interests of national security.[40]

---

34 *Youngstown*, 343 U.S. at 641 (Jackson, J., concurring).

35 U.S. Dep't of Justice, *supra* note 13, at 7 (citing Dep't of the Navy v. Egan, 484 U.S. 518, 527 (1988); The Prize Cases, 67 U.S. (2 Black) 635, 668 (1863)); *see* United States v. Brown, 484 F.2d 418, 426 (5th Cir. 1973) ("[B]ecause of the President's constitutional duty to act for the United States in the field of foreign relations, and his inherent power to protect national security in the context of foreign affairs, we reaffirm . . . that the President may constitutionally authorize warrantless wiretaps for the purpose of gathering foreign intelligence.").

36 *See infra* notes 37–39 and accompanying text.

37 *Youngstown*, 343 U.S. at 645–46 (Jackson, J., concurring).

38 *Wartime Executive Power and the National Security Agency's Surveillance Authority: Hearings Before the S. Comm. on the Judiciary*, 109th Cong. 1 (2006) (opening statement of Sen. Arlen Specter).

39 *Id.* at 58 (statement of Sen. Lindsay Graham).

40 Hamdi v. Rumsfeld, 542 U.S. 507, 581–82 (2004) (Thomas, I, dissenting) ("The Court has acknowledged that the President has the authority to 'employ [the Nation's Armed Forces]

As opposed to the Executive's broad grant of power in Article II, Section 1, Article I sets forth a few powers through which Congress may claim authority[41] Proponents of congressional power note that the Constitution provides Congress the power: "To declare War,"[42] "To raise and support Armies,"[43] "To provide and maintain a Navy,"[44] "To make Rules for the Government and Regulation of the land and naval Forces,"[45] and "To provide for calling forth the Militia to execute the Laws of the Union."[46] Congress further derives its authority from its power to conduct hearings,[47] as well as the power of the purse.[48] Through a combination of these enumerated powers, Congress has maintained a role in intelligence operations, albeit one periodically ignored by a disinterested Congress.

When interested, Congress has expressed this power through various approaches including hearings, investigations, legislation, and appropriations[49] Congressional participation, however, has been exclusively limited to oversight of intelligence operations; that is, "ensur[ing] that intelligence resources are not misused and that intelligence activities are conducted lawfully."[50] The actual execution of the operations has been reserved exclusively to the Executive.[51]

B. The Courts

In defending the NSA Surveillance program, the DOJ concluded that "the Supreme Court has consistently recognized the President's authority to conduct

in the manner he may deem most effectual to harass and conquer and subdue the enemy.'" (quoting Fleming v. Page, 50 U.S. 603, 615 (1850))).

41 U.S. Const, art. II, § 1; *see id.* art. I.

42 *Id.* art. I, § 8, cl. 11.

43 *Id.* art. I, § 8, cl. 12.

44 *Id.* art. I, § 8, cl. 13.

45 *Id.* art. I, § 8, cl. 14.

46 *Id.* art. I, § 8, cl. 15.

47 *See infra* notes 293-301 and accompanying text.

48 U.S. Const, art. I, § 8, cl. 1.

49 *See infra* Part V.

50 U.S. House of Representatives, Permanent Select Committee on Intelligence, About the Committee: Committee History, http://intelligence.house.gov/abouttheCommittee.aspx?Section=1 (last visited Jan. 25, 2007).

51 *See, e.g.*, Chi. & S. Air Lines, Inc. v. Waterman S.S. Corp., 333 U.S. 103 *passim* (1948) (recognizing the President's authority to determine which intelligence reports are published); Totten v. United States, 92 U.S. 105, 106 (1875) (recognizing the President's authority to hire spies).

intelligence activities."[52] This power is fairly settled.[53] Legal uncertainty arises, however, regarding the extent to which Congress may monitor, direct, and approve or disapprove such operations.[54] This issue, however, has never been squarely addressed by the judiciary.[55] The issue was, however, tangentially addressed in *Webster v. Doe,* a decision concerning the Administrative Procedure Act.[56] In a separate opinion, Justice O'Connor found: "The functions performed by the Central Intelligence Agency [(CIA)] and the Director of Central Intelligence [(DCI)] lie at the core of 'the very delicate, plenary and exclusive power of the President as the sole organ of the federal government in the field of international relations.'"[57]

The propriety of conducting intelligence operations domestically was tangentially addressed in *Laird v. Tatum,* where the United States Supreme Court examined an Army intelligence program directed at U.S. citizens.[58] The United States Court of Appeals for the District of Columbia Circuit, however, had addressed the scope of the executive in employing a domestic surveillance program run by the Army[59]

---

52 U.S. DEP'T OF JUSTICE, *supra* note 13, at 14 (citing Tenet v. Doe, 544 U.S. 1 (2005); *Chi. & S. Air Lines,* 333 U.S. at 111; United States v. Curtiss-Wright Exp. Corp., 299 U.S. 304, 320 (1936)).

53 Cumming, *supra* note 9, at 2 ("[A]s the head of the executive branch, the President generally is acknowledged to be 'the owner' of national intelligence."). For an extensive discussion of this power, see STEPHEN F. KNOTT, SECRET AND SANCTIONED: COVERT OPERATIONS AND THE AMERICAN PRESIDENCY 148-49 (1996); Russell J. Bruemmer, *Intelligence Community Reorganization: Declining the Invitation To Struggle,* 101 YALE L.J. 867, 878 (1992); William S. Cohen, *Congressional Oversight of Covert Actions: The Public s Stake in the Forty-Eight Hour Rule,* 12 HARV. J.L. & PUB. POL'Y 285, 294-95 (1989); Marcus Eyth, *The CIA and Covert Operations: To Disclose or Not To Disclose—That Is the Question,* 17 BYU J. PUB. L. 45, 45-47 (2002); Marshall Silverberg, *The Separation of Powers and Control of the CIA's Covert Operations,* 68 TEX. L. REV. 575, 609-13 (1990); and David Everett Colton, Comment, *Speaking Truth to Power: Intelligence Oversight in an Imperfect World,* 137 U. PA. L. REV. 571, 590-94 (1988).

54 *See* President George W. Bush, Press Conference of the President (Jan. 26, 2006) (transcript available at http://www.whitehouse.gov/news/releases/2006/01/20060126.html) ("I would say that there has been a historical debate between the executive branch and the legislative branch as to who's got what power.").

55 *See* Mendelsohn v. Meese, 695 F. Supp. 1474, 1483 (S.D.N.Y. 1988) ("We are aware of no case striking down federal legislation as an encroachment of the executive's authority to conduct foreign affairs. . . . There appears, therefore, no jurisprudence in this area, despite the existence of much legislation which has been criticized as an encroachment upon presidential authority to conduct foreign affairs."); *see also* National Security Act of 1947, Pub. L. No. 80-253, 61 Stat. 495 (establishing a comprehensive national security program, including the Department of Defense (DoD), Central Intelligence Agency (CIA), and National Security Counsel (NSC), and providing for congressional oversight of these agencies).

56 Webster v. Doe, 486 U.S. 592, 601 (1988); Administrative Procedure Act, 5 U.S.C. § 706 (2000).

57 *Webster,* 486 U.S. at 605–06 (O'Connor, J., concurring in part and dissenting in part) (quoting *Curtiss-Wright,* 299 U.S. at 320).

58 *See* Laird v. Tatum, 408 U.S. 1, 1-2 (1972).

59 *See* Tatum v. Laird, 444 F.2d 947, 947 (D.C. Cir. 1971), *rev'd,* 408 U.S. 1 (1972).

The court found that "[w]hen force is employed it should be intelligently directed, and this depends upon having reliable information—in time."[60] Continuing, the court concluded that it is "undeniable that the military . . . need[s] a certain amount of information in order to perform their constitutional and statutory missions."[61]

The issue presented on appeal to the Supreme Court was significantly more narrow; that is, whether "a complainant [may] allege[] that the exercise of his First Amendment rights [are] being chilled by the mere existence, without more, of a governmental investigative and data-gathering activity that is alleged to be broader in scope than is reasonably necessary for the accomplishment of a valid governmental purpose."[62] On appeal, the Supreme Court answered this question in the negative and did not address the broader issue of the propriety of the program.[63] Though, the court did acknowledge the sensitivity of the issue: "The concerns of the Executive and Legislative Branches in response to disclosure of the Army surveillance activities—and indeed the claims alleged in the complaint—reflect a traditional and strong resistance of Americans to any military intrusion into civilian affairs."[64] The case drew a harsh dissent authored by Justice Douglas and joined by Justice Marshall, which did focus on the propriety of the program.[65] The brunt of the critique focused on the domestic use of the military in any role, not just in an intelligence-specific role.[66] In closing, however, Justice Douglas issued a passionate defense of the Bill of Rights in the face of domestic surveillance:

> Army surveillance, like Army regimentation, is at war with the principles of the First Amendment. Those who already walk submissively will say there is no cause for alarm. But submissiveness is not our heritage. The First Amendment was designed to allow rebellion to remain as our heritage . . . The Bill of Rights was designed to keep agents of government and official eavesdroppers away from assemblies of people. The aim was to allow men to be free and independent and to assert their rights against government. There can be no influence more paralyzing of that objective than Army surveillance. When an intelligence officer looks over every nonconformist's shoulder in the library, or walks invisibly by his side in a picket line, or infiltrates his club, the America once extolled as the voice of liberty heard around the world no longer is cast

60 *Id.* at 952.

61 *Id.* at 953.

62 *Laird,* 408 U.S. at 10.

63 *See id.* at 15 ("We, of course, intimate no view with respect to the propriety or desirability, from a policy standpoint, of the challenged activities of the Department of the Army; our conclusion is a narrow one, namely, that on this record the respondents have not presented a case for resolution by the courts.").

64 *Id.*

65 *See id.* at 16 (Douglas, J., dissenting).

66 *See id.* at 19–20.

> in the image which Jefferson and Madison designed, but more in the Russian image, depicted in Appendix III to this opinion.[67]

Thus, while *Laird* did not squarely address the breadth of the power to conduct intelligence operations, it did invite increased public scrutiny and critique of the Intelligence Community's actions.[68]

III. THE INTELLIGENCE COMMUNITY GENERALLY

A. Pre-National Security Act of 1947

National leaders have conducted organized intelligence operations since the founding of the nation.[69] Early in the American Revolution, George Washington recognized the need for a system of secret communication and a network of spies.[70] Washington was not alone in his recognition of the importance of intelligence: Alexander Hamilton, John Jay, and Thomas Jefferson were all instrumental in securing support and funding for U.S. intelligence activities shortly after U.S. independence.[71] These four individuals were particularly instrumental in establishing both the need and viability of a coordinated U.S. intelligence effort, but were also critical in establishing the preeminence of the executive over the legislature in regard to the conduct of intelligence operations.[72]

The genesis of modern U.S. intelligence can be found in World War II.[73] On June 5, 1940, United States Army Intelligence, the United States Office of Naval Intelligence, and the Federal Bureau of Investigation (FBI) executed an agreement coordinating intelligence activities.[74] Shortly thereafter, under the direction of President Franklin Roosevelt, the FBI organized the Special Intelligence Service (SIS).[75] Dissatisfied with the SIS's intelligence and covert operations activities, President Roosevelt

---

67 *Id.* at 28–29.

68 *See, e.g.*, Fred P. Graham, *Court Bars Trial of Army over Civilian Surveillance,* N.Y. TIMES, June 27, 1972, at 1; Seymour M. Hersh, *Army Is Criticized on Civilian Spying,* N.Y. TIMES, Aug. 30, 1972, at 13.

69 *See* David M. Crane, *Divided We Stand: Counterintelligence Coordination Within the Intelligence Community of the United States,* ARMY LAW., Dec. 1995, at 26, 30 ("'There is one evil that I dread . . . and that is their spies. . . I think it a matter of some importance to prevent them from obtaining intelligence of our situation.'" (quoting Letter from George Washington to Josiah Quincy (Mar. 24, 1776), *in* THE PAPERS OF GEORGE WASHINGTON: 3 REVOLUTIONARY WAR SERIES 528, 529 (W.W. Abbot et al. eds., 1988))).

70 *See* KNOTT, *supra* note 53, at 15.

71 *See id.* at 27–48, 56–57.

72 *See id.*

73 *See generally* DAVID F. RUDGERS, CREATING THE SECRET STATE: THE ORIGINS OF THE CENTRAL INTELLIGENCE AGENCY, 1943–1947, at 149–80 (2000) (detailing the history of the CIA and its roots in World War II).

74 *Id.* at 7.

75 *See id.*

created the Office of Strategic Services (OSS) in 1942.[76] Falling under the ambit of the Joint Chiefs of Staff, the OSS was tasked with (1) research and analysis, (2) foreign espionage, and (3) counterespionage and security.[77]

Despite recognition of the need for a coordinated intelligence activity (and the resounding success of the OSS throughout World War II), President Harry Truman disbanded the OSS in 1945.[78] In 1946, President Truman created the Central Intelligence Group (CIG) and the National Intelligence Authority, which was established as a senior-level body tasked with coordinating, overseeing, and directing the CIG[79] With both the conclusion of World War II and the increasing tensions with the Soviet Union, senior government officials realized a need to restructure the entire defense establishment and centralize the Intelligence Community.[80] On July 26, 1947, President Truman signed the National Security Act of 1947 (National Security Act or Act)[81] and issued Executive Order 9877.[82]

B. National Security Act

The National Security Act sought "to provide a comprehensive program for the future security of the United States."[83] The Act created the Department of Defense (DoD), the CIA, and the National Security Council (NSC).[84] In effect, it created a national security super-structure under which the Intelligence Community was destined to operate.[85] The breadth of the Act was such that it provided no mandates concerning the composition or conduct of the Intelligence Community or its individual components.[86] As the focus was on defense generally, the intelligence

---

76 *See id.* at 10.

77 *See* Sherri J. Conrad, Note, *Executive Order 12,333: "Unleashing" the CIA Violates the Leash Law*, 70 Cornell L. Rev. 968, 969 (1985).

78 *See* Rudgers, *supra* note 73, at 43 (noting that Executive Order 9621 dissolved the OSS and temporarily folded its personnel into the United States Department of State as the Interim Research and Intelligence Service).

79 *See* John Prados, Presidents' Secret Wars: CIA and Pentagon Covert Operations from World War II Through the Persian Gulf 19 (Elephant Paperbacks 1996) (1986). Prados notes that the CIG had "no basis in the law of the land." *Id.* at 20. Thus the need for the restructuring that took the form of the National Security Act of 1947. *See id.*

80 *See id.*

81 National Security Act of 1947, Pub. L. No. 80-253, 61 Stat. 495 (codified as amended in scattered sections of 10 & 50 U.S.C.).

82 *See* Rudgers, *supra* note 73, at 148 (stating that Executive Order 9877 established "the missions of the armed services and nominat[ed]" James Forrestal, one of the principal authors of the National Security Act, as Secretary of Defense); Exec. Order No. 9877, 12 Fed. Reg. 5005 (July 29, 1947).

83 National Security Act of 1947 § 2, 61 Stat. at 496 (codified as amended at 50 U.S.C. § 401 (2000)).

84 *See id.* §§ 101-214, 61 Stat. at 496–507.

85 *See id.*

86 *See* Bruemmer, *supra* note 53, at 871.

aspects of the legislation were largely overlooked during the congressional debate concerning the Act.[87]

Through the ensuing decades, the Intelligence Community evolved with an assortment of agencies being created to fill an assortment of roles. The first major addition to the Intelligence Community came with the organization of the signals-intelligence discipline into the NSA in 1952.[88] Nine years later, the Defense Intelligence Agency (DIA) was organized under the DoD as part of an effort to consolidate and centralize military intelligence operations.[89] Presently, there are fifteen intelligence organizations comprising the Intelligence Community in addition to countless committees, councils, and offices associated with intelligence oversight and/or support.[90]

Anticipating complications arising from a vibrant, highly populated Intelligence Community, the Act created the position of the DCI.[91] It gave the DCI a host of

---

87 *See* RUDGERS, *supra* note 73, at 148 ("'One of the final steps before adjournment, largely overlooked in the avalanche of last-minute legislation, was the stamp of approval Congress placed on the creation, for the first time in American history, of an effective worldwide American intelligence service of its own.'" (quoting Samuel A. Tower, *Intelligence Net To Be World-Wide: For First Time in History This Country Plans an Effective and Permanent Service,* N. Y. TIMES, Aug. 3, 1947, at E5)); *see also* PRADOS, *supra* note 79, at 20 ("[M]ost congressmen concerned themselves mainly with those parts of the bill that were not about intelligence.").

88 *See* Memorandum from President Harry S. Truman to the Secretary of State and the Secretary of Defense, Communications Intelligence Activities (Oct. 24, 1952) (available at http://www.gwu.edu/~nsarchiv/NSAEBB/NSAEBB23/02-01.htm); *see also* NAT'L SEC. AGENCY/CENT. SEC. SERV. CTR. FOR CRYPTOLOGIC HISTORY, THE ORIGINS OF NSA, *available at* http://www.nsa.gov/publications/publi00015.cfm, *cited in* JEFFREY T. RICHELSON, THE U.S. INTELLIGENCE COMMUNITY 30-31 (4th ed. 1999) (describing Truman's top secret directive, which abolished the NSA's predecessor, the Armed Forces Security Agency, and created the NSA).

89 *See* DEP'T OF DEF., DIRECTIVE NO. 5105.21, DEFENSE INTELLIGENCE AGENCY 2-3 (Oct. 1, 1961); DEF. INTELLIGENCE AGENCY, DEFENSE INTELLIGENCE HISTORY 2007, at 2 (2007).

90 As defined by 50 U.S.C. § 401a(4) (2000), the Intelligence Community includes: the CIA; the DIA, under the DoD; NSA, under the DoD; the National Reconnaissance Office, under the DoD; Army Intelligence, under the DoD; the Office of Naval Intelligence, under the DoD; Air Force Intelligence, under the DoD; Marine Intelligence, under the DoD; the Bureau of Intelligence and Research, under the State Department; the Department of Energy; the Office of Intelligence Support, under the Department of the Treasury; the FBI, under the DOJ; staff elements of the DCI; the National Geospatial-Intelligence Agency, originally titled the National Imagery and Mapping Agency; and the Office of Intelligence and Analysis, under the Department of Homeland Security. On February 17, 2006, the Office of National Security Intelligence, an element of the Drug Enforcement Administration was designated as a member of the Intelligence Community, though this status is not yet reflected in the United States Code. News Release, Office of the Dir. of Nat'l Intelligence, Drug Enforcement Administration Element Becomes 16th Intelligence Community Member (Feb. 17, 2006) (available at http://www.dni.gov/press_releases/20060217_release.htm).

91 *See* 50 U.S.C. § 401a(4). The position, and accompanying responsibilities, are technically distinct from the duties and responsibilities of the Director of the CIA. *Compare id.* § 403–3 *with id.* § 403–1 (as currently dictated in the Act, the same individual has always been both the DCI and the Director of the CIA). In practice, said individual operates mainly as the DCI and delegates responsibility for the day-to-day operations of the CIA to the Deputy Director of

responsibilities including: (1) "as the primary [intelligence] advisor to the President and the NSC";[92] (2) for "[d]evelop[ing] ... objectives and guid[elines] for the Intelligence Community";[93] (3) "for production and dissemination of national foreign intelligence";[94] and (4) for coordinating with the Secretary of Defense to ensure no overlap of intelligence activities.[95]

It took little time for the CIA to assume this mandate and aggressively initiate operations throughout the world.[96] Indeed, all elements of the Intelligence Community quickly established themselves and remained very active through the early years of the Cold War.[97] From 1947 into the early 1970s, the Intelligence Community received little attention outside of the President, the NSC, and the other executive bodies charged with oversight or operation of intelligence activities.[98] Beginning in 1966, however, a series of events cast the Intelligence Community into the spotlight of public scrutiny.[99]

IV. INTELLIGENCE IMPROPRIETIES AND PUBLIC BACKLASH

The first public suggestion of intelligence impropriety came with a series of revelations of the United States Army surveilling antiwar dissidents.[100] Parallel reports implicated the FBI and CIA in similar activities.[101] The CIA was further implicated in the overthrow or attempted overthrow of a number of world leaders, including

---

the CIA. *See* RICHELSON, *supra* note 88, at 387–88. The role of the DCI was recently changed with the passage of the Intelligence Reform and Terrorism Prevention Act of 2004 (IRTPA), Pub. L. No. 108-458, §§ 1001–1020, 118 Stat. 3638, 3643–72 (codified in scattered sections of 50 U.S.C. (Supp. 2005)). *See also infra* notes 288-292 and accompanying text.

92 Exec. Order No. 12,333, 3 C.F.R. 200, 202 (1982), *reprinted as amended in* 50 U.S.C. § 401(2000).

93 *Id.* at 203.

94 *Id.*

95 *Id.* at 204.

96 *See* S. REP. No. 94-755 bk. 1, at 21–22 (1976). This report, known as the Church Committee Report, provides a very extensive overview of nearly all of the Intelligence Community activities ever undertaken by the United States. *See id.* at 48–57. The report focuses on occurrences dated after the conclusion of World War II. *Id.* at 1. The report addresses, in great detail, the efforts of the FBI and the CIA to spy on domestic antiwar groups throughout the course of the Vietnam War. *See id.* at 179–204. Discussion in this Article of this report is limited to the first three books.

97 *See generally* RICHELSON, *supra* note 88, at 30–31.

98 *See* KNOTT, *supra* note 53, at 160–61.

99 *See infra* Part IV.

100 *See generally* Paul M. Peterson, *Civilian Demonstrations Near the Military Installation: Restraints on Military Surveillance and Other Intelligence Activities*, 140 MIL. L. REV. 113, 117-18 (1993) (describing the history of Army intelligence operations during the Vietnam War era and the public's reaction to disclosure of the operations).

101 *See* S. REP. No. 94-757, bk. 1, at 179–81, 184 n.4, 185–87 (describing the CIA and FBI's covert funding of the National Student Association and the ensuing discovery by the American public).

Salvatore Allende in Chile,[102] Fidel Castro in Cuba,[103] Rafael Trujillo in the Dominican Republic,[104] and Patrice Lumumba in the Democratic Republic of the Congo.[105]

Public exposure to such activities played an absolutely critical role in bringing about congressional hearings, and later, congressionally mandated reform.[106] As the Church Committee[107] noted, "[i]n the few years prior to the establishment of this Committee . . . the public's awareness of the need to examine intelligence issues was heightened."[108] The Committee further noted:

> The consensus that had existed among the press, the informed public, the Congress, and the Executive branch and that had both supported and protected the CIA broke down. As conflicting policy preferences emerged and as misconduct in the Executive branch was revealed, the CIA, once exempt from public examination, became subject to close scrutiny.[109]

The importance of the following revelations cannot be overstated; they proved to be the impetus for what can only be described as a paradigm shift in how the public, and Congress, treated intelligence activities and organizations.

A. Vietnam

The first such revelation came in 1966, with a story in a small, liberal periodical entitled *Ramparts*.[110] The article disclosed that the CIA was operating a twenty-five-million-dollar project at Michigan State University, which, unbeknownst to most university officials and the American public in general, was designed to train South Vietnamese police.[111] Further, the article disclosed that a large cache of weapons associated with the program were at the time being stockpiled at the university.[112]

---

102 *See id.* at 54, 64.

103 *Id.* at 25.

104 *Id.*

105 *See* John M. Oseth, Regulating U.S. Intelligence Operations: A Study in Definition of the National Interest 59–60 (1985).

106 *See* S. Rep. No. 94-757, bk. 1, at 185–88 (describing the discovery of the CIA's funding of the National Student Association, the Katzenbach Committee, and the ensuing reforms).

107 So called because Senator Frank Church was the Chairman of the Senate Select Committee that authored the report. *See id.* at (II).

108 *Id.* at 11.

109 *Id.* at 122.

110 *See* Angus Mackenzie, Secrets: The CIA'S War at Home 16-19(1997) (citing Warren Hinckle, Robert Scheer & Sol Stern, *Michigan State: The University on the Make,* Ramparts, Apr. 1966, at 80 (with an introduction by Stanley K. Scheinbaum)).

111 *See id.*

112 *See id.* at 16.

Upon publication, the article caused such public outcry that President Lyndon Johnson established a task force comprised of cabinet-level officials to ensure the government did not violate "the integrity of the educational community."[113] CIA's Director of Security, Howard J. Osborn, was secretly assigned the responsibility of investigating *Ramparts* and keeping tabs on the magazine.[114] The *Ramparts* article shattered the illusion of an intelligence structure operating without fault in the name of national security.[115] The impact of the article was such that it was the only article referenced by name in the Church Committee report as an impetus for changing public sentiment and increasing public scrutiny of the Intelligence Community.[116]

A similar effect was felt after the publication of another magazine article in 1970 detailing domestic Army intelligence operations directed against the civil rights movement.[117] This article detailed a program that began in the late 1950s and continued through the 1960s.[118] At the outset, the program was directed at collecting intelligence against leaders in the civil rights movement; however, as the Vietnam War progressed and antiwar activities intensified, the Army shifted its focus to the antiwar movement.[119] During this time, the Army took steps to collect a wide range of information, including personal and political information concerning the individuals and the groups involved.[120] The public reaction led to congressional investigations into Army intelligence activities with the Senate subcommittee subsequently finding the Army's activities to be illegal.[121]

The full extent of the Army's antiwar activities did not become fully known until the hearings by the Church Committee in 1975.[122] At the hearings, reams of information exposed the Army's clandestine operations against antiwar activists, as well as similar operations conducted by the CIA (Operation CHAOS) and the FBI

113 *See id.* at 18.

114 *See id.* at 17–19.

115 *See* S. Rep. No. 94-757, bk. 1, at 10.

116 *See id.* ("During the last eight years, beginning with *Ramparts* magazine's exposure of CIA covert relationships with non-governmental organizations, there has been a series of allegations in the press and Congress which have provoked serious questions about the conduct of intelligence agencies at home and abroad.").

117 *See* Christopher H. Pyle, *CONUS Intelligence: The Army Watches Civilian Politics*, Wash. Monthly, Jan. 1970, at 4, *cited in* Peterson, *supra* note 100, at 118.

118 *See* Pyle, *supra* note 117, at 4.

119 *See* Peterson, *supra* note 100, at 117.

120 *See id.*

121 *See* Staff of the Subcomm. on Constitutional Rights of the S. Comm. on the Judiciary, 93d. Cong., Report on Military Surveillance of Civilian Politics 7 (Comm. Print 1973), *reviewed by* Peterson, *supra* note 100, at 118.

122 *See* S. Rep. No. 94-757, bk. II, at 66, 77, 84–85.

(Operation COINTELPRO).[123] All told, these three entities had files on more than 400,000 individuals and 100 domestic organizations.[124] The substantial size of these domestic intelligence operations coupled with the invasive means and methods utilized by the respective agencies proved a major emphasis of reform for the Church Committee.[125] Naturally, the public's response was tempered by the fact that these allegations did not surface until reform efforts were well underway.

B. The *New York Times* and the *Washington Post*

The public's reaction to Watergate, however, was markedly different.[126] On June 17, 1972, five men were arrested while attempting to break into the Democratic National Party headquarters at the Watergate building in Washington, D.C.[127] This event, of course, eventually led to President Nixon's resignation. Of concern to the Intelligence Community were the substantial connections between the break-in and the CIA.[128] Veterans of the Bay of Pigs-operation were involved, as were two individuals employed by or related to the CIA.[129]

Though association with Watergate was damning enough, the CIA's improprieties were seen not simply as misguided, but characteristic of a larger problem within the executive branch and the Intelligence Community. As noted by the Church Committee: "The Watergate disclosures raised additional questions concerning abuse of power by the executive branch, misuse of intelligence agencies, and the need to strengthen legal restraints against such abuses."[130] The impact was immediate and pervasive as to both the public and Congress, which convened twenty-eight days of congressional hearings.[131]

On the proverbial heels of the *Washington Post's* Watergate exposé came yet another damning news article.[132] On December 22, 1974, Seymour Hersh published a story

---

123 *See id.* at 10, 66, 77, 84–89, 99–102, 170, 211–16.

124 *Id.* at 6–7.

125 *See id.* at 5–21, 297–307, 310–12, 316–32.

126 *See* Jim Hougan, Secret Agenda: Watergate, Deep Throat, and the CIA, at xv–xvi (1984).

127 Carl Bernstein & Bob Woodward, All the President's Men 13 (1974).

128 *See* Hougan, *supra* note 126 (detailing the CIA's involvement), *discussed in* Phil Stanford, *Watergate—Was It Really a Sex Scandal,* Chi. Sun-Times, Mar. 30, 1986, at 40.

129 *See* Prados, *supra* note 79, at 324. Of particular controversy was the connection with Howard E. Hunt, a critical figure in the Watergate scandal. *See id.* Prados also notes the agency was found to have supplied "certain psychological profiles of Americans at the request of the White House." *Id.*

130 *See* S. Rep. No. 94-757, bk. II, at 10.

131 *See* Frank J. Smist, Jr., Congress Oversees the United States Intelligence Community: 1947–1994, at 148–49 (2d ed. 1994); *see also Misusing the CIA: A Final Report,* NY. Times, Nov. 4, 1973, § 4, at 2.

132 *See* Knott, *supra* note 53, at 165.

on the front page of the *New York Times* entitled "Huge CIA. Operation Reported in U.S. Against Antiwar Forces, Other Dissidents in Nixon Years."[133] Though some commentators have characterized the allegations made in the article as "vastly overstated,"[134] this was largely moot as the article created "'a press and political firestorm.'"[135] The validity of the allegations contained in the article quickly became a nonissue, as the article further devastated the public's perception of the CIA—and, more generally, their trust and confidence in the Intelligence Community as a whole.[136]

Thus, at the outset of 1975, the Intelligence Community found itself under increased public and congressional scrutiny. As detailed above, this was heretofore an unknown situation for the Intelligence Community[137] Since the establishment of the CIA in 1947, the Community enjoyed virtually unlimited amounts of respect and secrecy.[138] As the veil of secrecy was ripped away by the Church Committee, both public and congressional respect quickly evaporated.[139]

V. CONGRESSIONAL OVERSIGHT

Despite the diffuse nature of the Community, all agencies and organizations are subject to roughly the same oversight and regulation. Broadly stated, oversight mechanisms originate in either the executive or legislature. The executive exercises oversight though the use of Executive Orders, directives, and organization oversight mechanisms.[140] The legislature oversees intelligence operations though a combination of legislation, appropriations, and hearings; the legislative oversight is of primary concern in this Article.

133 Seymour M. Hersh, *Huge CIA. Operation Reported in U.S. Against Antiwar Forces, Other Dissidents in Nixon Years*, N.Y. Times, Dec. 22, 1974, at 1.

134 Knott, *supra* note 53, at 165.

135 *See* Prados, *supra* note 79, at 327 (quoting William Colby).

136 *See id.* at 326–27.

137 *See id.* at 332.

138 *See id.*

139 *See id.* at 326.

140 *See* Crane, *supra* note 69, at 30. Organizational oversight mechanisms refer primarily to each agency's Inspector General's office. This internal, independent office provides an "in house" check on activities. Further, organizations which come within the ambit of larger organizations are overseen by their Inspector General's office. *See* Inspector General Act of 1978 § 3, 5 U.S.C. app. 3 (2000). For instance, the DIA is a DoD Agency. Thus, DIA actions are implicitly overseen by the DoD General Counsel, Inspector General, and so on. *See* Def. Intelligence Agency, Introduction to DIA, http://www.dia.mil/ thisisdia/intro/index.htm (last visited Jan. 27, 2007); U.S. Dep't of Def., Office of Inspector Gen., Office of Deputy Inspector General for Intelligence, http://www.dodig.osd.mil/Ir/index. html (last visited Jan. 27, 2007).

A. Legislation

1. Pre-Church Committee

Prior to the passage of the National Security Act, intelligence and counterintelligence oversight functions were largely confined within the executive branch.[141] Though the Act marked the start of formal congressional involvement,[142] oversight functions of the Intelligence Community continued to be largely controlled by the President and the NSC.[143] Indeed, the Executive went to great lengths to self-regulate in an effort to forestall congressional intervention.[144]

The Act provides a loose foundation for all congressional regulation and oversight.[145] The Act was designed "to provide a comprehensive program for the future security of the United States."[146] In respect to the intelligence aspects of the Act, however, the provisions are exceptionally vague and noticeably devoid of regulations governing the structure and operation of components within the Intelligence Community.[147] Of particular note is the absence of a direct mandate to collect intelligence.[148] The CIA assumed this purpose to be inherent and engaged in numerous collection activities absent an express mandate authorizing such actions.[149] The ability of the CIA to collect foreign intelligence was not formally recognized until the report of the Church Committee.[150] Indeed, the Church Committee itself found that as of 1976, the Act provided an insufficient "framework for the conduct of America's intelligence activities."[151]

---

141 *See* CRANE, *supra* note 69, at 30.

142 *See id.*

143 *See* RUDGERS, *supra* note 73, at 149–80.

144 In a Congressional Research Service Report to Congress entitled *Proposals for Intelligence Reorganization, 1949–2004,* Richard A. Best, Jr., notes that President Eisenhower created the President's Board of Consultants on Foreign Intelligence Activities "to preempt closer congressional scrutiny of intelligence gathering." RICHARD A. BEST, JR., PROPOSALS FOR INTELLIGENCE REORGANIZATION, 1949–2004, at 12 (2004), *available at* http://www.fas.org/irp/crs/RL32500.pdf. On January 7, 1975, President Gerald Ford signed Executive Order 11,828 establishing a commission to investigate the above discussed relations of intelligence impropriety. Exec. Order No. 11,828, 3 C.F.R. 933 (1975).

145 *See* National Security Act of 1947, Pub. L. No. 80-253, §101, 61 Stat. 495, 496 (codified as amended at 50 U.S.C. § 401 (2000)).

146 *Id.*

147 *See id.* §§ 101-311, 61 Stat. at 495–510.

148 *See* CONRAD, *supra* note 77, at 970 ("[T]he [National Security Act] does not explicitly mention intelligence collection. . . .").

149 *See id.*

150 *See* S. REP. No. 94-757, bk. 1, at 127–28 ("[N]owhere does it specify that the [CIA] is authorized to engage in the direct collection of intelligence. . . . [However,] the Act can legitimately be construed as authorizing clandestine collection by the CIA.").

151 *See id.* at 426.

However, the Act does provide some degree of guidance. For instance, it empowers the CIA "to correlate and evaluate intelligence relating to the national security, and provide for the appropriate dissemination of such intelligence within the Government using where appropriate existing agencies and facilities."[152] The Act further defines the role of the CIA by prohibiting the Agency from acting with "police" or "law-enforcement powers" or from engaging in "internal-security functions."[153]

In regard to the Intelligence Community, the Act does not define or mention it.[154] The Act does provide that "the departments and other agencies of the Government shall continue to collect, evaluate, correlate, and disseminate departmental intelligence."[155] In regard to coordination of intelligence activities, it established the position of the DCI,[156] but "fail[ed] to address specifically the DCI's authority to lead and direct the Intelligence Community."[157] Beyond these provisions, the Act fails to provide any guidance to the Intelligence Community. Thus, an unbroken succession of Presidents has capitalized on this and sought to fill the gaps through a variety of presidential mechanisms.[158]

The first congressional foray into intelligence oversight after the Act came two years later with the final report of the Task Force on National Security Organization, which was organized in 1947 under the broader mandate of the Commission on Organization of the Executive Branch.[159] This task force and accompanying report, however, focused on an institutional review of the Intelligence Community rather than a review of the oversight role of Congress.[160] The Second Commission on Organization of the Executive Branch (commonly known as the Clark Task Force), organized four years later and squarely addressed the issue.[161] The Clark Task Force

152 National Security Act of 1947, Pub. L. No. 80-253, § 102(d)(3), 61 Stat. 495, 498 (codified as amended at 50 U.S.C. § 403-4a (2000)).

153 *See id.*

154 Bruemmer, *supra* note 53, at 871 ("The Intelligence Community has little statutory basis. It is not defined, or even mentioned, in the National Security Act of 1947.").

155 Pub. L. No. 80-253, § 102(d)(3), 61 Stat. at 498 (codified as amended at 50 U.S.C. § 403-4a).

156 *See id.* § 102(a), 61 Stat. at 497.

157 Bruemmer, *supra* note 53, at 872.

158 Most notably Executive Order 12,333 signed by President Reagan on December 4,1981, with a simple mandate: to provide the United States with "the best intelligence available." Exec. Order 12,333,3 C.F.R. 200, 200 (1982), *reprinted as amended in* 50 U.S.C. § 401. This order seeks to facilitate the collection of information by allowing autonomy of the Intelligence Community while providing a structure for oversight and coordination. This order remains in effect and continues to provide the principal body of rules regulating the Intelligence Community. *See id.*

159 *See* Best, *supra* note 144, at 4 (citing Comm'n on Org. of the Executive Branch of the Gov't, The Hoover Commission Report on Organization of the Executive Branch of the Government (1949)).

160 *See id.* at 4–6.

161 *See id.* at 8–9.

"foresaw the need for better oversight of intelligence activities and proposed a small . . . bipartisan commission, including Members of Congress and other 'public-spirited citizens,' to provide independent oversight of intelligence activities."[162]

Buoyed by findings of the Clark Task Force, in 1955 Senator Mike Mansfield introduced a bill designed to comprehensively regulate the Intelligence Community[163] However, the Intelligence Subcommittee of the Senate Armed Services Committee, with the support of President Eisenhower, ensured that the bill was soundly defeated.[164] President Eisenhower used this opportunity to forestall congressional intervention by implementing recommendations found in the Clark task-force report and establishing the President's Board of Consultants on Foreign Intelligence Activities.[165] Under the guise of assisting by not interfering, the Intelligence Subcommittee provided very little, if any, constructive oversight in the ensuing decades.[166]

Not surprisingly, the heyday of the Cold War proved a ripe time for intelligence operations.[167] Indeed it was largely operations conducted during this time that served as the impetus for later congressional hearings.[168] In response to a changing political climate in the United States (post-Vietnam) and later in response to the above-detailed revelations, intelligence oversight became a topic of increasing public concern and, thus, political concern.[169] Congress reasserted its control over

162 *Id.* at 9 (quoting COMM'N ON ORG. OF THE EXECUTIVE BRANCH OF THE GOV'T, INTELLIGENCE ACTIVITIES: A REPORT TO THE CONGRESS 71 (1955)).

163 *See* PRADOS, *supra* note 79, at 327.

164 *See id.* at 327–28.

165 *See id.* In 1961 this organization became the President's Foreign Intelligence Advisory Board. *See id.* at 327–29. This organization, comprised of private citizens, still exists and "provides advice to the President concerning the quality and adequacy of intelligence collection, of analysis and estimates, of counterintelligence, and of other intelligence activities." The White House, President's Foreign Intelligence Advisory Board, http://www.whitehouse.gov/pfiab/ (last visited Jan. 27, 2007) [hereinafter PFIAB].

166 *See* PRADOS, *supra* note 79, at 327–28. Between 1955 and 1964 the subcommittee was briefed an average of two times per year. *Id.* In 1965, the congressional intelligence-oversight apparatus was restructured. The successor committees tasked with intelligence oversight were briefed between 1965 and 1974 as follows: The Senate Armed Services Committee (SASC), three times a year; the House Armed Services Committee (HASC), four times a year; and the Senate Appropriations Committee (SAC), four times a year. *Id.* at 329; *see also* L. BRETT SNIDER, SHARING SECRETS WITH LAWMAKERS: CONGRESS AS A USER OF INTELLIGENCE (1997) ("As late as 1968, for example, CIA records reflect only one briefing that year to the HASC, three to the [House Appropriations Committee], and two each to the SASC and SAC. Attendance typically was limited to Members only, and often no record of the proceedings was kept. Sometimes, reportedly, no questions were asked at all.").

167 *See, e.g.*, PRADOS, *supra* note 79, at 32–33.

168 *See* S. REP. No. 94-757, bk. 1, at 22–27.

169 *See generally* KNOTT, *supra* note 53, at 164 (discussing the idea that the mid-1970s ushered in a new era of legislators eager to avoid the missteps of the Vietnam War by increasing transparency between Congress and the intelligence organization).

the Intelligence Community in 1974 with the passage of the Hughes-Ryan Amendment (Hughes-Ryan)[170] to the Foreign Assistance Act of 1961.[171]

Hughes-Ryan requires that before a covert action is undertaken, the President must make a "find[ing]" that ensures the activities are "important to the national security of the United States."[172] Further, Hughes-Ryan requires congressional notification of such activities.[173] A series of subsequent amendments passed shortly thereafter further limited the President's power to initiate covert operations in specific countries.[174] As discussed below, the reporting requirements of Hughes-Ryan were amended in 1981 and again in 1991.[175]

The requirement placed on the President to report certain intelligence activities to Congress is of particular importance in the instant issue regarding the NSA program. The debate will likely turn on the definition of the program as covert or noncovert.[176] At least one commentator has questioned the President's designation of the program as covert.[177] This in turn would determine the appropriate reporting requirements: if found to be noncovert, the program should be reported to the full committees. Though, it should be noted that the President's broad claims of executive power could easily encompass a claim against any reporting requirement.[178]

---

170 *See* Hughes-Ryan Amendment, Foreign Assistance Act of 1974, Pub. L. No. 93-559, § 32, 88 Stat. 1795, 1804 (codified at 22 U.S.C. §§ 2422-2423 (1976)), *repealed by* Pub. L. No. 102-88, 105 Stat. 429 (1991).

171 Foreign Assistance Act of 1961, Pub. L. No. 87-195, 75 Stat. 424 (codified as amended in scattered sections of 22 U.S.C. (2000)).

172 *See* Hughes-Ryan § 32, 88 Stat. at 1804, *repealed by* Pub. L. No. 102-88, 103 Stat. 429 (1991).

173 *See id.*

174 *See* Boland Amendment, Intelligence Authorization Act for Fiscal Year 1984, Pub. L. No. 98-215, § 108, 97 Stat. 1473, 1475 (limiting funding to the rebels in Nicaragua); Clark Amendment, International Security Assistance and Arms Export Control Act of 1976, Pub. L. No. 94-329, § 404, 90 Stat. 729, 757-58 (codified at 22 U.S.C. § 2293 note (1982)) (prohibiting assistance to paramilitary activity in Angola); Tunney Amendment, Department of Defense Appropriation Act of 1976, Pub. L. No. 94-212, tit. IV, 90 Stat. 153, 160-66 (codified at 40 U.S.C. § 255 (1982)) (prohibiting expenditure of funds for intelligence operations in Angola).

175 *See infra* notes 266–270 and accompanying text.

176 Covert actions are defined as activities designed "to influence political, economic, or military conditions abroad, where it is intended that the role of the United States Government will not be apparent or acknowledged publicly." Intelligence Authorization Act, Fiscal Year 1991, 50 U.S.C. § 413b(e) (2000).

177 *See* Alfred Cumming, Statutory Procedures Under Which Congress Is To Be Informed of U.S. Intelligence Activities, Including Covert Actions 7 (2006), *available at* http://www.epic.org/privacy/terrorism/fisa/crsll806.pdf ("Based upon publicly reported descriptions of the program, the NSA surveillance program would appear to fall more closely under the definition of an intelligence collection program, rather than qualify as a cover action program as defined by statute.").

178 *See* U.S. Dep't of Justice, *supra* note 13, at 30 ("Moreover, it is clear that some presidential authorities in this context are beyond Congress's ability to regulate.").

2. Church Committee

Reacting to Hersh's article, President Ford publicly "declared his administration would not tolerate illegal activities by intelligence agencies."[179] On January 4, 1975, President Ford established a commission, headed by Vice President Nelson Rockefeller, to investigate domestic CIA intelligence operations.[180] The Rockefeller Commission made numerous suggestions, including: (1) amending the CIA's charter to clarify that the CIAs activities were limited to matters of foreign intelligence, (2) signing an Executive Order prohibiting the CIA from conducting intelligence operations against U.S. citizens, (3) dividing intelligence regulation between the President and Congress, (4) retooling intelligence oversight, (5) constraining "intrusive" intelligence methodology, and (6) limiting human testing.[181]

On February 18, 1976, shortly after the Rockefeller Commission issued its report, President Ford issued Executive Order 11,905,[182] the first publicly known regulation concerning the operation and function of the Intelligence Community.[183] Predictably, President Ford's order echoed the findings of the Rockefeller Commission: the order continued the internal CIA prohibition on assassinations, created a number of entities designed to coordinate intelligence operations, limited human experimentation, and redefined covert operations.[184]

As one commentator noted, Executive Order 11,905 was not "an act of executive contrition."[185] It unequivocally sought to strengthen the intelligence capabilities of the United States in favor of the executive.[186] It also established a host of organizations designed to help facilitate intelligence gathering, coordination, and noncongressional oversight.[187] In short, President Ford's order made legitimate strides in clarifying and framing the powers of the Intelligence Community.[188]

179 *See* Prados, *supra* note 79, at 333 (quoting President Ford).

180 *See* Oseth, *supra* note 105, at 72 (citing Exec. Order No. 11,828,40 Fed. Reg. 1219 (Jan. 7, 1975)).

181 *See id.* at 85–87.

182 Exec. Order No. 11,905, 3 C.F.R. 90 (1977).

183 *See* Prados, *supra* note 79, at 349.

184 *See* Exec. Order No. 11,905, 3 C.F.R. 90, 101 (1977); Knott, *supra* note 53, at 171 (stating the prohibition of assassination likely came in response to the significant emphasis placed by the Church Committee on investigating the Castro assassination attempts); Richelson, *supra* note 88, at 375.

185 Oseth, *supra* note 105, at 92.

186 *See id.* at 92–93.

187 *Id.* at 93–95. The order created the following organizations: the Committee on Foreign Intelligence, the Operations Advisory Group, and the Intelligence Oversight Board. *See id;* Exec. Order No. 11, 905, 3 C.F.R. 90, 101 (1977).

188 *See* Oseth, *supra* note 105, at 93–95.

Critics point out, however, that President Ford's order merely reflected a desire "to protect ... presidential powers."[189]

President Ford's actions did not temper congressional intervention. Twelve days after the appointment of Rockefeller, Representative Michael Harrington introduced a resolution that would "create a select committee to investigate the [I]ntelligence [C]ommunity"[190] This was the genesis of the first substantive congressional participation in intelligence oversight since the National Security Act, and it marked what can only be described as a sea of change in congressional oversight of intelligence operations.[191] Accordingly, the Church Committee and the corresponding House Select Committee on Intelligence, known as the Pike Committee, were organized in 1975.[192]

Whereas previous congressional attempts to regulate the Intelligence Community proved incomplete, the Church Committee marked a watershed of congressional oversight and regulation. L. Britt Snider, former General Counsel of the Senate Select Committee on Intelligence and Inspector General of the CIA, summarized the importance of the Church Committee by dividing congressional oversight into two periods: before the Church Committee and after the Church Committee.[193] Operating under a broad mandate fueled by public backlash, the Church Committee sought to inquire into a myriad of intelligence functions and activities.[194] After fifteen months of investigation, the Church Committee announced their findings in a six-volume report, which was released on April 14, 1976.[195] The report detailed investigations into every element of the U.S. intelligence establishment, which included: foreign and military intelligence operations;[196] the constitutional framework

---

189 *Id.* at 102.

190 Smist, *supra* note 131, at 134. This resolution would later become the Nedzi Committee and then, finally, the Pike Committee. *Id.* at 134–38.

191 *See* Prados, *supra note 19,* at 348.

192 *See* Smist, *supra* note 131, at 136–37; S. Rep. No. 94-757, bk. 1, at (III). "The inquiry arose out of allegations of substantial, even massive wrong-doing within the 'national intelligence' system." *Id.* at 1. The effectiveness of the Pike Committee was grossly degraded by institutional infighting; thus, the Church Committee had a greater impact on the reassertion of congressional participation in intelligence oversight. In evaluating both the Nedzi and Pike Committees, Frank Smist has characterized both as committees plagued by "failures whose significance has still not been fully appreciated." Smist, *supra* note 131, at 211. In addition to internal institutional failings, Smist identifies interference from the executive as a major cause for failure. *See id.* at 213. He notes, "the executive branch went out of its way to hinder, frustrate, and ultimately destroy the House investigation." *Id.*

193 Silverberg, *supra* note 53, at 622 (citing *Remarks ofL. Britt Snider,* 11 Hous. J. Int'l L. 47, 48(1988)).

194 *See* S. Rep. No. 94-757, bk. 1, at 2–4.

195 *Id.* at (I), (III).

196 *Id.* at 15–30.

for intelligence activities;[197] the roles of the President and the DCI;[198] covert action;[199] counterintelligence;[200] use of intelligence proprietaries;[201] intelligence activities of the DoD,[202] the Department of State,[203] and FBI;[204] and the domestic intelligence operations.[205]

The domestic "misdeeds" of the Intelligence Community disclosed by the Church Committee included: the CIA's index of nearly 1.5 million names taken from letter openings; the CIA's files on more than 7200 American citizens and 100 domestic groups; the NSA's interception of "[m]illions" of telegrams; the United States Army's files on 100,000 American citizens; and the intelligence activities of those agencies directed at groups, including the Women's Liberation Movement, the Conservative American Christian Action Council, the John Birch Society, the NAACP, the Socialist Workers Party, Students for a Democratic Society, "'every Black Student Union'" in the country, and the New Left.[206] The Church committee labeled the most extensive counterintelligence program, the FBI's COINTELPRO, a "covert action," that is, an action designed "to influence political choices and social values."[207] The FBI devoted tremendous resources to COINTELPRO, attempting to protect national security by spying on, and interfering with, groups such as the U.S. Communist Party, the Socialist Workers Party, the White Hate Group, the Black Nationalist-Hate Group, and the New Left.[208]

Perhaps most disturbing were the revelations regarding the Civil Rights Movement. The NAACP, for instance, was investigated by the FBI over a period of twenty-five years.[209] Dr. Martin Luther King, Jr., was investigated from 1963 until his death in 1968.[210] The FBI saw Dr. King as a "'messiah'" who had the

197 *Id.* at 31–40.

198 *Id.* at 41–96.

199 *Id.* at 141–62.

200 *Id.* at 163–78.

201 *Id.* at 205–56. Proprieties in this context includes, for instance, the use of government-created corporations in intelligence operations. *Id.*

202 *Id.* at 319–66.

203 *Id.* at 305–18.

204 *See generally id.* bks. 1-3 passim.

205 *Id.* bk. II.

206 *Id.*

207 *See id.* bk. 3, at 4.

208 *See id*

209 *Id.* bk. 2, at 8.

210 *Id.* at 116.

potential to lead a "'black nationalist movement.'"[211] Seeing a threat, the FBI sought to "'neutralize'" Dr. King "as an effective civil rights leader."[212]

The foreign intelligence "misdeeds" catalogued by the Church Committee included inappropriate use of academic, voluntary, religious, and media organizations.[213] After wading through hundreds of CIA covert operations and proposed operations, the report found the use of covert operations to have been more than "an exceptional instrument used only in rare instances."[214] The most damning disclosures to the Intelligence Community were the revelations concerning the CIA's involvement in the assignation or overthrow of a number of world leaders.[215] It is not difficult to see why Senator Frank Church famously characterized the CIA as a "'rogue elephant.'"[216]

Though thoroughly critical of the executive, the committee was no less rigorous themselves. Among the many formal conclusions, the committee found:

> Congress, which has the authority to place restraints on domestic intelligence activities through legislation, appropriations, and oversight committees, has not effectively asserted its responsibilities until recently. . . .
>
> . . . .
>
> Congress has failed to establish precise standards governing domestic intelligence. . . .
>
> . . . .
>
> Congress has helped shape the environment in which improper intelligence activities were possible. . . .
>
> . . . .
>
> During most of the 40-year period covered in this report, congressional committees did not effectively monitor domestic intelligence activities.[217]

This introspective examination differs markedly from recent congressional investigations.[218]

3. Post-Church Committee

In 1976 and 1977, on recommendation of the Church and Pike Committees, the Senate Select Committee on Intelligence (SSCI) and the House Permanent Select

211 *See id.*

212 *See id.*

213 *See id.* bk. 1, at 181–203, 451–55.

214 *See id.* at 425.

215 *See supra* notes 102-105 and accompanying text.

216 *See* OSETH, *supra* note 105, at 59.

217 S. REP. No. 94-757, bk. 2, at 277–78.

218 Such as the congressional investigation into the events of 9/11. *See* S. REP. No. 107-351, H.R. REP. No. 107-792 (2002); *see also infra* notes 323–325 and accompanying text.

Committee on Intelligence (HPSCI) were established.[219] In 1979, Congress reorganized intelligence appropriations and required intelligence agencies to seek funding in the same manner as other federal agencies.[220] These congressional committees presently oversee all agencies within the Intelligence Community.[221] Of these agencies, only the CIA was created by statute and only the CIA reports directly to the President.[222] The remaining organizations were created by their respective departments and report directly to the same.[223]

Following the establishment of the intelligence-oversight committees, Congress attempted to pass omnibus legislation to completely reorganize and reform intelligence operations.[224] This legislation, however, "was strongly criticized from all sides in hearings; some arguing that it would legitimize covert actions inconsistent with American ideals and others suggesting that its complex restrictions would unduly hamper the protection of vital American interests."[225]

Support was found, however, in a smaller subset of the omnibus legislation concerning foreign intelligence surveillance.[226] The Church Committee expressly addressed this issue, noting "that every President since Franklin D. Roosevelt asserted the authority to authorize warrantless electronic surveillance and exercised that authority."[227] Addressing these concerns, the Senate Judiciary Committee, in their report accompanying the proposed legislation, noted the Church Committee found "firm evidence that foreign intelligence electronic surveillances involved abuses and that checks upon the exercise of these clandestine methods were clearly necessary."[228] Thus, in 1978, the President signed into law FISA, which provides the statutory framework governing the electronic collection of foreign intelligence.[229]

---

219 HPSCI was established by H.R. Res. 658, 95th Cong., 123 Cong. Rec. 22,932 (1977), and SSCI was established by S. Res. 400, 94th Cong., 122 Cong. Rec. 4754 (1976).

220 Intelligence and Intelligence-Related Activities Authorization Act for Fiscal Year 1979, Pub. L. No. 95-370, 92 Stat. 626; *see* BRUEMMER, *supra* note 53, at 874; Note, *The CIA's Secret Funding and the Constitution,* 84 YALE L.J. 608, 616–19 (1975) (describing the funding procedures of the CIA before the Intelligence and Intelligence-Related Activities Authorization Act for Fiscal Year 1979).

221 *See* RICHELSON, *supra* note 88, at 74–75, 453.

222 *See* BRUEMMER, *supra* note 53, at 872.

223 *See id.*

224 *See* National Intelligence Reorganization and Reform Act of 1978, S. 2525, 95th Cong. (1978); National Intelligence Reorganization and Reform Act of 1978, H.R. 11,245, 95th Cong. (1978).

225 BEST, *supra* note 144, at 26.

226 *See infra* notes 229–232 and accompanying text.

227 S. REP. No. 95-604, pt. I, at 7 (1978), *as reprinted in* 1978 U.S.C.CA.N. 3904, 3908 (referring to the Church Committee report).

228 S. REP. No. 95-701, at 9 (1978), as reprinted in 1978 U.S.C.C.A.N. 3973, 3977.

229 Foreign Intelligence Surveillance Act of 1978, Pub. L. No. 95-511, 92 Stat. 1783 (codified as amended in scattered sections of 50 U.S.C. (2000)).

FISA directed that the collection of electronic foreign intelligence need not be supported by a traditional warrant, but rather only authorization from the Foreign Intelligence Surveillance Court—established by the same legislation.[230] FISA remained largely unchanged until the events of 9/11,[231] when the USA PATRIOT Act significantly amended FISA.[232]

The early 1980s marked a time of further international unrest. International acts of terrorism rose from 1980 until 1987.[233] International groups, such as the Baader-Meinhof Gang (or Group and also known as the Red Army Faction), the Italian Red Brigades, and the Palestine Liberation Front, focused a great deal of their terror on American allies.[234] Acts, such as the kidnapping of General James L. Dozier in 1981 by the Italian Red Brigades, the hijacking of the ACHILLE LAURO in 1985 by the Palestine Liberation Front, the hijacking of TWA flight 847 in 1985, and the bombing of the La Belle disco in West Berlin in 1986, all garnered a great deal of publicity in the American press.[235] These events, along with the Soviet invasion of Afghanistan in 1979 and the bombing of the U.S. Marine Barracks in Beirut in 1983, facilitated an intelligence/military friendly environment.[236] This climate,

230 *See* 50 U.S.C. § 1803(a).

231 Before these events, FISA had been only slightly amended. *See* Intelligence Authorization Act for Fiscal Year 1999, Pub. L. No. 105-272, § 603, 112 Stat. 2396, 2412 (codified at 50 U.S.C. § 1801 note) (amending FISA to provide for FISA court orders on a wider range of intelligence techniques; such as pen registers, trap and trace devices, and business records of suspected agents of a foreign power); Intelligence Authorization Act for Fiscal Year 2000, Pub. L. No. 106-120, §601, 113 Stat. 1606, 1619-20 (extending the definition of "agent of a foreign power"); Intelligence Authorization Act for Fiscal Year 2001, Pub. L. No. 106-567, §§ 602-603, 114 Stat. 2831, 2851-53 (clarifying who could authorize applications for a FISA-court search authorization).

232 Uniting and Strengthening America by Providing Appropriate Tools Required To Intercept and Obstruct Terrorism (USA PATRIOT ACT) Act of 2001, Pub. L. No. 107-56, 115 Stat. 272 (codified in scattered sections of the U.S.C). For examples of how FISA changed, see *id.* § 206, 115 Stat. at 282 (allowing for roving search authorizations that are not fixed to a particular geographic location); *id.* § 225, 115 Stat. at 295–96 (amending FISA to provide third-party immunity for compliance with a FISA court order); and *id.* § 218, 115 Stat. at 291 (amending the primary purpose of the requested search, and now it need not be the collection of foreign intelligence).

233 Instances of terrorism rose through the early 1980s and peaked in 1987 with 666 acts of terrorism that occurred internationally. U.S. Dep't of State, Patterns of Global Terrorism: 1999, app. C (2000), *available at* http://www.state.gov/www/global/terrorism/1999report/patterns.pdf.

234 U.S. Dep't of State, Patterns of Global Terrorism: 1986, at 10, 15, 27–28 (1988), *available at* http://www.terrorisminfo.mipt.org/pdl71986pogt.pdf.

235 *See id.* at 5, 10; U.S. Dep't of State, Patterns of Global Terrorism: 1994, at 43, 58 (1995), *available at* http://www.terrorisminfo.mipt.org/pdf/1994pogt.pdf

236 Stephen E. Ambrose & Douglas G. Brinkley, Rise to Globalism: American Foreign Policy Since 1938, at 287–89, 311–12 (8th rev. ed. 1997).

paired with a like-minded President, created a ripe era for intelligence operations and misdeeds.[237]

For the Intelligence Community, the 1980s opened in dramatic fashion. At the outset of the decade, the U.S. Army established a number of organizations to address the hostage crisis in Iran. Among those organizations was the Intelligence Security Activity (ISA), an organization designed to provide high-risk intelligence to military special-operations forces.[238] The ISA enjoyed an unusually high degree of secrecy, remaining virtually unknown outside an extraordinarily small group of officials within the Army.[239] In 1981, the ISA contacted retired Army Special Forces Lieutenant Colonel James "Bo" Gritz concerning providing support to his private attempts to locate prisoners of war reportedly being held in Laos.[240] This arrangement was brokered absent approval from the Joint Chiefs of Staff.[241] On March 22, 1983, Gritz testified as to this arrangement to the House Subcommittee on Asian and Pacific Affairs.[242] The interests of both Congress and the press were peaked by the disclosure of this murky organization with an innocuous title.[243] These disclosures in turn caused the senior military leadership to question the activities of the ISA.[244]

An ensuing report by the DoD Inspector General found serious deficiencies in the conduct of the organization.[245] Deputy Defense Secretary, Frank C. Carlucci, characterized the organization as "uncoordinated and uncontrolled."[246] Seeking to forestall congressional intervention, the Army implemented a number of reforms designed to provide accountability for the ISA.[247]

The ISA experience did not, however, fully contain Army intelligence efforts to maintain robust operations in the face of increasing congressional scrutiny.

237 *See* Emerson, *supra* note 23, at 36–37. *See generally* Ambrose & Brinkley, *supra* note 236, at 331 ("Terrorism was important, mostly because the Reagan administration said it was.").

238 *See* Emerson, *supra* note 23, at 51; *see also* William M. Arkin, *The Secret War,* L.A. Times, Oct. 27, 2002, at M1.

239 *See* Emerson, *supra* note 23, at 50.

240 *See id.* at 79–80.

241 *See id.* at 80.

242 *New Information on U.S. MIA-POW's in Indochina?: Hearing Before the Subcomm. on Asian and Pacific Affairs of the H. Comm. on Foreign Affairs,* 98th Cong. 32–33 (1983) [hereinafter *Indochina Hearings*] (testimony of James Gritz, U.S. Army Retired); see Emerson, *supra* note 23, at 80–81.

243 *See Indochina Hearings, supra note* 242, at 32–33; *see also* Raymond Bonner, *Secret Pentagon Intelligence Unit Is Disclosed,* N. Y. Times, May 11, 1983, atA13.

244 *See* Emerson, *supra* note 23, at 81.

245 *See id.* The concerns of the DoD are reflected in a memorandum from the Deputy Defense Secretary. Memorandum from Frank C. Carlucci, Deputy Def. Sec'y, to the Deputy Undersecretary for Policy (May 26, 1982) (available at http://www.gwu.edu/~nsarchiv/NSAEBB/NSAEBB46/documenf7.pdf).

246 Memorandum from Frank C. Carlucci, *supra* note 245.

247 *See* Emerson, *supra* note 23, at 153.

During 1982, the press began reporting on substantial covert U.S. activities in El Salvador, Honduras, and Nicaragua.[248] In reaction, on December 8, 1982, Congress passed the first Boland Amendment, which prevented covert assistance to Nicaragua.[249]

With the passage of the first Boland Amendment, Army intelligence realized its ability to operate in this country was greatly reduced.[250] In reaction, an intelligence covert corporation was established with the express purpose of being beyond the appropriation powers of Congress.[251] This operation was entitled Yellow Fruit.[252] Being beyond the scope of appropriation's restrictions, Yellow Fruit was largely funded covertly with cash.[253] In the spring of 1983, supervisors within the unit began receiving reports of gross financial improprieties.[254] This sparked a series of audits, followed by an Army criminal investigation and a DOJ investigation.[255] The investigations eventually resulted in four courts martial and a number of nonjudicial punishments.[256] The Yellow Fruit scandal demonstrated the inclination of elements within the executive to operate far beyond the bounds of the law in pursuit of its self-identified national security goals, particularly in the absence of independent oversight. As with the ISA, the Army proactively addressed the problems resulting from Yellow Fruit in an effort to preclude congressional intervention.[257]

The lack of congressional oversight quickly came to a head on October 5, 1986, when an ancient Fairchild C-123 "Provider" cargo plane was shot down by the

248 *See, e.g.*, Editorial, *A Path Out of the Secret War*, N.Y. TIMES, May 1, 1983, at E20; John Brecher, John Walcott & David Martin, *A Secret War for Nicaragua*, NEWSWEEK, Nov. 8, 1982, at 42; *Not-So-Secret War in Honduras*, N.Y. TIMES, Nov. 5, 1982, at A26; *Secret Operations Can Go Awry, Says Former U.S. Ambassador*, CHRISTIAN SCI. MONITOR, Dec. 3, 1982, at 10; Philip Taubman, *U.S. Backing Raids Against Nicaragua*, N.Y. TIMES, Nov. 2, 1982, at A6; Editorial, *The Worst-Kept Secret War*, N.Y. TIMES, Dec. 8, 1982, at A30.

249 Further Continuing Appropriations Act of 1983, Pub. L. No. 97-377, § 793, 96 Stat. 1830, 1865 ("None of the funds provided *in this Act* may be used by the or the [DoD] to furnish military equipment, military training or advice, or other support for military activities, to any group or individual, not part of a country's armed forces, *for the purpose of overthrowing the Government of Nicaragua or provoking a military exchange between Nicaragua and Honduras*." (emphasis added)).

250 *See* EMERSON, *supra* note 23, at 150.

251 *See id.* at 153–54 ("In the fall of 1983, the structure set up by the [CIA Special Operations] Division and Yellow Fruit was being prepared, Army investigators later concluded, to become part of the 'enterprise' that, once Congress cut off all aid, could assist in the covert resupply of the contras.").

252 *See id.*

253 *See id.* at 151; *see also* PRADOS, *supra* note 79, at 391.

254 *See* PRADOS, *supra* note 79, at 391.

255 *Id.*

256 *Id.*

257 *See* Susan J. Crawford, General Counsel of the Army, Opening Remarks for the General Counsel's Conference (June 1988), *in* ARMY LAW., July 1988, at 13, 14 ("From the Yellow Fruit scandal to the Iran-Contra affair, the Army has taken the lead in reforming its own regulations and procedures.").

Sandinistas over Nicaragua.[258] This event was not altogether unusual, except that the lone survivor was an American citizen claiming to work for the CIA.[259] This was followed less than a month later by an article published in the Lebanese news magazine, *Ash-Shiraa*, detailing U.S. efforts to free hostages held in Iran in exchange for weapons.[260] These revelations, collectively known as the Iran-Contra Affair, sparked a significant public and congressional response, which focused largely on the executive's conduct in relation to congressional oversight and guidance.[261] The findings of independent counsel during this time focused on the actions of members of the executive acting under guidance from the President in contravention of congressional guidance.[262] In his concluding remarks, the independent counsel found:

> The lesson of the Iran/contra is that if our system of government is to function properly, the branches of government must deal with one another honestly and cooperatively. When disputes arise between the Executive and Legislative branches, as they surely will, the laws that emerge from such disputes must be obeyed. . . . Congress has the duty and the power under our system of checks and balances to ensure that the President and his Cabinet officers are faithful to their oaths.[263]

In addition to independent counsel's investigation, Congress formed a select joint committee to investigate the affair.[264] The congressional committees produced a report with similar findings and specific recommendations regarding the conduct of intelligence operations, particularly with regard to reporting the conduct of covert operations to Congress.[265] These recommendations were adopted in the Intelligence Authorization Act, Fiscal Year 1991,[266] which modified and expounded on reporting requirements established in the Intelligence Authorization Act for Fiscal Year 1981 by requiring that reports of covert actions be made to Congress

258 *See* Ambrose & Brinkley, *supra* note 236, at 338.

259 *See id.*

260 *See id.*

261 *See* 1 Lawrence E. Walsh, Final Report of the Independent Counsel for Iran/Contra Matters 555 (1993) ("The Iran/contra prosecutions illustrate in an especially stark fashion the tension between political oversight and enforcement of existing law").

262 *See* Knott, *supra* note 53, at 5.

263 Walsh, *supra* note 261, at 566.

264 *See* Ambrose & Brinkley, *supra* note 236, at 339.

265 *See* S. Rep. No. 100-216 (1987); H.R. Rep. No. 100-433 (1987). Prior to this report, the CIA, rather than the President, was required to provide Congress notice of covert actions "in a timely fashion." Intelligence Authorization Act for Fiscal Year 1981, Pub. L. No. 96-450, § 501, 94 Stat. 1975, 1982 (codified at 50 U.S.C. § 413 (1982)). This provision was a major issue in the Iran-Contra hearings. *See* Walsh, *supra* note 261, at 555–60.

266 Intelligence authorization Act, Fiscal Year 1991, Pub. L. No. 102-88, 105 Stat. 429 (codified as amended in scattered sections of 50 U.S.C).

"as soon as possible" and "before the initiation of the covert action."[267] Furthermore, it prohibited retroactive presidential findings.[268] Finally, the notice requirement extended to "significant anticipated intelligence activity"[269] This marked the first time Congress imposed a statutory obligation on the President to keep the intelligence committees informed.[270]

These reporting requirements, however, applied only to the "gathering of information."[271] This is distinguished from covert intelligence activities, defined as those activities designed "to influence political, economic, or military conditions abroad, where it is intended that the role of the United States Government will not be apparent or acknowledged publicly."[272] In regard to covert actions, the President may limit congressional notification where he "determines such an action is necessary to support identifiable foreign policy objectives of the United States and is important to the national security of the United States."[273] In these rare circumstances, the President is only obligated to inform the House and Senate majority and minority leaders and the chair and ranking members of the House and Senate intelligence committees—the so-called "gang of eight."[274]

The 1990s represented a quiet period for both intelligence operations and oversight. As the Cold War rapidly came to a close, the United States found itself the lone superpower.[275] The omnipresent threat of the Soviet Union had faded along with associated proxy wars, which for so long provided a rich operational intelligence environment.[276] Intelligence operations did not, of course, end but, rather, gradually began adapting to the "new world order."[277] During this time, intelligence activities supported major U.S. military operations in Bosnia, Kosovo, Haiti, Iraq, Panama, and Somalia.[278]

Congressional oversight during this time proved relatively quiet. Perhaps the most significant action during this decade was the decision of the DCI to publicly release the budget of the Intelligence Community. This occurred first in 1997 in response

---

267 *See id.* § 503(c)(1), 105 Stat. at 443 (codified as amended at 50 U.S.C. § 413b (2000)).

268 *Id.* § 503(a), 105 Stat. at 442 (codified as amended at 50 U.S.C. § 413b).

269 *Id.* § 603(d)(1)(B), 105 Stat. at 445 (codified as amended at 50 U.S.C. § 414).

270 *See* CUMMING, *supra* note 177, at 2 n.2.

271 S. REP. No. 102-85, at 33–34 (1991), *as reprinted in* 1991 U.S.C.C.A.N. 193, 227.

272 Intelligence Authorization Act, Fiscal Year 1991, § 503(e), 105 Stat. at 443 (codified as amended at 50 U.S.C. § 413b).

273 *See id.* § 503(a), 105 Stat. at 442 (codified as amended at 50 U.S.C. § 413b(a)).

274 *See supra* note 9 and accompanying text.

275 *See* AMBROSE & BRINKLEY, *supra* note 236, at 378.

276 *See* SMIST, *supra* note 131, at 301–02.

277 *See* AMBROSE & BRINKLEY, *supra* note 236, at 377–80.

278 *See id.* at 379–99.

to a Freedom of Information Act request,[279] and then again in 1998.[280] Though the Intelligence Community continues to face pressure from both Congress and the public concerning the disclosure of the annual intelligence budget, these were the only two public exposures in the history of the Intelligence Community.

4. Post-9/11

Not since December 7, 1941, had the United States been struck with such a devastating act of violence. The shock of the attack was compounded by the surprise with which it occurred. The public's critical gaze quickly fell on the Intelligence Community after it was revealed that the attacks were conducted by al-Qaeda—an organization responsible for a series of major terrorist attacks under very close intelligence observation since 1996.[281] The 9/11 Commission convened on November 27, 2002, and had the simple responsibility of determining how 9/11 happened and how to prevent such a tragedy in the future.[282] The resulting report largely concerned the conduct of the Intelligence Community, though it did address the oversight role of Congress.

The report did so, in fact, in a damning manner. Summarizing their findings with regard to congressional oversight, the report concluded that as "long as oversight is governed by current congressional rules and resolutions, we believe the American people will not get the security they want and need."[283] The commission did, however, recognize the need for congressional oversight: "The United States needs a strong, stable, and capable congressional committee structure to give America's national intelligence agencies oversight, support, and leadership."[284] The commission's recommendations in this regard focused on unity of effort and efficient committee structure.[285] The commission proposed two solutions: "[A] joint committee for

279 CIA Press Release No. 13-97, Statement of the Director of Central Intelligence Regarding the Disclosure of the Aggregate Intelligence Budget for Fiscal Year 1997 (Oct. 15, 1997) (available at https://www.cia.gov/cia/public_affairs/press_release/1997/prl01597. html).

280 CIA Press Release, Statement by the Director of Central Intelligence Regarding the Disclosure of the Aggregate Intelligence Budget for Fiscal Year 1998 (Mar. 20, 1998)(available at https://www.cia.gov/cia/public_affairs/press release/1998/ps032098.html).

281 *See* The 9/11 Comm'n, The 9/11 Commission Report: Final Report of the National Commission on Terrorist Attacks upon the United States 109 (2004). In 1996, a group within the CIA was specifically organized to combat the threat posed by al-Qaeda. *Id.* Further, in 1998, President Clinton issued a Memorandum of Notification authorizing the CIA to use force to capture Osama bin Laden. *See id.* at 126.

282 *See id.* at xv; *see also* Intelligence Authorization Act for Fiscal Year 2003 §§ 601-611, Pub. L. 107-306, 116 Stat. 2383, 2408 (codified as amended at 6 U.S.C. § 101) (creating the National Commission on Terrorist Attacks upon the United States).

283 The 9/11 Comm'n, *supra* note 281, at 419.

284 *Id.*

285 *Id.* at 419–20.

intelligence . . . or [the creation of] House and Senate committees with combined authorizing and appropriations powers."[286] Other recommendations made by the commission included: publicizing the budget of the Intelligence Community, creating an intelligence-oversight subcommittee, abolishing term limits on the proposed committees, and reducing the size of the proposed intelligence committees.[287]

Acting in part on the recommendations of the 9/11 Commission, the Intelligence Reform and Terrorism Prevention Act of 2004 (IRTPA) was signed into law on December 17, 2004.[288] While IRTPA did not adopt the aforementioned recommendations, it did modify the executive's requirement to report to Congress regarding the conduct of intelligence operations.[289] Specifically, IRTPA requires the Director of National Intelligence (DNI) to ensure that "national intelligence is provided . . . to the Senate and House of Representatives and the committees thereof"[290] IRTPA further specifies that such intelligence "should be timely, objective, [and] independent of political considerations."[291] This provision considerably strengthened the previous reporting requirement, which required only that the DCI (predecessor to the DNI) provide national intelligence when "appropriate."[292]

B. Hearings

The congressional power to hold public hearings is closely related to the power to legislate reporting requirements. Though not an enumerated power, the Court has consistently upheld Congress's ability to conduct hearings.[293] Hearings serve two vital roles: (1) a fact-finding tool that informs the legislative process and (2) a forum through which the public may be informed of government improprieties.[294] Congress has embraced this power warmly. In 2005, Congress conducted dozens of intelligence-related hearings regarding the Intelligence Community's

286 *Id.* at 420.

287 *Id.* at 420–21.

288 IRTPA, Pub. L. No. 108-458, 118 Stat. 3638 (codified as amended in scattered sections of 50 U.S.C.).

289 *Id.* § 102A, 118 Stat. at 3644–55 (amending 50 U.S.C. § 403-1 (2000)).

290 *Id.* § 102A(a)(1)(D), 118 Stat. at 3644 (amending 50 U.S.C. § 403-1).

291 *Id.* § 102A(a)(2), 118 Stat. at 3644 (amending 50 U.S.C. § 403-1).

292 National Security Act of 1947, Pub. L. No. 80-253, § 102(d)(3), 61 Stat. 495, 498 (codified as amended in scattered sections of 10 & 50 U.S.C).

293 *See,* e.g., Foremost Ins. Co. v. Richardson, 457 U.S. 668, 685 n.8 (1982) (Powell, J., dissenting) ("Congress has the power to hold hearings. . . ."); McGrain v. Daugherty, 273 U.S. 135, 174 (1927) ("We are of opinion that the power of inquiry—with process to enforce it—is an essential and appropriate auxiliary to the legislative function.").

294 *See McGrain,* 273 U.S. at 174.

capabilities,[295] conduct of intelligence operations,[296] and the confirmation of Intelligence Community officials.[297]

The public is rarely afforded a glimpse into the murky world of complex and classified intelligence operations. Thus, hearings and subsequent written reports relating to intelligence improprieties have historically sparked widespread public interest.[298] For instance, shortly after its release, the 9/11 Commission report rocked to the top of various best sellers' lists, eventually selling more than 600,000 copies.[299] Similarly, the hearings, which led to the exposure of the ISA, sparked a series of newspaper articles causing the DoD and the Army to aggressively self-regulate.[300]

Executive response to congressional intelligence hearings covers the spectrum from toleration to borderline contempt.[301] The executive has frequently cited two reasons for their hostility towards congressional hearings: (1) public hearings have the potential to expose classified aspects of the intelligence practice, and (2) appearing before dozens of hearings a year places an undue burden on senior intelligence officials.[302] Both issues present legitimate critiques that are addressed in the recommendations below.

C. Appropriations

Despite expansive claims of executive power, Congress has undeniably retained, and freely exercised, the power of the purse. This is most graphically illustrated in the yearly intelligence authorization bills wherein congressional requirements and

---

295 *See, e.g., Federal Initiatives for Homeland Security Information Sharing: Hearing Before the Subcomm. on Intelligence, Information Sharing, and Terrorism Risk Assessment of the H. Comm. on Homeland Security*, 109th Cong. (2005).

296 *See, e.g.*, Able Danger and Intelligence Information Sharing: Hearing Before the S. Comm. on the Judiciary, 109th Cong. (2005).

297 *See, e.g.*, Nomination of Vice Admiral John Scott Redd To Be Director, National Counterterrorism Center: Confirmation Hearing Before the S. Select Comm. on Intelligence, 109th Cong. (2005); Nomination of Benjamin A. Powell To Be General Counsel of the Office of the Director of National Intelligence: Confirmation Hearing Before the S. Select Comm. on Intelligence, 109th Cong. (2005).

298 On November 18, 1987, the major news networks devoted almost half of their programs to cover the release of the Iran-Contra report. *See* Tim Graham, *Who Makes or Breaks a Scandal?: The Cox Report vs. The Iran-Contra Report*, Media Res. Center, July 6, 1999, http://www.mediaresearch.org/specialreport/1999/sum/srl9990706-asp.

299 *See* Bob Minzesheimer, *Panel's '9/11 Report' Becoming a Big Seller*, USA Today (Wash., D.C.), July 27, 2004, at D1.

300 *See supra* notes 241–244 and accompanying text.

301 *See* Todd D. Peterson, *Prosecuting Executive Branch Officials for Contempt of Congress*, 66 N.Y.U. L. Rev. 563, 568-74 (1991) (detailing, in part, historical incidents of the tension between congressional requests for testimony and information and executive reluctance to provide such).

302 *See id.* at 571–74.

desires are expressly tied to funding.[303] These requirements have at times extended into the realm of directing U.S. foreign policy.[304] Indeed, the executive actions at issue in the Iran-Contra Affair were taken in response to a congressional restriction of funding for the Contras.[305]

The extent to which Congress may flex the power of the purse is a matter of continuing debate. It is generally acknowledged that the power is not unlimited.[306] Plainly, Congress may not restrict spending to achieve unconstitutional results.[307] The issue turns on what constitutes unconstitutional results, which, in turn, restates the original question concerning the respective powers of Congress and the President.

Some commentators have argued that "[w]here Congress prohibits use of any appropriated funds for an activity, the Executive simply has no authority to finance the prohibited activity with either private or public funds."[308] Others have come to wholly contradictory conclusions: "The Constitution does give Congress the power to appropriate money for the government's activities, presumably including intelligence operations. That does not, however, as the intelligence committees have claimed, give Congress carte blanche to 'restrict[] or condition[] the use of appropriated funds.'"[309] A full exploration of this debate is beyond of the scope of this essay; it is sufficient for the purposes here simply to acknowledge the ongoing

303 *See, e.g.*, Intelligence Authorization Act for Fiscal Year 2001, Pub. L. No. 106-567, § 103(e)(3), 114 Stat. 2831, 2834 (prohibiting use of funds in violation of the National Security Act).

304 For a fascinating, and somewhat whimsical, account of congressional appropriations power over the conduct of intelligence operations, see George Crile, Charlie Wilson's War: The Extraordinary Story of the Largest Covert Operation in History 19–20 (2003), which details how Congressman Charlie Wilson was able to almost single-handedly initiate and escalate the CIA's operations in Afghanistan during the 1979 Soviet invasion. Crile attributes Congressman Wilson's extraordinary achievement to his place on the Defense Appropriations subcommittee. *See id.*

305 *See* Deficit Reduction Act of 1984, Pub. L. No. 98-369, §2907, 98 Stat. 494, 1210 ("It is the sense of the Congress that no funds heretofore or hereafter appropriated in any Act of Congress shall be obligated or expended for the purpose of planning, directing, executing, or supporting the mining of the ports or territorial waters of Nicaragua.").

306 *See, e.g.*, Louis Fisher, *How Tightly Can Congress Draw the Purse Strings?*, 83 Am. J. Int'l L. 758, 762 (1989) ("The congressional power of the purse is not unlimited. Congress cannot use appropriations bills to enact bills of attainder, to restrict the President's pardon power or to establish a national religion. The Constitution prohibits Congress from diminishing the salaries of the President or federal judges. Congress would overstep its boundaries if it 'refused to appropriate funds for the President to receive foreign ambassadors or to make treaties.'" (citations omitted)).

307 *See id.*

308 Kate Stith, *Congress' Power of the Purse*, 97 Yale L.J. 1343, 1363 (1988) (citation omitted).

309 *See* James E. Gauch, Restoring Congress's Proper Role in Oversight of Covert Intelligence Operations 11 (May 2002), *available at* http://www.fed-soc.org/Publications/Terrorism/CIA.pdf (quoting S. Rep. No. 100-276, at 20 (1988) (alteration in original)); *see also* J. Gregory Sidak, *The President's Power of the Purse*, 1989 Duke L.J. 1162, 1163 ("[T]he President, without violating the Constitution or statutory law, may obligate the Treasury provided that Congress

constitutional debate. Pragmatically scrutinized, however, it is clear that Congress does indeed exercise considerable control through their appropriations power over the conduct of intelligence operations.

VI. THE FUTURE OF INTELLIGENCE OVERSIGHT

A. Current Proposals for Intelligence Oversight Reform

As many commentators have agreed (and at least one noted), "[t]he American intelligence infrastructure is in the midst of its most radical overhaul since the formation of the modern [I]ntelligence [C]ommunity following World War II."[310] Unlike intelligence reform seeking to reign in the rouge elephant, today's reform concerns "how to get [intelligence] agencies to be more aggressive—and how to get policymakers to use the results to better effect."[311] Hence, the debate over intelligence reform has centered on reforming those institutions or organizational impediments that hinder intelligence operations, rather than creating and empowering structures to ensure operations are conducted within the bounds of the law.[312]

Oversight, however, is intrinsically tied to the conduct of intelligence operations. Conventional wisdom establishes an inverse relationship between oversight and operations: the more oversight, the more restricted the operations. This is not, however, a universal tenet. As an initial matter, oversight offers a broader perspective on the development and execution of intelligence operations. That is to say, the inclusion of a neutral party offers a check on the dangers of organizational groupthink. This quality of oversight was recognized as early as 1956 when President Eisenhower organized the predecessor to the President's Foreign Intelligence Advisory Board, whose purpose is to provide "advice to the President concerning the quality and adequacy of intelligence collection, of analysis and estimates, of counterintelligence, and of other intelligence activities."[313]

Oversight also serves the less intuitive role of actually facilitating intelligence operations. The American public is much more willing to permit unfettered and robust intelligence operations when they know institutional checks are in place to ensure operations are conducted in accordance with applicable laws and generally accepted

---

has failed to appropriate the minimum amount necessary for him to perform the duties and exercise the prerogatives given him by article II of the Constitution.").

310 *See* Grant T. Harris, *The CIA Mandate and the War on Terror*, 23 Yale L. & Pol'y Rev. 529, 529 (2005); *see also* Deborah G. Barger, Rand, Toward a Revolution in Intelligence Affairs (2005).

311 See Richard K. Betts, *The New Politics of Intelligence:* Will Reforms Work This Time?, Foreign Afr., May/June 2004, at 2, 3.

312 *See* Barger, *supra* note 310, at 1 ("[T]he focus during this period was on reorganization of the Intelligence Community and the political issues surrounding the authorities and responsibilities of the director of Central Intelligence.").

313 *See* PFIAB, *supra* note 165; *see also supra* note 165 and accompanying text.

public mores.[314] As discussed at length above, when this assumption of legality and morality is corrupted, the public reaction has proven formidable.[315] Thus, it is in the interests of the Intelligence Community to be subjected to a certain degree of oversight.[316]

Congress, as a representative of the people, necessarily serves as the Intelligence Community's "honest broker." In this role, Congress must walk a fine line between beneficial and detrimental oversight. The history of congressional oversight, marked by wild oscillations of interest, demonstrates the inherent difficulty in this task. Following 9/11, various commissions and commentators found a myriad of issues with Congress's role in intelligence oversight, suggesting Congress has not yet found the appropriate balance.

1. 9/11 Commission Recommendations and Legislation

As noted above, Congress failed to adopt virtually any of the 9/11 Commission recommendations concerning congressional-oversight reform.[317] This failure was largely the result of organizational "turf wars" and partisan squabbling.[318] Many of the commission's recommendations, however, continue to receive support in Congress. The Senate version of the IRTPA passed the Senate ninety-six to two and would have implemented many of the 9/11 Commission's recommendations.[319] Most critically, the report urged the combination of congressional authorization and appropriation authorities.[320]

---

314 *See* James E. Knott, *Secrecy and Intelligence in a Free Society* 19 STUD. INTELLIGENCE 1, 1 (1975) ("The free society as a whole cannot make the judgment as to whether or not individual matters are legitimately kept secret. It must place its trust in an oversight body or bodies to act in its behalf.").

315 *See supra* notes 100-135 and accompanying text.

316 *See* Joel F. Brenner, *Information Oversight: Practical Lessons from Foreign Intelligence,* HERITAGE LECTURES, Sept. 30, 2004, at 1, 12, *available at* http://www.heritage.org/Research/National Security/upload/69877_1.pdf ("First, for our existing intelligence agencies, the trick will be to keep them on the law's leash without drawing their claws. Failure to encourage robust and imaginative intelligence will place the nation in continual jeopardy of further attack, and failure to do so in accordance with the law will produce the kind of backlash against the agencies that came after 1976.").

317 *See supra* note 255 and accompanying text.

318 For an in-depth discussion of the failure of Congress to implement fully the 9/11 Commission's recommendations, see Helen Fessenden, *The Limits of Intelligence Reform,* FOREIGN AFF., Nov./Dec. 2005, at 106.

319 *See* National Intelligence Reform Act of 2004, S. 2845, 108th Cong. (2004) (enacted as Pub. L. No. 108-458, 118 Stat. 3638).

320 *See* THE 9/11 COMM'N, *supra* note 281, at 420 ("A single committee in each house of Congress, combining the authorizing and appropriating authorities, is another [recommendation]." (emphasis omitted)).

The 9/11 Commission's report must be distinguished from the report produced by the congressional committee examining the events of 9/11. This latter report, entitled Joint Inquiry into Intelligence Community Activities Before and After the Terrorist Attacks of September 11, 2001 (Joint Inquiry Report), provided markedly different recommendations.[321] Absent among their findings, however, is any critical self-analysis. Of the report's sixteen "systemic findings" and four "related findings," none expressly discuss congressional failings or inefficiencies.[322] Further, one commentator has criticized the report as "a dismal failure."[323]

The report is not, however, without merit. As an initial matter, the very presence of a robust report indicates a congressional wiliness to engage in some degree of oversight. The 9/11 Commission fulfilled the desires of the vast majority of the American public; thus, the Joint Inquiry Report could have easily been written off as surplusage. Secondly, as discussed below, the Joint Inquiry Report does provide some valuable recommendations. And finally, the Joint Inquiry Report provides valuable insight into the mechanics of the intelligence committees. Through the individual statements of a number of junior senators, one can readily identify dissent and inefficiencies within the committees.[324]

2. Commission on the Intelligence Capabilities of the United States Regarding Weapons of Mass Destruction

The Weapons of Mass Destruction Commission (WMD Commission), a bipartisan commission, had two tasks: "[T]o assess the intelligence capabilities of the United States with respect to weapons of mass destruction 'and related threats' of the 21st century, and to recommend ways to improve those capabilities."[325] Before discussing both congressional and executive oversight, the WMD Commission's report first discussed the merits of oversight:

> Many—perhaps most—of the recommendations contained in this report have been made before. That we find ourselves proposing several sensible changes that former Secretary of Defense and Director of Central Intelligence James Schlesinger endorsed in 1971 suggests to us either that the Intelligence Community is inherently resistant to outside recommendations, or that it does not have the institutional capacity to implement them. In either case, we are left with the distinct impression that

---

321 *See* S. Rep. No. 107-351, H.R. Rep. No. 107-792, at xv–xviii (2002).

322 *See id.* at vx–xix.

323 Robert F. Blomquist, *Congressional Oversight of Counterterrorism and Its Reform,* 11 Roger Williams U. L. Rev. 1, 5 (2005) ("[T]he 9/11 oversight failure of Congress was due to a deficiency of institutional competence in matching and reining in the executive branch's effort to stonewall and obfuscate.").

324 *See* S. Rep. No. 107-351, H.R. Rep. No. 107-792 apps. (Additional Views).

325 Staff of Comm. on the Intelligence Capabilities of the U.S. Regarding Weapons of Mass Destruction (2005).

> meaningful intelligence reform proposals are only likely to become reality if the Intelligence Community receives sustained, senior level attention from knowledgeable outside observers.[326]

The WMD Commission's recommendations in this regard concerned proposals for executive action. The observation, however, underscores the beneficial nature of oversight. In addressing congressional oversight specifically, the WMD Commission endorsed the recommendations of the 9/11 Commission and further provided "a number of more modest suggestions."[327] Among the WMD Commission's suggestions were to: "[l]imit the activities of new intelligence oversight subcommittees to strategic oversight"; eliminate term limits; make numerous budget changes; foster bipartisanship within the committees; encourage a stronger relationship "between the Intelligence Community and its congressional overseers"; and create an intelligence-appropriations subcommittee.[328]

A related observation should give overseers pause. In an aside, under discussions concerning leadership and management, the WMD Commission noted that during the investigation, they "came across Intelligence Community leaders, operators, and analysts who claimed that they couldn't do their jobs because of a 'legal issue.'... [Q]uite often the cited legal impediments ended up being either myths that over-cautious lawyers had never debunked or policy choices swathed in pseudo-legal justifications."[329] As the report notes, the issue for overseers is these misconceptions "can breed uncertainty about *real* legal prohibitions."[330] There is presently no legislation or program designed to address this very real issue.

3. The SAFE Act and the USA PATRIOT Improvement and Reauthorization Act of 2005

By its original construction, portions of the USA PATRIOT Act were designed to sunset on December 31, 2005.[331] Numerous temporary extensions have been agreed to pending the passage of a permanent solution.[332] The USA PATRIOT Improvement and Reauthorization Act of 2005 seeks to address these sunset provisions

326 *Id.* at 336 (citation omitted).

327 *See id.* at 337 ("While we echo the 9/11 Commission's support for these [congressional reform] proposals, we also recommend a number of more modest suggestions for improving Congressional oversight of intelligence.").

328 *Id.* at 338–40.

329 *See id.* at 335.

330 *Id.*

331 USA PATRIOT Act, Pub. L. No. 107-56, § 224, 115 Stat. 272, 295 (codified as amended at 18 U.S.C. § 2501 (Supp. 2005)).

332 *See, e.g.*, USA PATRIOT Improvement and Reauthorization Act of 2005, Pub. L. No. 109-177, 120 Stat. 192 (codified as amended in scattered sections of 10 & 50 U.S.C).

by permanently extending some provisions and temporarily extending others.[333] Meanwhile, a competing piece of legislation that was under consideration in the Senate was known as the Security and Freedom Enhancement Act of 2005 (SAFE Act).[334]

The SAFE Act provides little in the way of increased congressional oversight; though, it would require the attorney general to notify the Senate and House judiciary committees regarding the DOJ's use of FISA search authorizations.[335] Despite this omission, the SAFE Act does create numerous procedures designed to limit the ability of intelligence officials to operate unrestrained. For instance, the search authorization granted by the FISA court would have to expressly identify the target of the search.[336] Additionally, the ability of law enforcement and intelligence officials to conduct sneak-and-peek searches would be limited to exigent circumstances.[337] Further, the SAFE Act would expand safeguards regarding the use of certain intelligence-gathering techniques.[338]

The SAFE Act's proposed oversight is largely judicial in nature.[339] Similarly, the SAFE Act empowers the judiciary to oversee the issuance of "National Security Letters."[340] The SAFE Act increases the standard of proof necessary to issue a National Security Letter and would provide a judicial avenue through which a person subject to a letter could challenge the search in a federal district court.[341] These provisions, however, are perhaps rendered somewhat moot by a pair of recent

---

333 *See* Brian T. Yeh & Charles Doyle, USA PATRIOT Improvement and Reauthorization Act of 2005 (H.R. 3199): A Brief Look (2005), *available at* http://www.fas.org/sgp/crs/intel/RS22348.pdf.

334 S. 737, 109th Cong. (2005). A companion piece of legislation in the House was entitled the Security and Freedom Enhancement Act of 2005 (SAFE Act). H.R. 1526, 109th Cong. (2005). Both versions of the SAFE Act provided for widespread reforms; however, the Senate version was somewhat more robust. Thus, this discussion will focus on the Senate bill. For an extensive discussion comparing S. 737 with H.R. 1526, see Charles Doyle, Security and Freedom Ensured Act (SAFE Act) (H.R. 1526) and Security and Freedom Enhancement Act (SAFE Act) (S. 737): Section by Section Analysis (2005), *available at* http://www.au.af.mil/au/awc/awcgate/crs/rl32907.pdf.

335 *See* S. 737, 109th Cong. § 4(d) (2005).

336 *Id.* § 2(1).

337 *Id.* § 4(c). A sneak-and-peek search is a search executed under judicial authorization but conducted in such a way that the subject of the search is not aware they have been searched. *See* Kevin Corr, *Sneaky but Lawful: The Use of Sneak and Peek Search Warrants,* 43 U. Kan. L. Rev. 1103, 1103 (1995).

338 S.737, 109th Cong. § 6.

339 *See id.* § 5.

340 The term "National Security Letters" refers to four federal statutory provisions which allow federal intelligence agents to demand the production of certain information in the absence of a court order. *See* 18 U.S.C. §2709 (2000); 12 U.S.C. §3414 (2000); 15 U.S.C. §1681u (2000).

341 S. 737, 109th Cong. § 5.

federal cases: *Doe v. Gonzales*[342] and *Doe v. Ashcroft*.[343] Both involved First and Fourth Amendment challenges to the issuance of a National Security Letter pursuant to 18 U.S.C. § 2709.[344] Both district courts found for the plaintiff—in *Ashcroft* on both grounds and in *Gonzales* on First Amendment grounds.[345]

4. The National Security Agency Program Solution

On March 8, 2006, the SSCI announced a compromise solution with the administration regarding the oversight of the NS A program.[346] Under the solution, the committee would create a seven-member subcommittee specifically designated to oversee the program.[347] Under the present plan, the NSA would be able to continue operations and Congress would decline to conduct a formal investigation.[348]

The Democrats on the SSCI harshly criticized the plan as an abdication of "responsibility to oversee the intelligence activities of the United States."[349] The *New York Times* editorial board was no less kind, noting the compromise leaves the SSCI on its "deathbed" and unable to "manage to do its basic job."[350] The SSCI's decision not to pursue a formal investigation presents a missed opportunity to reestablish the propriety of their role in intelligence oversight. This decision is particularly striking considering Congress's own research arm, the Congressional Research Service, had indicated the program was unconstitutional.[351]

B. Recommendations

Clearly the need for oversight reform in Congress is great. Congress's role in the oversight process is crucial in both ensuring compliance with the law and in facilitating a functional, aggressive, and efficient Intelligence Community. An inefficient oversight structure impairs intelligence operations. The recommendations contained herein

342 386 F. Supp. 2d 66 (D. Conn. 2005).

343 334 F. Supp. 2d 471 (S.D.N.Y. 2004).

344 *See Gonzales*, 386 F. Supp. 2d at 68–69; *Ashcroft*, 334 F. Supp. 26 at 474.

345 *See Ashcroft*, 334 F. Supp. 2d at 526–27; *Gonzales*, 386 F. Supp. 2d at 82.

346 Walter Pincus, *Senate Panel Blocks Eavesdropping Probe*, Wash. Post, Mar. 8, 2006, at A3.

347 *See* Scott Shane & David D. Kirkpatrick, *G.O.P. Plan Would Allow Spying Without Warrants*, N.Y. Times, Mar. 9, 2006, at A20.

348 *See id.*

349 Press Statement, Jay Rockefeller, Senator, Vice Chairman Rockefeller's Statement on the Senate Intelligence Committee's Failure To Vote on Whether To Authorize an Investigation into the NSA Surveillance Program (Feb. 16, 2006) (available at http://rockefeller.senate.gov/news/2006/pr021606a.html).

350 Editorial, *The Death of the Intelligence Panel*, N.Y. Times, Mar. 9, 2006, at A22; *see* Editorial, *Authorizing Surveillance*, Wash. Post, Mar. 9, 2006, atA18.

351 *See* Bazan & Elsea, *supra* note 16.

are neither unique nor revolutionary, but rather a common sense distillation of various examinations of Congress's role.

1. Committee Reorganization

ongressional intelligence committees are presently operating at a suboptimal level of efficiency. A number of bureaucratic constructs have markedly reduced the ability of the committees to both ensure legal compliance and facilitate an aggressive and effective Intelligence Community. To wit, Congress should seek to address three internal areas for reform: (1) appropriations authority, (2) committee organization, and (3) classification and secrecy.

a. Appropriations Authority

Congress should adopt the recommendations of both the 9/11 Commission and the WMD Commission, and establish either a bicameral intelligence committee or combine the appropriations and authorizations authorities into a single committee in each chamber.[352]

Presently, the authorizing authorities (i.e., the intelligence committees) have little say in the appropriation of intelligence monies. Due to the classified nature of the intelligence budget, the vast majority of the money is "hidden" within the DoD budget and is thus controlled by the defense committees rather than intelligence committees.[353] This arrangement presents a number of problems, summarized by one commentator as follows:

> First, the continuation of the stares quo keeps intact the unusual degree of control over the intelligence budget by appropriators (who write the checks in the end) rather than authorizers (who write the bills outlining their respective budgets), even though only the latter have a full staff of experts at their disposal. Second, the continuation of the stares quo makes it more difficult for Negroponte and his successors to count on a unified budget process, since it forces the DNI to deal with multiple actors rather than a few individuals. That splintering of jurisdiction, in turn, will make any future attempts at intelligence reform more difficult to push through Congress. Third and last, the decision to keep the intelligence budget split up among separate, classified accounts means that appropriators themselves cannot transfer money among their respective subcommittees—say, from Defense over to the State Department's Bureau of Intelligence and Research or to the FBI to aid its counterterrorism efforts—even if they decide that such a transfer reflects an important priority.[354]

---

352 *See supra* notes 222–226, 258–261 and accompanying text.

353 *See* Richard A. Best, Jr., Intelligence Issues for Congress 7 (2006), *available at* http://www.fas.org/sgp/crs/intel/RL33539.pdf.

354 Fessenden, *supra* note 318, at 106.

The House Committee on Rules is presently considering House Resolution 25, which would create an appropriations subcommittee for intelligence.[355] This bill was referred to the House Committee on Rules on January 9, 2007.[356] There has been no action on this issue since. Indeed, the Intelligence Authorization Act for Fiscal Year 2006 did not address this issue.[357] The Senate bill is not entirely without merit as it: requires a response to a committee request for intelligence within fifteen days of the request, establishes the Office of the Inspector General of the Intelligence Community, and empowers nonstatutorily established inspectors general.[358]

b. Committee Organization

Beyond the appropriations issues, Congress must address other lingering organizational issues such as internal information-sharing and term limits. The Joint Inquiry Report issued by Congress following the 9/11 attacks contained 190 pages of "additional views."[359] These comments were not so much notable for the additional, independent views on the Intelligence Community, but rather for their illustration of internal strife within the committees. Senators John Kyl and Pat Roberts detailed at length organizational issues with the manner in which the committee conducted its investigation.[360] Their comments bear a direct importance to both future investigations and the conduct of the committee operations generally. Their concerns dealt primarily with the hierarchical nature of the investigation and the retention of information and decision making by the "Big Four"—the Chairman and Vice Chairman of the Senate Select Committee on Intelligence and the Chairman and Raking Member of the House Permanent Select Committee on Intelligence.[361] They note:

> It is difficult, however, for rank-and-file Members of the two committees to know how thorough or accurate the Report is because of the way the JIS and the 'Big Four' conducted the inquiry, withholding information and decisions from the Members and SSCI and HPSCI staff throughout the process. . . .
>
> . . . .
>
> The inquiry was conducted and overseen in a way that left rank-and-file Members at a distinct disadvantage. . . .[362]

355 H.R. 334, 110th Cong. (2007) (recently referred to the House Committee on Rules).

356 *Id.*

357 H.R. 2475, 109th Cong. (2005). This bill passed in the House of Representatives on June 21, 2005, with a vote of 409 for and 6 against. *Id.* Senate Resolution 1803, 109th Cong. (2005) was placed on the Senate Legislative Calendar on November 16, 2005. Together these bills made up the Intelligence Authorization Act for Fiscal Year 2006.

358 S. Res. 1803, § 435, 109th Cong.

359 S. Rep. No. 107-351, H.R. Rep. No. 107-792 apps. (Additional Views).

360 *See id.* app. at 1–4 (Additional Views of Senator Jon Kyl and Senator Pat Roberts).

361 *See id.* app. at 1–2 (Additional Views of Senator Jon Kyl and Senator Pat Roberts).

362 *Id.* app. at 1–2 (Additional Views of Senator Jon Kyl and Senator Pat Roberts).

The Senators then proceed to provide specific examples of "irregularities" in the conduct of the inquiry.[363] Plainly, if senators are publicly chastising the leadership, there must be major organizational issues to be addressed by the committees.

This problem is further exasperated by the term limits applicable to both committees, which deny the congressmen the opportunity to forge stronger working relationships. These term limits were originally introduced to prevent congressional overseers from being co-opted by the organizations they were overseeing.[364] This prophylactic measure, however, presents a number of issues. The Intelligence Community is enormous in both terms of personnel and budget, and intelligence operations can be complex affairs running for many years. Furthermore, the oversight rules applying to different aspects of the Intelligence Community are highly specialized to intelligence law and are exceedingly complex.[365] Thus, by the time a new committee member has read into all the intelligence operations fully understands the oversight rules, it is time for that member to leave.

While the original reason for term limits remains a legitimate concern, the efficiencies wrought by this change would likely outweigh any potential for impropriety. Such improprieties could further be guarded against by providing for term limits on a small number of seats, thereby ensuring unbiased rotation of members on a regular basis. Such a scheme would only work, however, where the rotating members were afforded the same rights and privileges as the permanent members.

c. Secrecy

A comment from Congressman Tim Roemer concurrently illustrates two problems—information sharing within the committees and the overclassification of information:

> One of my great frustrations during my service on the Permanent Select Committee on Intelligence has been the degree to which access to information is restricted, either from the committee or within the committee, often for reasons that have little or no correlation to national security. Many times, these restrictions have the effect of impairing the ability of members of the committee to make fully informed decisions on important budgetary or policy matters.... [C]lassification should be for important national security reasons....[366]

---

363 *See id.* app. at 2 (Additional Views of Senator Jon Kyl and Senator Pat Roberts).

364 *Cf.* Thomas B. Edsall, *Coming to Term Limits,* WASH. POST, May 12, 1998, at A4; Edward Walsh, *Term-Limit Pledges Are Coming Due,* WASH. POST, Mar. 15, 1999, at A1.

365 *See* THE 9/11 COMM'N, *supra* note 281, at 103 ("Many members believe these limits prevent committee members from developing the necessary expertise to conduct effective oversight.").

366 S. REP. NO. 107-351, H.R. REP. NO. 107-792 app. at 1 (Additional Views of Congressman Tim Roemer).

Congressman Roemer is not alone in his criticism. The Intelligence Community has been roundly criticized for overclassifying information.[367] Millions of documents are classified every year.[368] By some accounts, a majority of the classified information should not be classified.[369] Most obviously, this has a tendency to reduce the transparency of government—a principal the Court has strongly criticized.[370] Further, overclassification has the tendency to dilute the meaning of "secret." The idea is that, when everything is secret, nothing is secret.

Finally, the costs associated with safekeeping, declassifying, or destroying such a volume of documents are tremendous. This issue was recently addressed by the Subcommittee on National Security, Emerging Threats, and International Relations in the House Committee on Government Reform; it succinctly summarized the problems arising from this issue:

> Overclassification ultimately incurs avoidable fiscal costs and compromises national security. Adversarial, versus automatic, declassifications procedures are cumbersome and time consuming. Safeguards for voluminous classified material require costly security measures. And government officials confronted with dizzyingly complex rules for numerous categories of classified information often cannot or do not distinguish truly significant security matters from routine material market secret out of an excess of caution or zeal.[371]

Reducing the classification of documents and programs would thus produce significant cost savings and increased efficiency. A similar effect could be found by implementing more automatic declassification protocols.

---

367 *See, e.g.*, THE 9/11 COMM'N, *supra* note 281, at 417 ("But the security concerns need to be weighed against the costs. Current security requirements nurture overclassification and excessive compartmentation of information among agencies.").

368 Memorandum from Lawrence J. Halloran to Members of the Subcomm. on Nat'l Security, Emerging Threats, & Int'l Relations 4 (Feb. 24, 2005) (available at http://www.fas.org/sgp/congress/2005/halloran.pdf) ("The [Information Security Oversight Office] 2003 Report to the President noted that 3,978 separate offices or individuals made 238,030 classification decisions in [Fiscal Year] 2003 affecting more than 14 million documents.").

369 *Emerging Threats: Overclassification and Pseudo-Classification: Hearing Before the Subcomm. on National Security, Emerging Threats, and International Relations of the H. Comm. on Government Reform*, 109th Cong. 2 (2005) (statement of Thomas S. Blanton, Executive Director of the National Security Archive at George Washington University) ("My own estimate of overclassification in the United States today tends towards the high end of [the] 90% range. . . .").

370 N.Y. Times Co. v. United States, 403 U.S. 713, 724 (1971) (Douglas, I, concurring) ("Secrecy in government is fundamentally anti-democratic, perpetuating bureaucratic errors. . . . On public questions there should be 'uninhibited, robust, and wide-open' debate." (quoting N.Y. Times Co. v. Sullivan, 376 U.S. 254, 269-270 (1964))). *But cf. N.Y. Times Co.*, 403 U.S. at 728 (Stewart, J., concurring) ("Yet it is elementary that the successful conduct of international diplomacy and the maintenance of an effective national defense require both confidentiality and secrecy.").

371 Memorandum from Lawrence J. Halloran to Members of the Subcomm. on Nat'l Security, Emerging Threats, & Int'l Relations, *supra* note 368, at 8.

Closely related to the problem of overclassifying information is the exact opposite—"leaks" of national security information. As noted above, one of the traditional fears of the Executive is the leaking of information through Congress. This fear, of course, causes the executive to err on the side of caution when sharing sensitive information. As with free speech, this unnecessarily "chills" communication between Congress and the executive. As noted by a member of the Senate Committee composing the Joint Inquiry Report: "Congress should take decisive steps to help stem our contemporary culture of endemic 'leaking' of national security information to the media, so as better to ensure that our analysts remain better informed about terrorists than the terrorists do about them."[372] Again, this demands aggressive internal checks.

2. Uniformity of Oversight

In his testimony before the 9/11 Commission, former Congressman and co-chair of the 9/11 Commission, Lee Hamilton, succinctly identified a systemic problem in the Intelligence Community—a lack of unity[373] The Joint Inquiry Report quoted his testimony as follows:

> "U.S. intelligence is governed by a set of disparate laws and executive orders produced over the last fifty-five years. No single one of these laws provides a comprehensive legal foundation for our massive intelligence establishment. This is a remarkable state of affairs in a country that takes the rule of law so seriously.... [W]e need a statutory foundation for U.S. intelligence."[374]

All executive agencies operate under the rubric of Executive Order 12,333; however, each agency has implemented it differently, thereby creating a patchwork of regulations that vary from agency to agency. The divergences between agencies are further exasperated by different education-oversight programs for each agency.[375] This, then, seriously hampers the ability of agencies to work with one another. Where oversight education is lacking, incomplete, or incorrect, legal misconceptions develop within the agency regarding what is and is not "legal." This issue is

---

372 S. Rep. No. 107-351, H.R. Rep. No. 107-792 app. at 8 (2002) (Additional Views of Senator Richard C. Shelby).

373 *Joint Inquiry into Intelligence Community Activities Before and After the Terrorist Attacks of September 11, 2001: Hearing Before the S. Select Comm. on Intelligence and H. Permanent Select Comm. on Intelligence,* 107 Cong. (2002) (statement of Lee H. Hamilton, Former Chairman, H. Permanent Select Comm. on Intelligence).

374 S. Rep. No. 107-351, H.R. Rep. No. 107-792, at 353.

375 *See, e.g.,* Dep't of Defense, Procedures Governing the Activities of DoD Intelligence Components that Affect United States Persons, Instruction No. 5240.1-R (1982) (implementing Exec. Order 12,333, 3 C.F.R. 200 (1981), *reprinted in* 50 U.S.C. § 401).

further complicated by the insular nature of the intelligence establishment, where each agency perpetuates its own misconceptions.[376]

Congress should establish a uniform framework for intelligence oversight. This recommendation can take one of two forms. The first, recommended by Congressman Hamilton, would establish a "statutory foundation for U.S. intelligence."[377] The second would require Congress to establish organizations that would then ensure Community uniformity. The establishment of an inspector general and general counsel in the Office of the DNI, for instance, should significantly facilitate this effort.

Further, in establishing a uniform framework for oversight rules, Congress should strive to issue clear guidance, free to the greatest extent possible from legalistic terms and textual constructs.[378] Congress should mandate and fund annual training on these regulations. Finally, Congress should establish a bipartisan task force, and require the DNI to do the same, designed to identify and address "legal misconceptions" that pervade the Intelligence Community.

3. Uniformity of Operations

Perhaps the most damning critique by the 9/11 Commission concerned the inability of the Intelligence Community to achieve "unity of effort" in the conduct of intelligence operations.[379] This was partially the result of legal impediments, such as the prohibitions on the use of intelligence to obtain information on domestic law enforcement—the so-called "wall" between the CIA and FBI. This was addressed in the IRTPA.[380] Beyond the legal impediments to cooperation, individual agencies are characteristically insular and wary of outside assistance from other agencies.

Similar problems plagued the U.S. military until the passage of the Goldwater-Nichols Department of Defense Reorganization Act of 1986 (Goldwater-Nichols Act), which forced the unity of the DoD.[381] Before the passage of the Goldwater-Nichols Act, each branch operated largely independently of the others. The Joint Inquiry

376 The author experienced this phenomenon personally while serving as a Judge Advocate in Iraq. During the course of operations, it became necessary to question a U.S. citizen. Relying on extensive oversight training they had received, the intelligence officers refused to question the citizen, even though Executive Order 12,333 clearly permitted the questioning.

377 *See supra* note 374 and accompanying text.

378 The vast majority of individuals to whom these rules are applicable are not lawyers. Further, operational environments frequently limit or negate the possibility of seeking legal counsel.

379 *See* The 9/11 Comm'n, *supra* note 281, at 407.

380 IRTPA, Pub. L. No. 108-458, §§ 1013, 2001, 118 Stat. 3638, 3662-63, 3700-02; *see* S. Rep. No. 107-351, H.R. Rep. No. 107-792 app. at 8 (2002) (Additional Views of Sen. Shelby) ("Congress and the Administration have made progress since September 11 in breaking down some of the mythologies that impeded coordination.").

381 Goldwater-Nichols Department of Defense Reorganization Act of 1986, Pub. L. No. 99-433, 100 Stat. 992 (codified as amended in scattered sections of 10 U.S.C.).

Report and the 9/11 Commission report identified this analogy and recommended reforms to address the same issues addressed in the Goldwater-Nichols Act. The Joint Inquiry Report reads:

> Congress should give serious consideration, in its intelligence reform efforts, to developing an approach loosely analogous to that adopted by the Goldwater-Nichols Act in reforming the military command structure in order to overcome entrenched bureaucratic interests and forge a much more effective "joint" whole out of a motley and disputatious collection of parts. . . .
>
> . . . .
>
> This landmark legislation—which reformed the roles of the Chiefs of Staff and created an entirely new system of regional unified commanders—tilted at what were thought to be bureaucratic windmills and ran into fearsome bureaucratic opposition, but it succeeded brilliantly and helped our armed forces find new strength and coherence in war-winning "joint" operations.[382]

Clearly this recommendation would require a Herculean legislative effort, as well as support from the various agencies and the President. The need for such legislation, however, may have been rendered moot by the establishment of the DNI, which was the solution proposed by the 9/11 Commission.[383] Given adequate authority, as promised in the bill establishing the position, the DNI should have the ability to effectuate such changes across the Intelligence Community.[384]

4. Increased Aggressiveness

As noted by Richard Betts, the present intelligence reform efforts are not directed at punishing or restricting the Intelligence Community, but rather at envisioning ways to make the Intelligence Community more aggressive.[385] In additional comments accompanying the Joint Inquiry Report, Senators Jon Kyl and Pat Roberts remarked that "[c]hanging the culture of risk aversion in these agencies is a major undertaking. It should be a central focus of any corrective actions we may attempt following this investigation."[386] Senators Kyl and Roberts intimate that the Intelligence Community's aversion to risk may be a result of the Church and Pike committees:

> Many comments on risk aversion alluded to congressional oversight and/or investigations dating back to the Church and Pike investigations of the 1970s. . . . It is quite possible—though this theme was not fully explored by the [Joint Inquiry Staff]—that

---

382 S. Rep. No. 107-351, H.R. Rep. No. 107-792 app. at 5, 26 (Additional Views of Sen. Shelby).

383 *See supra* note 285 and accompanying text.

384 *See supra* notes 286–290 and accompanying text.

385 Betts, *supra* note 311, at 3.

386 S. Rep. No. 107-351, H.R. Rep. No. 107-792 app. at 8 (Additional Views of Senator Jon Kyl and Senator Pat Roberts).

> a legacy of caution left by these historical episodes contributed to timidity in tackling the Al-Qaeda problem before Al-Qaeda struck on 9/11.[387]

Similar issues were addressed by Senator Richard Shelby, the Committee Vice Chairman: "[G]iven the unpleasant history of covert action scandals that have affected the CIA, one should not be surprised to find that—ironically, perhaps—the covert action infrastructure is a relatively cautious one."[388] This issue could be largely addressed through the adoption of uniform oversight regulations and oversight-education programs.[389]

There is, however, a related fear which is not addressed by these measures: the fear of criminal prosecution or civil liability for official acts committed in the course of intelligence operations. This fear has caused many CIA officials to take out personal liability insurance.[390] Few question the necessity of operating within the law; concerns arise, however, when the parameters of the law are not clear. Various agencies within the executive have issued extensive guidance on the conduct of interrogations as related to domestic and international law.[391] Thus, the question is posed: when a new administration comes into power, what happens if they adopt a stricter reading of these legal operations, thereby effectively criminalizing conduct that was previously permissible? Senator Shelby has identified these concerns:

> Intelligence officers will often, and with good reason, hesitate to take operational risks or to push aggressively to accomplish their missions if they are operating under ambiguous or convoluted legal authorities and always suspect that they may be prosecuted or hauled before a hostile inquiry for any actual or perceived missteps.[392]

---

387 *Id.* app. at 7.

388 *Id.* app. at 129 (ADDITIONAL VIEWS OF SEN. SHELBY).

389 *See supra* notes 379–384 and accompanying text.

390 NAT'L COMM'N ON TERRORISM, COUNTERING THE CHANGING THREAT OF INTERNATIONAL TERRORISM 12 (2000).

391 *See, e.g.*, Memorandum from George W. Bush on Humane Treatment of Taliban and al-Qaeda Detainees (Feb. 7, 2002). This memorandum notes the inapplicability of the Geneva Conventions to the war on terror, but requires executive agencies to act "consistent" with the conventions. *Id.* at 1; *see* Memorandum from Alberto R. Gonzales to George W. Bush on the Decision Re Application of the Geneva Convention on Prisoners of War to the Conflict with al-Qaeda and the Taliban (Jan. 25, 2002) (providing the legal analysis for the President's February 7 memorandum regarding application of the Geneva Conventions to the war on terror); Memorandum from William J. Haynes II, Dep't of Def. Gen. Counsel, to the Sec'y of Def. on Counter-Resistance Techniques (Nov. 27, 2002) (providing guidance to the DoD on interrogation polices); *see also* U.S. ARMY, FM [FIELD MANUAL] 34-52: INTELLIGENCE INTERROGATION (1992), *available at* http://www.fas.org/irp/doddir/army/fm34-52.pdf.

392 S. REP. NO. 107-351, H.R. REP. NO. 107-792 app. at 129 (ADDITIONAL VIEWS OF SEN. SHELBY).

Regardless of the legal treatment of this query, the very question is causing officials to artificially restrict their operations. In an effort to eliminate this fear (and the resulting operational inefficiency), Congress should consider legislation that would immunize official conduct from civil liability.[393] This is, however, distinct from the recent Graham-Levin-Kyl Amendment to the National Defense Authorization Act for Fiscal year 2006, which removed jurisdiction from all courts to consider writs of habeas corpus and judicial actions brought by individuals detained at Guantanamo Bay, Cuba.[394] Whereas the Graham-Levin-Kyl Amendment is designed to limit a detainee's ability to challenge their detention,[395] the recommendation proposed here simply seeks to remove the threat of civil liability.

VII. CONCLUSION

Quite plainly, the balance of executive autonomy and legislative oversight has not been resolved. The revelation of the NSA program plainly illustrates this and perfectly reflects recent history which finds a predictable sequence: public support for operations followed by either an intelligence/military failure or revelations of intelligence improprieties, followed by public demands for regulation and restraints. International and domestic events, the conduct of the intelligence agencies, and the perceived threat to national security combine to fuel the public climate that in turn shapes the political response. The key to effective policy making in regard to intelligence regulations is striking a balance between the short-term national security needs of the country, the long-term national security needs of the country, the liberties guaranteed by our Constitution, and the desires of the American public.

Congress serves an undeniably vital role in ensuring both lawful and efficient intelligence operations. In order to fulfill both roles most effectively, Congress must continuously and consistently exercise its powers in an efficient and responsible manner. Continuity and consistency are gained through a Congress interested in oversight in the absence of an intelligence failure or impropriety. Efficiency is gained through the adoption of any number of recommendations made by any number of organizations. In the end, however, Congress and the President, and ultimately the courts, will again be forced to reconcile the seemingly endless debate over separation of power and the conduct of intelligence operations.

---

393 *See* NAT'L COMM'N ON TERRORISM, *supra* note 390, at 12 ("Congress should . . . mandate full reimbursement of the costs of personal liability insurance for Federal Bureau of Investigation special agents and Central Intelligence Agency officers in the field who are combating terrorism.").

394 National Defense Authorization Act for Fiscal Year 2006, Pub. L. 109-163, § 1405, 119 Stat. 3136, 3476–78.

395 *Id.*

THE WAR AGAINST FUNDAMENTAL RIGHTS: FRENCH COUNTERTERRORISM POLICY AND THE NEED TO INTEGRATE INTERNATIONAL SECURITY AND HUMAN RIGHTS AGREEMENTS

Calliope Makedon Sudborough

Originally published in *Suffolk Transnational Law Review*, Vol. 30 (Summer 2007)

> Those who would give up essential liberty, to purchase a little temporary safety, deserve neither liberty nor safety.[1]

I. INTRODUCTION

At 8:50 am on July 7, 2005, three native Londoners trained in radical Islamist propaganda, simultaneously detonated bombs in their backpacks on London's underground metro system.[2] The terror resulting from the attacks fundamentally undermined London's traditionally tolerant society.[3] In the attack's aftermath, British and other European officials sought to enforce stricter security measures, attempting to borrow policies from the French approach to counterterrorism.[4] Both American and British officials have acknowledged that France was the first country to recognize the threat of, and pioneer a successful response to, radical

1 Letter from Benjamin Franklin to the Governor on behalf of the Pennsylvania Assembly (Nov. 11, 1755), *available at* http://www.ushistory.org/franklin/quotable/quote04.htm.

2 *See* Front Page, *Seven Days of Shock: How the Drama Unfolded,* FIN. TIMES, July 14, 2005, at 3 (describing logistics of July 7, 2005 terrorist attacks on London).

3 *See generally* Roger Blitz et. al., *The Politics of Policing: Americans and British Encounter Tensions over Terrorism After the London Bombs,* FIN. TIMES, Aug. 17, 2005, at 15 (describing London's history of tolerance allowing dissidents to live freely within city); Christopher Adams, *Sweeping Anti-terrorism Laws Planned,* FIN. TIMES, July 16, 2005 (describing British Prime Minister's new zero tolerance approach to resident radicals).

4 *See* Roger Blitz, *Blair Looks to France For Lessons on Expelling Islamist Extremists: The Prime Minister Wants Similar Powers to Other Governments*, FIN. TIMES, Aug. 9, 2005, at 3 (publicizing British prime minister's push to expand police and judiciary powers to match policies in France); *cf.* Jimmy Burns, Daniel Dombey & Frederick Studemann, *Human rights 'key to winning terror battle'*, FIN. TIMES, Jan. 22, 2006, at 8 (recounting European Union's antiterrorism coordinator's appeal to employ counterterrorism policies respecting human rights and civil liberties).

Islamist terrorists.[5] When, however, an innocent Brazilian man mistaken for a terrorist was shot seven times in the head by British security forces under a shoot-to-kill man-date, many questioned whether the quest for security had gone too far.[6] As Britain and other European countries struggling to fight the war on terrorism turn to France for bold counterterrorism solutions, some are wary of the implications on civil liberties.[7]

This Note examines French counterterrorism policy, in light of recent favorable recognition it has received, and argues that rather than being a model of a successful response to terrorism, French policy reflects international counter-terrorism law's failure to protect the human rights obligations essential to a free, democratic society.[8] Part II describes current international and French counter-terrorism policy, introduces France's civil liberties climate, and briefly surveys counterterrorism policies elsewhere in Europe and the United States.[9] Part III traces the development of the international legal framework on terrorism and human rights law.[10] Part IV contends that the international framework on terrorism undermines international human rights law and the freedoms of democratic society by dividing human rights law and counterterrorism law into disconnected spheres.[11]

---

5 *See* Blitz, *supra* note 4, at 3 (quoting CIA official's opinion that both U.S. and U.K have lagged behind France).

6 *See generally* Cathy Newman & Bob Sherwood, *Met Chief Faces Calls to Quit Over Shooting,* FIN. TIMES, Aug. 18, 2005, at 2 (describing gross logistical errors committed under British police force's shoot-to-kill policy).

7 *See* Blitz, *Blair Looks to France for Lessons, supra* note 4, at 3 (noting France's circumvention of human rights norms and negative implications if other European governments follow suit). *See also* Edith Y. Yu, *Domestic Spying and Why America Should Avoid the Slippery Slope,* 16 S. CAL. REV. OF L. & SOC. JUST. 3, 7-8 (2006) (suggesting civil liberties essential to survival of democracy); Kelly R. Cusick, Note, *Thwarting Ideological Terrorism: Are we Brave Enough to Maintain Civil Liberties,* 35 CASE W. RES. J. OF INT'L L. 55, 60 (describing importance of well-protected civil liberties to American society); Emanuel Gross, *The Struggle of a Democracy Against the Terror of Suicide Bombers: Ideological and Legal Aspects,* 22 WIS. INT'L L. J. 569, 659 (linking continued democracy and respect for civil liberties); [U.S. DEPT. OF STATE, The Terrorist Enemy], http://www.state.gov/s/ct/enemy (last visited March 1, 2007) (stating terrorist networks pose greatest threat to national security); [OFFICE OF THE COORDINATOR FOR COUNTERTERRORISM U.S. DEPT. OF STATE, Chapter 6 Terrorist Groups], http://www.state.gov/documents/organization/45323.pdf (last visited March 1, 2007) (listing and describing foreign terrorist organizations).

8 *See infra* Parts I-IV and accompanying notes (analyzing French counterterrorism policy in light of international security and human rights agreements).

9 *See infra* Part II (unfolding French counterterrorism measures and social climate).

10 *See infra* Part III (tracing international counterterrorism and human rights legal system).

11 *See infra* Part IV (arguing for integration of international counterterrorism law and human rights law).

II. THE CIVIL LIBERTIES CLIMATE IN FRANCE AND CURRENT COUNTERTERRORISM POLICY

A. French Society and Civil Liberties

To understand the French attitude towards civil liberties, one must first appreciate the importance of *l'État* in France, which essentially means the French "State."[12] France was once a highly fractious society that struggled to unify and acquiesce to a stable, democratic government for over one thousand years.[13] Today's France is a leading democratic nation in which almost every aspect of French life is provided for and controlled by the government in Paris.[14] Mindful of the stability *l'État* provides, the French are generally inclined to support an ultra-centralized government and ignore its excessive abuse of power.[15] Thus, the concept and culture of vigilantly protecting civil liberties from government infringement is not as fervent in France as it is elsewhere.[16] French citizens are more willing to give up greater degrees of

---

12 *Cf.* JEAN-BENOIT NADEAU & JULIE BARLOW, SIXTY MILLION FRENCHMEN CAN'T BE WRONG (WHY WE LOVE FRANCE BUT NOT THE FRENCH) 126 (Sourcebooks, Inc. 2003) (2003) (asserting French State's status as essence of French identity and difficulty in defining *État).* Unlike the State in Anglo-Saxon government, *lÉtat* not only regulates the economy and guarantees national security, but it defines culture, language, the "common good" and equalizes socio-economic disparities. *Id.* (elucidating meaning of *l'État* and its functions).

13 *See* NADEAU, *supra* note 12, at 126, 128, 314 (tracing political development of French nation and government). A millenium ago, a "French" people did not exist, but rather France resembled the Balkans in that people spoke different languages and had different customs and political allegiances. *Id.* at 128 (characterizing French ancestors' society as Balkan-like). France's divisiveness persisted after the French Revolution of 1789, during which time there were, "[F]ive Republics, two empires, three monarchies, and one fascist dictatorship." *Id* at 314 (listing French governments since French Revolution).

14 *See* NADEAU, *supra* note 12, at 127, 144–145, 158, 180–182 (describing *l'État's* superiority and control over local government, education, culture, and language).

15 *See* NADEAU, *supra* note 12, at 127 (describing French attitude towards central government). The French credit the State with unifying the nation, providing democratic stability, a common language, and vital services such as quality education and health care. *Id.* at 11. *See also* NADEAU, *supra* note 12, at 126–127, 136, 179 (describing State's role in developing government institutions and social services and quality thereof). A U.N. study ranked the French healthcare system first in the world while the U.S. system ranked thirty-seventh. *Id.* at 136. Additionally, a study conducted by the Organization for Economic and Cooperative Development ranked French students in the top quarter for math skills. *Id.* at 179. Canadian journalists who authored an ethnological book on France described the French attitude toward the State in this way:

> The French strongly believe in the common good and happily grant the State all the powers and privileges it requires to act for the common good. They affirm the State's role in virtually everything—culture, language, welfare, and the economy.

Id. at 282.

16 *See generally* Henri Astier, *Profile: France's Top Anti-Terror Judge,* BBC NEWS ONLINE (2003), http://news.bbc.co.Uk/go/pf/fr/-/2/hi/europe/3031640.stm (last visited Feb. 12, 2007) (explaining lack of civil liberties-related protest stems from small size of active French human rights community).

fundamental liberties, such as privacy and freedom of speech, in exchange for the services, safety, and stability that their government provides.[17]

Apart from the French state's political history, the changing ethnic composition of France has also shaped French attitudes toward civil liberties.[18] The largest Muslim and African populations in Europe reside in France, and the nation's second most popular religion is Islam.[19] Arabic culture has established a mainstream presence in French television, cinema, music, and cuisine.[20] Nevertheless, the emergence of the xenophobic political party, *Front National*, illustrates that Muslim immigrants are not entirely welcome in France.[21] Moreover, multiculturalism is not a positive term in France because the nation is founded on an assimilation doctrine, in which the principle of *égalité*, or "equality," depends upon the elimination of cultural, educational, linguistic, and economic differences.[22] As a consequence of assimilation,

---

> The French public is accustomed to and willing to tolerate a police bureaucracy that would certainly be viewed as invasive in the US, even taking into account the change in attitudes after the 9/11 attacks. While there is concern over the effect of this system on civil liberties, particularly to the left of the political spectrum, there seems to be a consensus that the freedom to walk the street or to take the subway without fear of bombs lies at the base of other civil liberties.

Jeremy Shapiro & Bénédicte Suzan, *The French Experience of Counterterrorism*, SURVIVAL, Spring 2003 at 67, 88, *available at* http://www.brookings.edu/views/articles/fellows/shapiro 20030301.pdf.

17 *See generally* NADEAU, *supra* note 12, at 127; Shapiro & Suzan, *supra* note 16, at 88. "[T]he French are willing to overlook almost anything [the state has] done because of one splendid thing it accomplished: creating France. It's a political reflex absolutely alien to North Americans." NADEAU, *supra* note 12, at 127.

18 *See* NADEAU, *supra* note 12, at 295–311 (discussing immigrant populations' effects on French politics and society).

19 *See* NADEAU, *supra* note 12, at 295 (stating France ranks as biggest Muslim nation in Europe); KAREN ARMSTRONG, ISLAM: A SHORT HISTORY, 148 (Random House Inc 2002) (2000) (tracing France's colonization of African countries during 19–20th centuries). The large Arab and African populations in France are due to France's colonization of Algeria, Tunisia, Egypt, Sudan, Libya, and Morocco. *Id.* After de-colonization, waves of immigrants from the former colonies sought work and settled in France. *See* NADEAU, *supra* note 12, at 112 (describing volume of Algerian nationals immigrating to France after Algerian independence).

20 *See* NADEAU, *supra* note 12, at 295 (pointing to evidence of Arab infusion in French popular culture). After the French soccer team, whose star player was of Algerian descent, won the 1998 World Cup tournament, the "Beurs," second-generation North Africans, asserted and popularized Arabic culture in France. *Id.* at 295–296.

21 *See* NADEAU, *supra* note 12, at 305 (stipulating rising popularity of *le Front National* relates to French resentment towards immigrants). Before the 1980's, *le Front National* could not garner one percent of the vote, but in 2002, the party won almost twenty percent of the popular vote. *Id.* at 305–307.

22 *See* NADEAU, *supra* note 12, at 301, 309 (expounding on French assimilation doctrine and societal attitude towards multiculturalism); French Government Portal, *Immigration: A Policy Built on Clearer Rules* (2005), *available at* http://www.premierministre.gouv.fr/en/chantiers/major_projects_94/policy_built_on_clear_56775.html (last visited Feb. 15, 2007) (describing France's integration policy with respect to immigrants).

statistics relating to race and immigration in France—and any abuses related thereto—are "black holes" because official questionnaires on race, religion, native language, and other socio-economic factors are illegal.[23]

B. Current French Counterterrorism Policy

Having successfully protected French soil from terrorist attacks since 1996, France serves as an attractive model for countries seeking to increase their domestic counterterrorism measures' effectiveness.[24] The French counterterrorism strategy is a pre-emptive approach that employs both domestic and international legal tools to carry out the government's zero tolerance approach.[25] The French government maintains that its counterterrorism policy is obliged to comply with human rights principles and respect for fundamental liberties.[26] At the same time, however, the architect of France's counterterrorism policy, Charles Pasqua, stated, "one must terrorize the terrorists."[27]

Current French counterterrorism policy originated in sweeping legislation adopted by the French government in 1986.[28] The 1986 Act defined terrorism as "an individual or collective enterprise intending to gravely trouble public order by means of intimidation

23 *See* Nadeau, *supra* note 12, at 301–302 (describing illegality of ethnicity, race, or religious identification questions in French census).

24 *See* Shapiro & Suzan, *supra* note 16, at 67–68 (recalling instances of successful terrorist attack prevention and suggesting ways United States can learn from French experience); Martin Arnold, *'Le Sheriff' Warns on Globalization of Terrorism*, Fin. Times, Aug. 25, 2005, at 6 (quoting top French investigatory magistrate statement and discussing U.K.'s ability to adopt French policies). French authorities foiled planned attacks on the French World Cup in 1998, the Cathedral in Strasbourg in 2000, and the American Embassy in Paris in 2001, among others. *See* Shapiro & Suzan, *supra* note 16, at 68.

25 *See* Craig Whitlock, *French Push Limits in Fight on Terrorism: Wide Prosecutorial Powers Draw Scant Public Dissent*, Wash. Post, Nov. 2, 2004, at A01 (describing French law enforcement's strategy as "preemptive"). The government characterizes French counterterrorism policy as an "unequivocal condemnation" of terrorism. *See* Ministère des Affaires Étrangères, *Terrorism: National Instruments*, http://www.diplomatie.gouv.fr/en/france-priorities_l/terrorism_1944/national-instruments_1344.html (last visited April 10, 2007) (describing French law enforcement strategy). *See generally* Ministère des Affaires Étrangères, *Terrorism: Multilateral Initiatives*, http://www.diplomatie.gouv.fr/en/france-priorities_l/terrorism_1944/multilateral-initiatives_1345.html (last visited April 10, 2007) (articulating International counterterrorism legislation).

26 *See* Ministère des Affaires Étrangères, *supra* note 25. The French government avows that "France considers that the unequivocal fight against terrorism must be fought in compliance with human rights and public freedoms." *Id.*

27 *See* Michaël McColgan & Attanasio and Alessandro Attanasio, *Mission Internationale D'Enquete: France "La Porte Ouverte à L'Arbitraire*, Fédération Internationale des Ligues des Droits de l'Homme, Rapport No. 271, (Jan. 1999) *available at* http://www.fidh.org/rapports/r271.htm (quoting author of French counterterrorism laws on legislative goals).

28 *See* Shapiro & Suzan, *supra* note 16, at 76 (describing legislation's innovations and shift in direction). The legislation represented a shift in counterterrorism policy that moved away from accommodating diplomacy towards a hard-line judicial approach. *Id.*

or terror."[29] The Act also criminalized "association with wrongdoers involved in terrorist enterprises."[30] This new law allows French authorities to conduct raids, in which the police may arrest hundreds of persons for questioning, without requiring authorities to present evidence that any particular individual has contributed to a terrorist plot.[31] This law also permits courts to convict persons under a lesser burden of proof because to prove a defendant guilty it is not necessary to show that the defendant somehow furthered the terrorist conspiracy.[32] Rather, it is sufficient to show that the defendant interacted with, and was somehow linked to, a terrorist.[33]

In addition, the 1986 legislation centralized investigatory, prosecutorial, and judicial procedures.[34] The new laws created a group of "investigatory magistrates."[35]

---

29 Legifrance.gouv.fr, C. Pr. Pen. Art. 41, Nov. 3, 2005, *available at* http://195.83. 177.9/code/liste.phtml?lang=uk&c=33&r=3794 (defining conduct punishable as terrorism under French penal code); Shapiro & Suzan, *supra* note 16, at 77 (citing terrorism definition in Sept. 9, 1986 legislation); Ministère de l'Intérieur, *Le Terrorisme,* Oct. 3, 2005, http://www.interieur.gouv.fr/rubriques/c/c3_police_nationale/c332_dcpj/Le_terrorisme_et_les_trafics_d_armes (citing terrorism definition in Sept. 9, 1986 legislation).

30 C. Pr. Pen. Art. 41, *supra* note 29, at Art. 421–1 (defining terrorism under new laws); *Le Terrorisme, supra* note 29 (explaining definitions under new terrorism laws); Bruce Crumley, *Targeting Terrorism,* FRANCE MAGAZINE, Spring 2004, *available at* www.francemagazine.org/articles/issue69/article88.asp?issuue_id=69&article_id=88 (summarizing new crime established by 1986 legislation). Currently, a suspect convicted of association with terrorists may be charged with a maximum sentence of ten years. *See* Piotr Smolar, *Le Gouvernement Veut Punir Plus Sévèrement les Terroristes,* LE MONDE, Sept. 7, 2005, *available at* http://www.lemonde.fr/web/imprimer_element/0,40–0@2-3226, 50-686442,0.html (expounding sentencing changes proposed by new counterterrorism legislation). New legislation that the French parliament debated in October 2005 contemplated extending the maximum penalty for associating with terrorists from ten years to twenty, and the maximum penalty for the leaders of terrorist networks could be expanded from twenty to thirty years. *Id.*

31 *See* Shapiro & Suzan, *supra* note 16, at 85 (describing sweeping round-ups French police can conduct under association with terrorist wrongdoers law). The police often arrest persons who merely happen to be present at the scene, even though only a few persons are actually documented suspects. *Id.* at 84–85.

32 *See* Shapiro & Suzan, *supra* note 16, at 85 (arguing association with terrorist wrongdoers law imposes lesser burden of proof on prosecutors).

33 *See* McColgan & Attanasio & Attanasio, *supra* note 27, at 3–6 (quoting judicial decision convicting detainee despite no evidence of misconduct for association with terrorist collaborators). In convicting a suspect who allegedly assisted a convicted terrorist, the court based its decision on speculation, stating that it was unrealistic to expect that the suspect could associate with so many terrorist operatives without being aware of their actions and objectives. *Id.* at 3–6 (quoting judicial decision convicting suspect for association with wrongdoers).

34 *See* Shapiro & Suzan, *supra* note 16, at 77 (describing centralized judicial proceedings related to terrorism created by 1986 legislation); Crumley, *supra* note 30, (describing organizational bodies and relationships created by 1986 legislation). The 1986 legislation combines the efforts of investigatory magistrates with secret intelligence agencies called the Renseignements Généraux and the Directorate of Territorial Security (DST). *See* Crumley, *supra* note 30 (setting forth the antiterror unit structure created by the 1986 legislation).

35 Shapiro & Suzan, *supra* note 16, at 78 (defining *juge d'instruction).*

These are officials bestowed with the combined functions of a prosecutor and a judge, whose purpose is to conduct an impartial investigation as a neutral party.[36] Under these measures, investigatory magistrates have wide prosecutorial powers that allow them to launch investigations, issue search warrants, wiretaps, and subpoenas without further authorization.[37]

The 1986 legislation also permits authorities to detain terrorist suspects for up to ninety-two hours, which amounts to four days, before allowing them access to counsel; and, in some instances, suspects may be detained for years before authorities initiate a trial.[38] This measure, called "preventive detention," facilitates police investigations by allowing the police to hold a suspect in prison until more persuasive evidence can be obtained for a conviction.[39] In one instance, French authorities detained an acquaintance of Richard Reid, the British shoe-bomber, in a French prison from June 2002 until November 2004 without filing formal charges against him.[40] Police threaten preventative detention as a strategic investigatory tool in persuading suspects to become informants.[41] Occasionally, however, the preventive detention strategy has resulted in dangerous effects on detainees, including suicide.[42]

---

36 *See* Shapiro & Suzan, *supra* note 16, at 78 (explaining functions of *juge d'instruction* and lack of similar concept in Anglo-Saxon law). *See* Crumley, *supra* note 30 (articulating permitted maximum lengths of detention for terrorist suspects under 1986 legislation).

37 *See* Shapiro & Suzan, *supra* note 16, at 78 (highlighting investigatory magistrates' judicial and investigatory powers).

38 *See* Shapiro & Suzan, *supra* note 16, at 84 (delineating investigatory magistrates' authority to detain suspects in terrorist cases); Arnold, *supra* note 24, at 6 (noting government's ability to detain suspects for ninety-two hours before suspect is charged or has access to counsel). Authorities have the power to detain terrorist suspects for ninety-two hours prior to filing charges and imprison them for up to three years before authorities decide whether their investigations have gathered sufficient information to launch a trial. *See* Shapiro & Suzan, *supra* note 16, at 84 (describing investigatory magistrates' power to detain terrorist suspects); *see also* Astier, *supra* note 16 (describing detention of terrorist suspects under 1986 legislation); Whitlock, *supra* note 25 (asserting French authorities may detain terrorist suspects for up to three years before start initiating trial); Crumley, *supra* note 30, at 6 (asserting 1986 legislation allows officials to detain terrorist suspects before trial for over three years).

39 *See* Astier, *supra* note 16 (describing lengthy detentions as "preventive detention"); *cf.* Crumley, *supra* note 30, at 6 (suggesting preventive detention method has successfully prevented bombing plots).

40 *See* Whitlock, *supra* note 25 (documenting Hakim Mokhfi's detention). Mokhfi was eventually released in 2005. *See France Jails Shoe-Bomber Contact,* BBC News, May 16, 2005, http://news.bbc.co.Uk/2/hi/europe/4100102.stm (stating jailed contact not accessory to attempted shoe-bombing).

41 *See* Whitlock, *supra* note 25, at A01 (stating police threaten pre-emptive arrest as reconnaissance strategy).

42 *See* McColgan & Attanasio, *supra* note 27, at VI (narrating detention of Kurdish political refugee for ties to PKK). For example, French authorities detained a Kurdish political refugee, M. Alpaslan, in a French prison for suspected association with high-ranking members of the P.K.K., a Kurdish terrorist group seeking an independent state in Turkey. *Id.* Alpaslan remained imprisoned for over a year while police investigated his case, although the only proof that

The mastermind behind French judicial efforts to fight terrorism is investigating magistrate Jean-Louis Bruguière.[43] Having hunted Middle Eastern and radical Islamist terrorists for over twenty years, Bruguière's expertise has drawn the attention of many foreign governments.[44] Bruguière's methodology is to unravel the logistical and financial networks that support international terrorists.[45] Beyond his expertise in dismantling international terrorist cells, Bruguière's investigatory tactics are also widely publicized.[46] He is known for arresting and questioning hundreds of persons at a time.[47]

III. THE INTERNATIONAL LEGAL FRAMEWORK

A. International Counterterrorism Law

U.N. conventions and resolutions form "pillars of the international legal order" and are among the principal international legal tools for responding to the security threat posed by terrorism.[48] On September 28, 2001, the UN Security Council passed Resolution 1373, which pronounced terrorism a threat to "international peace and security" and imposed compulsory responsibilities on all UN member states to enact domestic legislation.[49]

Alpaslan collaborated in the PKK's efforts was supplied by Turkey, the country from which Alpaslan had sought political asylum and a country whose reputation for respecting human rights has long been questioned. *Id.* The day before the French authorities finally decided to release Alpaslan on bail, he committed suicide in his jail cell at age 28. *Id.*

43 *See* Crumley, *supra* note 30 (describing Bruguière as "emblematic" of French war on terrorism); Arnold, *supra* note 24, at 6 (describing Bruguière as "best-known" anti-terror judge); Astier, *supra* note 16 (quoting American terrorist-expert describing Bruguière as representing "forefront" of war on terrorism).

44 *See* Astier, *supra* note 16 (tracing Bruguière's growing reputation for terrorist tracking expertise and foreign government interest); Crumley, *supra* note 30 (describing foreign government interest in Bruguière's expertise after September 11, 2001). A French security official stated that Bruguière's "invented the specialty of identifying and cracking Islamist terror networks," and that after September 11, 2001, foreign colleagues stopped regarding Bruguière's mission to pursue Middle Eastern terrorists as "some sort of odd French obsession." *See* Crumley, *supra* note 30.

45 *See* Crumley, *supra* note 30 (describing Bruguière's investigations).

46 *See* Astier, *supra* note 16 (describing public reaction to Bruguière's use of investigatory powers); Crumley, *supra* note 30 (describing publicity generated by Bruguière's investigatory methods).

47 *See* Astier, *supra* note 16 (describing Bruguière's large roundups of terrorist suspects).

48 *See E. U. Network of Independent Experts in Fundamental Rights, The Balance Between Freedom and Security in the Response by the European Union and its Member States to the Terrorist Threats*, at 7, (Mar. 31, 2003) *available at* http:// www.statewatch.org/news/2003/apr/CFR-CDG. ThemCommentl.pdf [hereinafter, "CFR-CDF"] (citing U.N. conventions in discussion of international law on terrorism); Ministère des Affaires Étrangères, supra note 25 (recognizing U.N. resolutions as primary sources of international cooperation against terrorism).

49 *See* CFR-CDF, *supra* note 48, at 9 (highlighting Resolution 1373's role in creation of anti-terrorism legislation among EU member states). *See generally* S.C. Res. 1566, U.N. Doc. S/RES/1566 (Oct. 8, 2004), *available at* http://daccessdds.un.org/doc/UNDOC/GEN/N04/542/82/PDF/N0454282.pdf?OpenElement (calling for development of best practices

Furthermore, Resolution 1373 incorporates provisions from existing UN counter-terrorism conventions that had not been universally adopted and, by integrating them into Resolution 1373, made them binding on all UN member states.[50] UN conventions on terrorism, such as the International Convention for the Suppression of Terrorist Bombings, among others, seek to condemn various forms of terrorism and call upon state-parties to adopt domestic and cooperative measures aimed at preventing and punishing terrorists.[51] Although various forms of terrorism are condemned, Resolution 1373, and the conventions it incorporates, do not contain a definition of terrorism, but leave member states to define terrorism under their domestic laws.[52]

---

guidelines for member state implementation of Resolution 1373); S.C. Res. 1526, U.N. Doc. S/RES/1526 (Jan. 30, 2004), *available at* http://daccessdds.un.org/doc/UNDOC/GEN/N04/226/69/PDF/N0422669.pdf?OpenElement (calling for special implementation of Resolution 1373 with respect to Taliban and Al-Qaida); S.C. Res. 1373, U.N. Doc. S/RES/1373 (Sept. 28, 2001), *available at* http:// www.unodc.org/images/resolution%201373.pdf (last visited Feb. 15, 2007) [hereinafter "Resolution 1373"] (delineating strategies member states must employ to prevent and suppress terrorism); S.C. Res. 1267, U.N. Doc. S/RES/1267 (Oct. 15, 1999), *available at* http://daccessdds.un.org/doc/UNDOC/GEN/N99/300/44/PDF/N9930044.pdf?Open Element (calling on member states to impede Taliban use of national resources and services). Resolution 1373 and the subsequent reaffirming resolutions call on UN member states to criminalize and prevent the financing of terrorist acts, prevent assistance to terrorist perpetrators, cooperate in criminal investigations and proceedings relating to terrorism, implement effective border controls to prevent the movement of terrorist groups, and improve inter-state information exchanges on terrorism-related developments. *See* Resolution 1373, *supra*, at ¶¶ 1–3 (listing policies member states should adopt for prevention and suppression of terrorist acts).

50 *See* Eric Rosand, *Security Council Resolution 1373, the Counterterrorism Committee, and the Fight Against Terrorism*, 97 A.J.I.L. 333, 333-334 (2003) (introducing UN Resolution 1373, its goals, and modus operandi).

51 *See* International Convention for the Suppression of Acts of Nuclear Terrorism, Apr. 13, 2005, UN. GAOR 59th Sess., UN Doc. A/59/766 *available at* http://untreaty.un.org/English/Terrorism/English_18_15.pdf (criminalizing possession of radioactive material with intent to cause serious injury on civilians or environment); International Convention for the Suppression of the Financing of Terrorrism, G.A. Res. 54/109, U.N. Doc. A/RES/54109 *available at* http://untreaty.un.org/English/Terrorism/Convl2.pdf (criminalizing provision or collection of funds with intent to carry out serious injury on civilians); International Convention for the Suppression of Terrorist Bombings, Jan. 12, 1998, G.A. Res. 52/164, U.N. DOC. A/RES/52/164 *available at* http://untreaty.un.org/English/Terrorism/Convll.pdf (criminalizing possession or detonation of explosives with intent to seriously injure civilians); International Convention against the Taking of Hostages, Dec. 17, 1979, T.I.A.S. No. 11,081, 1 316 U.N.T.S. 205 *available at* http://untreaty.un.org/English/Terrorism/Conv5.pdf (criminalizing detention and threats to kill persons to compel third parties to act or abstain therefrom); Convention on the Prevention and Punishment of Crimes against Internationally Protected Persons, Including Diplomatic Agents, Dec. 14, 1973, 28 U.S.T. 1975, 1035 U.N.T.S. 167 *available at* http://untreaty.un.org/English/Terrorism/Conv4.pdf (criminalizing any infringement on liberty or life of internationally protected persons).

52 *See* Rosand, *supra* note 50, at 339 (noting absence of definition of terrorism under UN counterterrorism framework).

Resolution 1373 also created the Counterterrorism Committee (CTC) within the Security Council to supervise member states' adoption of the Resolution.[53] The CTC reviews member states' reports on domestic progress in implementing Resolution 1373 and consults with independent "Expert Advisers" in advising member states on such issues as legislative drafting, various areas of law, and law enforcement.[54] Although Resolution 1373's scope and the oversight of the CTC are very broad, the CTC does not monitor states' compliance with human rights norms in the counterterrorism arena.[55] Despite the UN High Commissioner for Human Rights' efforts to compel the CTC to appoint an expert on human rights compliance, the CTC has maintained the position that monitoring adherence to human rights obligations in the war against terrorism falls outside the CTC's scope and purpose.[56] The refusal to explicitly link human rights compliance with Resolution 1373 adherence was made clear by a former CTC chairman who stated,

> The Counterterrorism Committee is mandated to monitor the implementation of resolution 1373[]. Monitoring performance against other international conventions, including human rights law, is outside the scope of the Counterterrorism Committee's mandate. But we will remain aware of the interaction with human rights concerns, and we will keep ourselves briefed as appropriate.[57]

Since France is a European Union (EU) member, and EU law is binding on member states and takes precedence over member states' national laws, it is important to describe EU counterterrorism law here.[58] The EU is a supranational entity with twenty-seven member states that comprises a common market and currency,

---

53 *See* Resolution 1373, *supra* note 49, at ¶ 6 (deciding to establish a committee of the Security Council to monitor Resolution 1373 implementation). Paragraph 6 states that the Security Council,

> *Decides* to establish . . . a Committee of the Security Council, consisting of all the members of the Council, to monitor implementation of this resolution, with the assistance of appropriate expertise, and *calls upon* all States to report to the Committee . . . on the steps they have taken to implement this resolution, (emphasis in original)

Id. See Counterterrorism Committee, U.N. Security Council, *How does the CTC work with States?* (2003), http://www.un.org/Docs/sc/committees/1373/work.html [hereinafter CTC] (describing relationship between CTC and member states and CTC's functions).

54 *See* CTC, *supra* note 53 (explaining specific utilities of CTC).

55 *See* Rosand, *supra* note 50, at 340 (describing efforts to include a human rights compliance expert in CTC). Resolution 1373 encompasses a range of measures from border security and financing terrorists to weapons trade. *Id.*

56 *See* Rosand, *supra* note 50, at 340 (reiterating CTC position on monitoring human rights compliance within fight against terrorism).

57 Kim Lane Scheppele, *Other People's Patriot Acts: Europe's Responses to September 11*, 50 Loy. L. Rev. 89, 92-93 (2004) (quoting first CTC chairman's position on gap between Resolution 1373 compliance and human rights compliance).

58 *See* Europa, *The EU at a Glance – European Countries*, http://europa.eu/abc/european_countries/index_en.htm (mapping EU member states); Desmond Dinon, Ever Closer Union: An Introduction to European Integration 304 (Lynne Rienner Publishers 1999)

legislative political institutions, a judicial branch, and a cooperative framework for defense and security.[59] The EU has issued numerous measures addressing general security needs relevant to the fight against terrorism.[60] In 2002, the EU's main decision-making body issued the Council Framework Decision on Combating Terrorism, creating a common definition of terrorism and mandating member states to adopt terrorism prevention and penalization legislation.[61] Article 1 of the Terrorism Framework Decision defines terrorist offenses as

> [I]ntentional acts . . . which . . . may seriously damage a country or an international organization . . . where committed with the aim of:
>
> - seriously intimidating a population, or
> - unduly compelling a Government or international organisation to perform or abstain from performing any act, or seriously destabilising or destroying the fundamental political, constitutional, economic or social structures of a country or an international organisation.[62]

(stating European Court of Justice has determined EU law is supreme over contradictory national laws).

59 *See* Europa, *The EU at a Glance – How is the EU organized?* (2007) http:// europa.eu/abc/panorama/howorganised/index_en.htm (last visited Feb. 15, 2007) (describing European Union's organization); Europa, *The EU at a Glance – The History of the European Union* (2007) http://europa.eu/abc/history/index_en.htm (describing European Union's history). Following World War II, France, Germany, Italy, Belgium, Luxembourg, and the Netherlands believed economic integration and prosperity would make another war on the continent impossible, and in 1958, signed the Treaty of Rome creating the European Community. *Id.* (describing first signatories' motivations for adhering to Treaty of Rome). After several revisions to the Treaty of Rome and the adoption of the Treaty of Maastricht on European Union, the European Community evolved into the European Union consisting of three "pillars": European Economic Community, Common Foreign and Security Policy, and Justice and Home Affairs, and created a common currency and EU citizenship. *See* Europa, Treaty of Maastricht on European Union, http://europa.eu/scadplus/treaties/maastricht_en.htm (last visited Feb. 15, 2007); Europa, *The EU at a Glance – The History of the European Union, supra* note 58 (summarizing Treaty of Maastricht's principal modifications).

60 *See* Council Framework Decision of 13 June 2002 on Combating Terrorism 2002/475/JHA, preamble ¶ 5, 2002 O.J. (L 164) 3 (EU) [hereinafter Council Framework Decision] (listing EU counterterrorism measures). These measures, as a general matter, created organizational authorities to oversee and coordinate various terrorism-related security and prosecutorial needs. *Id.* Many post-9/11 measures implemented by the EU were not related to terrorism directly but were more general, having to do with police and judicial cooperation. *See* Jan Wouters, *The European Union and "September 11"*, 13 IND. INT'L & COMP. L. REV. 719, 726 (2003) (describing general nature of many of EU's post-9/11 security measures).

61 *See* Council Framework Decision, *supra* note 60, at art. 1–11 (requiring member states to ensure adoption and implementation of legislation defining and penalizing certain terrorist conduct); Europa, The Council of the European Union, http://europa.eu/institutions/inst/council/index_en.htm (last visited Feb. 28, 2007) (describing EU Council's composition and functions).

62 Council Framework Decision, *supra* note 60, at art. 1 (harmonizing EU member states' definitions of terrorism).

Article 1.2 attempts to limit the potential for interpreting this definition too broadly, stating, "This Framework Decision shall not have the effect of altering the obligation to respect fundamental rights and fundamental legal principles as enshrined in Article 6 of the Treaty on European Union."[63]

B. International Human Rights Law

The UN legal framework on human rights is vast, but is spearheaded by two important treaties.[64] In 1948, the UN General Assembly adopted the Universal Declaration of Human Rights (UNDHR), which is the foundational legal instrument for protecting fundamental rights.[65] This document, and the subsequent International Covenant on Civil and Political Rights of 1966 (ICCPR), codify fundamental liberties norms such as the right to a presumption of innocence until proven guilty, the right to counsel, the right to only be held guilty of crimes that have been enacted and defined legislatively, the right to a trial without unreasonable delay, the right to privacy, and the right to peaceful assembly and association.[66] The ICCPR's content largely duplicates the UNDHR provisions except that it contains additional remedies for violations of the Covenant.[67] For instance, States must periodically provide reports to the Human Rights Commission, describing measures ensuring protection of the rights embodied by the ICCPR and cataloguing any progress.[68] In addition, States and individuals may

63 Council Framework Decision, *supra* note 60, at art. 1.2 (stating Council Framework Decision shall not derogate from EU human rights principles). *See also* Wouters, *supra* note 60, at 738 (suggesting Article 1.2 of Council Framework Decision limits over-broad scope of its definition of terrorism).

64 *See generally* Christyne J. Vachon, *Hong Kong's 1997 Transition: UN Enforcement Mechanisms to Guarantee Hong Kong's Human Rights Will Endure After the Transition*, 28 Denv. J. Int'l L. & Pol'y 97, 112-114 (1999) (discussing two most influential human rights treaties regarding Hong Kong's transition in government).

65 *See* Universal Declaration of Human Rights, G.A. Res. 217A (III), U.N. GAOR, 3d Sess., U.N. Doc. A/810 (1948), at introduction (listing human rights principles to which member states are bound to observe and implement); Office of the U.N. High Commissioner for Human Rights, *International Law,* November 3, 2005, http://www.ohchr.org/english/law/index.htm (last visited Feb. 15, 2007) (pointing to sources of international law on human rights beginning with Universal Declaration of Human Rights).

66 *See* Universal Declaration of Human Rights, *supra* note 65, at art. 11–12, 18–20 (adopting individual rights to fair adjudication, privacy, personal freedom, and freedom to peaceful assembly and association); International Covenant of Civil and Political Rights, G.A. Res. 2200A, U.N. GAOR Supp. (No. 16), U.N. Doc A/6316 (1996), at art. 14–15 (adopting and delineating individual rights to fair adjudication).

67 *See* Vachon, *supra* note 64, at 114 (introducing nature and content of International Covenant on Civil and Political Rights). The ICCPR has been described as "one of the fundamental instruments created by the international community for the global promotion and protection of human rights" and is binding on state parties to the Covenant. *Id.*

68 *See* Vachon, *supra* note 64, at 115 (describing ICCPR Article 40 requirements for State reporting on civil liberties protection progress).

file complaints with the Human Rights Commission alleging a State's violation of the ICCPR.[69]

Regarding the EU, human rights principles are "recognized" by the Charter of Fundamental Rights of the European Union.[70] These principles are not yet legally binding on the member States but set out common standards for fundamental rights among the various EU members.[71] In content, the Charter's provisions largely resemble the UNDHR and ICCPR.[72]

IV. DECLINE OF FUNDAMENTAL RIGHTS IN FRANCE

A. Vague Terminology in Definition of Terrorism-Related Crimes Perpetuate Indiscriminate Arrests

According to French law, terrorism is defined as "an individual or collective enterprise intending to gravely trouble public order by means of intimidation or terror."[73] This definition lacks sufficient specificity and, consequently, fails to exclude lesser crimes from its umbrella.[74] Such a definition, for example, does not exclude protest movements that involve urban violence, rioting, and looting.[75] The lacking specificity in the French definition of terrorism reflects international

---

69 *See* Vachon, *supra* note 64, at 116–117 (describing additional ICCPR enforcement mechanisms).

70 *See* Charter of Fundamental Rights of the European Union, Preamble, 2000/C 364/01, 2000 O.J. (C 364) 8 (EU) (expounding principles recognized by EU Council, Commission, and Parliament).

71 *See generally* European Parliament, *The Charter of Fundamental Rights of the European Union,* www.europarl.eu.int/charter/default_en.htm (last visited March 1, 2007) (noting legal status of Charter not yet binding).

72 *Compare* Charter of Fundamental Rights of the European Union, *supra* note 70, at art. 1–26 (listing principles of fundamental rights), *with* Universal Declaration of Human Rights, *supra* note 65, at art. 1–30 (listing human rights principles), *and* International Covenant on Civil and Political Rights, *supra* note 66, at art. 1–53 (listing protected fundamental liberties).

73 *See* Shapiro & Suzan, *supra* note 16, at 77 (citing definition of terrorism in September 9, 1986 legislation).

74 *See generally* CFR-CDF, *supra* note 48 (stating international legal instruments have not succeeded in defining terrorism clearly). For example, according to the French definition, the youth riots that gripped Paris during the fall of 2005 could be classified as acts of terrorism. *Id.* During these riots, disaffected youth burned thousands of cars in the Paris suburbs in response to perceived discrimination by the French government. Craig Smith and Ariane Bernard, *Angry Immigrants Embroil France in Wider Riots,* N.Y. Times, Nov. 5, 2005, at 1. The riots severely disturbed public order in and around Paris. *Id.*

75 *See* Tony Bunyan, *The War on Freedom and Democracy: An Analysis of the Effects on Civil Liberties and Democratic Culture in the EU,* Statewatch, Sept. 6, 2002, at 3, *available at* http://www.statewatch.org/news/2002/sep/analyl3.pdf (noting initial EU definition of terrorism encompassed protests in form of urban violence).

law's failure to successfully distinguish terrorism from other crimes.[76] U.N. counterterrorism conventions condemn terrorist crimes including kidnapping, bombing, hostage-taking, and financing of attacks, but never specifically define terrorism; they merely suggest that a certain mindset is necessary for such acts to constitute terrorism.[77] Both U.N. counterterrorism conventions and the European Framework Decision only go so far as to indicate that terrorism is conduct seeking to manipulate government policy by provoking public disorder.[78]

The lack of legal specificity in the French definition of terrorism violates human rights principles and undermines the lawfulness of counterterrorism measures.[79] International human rights law prohibits states from holding persons guilty of conduct that does not constitute a criminal offense under national or international law.[80] The French definition of terrorism fails to meet basic definitional elements of a crime under general principles of law because it lacks an intent element that sufficiently distinguishes terrorism from lesser crimes.[81] Similarly, international

---

76 *See* CFR-CDF, *supra* note 48, at 7 (stating international law has not succeeded in overcoming lack of specificity in definition of terrorism).

77 *See* International Convention for the Suppression of Acts of Nuclear Terrorism, *supra* note 51 (criminalizing possession of radioactive material with intent to cause serious injury on civilians or environment); International Convention for the Suppression of the Financing of Terrorism, *supra* note 51 (criminalizing provision or collection of funds with intent to carry out serious injury on civilians); International Convention for the Suppression of Terrorist Bombings, *supra* note 51 (criminalizing possession or detonation of explosives with intent to seriously injure civilians); International Convention Against the Taking of Hostages, *supra* note 51 (criminalizing detention and threats to kill persons to compel third parties to act or abstain therefrom); Convention on the Prevention and Punishment of Crimes Against Internationally Protected Persons, Including Diplomatic Agents, *supra* note 51 (criminalizing any infringement on liberty or life of internationally protected persons).

78 *See* International Convention for the Suppression of Terrorist Bombings, *supra* note 51, at art. 5 (requiring signatories to criminalize conduct intended to provoke terror); International Convention for the Suppression of the Financing of Terrorism, *supra* note 51, at art. 2(b) (condemning conduct intended to cause civilian death or injury to achieve government intimidation or influence); International Convention for the Suppression of Acts of Nuclear Terrorism, *supra* note 51, at art. 2(1) (hi) (condemning as contrary to Convention conduct intending to compel government conduct or abstention therefrom).

79 *See* CFR-CDF, *supra* note 48, at 7 (stating vague terrorism definition jeopardizes legality of counterterrorism measures); Council of Europe, *Guidelines of the Committee of Ministers of the Council of Europe on Human Rights and the Fight Against Terrorism,* 804th meeting of Delegates, Principle III, (2002), *available at* http://portal.coe.ge/downloads/terrorism.en.pdf (requiring precision for lawfulness of counterterrorism measures).

80 *See* International Covenant on Civil and Political Rights, *supra* note 65, at art. 15 (prohibiting criminal convictions for conduct not criminal under national or international law); Universal Declaration of Human Rights, *supra* note 65, at art. 7 (prohibiting criminal convictions for conduct not criminal under national or international law); Charter of Fundamental Rights of the European Union, *supra* note 70, at art. 49 (prohibiting criminal convictions for conduct not criminal under national or international law).

81 *See* McColgan & Attanasio, *supra* note 27, at 3 (highlighting intent as essential criminal element and lack thereof in French definition of terrorist crimes).

law, as mentioned previously, categorizes certain conduct as terrorist crimes but fails to distinguish the intent necessary for such conduct to constitute terrorism in a manner that excludes less severe offenses.[82] As neither French nor international law meet definitional standards for establishing a crime, counterterrorism measures' legality according to human rights law is doubtful.[83]

In addition, French law criminalizes association with people who are "involved in terrorist enterprises."[84] This vague language fails to distinguish criminal from innocent association, potentially implicating a vast number of people who may harmlessly interact with a person suspected of wrongdoing.[85] Moreover, the "association with wrongdoers" law does not even require that a person have somehow meaningfully contributed to the terrorist enterprise before being arrested, but rather criminalizes mere association with a terrorist suspect.[86] As noted before, the French media has recorded and publicized many incidents where the police have arrested over a hundred people at a time, although only a few persons were actually alleged to be involved in the suspected terrorist activity.[87] The majority of those arrested were subsequently released after enduring many hours or even several days of police questioning.[88]

Such arrests, made possible by the vague terminology of the French definition of terrorism and terrorism-related laws, violate human rights principles.[89] Article 12 of the UNDHR and Article 17 of the ICCPR state, "[n]o one shall be subjected to arbitrary interference with his privacy . . . nor to attacks upon his honour and reputation."[90] The French "association with wrongdoers" law violates this principle by allowing law enforcement officials to arrest people who may merely have come

82 *See, e.g. supra* note 63 and accompanying text (discussing definition of terrorism under Terrorism Framework Decision).

83 *Cf.* CFR-CDF, *supra* note 48, at 11 (concluding European definition of terrorism falls short of lawfulness requirement under human rights law).

84 *See* Legifrance.gouv.fr, *supra* note 29 (setting forth conduct punishable under French terrorism law).

85 *See* Shapiro & Suzan, *supra* note 16, at 84–85 (describing sweeping arrests of persons with unsubstantiated relationships to terrorist networks). The Fédération Internationale des Ligues des Droits de l'Homme, a civil liberties organization in France, has criticized French antiterror laws as being excessive in scope and vague. *Id.*

86 *See* Shapiro & Suzan, *supra* note 16, at 85 (describing how mere association with participant in terrorist enterprise suffices under "association with wrongdoers" law).

87 *See, e.g.* Astier, *supra* note 16 (recounting antiterror raid arresting 160 persons and subsequently releasing majority after four days); Crumley, *supra* note 30 (describing Bruguière's counterterrorism method involving excessive arrests for small number of suspects).

88 *See* Astier, *supra* note 16 (quoting French human rights activist's description of antiterror raid near Paris).

89 *See* Shapiro & Suzan, *supra* note 16, at 86 (discussing arguments characterizing French counterterrorism laws as violating public liberties).

90 *See* Universal Declaration of Human Rights, *supra* note 65, at art. 12; International Covenant on Civil and Political Rights, *supra* note 66, at art. 17 (declaring protection from arbitrary interference with, inter alia, one's privacy, family, home, and reputation).

into contact with a terrorist suspect, without requiring more meaningful involvement or criminal intent.[91] Moreover, such arrests are often widely publicized, a fact that directly undermines the right to freedom from arbitrary interference with one's privacy and attacks on one's reputation.[92]

The vagueness of this law potentially derogates from another fundamental liberties principle: the freedom of peaceful assembly and association.[93] Human rights law protects the freedom to associate with others as long as such association is peaceful.[94] Yet, French counterterrorism law, by criminalizing association without requiring some form of culpable intent or strategic participation in the terrorist enterprise, renders this civil liberties principle void.[95] Indeed, French authorities have convicted persons of this crime, which carries a maximum penalty of ten years, merely because those convicted associated too frequently with people who had terrorist objectives.[96] The French authorities based these convictions solely on the fact of association and never provided evidence showing that, beyond their acquaintance, the suspects participated in the terrorist enterprise.[97]

B. Excessive Detention and Slow Justice Deprive People of their Right to Liberty

In addition to the ease with which a person may be arrested for suspected violation of a French antiterrorism law, one might remain in prison for years before the police complete investigations and initiate a trial.[98] In essence, the French system

91 *See* Shapiro & Suzan, *supra* note 16, at 86 (quoting human rights activist's perspective on arbitrary enforcement made possible by French counterterrorism laws); Astier, *supra* note 16 (quoting human rights activist's description of indiscriminate arrests made possible by French counterterrorism laws); Whitlock, *supra* note 25, at A01 (noting position that majority of persons arrested under antiterrorism laws are released without charges).

92 *See* Universal Declaration of Human Rights, *supra* note 65, at art. 12 (stating persons have right to freedom from arbitrary invasions of privacy and attacks on reputation); Crumley, *supra* note 30 (describing media coverage of antiterror raids).

93 *See* McColgan & Attanasio, *supra* note 27, at 3–6 (suggesting peaceful association among Muslims or participation in Islamic instruction jeopardized by French counterterrorism law).

94 *See* Universal Declaration of Human Rights, *supra* note 65, at art. 20; International Covenant on Civil and Political Rights, *supra* note 66, at art. 22; Charter of Fundamental Rights of the European Union, *supra* note 70, at art. 12; Convention for the Protection of Human Rights and Fundamental Freedoms, *supra* note 65, at art. 11.

95 *See* McColgan & Attanasio, *supra* note 27, at 3–6 (quoting judicial decision convicting detainee for associating with terrorist collaborators despite no evidence of misconduct). In the conviction of a suspect who allegedly assisted a convicted terrorist, the court based its decision on speculation, stating that it was unrealistic to expect that the suspect could associate with so many terrorist operatives without being aware of their actions and objectives. *Id.*

96 *See supra* note 33 and accompanying text.

97 *See supra* note 33 and accompanying text.

98 *See* Whitlock, *supra* note 25, at A01 (recounting instances in which suspects remain detained for years while police conduct investigation); Crumley, *supra* note 30 (stating suspects may be

locks up suspicious persons as a form of preemptive detention until the police can locate more persuasive evidence for a conviction.[99]" Furthermore, the police threaten suspects with preventive detention, in which the police interrogate suspects for 92 hours without the intervention of legal defense, as a strategic tool in persuading suspects to become informants.[100]

Fundamental rights law guarantees that every person charged with a crime shall be promptly informed of the specific nature of the charge in a detailed way and in a manner that the accused understands.[101] Civil liberties laws also guarantee the right to have access to counsel of one's choosing and to be tried without excessive delay.[102] French preemptive detention practices contravene these rights.[103] As mentioned earlier, suspects may be detained for four days before consulting with a lawyer.[104] Furthermore, the police may imprison suspects for years, while they continue to conduct their investigation, before an indictment is filed and a trial is commenced.[105] Moreover, all of this is possible under laws that fail to adequately distinguish terrorism from lesser crimes.[106]

These gaps between enforcing counterterrorism laws and failure to comply with human rights norms reflect the lack of fundamental rights provisions in counterterrorism agreements.[107] Neither Resolution 1373 nor the European Framework Decision include clauses ensuring that their counterterrorism provisions comply with human rights law beyond general statements that fundamental rights are to be "respected" in

---

detained for days before police file charges and years before trial); Astier, *supra* note 16 (describing lengthy detentions as "preventive detention").

99 *See* Astier, *supra* note 16 (discussing "preventive detention"); *cf.* Crumley, *supra* note 30 (suggesting preventive detention method has successfully prevented bombing plots).

100 *See* Whitlock, *supra* note 25, at A01 (stating police threaten preemptive arrest as intelligence strategy).

101 *See* International Covenant on Civil and Political Rights, *supra* note 66, at art. 9 (guaranteeing accused persons universal right to prompt information of charge); Convention for the Protection of Human Rights and Fundamental Freedoms, *supra* note 65, at art. 6 (granting accused persons universal right to prompt information of charge).

102 *See* International Covenant on Civil and Political Rights, *supra* note 66, at art. 14 (guaranteeing accused persons right to defense counsel and trial without undue delay); Convention for the Protection of Human Rights and Fundamental Freedoms, *supra* note 65, at art. 6 (assuring accused persons right to defense counsel).

103 *Cf.* McColgan & Attanasio, *supra* note 27 (suggesting preventive detention violates Article 6 of Convention for the Protection of Human Rights and Fundamental Freedoms).

104 *See supra* notes 38-42 and accompanying text (describing detaining powers of French counterterrorism authorities).

105 *See supra* notes 38–42 and accompanying text (observing length of terrorist suspects' detention).

106 *See supra* notes 29–33 and accompanying text (summarizing wide scope of French definition of terrorism).

107 *See supra* notes 48–63 and accompanying text (recalling substance of fundamental rights provisions in international counterterrorism agreements).

security provision implementation.[108] In essence, the international agreements grant full discretion to the states to individually decide what "respect" for fundamental rights means when faced with the security threats posed by terrorism.[109]

C. Counterterrorism Agreements Must Integrate and Reflect a Balance Between Human Rights Principles and Security Measures

The French counterterrorism system not only demonstrates that fundamental rights have been sacrificed for security in France, but also demonstrates the French people's willingness to accept such a sacrifice.[110] Such acceptance is partially due to the French public's societal deference towards *l'État*.[111] Public acquiescence also largely results from a lack of information because the government does not reveal statistics on French terrorism prosecutions.[112] The lack of protest and debate in France regarding counterterrorism law's effect on civil liberties and human rights is dangerous because the antiterrorism laws themselves do not have built-in safeguards against abuse.[113]

The decline of fundamental rights in France today, as a result of the pressures exerted by the war on terrorism, demonstrates that the international legal framework is flawed and must adapt to include human rights considerations.[114] Although international counterterrorism law mentions human rights principles, such references are only in the form of reminders urging states to create security measures that comply with human rights.[115] Although seemingly noble, the references to human rights principles

108 *See supra* notes 48–63 and accompanying text (describing human rights content of counterterrorism agreements).

109 *See supra* notes 48–63 and accompanying text (recounting substance of human rights measures in international security agreements).

110 *See* Shapiro & Suzan, *supra* note 16, at 88 (arguing French are more tolerant than Americans of security at expense of civil liberties).

111 *See supra* notes 12–17 and accompanying text (describing French deference to state government).

112 *See* Whitlock, *supra* note 27, at A01 (stating official statistics on French terrorism prosecutions are unavailable); *cf.* NADEAU, *supra* note 12, at 301 (describing difficulty in collecting statistical data in France due to government practices).

113 *See* Shapiro & Suzan, *supra* note 16, at 85 (discussing lack of controlling authority over investigatory magistrates); McColgan & Attanasio, *supra* note 27, at 2 (highlighting concentration of power in four counterterrorism judges who are not accountable). The 1986 anti-terrorism laws centralized many aspects of counterterrorism procedures under the control of four investigatory magistrates, whose decisions are not subject to judicial review on issues of fact and law. *See* Shapiro & Suzan, *supra* note 16, at 85 (describing counterterrorism judicial procedure). *See also* McColgan & Attanasio, *supra* note 27, at 2 (discussing concentration of counterterrorism powers in hands of four magistrates).

114 *See* CFR-CDF, *supra* note 48, at 7–8, 11 (arguing state compliance with international counterterrorism law has undermined compliance with human rights law).

115 *See* International Convention for the Suppression of Terrorist Bombings, *supra* note 51, art. 14 (requiring treatment in compliance with human rights for persons detained under terms of agreement); International Convention for the Suppression of the Financing of Terrorism, *supra* note 51,

in antiterrorism law are so vague that they essentially become irrelevant.[116] These short, sentence-long references allude to entire bodies of human rights law and to general fairness principles rather than to specific protections that are particularly pertinent to the law created by the counterterrorism agreements.[117] For example, the International Convention for the Suppression of Terrorist Bombings calls upon states to investigate, detain, and prosecute terrorist bombers.[118] In light of the previous discussion regarding the potential for excessive detention during antiterrorism investigations, the Convention would more effectively protect fundamental liberties by specifically obliging signatories to indict and commence a trial without undue delay—rather than making an exhortation to respect human rights generally.[119]

D. The Threat to Democratic Society

Terrorist groups aim to overthrow democratically elected governments and to replace them with authoritarian regimes to force the effectuation of their political or religious agendas upon society.[120] By ignoring or undermining civil liberties laws in the fight against these terrorist groups, society is unknowingly aiding and abetting the terrorists' objectives.[121] The protections and rights that characterize a free society have been the glue that has maintained the loyalty and faith of people living under

art. 17 (requiring humane treatment for persons detained under terms of agreement); International Convention for the Suppression of Acts of Nuclear Terrorism, *supra* note 51, art. 12 (requiring treatment in compliance with human rights for persons detained under terms of agreement); Council Framework Decision, *supra* note 60, ¶ 1, ¶ 10, art. 1 (2) (declaring respect for, and promising not to derogate from, foundational human rights principles). Each U.N. countererrorism treaty contains the same language stating, "[a]ny person who is taken into custody . . . pursuant to this Convention shall be guaranteed . . . all rights . . . in conformity with . . . international law of human rights." International Convention for the Suppression of Terrorist Bombings, *supra* note 51, art. 14. *See also* International Convention for the Suppression of the Financing of Terrorism, *supra* note 51, at art. 17; International Convention for the Suppression of Acts of Nuclear Terrorism, *supra* note 51, at art. 12. The EU Council Framework Decision repeatedly recognizes human rights as an important principle in effectuating counterterrorism measures and specifically states that the Framework Decision, "shall not have the effect of altering the obligation to respect fundamental rights." Council Framework Decision, *supra* note 60, art. 1 (2).

116 *See generally supra* notes 78–89 and accompanying text (illustrating examples where international antiterror laws containing general human rights provisions failed to stem abuses).

117 *See supra* note 54–56 and accompanying text (indicating limited human rights protections built in to international counterterrorism laws).

118 *See* International Convention for the Suppression of Terrorist Bombings, *supra* note 51, at art. 4, 6–7 (obliging signatories to treaty to create criminal legislation for prosecution of terrorist bombings).

119 *See generally supra* notes 78–89 and accompanying text (demonstrating how general exhortations to respect human rights lack effectiveness).

120 *See* [U.S. Deft, of State, The Terrorist Enemy], *supra* note 7 (describing agenda of primary terrorist enemy of United States). *See generally* [U.S. Deft, of State, Chapter 6 Terrorist Groups], *supra* note 7 (containing State Department's annual report on foreign terrorist groups and describing their objectives and operations).

121 *See infra* notes 122–124 and accompanying text (arguing counterterrorism laws impinging on fundamental liberties undermine strength of democratic government, as desired by terrorists).

democratic governments.[122] Indeed, civil liberties are the life-blood of democracies and must be protected at all times; "[f]undamental democratic principles, [such as] the rule of law, the separation of powers, the independence of judicial authority . . . are not luxuries of peace time . . . [but r]ather, without them the democracy does not exist."[123] Counterterrorism laws that do not comply with international human rights standards and civil liberties may appear to be effective methods to fight terrorism.[124] Yet, these tactics will ultimately fail because such unbalanced security measures strip governments of their democratic character and of the moral fabric of their society, furthering the goals of the terrorists they are trying to stop.[125]

V. CONCLUSION

States seeking to protect themselves against terrorist attacks may admire the effectiveness of the French government in preventing radical Islamist terrorist plots, particularly considering that France is the most Islamic nation of Europe.[126]

---

122 *See* Edith Y. Yu, *supra* note 7, at 7–8 (explaining American people's faith rests on belief that U.S. government will continue to protect civil liberties).

> Only because "governments have endorsed the idea that civilians should enjoy special legal protections from attack" do Americans continue to have faith in the U.S. government to "do the right thing." In order to maintain this faith in government, Americans must be able to trust that constitutional and other legal protections will be enforced and that the United States will not resort to employing the same military tactics and faulty criminal justice systems that characterize the war on terror in foreign lands. The American government must not lose sight of the way of life and civil liberties we are defending.

Id. at 8. *See also* Kelly R. Cusick, *supra* note 7, at 60 (arguing civil liberties built into U.S. Constitution have glued American society together over 200 years).

> The values of the Constitution of the United States have united the country for more than 200 years. The framers designed the Constitution to protect civil liberties in times of war as well as in times of peace . . . American ideals and values must be respected to maintain the strength of the United States. Commitment to the principles of the Constitution in the face of terrorist atrocities will serve justice and demonstrate the strength of the United States to the world.

Id. at 60–61. *See also* Emanuel Gross, *supra* note 7, at 659 (describing importance of protecting civil liberties in preserving democratic character of states).

> An unconstitutional violation of the constitutional liberties of the individual, even if he is suspected of involvement in terrorist activities, impairs the rule of law (in the substantive sense) and the steadfastness of the democracy in precisely the same way as according overly heavy weight to individual rights at the expense of the security interest infringes them.

Id.

123 Gross, *supra* note 7, at 655.

124 *See, e.g.*, *supra* notes 5, 24 and accompanying text (describing success of strict French counter-terrorism measures).

125 *See* Cusick, *supra* note 7, at 61 (arguing erosion of civil liberties could have profound implications on U.S. democracy).

126 *See* Nadeau, *supra* note 12, at 295 (describing size of Muslim population and significance in French culture); Whitlock, *supra* note 25 (noting importance of France's large Muslim population in Europe with regard to anti-terror and immigration law).

Nevertheless, the French fight against terrorism is causing a lamentable decline in human rights guaranties and fundamental liberties within France.[127] The French security system's effect on fundamental rights, however, is only a reflection of the flaws within the international framework on counterterrorism.[128] If the fundamental rights essential to a democratic society are to survive the war on terrorism, counter-terrorism laws must integrate specific human rights protections into the security measures proposed by international treaties.[129]

International counterterrorism laws serve as a springboard for State domestic laws.[130] At the same time, international law has also been the impetus for domestic human rights improvements in many states.[131] If these essential sources of law continue to act on parallel fields, in which counterterrorism and human rights law merely cross-reference, but fail to meaningfully integrate the other's principles, it is not surprising that gaps will be reflected in states' domestic law.[132] Accordingly, international counterterrorism agreements bear the burden of ensuring that human rights principles are not sacrificed by the climate of fear created by the war on terrorism.[133] Indeed, protecting and respecting civil liberties in a tolerant society might be the only effective weapon in the war on terrorism.[134]

Calliope Makedon Sudborough

---

127 *See* Whitlock, *supra* note 25 (detailing detention of terrorism suspects and human rights advocates' responses). Michel Tubiana, president of the Human Rights League in France, acknowledged the effect of French counterterrorism policy on civil liberties, stating, "[t]here has been a definite erosion of civil liberties in France . . . We're seeing things that would have been unthinkable 10 years ago." *Id.*

128 *See supra* Part IV and accompanying notes (drawing parallels between French and international counterterrorism frameworks).

129 *See supra* Part IV and accompanying notes (arguing for incorporation of human rights norms into counterterrorism legal framework).

130 *See* Ministère des Affaires Étrangères, *supra* note 25 (stating U.N. anti-terrorism security agreements form basis of French system).

131 *See generally supra* notes 66–70 and accompanying text (describing ICCPR as basis for many state civil liberties laws).

132 *See generally supra* Part IV Section A and accompanying notes.

133 *Cf.* Shapiro & Suzan, *supra* note 16, at 88 (describing French public's willingness to accept loss of civil liberties as price of safety).

134 *See* Jimmy Burns, Daniel Dombey & Frederick Studemann, *supra* note 4 (quoting EU counterterrorism minister's argument on key part of global anti-terrorism strategy). Gijs de Vries, the European Union's counterterrorism coordinator stated, "We need to engage with them ([moderate] Muslims) on the basis of the values we share: respect for human life, respect for democratic standards, respect for individual liberty and dignity . . . This means our policies to combat terrorism must respect the rights and values we have pledged to defend, including the rights of prisoners." *Id.*

COMPARATIVE PERSPECTIVES ON THE DETENTION OF TERRORIST SUSPECTS

John Ip[†]

Originally published in *Transnational Law and Contemporary Problems*, Vol. 16 (Spring 2007)

I. INTRODUCTION

The "Global War on Terror" that began after September 11, 2001 has triggered a re-examination of the appropriate balance between security and individual rights in multiple contexts. Is speech that glorifies terrorism still within the realm of protected speech? Is racial profiling justified in the context of airport security? Is the use of torture ever justified? In each case, our commitment to certain values—freedom of expression, non-discrimination, and respect for human dignity—is tested. The subject of this Article is the detention of suspected terrorists, a context in which the cherished right to liberty comes into conflict with the need for security.

The United States is currently detaining several hundred alleged terrorists, many at Guantánamo Bay Naval Base in Cuba. However, the United States is not the only nation detaining terrorist suspects. Other Western countries, including the United Kingdom, Canada, and New Zealand, have all detained suspected terrorists. In Part II, this Article outlines the detention regimes of these Anglo-common law countries as they have operated over the past five years, as well as the relevant court decisions that have affected them. In Part III, this Article discusses the differences between American and non-American detention regimes. In short, the American detention model differs from that adopted in other jurisdictions in that the U.S. model is executive-dominated and purports to exclude all human rights norms.[1]

At the same time, certain commonalities emerge. Each jurisdiction distinguishes between citizen and non-citizen terrorist suspects.[2] Each jurisdiction also has had to determine the level of procedural safeguards to which terrorist suspects are entitled.[3] Finally, the courts in each jurisdiction have generally been surprisingly willing to

† Lecturer, Faculty of Law, University of Auckland, New Zealand. My thanks to Kevin Jon Heller, Treasa Dunworth, and An Hertogen for their comments on earlier drafts. Any errors remain my own.

1 *See infra* notes 18–33 and accompanying text.

2 *See* discussion *infra* Part IV.A.

3 *See* discussion *infra* Part IV.B.

intervene in an area where they historically have not.[4] These common themes are discussed in Part IV.

II. THE REGIMES FOR DETAINING TERRORIST SUSPECTS POST 9/11

A. The United States

1. The Creation of a Legal Vacuum

Guantánamo Bay Naval Base in Cuba (Guantánamo) has a land area of thirty-one square miles, making it larger than the island of Manhattan.[5] It has a population of approximately 6,000. It is self-sufficient, with its own water plant, schools, a four-year college, and the usual accoutrements of American suburbia: McDonald's, Pizza Hut, Subway, and Kentucky Fried Chicken.[6]

In January 2002, several months after the American campaign in Afghanistan against al Qaeda and the Taliban regime had begun, the first captives arrived at Guantánamo. The United States detained them at Camp X-Ray, at the time nothing more than a makeshift collection of exposed wire cages which would serve as the backdrop for the now-iconic image of kneeling detainees clad in orange jumpsuits.[7] In April 2002, the camp was replaced by Camp Delta, a more permanent establishment. Camp Delta is divided into five camps, with more compliant detainees held in a lower security camp with better conditions and less compliant detainees held in maximum security.[8] In 2006, the United States completed construction of another permanent detention facility at Guantánamo, Camp Six.[9] Despite numerous calls for its closure over the past five years, Guantánamo continues to hold about 400 detainees.[10]

The decision to detain terrorist suspects at Guantánamo was a deliberate choice to place detainees in a legal vacuum, a decision made possible by Guantánamo's unique

4 *See* discussion *infra* Part IV.C.

5 Gerald L. Neuman, *Closing the Guantánamo Loophole*, 50 Loy. L. Rev. 1, 34–35 (2004).

6 *Id.*

7 *See In Pictures: Camp X-Ray Prisoners*, BBC News Online, Jan. 20, 2002, http://news.bbc.co.uk/2/hi/americas/1771816.stm.

8 Tung Yin, *Ending the War on Terrorism One Terrorist at a Time: A Non-Criminal Detention Model for Holding and Releasing Guantánamo Bay Detainees*, 29 Harv. J.L. & Pub. Pol'y 149, 161–62 (2005).

9 Ben Fox, *Guantanamo Remains Source of Outrage*, CBS NEWS, Jan. 10, 2007, http://www.cbsnews.com/stories/2007/01/10/ap/world/mainD8MIM5IO0.shtml.

10 In September 2006, President Bush announced that fourteen high value CIA captives, previously held at unknown "black sites" around the world, were being moved to Guantánamo to face trial. *See* Tim Golden, *The Battle for Guantánamo*, N.Y. Times Magazine, Sept. 17, 2006, at 60; Dafna Linzer & Glenn Kessler, *Decision to Move Detainees Resolved Two-Year Debate Among Bush Advisers*, Wash. Post, Sept. 8, 2006, at A1. On "black sites", see Leila Nadya Sadat, *Ghost Prisoners and Black Sites: Extraordinary Rendition Under International Law*, 37 Case W. Res. J. Int'l L. 309 (2006).

legal status. Guantánamo has been an American possession since the Spanish-American War in 1898. The United States holds Guantánamo under a lease agreement that continues indefinitely unless terminated with the consent of both Cuba and the United States.[11] Under the terms of the lease, the United States exercises complete jurisdiction and control over the base, although ultimate sovereignty remains with Cuba. After Castro came to power, the United States surrounded the base with a cactus barrier, and later a minefield.[12]

Guantánamo's geographic isolation means that those detained there can be detained largely in secret, away from the eyes of the media and public. Thus, in 1991, the United States used Guantánamo as a center for processing refugees free of some of the legal protections they would otherwise have enjoyed.[13] It is unsurprising, then, that Guantánamo would be chosen as the site for detaining suspected terrorists some ten years later. Even more significant than its physical remoteness, however, is its status as a legal twilight zone. It is clear that Cuban law does not apply to Guantánamo. At the same time, it is not formally part of the United States. Thus, the Bush administration thought that incarcerating terrorist suspects at Guantánamo would put those suspects beyond the jurisdiction of American federal courts.[14]

Having ostensibly avoided the application of U.S. domestic law, the next step was to deny the detainees the protection of international law. The law of war regulates conduct during armed conflict.[15] It can be divided into two general areas: Hague law, which concerns the conduct of armed forces on the battlefield, and Geneva law, which concerns the protection of persons affected by war.[16] Of particular relevance to Guantánamo is the Third Geneva Convention (GCIII), which deals with the treatment of prisoners of war (POWs).[17] As the United States alleged that many Guantánamo detainees were enemy fighters captured on the battlefield, GCIII appeared applicable. This posed some difficulties for the Bush administration because POWs are entitled to certain protections under GCIII. For example, a POW cannot be tried for merely participating in battle, as he is protected by combatants' privilege.[18] Although POWs can be tried for war crimes, the detaining

11 Neuman, *supra* note 5, at 35–38; Owen Fiss, *The War Against Terrorism and the Rule of Law*, Ox. J. Legal Stud. 235, 246 (2006).

12 Neuman, *supra* note 5, at 38.

13 Gerald L. Neuman, *Anomalous Zones*, 48 Stan. L. Rev. 1197, 1228–29 (1996).

14 *See* Memorandum from Patrick F. Philbin & John C. Yoo, Deputy Att'y Gens., on Possible Habeas Jurisdiction over Aliens Held in Guantánamo Bay Cuba, to William J. Haynes, II, Gen. Counsel, Dep't of Defense, (Dec. 28, 2001), *available at* http://www.msnbc.msn.com/id/5022 681/site/newsweek/.

15 *See generally* Ingrid Detter, The Law of War (2d ed. 2000).

16 *Id.* at 158.

17 Geneva Convention (III) Relative to the Treatment of Prisoners of War, Aug. 12, 1949, 6 U.S.T. 3316, 75U.N.T.S. 135 [hereinafter GCIII].

18 Derek Jinks, *The Declining Significance of POW Status*, 45 Harv. Int'l L. J. 367, 376 (2004).

power must ensure that the court trying a POW is equivalent to the court that the country would use to try its own forces.[19] The court must also meet certain basic procedural standards.[20] The military commissions envisaged by President Bush's military order of November 13 2001[21] would plainly have been precluded by GCIII. Moreover, Article 17 of the Third Geneva Convention famously states that POWs need only state their name, rank and serial number.[22] Contrary to popular perception, there is nothing that prevents a detaining power from interrogating a POW. However, a POW cannot be tortured or coerced into giving up information.[23]

When the United States initially considered the issue of the treatment of war-on-terror detainees in January 2002, there was no move to deviate from the Geneva Conventions. However, Department of Justice lawyers sought to establish that the Geneva Conventions did not apply to the conflict with al Qaeda and the Taliban as a legal matter,[24] a position the State Department strenuously opposed.[25] President Bush eventually determined that the Geneva Conventions applied to Taliban detainees but not to al Qaeda detainees.[26] The Taliban detainees, however, were not entitled to POW status because they did not qualify under the terms of GCIII. Nonetheless, Bush ordered that all Guantánamo detainees be treated "humanely,"

19 GCIII, *supra* note 17, at art. 102.

20 *Id.* at arts. 82–88, 99–107.

21 Military Order, 66 Fed. Reg. 57,833 (Nov. 13, 2001) [hereinafter Nov. 13 Order].

22 GCIII, *supra* note 17, at art. 17.

23 *Id.* at arts. 13 & 17.

24 Memorandum from John Yoo, Deputy Assistant Att'y Gen., & Robert J. Delahunty, Special Counsel, on Application of Treaties and Laws to al Qaeda and Taliban Detainees, to William J. Haynes II, Gen. Counsel, Dep't. of Defense (Jan. 9, 2002), *available at* http://www.gwu.edu/~nsarchiv/NSAEBB/NSAEBB127/02.01.09.pdf. Memorandum from Alberto R. Gonzales, Att'y Gen., on Decision Re Application of the Geneva Convention on Prisoners of War to the Conflict with Al Qaeda and the Taliban, to the President (Jan. 25, 2002), *available at* http://www.gwu.edu/~nsarchiv/NSAEBB/NSAEBB127/02.01.25.pdf. *See also* William H. Taft IV, *A View From the Top: American Perspectives on International Law After the Cold War*, 31 Yale J. of Int'l L. 503, 507 (2006).

25 Memorandum from William H. Taft, IV, Legal Advisor, Dep't of State, on Your Draft Memorandum of January 9, to John C. Yoo, Deputy Assistant Att'y Gen. (Jan. 11, 2002), *available at* http://www.cartoonbank.com/newyorker/slideshows/01TaftMemo.pdf. Memorandum from Colin L. Powell, on Draft Decision Memorandum for the President on the Applicability of the Geneva Convention to the Conflict in Afghanistan, to Counsel to the President, Dep't of State (Jan. 26, 2002), *available at* http://www.gwu.edu/~nsarchiv/NSAEBB/NSAEBB127/02.01.26.pdf. Memorandum from William H. Taft, IV, Legal Advisor, Dep't of State, on Comments on Your Paper on the Geneva Convention, to Counsel to the President (Feb. 2, 2002), *available at* http://www.nytimes.com/packages/html/politics/20040608_DOC.pdf.

26 Press Release, Office of the Press Sec'y, The White House, Fact Sheet, Status of Detainees at Guantánamo (Feb. 7, 2002), *available at* http://www.whitehouse.gov/news/releases /2002/02/20020207-13.html [hereinafter Fact Sheet, Status of Detainees at Guantánamo].

and "to the extent appropriate and consistent with military necessity, in a manner consistent with the principles of the Third Geneva Convention of 1949."[27]

Just one obstacle remained: international human rights law. The basic idea of human rights, that all people have certain rights simply by virtue of being human,[28] has gained great currency since World War II, resulting in an explosion of international human rights treaties beginning with the Universal Declaration of Human Rights in 1948.[29] The most important for present purposes is the International Covenant on Civil and Political Rights (ICCPR), one of two treaties intended to set out the principles enunciated in the Universal Declaration.[30] The ICCPR was signed by the United States in 1977 and ratified in 1992.[31] The Covenant contains several provisions that are relevant to the Guantánamo detainees. Article 9 affirms the right to liberty and security of the person, and the right to have the lawfulness of one's detention considered by a court without delay.[32] Article 7 prohibits the use of torture.[33] Article 14 stipulates a series of minimum fair trial requirements.[34]

It is axiomatic that rights do not prevail in all instances. Article 4 of the ICCPR itself permits derogation from many rights during a "public emergency which threatens the life of the nation."[35] The United States has made no such provision for derogation, and it is unclear whether it could do so under Article 4.[36] Instead, the Bush administration has relied on two arguments to avoid the application of international human rights law altogether.

The first argument the Bush administration employs is a jurisdictional argument similar to that employed to preclude judicial review by American courts. Article 2 of the ICCPR obligates states to afford the rights recognized by the Covenant to "all individuals within its territory and subject to its jurisdiction."[37] This could mean that a state must respect the rights of individuals who are both within its territory

27 *Id.*

28 *See* RESTATEMENT (THIRD) OF THE FOREIGN RELATIONS LAW OF THE U.S. § 701 (1987).

29 Universal Declaration of Human Rights, G.A. Res. 217A (III), at 71 U.N. Doc A/810 (Dec. 12, 1948).

30 International Covenant on Civil and Political Rights, Dec. 9, 1966, 999 U.N.T.S. 171 [hereinafter ICCPR].

31 United Nations High Commission for Human Rights, Ratifications and Reservations of the International Covenant on Civil and Political Rights, *available at* http://www.ohchr.org/english/countries/ratification/4.htm (last visited Mar. 6, 2007).

32 ICCPR, *supra* note 30, at art. 9 §§ 1, 4.

33 *Id.* at art. 7.

34 *Id.* at art. 14.

35 *Id.* at art. 4 § 1.

36 Derek Jinks, *International Human Rights Law and the War on Terrorism,* 31 DENV. J. INT'L L. & POL'Y 58, 67(2002).

37 ICCPR, *supra* note 30, at art. 2 § 1.

and subject to its jurisdiction. Alternatively, it could mean that a state must respect the rights of individuals who are within its territory and individuals who are outside its territory but nonetheless subject to its jurisdiction.[38] The Bush Administration has taken the former view. It has insisted that, even though the Guantánamo detainees are subject to American jurisdiction and control, they are outside the territory of the United States and hence not covered by the ICCPR.[39]

The idea that there can be geographical areas where human rights law does not apply because of jurisdictional issues is anathema to the very idea of human rights. Unsurprisingly, the prevailing view among international lawyers and the United Nations Human Rights Committee is that the duty of a state to respect human rights extends beyond a state's territorial borders. The relevant question is whether the state has control and authority over the person in instances where the person is physically outside the state.[40]

The Bush administration's second argument is that human rights law is inapplicable "to the conduct of hostilities or the capture and detention of enemy combatants" because such matters are "governed by the more specific laws of armed conflict."[41]

---

38 David W. Glazier, *Full and Fair by What Measure?: International Law Standards Regulating Military Commission Procedure,* B.U. INT'L L.J. (forthcoming) (manuscript at 56, on file with Social Science Research Network), *available at* http://ssrn.com/abstract=896643 (last visited Mar. 20, 2007).

39 U.S. DEPARTMENT OF STATE, SECOND AND THIRD PERIODIC REPORT OF THE UNITED STATES OF AMERICA TO THE U.N. COMMITTEE ON HUMAN RIGHTS CONCERNING THE INTERNATIONAL COVENANT ON CIVIL AND POLITICAL RIGHTS, CCPR/C/USA/3, para. 130, (Nov. 28, 2005), *available at* http://www.unhchr.ch/tbs/doc.nsf/(Symbol)/CCPR.C.USA.3.En?Opendocument.

> The United States recalls its longstanding position that . . . the obligations assumed by the United States under the Covenant apply only within the territory of the United States. In that regard, the United States respectfully submits that this Committee request for information is outside the purview of the Committee. The United States also notes that the legal status and treatment of such persons is governed by the law of war.

Id.

40 U.N. Human Rights Comm., International Covenant on Civil and Political Rights, *General Comment No. 31 [80]: The Nature of the General Legal Obligation Imposed on States Parties,* CCPR/C/21/Rev. 1/Add. 13 (Apr. 29, 2004), *available at* http://www.unhchr.ch/tbs/doc.nsf/(Symbol)/CCPR.C.21.Rev.1.Add.13.En?Opendocument; U.N. Comm. Against Torture, *Consideration of Reports Submitted by States Parties under Article 19 of the Convention: Conclusions and Recommendations of the Committee Against Torture,* para. 15, 36th Sess., CAT/C/USA/CO/2 (July 25, 2006), *available at* http://www.unhchr.ch/tbs/doc.nsf/(Symbol)/CAT.C.XXVII.Concl.5.En?Opendocument; Legal Consequences of the Construction of a Wall in the Occupied Palestinian Territory, Advisory Opinion, 2004 I.C.J. 136, paras. 102–11 (July 9, 2004) (rejecting Israel's contention that international human rights conventions such as the ICCPR were inapplicable in occupied Palestinian territory); Ilascu and others v. Moldova and Russia 40 Eur. H.R. Rep. 1030 (2005); Loizidou v. Turkey, 20 Eur. H.R. Rep. 99 (1995) (stating that the responsibility of a party to comply with the European Convention on Human Rights can extend to areas outside its territory but within its effective control).

41 *Response of the United States to Request for Precautionary Measures—Detainees in Guantánamo Bay, Cuba,* July 2002, 41 I.L.M. 1015, 1020–21 (2002).

This is an incorrect statement of the law. The existence of armed conflict or hostilities does not result in the wholesale abrogation of human rights protections. Nor does the application of the law of war to a certain situation necessarily exclude the operation of human rights law,[42] although in some instances the precise content of particular human rights may differ because of the contemporaneous applicability of certain rules from the law of war.[43]

Having denied the application of any body of law to the detainees, the Bush administration's creation of a legal vacuum was complete. The administration had effectively transformed the Guantánamo detainees into persons with no legal rights, held at a place where no law applied. Then-Deputy Assistant Attorney General John Yoo was quite candid about the administration's aims at the time: "What the Administration is trying to do is create a new legal regime."[44] That was a regime where the executive was constrained by law only to the extent of its own choosing.

This complete discretion fulfilled several purposes for the Bush administration. To begin with, it facilitated plans for swiftly bringing the worst terrorists to justice before military commissions.[45] Placing the detainees beyond the reach of American civilian courts ensured that the military commissions could operate without the interference of judicial review.[46] However, the paucity of information about many detainees soon undermined prosecution as a rationale for detention. In addition to establishing military commissions, the President's military order of November 13, 2001 also authorized the detention and prosecution of any foreign national whom the President determined to be a terrorist or to have terrorist links.[47] Then-White House Counsel Alberto Gonzales directed intelligence officers at Guantánamo to

---

42 U.N. Human Rights Comm., *supra* note 40, para. 11.

> [T]he Covenant applies also in situations of armed conflict to which the rules of international humanitarian law are applicable. While, in respect of certain Covenant rights, more specific rules of international humanitarian law may be specially relevant for the purposes of the interpretation of Covenant rights, both spheres of law are complementary, not mutually exclusive.

Id. U.N. Comm. Against Torture, *supra* note 40, para. 14 ("The State party should recognize and ensure that the Convention applies at all times, whether in peace, war or armed conflict, in any territory under its jurisdiction."); Legal Consequences of the Construction of a Wall in the Occupied Palestinian Territory, *supra* note 40, para. 106 ("[T]he Court considers that the protection offered by human rights conventions does not cease in case of armed conflict, save through the effect of provisions for derogation of the kind to be found in Article 4 of the International Covenant on Civil and Political Rights.").

43 Silvia Borelli, *Casting Light on the Legal Black Hole: International Law and Detentions Abroad in the "War on Terror"*, 857 Int'l Rev. Red Cross 39, 54–55 (2005).

44 Warren Richey, *How Long Can Guantánamo Prisoners Be Held?*, Christian Sci. Monitor, Apr. 9, 2002, at 01.

45 Tim Golden & Don Van Natta Jr., *Administration Officials Split Over Stalled Military Tribunals*, N.Y. Times, Oct. 25, 2004, at A1.

46 Neal Katyal, *Executive and Judicial Overreaction in the Guantánamo Cases*, 2004 Cato S. Ct. Rev. 49, 66 (2004).

47 Nov. 13 Order, *supra* note 21.

complete a one-page form for each detainee stating the President's reason for believing that the detainee was involved in terrorism. The intelligence officers soon reported that they did not have sufficient evidence about most prisoners to complete the form.[48] Consequently, by March 2002, Pentagon officials justified the indefinite detention at Guantánamo on the grounds that the detainees were "enemy combatants" locked in a war with the United States, and as such, could be detained by the United States for the duration of hostilities.[49]

Complete discretion also ensured operational flexibility for the gathering of intelligence from the detainees. Accordingly, a further ground the Bush administration emphasized to justify detention was that the detainees were a valuable source of intelligence which had to be preserved in order to forestall future attacks.[50] So long as the detainees remained at Guantánamo, the Bush administration thought that interrogation could continue without concerns about prosecutions under the War Crimes Act of 1996[51] for grave breaches of Geneva Conventions.[52]

2. The 2004 Supreme Court Cases

In June 2004, the U.S. Supreme Court decided a trilogy of cases with important ramifications for the War on Terror and the detention of terrorist suspects.[53] Two cases, *Hamdi v. Rumsfeld*[54] and *Rumsfeld v. Padilla,*[55] concerned the position of two enemy combatants who were American citizens. The third case, *Rasul v. Bush,*[56] directly addressed the position of the Guantánamo detainees.

a) Hamdi

In November 2001, the Northern Alliance captured Yaser Hamdi in Afghanistan and turned him over to American forces. The military initially detained Hamdi at Guantánamo until the discovery in April 2002 that he was an American citizen. The military then moved Hamdi to naval brigs in Virginia and South Carolina,

48 Golden & Van Natta, *supra* note 45.

49 *Id.; see, e.g.,* President George W. Bush, Remarks Discussing the Creation of Military Commissions to Try Suspected Terrorists (Dec. 16, 2006), *available at* http://www.whitehouse.gov/news/releases/2006/09/20060906-3.html ("We have a right under the laws of war . . . to detain these enemies and stop them from rejoining the battle.").

50 Golden & Van Natta, *supra* note 45.

51 *See* War Crimes Act of 1996, 18 U.S.C. § 2441 (2006). The Act has since been amended by the Military Commissions Act of 2006. *See infra* note 141 and accompanying text.

52 *See* Memorandum from Alberto R. Gonzales, *supra* note 24.

53 *See* Fiss, *supra* note 11; Daniel Moeckli, *The US Supreme Court's 'Enemy Combatant' Decisions: A Major Victory for the Rule of Law?*, 10 J. of Conflict & Security L. 75 (2005).

54 Hamdi v. Rumsfeld, 542 U.S. 507 (2004).

55 Rumsfeld v. Padilla, 542 U.S. 426 (2004).

56 *Rasul,* 542 U.S. at 510.

where it held him as an enemy combatant.[57] Hamdi s father filed a writ of habeas corpus on his behalf.[58] A key issue was the extent to which Hamdi should be able to contest his enemy combatant status. The District Court ordered the government to produce further information showing that Hamdi was an enemy combatant so that meaningful judicial review could take place.[59] The government successfully appealed to the Fourth Circuit Court of Appeals, which held that a declaration made by a government official was sufficient to establish the legality of Hamdi's detention.[60]

The Supreme Court ruled five-to-four that the military could detain Hamdi as an enemy combatant because Congress had impliedly authorized such detention with the Authorization for the Use of Military Force (AUMF).[61] However, Justice O'Connor's plurality opinion also concluded that the government's evidence was insufficient support for Hamdi's detention, meaning that further process in the form of a hearing was necessary.[62] The opinion then outlined a rudimentary due process framework for conducting such a hearing. Significantly, Justice O'Connor suggested that due process permitted the use of hearsay evidence, a presumption in favor of government evidence, and the use of military tribunals.[63]

b) Padilla

In May 2002, FBI agents arrested Jose Padilla at Chicago's O'Hare Airport. The government alleged that Padilla was plotting a radiological "dirty bomb" attack on unknown targets within the United States.[64] The government initially detained Padilla as a material witness, but later President Bush designated him an enemy combatant. The government then transferred Padilla into military custody and detained him incommunicado.[65]

Padilla's lawyer, who had been appointed to represent him while he was detained as a material witness, sought a writ of habeas corpus on his behalf. The District Court

57 Hamdi v. Rumsfeld, 542 U.S. 507, 510 (2004).

58 *Id.* at 511.

59 Hamdi v. Rumsfeld, 243 F. Supp. 2d 527 (E.D. Va. 2002).

60 Hamdi v. Rumsfeld, 316 F.3d 450 (4th Cir. 2003).

61 Authorization for Use of Military Force of Sept. 18, 2001, 107 Pub. L. No. 107-40, 115 Stat. 224. Five justices accepted that the AUMF justified Hamdi's detention. *Hamdi,* 542 U.S. at 507.

62 *Hamdi,* 542 U.S. at 509 ("Due process demands that a citizen held in the United States as an enemy combatant be given a meaningful opportunity to contest the factual basis for that detention before a neutral decisionmaker.").

63 *Id.* at 533–34.

64 Jennifer Elsea, Cong. Res. Service, CRS Rep. for Congress, Detention of American Citizens as Enemy Combatants 2 (Mar. 31, 2005), http://www.fas.org/sgp/crs/natsec/RL317 24.pdf.

65 *Id.* at 2–3.

ruled that the President had the authority to detain Padilla, but that the court would examine whether there was some evidence to support the finding that he was an enemy combatant.[66] On appeal, the Second Circuit held that neither the President's inherent constitutional powers nor any act of Congress had authorized the detention of an American citizen captured inside the United States as an enemy combatant.[67] The Supreme Court disposed of the case and ducked the substantive issue. In a five-to-four decision, the Court ruled that Padilla's petition should have been brought not in New York but in South Carolina, the state where Padilla—unbeknownst to his lawyer—was physically being held.[68]

c) Rasul

The petitioners were two Australian and twelve Kuwaiti detainees who had been captured during the Afghanistan conflict and detained at Guantánamo.[69] In the D.C. District Court and D.C. Circuit Court of Appeals, the Bush administration successfully argued that the courts had no jurisdiction to hear claims from Guantánamo detainees as they were non-citizens detained by the military outside American territory.[70] The authority for this position was *Johnson v Eisentrager*,[71] a case where German citizens captured and tried by American forces in China, and then imprisoned in occupied Germany, unsuccessfully petitioned for habeas corpus.

Overruling the lower courts, the Supreme Court held six-to-three that the Guantánamo detainees were entitled to petition American courts under the habeas corpus statute.[72] Although it did not overrule *Eisentrager*, the Court factually distinguished that case in several respects: these detainees came from countries that were not at war with the United States, the detainees all denied engaging in hostile acts against the United States, none of the detainees had ever been tried or convicted of any wrongdoing, and all of them had been detained for more than two years on territory over which the United States has exclusive jurisdiction and control.[73] Yet these factual distinctions were not the basis of *Rasul*. Rather, Justice Stevens' majority opinion stated that *Eisentrager* concerned the constitutional rather than statutory right to habeas corpus. The habeas corpus statute had been reinterpreted since *Eisentrager* to allow petitions from detainees of the United States held overseas,

66 Padilla v. Rumsfeld, 233 F. Supp. 2d 564 (S.D.N.Y. 2002).

67 Padilla *ex rel.* Newman v. Bush, 352 F.3d 695 (2d Cir. 2003).

68 Rumsfeld v. Padilla, 542 U.S. 426 (2004).

69 Rasul v. Bush 542 U.S. 466, 470–71 (2004).

70 Rasul v. Bush, 215 F. Supp. 2d 55 (D.D.C. 2002); Al Odah v. United States, 321 F.3d 1134 (D.C. Cir. 2003).

71 Johnson v. Eisentrager, 339 U.S. 763 (1950).

72 28 U.S.C. § 2241 (2006); Rasul v. Bush, 542 U.S. 466 (2004).

73 *Rasul*, 542 U.S. at 476.

provided that the custodian could be reached by service.[74] Accordingly, the courts had jurisdiction to hear statutory habeas petitions from Guantánamo detainees.[75]

Justice Kennedy's concurrence was more narrow. He agreed that the federal courts had jurisdiction over the Guantánamo detainees on the basis that Guantánamo was effectively American territory, that it was far from the battlefield, and that the detainees were being held without the benefit of any legal hearing about their status.[76] Both opinions signaled a decisive rejection of the "Guantanamo fiction."[77]

3. Aftermath of the 2004 Cases

Padilla duly filed his case in South Carolina. The District Court ruled that the President had no power to hold Padilla as an enemy combatant, and that the Non-Detention Act prohibited Padilla's detention.[78] The court ordered Padilla be released.[79] The Fourth Circuit overruled the lower court's decision holding that the government did have the power to detain Padilla as an enemy combatant.[80] In November 2005, shortly before a response to Padilla's petition for a second Supreme Court hearing was due, the Bush administration reversed course and transferred Padilla into the civilian court system. The purpose of this strategy was likely to avoid the creation of unfavorable Supreme Court precedent.[81] Padilla is currently facing criminal charges unrelated to either the original "dirty bomb" plot or the later alleged plan to blow up apartments with natural gas.[82]

Hamdi's hearing before a neutral decision maker never took place because the U.S. government subsequently negotiated a deal that allowed him to return to Saudi Arabia.[83]

---

74 *Id.* at 476–80.

75 *Id.* at 483–84.

76 *Id.* at 487–88.

77 This phrase was coined by Joseph Margulies to describe the argument that Guantánamo was not part of U.S. territory. JOSEPH MARGULIES, GUANTÁNAMO AND THE ABUSE OF PRESIDENTIAL POWER 51 (2006).

78 18 U.S.C. § 4001(a) (2000).

79 Padilla v. Hanft, 389 F. Supp. 2d 678 (D.S.C. 2005).

80 Padilla v. Hanft, 423 F.3d 386 (4th Cir. 2005).

81 *See* Padilla v. Hanft, 432 F. 3d. 582, 585 (4th Cir. 2005) ("First, the government's actions since this court's decision . . . have given rise to at least an appearance that the purpose of these actions may be to avoid consideration of our decision by the Supreme Court."); *see also* David Stout, *U.S. Indicts Padilla After 3 Years in Pentagon Custody,* N.Y. TIMES, Nov. 22, 2005, http://www.nytimes.com/2005/11/22/politics/22cnd-terror.html?ex=1290315600&en=43073b0d4533c7c1&ei=5090&partner=rssuserland&emc=rss.

82 *See* Dan Eggen, *Padilla Case Raises Questions About Anti-Terror Tactics,* WASH. POST, Nov. 19, 2006, at A3 (discussing the difficulties the government is facing in prosecuting Padilla in the ordinary court system).

83 Joel Brinkley & Eric Lichtblau, *U.S. Releases Saudi-American It Had Captured in Afghanistan,* N.Y. TIMES, Oct. 12, 2004, at A15.

Hamdi was allegedly so dangerous that he had to be detained without trial or access to a lawyer. Yet upon being asked to meet fairly rudimentary due process requirements, the Bush administration released him. According to a Pentagon statement, "considerations of United States national security did not require his continued detention."[84]

Nevertheless, the *Hamdi* decision is still important because its due process framework was interpreted and applied to the Guantánamo detainees. In July 2004, the Department of Defense established a process whereby Guantánamo detainees could challenge their status as enemy combatants before Combatant Status Review Tribunals (CSRTs).[85] These tribunals, composed of three military officers, determine whether a preponderance of evidence supports the detention of the detainee as an enemy combatant.[86] There is a rebuttable presumption in favor of the government's evidence.[87] Instead of lawyers, each detainee is assigned a personal representative, a military officer whose job is to assist with the process.[88] The United States releases detainees whom the Tribunals determine are not enemy combatants.[89] There were 558 such tribunals between July 30, 2004 and January 12, 2005.[90] Of the 558 detainees, the tribunals confirmed the enemy combatant status of 520. Thirty eight detainees were found to no longer meet the criteria for designation as enemy combatants.[91]

Rasul was a deliberately narrow decision in that it only established that the courts had jurisdiction to hear habeas petitions from Guantánamo detainees. But *Rasul* raised further questions, such as whether it applied to terrorist suspects held by the United States outside of Guantánamo.[92] Most obviously, the decision said little

---

84 Jerry Markon, *Hamdi Returned to Saudi Arabia,* WASH. POST, Oct. 12, 2004, at A2.

85 Memorandum from Gordon England, Secretary of the Navy, on Implementation of Combatant Status Review Tribunal Procedures for Enemy Combatants Detained at Guantánamo Bay Naval Base, Cuba, for distribution (July 29, 2004), *available at* http://www.defenselink.mil/news/Jul2004/d20040730comb.pdf [hereinafter England Memorandum].

86 *Id.*

87 *Id.*

88 *Id.* The infirmities of the CSRT process are discussed below. *See infra* text accompanying notes 406–427; *see also* Moeckli, supra note 53, at 94–96.

89 England Memorandum, *supra* note 85.

90 Kent Roach & Gary Trotter, *Miscarriages of Justice in the War Against Terror,* 109 PENN ST. L. REV. 967, 1027 (2005).

91 Gordon England, Secretary of the Navy, Defense Department Special Briefing on Combatant Status Review Tribunals (Mar. 29, 2005), http://www.defenselink.mil/transcripts/transcript.aspx?transcriptid=2504. The logical contortion evident in the term "no longer an enemy combatant" was adopted to reduce the chance of detainees suing for wrongful imprisonment. Tim Golden, *For Guantánamo Review Boards, Limits Abound,* N.Y. TIMES, Dec. 31, 2006, at A1.

92 The dissent of Justice Scalia suggests that, under *Rasul,* habeas jurisdiction would extend to parts of Iraq and Afghanistan. Rasul v. Bush, 542 U.S. 466, 501 (2004).

about the substantive claims detainees might raise, although a tantalizing hint appeared in the last footnote of the majority opinion:

> Petitioners' allegations—that, although they have engaged neither in combat nor in acts of terrorism against the United States, they have been held in Executive detention for more than two years in territory subject to the long-term, exclusive jurisdiction and control of the United States, without access to counsel and without being charged with any wrongdoing—unquestionably describe "custody in violation of the Constitution or laws or treaties of the United States."[93]

It fell to the lower courts to begin resolving these questions. The two D.C. District Court decisions that considered these issues came to quite different conclusions. In *Khalid v. Bush,* Judge Leon considered the cases of seven Guantánamo detainees who had been captured outside of Afghanistan.[94] Judge Leon found that the AUMF authorized the President to detain enemy combatants regardless of where they were apprehended,[95] and that neither the Constitution, federal law, nor international law could serve as the basis for issuing a writ of habeas corpus.[96] By contrast, another D.C. District Court decision, *In re Guantánamo Detainee Cases,* held that the Guantánamo detainees had rights under the Constitution, and that the CSRT procedures did not satisfy the standards of due process under the Fifth Amendment.[97] There, Judge Green also ruled that some of the detainees had stated valid claims under GCIII.[98]

The third case that came before the D.C. Circuit concerned the President's military commissions. By this time, the "bringing terrorists to justice" rationale for Guantánamo had become largely untenable. As previously noted, that rationale had been quietly replaced by the alternative "law of war" rationale under which "enemy combatants" could be detained for the duration of hostilities. The Bush administration did not, however, entirely abandon its plans to try certain suspects before military commissions. In July 2003, some eighteen months after the November 2001 Presidential order, the first detainees were designated for trial before military commissions.[99] To date, only a handful of detainees have ever been designated for trial. No trial has yet been completed.

---

93 *Id.* at 483 n. 15. This footnote has been interpreted as suggesting that non-citizens detained outside of the United States possess certain fundamental constitutional rights. *See* Katyal, *supra* note 46, at 55.

94 Khalid v. Bush, 355 F. Supp. 2d 311 (D.D.C. 2005).

95 *Id.*

96 *Id.*

97 In re Guantánamo Detainee Cases, 355 F. Supp. 2d 443 (D.D.C. 2005).

98 *Id.* at 480.

99 Hamdan v. Rumsfeld, 126 S. Ct. 2749, 2760 (2006).

Thanks to the professionalism and determination of the military lawyers appointed to defend the few detainees initially designated for trial,[100] the system of military commissions—widely regarded as unfair[101]—was challenged in the courts. The case of Salim Hamdan, a Yemeni captured by militia forces and handed over to U.S. forces during the Afghanistan conflict, worked its way through the federal court system. Hamdan had been detained at Guantánamo since June 2002.[102] In July 2003, he was among the first detainees designated for trial by military commission.[103] A year later the United States charged Hamdan, who was alleged to be Osama Bin Laden's bodyguard and driver, with conspiracy to commit various war crimes.[104]

The military commission's procedures severely handicapped Hamdan's defense. For example, Hamdan and his civilian counsel could be excluded from portions of the trial, and could even be prevented from finding out what evidence was presented during those portions.[105] The commission's evidentiary standards were lax: any evidence that would have any probative value to a reasonable person, including hearsay and coerced testimony, was admissible.[106] Hamdan also faced the problem of "moving goalposts" in that the commission's procedures continued to change even after proceedings had begun.[107]

---

100 Hamdan's lawyer, Charles Swift, was initially told that he could only negotiate a guilty plea. Swift instead mounted a spirited defense. David Johnston & Neil A. Lewis, *Lawyer Says Military Tried to Coerce Detainee's Plea,* N.Y. TIMES, June 16, 2005, at A25. Swift was subsequently passed over for promotion and forced out of the navy. *See* The Associated Press, *Paper: Detainee Lawyer Must Leave Navy,* WASHINGTONPOST.COM, Oct. 8, 2006, http://www.washingtonpost.com/wp-dyn/content/article/2006/10/08/AR2006100800603.html; Editorial, *The Cost of Doing Your Duty,* N.Y. TIMES, Oct. 11, 2006, at A26.

101 Neil A. Lewis, *Two Prosecutors Faulted Trials for Detainees,* N.Y. TIMES, Aug. 1, 2005, at A1 (discussing comments from two senior prosecutors critical of the military commissions). *See also* Neal K. Katyal, *Hamdan v. Rumsfeld: The Legal Academy Goes to Practice,* 120 HARV. L. REV 65, 87–90 (2006); SERRIN TURNER & STEPHEN J. SCHULHOFER, THE BRENNAN CENTER FOR JUSTICE, THE SECRECY PROBLEM IN TERRORISM TRIALS (2005), *available at* http://www.brennancenter.org/dynamic/subpages/download_file_34654.pdf.

102 Hamdan v. Rumsfeld, 126 S. Ct. at 2759.

103 *Id.* at 2760.

104 *See* Jonathan Miller, *The Bush Administration vs. Salim Hamdan,* N.Y. TIMES MAGAZINE, Jan. 8, 2006, at 44.

105 Hamdan v. Rumsfeld, 126 S. Ct. at 2786.

106 *Id.*

107 *Id.; see also* Katyal, *supra* note 101, at 89. The malleability of the procedures for the military commissions is further illustrated by the special arrangements made for the designated detainees of certain countries. *See* JENNIFER ELSEA, CONG. RES. SERVICE, CRS REP. FOR CONGRESS, THE DEPARTMENT OF DEFENSE RULES FOR MILITARY COMMISSIONS: ANALYSIS OF PROCEDURAL RULES AND COMPARISON WITH PROPOSED LEGISLATION AND THE UNIFORM CODE OF MILITARY JUSTICE, 2 (Aug. 4, 2005), *available at* http://www.fas.org/irp/crs/RL31600.pdf (discussing the exemption of certain designated detainees from the death penalty following negotiations with the Australian and British governments).

In November 2004, a D.C. District Court judge ruled that Hamdan's military commission proceedings were illegal and stayed the commission proceedings.[108] The Court of Appeals for the D.C. Circuit overturned this decision.[109] In November 2005, the Supreme Court granted certiorari.[110] One month later, Congress enacted the Detainee Treatment Act of 2005 (DTA).[111] In addition to imposing certain minimum standards for the treatment of detainees, the DTA purported to strip the courts of jurisdiction to hear habeas corpus applications from Guantánamo detainees.[112] Instead, the DTA provided for limited appeals of CSRT determinations and decisions of military commissions.[113]

In June 2006, the Supreme Court ruled five-to-three in favor of Hamdan.[114] The Court rejected the contention that the DTA left it without jurisdiction to review habeas corpus cases pending at the time of the DTA's enactment.[115] On the merits of the case, Justice Stevens ruled that Hamdan's military commission could not proceed because it violated the Uniform Code of Military Justice (UCMJ) and the 1949 Geneva Conventions.[116]

Justice Stevens' opinion rejected the Bush administration's argument that certain Congressional Acts, most notably the AUMF, had expanded the President's authority to convene military commissions beyond the authorization contained in the UCMJ.[117] Consequently, the rules governing Hamdan's military commission had to be the same as those for courts-martial "insofar as practicable."[118] Justice Stevens held that, absent a showing of impracticality, the rules for Hamdan's military commission, which deviated significantly from the rules of courts-martial, were illegal.[119]

Additionally, Justice Stevens held that the military commission's procedures violated the 1949 Geneva Conventions.[120] The Conventions were applicable because the UCMJ's authorization for military commissions was contingent upon

108 Hamdan v. Rumsfeld, 344 F.Supp.2d 152, 173 (D.D.C. 2004).

109 Hamdan v. Rumsfeld, 415 F.3d 33, 43 (D.C. Cir. 2005).

110 Hamdan v. Rumsfeld, 126 S. Ct. at 2762.

111 Detainee Treatment Act 2005, Pub. L. No. 109-148, 119 Stat. 2739, §§ 1002, 1003 (2005) [hereinafter DTA]. *See* Arsalan M. Suleman, *Detainee Treatment Act of 2005,* 19 Harv. Hum. Rts. J. 257 (2006).

112 *Id.* § 1005(e)(1).

113 *Id.* § 1005(e)(2), (3).

114 *Hamdan,* 126 S. Ct. 2749.

115 *Id.* at 2787. Chief Justice Roberts, having earlier heard the case as a judge on the D.C. Circuit, did not participate.

116 *Id.* at 2792–93.

117 *Id.* at 2792.

118 *Id.* at 2790.

119 *Hamdan,* 126 S. Ct. at 2792–93.

120 *Id.* at 2793.

compliance with the law of war, of which the Geneva Conventions form a major part.[121] Justice Stevens held that Hamdan's military commission violated Common Article 3 of the Geneva Conventions (CA3).[122] Common Article 3 applies to situations of "armed conflict not of an international character occurring in the territory of one of the High Contracting Parties."[123] Because CA3 may apply even if the conflict is not one between parties to the Conventions, Justice Stevens was able to sidestep arguments that the Geneva Conventions were inapplicable to al Qaeda detainees because al Qaeda was not a party to the Conventions.[124]

The Bush administration maintained that CA3 was inapplicable to the conflict between the United States and al Qaeda because it was transnational, and therefore "of an international character."[125] Justice Stevens, however, held that the armed conflict between the United States and al Qaeda was not between two nations, and was therefore "not of an international character," making CA3 applicable.[126]

4. After Hamdan

Although *Hamdan* concerned the legality of military commissions, the ruling that CA3 applied to the conflict with al Qaeda had wider ramifications for the War on Terror. The requirements of Common Article 3 that detainees be "treated humanely" and be protected from "violence to life and person, in particular murder of all kinds, mutilation, cruel treatment and torture," and "outrages upon personal dignity, in particular humiliating and degrading treatment" directly implicated American interrogation practices such as water-boarding and exposure to extreme temperatures.[127] Further, as Justice Kennedy's concurring opinion emphasized, not only had the United States ratified CA3 and "thus accepted [it] as binding law," but violations of it were punishable under the War Crimes Act.[128]

---

121 *Id.* at 2794.

122 *Id.* at 2798. CA3 prohibits "the passing of sentences and the carrying out of executions without previous judgment pronounced by a regularly constituted court affording all the judicial guarantees which are recognized as indispensable by civilized peoples." *Id.* at 2795.

123 GCIII, *supra* note 17, at art. 3.

124 *Hamdan,* 126 S. Ct. at 2794–96.

125 *Id.* at 2795.

126 *Id.* at 2795–96.

127 *Id.* It has been widely reported that certain al Qaeda suspects at Guantánamo and other secret locations have been exposed to such techniques. *See* Adam Zagorin & Michael Duffy, *Inside the Interrogation of Detainee 063,* TIME MAG., June 12, 2005, at 26; Michael Isikoff, *Secret Memo—Send to Be Tortured,* NEWSWEEK, Aug. 8, 2005, at 7; *see also* RON SUSKIND, THE ONE PERCENT DOCTRINE (2006); JAMES RISEN, STATE OF WAR (2006).

128 *Hamdan,* 126 S. Ct. at 2802 (Kennedy J., concurring).

Eight days after the Court decided *Hamdan,* the Pentagon issued a memorandum directing that all detainees be treated in accordance with CA3.[129] However, the Bush administration quickly made plans to have Congress enact a statutory regime that would establish new military commission procedures and limit the scope of *Hamdan's* ruling on CA3. *Hamdan* plainly did not affect the ability of the Bush administration to continue to detain terrorist suspects.[130] However, nearly five years after 9/11, it suddenly became urgent for Congress to pass a new law that would enable the trial of a small number of detainees. In this environment of artificial exigency,[131] Congress responded with a hastily drawn up and draconian law—the Military Commissions Act of 2006 (MCA).[132] The MCA addresses the two grounds on which the *Hamdan* decision invalidated the President's military commissions.[133] The MCA also makes considerable changes to the procedures for military commissions, which, while hardly flawless, nonetheless represent progress.[134] For example, the rules on excluding defendants from trial,[135] the use of testimony obtained through torture,[136] and the appeals process are all improved under the MCA.[137] More fundamentally, the enactment of the MCA at least means that the military commissions will operate under fixed rules and not executive caprice.[138]

But despite its title, the most significant aspects of the MCA are not directly concerned with military commissions. In addition to altering the procedures for military commissions, the MCA makes three very significant changes. First, it prohibits the invocation of the Geneva Conventions in American courts during any proceedings[139] and gives the President the authority to interpret the Geneva Conventions.[140]

---

129 Memorandum from Gordon England, Deputy Secretary of Defense, on Application of Common Article 3 of the Geneva Conventions to the Treatment of Detainees in the Department of Defense, to Secretaries of the Military Departments (July 7, 2006), *available at* http://jurist.law.pitt.edu/pdf/genevaconsmemo.pdf.

130 *Hamdan,* 126 S. Ct. at 2798 ("It bears emphasizing that Hamdan does not challenge, and we do not today address, the Government's power to detain him for the duration of active hostilities.").

131 Editorial, *A Sudden Sense of Urgency,* N.Y. Times, Sept. 7, 2006, at A30; Editorial, *Profiles in Cowardice,* Wash. Post, Oct. 1, 2006, at B6.

132 Military Commissions Act of 2006, Pub. L. No. 109-336, 120 Stat. 2600 (2006).

133 *Id.* §§ 4(a)(2), (3) (amending the portions of the UCMJ on which *Hamdan* was based). Some commentators have seen this as vindication of the pre-*Hamdan* position. *See* John Yoo, *Congress to Courts: Get Out of the War on Terror,* Wall St. J., Oct. 19, 2006, at A18.

134 Stephen J. Ellmann, *The "Rule of Law" and the Military Commission,* 51 N.Y.L. Sch. J. Int'l L. Rev (forthcoming 2007) (manuscript at 29–32), *available at* SSRN: http://ssrn.com/abstract=939603.

135 Military Commissions Act § 3, creating 10 U.S.C. § 949d(e) (2006).

136 *Id.* § 3, creating 10 U.S.C. § 948r (2006).

137 *Id.* § 3, creating 10 U.S.C. §§ 950a–950j (2006).

138 Katyal, *supra* note 101, at 98.

139 Military Commissions Act § 5(a).

140 *Id.* § 6(a)(3).

Second, the MCA amends the War Crimes Act of 1996 to criminalize only the commission of certain narrowly defined acts, rather than breaches of CA3.[141] The effect is to allow American interrogators more leeway in the use of coercive interrogation techniques. This amendment is also given retroactive application.[142] Finally, the MCA removes the right of a non-citizen who has been detained by the United States as an enemy combatant, or who is awaiting such a determination, to seek habeas corpus.[143] Therefore, while the MCA affords greater procedural protections to a small number of Guantánamo detainees who face trial by military commission, it cuts off access to the courts for the majority of detainees who have no prospect of trial.[144]

In February 2007, the D.C. Circuit Court of Appeals decided *Boumediene v. Bush.*[145] *Boumediene,* the successor to the two opposing D.C. District Court decisions on the rights of Guantánamo detainees,[146] was the first judgment to consider the effect of the MCA. The Court unanimously held that the MCA had eliminated the jurisdiction of the courts to hear habeas corpus claims from detainees.[147] A majority then held that the MCA's elimination of jurisdiction was not unconstitutional.[148]

Further legal challenges to the MCA appear inevitable; the Supreme Court is almost certain to hear *Boumediene* in the near future.[149] Further, now that the MCA appears to have foreclosed all statutory avenues, the Supreme Court will have to address the issue of whether certain constitutional rights can apply extra-territorially to the Guantánamo detainees.

B. The United Kingdom

Just prior to 9/11, the United Kingdom enacted a major anti-terrorism law in the form of the Terrorism Act 2000.[150] This Act criminalizes a range of activities relating to terrorism, such as the financing of terrorism and belonging to or inviting

---

141 *Id.* § 6(b)(1).

142 *Id.* § 6(b)(2).

143 *Id.* § 7.

144 *See* Adam Liptak, *Detainee Deal Comes with Contradictions,* N.Y. Times, Sept. 23, 2006, at A1.

145 Boumediene v. Bush, 476 F.3d 981 (D.C. Cir. 2007).

146 *See supra* text accompanying notes 94–98.

147 Boumediene v. Bush, 476 F.3d 981, at 988, 994.

148 *Id.* at 26.

149 Ali Saleh Kahlah Al-Marri's case is also pending in the Fourth Circuit. Following the District Court's dismissal of his habeas corpus petition, Al Marri filed an appeal brief with the Fourth Circuit that addresses the effect of the MCA. *See* Brief of Petitioner-Appellant, United States v. Ali Saleh Kahlah Al-Marri, No. 06-7427 (4th Cir. Nov. 2006), *available at* http://jurist.law.pitt.edu/pdf/al-marriappealbrief.pdf.

150 Terrorism Act, 2000, c. 11 (Eng.).

support for a proscribed terrorist organization.[151] However, it was an Act that was passed after 9/11, the Anti-terrorism, Crime and Security Act 2001 (ATSCA), that authorized the indefinite detention of terrorist suspects.[152]

1. Indefinite Detention Under the ATSCA

Prior to its eventual repeal, Part IV of the ATSCA provided for the detention without trial of non-citizens. If the Secretary of State for the Home Department (Home Secretary) reasonably believed that a person's presence in the United Kingdom was a risk to national security, and suspected that the person was a terrorist, then a certificate could be issued against that person.[153] The ATSCA broadly defined the term "terrorist" as someone who "is or has been concerned in the commission, preparation or instigation of acts of international terrorism" or "is a member of or belongs to an international terrorist group" or "has links with an international terrorist group."[154] The ATSCA further defined "[having] links with an international terrorist group" as denoting support or assistance for the group.[155]

A person so certified by the Home Secretary became a "suspected international terrorist" for the purposes of the Act.[156] In cases where legal or practical considerations barred the United Kingdom from removing a non-citizen certified as a suspected international terrorist,[157] Section 23 of the ATSCA authorized indefinite detention without trial.[158]

Appeals from the Home Secretary's certification were heard by the Special Immigration Appeals Authority (SIAC),[159] a body composed of a High Court judge, one

---

151 *See* Ben Brandon, *Terrorism, Human Rights and the Rule of Law: 120 Years of the UK's Legal Response to Terrorism*, 2004 Crim. L. Rev. 981, 986–90 (2004); *see also* J. J. Rowe, *The Terrorism Act 2000*, 2001 Crim. L. Rev. 527 (2001).

152 Anti-terrorism, Crime and Security Act, 2001, c. 24 (Eng.). For an overview of the ATSCA, see Adam Tomkins, *Legislating Against Terror: the Anti-Terrorism, Crime and Security Act 2001*, [2002] Pub. L. 205.

153 Anti-terrorism, Crime and Security Act § 21(1).

154 *Id.* § 21(2).

155 *Id.* § 21(4).

156 *Id.* § 21(5).

157 Typically, this barring of removal arose where criminal prosecution was difficult and where deportation from the United Kingdom was not feasible because of concerns that the certified person's right to be free from torture might be violated upon return to his home country. *See* Chalal v. United Kingdom 12 Eur. H.R. Rep. 413, para. 74 (1996) (holding that it violates Article 3 of the European Convention on Human Rights to deport or extradite a person where "substantial grounds have been shown for believing that the person in question, if expelled, would face a real risk of being subjected to treatment contrary to Article 3 in the receiving country").

158 Anti-terrorism, Crime and Security Act § 23(1).

159 *Id.* § 21(8)–(9).

expert on immigration matters, and one expert on national security matters.[160] The SIAC could cancel a certification if it concluded that there were no reasonable grounds for suspecting the person to be a terrorist as defined in Section 21(1),[161] although this did not prevent the Home Secretary from issuing another certificate.[162]

Part IV of the ATSCA was controversial. Its indefinite detention regime was plainly inconsistent with Article 5 of the European Convention for the Protection of Human Rights and Fundamental Freedoms 1950 (ECHR),[163] which protects the right to liberty and security of the person. Part IV required the British government to lodge a formal derogation from Article 5 in accordance with Article 15, the ECHR's derogation provision.[164] Despite recommendations to the contrary from a number of different bodies,[165] the Blair government persisted with indefinite detention under Part IV of the ATSCA.

Sixteen persons suspected of various terrorism-related activities were certified by the Home Secretary and detained at Belmarsh Prison in London (the Belmarsh detainees).[166] Nine of the detainees challenged the lawfulness of Part IV of the ATSCA and the derogation from the United Kingdom's human rights obligations under the ECHR. Of those nine detainees, one was released after his certification was revoked by the Home Secretary, one was released on strict bail conditions, one

---

160 *See* Special Immigration Appeals Commission Act, 1997, c. 68 (Eng.); *see also* Constitutional Affairs Committee, The Operation of the Special Immigration Appeals Commission (SIAC) and the Use of Special Advocates (Seventh Report of Session 2004–2005, Vol. I), Mar. 22, 2005, H.C. 323-I, *available at* http://www.publications.parliament.uk/pa/cm200405/cmselect/cmconst/323/323i.pdf.

161 Anti-terrorism, Crime and Security Act §§ 25(2), (5).

162 *Id.* § 27(9).

163 Most of the ECHR is enforceable by virtue of its incorporation into the Human Rights Act 1998, ch. 42. Human Rights Act (Designated Derogation Order), 1998, S.I. 2001/3644 (Eng.).

164 *Id.* Formal notice of derogation was lodged on 18 Dec. 2001. The United Kingdom also derogated from Article 9 of the ICCPR: *see* A and others v. Secretary of State for the Home Department, [2005] 2 A.C. 68, para. 11 (U.K.).

165 Privy Counsellor Review Committee, Anti-terrorism, Crime and Security Act 2001 Review Report, Dec. 18, 2003, H.C. 100, paras. 205–43, *available at* http://www.archive2.official-documents.co.uk/document/deps/hc/hc100/100.pdf [hereinafter Newton Report]; Joint Committee on Human Rights, Review of Counter-terrorism Powers (Eighteenth Report of Session 2003–2004), Aug. 4, 2004, H.L. 158/ H.C. 713, paras. 52–64, *available at* http://www.publications.parliament.uk/pa/jt200304/jtselect/jtrights/158/158.pdf; Joint Committee on Human Rights, Counter-Terrorism Policy and Human Rights: Prosecution And Pre-Charge Detention (Twenty-fourth Report of Session 2005–2006), July 24, 2006, H.L. 240, H.C. 1576, *available at* http://www.publications.parliament.uk/pa/jt200506/jtselect/jtrights/240/240.pdf.

166 Sangeeta Shah, *The UK's Anti-Terror Legislation and the House of Lords: The First Skirmish*, 5 Hum. Rts. L. Rev. 403, 405–06 (2005).

was transferred to a hospital after suffering a mental illness, and two chose to leave the United Kingdom.[167]

The SIAC ruled in favor of the detainees, but was then overruled by the Court of Appeal.[168] In December 2004, the House of Lords decision *A v. Secretary of State for the Home Department (A v. Secretary of State)* dealt the Blair government's detainee policy a setback by reversing the Court of Appeal's judgment.[169] Although eight Law Lords were satisfied that the government was entitled to its view that there was a public emergency justifying derogation from the ECHR, a majority held that Section 23 of the ATSCA was nonetheless illegal on two grounds. First, the Lords held that indefinite detention under the ATSCA was a disproportionate response that exceeded what was "strictly required by the exigencies of the situation" under Article 15, and thus infringed Article 5 of the ECHR.[170] Second, the Lords held that Section 23 violated Article 14 of the ECHR—the right to be free from discrimination—in that it treated citizens and non-citizens differently without a rational and objective justification.[171] The House of Lords quashed the derogation order and declared Section 23 of the ATSCA incompatible with Articles 5 and 14 of the ECHR.[172]

2. The Aftermath of *A v. Secretary of State*

Although English courts do not have the power to strike down legislation, *A v. Secretary of State* forced the Blair government to change course. The government's post-*A* approach was to seek to deport non-citizen terrorist suspects and to obtain diplomatic assurances from receiving states to satisfy human rights requirements.[173] Those who could not be deported would be detained under a new legislative framework.[174] On March 11, 2005, Parliament enacted the Prevention of Terrorism

---

167 A v. Secretary of State for the Home Department, [2004] UKHL 56,, [2005] 2 A.C. 68 para. 2 (appeal taken from Eng.) (U.K.), [Hereinafter A v. Secretary of State].

168 A and others v. Secretary of State for the Home Department, [2003] 2 W.L.R. 564 (U.K.).

169 A v. Secretary of State, [2004] UKHL 56, [2005] 2 A.C. 68 (appeal taken from Eng.) (U.K.). *See generally* Shah, *supra* note 166.

170 *See* A v. Secretary of State, [2004] UKHL 56, [2005] 2 A.C. 68, paras. 43 (Lord Bingham), 81 (Lord Nicholls), 132–33 (Lord Hope), 156 (Lord Scott), 189 (Lord Rodger) & 231 (Baroness Hale).

171 *See id.* paras. 68 (Lord Bingham), 138 (Lord Hope), 159 (Lord Scott), 189 (Lord Rodger) & 232 (Baroness Hale).

172 *See id.* paras. 73 (Lord Bingham), 85 (Lord Nicholls), 139 (Lord Hope), 160 (Lord Scott), 190 (Lord Rodger), 239 (Baroness Hale) & 240 (Lord Carswell).

173 *See supra* text accompanying notes 132–33. For a discussion of the use of diplomatic assurances, see Joint Committee on Human Rights, Counter-Terrorism Policy And Human Rights: Terrorism Bill and Related Matters, 2005–2006, H.L. 75-I/ H.C. 561-I, paras. 120–46, *available at* http://www.publications.parliament.uk/pa/jt200506/jtselect/jtrights/75/75i.pdf.

174 *See* Mary Arden, *Human Rights in the Age of Terrorism,* 121 L.Q.R. 604, 609 (2005).

Act 2005 (PTA),[175] which repealed Part IV of the ATSCA and created the new detention regime.[176] The PTA allows the Home Secretary to impose "control orders" upon both citizen and non-citizen terrorist suspects who have "involvement in terrorist-related activity" as defined by the Act.[177] Control orders—perhaps best analogized to sets of strict bail conditions—impose certain restrictions on the liberty of their target, the controlee, in order to restrict or prevent involvement in terrorism-related activity. It is an offense to breach an obligation in a control order without reasonable excuse.[178]

The PTA provides for two types of control order. Derogating control orders are for individuals who represent a serious risk to public safety.[179] The degree of infringement on an individual's liberty imposed by this type of control order—for example, house arrest—is sufficiently onerous to require derogation from Article 5 of the ECHR.[180] Derogating control orders can only be imposed by the High Court upon application by the Home Secretary.[181] The High Court must be satisfied on the balance of probabilities that the controlee is or has been involved in "terrorism-related activity", and must consider that the imposition of obligations on the subject is necessary for the protection of the public.[182] Further, it must appear to the court that the risk arises out of, or is associated with, a public emergency in respect of which there has been a derogation from Article 5, and that the obligations are described in the designation order.[183] A derogating control order ceases after six months unless renewed.[184]

Non-derogating control orders impose specific combinations of restrictions upon individuals such as curfew, electronic tagging, searches of residences and other premises, restrictions on association, and restrictions on the use of telephones and Internet.[185] Non-derogating control orders, which last for twelve months unless renewed,[186] may be imposed in cases where the Home Secretary has reasonable grounds for suspecting that an individual is or has been involved in terrorism-related

175 Prevention of Terrorism Act 2005, c. 2 (Eng.).

176 Arden, *supra* note 174, at 627.

177 Prevention of Terrorism Act 2005 § 1(9).

178 *Id.* § 9.

179 Shah, *supra* note 166, at 418.

180 Prevention of Terrorism Act 2005 §§ 4(3)(c), 4(7)(c), 4(10)(c); *see generally* Shah, *supra* note 166, at 417–20.

181 Prevention of Terrorism Act 2005 § 1(2)(b).

182 *Id.* § 4(7).

183 *Id.* A "designation order," per § 1(1), is the order under § 14(1) of the Human Rights Act 1998 by which the derogation is designated.

184 *Id.* §§ 4(8), 4(9).

185 *Id.* § 1(4).

186 Prevention of Terrorism Act 2005 §§ 2(4), 2(6).

activity and considers it necessary to make a control order imposing obligations on that individual in order to protect the public.[187] Except in emergencies, the Home Secretary must have the High Court's permission to make a non-derogating control order.[188] The High Court then reviews the Home Secretary's decision.[189]

Upon release, the Belmarsh detainees were immediately made subject to non-derogating control orders.[190] Nine detainees were later served with notices of intention to deport and had their control orders revoked in August 2005. Two detainees remained subject to control orders.[191] As of September 2006, there were fifteen control orders in force, with six of those applying to British citizens.[192]

Non-derogating control orders have since been challenged in the courts. The relevant human rights issues had already been flagged.[193] The first challenge to non-derogating control orders was based on Article 6 of the ECHR, which protects the right to a fair trial. In *Secretary of State for the Home Department v. MB,* the Court of Appeal overruled a High Court decision that held that the procedure for imposing non-derogating control orders violated Article 6.[194] At issue was Section 3(10) of the PTA, which states that the court is to determine whether the Home Secretary's decision to impose a control order "was flawed." The High Court Judge concluded that Section 3(10) limited the court to considering material that was available to the Home Secretary at the time the decision was made.[195] Consequently, judicial supervision was in actuality so weak as to breach Article 6 of the ECHR. In contrast, the Court of Appeal interpreted the section to mean flawed at the time of the court hearing, which allowed consideration of a wider range of information, including

187 *Id.* § 2(1).

188 *Id.* § 3(1).

189 *Id.* § 3.

190 Clive Walker, *Intelligence and Anti-terrorism Legislation in the United Kingdom,* 44 Crime, L. & Soc. Change 387, 407 (2005); Constitutional Affairs Committee, *supra* note 160, para. 30.

191 Lord Carlisle, First Report of the Independent Reviewer Pursuant to Section 14(3) of the Prevention of Terrorism Act 2005, Feb. 2, 2006, para. 18, http://security.homeoffice.gov.uk/news-publications/publication-search/independent-reviews/laws-against-terror.pdf?view=Binary.

192 Tony McNutly, Minister for Policing, Security and Community Safety, Written Ministerial Statements for 11 Sept. 2006, *available at* http://www.publications.parliament.uk/pa/cm/cmtoday/cmwms/archive/060911.htm#hddr_27 (last visited Mar. 20, 2007).

193 *See* Joint Committee of Human Rights, Counter-Terrorism Policy and Human Rights: Draft Prevention of Terrorism Act 2005 (Continuance in force of sections 1 to 9) Order 2006, 2005–2006, H.L. 122/H.C. 915, *available at* http://www.publications.parliament.uk/pa/jt200506/jtselect/jtrights/122/122.pdf.

194 Secretary of State for the Home Department v. MB, [2006] EWCA (Civ) 1140 (U.K.).

195 *Re: MB,* [2006] EWHC 1000 (U.K.).

the response of the individual concerned.[196] Accordingly, the court held there was no breach of Article 6.

A second decision concerned whether the cumulative effect of restrictions imposed by non-derogating control orders were sufficiently onerous so as to breach Article 5 of the ECHR. In *Secretary of State for the Home Department v. JJ and others*,[197] the Court of Appeal considered whether the obligations imposed by six control orders—daily eighteen-hour curfew, random searches by authorities, restrictions on visitors, electronic tagging, reporting requirements, geographical restrictions on travel outside of curfew, and prohibitions on using cellular phones and the Internet—in effect deprived the controlees of their liberty.[198] The Court of Appeal ruled that the obligations imposed by these non-derogating control orders were collectively severe enough to amount to a deprivation of liberty in breach of Article 5 and, as such, could not be validly made by the Home Secretary.[199] The Home Secretary has indicated that he intends to appeal this decision to the House of Lords.[200]

C. Canada

As was the case in the United Kingdom, 9/11 led to the swift enactment of a new anti-terrorism law in Canada, the Anti-Terrorism Act.[201] This Act contains some prosaic provisions, such as those concerned with the financing of terrorism, along with controversial measures such as preventive arrest and compelled testimony before investigative hearings.[202] However, terrorist suspects in Canada have been detained using another statute, the Immigration and Refugee Protection Act (IRPA).[203] The IPRA specifies several bases on which non-citizens are inadmissible to Canada, one of which is security. A non-citizen may be inadmissible on security grounds in a number of ways. These include being engaged in terrorism, being a danger to the security of Canada, engaging in violence that might endanger

196 [2006] EWCA (Civ.) 1140, para. 46.

197 Secretary of State for the Home Department v. JJ and others, [2006] EWCA (Civ) 1141 (U.K.).

198 These requirements are described in the High Court judgment. *See* Secretary of State for the Home Department v. JJ and others, [2006] EWHC (Admin) 1623, paras. 60–71 (Eng.).

199 [2006] EWCA (Civ.) 1141, para. 23.

200 Alan Travis, *Reid's Curfew Orders on Six Terror Suspects Are Illegal, Say Judges*, THE GUARDIAN, Aug. 2, 2006, at 13, *available at* http://www.guardian.co.uk/frontpage/story/0,1835412,00.html.

201 Anti-Terrorism Act, 2001 S.C., ch. 41 (Can.).

202 *See* Reg Whitaker, *Keeping Up with the Neighbours? Canadian Reponses to 9/11 in Historical and Comparative Context*, 41 OSGOODE HALL L.J. 241, 261 (2003). These two temporary measures have since been allowed to expire. *See* Ian Austen, *Canadian Parliament Decides to Let 2 Measures Passed After 9/11 Expire*, N.Y. TIMES, Feb. 28, 2007, at A8.

203 Immigration and Refugee Protection Act, 2001 S.C. ch. 27, §§ 77–88 (Can.). *See generally* Kent Roach, *Canada's Response to Terrorism*, *in* GLOBAL ANTI-TERRORISM LAW AND POLICY 511 (Victor V. Ramraj et al. eds., 2005).

the lives or safety of people in Canada, or being a member of an organization that there are reasonable grounds for believing has engaged, engages, or will engage in terrorist acts.[204]

If an inadmissible non-citizen is present in Canada, that person may be deported.[205] The deportation of non-citizens considered inadmissible on security grounds occurs via the IRPA's security certificate process. This process permits non-citizens considered to be security risks to be made subject to security certificates, and then detained until such time as removal from Canada can occur.[206]

Security certificates have existed as a part of Canadian law since the 1990s.[207] About twenty-seven such certificates, which are now signed by the Minister of Citizenship and Immigration and the Minister of Public Safety and Emergency Preparedness, have been issued.[208] Five have been issued since 9/11.[209] The five men that have been indefinitely detained under the security certificate regime since 9/11 are Mohamed Harkat, an Algerian refugee detained from December 2002; Syrian-born Hassan Almrei, imprisoned since October 2001; Mohammed Mahjoub, an Egyptian arrested in June 2000; Moroccan Adil Charkaoui, held from May 2003; and Mahmoud Jaballah, also an Egyptian, held since August 2001.[210] Charkaoui, Harkat, Mahjoub, and Jaballah were released on conditions in February 2005, June 2006, February 2007, and March 2007, respectively.[211] Almrei remains held in a special unit established in April 2006 at Millhaven Penitentiary in Ontario. Critics have dubbed the Millhaven unit "Guantanamo North."[212]

---

204 Immigration and Refugee Protection Act, ch. 27, § 34(1).

205 Hamish Stewart, *Is Indefinite Detention of Terrorist Suspects Really Constitutional?*, 54 U.N.B.L.J. 235, 236 (2005).

206 Immigration and Refugee Protection Act, ch. 27, §§ 34, 77–84.

207 Roach & Trotter, *supra* note 90, at 1003.

208 *Id.*

209 Canada Border Services Agency, Security Certificates under the Immigration and Refugee Protection Act, Apr. 2005, *available at* http://www.cbsa-asfc.gc.ca/newsroom/factsheets/2005/certificate.pdf.

210 Timothy Appleby, *High-Security Centre to House Terror Suspects*, Globe And Mail, Feb. 2, 2006, at A2, *available at* http://www.theglobeandmail.com/servlet/story/RTGAM.20060202.wxprison02/BNStory/National.

211 Michelle Shephard, *Terror Suspect Ordered Freed*, Toronto Star, March 7, 2007, http://www.thestar.com/News/article/189036; *Court Orders Release of Suspected Terrorist on Hunger Strike*, CBC News Online, Feb. 15, 2007, http://www.cbc.ca/canada/story/2007/02/15/court-mahjoub.html?ref=rss; *Top Court Rules Against Security Certificates*, CBC News Online, Feb. 23, 2007, http://www.cbc.ca/canada/story/2007/02/23/security-certificate.html.

212 Michelle Shephard, *Inside Gitmo North*, Toronto Star, Jan. 6, 2007, *available at* http://www.thestar.com/printArticle/168467; John Gray, *Canada's prisoners of secret evidence*, CBC News Online, May 29, 2006, http://www.cbc.ca/news/background/realitycheck/gray/20060529.html.

Once a security certificate is issued, detention may ensue.[213] The certificate is then referred to a designated Federal Court judge for a review of its reasonableness.[214] The review in Federal Court operates under special rules of procedure. The judge may be required to hear the evidence in support of the security certificate's reasonableness in camera and ex parte if the judge considers this necessary to protect national security or the safety of any person.[215] In such cases, the judge must provide the certified person a summary of information that allows that person to be "reasonably informed of the circumstances giving rise to the certificate," but this cannot include anything that, if disclosed, would harm national security or public safety.[216] A determination by the Federal Court that a security certificate is reasonable is conclusive proof that the certified person is inadmissible on security grounds and constitutes a removal order.[217] The decision is not subject to appeal.[218]

The IRPA security certificate process results in indefinite detention because of the time delay inherent in the review process, and because of the difficulties surrounding the removal of a non-citizen to a state where he might face torture.[219] The second issue is the same as that faced by the United Kingdom, and was one of the reasons for the express provision of indefinite detention under Part IV of the ATSCA. Canada, however, has been less categorical in respecting its obligation not to return non-citizens to states where they could face torture. The IRPA affirms the principle of non-refoulement, which prohibits the removal of a person to a country where they would be at risk of persecution, torture, or cruel and unusual treatment or punishment.[220] However, Canada makes an exception for a person inadmissible on security grounds if, in the opinion of the Minister of Citizenship and Immigration, that person should not be allowed to remain because of "danger to the security of Canada."[221]

---

213 Immigration and Refugee Protection Act, 2001 S.C., ch. 27, §§ 82(2) (providing for mandatory detention of certified foreign nationals), 82(1) (providing for discretionary detention of permanent residents).

214 *Id.* §§ 77(1), 80.

215 *Id.* § 78(e).

216 *Id.* § 78(h).

217 *Id.* § 81.

218 Immigration and Refugee Protection Act § 80(3).

219 Charkaoui v. Canada, [2007] S.C.C. 9, para. 105 (Can.).

220 Immigration and Refugee Protection Act § 115(1).

221 *Id.* § 115(2). A number of the five recent security certificate detainees have faced this very situation. *See* Almrei v. Canada, [2005] 251 D.L.R. 4th 13; *see also* HUMAN RIGHTS WATCH, STILL AT RISK: DIPLOMATIC ASSURANCES NO SAFEGUARD AGAINST TORTURE 49–54, (Apr. 2005) http://hrw.org/reports/2005/eca0405/eca0405.pdf (describing moves by the Canadian government to deport Charkaoui and Mahjoub to countries with dubious human rights records).

Significantly, the Supreme Court decision of *Suresh v. Canada* leaves open the possibility of deportation to a state where the deported person may face torture.[222] In *Suresh,* the Court considered the Minister of Citizenship and Immigration's decision that Suresh, who had alleged links to the Tamil Tigers, constituted a "danger to the security of Canada" under earlier legislation.[223] While accepting that deporting a person certified as inadmissible on security grounds to a situation where they would face a substantial risk of torture would generally violate the guarantee of fundamental justice under Section 7 of the Canadian Charter of Rights and Freedoms (the Charter), the Court left open the possibility of justifiable deportation to torture in unspecified exceptional circumstances.[224]

In February 2007, a unanimous Canadian Supreme Court ruled in *Charkaoui v. Canada* that the IRPA's security certificate process violated the Charter.[225] The Court held that the use of evidence not disclosed to the certified person, and the failure to provide an adequate mechanism for alleviating the ensuing prejudice, resulted in a violation of the Charter's section 7 guarantee of fundamental justice.[226] The Court also held that the IRPA's denial of prompt hearings for applications of release from certified foreign nationals violated Section 9's guarantee against arbitrary detention and section 10(c)'s right to a prompt review of detention.[227]

Because it violated the Charter, the Court ruled that the IRPA's security certificate process was "of no force or effect."[228] However, the Court suspended its declaration for one year in order to allow the Canadian Parliament to devise a new regime that would pass constitutional muster.[229]

D. New Zealand

As with the other jurisdictions considered in this Article, 9/11 was a catalyst for the enactment of new counterterrorist legislation in New Zealand. Most notable was the Terrorism Suppression Act 2002, which, like its equivalents in the United Kingdom and Canada, sets out a definition of terrorism and prohibits certain terrorist-related activities such as the financing of terrorism and the harboring or

222 Suresh v. Canada, [2002] 1 S.C.R. 3 (Can.); *see also* Craig Forcese, *Through a Glass Darkly: The Role and Review of "National Security" Concepts in Canadian Law*, 43 Alta. L. Rev. 963 (2006).

223 Suresh v. Canada, [2002] 1 S.C.R. 3, para. 16 (Can.).

224 *Id.* para. 78.

225 Charkaoui v. Canada, [2007] S.C.C. 9 (Can.).

226 *Id.* para. 139.

227 *Id.* paras. 93–94. The Court rejected the two other claims based on Section 12's guarantee against cruel and unusual punishment, and Section 15(1)'s guarantee against discrimination. *See id.* paras. 110, 129–32.

228 *Id.* para. 140.

229 *Id.*

concealing of terrorists.[230] However, the single terrorist suspect detained in New Zealand, Ahmed Zaoui, has been held under a pre-existing amendment to the Immigration Act 1987.

Zaoui is an Algerian national who fled his native country following a military coup d'état. He arrived in New Zealand in December 2002.[231] Upon arrival, he sought refugee status, which he gained in August 2003.[232] By this time, details of his past, including criminal convictions in France and Belgium, had come to the attention of the New Zealand Security Intelligence Service (NZSIS). This led the NZSIS Director to issue the first-ever security risk certificate against Zaoui in March 2003.[233] This certificate stated that Zaoui's presence was "a threat to national security," and that there were "reasonable grounds for regarding [Zaoui] as a danger to the security of New Zealand."[234]

Once the NZSIS Director issues a security risk certificate, the Minister of Immigration makes a preliminary decision whether to rely on it.[235] The decision to rely on the certificate has a number of consequences, including mandating the certified person's detention if that person is in New Zealand[236] and potentially removal or deportation from New Zealand down the line.[237] The Act provides the certified person the right to seek review of the decision to issue the certificate before the Inspector General of Intelligence and Security, a retired High Court Judge.[238] If the Inspector General decides the certificate was not proper, the government must release the detainee.[239] If the Inspector General confirms the certificate as proper, then the Minister makes a final decision as to whether to rely on the certificate. A decision to rely on the certificate results in the cancellation of any visa or permit still held and the issuance of a removal or deportation order.[240]

---

230 Terrorism Suppression Act 2002, §§ 8, 13A; *see also* Treasa Dunworth, *Review: Public International Law,* N.Z. L. Rev. 411, 418–22 (2004).

231 Refugee Appeal No. 74540, Aug. 1, 2003, paras. 2–5, *available at* http://www.humanrights.co.nz/documents/RSAAdecision_001.pdf.

232 Refugee Appeal No. 74540, Aug. 1, 2003, *available at* http://www.humanrights.co.nz/documents/RSAAdecision_001.pdf.

233 Immigration Act 1987, 1987 S.N.Z. No. 43, § 114D; *see generally id.* at Part 4A.

234 The certificate is reproduced in Zaoui v. Attorney-General, [2006] 1 N.Z.L.R. 289 S.C., para. 3; *see also* Immigration Act 1987, 1987 S.N.Z. No. 43, §§ 114C(6)(a), (4)(a).

235 Immigration Act 1987, 1987 S.N.Z. No. 43, § 114F.

236 *Id.* §§ 114G(3)(c), (5).

237 *Id.* § 114K.

238 *Id.* § 114H.

239 *Id.* § 114J(2).

240 Immigration Act 1987, 1987 S.N.Z. No. 43, §114K.

Zaoui has now been in New Zealand for more than four years. During that time, in addition to polarizing public opinion,[241] he has initiated several sets of court proceedings, two of which have reached New Zealand's Supreme Court. The first case sought his release from custody.[242] Zaoui had been detained upon his arrival because he arrived without travel documents. He spent two years in prison, including ten months in solitary confinement.[243] Ordinarily, the granting of refugee status would have permitted Zaoui's release.[244] However, he remained in custody because he was already subject to the security risk certificate.[245] Zaoui was successful in the Supreme Court. The Court first ruled that the relevant provisions of the Immigration Act did not exclude the inherent jurisdiction of the courts to grant release on bail,[246] and then, remarkably, heard and granted Zaoui's subsequent bail application itself.[247]

The second case concerned the parameters of the Inspector General's review of Zaoui's security risk certificate.[248] In October 2003, the Inspector General issued a preliminary decision concerning the procedure and scope of his review, aspects of which Zaoui challenged.[249] The issue for the Supreme Court was whether the Inspector General had to consider the risks Zaoui might face if New Zealand were to deport him. The Court held that the Inspector-General was only to determine whether the statutory security criteria were satisfied; he was not to determine whether Zaoui was subject to a threat that would or might prevent his removal because of New Zealand's human rights obligations.[250]

Although this decision went in the government's favor, it significantly circumscribed the government's ability to deport Zaoui if the security risk certificate were to be confirmed and relied on. The Court concluded that the executive's power to deport Zaoui was to be interpreted and applied consistently with rights that are affirmed in both domestic[251] and international law,[252] namely the right to life and the right to be free from torture or cruel, inhuman, or degrading treatment.

241 *See NZ's Lone Terror Suspect Splits Country*, BBC NEWS ONLINE, Oct. 25, 2006, http://news.bbc.co.uk/2/hi/asia-pacific/6066678.stm.

242 Zaoui v. Attorney-General, [2005] 1 N.Z.L.R. 577.

243 Catherine Masters, *Zaoui a Reluctant Celebrity*, N.Z. HERALD, June 25, 2005, http://www.nzherald.co.nz/search/story.cfm?storyid=4992EF1C-39E4-11DA-8E1B-A5B353C55561.

244 Treasa Dunworth, *Review: Public International Law*, N.Z. L. REV. 367, 370 (2006).

245 Immigration Act, §§ 114G(3)(c), (5).

246 Zaoui v. Attorney-General, [2005] 1 N.Z.L.R. 577.

247 *Id.* at 662. Since his release on bail, Zaoui has been living at a Dominican priory.

248 Zaoui v. Attorney-General, [2006] 1 N.Z.L.R. 289.

249 *Id.* para. 6.

250 *Id.* para. 73.

251 New Zealand Bill of Rights Act 1990, 1990 S.N.Z. No. 109, §§ 8, 9.

252 ICCPR, *supra* note 30 at arts. 6, 7; Convention Against Torture and Other Cruel, Inhuman or Degrading Treatment or Punishment Dec. 10, 1984, 1465 U.N.T.S. 85, art. 3 (hereinafter CAT).

Therefore, even if the government considered Zaoui a threat to national security, it could not lawfully deport him if the relevant executive decision makers were satisfied that there were substantial grounds for believing deportation would put Zaoui in danger of being arbitrarily deprived of life, subjected to torture, or subjected to cruel, inhuman, or degrading treatment.[253] This further implied an obligation on the executive's part to conduct a sufficiently thorough inquiry into the human rights implications of deporting Zaoui.[254]

Although the Supreme Court resolved the issue of the Inspector General's scope of review in mid-2005, at the time of writing, Zaoui's review remains pending. It is currently scheduled to take place in mid-2007.

III. DIFFERENCES IN THE REGIMES FOR THE DETENTION OF TERRORIST SUSPECTS

All four jurisdictions examined are Western democracies sharing a common legal heritage. Nonetheless, certain broad differences between the American and non-American regimes for detaining terrorist suspects are discernible. First, the model or paradigm that serves as the basis for the detention of terrorist suspects differs. The United States has relied on a model roughly based on the law of war, while the other jurisdictions have relied on a detention model based on immigration law. Second, the detention of terrorist suspects by the United States has been an issue dominated by discretionary executive decisions. By contrast, the other detention regimes have been set out by the respective legislatures. A third difference is the varying attitudes towards human rights norms. The American approach has been to attempt to exclude them altogether, while the approach in the other jurisdictions has been to work within the human rights paradigm, arguing, where necessary, that exceptional circumstances justify the limitation of rights.

A. Models of Detention: Terrorists as Criminals, Enemy Belligerents, or Illegal Aliens?

Since terrorist acts almost invariably involve violations of the criminal law, the most obvious course is to treat terrorists as we treat others who violate the law. This would involve the use of the criminal justice system to try suspected terrorists. If a terrorist suspect were tried and convicted, the state could then take away his liberty. But there are difficulties in using the criminal law as a counter-terrorism tool. Counter-terrorism ideally prevents a terrorist act from taking place at all. This prospective orientation is at odds with the criminal law's primarily retrospective focus on punishing individuals' past acts.

253 Zaoui v. Attorney-General, [2006] 1 N.Z.L.R. 289, paras. 90–91, 93.

254 *Id.* para. 92. On the situation in Algeria, see Paul Buchanan, *Zaoui Between a Rock and a Hard Place,* N.Z. Herald, Oct. 5, 2005, *available at* http://www.nzherald.co.nz/search/story.cfm?storyid=C22FBD56-39E4-11DA-8E1B-A5B353C55561.

There may also be difficulties in bringing criminal prosecutions against terrorist suspects due to evidentiary and procedural issues. For example, statements made by certain high-level al Qaeda detainees during interrogations would almost certainly be inadmissible under standard rules of evidence, as such statements may have been procured through torture or coercion.[255] Thus the imperatives of intelligence gathering may conflict with those of prosecution.[256] Further, the majority of the Guantánamo detainees are not high-level terrorist suspects. Many were scooped up off the battlefield in Afghanistan, and in some cases, from various other locales.[257] There simply may be insufficient evidence to satisfy the high standard of proof applicable in ordinary criminal proceedings.[258]

This is not to say, however, that only those convicted of crimes can be deprived of liberty. For example, so long as a certain level of due process is provided, the law allows pre-trial detention, the detention of the mentally ill, and the preventive detention of dangerous sexual predators.[259] Another option is to adopt a war paradigm, where the terrorist is treated as an enemy in armed conflict. Rather than focusing on whether certain acts of a terrorist constitute crimes, it is the terrorist's status as the enemy that is controlling.[260] Under the law of war, captured enemies may be detained without trial for the duration of hostilities.[261] In this case, the purpose of detention is purely to incapacitate, rather than to punish.[262] Additionally, procedural protections that are part and parcel of the Western criminal model—the presumption of innocence, the right to a fair trial, and the assistance of counsel—are inapplicable.[263]

Immigration law provides another scheme for permitting the detention of terrorists.[264] Immigration law permits detention while not affording detainees the full panoply of procedural protections characteristic of criminal law. Like the law of war, immigration law focuses on status rather than on conduct. The United Kingdom,

255 Helen Duffy, The 'War on Terror' and the Framework of International Law 123 (2005).

256 *See* Bill Dedman, *Gitmo Interrogations Spark Battle over Tactics,* MSNBC News, Oct. 23, 2006, http://www.msnbc.msn.com/id/15361458.

257 *See infra* text accompanying notes 433–39.

258 Duffy, *supra* note 255, at 122.

259 Yin, *supra* note 8, at 22–26; Benjamin J. Priester, *Return of the Great Writ: Judicial Review, Due Process, and the Detention of Alleged Terrorists as Enemy Combatants,* 37 Rutgers L.J. 39, 43–51 (2005).

260 Stephen C. Neff, War and the Law of Nations 384 (2005).

261 Geneva Convention Relative to the Treatment of Prisoners of War, art. 118, Aug. 12, 1949; 6 U.S.T. 3316.

262 Yin, *supra* note 8, at 9–11.

263 Neff, *supra* note 260, at 390.

264 Kent Roach, *The Criminal Law and Terrorism, in* Global Anti-Terrorism Law And Policy 129, 142–43 (Victor V. Ramraj et al. eds., 2005).

Canada, and New Zealand have all used immigration law as the basis for their detention regimes. The United States has used a model based on the law of war. Both models are discussed further below.

1. United States: The Quasi Law-of-War Model

Before 9/11, the United States' skirmishes with al Qaeda featured the use of both the criminal-justice and war paradigms. For example, agents of al Qaeda were indicted, and in some cases successfully tried, for their roles in various bombings of American interests.[265] Conversely, after the bombings of American embassies in Kenya and Tanzania, cruise missiles struck al Qaeda targets in Sudan and Afghanistan.[266]

In the immediate aftermath of 9/11, the United States used immigration law to indiscriminately detain Arab and Muslim non-citizens.[267] The United States detained some 1000 non-citizens, although it never brought any charges relating to the attacks.[268] However, by the time hostilities commenced in Afghanistan one month later, the contest was between the criminal justice and war paradigms. An illustration of this is the treatment of certain terrorist suspects apprehended in 2001 and early 2002. John Walker Lindh, an American citizen captured in Afghanistan in November 2001, was tried under the criminal law in federal court. He pleaded guilty to one charge of providing service to the Taliban and a further charge of carrying explosives. He was sentenced to twenty years' imprisonment.[269] Yaser Hamdi, another American citizen captured in Afghanistan, was detained for several years as an enemy combatant before his eventual release.[270] Jose Padilla, an American citizen arrested in Chicago, was also detained for several years as an enemy combatant before eventually reentering the criminal justice system.[271]

Ali Saleh Kahlah Al-Marri, a Qatari national, was arrested and detained in the United States in December 2001 as a material witness in relation to the 9/11 investigation.[272] The United States subsequently charged him with various crimes, but then designated him as an enemy combatant before his trial.[273] Al-Marri remains

---

265 Neff, *supra* note 260, at 387.

266 *Id.*

267 *See* Margaret H. Taylor, *Dangerous by Decree: Detention Without Bond in Immigration Proceedings*, 50 Loy. L. Rev. 149 (2004); David Cole, Enemy Aliens 26–35 (2003).

268 Roach & Trotter, *supra* note 90, at 970.

269 Neil A. Lewis, *Admitting He Fought in Taliban, American Agrees to 20-Year Term*, N.Y. Times, Jul. 16, 2002, at A1.

270 *See supra* text accompanying notes 83–84.

271 *See supra* text accompanying notes 78–82.

272 Elsea, *supra* note 64, at CRS-32.

273 *Id.*

detained at a naval brig in South Carolina.[274] Zacarias Moussaoui, a French-born al Qaeda member captured in August 2001, was tried and convicted by a federal jury and is currently serving six life sentences.[275] Richard Reid, the British "shoe-bomber" arrested in December 2001, was also convicted in federal court and sentenced to life imprisonment.[276] The disparate treatment of these men suggests that who is detained as an enemy combatant and who is detained as a criminal is a matter of pure discretion.[277]

Despite the occasional countervailing example,[278] the war paradigm has come to dominate, and detention under the rubric of the law of war has become the primary means of incapacitating terrorist suspects. Since the U.S. military established Guantánamo Bay as a detention camp, hundreds of terrorist suspects have been detained there indefinitely.

Despite some claims to the contrary,[279] it bears emphasizing that the Bush administration's approach to the detention of terrorist suspects is only loosely based on the law of war. It is more accurately described as the "quasi law-of-war model," a model which selectively utilizes aspects of the law of war to incarcerate terrorist suspects, but which denies certain rights and protections that the same body of law normally affords detainees. This selective application of the law of war can be seen with the use of the term "enemy combatant" and the administration's sporadic application of the Geneva Conventions.

a) The Expanding Notion of "Enemy Combatant"

In the War on Terror, categorization as an "enemy combatant" is the trigger for indefinite incommunicado detention. Despite the impression conveyed by

---

274 Al-Marri v. Wright, 443 F.Supp.2d 774 (2006) (denying Al-Marri's petition for writ of habeas corpus).

275 Associated Press, *Moussaoui Formally Sentenced, Still Defiant,* May 4, 2006, http://www.msnbc.msn.com/id/12615601/; Neil A. Lewis, *Moussaoui Given Life Term by Jury Over Link to 9/11,* N.Y. Times, May 4, 2006, at A1.

276 Pam Belluck, *Unrepentant Shoe Bomber Is Given a Life Sentence for Trying to Blow Up Jet,* N.Y. Times, Jan. 31, 2003, at A13.

277 Adam Liptak, *In Terror Cases, Administration Sets Own Rules,* N. Y. Times, Nov. 27, 2005; Golden & Van Natta, *supra* note 45 (quoting former Justice Department official Viet Dinh as stating, "[t]here was not a real process for determining who was an enemy combatant . . . [a]nd the ad hoc nature of that process gave a lot of power to the Pentagon"); *see also* Tung Yin, *Coercion and Terrorism Prosecutions in the Shadow of Military Detention,* 2006 B.Y.U. L. REV. 1255 (2006); Jesselyn A. Radack, *You Say Defendant, I say Combatant: Opportunistic Treatment of Terrorism Suspects Held in the United States and the Need for Due Process,* 29 N.Y.U. Rev. L. & Soc. Change 525 (2005).

278 *See, e.g.*, Michael Powell, *No Choice but Guilty,* Wash. Post, Jul. 29, 2003, at A1 (discussing the prosecution of the "Lackawanna six").

279 *Response of the United States to Request for Precautionary Measures, supra* note 41, at 1024 ("The detainees are being treated humanely. In fact, the United States is treating the detainees consistent with applicable international humanitarian law.").

American officials,[280] the term does not originate from law-of-war terminology. The law of war does, however, recognize the notion of unlawful or unprivileged belligerency. An unlawful combatant or unprivileged belligerent is someone who takes part in hostilities when not entitled to do so.[281] Upon capture, such a person may be denied POW status and tried for mere participation in hostilities.[282] President Bush's memorandum outlining his decision regarding the status of Taliban and al Qaeda detainees actually used the term "unlawful combatant,"[283] as did other official statements from the administration.[284] However, this term was soon replaced by "enemy combatant."[285]

The stock response to queries about the provenance of the term "enemy combatant" is a reference to *Ex Parte Quirin,* a World War II-era Supreme Court precedent concerning the legality of the trial by military commission of German saboteurs captured in the United States.[286] In contrast to "unlawful combatant," "unlawful belligerent," "unlawful enemy belligerent," and "enemy belligerent," each of which appears multiple times in *Quirin,* the term "enemy combatant" appears just once:

> Unlawful combatants are likewise subject to capture and detention, but in addition they are subject to trial and punishment by military tribunals for acts which render their belligerency unlawful. The spy who secretly and without uniform passes the military lines of a belligerent in time of war . . . or an enemy combatant who without uniform comes secretly through the lines for the purpose of waging war by destruction of life or property, are familiar examples of belligerents who are generally deemed

---

280 *See* Dana Priest & Joe Stephens, *Secret World of U.S. Interrogation: Long History of Tactics in Overseas Prisons is Coming to Light,* Wash. Post, May 11, 2004, at A1 (quoting Alberto Gonzales, then Counsel to the President, as stating, "[u]nder these rules [the law of war], captured enemy combatants, whether soldiers or saboteurs, may be detained for the duration of hostilities").

281 Adam Roberts, *Counter-terrorism, Armed Force and the Laws of War,* 44 Survival 7, 22–23 (2002).

282 *Id.*; *see also* Knut Dörmann, *The Legal Situation of "Unlawful/Unprivileged Combatants,"* 85(849) Int'l Rev. Red Cross 45, 46–47 (2003).

283 Memorandum from President George W. Bush on Humane Treatment of al Qaeda and Taliban Detainees to the Vice President et al. (Feb. 7, 2002), *available at* http://www.gwu.edu/~nsarchiv/NSAEBB/NSAEBB127/02.02.07.pdf.

284 *See* Serge Schmemann, *Prisoners, Surely. But P.O.W.s?,* N.Y. Times, Jan. 27, 2002, at C14; Katharine Q. Seelye, *Detainees Are Not P.O.W.'s, Cheney and Rumsfeld Declare,* N.Y. Times, Jan. 28, 2002, at A6.

285 *See* Katharine Q. Seelye, *Pentagon Says Acquittals May Not Free Detainees,* N.Y. Times, Mar. 22, 2002, at A13. Certain official statements continue to use "enemy combatant" interchangeably with "unlawful combatant" and "unprivileged combatant." *See* U.S. Dep't of State, Second Periodic Report of the United States of America to the Committee Against Torture, 52 (2005), *available at* http://www.state.gov/documents/organization/62175.pdf.

286 *Ex Parte* Quirin v. Cox, 317 U.S. 1 (1942).

> not to be entitled to the status of prisoners of war, but to be offenders against the law of war subject to trial and punishment by military tribunals.[287]

It is clear from this passage that the term "enemy combatant" is not a term of art. Rather, the phrase in which it appears was simply used as an example of unlawful or unprivileged belligerency. However, it is the words that follow "enemy combatant," not the term itself, which are doing the work. Taken in isolation, "enemy combatant" simply refers to a combatant of the enemy. It tells us nothing about the status of the combatant.

Moreover, as employed by the Bush administration, the term "enemy combatant" lacks a stable definition and casts a considerably wider net than the law of war. The law of war permits the detention of captured enemies, typically those who fought on the battlefield during an armed conflict. This roughly aligns with the definition of "enemy combatant" the government proposed in *Hamdi:*

> There is some debate as to the proper scope of this term, and the Government has never provided any court with the full criteria that it uses in classifying individuals as such. It has made clear, however, that, for purposes of this case, the "enemy combatant" that it is seeking to detain is an individual who, it alleges, was "part of or supporting forces hostile to the United States or coalition partners" in Afghanistan and who "engaged in an armed conflict against the United States" there.[288]

However, many Guantánamo detainees held as enemy combatants were not captured in Afghanistan nor on any battlefield in any conventional sense. The power under the law of war to detain for the duration of hostilities, relied on by Justice O'Connor's *Hamdi* opinion, does not obviously apply to such persons.[289] For example, Mustafa Ait Idir was one of six Algerians who had lived in Bosnia for several years before being arrested on suspicion of plotting to bomb the American and British embassies in Sarajevo. The six were held for three months before the Bosnian Supreme Court acquitted them.[290] Upon release, they were re-arrested by Bosnian and American officials and sent to Guantánamo.[291] The same point can be made about Padilla and Al-Marri, both of whom were apprehended inside the United States.

---

287 *Id.* at 31.

288 Hamdi v. Rumsfeld, 542 U.S. 507, 516 (2004) (O'Connor J., citing Brief for Respondents).

289 *Id.* at 521:

> Further, we understand Congress' grant of authority for the use of 'necessary and appropriate force' to include the authority to detain for the duration of the relevant conflict, and our understanding is based on longstanding law-of-war principles. If the practical circumstances of a given conflict are entirely unlike those of the conflicts that informed the development of the law of war, that understanding may unravel.

Id.

290 Jackie Northam, *Tapes Provide First Glimpse of Secret Gitmo Panels,* NAT'L PUB. RADIO, Nov. 21, 2006, http://www.npr.org/templates/story/story.php?storyId=6514923.

291 *Id.*

Nonetheless, the Bush administration has had no trouble invoking the law of war to justify the detention of all these men as enemy combatants. This is because the administration has adapted and expanded the definition of "enemy combatant" to suit its needs. For instance, the definition used for the Combatant Status Review Tribunals (CSRT) differed considerably from the definition put forward in *Hamdi*:

> [A]n individual who was part of or supporting Taliban or al Qaeda forces, or associated forces that are engaged in hostilities against the U.S. or its coalition partners. This includes any person who has committed a belligerent act or has directly supported hostilities in aid of enemy armed forces.[292]

Under this definition, individuals who have neither fought against nor directly supported hostilities against the United States or its allies can nonetheless be indefinitely detained as enemy combatants.[293] This astonishingly broad definition was discussed during the oral arguments in *In re Guantánamo Detainee Cases.* Government counsel argued that the United States could justifiably detain the following people for the duration of hostilities:

> [a] little old lady in Switzerland who writes checks to what she thinks is a charity that helps orphans in Afghanistan but [what] really is a front to finance al-Qaeda activities, a person who teaches English to the son of an al Qaeda member, and a journalist who knows the location of Osama Bin Laden but refuses to disclose it to protect her source.[294]

The latest definition contained in the MCA is similar. The MCA's term, "unlawful enemy combatant,"[295] covers two groups of detainees. The first are those who have either engaged in hostilities or have "purposefully and materially supported hostilities" against the United States and its allies and who are not lawful combatants.[296] While this definition would exclude those who provide unknowing or inadvertent support, it remains to be seen how widely the government will apply the phrase "materially supported." Even if the first prong of the MCA definition is not satisfied, a detainee may still be an "unlawful enemy combatant" under the MCA, provided that the detainee has been determined to fall into that category by a CSRT or other competent tribunal at some point in time.[297] This has the effect of legislatively

292 Memorandum from Paul Wolfowitz, U.S. Deputy Sec'y of Defense, on Combatant Status Review Tribunal to the Secretary of the Navy 1 (July 7, 2004), *available at* http://www.defenselink.mil/news/Jul2004/d20040707review.pdf.

293 In re Guantánamo Detainee Cases, 355 F. Supp. 2d at 443, 475 (2005).

294 *Id.* (internal citations omitted).

295 *See* Military Commissions Act, S. 3930 § 3 (2006), codified at 10 U.S.C. § 948a(1) (defining "unlawful enemy combatant") and § 948a(2) (defining "lawful enemy combatants"). Only alien unlawful combatants are subject to trial by the MCA's military commissions. *See Id.* § 948c.

296 10 U.S.C. § 948a(1)(i).

297 10 U.S.C. § 948a(1)(ii).

ratifying the results of the CSRTs, and by extension, the CSRT's definition of "enemy combatant."

The point that emerges is that a person does not have to commit a belligerent act against the United States or directly support hostilities in order to be classified as an "enemy combatant." Conduct that would not qualify someone as a combatant under the law of war may be nonetheless sufficient to qualify one as an enemy combatant subject to indefinite detention.[298] The merits of the Bush administration's view that the whole world is a battlefield[299] and that support of terrorism, broadly defined, is sufficient to justify indefinite detention in military custody is debatable. But it is wrong to say that the law of war supports such a position.

b) A Selective Understanding of the Law of War

The Bush administration's interpretation of GCIII provides a further illustration of the administration's selective use of the law of war. According to the Bush administration's view of GCIII, terrorist suspects are subject to the burden of detention for the duration of hostilities, however long that might be.[300] At the same time, they are denied the benefits of GCIII, as well as the protection of other parts of the law of war. Justice Souter's opinion in *Hamdi* recognized this selectivity. Justice Souter accepted that the AUMF might implicitly allow the President to deal with and detain "enemy belligerents according to the treaties and customs known as the laws of war."[301] However, the government could not avail itself of this argument because it was not complying with the law of war itself.[302]

The Bush administration argues that the Taliban are covered by the Geneva Conventions but do not qualify for POW status, and that al Qaeda is not a party to the Conventions and thus its members are not entitled to POW status.[303] This assumes the existence of an international armed conflict under common Article 2;

298 Ryan Goodman & Derek Jinks, *Replies to Congressional Authorization: International Law, U.S. War Powers, and the Global War on Terrorism*, 118 Harv. L. Rev. 2653, 2655–59 (discussing the requirement of direct participation in hostilities and concluding that "the President's notion of enemy combatants'. . . exceeds the scope of [the law of armed conflict]").

299 This claim has been accepted in Khalid v. Bush, 355 F. Supp. 2d 311, 320 (D.D.C. 2005) ("The fact that the petitioners in this case were not captured on or near the battlefields of Afghanistan, unlike the petitioner in Hamdi, is of no legal significance to this conclusion because the AUMF does not place geographic parameters on the President's authority to wage this war against terrorists."). *See also* Padilla v. Hanft, 423 F.3d 386, 393–94 (4th Cir. 2005) (finding that the AUMF authorized Padilla's detention even though he was apprehended inside the United States).

300 GCIII, *supra* note 17 at art. 118.

301 Hamdi v. Rumsfeld, 542 U.S. 507, 548–49 (2004).

302 *Id.* at 551 ("[T]he Government has not made out its claim that in detaining Hamdi in the manner described, it is acting in accord with the laws of war authorized to be applied against citizens by the Force Resolution." (Souter, J.)).

303 Fact Sheet, Status of Detainees at Guantánamo, *supra* note 26.

otherwise POW status and much of the Geneva Conventions are inapplicable.[304] The administration's understanding of the Conventions, however, is suspect.

Article 4 of GCIII specifies six categories of persons who qualify as POWs, three of which might be relevant to the status of captured al Qaeda or Taliban fighters. Article 4 provides in relevant part:

> A. Prisoners of war, in the sense of the present Convention, are persons belonging to one of the following categories, who have fallen into the power of the enemy:
>
> (1) Members of the armed forces of a Party to the conflict, as well as members of militias or volunteer corps forming part of such armed forces.
>
> (2) Members of other militias and members of other volunteer corps, including those of organized resistance movements, belonging to a Party to the conflict and operating in or outside their own territory, even if this territory is occupied, provided that such militias or volunteer corps, including such organized resistance movements, fulfil the following conditions:
>
> (a) that of being commanded by a person responsible for his subordinates;
>
> (b) that of having a fixed distinctive sign recognizable at a distance;
>
> (c) that of carrying arms openly;
>
> (d) that of conducting their operations in accordance with the laws and customs of war.
>
> (3) Members of regular armed forces who profess allegiance to a government or an authority not recognized by the Detaining Power.[305]

An al Qaeda or Taliban fighter captured in the Afghanistan conflict could theoretically be entitled to POW status in a number of ways. A Taliban fighter could be considered the "armed forces of a Party to the conflict" under GCIII Article 4(A)(1) or a "member of regular armed forces . . . profess [sing] allegiance to a government or an authority not recognized by the Detaining Power" under Article 4(A)(3). An al Qaeda fighter might fall under either Article 4(A)(1) or 4(A)(2)'s reference to militias or volunteer corps.

Based on the text of Article 4, militias, volunteer corps, and organized resistance movements must satisfy the four requirements of Article 4(A)(2); the armed forces referred to in Articles 4(A)(1) and 4(A)(3) do not. Therefore, Article 4(A)(1) or

---

304 Derek Jinks, *The Applicability of the Geneva Conventions to the "Global War on Terrorism"*, 46 VA. J. INT'L L. 165, 181 (2006). A number of commentators have described the Afghanistan conflict as an international armed conflict between the U.S.-led coalition and Taliban/al Qaeda forces. *See, e.g.*, Robert Cryer, *The Fine Art of Friendship: Jus in Bello in Afghanistan,* 7 J. OF CONFLICT AND SECURITY L. 37, 41 (2002); Adam Roberts, *The Laws of War in the War on Terror, in* 32 ISR. Y.B. ON HUM. RTS 193, 230 (Yovam Dinstein & Fania Domb eds. 2002).

305 GCIII, *supra* note 17, art. 4.

4(A)(3) may entitle al Qaeda and Taliban to POW status.[306] There appears to be genuine disagreement over whether the four requirements of Article 4(A)(2) also extend to the other categories of persons eligible for POW status. The view taken here is that the requirements do not extend to Articles 4(A)(1) and 4(A)(3).[307] As will become apparent, however, this point is not of great significance.

President Bush's decision on the applicability of GCIII categorically excludes al Qaeda fighters from POW status and excludes the Taliban on the terms of the Convention.[308] Denying the Taliban POW status is problematic. Taliban fighters were members of the armed forces of Afghanistan, a party to the conflict. The United States denied them POW status because of their alleged failure to satisfy the requirements of Article 4(A)(2).[309] If those requirements do not apply to Article 4(A)(1) or 4(A)(3), then the denial of POW status is plainly wrong. Furthermore, even if those requirements do apply, the Taliban may still qualify. First, the Taliban must have had some form of command structure that allowed them to field an army that controlled most of Afghanistan, although they may not have had the organized hierarchy of a modern army.[310] Second, photographs show Taliban forces carrying their arms openly and wearing distinctive military vests and black headgear that could conceivably qualify as a "fixed distinctive sign."[311]

Much has been made of the fourth requirement of compliance with the laws and customs of war. This requirement is addressed collectively to a fighting force as well as to individual fighters.[312] If a fighting force consistently disregards the laws and customs of war, then all members of that group may be denied POW status

---

306 Moeckli, *supra* note 53, at 78.

307 George H. Aldrich, *The Taliban, Al Qaeda, and the Determination of Illegal Combatants,* 96 Am. J. Int'l L. 891, 894 (2002); Jordan Paust, *Judicial Power to Determine the Status and Rights of Persons Detained Without Trial,* 44 Harv. Int'l L.J. 503, 510–11 (2003); Borelli, *supra* note 43, at 49; c.f. William H. Ferrell III, *No Shirt, No Shoes, No Status: Uniforms, Distinction and Special Operations in International Armed Conflict,* 178 Mil. L. Rev. 94, 101 (2003); Glazier, *supra* note 38, at 34–35.

308 Fact Sheet, Status of Detainees at Guantánamo, *supra* note 26.

309 Donald H. Rumsfeld, Secretary, U.S. Dep't of Defense, Secretary Rumsfeld Media Availability en route to Camp X-Ray, Remarks on Ferry from Air Terminal to main Base, Guantánamo Bay, Cuba, (Jan. 27, 2002), (transcript available at http://www.defenselink.mil/transcripts/transcript.aspx?transcriptid=2338). Then Secretary Rumsfeld noted,

> With respect to the Taliban, the Taliban also did not wear uniforms, they did not have insignia, they did not carry their weapons openly, and they were tied tightly at the waist to al Qaeda.... I'm not a lawyer, but there isn't any question in my mind but that they are not, they would not rise to the standard of a prisoner of war.

310 Memorandum from William H. Taft IV, *supra* note 25, at 21.

311 Cryer, *supra* note 304, at 70; Rosa Ehrenreich Brooks, *War Everywhere: Rights, National Security Law, and the Law of Armed Conflict in the Age of Terror,* 153 U. Pa. L. Rev. 675, 734 (2004); Glazier, *supra* note 38, at 35–36.

312 G. I. A. D. Draper, *The Status of Combatants and the Question of Guerilla Warfare,* 45 Brit. Y.B. Int'l L. 173, 196 (1971) (stating that the obligations to carry arms openly, wear a fixed distinctive

regardless of compliance by individual members.[313] However, a collective violation cannot be inferred from sporadic instances of individual violations. Thus, in World War II, violations of the law of war by some Japanese and German troops could not justify denying POW status to all captured Japanese and German soldiers.[314] Rosas suggests a consistent practice of violation from a significant part of the group is required.[315] Draper states that a majority of the group must fail to observe the requirement.[316]

At the time of the Afghanistan conflict, there were no specific allegations of the Taliban's failure to comply with the laws and customs of war.[317] Therefore, the United States should not deny a Taliban fighter POW status because some members of the Taliban violated the laws and customs of war, unless it can be demonstrated that at least a significant portion of the Taliban failed to observe the requirement.

As for al Qaeda fighters, the President excludes them on the basis that they are a terrorist group, and hence not a party to GCIII.[318] Nonetheless, it may still be problematic to deny all al Qaeda fighters POW status.[319] As noted above, al Qaeda fighters could theoretically qualify for POW status under either Article 4(A)(1) or 4(A)(2)'s reference to militias or volunteer corps. It has been reported that some al Qaeda fighters fought in Taliban units meaning that they might qualify under Article 4(A)(1).[320] It is, however, unlikely that al Qaeda fighters would qualify under Article 4(A)(2). News footage from Afghanistan in August 2002 indicates that at least some al Qaeda fighters wore uniforms and carried their arms openly.[321] This could have continued during the Afghanistan conflict. However, al Qaeda is

---

sign, and comply with the laws and customs of war are both collective and individual); *see also* ALLAN ROSAS, THE LEGAL STATUS OF PRISONERS OF WAR 305, 334–35 (1976).

313 Draper, *supra* note 312, at 197–98; ROSAS, *supra* note 312, at 335.

314 Glazier, *supra* note 38, at 31.

315 ROSAS, *supra* note 312, at 335.

316 Draper, *supra* note 312, at 198.

317 Aldrich, *supra* note 307, at 895.

318 Fact Sheet, Status of Detainees at Guantánamo, *supra* note 26.

319 *See* Jinks, *supra* note 304, at 182 (discussing how Al Qaeda fighters could theoretically qualify for POW status).

320 Thom Shanker & Steven Lee Myers, *A Nation Challenged: Pentagon; U.S. Special Forces Step up Campaign in Afghan Areas,* N.Y. TIMES, Oct. 19, 2001, at A1; *see also* Roberts, *supra* note 304, AT 225; ROBERT K. GOLDMAN & BRIAN D. TITTEMORE, AM. SOC'Y INT'L L., TASK FORCE ON TERRORISM, UNPRIVILEGED COMBATANTS AND THE HOSTILITIES IN AFGHANISTAN: THEIR STATUS AND RIGHTS UNDER INTERNATIONAL HUMANITARIAN AND HUMAN RIGHTS LAW, (Dec. 2006), *available at* http://www.asil.org/taskforce/goldman.pdf.

321 Glazier, *supra* note 38, at 35.

a terrorist group which conducts its operations outside of the law of war,[322] and as such, is unlikely to satisfy Article 4(A)(2)(d).

Furthermore, the blanket exclusion of Taliban and al Qaeda fighters from protection is also incompatible with Article 5 of GCIII which provides that in cases of doubt, captives are to be treated as POWs "until such time as their status has been determined by a competent tribunal."[323] The Department of Defense reportedly had planned to conduct these hearings in Afghanistan but was overruled by the White House.[324] The Bush administration believed that after the President's determination that al Qaeda and Taliban detainees did not qualify for POW status, there was no doubt as to their status, and therefore no need to hold Article 5 hearings.[325]

Even if one assumes that al Qaeda and Taliban fighters are properly denied POW status, the government must still establish that a particular detainee is actually a member of al Qaeda or the Taliban. In the chaos of an armed conflict, errors are likely. For example, during the first Gulf War, some 1200 Article 5 hearings were held to determine the status of various detainees in American custody. About two-thirds of these detainees were subsequently found to be civilians or refugees.[326]

Moreover, even if some actual al Qaeda or Taliban fighters have been legitimately denied POW status under GCIII—contrary to what appears to be the Bush administration's view—this does not mean that the law of war affords them no protection.[327] Such persons, although not POWs, could still benefit from the protection of other parts of the law of war. First, according to the International Committee of the Red Cross, detainees who are denied POW status should be considered civilians protected by the Fourth Geneva Convention (GCIV).[328] This Convention provides

322 See William H. Taft IV, *The Law of Armed Conflict After 9/11: Some Salient Features*, 28 Yale J. Int'l L. 319, 320–21 (2003); Jiri Toman, *The Status of Al Qaeda/Taliban Detainees under the Geneva Conventions*, *in* 32 Isr. Y.B. on Hum. Rts 271, 294 (Yovam Dinstein & Fania Domb eds., 2002); Christopher Greenwood, *International Law and the "War against Terrorism,"* 78 Int'l Aff. 301, 316(2002).

323 GCIII, *supra* note 17 at art. 5.

324 *See* Jane Mayer, *The Hidden Power,* The New Yorker, July 3, 2006, *available at* http://www.newyorker.com/fact/content/Articles/060703fa_fact1.

325 Brief for the Respondents at 23–24, Hamdi v. Rumsfeld, 542 U.S. 507 (2004), *available at* http://www.jenner.com/files/tbl_s69NewsDocumentOrder/FileUpload500/216/Brief_Respondents.pdf. The Combatant Status Review Tribunals (CSRTs) created in the wake of the 2004 Supreme Court decisions are not a substitute for Article 5 hearings since they consider different questions. Ironically, the decisions of the CSRTs that the vast majority of Guantánamo detainees were enemy combatants is in no way incompatible with a finding of POW status. *See* Joseph Blocher, *Combatant Status Review Tribunals: Flawed Answers to the Wrong Question,* 116 Yale L.J. 667 (2006).

326 Roach & Trotter, *supra* note 90, at 1012.

327 Cryer, *supra* note 304, at 72; Jinks, *supra* note 18; Roberts, *supra* note 282, at 23.

328 Commentary On Geneva Convention IV 51 (Jean S. Pictet Ed., 1958); *see also* Hans-Peter Gasser, *Acts of Terror, Terrorism and International Humanitarian Law,* 84 Int'l Rev. Red

protection to "those who, at a given moment and in any manner whatsoever, find themselves, in case of a conflict or occupation, in the hands of a Party to the conflict or Occupying Power of which they are not nationals."[329] Its coverage theoretically includes unlawful combatants,[330] and even permits the detention of individuals "if the security of the detaining power makes it absolutely necessary."[331] However, the coverage of GCIV has a number of exceptions, one of which is relevant to the Guantánamo detainees. Article 4 does not protect nationals of states with which the detaining power has normal diplomatic relations.[332] This would exclude from the protection of GCIV Guantánamo detainees who are nationals of states with which the United States has normal diplomatic relations.

Second, Common Article 3 may be applicable. As noted above, CA3 provides a minimum set of protections applicable in any conflict that is not of an international character.[333] The Bush administration's position was that CA3 was inapplicable to the Afghanistan conflict since the conflict was "of an international character."[334] The Supreme Court rejected this view in *Hamdan*.[335] In any event, the characterization of the conflict is immaterial, as CA3 also states the minimum protection applicable to international armed conflicts as a matter of customary international law.[336]

Third, Article 75 of the first Additional Protocol to the Geneva Conventions (AP1) specifies certain minimum guarantees to "persons who are in the power of a Party to the conflict and who do not benefit from more favourable treatment. . . . "[337]These guarantees include ten specified criteria for a fair trial and prohibitions on mistreatment of detainees.[338] Although the United States has not ratified the two Additional Geneva Protocols of 1977, Article 75 of AP1 is nonetheless applicable as the United States accepts that it is declaratory of customary international law.[339]

Cross 547, 568 (2002); David L. Sloss, *International Decision: Availability of U.S. Courts to Detainees at Guantanamo Bay Naval Base,* 98 Am. J. Int'l L. 788, 795–96 (2004).

329 Geneva Convention Relative to the Protection of Civilian Persons in Time of War, Aug. 12, 1949, 6 U.S.T. 3516, 75 U.N.T.S. 287 (hereinafter "GCIV").

330 Jinks, *supra* note 18, at 381–99; Dörmann, *supra* note 282, at 64; Duffy, *supra* note 255, at 401–02.

331 GCIV, *supra* note 329, art. 5.

332 *Id.* art. 4.

333 *See supra* text accompanying note 122.

334 *Hamdan,* 126 S. Ct. at 2795.

335 *Id.* at 2795–96.

336 Military and Paramilitary Activities in and against Nicaragua (Nicar. v. U.S.), Merits, 1986 I.C.J. Rep. 4, 103–05, paras. 218–20 (June 27); *see also* George H. Aldrich, *The Laws of War on Land,* 94 Am. J. Int'l L. 42, 60 (2000); Roberts, *supra* note 282, at 230; Jinks, *supra* note 18, at 402–03.

337 Protocol Additional to the Geneva Conventions of 12 Aug. 1949, and Relating to the Protection of Victims of International Armed Conflicts, (Protocol I), art. 75, 8 June 1977, 1125 U.N.T.S. 13 (1979).

338 *Id.* at art. 75(4).

339 Taft, *supra* note 322, at 322; Roberts, *supra* note 304, at 230–31; *Hamdan,* 126 S. Ct. at 2797.

So far, the discussion has proceeded on the assumption that an international armed conflict exists, triggering the full application of the Geneva Conventions. However, *Hamdan's* ruling that CA3 applied to the conflict with al Qaeda suggests that the Supreme Court considers the conflict to be of a non-international character. Even assuming all facets of the Afghanistan conflict are correctly characterized as non-international,[340] detainees would still be entitled to protection under the law of war. Common Article 3 would, of course, apply by its terms, and the content of Article 75 of AP1 might also apply as customary international law.[341]

2. The Immigration Law Model

Section 412 of the U.S.A. Patriot Act permits the certification and detention of non-citizen terrorist suspects.[342] Under the Act, non-citizens may be detained for up to seven days, after which they must either be placed in removal proceedings, charged with an offense, or released.[343] Removal of the certified person usually occurs within ninety days.[344] However, in cases where removal is unlikely "in the reasonably foreseeable future," and where release would threaten "the national security of the United States or the safety of the community or any person" the government may order additional detention periods of six months.[345] As originally conceived by the Bush administration, this section would have allowed indefinite detention, but the administration made some compromises, such as the requirements of periodic reconsideration and judicial review.[346] It appears as though the administration has not used Section 412.[347] A likely reason is that the United States has instead used the quasi-law of war model to detain most terrorist suspects. However, the detention regimes for terrorist suspects in the United Kingdom, Canada, and New Zealand either are, or have been, based on immigration law. These regimes are broadly similar to that set up by Section 412.

The legal ancestor of Part IV of the ATSCA was the Immigration Act of 1971 which included the power to deport non-citizens who were considered national security risks.[348] Part IV of the ATSCA was titled "Immigration and Asylum."

340 International and non-international armed conflicts are not mutually exclusive situations. It is possible for both to simultaneously exist: *see* Jinks, *supra* note 304, at 182 n. 32.

341 This is the view of the International Red Cross. *See* JEAN-MARIE HENCKAERTS & LOUISE DOSWALD-BECK, CUSTOMARY INTERNATIONAL HUMANITARIAN LAW: VOLUME I: RULES 306 (2005).

342 U.S.A. Patriot Act, Section 412(a)(3), *codified at* 8 U.S.C. § 1226a(a) (2001).

343 *Id.* § 412(a)(5).

344 *Id.* § 412(a)(6).

345 *Id.*

346 *See* Taylor, *supra* note 267, at 152.

347 *Id.* at 154; *See* Shirin Sinnar, Note, *Patriotic or Unconstitutional? The Mandatory Detention of Aliens Under the USA Patriot Act*, 55 STAN. L. REV. 1419 (2003).

348 Brandon, *supra* note 151, at 991.

Canada's IRPA and the relevant part of New Zealand's Immigration Act also transparently operate under an immigration law-based model. Like a detention model based on the law of war, an immigration law-based model permits detention based on status rather than on conduct. Thus, rather than requiring proof that a certain non-citizen has perpetrated terrorist acts, it is enough that the government consider that person a "national security risk," or a "terrorist," or someone who has "links to terrorist organizations." As a non-citizen, that person is then subject to immigration control, such as removal or deportation, and detention pending removal or deportation.[349]

These detention regimes are said to create a "three walled prison." The detainee faces the prospect of a long detention, with the only immediate prospect of freedom being voluntary departure from the detaining jurisdiction to the detainee's country of origin.[350] However, as the experiences of the United Kingdom, Canada, and New Zealand demonstrate, the immigration law-based detention regimes, despite the "three walled prison" metaphor, generally result in prolonged and indefinite detention due to the legal difficulties of transferring terrorist suspects to countries where their human rights might be violated.[351] Only the ATSCA openly acknowledged this reality by including a specific provision authorizing indefinite detention. However, in practice, the regimes in Canada and New Zealand authorize indefinite detention as well, even if this is not explicitly stated.

B. Executive Discretion Versus Legislative Frameworks

In addition to employing a distinct model of detention, the non-American jurisdictions demonstrate a contrasting level of legislative involvement. American detention policy has been an executive-dominated affair. In addition to attempting to avoid judicial scrutiny of its detention policies, the Bush administration has also successfully marginalized the legislative branch.[352] Congress has been sidelined, even though it has hardly been unwilling to arm the executive with counter-terrorism tools.[353] Instead, the President has repeatedly asserted his constitutional prerogative to prosecute the War on Terror in the manner he thinks fit. This includes matters relating to the detention of terrorist suspects as enemy combatants at Guantánamo and elsewhere.[354]

---

349 *See* Roach, *supra* note 264, at 143.

350 *See infra* text accompanying notes 402–405.

351 *See supra* text and accompanying notes 157–158, 220–224, and 248–254.

352 Kim Lane Scheppele, *Law in a Time of Emergency: States of Exception and the Temptations of 9/11*, 6 U. Pa. J. Const. L. 1001, 1051–52 (2004).

353 Stephen I. Vladeck, *The Detention Power*, 22 Yale Law & Pol'y Rev. 153, 191 (2004); Harold H. Koh, *Setting the World Right*, 115 Yale L. J. 2350, 2359 (2006).

354 *See* Jeffrey Toobin, *Killing Habeas Corpus*, The New Yorker, Nov. 27, 2006, *available at* http://www.newyorker.com/fact/content/Articles/061204fa_fact (discussing the Bush administration's unilateralist approach to issues relating to Guantánamo).

The Supreme Court in *Hamdi* conspicuously left unaddressed the issue of whether the detention of enemy combatants could be justified by the President's inherent constitutional powers. Instead, a majority construed the AUMF as an implied legislative authorization for the detention of enemy combatants.[355] Constrained by only the *Hamdi* plurality's minimalist suggestions as to the applicable level of due process, the administration was able to continue its detention regime with minor modifications. The Supreme Court's institutional limitations as an inherently reactive body, together with Congressional silence, left the administration with considerable latitude.

It was not until the enactment of the DTA and later the MCA that Congress finally entered the debate on the detention of terrorist suspects. Then again, the DTA and the MCA amount to little more than tinkering at the edges of the issue.[356] The DTA prohibits mistreatment of detainees, purports to strip the courts of habeas jurisdiction, and prescribes procedures for the limited review of decisions of CSRTs and military commissions.[357] The MCA covers some of the same areas, and prescribes new procedures for the conduct of military commissions.[358] Neither act addresses the key concerns in this area: who can be legitimately detained as a terrorist suspect and under what circumstances? Rather, both the DTA and MCA assume the existence of the power to detain and do no more than supplement or qualify it in minor ways.

In the United Kingdom, Canada, and New Zealand, there has been much heavier legislative involvement in determining the appropriate framework for detaining terrorist suspects. The legislative frameworks in these jurisdictions at least attempt to address the key issues of who can be detained and when, even if terms such as "support," "links to terrorism," and "terrorist" are notoriously open-textured. These frameworks also contain provisions setting out the procedural safeguards available to detainees.[359] For example, the ATSCA, while permitting detention with fewer procedural protections than the criminal law, nonetheless afforded detainees safeguards such as a review before the SIAC, special advocates, and appeals to the ordinary courts.[360] This was far more than what the United States has provided to Guantánamo detainees.[361] As Baroness Hale remarked in *A v. Secretary of State*, "[t]here are safeguards, as the Attorney General has rightly pointed out, greater than under any

355 Hamdi v. Rumsfeld, 542 U.S. 507, 519, 579 (2004).

356 *See* Kenneth Anderson, *Law and Terror,* 139 Pol'y Rev. 3, 4–5 (2006); Kenneth Anderson, *It's Congress's War, Too,* N.Y. Times, Sept. 3, 2006, at 20.

357 *See supra* text and accompanying notes 111–113.

358 *See supra* text and accompanying notes 132–144.

359 *See* Arden, *supra* note 174, at 621.

360 *See supra* text and accompanying notes 159–162.

361 Connor Gearty, *11 Sept. 2001, Counter-terrorism, and the Human Rights Act*, 32 J.L. & Soc. 18, 24–25 (2005).

earlier internment powers. Belmarsh is not the British Guantánamo Bay."[362] Similarly, the PTA makes reasonably clear who can be made subject to a control order, clearly provides for review before the courts, and specifies the procedures for court hearings in detail.[363]

In Canada, the IRPA specifies who is inadmissible on security grounds. It sets out the procedures for the review of the security certificate, as well as possible outcomes.[364] New Zealand's Immigration Act also specifies certain criteria that, if met, may subject a person to a security risk certificate. While the Act does not spell out the procedural minutiae for the Inspector General's review in quite the same way that the PTA or the IRPA does, there is nonetheless explicit statutory provision for matters such as the right to seek review, the right to be represented, the right to access non-classified information, and the right to appeal on points of law.[365]

Therefore, one clear distinction between the United Kingdom, Canada, and New Zealand on the one hand, and the United States on the other, is the level of involvement of their respective legislatures. In the non-American jurisdictions, relatively clear legislative frameworks spell out, ex ante, key substantive and procedural issues related to the detention of terrorist suspects. By contrast, in the United States, the detention of terrorist suspects remains largely a discretionary area for the executive. The belated Congressional input thus far still amounts to little more than marginal qualifications of the executive's policy choices.

C. Acceptance of the Applicability of Human Rights Norms

A further difference between the detention regimes of the United States and the other jurisdictions is their respective attitudes towards human rights norms. Arguing that such norms impede the War on Terror, the Bush administration has asserted that the United States is only obligated to respect human rights within its territory, which excludes Guantánamo, and that the operation of human rights law is displaced by the law of war.[366] As discussed previously in this Article, such arguments seek to avoid the application of human rights norms altogether.[367]

In the United Kingdom, Canada, and New Zealand, detention regimes are set out in advance by legislative frameworks which contemplate and accept, on some level, the applicability of human rights norms. With the ATSCA, the British government recognized that indefinite detention under Section 23 would violate the right to liberty affirmed by Article 5 of the ECHR. The government accordingly lodged a

362 A v. Secretary of State, [2004] UKHL 56, [2005] 2 A.C. 68, para. 223 (U.K.).

363 *See supra* Part II.B.2.

364 *See supra* Part II.C.

365 Immigration Act, 1987 S.N.Z. No. 74, §§ 114H, 114P.

366 *See supra* text at accompanying notes 37–43.

367 *See* discussion *supra* Part II.A. 1.

formal derogation in accordance with Article 15.[368] One can disagree as to whether the threshold for derogation was met, or whether the exigencies of the situation necessitated the measures taken,[369] but it is clear that the United Kingdom operated within a human rights paradigm. This has continued with the PTA, which exhibits the influence of the ECHR, most notably in the distinction it makes between derogating and non-derogating control orders.[370]

The Canadian litigation over the IRPA has focused on whether the security certificate process comports with the requirements of fundamental justice under Section 7 of the Charter. Fundamental justice includes the right to a fair hearing,[371] a right clearly implicated by the security certificate process. This process clearly differs from an ordinary court hearing, and places the detainee at a considerable disadvantage. In defending this process, the Canadian executive has noted the procedural protections that the security certificate provides and emphasized the need to balance the rights of individual detainees against national security imperatives.[372] For example, in cases concerning the deportation of non-citizens to countries where they are at risk of being tortured (such as *Suresh),*[373] the courts have balanced security and individual rights.[374] Thus, it is not the case that the detainees lack rights, but simply that the executive believes that countervailing security concerns outweigh those rights.

In New Zealand, the executive did not deny that Zaoui had certain human rights. There was no dispute that Zaoui had the right to be heard by the Inspector General upon the review of his case as this is expressly provided by statute.[375] The real dispute was what this right meant in the statutory context of Part 4A of the Immigration Act.[376] Likewise, there was no dispute that Zaoui had a right not to be

368 *See supra* text at accompanying notes 163–164.

369 Indeed the House of Lords did just this: *see A v. Secretary of State,* [2005] 2 A.C. 68 (appeal taken from Eng.) (U.K.).

370 David Bonner, *Responding to Crisis: Legislating Against Terrorism,* 122 L. Q. Rev. 602, 629 (2006). However, this distinction has not proven to be clear. *See* Secretary of State for the Home Department v. JJ and others, [2006] EWCA (Civ.) 1141, para. 23 (U.K.).

371 Stewart, *supra* note 205, at 242.

372 *See generally,* Dep't of Justice Canada, Newsroom, Joint Statement by the Hon. Anne McLellan, Deputy Prime Minister and Minister of Public Safety and Emergency Preparedness & the Hon. Irwin Cotler, Minister of Justice and Attorney General of Canada, on the Occasion of Appearances Before the Senate Special Committee On the Anti-terrorism Act and the House of Commons Subcommittee on Public Safety and National Security (Nov. 14, 2005), *available at* http://www.justice.gc.ca/en/news/sp/2005/doc_31726.html ("Our system incorporates due process even for the most extreme cases and seeks to strike a careful balance between the rights of individuals and the protection of society against threats to our safety and security.").

373 *See supra* text at accompanying notes 221–224.

374 Dep't of Justice Canada, *supra* note 372.

375 Immigration Act 1987, 1987 S.N.Z. No. 43, § 114H(2)(c); *see also* New Zealand Bill of Rights Act 1990, Section 27(1).

376 *Zaoui,* [2006] 1 N.Z.L.R. para. 18.

returned to a state where he was at risk of being tortured or deprived of life.[377] The issue was whether the Inspector General had to consider this in conducting his review, or whether, as the government contended, it was solely a matter for the Minister of Immigration.[378]

The difference between the American position and the positions of the other jurisdictions highlights the difference between the the wholesale suspension of rights and the limitation of rights. Even though the detention regimes of the non-American jurisdictions make serious inroads into the rights concerned, they still recognize that human rights norms apply to some degree. This position is qualitatively different from the Bush administration's position that human rights norms are inapplicable as soon as terrorist suspects are detained as enemy combatants.

IV. COMMON THEMES

Having examined differences between the various jurisdictions in the detention of terrorist suspects in Part III, this Part considers three common themes. The first is the emphasis placed on citizenship. In all four jurisdictions, there are certain advantages that a citizen terrorist suspect has over a non-citizen terrorist suspect. This differential treatment is arguably discriminatory and unjustifiable from a security standpoint. The second commonality is the question of the appropriate level of procedural protection due to terrorist suspects. Each jurisdiction has had to grapple with the competing concerns of fairness and national security. Finally, the courts in each jurisdiction have generally insisted on robust judicial scrutiny, often in spite of claims of executive exclusivity in the area of national security. This insistence leads to a discussion of the conventional wisdom about the utility of courts in times of crisis.

A. Distinctions in the Treatment of Citizens and Non-Citizens

All four states discussed here have drawn distinctions based on the nationality of terrorist suspects. Originally, the United States only detained non-Americans as enemy combatants. However, once the concept of an enemy combatant was established, it became a simple matter to apply the concept to American citizens as well.[379] A majority of the Supreme Court in *Hamdi* has since endorsed this extension, at least in the case of U.S. citizens captured on the field of battle.[380] In the case of a citizen captured inside the United States, the answer remains equivocal because the Supreme Court has not ruled on this point.[381] Regardless, there remain some differences in the American treatment of citizen enemy combatants and

377 *Id.* paras. 16, 75–77.

378 The Supreme Court decided this issue in favor of the government. Zaoui v. Attorney General (no. 2) [2006] 1 N.Z.L.R. 289, para. 73 (S.C.).

379 Cole, *supra* note 267, at 4–5.

380 Hamdi v. Rumsfeld, 542 U.S. 507, 533 (2004).

381 *See* discussion *supra* Part II.A.3.

non-citizen enemy combatants. Most obviously, the government only detains non-citizens at Guantánamo. The exception was Hamdi himself, who was detained at Guantánamo until his true citizenship came to light.[382] More significantly, only non-citizen enemy combatants were eligible for trial before the President's military commissions.[383] This distinction has carried over to the MCA, which states that only "alien unlawful enemy combatant[s]" are eligible for trial by military commission.[384] Additionally, the MCA only strips non-citizen enemy combatants of the ability to apply for habeas corpus.[385]

However, the United States draws relatively minor distinctions between citizen enemy combatants and non-citizen enemy combatants. By comparison, the detention models that the United Kingdom, Canada, and New Zealand employ place much greater emphasis on the citizen/non-citizen distinction. Indeed, this distinction is critical because of the immigration law roots of these detention regimes. Consequently, Section 23 of the ATSCA only authorized the indefinite detention of a certified "suspected international terrorist" who was not a British citizen.[386] The power to issue a security risk certificate under New Zealand's Immigration Act is only available in relation to "an identifiable individual who is not a New Zealand citizen."[387] The IRPA refers to a "permanent resident or a foreign national" as being inadmissible to Canada on security grounds.[388] The power to issue a security certificate under the IRPA is accordingly limited to non-Canadian citizens.[389] The effect of this, according to Roach, is to relegate non-citizens to an inferior system with "considerably lower standards of adjudicative fairness" than is applicable to Canadian citizens.[390] The same point can be made about any other detention regime based on the immigration law model.

There are two major weaknesses inherent in the detention regimes operated by the United Kingdom, Canada, and New Zealand. The first is under-inclusiveness. Using an immigration law model as a detention regime entails using the category of "citizen" as a proxy for "non-terrorist," and "non-citizen" as a proxy for "terrorist."

382 *See supra* text accompanying note 57.

383 Nov. 13 Order, *supra* note 21 (stating that only an "individual who is not a United States citizen" was eligible for trial).

384 10 U.S.C. § 948c (2006).

385 28 U.S.C. §§ 2241(e)(1)–(2) (2006). There would, of course, be constitutional problems in doing the same to an American citizen.

386 *See* A and others v. Secretary of State for the Home Department [2004] UKHL 56, [2005] 2 A.C. 68 (appeal taken from Eng.), (Lord Scott) (stating that "Detention under section 23 cannot be imposed on British nationals. It can only be invoked against immigrants who have no right of residence in this country").

387 Immigration Act 1987, 1987 S.N.Z. No. 43, § 114D(1)(a).

388 Immigration and Refugee Protection Act, 2001 S.C., ch. 27, § 34 (Can.).

389 *Id.* § 77(1).

390 Roach, *supra* note 203, at 528.

The accuracy of such equations is questionable. Excluding all citizens from the scope of a detention regime only makes sense if non-citizens are significantly more dangerous than citizens. However, as discussed by the House of Lords,[391] this is not necessarily the case. The different treatment afforded to British citizens involved with terrorist groups was a significant factor in the Lords ruling that indefinite detention under the ATSCA was disproportionate as well as discriminatory.[392] Lord Scott, for example, noted that, "[s]ome suspected terrorists may well be home-grown,"[393] but that those suspected terrorists could not be subject to detention under the ATSCA. This distinction in treatment based on citizenship was irrational because the important issue was not whether a person was a citizen, but whether that person was a threat to security.[394] Subsequent events have proven the majority view of the House of Lords correct. There is no necessary correlation between "citizen" and "non terrorist." Three of the four 7/7 London bombers were second-generation British citizens.[395] Likewise, of the seventeen persons arrested for the 2006 Toronto bomb plot some were long-term residents, but the majority were Canadian citizens.[396]

The restriction of harsh counter-terrorism measures to non-citizens is often a reflection not of security imperatives but of political expediency. For instance, prior to *A v. Secretary of State,* the Blair government defended ATSCA's differential treatment of citizens and non-citizens on three grounds: the two groups have different rights and responsibilities; citizens are not subject to immigration powers and deportation; and the detention of British citizens would be "draconian" and "difficult to justify."[397] The first two arguments beg the question. First, citizens and non-citizens have different rights and responsibilities because that is what the law provides. Even so, citizens and non-citizens nonetheless share the same interest

---

391 *A. v. Secretary of State*, [2005] 2 A.C. 68.

392 *Id.* paras. 33, 76, 132–33, 157–58, 183–86 & 228–31; *see also* Joint Committee On Human Rights, Review of Counter-terrorism Powers, *supra* note 165, para. 47; Newton Report, *supra* note 165, paras. 192–94.

393 *A v. Secretary of State,* [2005] 2 A.C. 68, para. 158.

394 *Id.* Lord Scott wrote, "In my opinion, however the Article 15 requirement does not justify a discriminatory distinction between different groups of people all of whom are suspected terrorists who together present the threat of terrorism and to all of whom the measures, if they really were 'strictly necessary' would logically be applicable." *Id.*

395 House of Commons, Report of the Official Account of the Bombings in London on 7th July 2005, 2005–6, H.C. 1087, at 13, *available at* http://www.official-documents.gov.uk/document/hc0506/hc10/1087/1087.pdf.

396 Doug Struck, *Canada Holds 17 In Alleged Bomb Plot,* Wash. Post, June 4, 2006, at A1; *Homegrown extremism,* CBS News Online, July 14, 2006, http://www.cbc.ca/news/background/toronto-bomb-plot/homegrown-extremism.html.

397 Secretary of State for the Home Department, Counter-terrorism Powers: Reconciling Security and Liberty in an Open Society, para. 36 (Feb. 2004) (discussion paper presented to Parliament), *available at* http://www.homeoffice.gov.uk/documents/cons-count-terror-powers-310804.

in liberty.[398] Second, although it is true that citizens may not be subject to immigration powers, the difference in treatment between citizens and non-citizens only arises because the government chose the immigration-law model as the basis of the ATSCA's detention regime. Hence the real reason is the third—it was simply not politically feasible to enact a law authorizing the indefinite detention of British citizens.

The difference between the enactment of the PTA and ATSCA reinforces this view. Although the Blair government managed to avoid a genuine debate on the merits of indefinite detention when it enacted the ATSCA in 2001, the same cannot be said of the passage of the PTA in 2005. In Parliament's longest sitting in ninety-nine years, Parliament vigorously debated the PTA, which permits the imposition of security measures on citizens and non-citizens alike.[399] The Act only passed after the government made concessions providing for increased judicial supervision and a review of the legislation a year later.[400] Similarly, in the immediate aftermath of 9/11, the roundup of non-citizens and the detention of non-citizen enemy combatants at Guantánamo barely registered in American popular consciousness. It was only after the government detained American citizens Hamdi and Padilla as enemy combatants that a chorus of objections ensued.[401]

The second weakness inherent in immigration-law based detention regimes is that they seek only to relocate the threat of terrorism. The "three walled prisons" created by these detention regimes can be circumvented by the voluntary departure of the detainee. Two persons certified by the Home Secretary under Section 21 of ATSCA did just this. One left for France, and the other left for Morocco. Thus two persons considered such serious security risks that they were subject to indefinite detention under the ATSCA were able to leave the United Kingdom to potentially carry on their dangerous activities nearby. Several of the Lords in *A v. Secretary of State* noted this paradoxical outcome.[402]

398 *A v. Secretary of State,* [2005] 2 A.C. 568, para. 132 (Lord Hope); Joint Committee On Human Rights, Review of Counter-terrorism Powers, *supra* note 165, para. 44.

399 Daniel Moeckli, *The Selective "War on Terror": Executive Detention of Foreign Nationals and the Principle of Non-Discrimination,* 31 Brook. J. Int'l L. 495, 533 (2006).

400 *Id.;* Patrick Wintour & Alan Travis, *The Longest Day: Both Sides Claim Victory as Tories Accept Blair Deal after Marathon Battle over Terror Bill,* The Guardian, Mar. 12, 2005, at 1, *available at* http://politics.guardian.co.uk/attacks/story/0,,1436086,00.html.

401 Moeckli, *supra* note 399, at 514.

402 *A v. Secretary of State,* [2005] 2 A.C. 68:

> But allowing a suspected international terrorist to leave our shores and depart to another country, perhaps a country as close as France, there to pursue his criminal designs, is hard to reconcile with a belief in his capacity to inflict serious injury to the people and interests of this country.

Id. para. 33. *See also id.* paras. 127 (Lord Hope) & 230 (Baroness Hale).

Even if the detainee does not leave voluntarily, the successful "endgame" of immigration-law based detention regimes is the removal or deportation of the detainee to another state.[403] Thus, if Canada or New Zealand detain an actual non-citizen terrorist and manage to resolve the difficulties of deporting such a person, that person will be deported to another state. Likewise, the other limb of the United Kingdom's post-*A v. Secretary of State* policy has been to find ways to deport non-citizen terrorist suspects.[404] The deportation of a terrorist suspect counts as a "successful" outcome, but the person deported, if truly a terrorist, can continue operating elsewhere. Given the reach of international terrorism, it is hard to see how this enhances security for the deporting state, or any other state for that matter. At best, it is displacement of terrorism.[405]

B. The Appropriate Level of Procedural Protection Due to Suspects

In the United States, one of the major issues in the debate over trying terrorist suspects with military commissions has been the appropriate level of procedural protection. For the time being, the MCA has settled this debate. However, only a small proportion of Guantánamo detainees face the prospect of trial. The bigger and largely overlooked issue concerns the level of procedural protection that is due before the government can designate someone as an enemy combatant. Put another way, even assuming that enemy combatants can legally be detained for the duration of hostilities, what procedures should there be for determining whether a certain person falls into that class? The United Kingdom, Canada, and New Zealand face a similar difficulty. The detention regimes in those countries permit the detention of terrorist suspects. But how sure must the government be that someone is a terrorist? To what extent should detainees be able to contest their status?

The existing processes for determining who can be detained as an enemy combatant or a terrorist suspect afford few procedural protections. This section identifies three common hallmarks: a reduced standard of proof, the use of secret evidence not disclosed to the detainee, and limited review by independent bodies. The cumulative effect of these features is a significant risk of error.

1. Minimal Procedural Protections

a) The United States

The Supreme Court has so far provided little guidance on the procedural protections due to a person designated as an enemy combatant. The *Hamdi* plurality suggests that a fairly rudimentary level of due process is sufficient, and that hearsay evidence, a presumption in favor of the government's evidence, and the use of military tribunals

403 Kent Roach, *Must we trade rights for security? The Choice Between Smart, Harsh, or Proportionate Security Strategies in Canada and Britain*, 27 CARDOZOL. REV. 2151, 2187 (2006).

404 *See supra* text accompanying note 173.

405 Newton Report, *supra* note 165, para. 195; Roach, *supra* note 403, at 2187.

are appropriate.[406] The CSRTs followed the minimalist contours of the *Hamdi* plurality.[407] According to the Implementation Guidance, CSRTs decide whether "a preponderance of evidence" supports the detention of the detainee as an enemy combatant. A CSRT may consider any evidence, including hearsay, which it considers helpful. There is also a rebuttable presumption that the Government's evidence is "genuine and accurate".[408] Detainees have no access to any classified material and the government only provides them with "a written statement of the unclassified factual basis" of their classification.[409]

In practice, this combination of non-disclosure of evidence, the presumption in favor of the government's evidence, and the acceptance of hearsay evidence put the detainees at a great disadvantage, and reduced the CSRT process to a pro forma affair.[410] For example, in September 2004, Farouq Ali Ahmed appeared in front of a CSRT and was confronted with four allegations. The first two were derived from his admissions during interrogation. The latter two, suggestive of links to al Qaeda, he denied. His denials were ineffective because he could not see the undisclosed details that formed the basis of these allegations.[411]

The CSRT hearing recounted in Judge Green's *In re Guantánamo Detainee Cases* decision has a similar ring to it. Mustafa Ait Idr was alleged to have associated with a known al Qaeda operative.[412] The following exchange then took place:

> Detainee: Give me his name.
>
> Tribunal President: I do not know.
>
> Detainee: How can I respond to this?
>
> Tribunal President: Did you know of anybody that was a member of Al Qaida?
>
> Detainee: No, no.
>
> Tribunal President: I'm sorry, what was your response?
>
> Detainee: No.
>
> Tribunal President: No?

---

406 Hamdi v. Rumsfeld, 542 U.S. 507, 534, 538 (2004).

407 Justice Souter, with Justice Ginsburg joining, agreed with the plurality in ordering the case remanded. However, they did not agree with the plurality's suggestions as to the applicable procedure: "I do not mean to imply agreement that the Government could claim an evidentiary presumption casting the burden of rebuttal on Hamdi, or that an opportunity to litigate before a military tribunal might obviate or truncate inquiry by a court on habeas." *Id.* at 553–54 (internal citations omitted).

408 England Memorandum, *supra* note 85.

409 *Id.*

410 Corine Hegland, *Guantánamo's Grip*, NAT'L J., Feb. 3, 2006, *available at* http://nationaljournal.com/about/njweekly/stories/2006/0203nj1.htm; *see also* Al Marri v. Wright, 443 F. Supp. 2d 774 (2006) (illustrating the operation of the evidential presumptions and use of hearsay evidence).

411 Hegland, *supra* note 410.

412 In re Guantánamo Detainee Cases, 355 F. Supp. 2d 443, 469 (D.D.C. 2005).

> Detainee: No. This is something the interrogators told me a long while ago. I asked the interrogators to tell me who this person was. Then I could tell you if I might have known this person, but not if this person is a terrorist. Maybe I knew this person as a friend. Maybe it was a person that worked with me. Maybe it was a person that was on my team. But I do not know if this person is Bosnian, Indian or whatever. If you tell me the name, then I can respond and defend myself against this accusation.
>
> Tribunal President: We are asking you the questions and we need you to respond to what is on the unclassified summary.[413]

An empirical study of the CSRT process by Mark and Joshua Denbeaux, based on records of the CSRTs released by the government and 102 full records disclosed during habeas litigation is consistent with the accounts of Farouq Ali Ahmed's and Mustafa Ait Idr's hearings.[414] The Denbeaux study indicates that detainees were denied access not only to classified information, but frequently unclassified information as well.[415] Coupled with the presumption in favor of the government's evidence, this non-disclosure of information made the government's allegations in CSRT hearings virtually irrefutable. It is not surprising, therefore, that the government had no need to introduce any witnesses during the CSRT process.[416] The 102 available full records indicate that in 52 percent of cases, the government produced neither witnesses nor any documentary evidence and relied solely on classified evidence.[417] Records also indicate that up to 96 percent of detainees began their hearings with nothing more than the perfunctory summary of the classified evidence.[418] These detainees had to make their case without knowledge of the facts they needed to refute.[419]

This pattern persists through other parts of the CSRT process. For example, the detainee's right to call witnesses was largely illusory. Most requests for witnesses were denied, including all requests for witnesses from outside of Guantánamo.[420] The 102 full records show no evidence that the reliability of hearsay evidence was considered, as required by the Implementation Guidance.[421]

---

413 *Id.* at 469.

414 Mark Denbeaux & Joshua Denbeaux, No-hearing Hearings CSRT: the Modern Habeas Corpus? 2–3 (Nov. 17, 2006) (unpublished manuscript), *available at* http://law.shu.edu/news/final_no_hearing_hearings_report.pdf .

415 *Id.*

416 *Id.* at 21.

417 *Id.* at 22.

418 *Id.* at 25.

419 Denbeaux & Denbeaux, *supra* note 414, at 25.

420 *Id.* at 28.

421 *Id.* at 33–34; *see also* Hegland, *supra* note 410; Corine Hegland, *Empty Evidence,* NAT'L J., Feb. 3, 2006, *available at* http://nationaljournal.com/about/njweekly/stories/2006/0203nj4.htm (describing instances of uncritical use of hearsay evidence against detainees).

In sum, the CSRT process amounted to very little; the government often adduced no witnesses or unclassified evidence to demonstrate that a certain detainee was an enemy combatant. In other cases, the government adduced some unclassified evidence that was not, in most cases, disclosed to the detainee.[422] In all cases, the government could simply rely on the presumptively valid classified evidence that the detainee could neither see nor rebut effectively.[423]

Once the CSRT has made its decision, review of that decision is limited. The CSRT's procedures provide that the CSRT Director may review a Tribunal's decision.[424] In at least three cases, detainees initially found by a CSRT not to be enemy combatants were subject to rehearings before new CSRTs, without their knowledge, until the new CSRT found each to be properly detained as an enemy combatant.[425] In terms of independent review, the DTA confers exclusive jurisdiction upon the D.C. Court of Appeals to review a CSRT's decision that an "alien is properly detained as an enemy combatant."[426] However, the scope of this review is limited to determining whether the CSRT's decision was consistent with the prescribed procedures for CSRTs, "including the requirement that the conclusion of the Tribunal be supported by a preponderance of evidence and allowing a rebuttable presumption in favor of the Government's evidence," and the laws and Constitution of the United States to the extent that they are applicable.[427] Thus, such a review would in all likelihood be largely pointless, as the reviewing court can only consider whether a CSRT complied with its own government-friendly procedures or the laws and Constitution which the Bush administration has maintained are inapplicable to alien enemy combatants detained at Guantánamo.

b) The United Kingdom

Under Part IV of the ATSCA, the standard of proof was low; indefinite detention only required a reasonable belief on the part of the Home Secretary that a certain person was a national security risk, and a reasonable suspicion that the person was a terrorist.[428] As Baroness Hale pointed out in *A v. Secretary of State,* neither threshold was difficult to satisfy: "belief involves thinking that something is true; suspicion involves thinking that something may be true."[429] Additionally, the definition of "terrorist" included those who supported or assisted an international terrorist group.[430]

422 Denbeaux & Denbeaux, *supra* note 414, at 22.

423 *Id.* at 19.

424 England Memorandum, *supra* note 85.

425 Denbeaux & Denbeaux, *supra* note 414, at 37–39.

426 Detainee Treatment Act of 2005, Pub. L. No. 109-48, § 1005(e)(2)(B).

427 *Id.* § 1005(e)(2)(C).

428 Anti-terrorism Crime and Security Act, 2001, c.24, § 21(1).

429 A. v. Secretary of State, [2005] 2 A.C. 68, para. 223 (U.K.).

430 Anti-terrorism Crime and Security Act, 2001, c.24, § 21(2).

The low standard of proof, combined with the openness of the definition of "terrorist," gave the ATSCA a broad scope.

While the SIAC had access to all of the material available to the Home Secretary, the detainee faced the additional hurdle of non-disclosure of certain sensitive information. As several Law Lords in *A v. Secretary of State* emphasized, a detainee had no right to know the basis of the Secretary of State's suspicion that he was a terrorist.[431] The provisions governing issues related to non-disclosure were complex. The statute establishing the SIAC empowered the Lord Chancellor to make certain procedural rules for the SIAC.[432] These included rules enabling the SIAC to hold closed proceedings without the detainee or the detainee's lawyer,[433] enabling the SIAC to give the appellant a summary of any evidence taken in his absence,[434] and outlining the functions of persons—the special advocates—who represent the interests of detainees in closed proceedings before the SIAC.[435] These provisions applied to the Belmarsh detainees' appeals to the SIAC against certification by virtue of Section 27(5) of the ATSCA.

The Special Immigration Appeals Commission (Procedure) Rules 2003 contains more detailed rules for the running of the SIAC.[436] In cases where the Home Secretary sought to rely on "closed material" that was not to be disclosed to the detainee, the Home Secretary would serve the appointed special advocate with a copy of the closed material, the reasons for its nondisclosure, and an unclassified summary of the material that could be served on the detainee.[437] The special advocate, a security-cleared lawyer, would then challenge the government's case during SIAC's closed proceedings by examining the undisclosed material, cross-examining witnesses, and making representations to the SIAC about the material, and in some cases ultimately persuading the SIAC that portions of the material should be disclosed to the detainee and to the detainee's counsel.[438]

Without the additional safeguard of a special advocate, a person certified and detained under the ATSCA would be in a roughly similar position to an alleged enemy combatant before a U.S. CSRT. However, the special advocate system represents a compromise, as the special advocate generally cannot take instructions or communicate with the detainee about the substance of proceedings once she has

431 A. v Secretary of State, [2005] 2 A.C. 68, paras. 87 (Lord Hoffman), 155 (Lord Scott) & 233 (Baroness Hale) (U.K.).

432 Special Immigration Appeals Commission Act, 1997, c. 68, § 5.

433 *Id.* § 5(3)(b).

434 *Id.* § 5(3)(d).

435 *Id.* §§ 5(3)(c), 6.

436 The Special Immigration Appeals Commission (Procedure) Rules, 2003, S.I. 2003/1034 (U.K.).

437 *Id.*, at rule 37(3).

438 *Id.*, at rule 35; *see also* CONSTITUTIONAL AFFAIRS COMMITTEE, *supra* note 160, paras. 56–61.

seen the undisclosed material.[439] This means that the special advocate cannot liaise with the detainee, who is probably the best source of information for refuting the government's allegations,[440] which will often include allegations based on hearsay.[441] Such allegations are difficult to refute without more detailed information about their factual basis.[442] In one case, a special advocate overcame these obstacles and contributed to the successful appeal of "M" against certification through submissions and cross-examination during the closed sessions.[443] At the same time, the Court, which rejected the Home Secretary's appeal in this case, was cognizant of the limitations of special advocates:

> [I]ndividuals who appeal to SIAC are undoubtedly under a grave disadvantage. So far as it is possible this disadvantage should be avoided or, if it cannot be avoided, minimised. However, the unfairness involved can be necessary because of the interests of national security. The involvement of a special advocate is intended to reduce (it cannot wholly eliminate) the unfairness which follows from the fact that an appellant will be unaware at least as to part of the case against him.[444]

As for independent review, although Part IV of the ATSCA provided some level of judicial review of the Home Secretary's decision, its scope was decidedly limited. The SIAC's only concern was whether the Home Secretary based his suspicion and belief on reasonable grounds.[445] This was plainly a quite distinct inquiry from determining whether a certified person actually was a terrorist.[446] As Baroness Hale

439 The Special Immigration Appeals Commission (Procedure) Rules, 2003, S.I. 2003/1034, rule 36 (U.K.). If the special advocate wishes to consult with the detainee or his lawyer, the SIAC must authorize it after notifying the Secretary of State, who may object. *Id.* rules 36(4), (5). Rule 36(6) permits the detainee to communicate in writing with the special advocate. But given that the detainee will be unaware of the contents of the closed proceedings, and given the special advocate cannot do more than acknowledge receipt of the materials, it is unclear what this communication actually achieves.

440 A v. Secretary of State, [2004] UKHL 56, [2005] 2 A.C. 68 (U.K.), paras. 155 (Lord Scott), 223 (Baroness Hale) (appeal taken from Eng.).

441 Special Immigration Appeals Commission (Procedure) Rules 2003, S.I. 2003/1034, rule 44(3) (U.K.) ("The Commission may receive evidence that would not be admissible in a court of law.").

442 *See* Michael Code & Kent Roach, *The Role of the Independent Lawyer and Security Certificates*, 52 CRIML. Q. 85, 99–100 (2006).

443 M v. Secretary of State for the Home Department, [2004] 2 All E.R. 863 (U.K.).

444 *Id.* para. 13. The special advocates themselves are acutely aware of the limitations of their role, how they are likely perceived by detainees, and their lack of support. *See* Joint Committee on Human Rights, *supra* note 160, paras. 40–41, 69–70 and 75–82. Human rights organizations have also expressed reservations about closed proceedings, even with the use of special advocates. *See* Amnesty International, *United Kingdom: Justice Perverted Under the Anti-terrorism, Crime and Security Act 2001,* 11–12 EUR 45/029/2003, Dec. 11, 2003, *available at* http://web.amnesty.org/library/pdf/EUR450292003ENGLISH/$File/EUR4502903.pdf.

445 Anti-terrorism, Crime, and Security Act, 2001, c. 11, §§ 25(2), 26(5) (Eng.).

446 A v. Secretary of State, [2004] UKHL. 56, [2005] 2 A.C. 68, para. 223 (U.K.).

observed in *A v. Secretary of State*, it was unsurprising that the SIAC had only cancelled the security certificate of one person detained under Section 23 of the ATSCA.[447]

The same issues arise with the PTA.[448] There, the standard of proof for the imposition of a control order remains low. Although derogating control orders require a court to be "satisfied, on the balance of probabilities" that the target of the control order "is or has been involved in terrorism-related activity,"[449] non-derogating control orders require only that the Home Secretary has "reasonable grounds for suspecting" that the individual is or has been involved in terrorism-related activity.[450] This is the same standard that applied under the ATSCA. Thus, it remains possible for serious impositions to be made on individual liberty based on only a minimal standard of proof.

Moreover, the issue of non-disclosure remains pertinent to the control order regime. The PTA provides powers for making procedural rules in proceedings concerning control orders.[451] The PTA authorized the creation of the Civil Procedure (Amendment No. 2) Rules.[452] These rules introduced a new Part 76 to the Civil Procedure Rules 1998.[453] Part 76 contains familiar provisions relating to the non-disclosure of sensitive information,[454] the holding of closed proceedings,[455] and the appointment and conduct of special advocates.[456] Therefore, the same difficulties that arose in relation to closed proceedings before the SIAC now arise in closed proceedings before the High Court.[457]

However, the non-disclosure issue did not trouble the Court of Appeal in *Secretary of State for the Home Department v. MB*.[458] The Court observed that Article 6 of the ECHR did not require full disclosure in every case provided that there were

---

447 *Id.*

448 These issues were heavily debated during the enactment of the PTA. *See* Stuart MacDonald, *The U.K.'s Response to the Threat of Terrorism: Control Orders—Two Recurring Themes, Two Apparent Contradictions*, Sept. 26, 2006, http://ssrn.com/abstract=932904; *see also* JOINT COMMITTEE OF HUMAN RIGHTS, *supra* note 193, paras. 55–78.

449 Prevention of Terrorism Act, 2005, c. 2, § 4(7)(a) (Eng.).

450 *Id.* § 2(1)(a).

451 *Id.* § 11(5), sched., para. 4.

452 The Civil Procedure (Amendment No. 2) Rules, 2005, S.I. 2005/656 (U.K.).

453 The Civil Procedure Rules, 1998, S.I. 1998/3132 (U.K.).

454 *Id.* at rule 76.2(2).

455 *Id.* at rule 76.22.

456 *Id.* at rules 76.23–25.

457 *See* David Bonner, *Checking the Executive? Detention Without Trial, Control Orders, Due Process and Human Rights*, 12 EUR. PUB. L. 45, 68–69 (2006).

458 Sec'y of State for the Home Dep't v. MB, [2006] EWCA (Civ.) 1140, [2006] 3 W.L.R. 839 (appeal taken from Q.B.) (U.K.).

adequate safeguards to reduce the prejudice of nondisclosure.[459] In the Court's view, providing special advocates sufficiently safeguarded against any prejudice.[460]

Finally, the court's supervisory role regarding non-derogating control orders is limited. The PTA requires that the Home Secretary obtain the High Court's permission to make a non-derogating control order, except in cases where the Home Secretary certifies that urgency precludes this. In such cases, the case must be referred immediately to court.[461] The court must decide whether the Home Secretary's decision to impose the control order was "obviously flawed."[462] This generally occurs in the context of an ex parte preliminary hearing.[463] Assuming the Home Secretary's decision passes this initial hurdle, the court then holds a full hearing to address whether the Home Secretary's decision regarding the requirements for imposing non-derogating control orders was "flawed" based on traditional principles of judicial review.[464] The PTA also makes plain that appeals in control order cases also proceed on this basis.[465]

However, in *Secretary of State for the Home Department v. MB,* the Court of Appeal interpreted the Act to give more latitude to judges to review the cases.[466] This interpretation seems to go beyond the statutory language. The Court held that the PTA did not restrict the reviewing court solely to the question of whether the Home Secretary's decision was flawed at the time the decision was made.[467] Rather, a reviewing court should consider "whether the continuing decision of the Secretary of State to keep the order in force is flawed."[468] The decision also suggests that a reviewing court must form its own view as to whether reasonable grounds existed for suspecting the controlee was involved in terrorism-related activities and whether the obligations imposed were necessary for protecting the public from the risk of terrorism.[469]

c) Canada

As with the ATSCA, the standard of proof to be satisfied under the IRPA's security certificate process is low. For a non-citizen to be certified as a security risk, it need

459 *Id.* paras. 80, 84.

460 *Id.* para. 86.

461 Prevention of Terrorism Act, 2005, c. 2, §§ 3(1), 3(3) (Eng.).

462 *Id.* §§ 3(2)(b), 3(3)(b).

463 *Id.* § 3(5).

464 *Id.* §§ 3(10), 3(11).

465 *Id.* §§ 10(4), 10(5), 10(6).

466 Sec'y of State for the Home Dep't v. MB, [2006] EWCA (Civ.) 1140, [2006] 3 W.L.R. 839 (appeal taken from Q.B.) (U.K.).

467 *Id.* paras. 40–46.

468 *Id.* para. 44.

469 *Id.* paras. 58–65.

not be proven that the person engaged in terrorism, is a danger to Canada, or that the person is a member of a terrorist organization.[470] It is sufficient that there are "facts for which there are reasonable grounds to believe that they have occurred, are occurring or may occur."[471] As Roach observes, this is less than a civil standard of proof.[472]

A non-citizen detained under the IRPA also faces the obstacle of nondisclosure of information during the review of the security certificate in Federal Court. The IRPA frequently puts the court in the position of reviewing what amounts to secret evidence. At the request of the relevant Ministers, the reviewing judge must hear all or part of the information or evidence ex parte if the judge determines that the disclosure of information or evidence would compromise national security or public safety.[473] The detainee is only entitled to a summary of the information or evidence which "enables them to be reasonably informed of the circumstances giving rise to the certificate," but that summary cannot include anything that the judge considers injurious to national security or to the safety of any person if disclosed.[474] Yet this could be the information that forms the basis of the allegations against the detainee. Further, the allegations in the summary could consist entirely of hearsay,[475] which, as discussed earlier, is difficult to challenge without further information. Thus, under the IRPA, the reasonableness of a security certificate may be determined without the detainee actually being able to see or respond to key portions of the government's case.[476]

The scope of judicial review under the IRPA is also limited and deferential. The Federal Court judge must merely determine "whether the certificate is reasonable."[477] Hence, rather than determining whether a certified person actually is a security risk, the judge effectively determines whether executive officials reasonably considered the person inadmissible on security grounds,[478] bearing in mind the government-friendly standard of proof for establishing inadmissibility.

Ultimately, the procedures under the IRPA place a heavy burden on the reviewing Federal Court judge, who must function without the security blanket of the

470 Immigration and Refugee Protection Act, § 34(1).

471 Immigration and Refugee Protection Act, § 33.

472 Roach, *supra* note 403, at 2186.

473 Immigration and Refugee Protection Act, § 78(e).

474 *Id.* §§ 78(g), 78(h).

475 *Id.* § 78(j) ("[T]he judge may receive into evidence anything that, in the opinion of the judge, is appropriate, even if it is inadmissible in a court of law.").

476 Charkaoui v. Canada, 2007 S.C.C. 9, paras 54–55; Roach, *supra* note 403, at 2190; *see also* Colleen Bell, *Subject to Exception: Security Certificates, National Security and Canada's Role in the "War on Terror"*, 21 CAN. J. L. & SOC'Y 63, 71–72 (2006).

477 Immigration and Refugee Protection Act, § 80(1).

478 Bell, *supra* note 476, at 68.

adversarial process and without the benefit of any inquisitorial powers.[479] Indeed, one Federal Court judge expressed discomfort about the IRPA's procedures with unusual candor. Speaking of the Federal Court's jurisdiction over security matters, Justice James Hugessen expressed his reservations about the one-sided, non-adversarial nature of proceedings under the IRPA, and then admitted, "I sometimes feel a little bit like a fig leaf."[480]

However, the Canadian Supreme Court found that the IRPA's security certificate process, properly followed, did not compromise judicial independence and impartiality.[481] The Court concluded that Section 80(1) of the IRPA contemplates a "searching"[482] and "non-deferential"[483] role for the reviewing Federal Court judge.

The *Charkaoui* decision's holding that Section 7's guarantee of fundamental justice was violated turned on the non-disclosure issue. Nondisclosure of certain evidence denied the person certified the ability to respond meaningfully to the government's allegations.[484] Thus, a reviewing Federal Court judge could be in the position of deciding a case on the basis of an incomplete view of the facts and potentially unreliable information.[485]

The Court endorsed the adoption of a British-style system of special advocates, an idea that has gained support in the Canadian academic commentary.[486] Although the Court was cognizant of the limitations of special advocates,[487] it recognized that a system of special advocates would still represent an improvement on the existing ex parte proceedings under the IRPA's security certificate process.[488]

d) New Zealand

The security risk certificate system does not operate under a clear standard of proof. Under Section 114D(1) of the Immigration Act, the Director of the NZSIS must be "satisfied" of certain specified matters before issuing a security risk certificate. The Director's certificate need only state that: 1) the Director is satisfied that the classified security information relates to a non-citizen; 2) the information is credible; 3) the information pertains to the relevant security criteria; and 4) the person meets

479 Code & Roach, *supra* note 442, at 95.

480 Roach & Trotter, *supra* note 90, at 1005.

481 Charkaoui v. Canada, [2007] S.C.C. 9, para. 46 (Can.).

482 *Id.* para. 39.

483 *Id.* para. 42.

484 *Id.* para. 54 ("Without this information, the named person may not be in a position to contradict errors, identify omissions, challenge the credibility of informants or refute false allegations.").

485 *Id.* para. 63.

486 *Id.* paras. 80–87.

487 *Id.* para. 86; *see also supra* notes 439, 444 and accompanying text.

488 *Id.* para. 86.

the criteria. The only reference to a standard of proof is in one of the relevant security criteria; Section 114C(6)(a) refers to the existence of "reasonable grounds" for regarding the person as a danger to the security of New Zealand.

The issue of non-disclosure also arises under New Zealand's security risk certificate regime.[489] The subject of the certificate does not have access to "classified security information."[490] Consequently, in his preliminary decision, the Inspector General had stated that he would consider certain information from the NZSIS that would not be disclosed to either Zaoui or his lawyers.[491] In his appeal concerning the parameters of the Inspector General's review, Zaoui successfully argued that he was entitled to an unclassified summary of the classified security information that formed the basis of the security risk certificate.[492] Additionally, the current Inspector General has, by analogy to the practice in the United Kingdom, appointed a special advocate who will be able to view and examine the classified evidence against Zaoui. It appears that the special advocate will operate under the same constraints as special advocates in the United Kingdom.[493] Therefore, even though there is no express provision for a summary of allegations or for a special advocate in New Zealand, the government ultimately provided Zaoui with both. This places him in a situation similar to that of terrorist suspects in the United Kingdom.

In contrast to its relative silence on other matters of procedure, Part 4A of the Immigration Act outlines the scope of the Inspector General's review in considerable detail. On review, the Inspector General must consider whether the certificate was "properly made."[494] Read in isolation, this suggests a fairly deferential level of scrutiny. However, the section goes on to require the Inspector General to assess the credibility of information and the relevance of information to the statutory security criteria, as well as to evaluate whether the certified person falls within one of the security criteria.[495] Consequently, the scope of the review appears, at least on paper, to be considerably more searching than under the PTA and the IRPA. However, given his close working relationship with the NZSIS, the Inspector

489 Immigration Act 1987, 1987 S.N.Z. No. 74, §§ 114B, 114D.

490 *Id.* § 114H(2)(b).

491 Zaoui v. Attorney-General, [2004] 2 N.Z.L.R. 339, para. 35 (H.C.).

492 *Id.* para. 110. *See Why Zaoui is Being Kept in Prison—a Summary,* N.Z. Herald, Feb. 23, 2004, *available at* http://www.nzherald.co.nz/search/story.cfm?storyid=EC280FE0-39E0-11DA-8E1B-A5B353C55561.

493 Gordon Campbell, *Pursuit of Justice,* N.Z. Listener, May 7–13 2005, *available at* http://www.listener.co.nz/issue/3391/features/3952/pursuit_of_justice.html; *see also* New Zealand Press Association, *Hearings on Zaoui to Be Held in Secret,* N.Z. Herald, May 3, 2006, *available at* http://www.nzherald.co.nz/search/story.cfm?storyid=0008A51E-47CD-1457-831C83027AF1010F.

494 Immigration Act 1987, 1987 S.N.Z. No. 74, § 114I(4).

495 *Id.* §§ 114I(4)(b), 114I(4)(c).

General lacks the same degree of institutional independence inherent in the reviewing bodies in Canada and the United Kingdom.[496]

2. The Risk of Error

The United Kingdom's experience with miscarriages of justice in terrorism trials—most notably the cases of the Birmingham Six, the Macguire Seven, and the Guildford Four—provide salutary history lessons about the dangers of not affording appropriate procedural protections when combating terrorism.[497] Government officials may be so convinced that they have the wrongdoers in custody that they engage in practices such as coercive interrogation and restricting the disclosure of information to the accused.[498] The government can subsequently turn out to be wrong, and this is all the more likely when it takes procedural shortcuts.[499]

All four regimes for detaining terrorist suspects exhibit similar procedural shortcuts: lenient standards of proof, non-disclosure of certain information, and limited review.[500] It is unclear whether anyone has been wrongfully detained as a terrorist suspect in Canada, the United Kingdom, or New Zealand. However, the cumulative effect of these features of the immigration-law-based detention regimes is a significant risk of error. This risk is likely exacerbated by the respective governments' lack of familiarity with the relevant political situations, the use of foreign intelligence sources, and translation issues.[501]

In the case of the Guantánamo detainees, there is a significant amount of evidence suggesting that the U.S. government has made mistakes. Early public statements from the Bush administration regarding the Guantánamo detainees exuded an air of infallibility. The detainees were collectively described as "the worst of the worst,"[502]

496 Paul G. Buchanan, *Of Myth and Reality in Terrorist Threat Assessment,* (Dep't of Political Studies, Univ. of Auckland, Working Paper No. 15, 2005), *available at* http://www.arts.auckland.ac.nz/FileGet.cfm?ID=5f858975%2D6018%2D4e66%2Da3c3%2D54eaed3b7d2e.

497 *See* Roach & Trotter, *supra* note 90, at 975–80.

498 *Id.* at 969.

499 Kent Roach, *Three Year Review of Canada's Anti-Terrorism Act: The Need for Greater Restraint and Fairness, Non-Discrimination and Special Advocates*, 54 U.N. BRUNSWICK L.J. 308, 329 (2005).

500 *See supra* Part IV.B. 1.

501 *See* Roach & Trotter, *supra* note 90, at 1006.

502 Katharine Q. Seelye, *Some Guantánamo Prisoners Will Be Freed, Rumsfeld Says,* N.Y. TIMES, Oct. 23, 2002, at A14; *see also* Ruth Wedgewood, *Countering Catastrophic Terrorism, in* ENFORCING INTERNATIONAL LAW NORMS AGAINST TERRORISM 103, 112 (Andrea Bianchi ed., 2004) (claiming there was a careful screening process that took place before detainees were sent to Guantánamo).

"the worst of a very bad lot,"[503] and terrorists dedicated to killing Americans.[504] Perhaps most hyperbolically, the administration described them as people so dangerous that they "would gnaw hydraulic lines in the back of a C-17 [transport plane] to bring it down."[505]

As more information has come to light, the inaccuracy of such sweeping claims is manifest. Among the detainees subsequently released by the United States were men claiming to be ninety years of age or older.[506] The United States eventually released the "Tipton Three" after British intelligence confirmed the impossibility of both the accusations against them and their false confessions.[507] There is no reason to suppose that these are isolated cases. Military sources soon revealed that the United States had not captured and detained the most important or dangerous terrorists, but rather those who were the slowest to leave the battlefield.[508] Other reports indicated that the government had overstated the dangerousness and intelligence value of the detainees.[509]

The findings of subsequent empirical studies are consistent with these anecdotal reports. They strongly suggest that the screening processes for detainees are undiscriminating and fallible, and also cast doubt upon the CSRTs. Another study by Mark and Joshua Denbeaux examined the government's records of its CSRTs and revealed some striking data. U.S. or coalition forces captured only 7 percent of

---

503 Tim Golden & Don Van Natta Jr., *U.S. Said to Overstate Value of Guantánamo Detainees,* N.Y. Times, June 21, 2004, at A1.

504 Patrick Jackson, *Life After Guantánamo,* B.B.C. News Online, Oct. 4, 2004, http://news.bbc.co.uk/2/hi/americas/3929535.stm (quoting Rear Admiral John D. Stufflebeem as stating, "They are bad guys and . . . if let out on the street, they will go back to the proclivity of trying to kill Americans and others.").

505 Donald H. Rumsfeld, U.S. Secretary of Defense, Department of Defense News Briefing (Jan. 11, 2002), http://www.defenselink.mil/transcripts/2002/t01112002_t0111sd.html.

506 Roach & Trotter, *supra* note 90, at 1013.

507 David Rose, *Revealed: The Full Story of the Guantanamo Britons,* The Observer (London), Mar. 14, 2004, at 1.

508 Golden & Van Natta, *supra* note 45. Many of the Guantánamo detainees turned out to be "low-level militants, Taliban fighters and men simply caught in the wrong place at the wrong time." *Id.* Lt. Col. Thomas S. Berg, a member of the original military prosecution team, said, "It became obvious to us as we reviewed the evidence that, in many cases, we had simply gotten the slowest guys on the battlefield. . . . We literally found guys who had been shot in the butt." *Id.*

509 Golden & Van Natta, *supra* note 503 (stating that government and military officials have "repeatedly exaggerated both the danger the detainees posed and the intelligence they have provided" and that only a small number of detainees were sworn al Qaeda members); Mayer, *supra* note 324 (describing the conclusions of a C.I.A. analyst sent to Guantánamo that more than half the detainees did not belong there); Hegland, *supra* note 421 (stating that by the fall of 2002, it was common knowledge around the C.I.A. that fewer than 10 percent of Guantánamo detainees were "high value terrorist operatives").

the detainees.[510] The Northern Alliance or Pakistani security forces captured 86 percent of the detainees and subsequently turned them over to the United States. At the time, the United States offered large bounties for the capture of Taliban or al Qaeda members.[511] 55 percent of the detainees were determined not to have committed any hostile act against the United States or its allies.[512] A mere 8 percent of the detainees were found to be al Qaeda or Taliban fighters.[513] 40 percent had no clear connection with al Qaeda, and 18 percent had no clear connection with either al Qaeda or the Taliban.[514] 60 percent of the detainees were detained because they were deemed to be "associated with" al Qaeda, the Taliban, or another terrorist organization.[515]

The study also reveals some of the evidence used to justify the continued detention of the Guantánamo detainees as enemy combatants. The evidence against certain detainees is acknowledged to be formidable, but these detainees constitute the exception rather than the rule. Evidence given as proof that certain detainees were enemy combatants included: the possession of Kalashnikov rifles; the use of guest houses; and the possession of Casio watches and olive drab clothing.[516] The probative value of these pieces of evidence is, at best, minimal.

Hegland's examination of the court documents filed by the Defense Department in relation to the habeas petitions of 132 detainees tells a similar story.[517] Seventy-five members of the group were not accused of participating in hostilities against the United States. Typically, detention was based on having links of varying strength to the Taliban or al Qaeda.[518] 115 of the files note the place of capture. Of these, 55 percent were apprehended by Pakistani security forces in Pakistan.[519]

C. Robust Judicial Scrutiny in the National Security Arena

Courts across the four jurisdictions, particularly the highest courts, have generally insisted on robust judicial scrutiny. Historically, the executive's use of emergency powers during times of crisis has generally met with little judicial resistance.

---

510 Mark Denbeaux & Joshua W. Denbeaux, *Report on Guantánamo Detainees: A Profile of 517 Detainees through Analysis of Department of Defense Data* 14–15, (Seton Hall Public Law Research Paper No. 46, 2006) *available at* http://ssrn.com/abstract=885659.

511 *Id.* at 3.

512 *Id.* at 6–7.

513 *Id.* at 9.

514 *Id.* at 8.

515 Denbeaux & Denbeaux, *supra* note 510, at 9.

516 *Id.* at 17–20.

517 Corine Hegland, *Who Is at Guantánamo Bay,* NAT'L J., Feb. 3, 2006, *available at* http://nationaljournal.com/about/njweekly/stories/2006/0203nj2.htm.

518 *Id.*

519 *Id.*

Since 9/11, despite familiar assertions about the need for executive exclusivity in matters of national security, this pattern has not repeated itself. This is a positive development that may require a qualification of the conventional wisdom about courts failing to protect rights in times of emergency. Indeed, courts can play a useful role in moderating the tendency of the elected branches of government to overreact in times of crisis.

1. A Brief History of Emergency Detention Laws in the Twentieth Century

a) The United States[520]

World War I resulted in the use of the Alien Enemy Act, a law originally enacted in 1798 as part of the Alien and Sedition Act.[521] The Alien Enemy Act conferred emergency authority upon the President to implement restrictions, including detention and deportation, on alien enemies.[522] Upon the United States' entry into World War I, President Wilson issued a proclamation under the Act warning alien enemies that they could be subject to such measures.[523] The United States used the Act again during World War II. President Roosevelt issued numerous proclamations ordering the internment of aliens deemed a danger to the public or a security risk.[524]

In 1942, Executive Order 9066[525] and supporting legislation subsequently enacted by Congress extended internment to certain citizens.[526] These measures formed the legal basis for the evacuation and eventual internment of more than 110,000 people of Japanese heritage, the majority of them American citizens.[527] This forced evacuation and internment was challenged most famously in *Korematsu v. United States*.[528] In *Korematsu*, the Supreme Court blithely accepted the executive's claims of military necessity and failed to rule the internment program unconstitutional.[529]

---

520 For wider treatments of the history of American civil liberties in times of crisis, see Frederic Block, *Civil Liberties During National Emergencies: The Interactions Between the Three Branches of Government in Coping with Past and Current Threats to the Nation's Security*, 29 N.Y.U. Rev. L. & Soc. Change 459, 481–89 (2005); Vladeck, *supra* note 353, at 167–81; Cole, *supra* note 267; Geoffrey R. Stone, Perilous Times (2004).

521 Act of July 6, 1798, §1, 1 Stat. 577.

522 Elsea, *supra* note 65, at CRS-17.

523 *Id.*

524 *Id.* at 20–21.

525 Exec. Order No. 9066, 7 Fed. Reg. 1407 (Feb. 19, 1942).

526 Act of March 21, 1942, 18 U.S.C.A. 1383, National Emergencies Act, 56 Stat. 173 (1942), *repealed by* Pub. L. No. 94-412, Title V, § 501(e), 90 Stat. 1255 (1976).

527 *See* Elsea, *supra* note 64, at CRS-21-22.

528 Korematsu v. United States, 323 U.S. 214 (1944).

529 *Id.; see also* Hirabayashi v. United States, 320 U.S. 81 (1943); Yasui v. United States, 320 U.S. 115 (1943); *ex parte* Endo, 323 U.S. 283 (1944).

The United States government would eventually apologize for its actions some forty years later.[530]

The end of World War II was followed by the onset of the Cold War, and the focus shifted to the threat of communism. To counter what was perceived as a worldwide communist movement dedicated to overthrowing the United States government, Congress enacted the Internal Security Act of 1950 over the veto of President Truman.[531] Title II of the Internal Security Act was the Emergency Detention Act,[532] which authorized the President to declare an internal security emergency in certain exigent circumstances.[533] The Act then authorized the creation of internment camps similar to those used in World War II.[534] Although no internal security emergencies were ever declared, the Act's continued existence on the statute books remained a concern. Even the Justice Department came to the view that the benefits of repealing the Act outweighed any potential advantages it might offer for dealing with emergencies.[535] Congress repealed the Emergency Detention Act in 1971 and replaced it with the Non-Detention Act—the law that would be central to the debate over the detention of enemy combatants after 9/11.[536]

b) The United Kingdom

During World War I, the Defence of the Realm Acts 1914–1915 delegated broad powers to the executive to make regulations to secure public safety or the defense of the realm.[537] For a time, in Simpson's words, "the executive became the legislature."[538] Driven by rumors of a German fifth column,[539] the executive introduced internment in 1915 through regulation 14B.[540] In addition to almost 30,000 enemy aliens, the government interned approximately 160 people using regulation 14B.[541] Regulation 14B was challenged in the courts, most notably in *R v. Halliday,*

530 Civil Liberties Act of 1988, Pub. L. No. 100-383, 102 Stat. 903 (1988) (codified as amended in scattered sections of 50 U.S.C.).

531 Internal Security Act of 1950, 64 Stat. 987 (1950).

532 *Id.* at Title II, 64 Stat. 1019–1031 (1950), *repealed by* Pub. L. 92-128 (1971), 18 U.S.C. § 4001(a) (2000).

533 *Id.* § 1021.

534 Block, *supra* note 520, at 465.

535 Elsea, *supra* note 64, at 30–31.

536 18 U.S.C. § 4001(a).

537 *See* Defence of the Realm Act 1914, 4 & 5 Geo. 5, c. 29; Defence of the Realm (no. 2) Act, 4 & 5 Geo. 5, c. 63; Defence of the Realm (Consolidation) Act, 1914, 5 Geo. 5, c. 8. For later Acts, see Cornelius P. Cotter, *Constitutionalizing Emergency Powers,* 5 Stan. L. Rev. 382, 387 n. 29 (1952–1953).

538 A. W. Brian Simpson, In the Highest Degree Odious 6 (1992).

539 *Id.* at 12.

540 Defence of the Realm (Consolidation) Act, 1914, 5 Geo. 5, c. 8 (Eng.).

541 Simpson, *supra* note 538, at 15–17.

ex parte Zadig.[542] In *Zadig*, a majority of the House of Lords ruled that general words of the Defence of the Realm Consolidation Act[543] were sufficient to impliedly authorize regulation 14B, hence justifying Zadig's detention.[544]

This pattern repeated itself in World War II. Immediately prior to the outbreak of hostilities, Parliament enacted the Emergency Powers (Defence) Act 1939.[545] Like its World War I predecessors, this Act delegated broad powers to the executive to make regulations that appeared necessary for a number of purposes including public safety, the defense of the realm, and the efficient prosecution of the war. Unlike its predecessors, it expressly provided for the power to intern.[546] The executive promulgated the infamous regulation 18B of the Defence (General) Regulations under the authority of this Act. In addition to some 28,000 enemy aliens detained by the government, about 2000 people were detained pursuant to regulation 18B.[547]

In *Liversidge v. Anderson*, the House of Lords rejected a challenge to regulation 18B.[548] On the face of it, regulation 18B permitted the Home Secretary to order a person detained "if he had reasonable cause to believe" the person was of hostile origin or associations.[549] A majority of the Lords held that the regulation only required the Home Secretary subjectively believe the detainee had hostile origins or associations. This decision was not to be second-guessed with an inquiry into the grounds of that belief.[550] Although bad faith or an error in formality could still theoretically be established,[551] the upshot of the Lords' decision was to make the Home Secretary's decision unreviewable.

From 1920 to 1960, the British government also extensively employed detention without trial to deal with the troubles in Northern Ireland.[552] However, it was not until the internments of 1971, originally authorized by regulations issued under

542 R v. Holliday, *ex parte* Zadig, [1917] A.C. 260 (U.K.); *see also* David Foxton, *R. v. Halliday* ex parte *Zadig in Retrospect,* 119 L.Q.R. 455 (2003).

543 Defence of the Realm (Consolidation) Act, 1914, 5 Geo. 5, c. 8 (Eng.).

544 *Id.*

545 Emergency Powers (Defence) Act, 1939, 2 & 3 Geo. 6, c. 62 (Eng.).

546 Joseph W. Bishop, *Jr., Law in the Control of Terrorism and Insurrection: The British Laboratory Experience*, 42 LAW & CONTEMP. PROBS. 140, 144(1978).

547 SIMPSON, *supra* note 538, at 1.

548 Liversidge v. Anderson, [1942] A.C. 206 (U.K.); *see also* SIMPSON, *supra* note 538, at 333–45, 355–66.

549 *Id.* at 220.

550 *Id.* at 224 (Viscount Maugham), 254, 258 (Lord MacMillian), 261 (Lord Wright), 282 (Lord Romer).

551 *Id.* at 224 (Viscount Maugham), 258 (Lord MacMillan), 261 (Lord Wright); *see* also SIMPSON, *supra* note 538, at 362.

552 Brandon, *supra* note 151, at 983.

emergency legislation dating from 1922, that the world took much notice.[553] The internment began in August 1971 when British soldiers arrested 342 persons in Northern Ireland as terrorist suspects.[554] By the time the internment program ceased in December 1975, between 500 and 1000 people had been detained without trial.[555] Because of faulty intelligence, many of those detained had no ties to the Irish Republican Army.[556]

The British government correctly surmised that this internment program violated Article 5 of the ECHR and derogated from the Convention in 1971. This derogation was unsuccessfully challenged in *Ireland v. United Kingdom.*[557] However, the court held that the interrogation techniques used on a select few detainees constituted inhumane or degrading treatment, and thus violated Article 3 of the ECHR.[558] The power to intern would remain on the statute books until 1998.[559]

c) Canada

The Canadian experience with executive detention revolves around the War Measures Act, which permitted the delegation of broad powers to the executive upon the proclamation of an emergency.[560] The Canadian Parliament enacted the Act in 1914 upon the outbreak of World War I. Regulations under the Act, including those permitting internment of enemy aliens, were swiftly promulgated.[561] During World War II, the Act was again used as the source of emergency powers, including the power to intern. After Pearl Harbor, the government "evacuated" 22,000 Japanese-Canadians from the Pacific coast under the authority of the War Measures Act.[562]

The Act was invoked for a third time in 1970. In October, a cell of Le Front de Liberation du Quebec (FLQ) kidnapped James Cross, the British Trade Commissioner, to draw attention to the group's demands for a separate state and the release of its members. Meanwhile, another FLQ cell kidnapped and subsequently murdered Pierre Laporte, the Quebec Minister of Labor.[563] The federal government responded by deploying troops in Quebec. The government also

553 *Id.* The internment was later authorized by newer legislation. *See* Ireland v. United Kingdom, 2 Eur. Ct. H.R. 25, paras. 58, 68 (1978).

554 Bishop, *supra* note 546, at 160.

555 Brandon, *supra* note 151, at 985.

556 *Id.* at 983.

557 Ireland v. United Kingdom, 2 Eur. Ct. H.R. 25, para. 224.

558 *Id.* paras. 165–68.

559 Clive Walker, *Prisoners of "War All the Time,"* [2005] Eur. Hum. Rts. L. Rev. 50, 53.

560 War Measures Act, ch. 2 (2d Session) (1914) (Can.).

561 Robert Martin, *Notes on Emergency Powers in Canada,* 54 U.N. B.L. J. 162, 164 (2005).

562 *Id.* at 167; Kim Lane Scheppele, *North American Emergencies: The Use of Emergency Powers in Canada and the United States,* 4 Int'l J. Const. L. 213, 224 (2006).

563 Martin, *supra* note 561, at 168.; Scheppele, *supra* note 562, at 230.

invoked the power of the War Measures Act to criminalize membership of the FLQ and to provide extraordinary powers to the executive, including the power to arrest and search without warrant, and the power to detain without charge.[564] More than three hundred people were detained in this way.[565] In December, the kidnappers released Cross and were granted passage to Cuba.[566] Three other FLQ members were charged with the kidnapping and murder of Laporte. Law enforcement apprehended them through the ordinary criminal investigation process rather than through the use of the extraordinary powers conferred by the Act. Two of the three were eventually convicted.[567] The 1970 crisis had many repercussions. One of the long term consequences was the eventual repeal of the War Measures Act in 1988.[568]

d) New Zealand

New Zealand's experience with emergency powers is similar to that of the United Kingdom and Canada—statutes conferred power upon the executive to make regulations as it saw fit.[569] During World War I, the War Regulations Act 1914 conferred power upon the executive to make emergency regulations. Among the many regulations promulgated were regulations authorizing the detention of enemy aliens.[570] At the time, more than 4000 persons of German birth lived in New Zealand. The government did not accept them for military service and interned those of uncertain loyalty.[571]

Upon the outbreak of World War II, emergency regulations were made pursuant to an existing statute, the Public Safety Conservation Act 1932.[572] Soon afterwards, New Zealand's Parliament enacted the Emergency Regulations Act 1939. This Act replaced the Public Safety Conservation Act as the legal basis for existing regulations, and served as the foundation of the Alien Emergency Regulations 1940, which imposed a host of requirements upon aliens, including potential internment

564 Martin, *supra* note 561, at 169–70; Scheppele, *supra* note 562, at 230; *see also* Whitaker, *supra* note 202, at 249.

565 W. H. McConnell, *Cutting the Gordian Knot: The Amending Process in Canada,* 44 LAW & CONTEMP. PROBS. 195, 200 (1981).

566 Martin, *supra* note 561, at 170.

567 *Id.* at 170–71.

568 Whitaker, *supra* note 202, at 251. The War Measures Act was replaced by the Emergencies Act, R.S.C., 1985, c. 22. This Act received royal assent in July 1988.

569 *See* Philip Joseph, *Delegated Legislation in New Zealand,* 18 STATUTE L. REV. 85, 89 (1997) (describing the First and Second World Wars as giving a "new purpose to delegated legislation").

570 War Regulations Act 1914, 1914 N.Z.G. No. 4021 (N.Z.).

571 PAUL BAKER, KING AND COUNTRY CALL: NEW ZEALANDERS, CONSCRIPTION AND THE GREAT WAR 223 (1988).

572 The executive also invoked powers under this Act to respond to a national strike by waterfront workers in the 1950s. *See* Waterfront Strike Emergency Regulations 1951, 1951 S.R. No. 24 (N.Z.). Before its eventual repeal in 1987, this Act was described as "potentially the most dangerous and repressive piece of legislation on the New Zealand statute books." *See* GEOFFREY PALMER, UNBRIDLED POWER 177 (1987).

or deportation.[573] At the time, approximately 7000 non-naturalized aliens lived in New Zealand. Despite some pressure to intern all aliens, the government selectively interned a total of 221 enemy aliens.[574]

2. Courts in the War on Terror

The conventional view is that during wartime or times of crisis, courts bow to the exigencies of the situation.[575] There is certainly a historical basis for this view. The failure of the U.S. Supreme Court to hold the government's evacuation and internment of Japanese unconstitutional in the face of claims about military necessity is well known.[576] The hands-off approach taken by the House of Lords in its wartime detainee cases has also met with subsequent criticism.[577]

Consequently, there was reason not to be overly optimistic about the chances of terrorist suspects succeeding in court, especially as governments made familiar claims about the need to defer to executive superiority in dealing with national security matters.[578] The Bush administration, in particular, has made bold claims

573 S. Res. 273, 76th Cong. (1940).

574 *See* Frederick Lloyd Whitfield Wood, The New Zealand People at War: Political and External Affairs 157–60 (1971).

575 *See* Oren Gross, *Chaos and Rules: Should Responses to Violent Crises Always Be Constitutional?*, 112 Yale L.J. 1011, 1034 (2003) ("Notwithstanding statements about the courts' role in safeguarding human rights and civil liberties precisely when those rights and liberties are most at risk, when faced with national crises, the judiciary tends to 'go[] to war.'"); Bishop, *supra* note 546, at 187 ("[I]t is more instructive to look at what the courts do than at what they say: in England, as in the United States, they have not been disposed straitly to confine the powers granted the executive by statute in what they perceive as a real emergency."); *see also* Jeremy Waldron, *Security and Liberty: "The Image of Balance"*, 11 J. of Pol. Phil. 191 (2003); David Cole, *Judging the Next Emergency: Judicial Review and Individual Rights in Times of Crisis*, 101 Mich. L. Rev. 2565, 2568–71 (2003); Bonner, *supra* note 457, at 51–52.

576 *See* Peter Irons, Justice at War (1983); Greg Robinson, By Order of the President (2001).

577 *See* Foxton, *supra* note 542, at 491 (describing the actions of the House of Lords in *Halliday* as illustrative of a "generally supine judicial performance"); Simpson, *supra* note 538, at 418–19 (concluding that "the courts did virtually nothing" for those detained under regulation 18B).

578 In *A. v Home Secretary*, the Blair government challenged the standard of review sought by the appellants. The Attorney General argued

> [T]hat as it was for Parliament and the executive to assess the threat facing the nation, so it was for those bodies and not the courts to judge the response necessary to protect the security of the public. . . . Matters of the kind in issue here fall within the discretionary area of judgment properly belonging to the democratic organs of the state. It was not for the courts to usurp authority properly belonging elsewhere.

A v. Secretary of State, [2004] UKHL 56, [2005] 2 A.C. 68, para. 37 (U.K.). Former Home Secretary Charles Clarke, speaking about anti-terrorism decisions that have gone against the government, alleged that the judiciary "bears not the slightest responsibility for protecting the public, and sometimes seems utterly unaware of the implications of their decisions for our security." *Clarke Criticises Lords on Terror*, BBC News Online, Jan. 17, 2007, http://news.bbc.co.uk/2/hi/uk_news/politics/6270599.stm.

asserting that the executive is not subject to any meaningful judicial scrutiny in the national security arena.[579] Yet in spite of such claims of executive exclusivity in matters of national security, most courts, particularly the highest courts in each jurisdiction, have so far insisted that they play a supervisory role.

a) The United States

In ruling for the government, a number of lower courts deferred to asserted national security concerns. For example, the Fourth Circuit held that no factual inquiry into Hamdi' s capture was necessary. Although courts were ordinarily in the business of adjudicating the legality of detentions by the executive, this was an exceptional case where "[a]ny effort to ascertain the facts concerning the petitioner's conduct while amongst the nation's enemies would entail an unacceptable risk of obstructing war efforts authorized by Congress and undertaken by the executive branch."[580] Similarly, Judge Leon, in rejecting the claims for relief of seven Guantánamo detainees in *Khalid v. Bush*[581] noted that "[t]he Founders allocated the war powers among Congress and the Executive, not the Judiciary. As a general rule, therefore, the judiciary should not insinuate itself into foreign affairs and national security issues."[582]

The Supreme Court, however, adopted a considerably less deferential stance. In holding that the Guantánamo detainees could file habeas corpus applications, *Rasul* stymied the Bush administration's attempt to insulate Guantánamo from judicial scrutiny.[583] The majority took this course in spite of government claims that national security would be imperiled.[584] Although enactment of the MCA

---

579 In its brief before the Fourth Circuit in *Hamdi,* the government argued that "[the court] may not review at all its designation of an American citizen as an enemy combatant—that its determinations on this score are the first and final word." *See* Hamdi v. Rumsfeld, 296 F.3d 278, 283 (4th Cir. 2002). In the Supreme Court, the government contended that Hamdi's status as an enemy combatant justified "holding him in the United States indefinitely—without formal charges or proceedings—unless and until it makes the determination that access to counsel or further process is warranted." Hamdi v. Rumsfeld, 542 U.S. 507, 510–11 (2004). The government also argued that "as long as a prisoner could challenge his enemy combatant designation when responding to interrogation during incommunicado detention he was accorded sufficient process to support his designation as an enemy combatant." *Id.* at 540–41. In a brief to the D.C. Circuit, the government argued that the very fact litigation was possible endangered national security: "By permitting captured enemies to continue their fight in our courts, the district court's holding threatens to undermine the President's power to subdue those enemies." *See* Brief for Appellants at 12, Hamdan v. Rumsfeld, 415 F.3d 33 (D.C. Cir. 2005), *available at* http://www.law.georgetown.edu/faculty/nkk/documents/hamdan-opening-brief2.pdf.

580 Hamdi v. Rumsfeld, 316 F.3d 450, 473–75 (4th Cir. 2003).

581 Khalid v. Bush, 355 F. Supp. 2d 311, 329 (D.D.C. 2005).

582 *Id.* at 329.

583 Rasul v. Bush, 542 U.S. 466 (2004).

584 In its Supreme Court brief, the Bush administration claimed that

> [a]ny judicial review of the military's operations at Guantanamo would directly intrude on those important intelligence-gathering operations. Moreover, any judicial demand that the Guanta-

nullified *Rasul's* holding, the decision has nonetheless been important in that it revealed some of what was going on at Guantánamo and raised awareness of the situation faced by detainees. Much of the information now known about Guantánamo and its detainees can be traced, directly or indirectly, to *Rasul.*

The *Hamdi* decision was equally important. To date it is the only Supreme Court decision to consider the level of due process to which an alleged enemy combatant is entitled.[585] Justice O'Connor's plurality opinion does not go as far as some of the other opinions.[586] However, in addition to containing the Court's most quotable sound-bite,[587] it rejected the most extreme claims made by the Bush administration. Justice O'Connor rejected the government's claims that no further fact-finding into the circumstances of Hamdi's capture was necessary,[588] and that "[r]espect for separation of powers and the limited institutional capabilities of courts in matters of military decision-making . . . ought to eliminate entirely any individual process."[589] Additionally, the plurality opinion pared down the amorphous definition of enemy combatant[590] and placed a narrower (albeit theoretical) limit on the permissible duration of detention.[591]

> namo detainees be granted access to counsel to maintain a habeas action would in all likelihood put an end to those operations—a result that not only would be very damaging to the military's ability to win the war, but no doubt be "highly comforting to enemies of the United States.

Brief for the Respondents at 54, Rasul v. Bush, 542 U.S. 466 (2004) *available at* http://www.ccrny.org/v2/legal/Sept._11th/docs/Brief_for_the_Respondents.pdf (Nov. 2006) (quoting Johnson v. Eisentrager, 339 U.S. 763, 779 (1950)).

585 Hamdi v. Rumsfeld, 542 U.S. 507 (2004).

586 Justices Scalia and Stevens dissented and held that the detention of an American citizen could only be legal after a conviction for a criminal charge or where the writ of habeas corpus had been suspended. *Id.* at 554–79. Justices Souter and Ginsburg joined the plurality opinion so as to vacate the lower court opinion. However, they disagreed with Justice O'Connor's conclusion that the AUMF impliedly authorized detention and her suggestions about what might satisfy her due process framework for enemy combatants. *Id.* at 540–54. Only Justice Thomas accepted the government's legal position in its entirety. *Id.* at 579–99.

587 Hamdi v. Rumsfeld, 542 U.S. 507, 536 (2004). ("[A] state of war is not a blank check for the President when it comes to the rights of the Nation's citizens.").

588 *Id.* at 526.

589 *Id.* at 527.

590 *Id.* at 526.

> [U]nder the definition of enemy combatant that we accept today as falling within the scope of Congress' authorization, Hamdi would need to be 'part of or supporting forces hostile to the United States or coalition partners' and 'engaged in an armed conflict against the United States' to justify his detention in the United States for the duration of the relevant conflict.

Id.

591 *Hamdi,* 542 U.S. at 521:

> Hamdi contends that the AUMF does not authorize indefinite or perpetual detention. Certainly, we agree that indefinite detention for the purpose of interrogation is not authorized. Further, we understand Congress' grant of authority for the use of "necessary and

The Court again rebuffed the President in its *Hamdan* decision. In addition to sending the Bush administration's plans for military commissions back to the drawing board, the majority also held that CA3 of the Geneva Conventions applied to the conflict with al Qaeda.[592] This had significant ramifications for U.S. detainee policy, especially in the areas of interrogation and treatment of detainees. Further, *Hamdan* has great significance for other aspects of the War on Terror. The idea that the President, as Commander-in-Chief, has constitutional carte blanche in prosecuting the War on Terror—even in the face of contrary legislation—underlies many of the administration's more notorious counterterrorism policies.[593] *Hamdan* repudiates these expansive claims about presidential power and reaffirms that the President, the commander-in-chief in wartime, must operate within the confines of the law.[594] Even though the MCA has largely cancelled out its holding, *Hamdan's* affirmation of separation of powers principles secures its place as a modern-day *Youngstown*.[595]

b) The United Kingdom

The case of *Secretary of State for the Home Department v. Rehman* concerned a decision by the Home Secretary to deport a Pakistani national on national security grounds because of his association with an organization involved in terrorist activities in the Indian subcontinent.[596] Rehman appealed to the SIAC. The SIAC ruled that "national security" had to involve a threat targeted at the United Kingdom and Rehman was not a threat to national security as defined.[597] The Court of Appeal allowed the Home Secretary's appeal, and Rehman's appeal to the House of Lords was dismissed. The House of Lords disagreed with the narrow view of "national

---

> appropriate force" to include the authority to detain for the duration of the relevant conflict, and our understanding is based on longstanding law-of-war principles.

Id.

592 Hamdan v. Rumsfeld, 126 S. Ct. 2749, 2794–96 (2006).

593 *See* U.S. Department of Justice, Legal Authorities Supporting the Activities of the National Security Agency Described by the President 34–35 (2006), *available at* www.usdoj.gov/opa/whitepaperonnsalegalauthorities.pdf (claiming inherent Presidential power to authorize warrantless eavesdropping on American citizens in the United States, even though the Foreign Intelligence Surveillance Act (50 U.S.C. §§ 1801–1862) ostensibly provides the exclusive means for engaging in such surveillance); *see also* Memorandum from Jay Bybee on Standards of Conduct for Interrogation Under 18 U.S.C. §§ 2340–2340A to Alberto R. Gonzales (Aug. 1, 2002), *available at* http://fl1.findlaw.com/news.findlaw.com/hdocs/docs/doj/bybee80102mem.pdf (asserting that the President, even in the face of domestic and international law to the contrary, has the inherent power to authorize torture).

594 Hamdan v. Rumsfeld, 126 S. Ct. 2749, 2774 n. 23 (2006) (citing Youngstown Sheet & Tube Co. v. Sawyer, 343 U.S. 579, 637 (1952) (Jackson J., concurring)).

595 *Youngstown Sheet*, 343 U.S. 579; Katyal, *supra* note 101, at 98 (emphasizing that the MCA, despite its many shortcomings, is still a defeat for the administration's views on executive power).

596 Secretary of State for the Home Department v. Rehman, [2003] 1 A.C. 153 (H.L.) (U.K.).

597 *Id.* paras. 4–6.

security" taken by the SIAC, and emphasized that this was an area where the courts should defer to the views of the executive.[598] This view was most clearly expressed by Lord Hoffman:

> I wrote this speech some three months before the recent events in New York and Washington. They are a reminder that in matters of national security, the cost of failure can be high. This seems to me to underline the need for the judicial arm of government to respect the decisions of ministers of the Crown on the question of whether support for terrorist activities in a foreign country constitutes a threat to national security. It is not only that the executive has access to special information and expertise in these matters. It is also that such decisions, with serious potential results for the community, require a legitimacy which can be conferred only by entrusting them to persons responsible to the community through the democratic process.[599]

The Court of Appeal decision upholding indefinite detention under Section 23 of the ATSCA predictably cited *Rehman* several times as authority for the proposition that courts should defer to the executive in matters of national security.[600] However, the the House of Lords took a more nuanced approach in *A v. Secretary of State.*[601] Most of the Law Lords were still deferential on the question of whether there was a public emergency threatening the life of the nation for the purposes of Article 15 of the ECHR.[602] Lord Scott, for example, expressed "very great doubt" as to whether a sufficiently grave state of affairs existed, but in the end gave the Home Secretary the benefit of the doubt.[603] Lord Hoffman, however, in a complete turnaround from his earlier paean to deference in *Rehman,*[604] dissented on this point:

> Terrorist violence, serious as it is, does not threaten our institutions of government or our existence as a civil community. . . . The real threat to the life of the nation, in the sense of a people living in accordance with its traditional laws and political values, comes not from terrorism but from laws such as these. That is the true measure of what terrorism may achieve.[605]

598 *Id.* paras. 17 (Lord Slynn), 31 (Lord Steyn).

599 *Id.* para. 62.

600 A v. Secretary of State, [2005] 2 A.C. 68, paras. 40, 44, 81 (U.K.).

601 *Id.*

602 *See Id.* para. 79 (Lord Nicholls):

> All courts are very much aware of the heavy burden, resting on the elected government and not the judiciary, to protect the security of this country and all who live here. All courts are acutely conscious that the government alone is able to evaluate and decide what counter-terrorism steps are needed and what steps will suffice. Courts are not equipped to make such decisions, nor are they charged with that responsibility.

Id. See also id. paras. 29 (Lord Bingham), 116 (Lord Hope), 226 (Baroness Hale).

603 *Id.* para. 154.

604 See Adam Tomkins, *Readings of A v. Secretary of State for the Home Department,* [2005] PUB. L. 259, 264.

605 A v. Secretary of State, [2005] 2 A.C. 68, paras. 96–97 (U.K.).

Regardless of their views on the existence of a public emergency, a clear majority of the Law Lords afforded the executive much less deference in determining whether Part IV of the ATSCA was strictly required by the exigencies of the situation.[606] Lord Rodger and Baroness Hale both emphasized that the power to review the legality of the derogation required them to do more than merely "rubber-stamp" the actions of the executive and Parliament.[607] The Lords' decision was, in Tomkins' words, "an extremely rare example of a British Court overturning the government's view of what was necessary in the interests of national security."[608]

c) Canada

The Federal Court of Appeal's *Charkaoui* decision noted that the IRPA procedures were a significant derogation from the adversarial process.[609] Adopting a deferential stance, the Court simply observed that rights were not absolute and swiftly concluded that the IRPA's procedures passed constitutional scrutiny.[610] The Supreme Court's own *Suresh* decision was also suggestive of "an approach to fundamental justice procedural protections quite accommodating of government security claims."[611]

In its *Charkaoui* decision, the Supreme Court acknowledged that protecting Canada's national security was an important objective,[612] and that the exigencies of national security considerations could justify some degree of limitation on rights:

> The principles of fundamental justice cannot be reduced to the point where they cease to provide the protection of due process that lies at the heart of [Section] 7 of the *Charter*. The protection may not be as complete as in a case where national security constraints do not operate. But to satisfy s. 7, meaningful and substantial protection there must be.[613]

---

606 *See* Shah, *supra* note 166, at 416–17.

607 A v. Secretary of State, [2005] 2 A.C. 68, paras. 164 (Lord Rodger), 226 (Baroness Hale).

608 Tomkins, *supra* note 604, at 259; *see also* David Feldman, *Proportionality and Discrimination in Anti-terrorism Legislation,* 64 CAMBRIDGE L.J. 271, 272 (2005) (describing the decision as unprecedented in that it examined "the legitimacy of measures adopted in good faith on national security grounds"); *but see* Walker, *supra* note 190, at 408:

> The headlines about *A and others v. Secretary of State for the Home Department* may create the impression of a judicial revolt. But one should be cautious about claims that an new era of judicial activism has dawned. First, this case must be set against the vast majority where executive decisions have been upheld.

Id.

609 Re. Charkaoui, [2005] 2 F.C.R. 299, [2004] 247 D.L.R. (4th) 405, para. 75 (Fed.C.A.).

610 *Id.* paras. 100–01, 122.

611 *See* Forcese, *supra* note 222, at 999.

612 Charkaoui v. Canada, [2007] S.C.C. 9, para. 68 (Can.).

613 *Id.* para. 58.

However, the Court stated unequivocally that the non-disclosure provisions of the IRPA's security certificate process went too far: "[A] person whose liberty is in jeopardy must know the case to meet. Here that principle has not merely been limited; it has been effectively gutted. How can one meet a case one does not know?"[614]

Strikingly, all nine Justices on the Court agreed that the security certificate process violated Section 7 of the Charter,[615] although the Court's declaration was suspended for one year to allow the Canadian Parliament to develop a new detention regime consistent with its decision.[616]

d) New Zealand

The Zaoui litigation showed that the New Zealand Supreme Court is also willing to intervene in a case with national security implications. In its first *Zaoui* decision, despite the government arguing that finding jurisdiction to grant bail to Zaoui would undermine the security risk certificate,[617] the Court held that Part 4A of the Immigration Act had not expressly nor impliedly excluded this jurisdiction. Thus, the High Court had inherent jurisdiction to grant Zaoui bail. For the Supreme Court, then the newly minted replacement for the Privy Council, to open the possibility of bail to a man the government considered a terrorist suspect was exceptional enough. Unlike the ATSCA and the IRPA, Part 4A of the Immigration Act has no specific provision dealing with bail or release of detainees on conditions.[618] However, the Supreme Court went further—it actually heard and granted Zaoui's application for bail.[619]

The Supreme Court's second *Zaoui* decision was similarly robust.[620] The outcome appeared to be a victory for the government. After all, the Court had endorsed the government's position that the Inspector General, in conducting his review of Zaoui's security risk certificate, only had to consider whether the statutory security criteria were satisfied.[621] However, the Court ruled that even if the security risk certificate were to be confirmed, Zaoui could not be deported if the relevant executive decisionmakers were satisfied that there were substantial grounds for believing that deportation would put him in danger of being arbitrarily deprived of life, or subject to torture or cruel, inhumane, or degrading treatment.[622] This was

614 *Id.* para. 64.

615 *Id.* para. 139.

616 *Id.* para. 140.

617 Zaoui v. Attorney General, [2004] 1 N.Z.L.R. 577, para. 66 (S.C.).

618 *See* Immigration and Refugee Protection Act § 84(2); Anti-terrorism, Crime and Security Act § 24.

619 Zaoui v. Attorney General, [2004] 1 N.Z.L.R. 577, at 662 (S.C.).

620 Zaoui v. Attorney-General (no. 2), [2005] 1 N.Z.L.R. 289 (S.C.).

621 *Id.* para. 73.

622 *Id.* paras. 90–91, 93.

because the power to deport had to be interpreted and applied consistently with human rights norms.[623] Additionally, the government was obliged to conduct a sufficiently meticulous factual inquiry into the human rights implications of deporting Zaoui.[624]

In essence, the Court imposed two restrictions on the executive.[625] The first is a substantive restriction that qualifies the power to deport those who pose a threat to national security.[626] The second restriction, an inquiry into the implications of deporting Zaoui, is procedural. Although desirable in terms of ensuring New Zealand carries out its human rights obligations under international law, both restrictions fit uncomfortably with the statutory language and context. First, Section 114C(6) of the Immigration Act directly incorporates Article 33.2 of the Refugee Convention.[627] On its terms, Article 33.2 permits the expulsion of a refugee "whom there are reasonable grounds for regarding as a danger to the security of the country."[628] It is difficult to square Article 33.2 with the Court's substantive restriction on the power to deport those who pose a threat to national security.

Second, once a security certificate is confirmed, the Minister has three working days to decide whether to rely on the security risk certificate.[629] If the Minister fails to make a final decision within that time, then the government must release the detainee.[630] The factual inquiry contemplated by the Supreme Court is likely to take much longer than three days. However, according to the Supreme Court, "there is no pressing prescriptive time requirement" for this inquiry.[631] In light of the statutory context, which suggests a swift and streamlined process once the security risk certificate has been confirmed by the Inspector General, the Court's insertion of an open-ended factual inquiry into the process is extraordinary. As Dunworth observes, "The effect . . . is that the three-day timeframe stipulated in Section 114K(1) has been erased."[632]

623 *Id.* para. 91.

624 *Id.* para. 92.

625 *See* Claudia Geiringer, *Zaoui Revisited,* [2005] N.Z.L.J. 285, 288.

626 Immigration Act 1987, 1987 S.N.Z. No. 43, § 72.

627 Convention Relating to the Status of Refugees 1951, Geneva, 28 July 1951, T.S. 39 (1954). Article 33.2 states that "[t]he benefit of the present provision may not, however, be claimed by a refugee whom there are reasonable grounds for regarding as a danger to the security of the country in which he is, or who, having been convicted by a final judgment of a particularly serious crime, constitutes a danger to the community of that country." *Id.*

628 *Id.*

629 Immigration Act 1987, § 114K(1).

630 *Id.* §§ 114L(1)(d), 114L(2).

631 Zaoui v. Attorney-General (no 2), [2005] 1 N.Z.L.R. 289, para. 92 (S.C.).

632 *See* Dunworth, *supra* note 244, at 376.

3. Reconsidering the Conventional View of Courts in Times of Crisis

Do these developments require a reappraisal of the conventional view about courts failing to protect civil liberties during times of crisis? The generally robust approach of the courts described in the previous section appears to be incompatible with this view. However, a number of commentators have pointed out that although there is a wealth of historical evidence that supports the conventional thesis, there are also historical instances of courts protecting civil liberties during times of emergency or perceived emergency.[633] Courts are not invariably ineffective defenders of rights during times of crisis. These counter-examples suggest that the conventional account, typically based on the most egregious judicial failures, is incomplete. A more complete historical account presents a more nuanced picture—sometimes the courts deliver a *Korematsu,* and sometimes they deliver a *Hamdan.* If one adopts this alternative account, then the recent run of post-9/11 War on Terror cases can readily be accommodated.

Further, discussions about the ineffectiveness of courts in times of crisis typically consider the judiciary in isolation. One cannot meaningfully assess the courts' performance as a check on governmental power without also considering the alternatives.[634] History demonstrates that neither the executive nor the legislature is reliable in this regard. The emergency laws that prompt the cases that the courts adjudicate have to originate somewhere. The legislature and executive often rashly enact these laws and, in the course of doing so, have proven quite willing to sacrifice civil liberties. The U.S. Congress, for example, historically has rallied around the flag and given the President whatever powers he has required in times of crisis and perceived crisis, whether that be funds to continue running internment camps, enacting the Internal Security Act during the McCarthy era, or passing a battery of new powers in the form of the USA PATRIOT Act.[635] The craven capitulation of Congress regarding the MCA provides the latest example.[636]

Legislatures in the United Kingdom, Canada, and New Zealand willingly enacted emergency statutes delegating broad powers to the executive to protect national security during both World Wars. These delegations of power were so broad that power became concentrated in the executive, and was exercised with little

633 Cole, *supra* note 575, at 2571–76; Mark A. Graber, *Counter-Stories: Maintaining and Expanding Civil Liberties in Wartime, in* The Constitution in Wartime: Beyond Alarmism and Complacency 95 (Mark Tushnet ed., 2005).

634 Cole, *supra* note 575, at 2591 ("But the real question to be asked when assessing the courts' performance is: Compared to what? The courts are undoubtedly highly imperfect; but the alternatives are worse.").

635 *Id.* at 2591–92; David Cole, *The Priority of Morality: The Emergency Constitution's Blind Spot,* 113 Yale L.J. 1753, 1764 (2004). *See* Jonathan Simon, Governing Through Crime 267 (2007) (observing that the Patriot Act had not been read by most of those who voted for it).

636 *See* Katyal, *supra* note 101, at 104 n.158 ("[T]he MCA was rushed through Congress with no deliberation and it suffers from myriad constitutional and other legal problems.").

Parliamentary oversight. In more recent times, the U.K. Parliament has been particularly prone to enacting reactionary anti-terrorism laws. For example, in the wake of the bombings of two Birmingham pubs in 1974, Parliament rushed the Prevention of Terrorism (Temporary Provisions) Act 1974 through the legislative process in forty-eight hours.[637] This Act was the first of a series of "temporary" Prevention of Terrorism Acts to introduce emergency powers to the mainland of the United Kingdom.[638] The ATSCA, which Tomkins describes as "the most draconian legislation Parliament has passed in peacetime" was also swiftly enacted[639]—the House of Commons passed the Act after sixteen hours of debate and the House of Lords passed it after nine days.[640] The ATSCA passed with the backing of most members of Parliament, including the opposition party.[641]

These examples, both historical and current, suggest that executives and legislatures have a tendency to respond to threats, real or perceived, with hastily enacted legislation. This legislation often turns out, in retrospect, to be unnecessarily harsh, ineffective, or even counterproductive. An explanation for this phenomenon lies in the psychology of risk perception.[642] In the case of seemingly uncontrollable, terrifying events such as a terrorist attack where media coverage usually amplifies the vividness, people exhibit "probability neglect." That is, people focus on the outcome—the terrible event—to the exclusion of the probability of its occurrence.[643] Therefore, a predictable consequence in the wake of a terrorist attack is a popular demand for a governmental response. As Sunstein observes, this may include "a demand for legal interventions that might not reduce risks and that might in fact make things worse."[644] For elected officials, the popular pressure for some kind of response means that the politically expedient course is to do something, or at least be seen as doing something, regardless of whether it is necessary or effective. An obvious candidate for that "something" is tough new legislation that appears to deal with the threat.[645] Other elected officials are likely to jump on the national security bandwagon because being perceived as "soft on terror" is a political kiss of death.

637 The Prevention of Terrorism (Temporary Provisions) Act, 1974, c. 56 (Eng.).

638 Brandon, *supra* note 151, at 985–86; *see also* Bonner, *supra* note 370.

639 Tomkins, *supra* note 152, at 205.

640 *Id.*

641 Helen Fenwick & Gavin Phillipson, *Legislative Over-Breadth, Democratic Failure and the Judicial Response: Fundamental Rights and the UK's Anti-Terrorist Legal Policy*, in GLOBAL ANTI-TERRORISM LAW AND POLICY 455, 457 (Victor v. Ramraj et al. eds., 2005).

642 *See* Victor V. Ramraj, *Terrorism, Risk Perception and Judicial Review, in* GLOBAL ANTI-TERRORISM LAW AND POLICY 107 (Victor V. Ramraj et al. eds., 2005).

643 Cass R. Sunstein, *Terrorism and Probability Neglect,* 26 THE J. OF RISK & UNCERTAINTY 121, 122 (2003); *see also* W. Kip Viscusi & Richard J. Zeckhauser, *Sacrificing Civil Liberties to Reduce Terrorism Risks,* 26 THE J. OF RISK & UNCERTAINTY 99, 99–100 (2003).

644 Sunstein, *supra* note 643, at 122.

645 *Id.; see also* Ramraj, *supra* note 642, at 113.

Thus, the phenomenon of probability neglect helps explain why elected government officials, during times of fear and stress, are susceptible to faulty risk assessment and frequently enact reactionary laws.[646] It also suggests that courts have a role to play as a counterweight. Given their relative institutional isolation, the courts may offer a better forum for cool reflection and evaluation of the relevant issues.[647] This point should not be overstated. Courts may be more insulated, but they are not immune from popular pressure. They will likely also suffer an informational disadvantage compared to the other branches of government.[648] However, the fact remains that detained terrorist suspects, like criminals convicted of the most heinous crimes, are unlikely to elicit much popular sympathy. Hence, it is unlikely that there will be any incentive for elected officials to change course—there is little electoral traction in the campaign slogan "More procedural rights for terrorist suspects." Courts, on the other hand, in addition to being less susceptible to political pressures, are very much in the business of hearing from people deprived of their liberty.[649]

In the last five years, many changes in counter-terrorism policy, both large and small, have been triggered by the courts. It has often taken litigation and adverse court decisions to compel further deliberation and reconsideration by government officials. For example, on the day the Bush administration's *Rasul* brief was due in the Supreme Court the Bush administration announced the creation of special annual review boards (ARBs) to consider whether Guantánamo detainees still constituted a threat and required continued detention.[650] Frank Dunham, who had been litigating for Hamdi for eighteen months, had been unable to see his client due to government claims that allowing Hamdi access to counsel would imperil national security.[651] Mysteriously, the night before briefs were due in the Supreme Court, the government called Dunham to say that Hamdi's intelligence value had decreased, meaning that he could now see his lawyer.[652] The government also belatedly allowed Padilla's lawyers, Donna Newman and Andrew Patel, to meet with their client just prior to the due date for the government's brief.[653] It is doubtful

646 Ramraj, *supra* note 642, at 119.

647 *Id.* at 121; *see also* Stone, *supra* note 520, at 543–44.

648 Cole, *The Priority of Morality*, *supra* note 635, at 2570–71.

649 Cole, *supra* note 635, at 1766.

650 Katyal, *supra* note 101, at 90. The ARB process resulted in recommendations to release fourteen detainees, transfer 120, and hold 329. *See* Dep't of Defense News Release, Guantánamo Bay Detainee Administrative Review Board Decisions Completed, Feb. 9, 2006, http://www.defenselink.mil/releases/2006/nr20060209-12464.html.

651 Margulies, *supra* note 77, at 101.

652 *Id.* at 144; see also Frank Dunham, *Where Hamdi Meets Moussaoui in the War on Terror*, 53 Drake L. Rev. 839 (2005).

653 Katyal, *supra* note 101, at 90.

that these eleventh-hour changes of heart would have taken place without the existence of pending court litigation.

The Supreme Court's actual decisions also precipitated change on a more macro level. The 2004 decisions rejected the Bush administration's position that terrorist suspects could be detained incommunicado and indefinitely in a place where no law applied. The rejection of the Guantánamo fiction in *Rasul*, together with the rejection of the argument that the President's say-so alone was sufficient to justify indefinite detention in *Hamdi*, resulted in changes at Guantánamo, most notably the creation of the CSRTs and multiple sets of habeas petitions. *Hamdan*, which rebuffed the President's plan to try terrorist suspects with military commissions, not only led to change, but expressly invited further deliberation and action from the elected branches.[654]

In the United Kingdom, it was only after the House of Lords ruled that indefinite detention under Part IV of the ATSCA was incompatible with the European Convention that the Blair government changed its detention regime for terrorist suspects. The Lords' *A v. Secretary of State* decision forced the government's hand. The result was the replacement of Part IV of the ATSCA with the PTA, which gave the executive the power to impose lesser (although still significant) limitations on liberty in the form of control orders.[655] Subsequently, aspects of the PTA's control order regime have been successfully challenged as well, and the House of Lords will likely consider the PTA in the near future.[656]

Similarly, the Canadian Supreme Court's *Charkaoui* decision has compelled the Canadian government to rethink its system of detention.[657] As noted above, the Court did not impose its own solution to the matter, but returned the issue to the legislature.[658] It did, however, endorse the use of special advocates,[659] which is likely to see their inclusion in any future system devised by the Canadian Parliament.

In New Zealand, the courts have been a driving force in the Zaoui saga. The High Court decision rejected the government's attempts to preclude court review, and ruled that the government had to provide Zaoui an unclassified summary of the allegations

654 Hamdan v. Rumsfeld, 126 S. Ct. 2749, 2798 (2006) (Breyer, J., concurring) ("Nothing prevents the President from returning to Congress to seek the authority he believes is necessary."); *id.* at 2809 (Kennedy, J., concurring) ("If Congress, after due consideration, deems it appropriate to change the controlling statutes, it has the power and prerogative to do so.").

655 *See supra* Part II.B.2.

656 *See supra* note 200 and accompanying text.

657 The Canadian government has indicated that it will abide by the Court's ruling. *See* Ian Austen, Linda Greenhouse, & Christopher Mason, *Canadian Court Limits Detention in Terror Cases*, N.Y. Times, Feb. 24, 2007, at A1.

658 *See supra* notes 228–229 and accompanying text.

659 *See supra* notes 486–488 and accompanying text.

against him.[660] This decision proved a harbinger of things to come, as the Supreme Court subsequently released Zaoui on bail and limited the power of the government to deport him even if his security risk certificate were to be confirmed.[661]

To sum up, the courts, particularly the highest courts, so far, have not been reluctant to assert their authority in the national security arena. Although there are plenty of historical examples of courts being overly deferential during wartime and times of crisis, this was not invariably the case, as these decisions from the highest courts are not unprecedented.[662] Further, the judicial record during times of crisis should not be considered in isolation. The record of elected officials in the executive and legislative branches is hardly flawless either. So, while the courts' spotty record in times of crisis may render judicial review an imperfect mechanism for the protection of liberty and other important rights, it is nonetheless superior to the alternatives.

V. CONCLUSION

This Article has examined the regimes for detaining terrorist suspects in the United States, the United Kingdom, Canada, and New Zealand, and has identified a number of differences and common themes. One further commonality is that each state faces its own "Guantanámo dilemma"—how can a detention regime minimize the incidence of both false positives—innocents being detained indefinitely as terrorists—and false negatives—genuine terrorists being set free? The existing procedures, perhaps understandably, skew towards avoiding false-negatives. Consequently, the risk of error has been borne heavily by detainees.

It might be thought that erring on the side of detaining terrorist suspects, even at the risk of false positives, by definition enhances security. The liberty interests of those wrongly detained are simply an unfortunate transaction cost. However, the United Kingdom's experience with terrorism in Northern Ireland suggests that the reality is more complex. The wrongful convictions in the United Kingdom's famous IRA terrorism cases were counterproductive in the long run because they encouraged deeper resentment amongst the Irish.[663] The United Kingdom's internment program that began in 1971 also demonstrates that overly general preventive measures can be counterproductive. This was true in the short-run, as internment failed to quell the violence that it was meant to prevent.[664] This also was true in the long

660 Zaoui v. Attorney-General, [2004] 2 N.Z.L.R. 339, paras. 50–73 (H.C.). The government unsuccessfully argued that Zaoui's judicial review proceedings should be precluded as the court lacked jurisdiction to review the powers of the Inspector General, and alternatively that it was inappropriate for the courts to intervene at the interlocutory stage. *See id.*

661 *See supra* notes 248–254 and accompanying text.

662 *See supra* text accompanying note 633.

663 Roach & Trotter, *supra* note 90, at 974–75.

664 *See* Ireland v. United Kingdom, 2 Eur. H.R. Rep. 25 (1978) paras. 42–44.

run, as the internment, which swept up many wholly innocent people, became a clarion call for a new generation of IRA recruits.[665]

Likewise, indiscriminate detention at Guantánamo has long-run costs as well. American detention policy has reportedly "contributed to a feeling of alienation and stigmatization among the Muslim and Arab communities in the United States."[666] These are the very communities whose cooperation and help is needed in the War on Terror.[667] Outside the United States, much of the ill-feeling towards American counter-terrorism policy, particularly in the Muslim world, is likely due at least in part to the detention at Guantánamo.[668] In fueling anti-American discontent, Guantánamo is a "propaganda gift to America's enemies."[669]

Some Guantánamo detainees have been detained for five years. Although the law of war permits detention for the duration of hostilities, it is not clear when the conflict between the United States and al Qaeda, or the "War on Terror" will end. This raises the troubling specter of permanent detention.[670] Therefore, it is even more important that the U.S. government put procedures in place to better ensure that it only detains the right people.

The United Kingdom once faced a similar problem with captured terrorist suspects during its campaign against terrorism in Northern Ireland. The British government's acceptance that standards applied to the treatment of detainees helped defuse the issue.[671] Eventually, the British treated detainees in accordance with "basic legal principles derived from the laws of war," even though the United Kingdom disclaimed both the entitlement of the detainees to POW status and the existence of an armed conflict for the purposes of the law of war.[672] Prior to 2001, the United States had a similar policy of acting in accordance with the Geneva Conventions regardless of whether the detainee was strictly entitled to its protection.[673]

---

665 Brandon, *supra* note 151, at 996–97; Bonner, *supra* note 457, at 50–51; Brice Dickson, *Law Versus Terrorism: Can Law Win?*, 10 Eur. Hum. Rts. L. Rev. 11, 24 (2005).

666 Moeckli, *supra* note 399, at 529.

667 *Id.*

668 *See* Francis Elliott & Raymond Whitaker, *Shameful: This is the World's View on Guantanamo. But Tony Blair Still Calls it 'An Anomaly'*, The Independent, February 19, 2006, http://news.independent.co.uk/world/politics/article346357.ece; Thom Shanker & David E. Sanger, *New to Pentagon, Gates Argued For Closing Guantanamo Prison*, N.Y. Times, March 23, 2007, at A1.

669 *Editorial: Un-American by Any Name*, N.Y. Times, June 5, 2005, at D13.

670 *See* Yin, *supra* note 8, at 16.

671 Adam Roberts, *The "War on Terror" in Historical Perspective*, 47 Survival 101, 111(2005).

672 *Id.*

673 Taft, Comments on Your Paper on the Geneva Convention, *supra* note 25; Powell, *supra* note 25; *see also* Taft, *supra* note 24, at 506–07.

Returning to this position, which is similar to the recommendation made by the 9/11 Commission,[674] would certainly be a step in the right direction.

Of course, aspects of the detention regimes of other states can be counterproductive too. In its discussion of Part IV of the ATSCA, the Newton Committee noted that the uneasiness amongst the local Muslim community caused by indiscriminate anti-terrorism laws was ultimately counterproductive to counter-terrorism efforts.[675] In this one respect, the extension of security measures to citizens as well as non-citizens in the PTA can be seen as a positive step—a step that has not been followed in Canada and New Zealand. In addition to blunting the force of the discrimination argument, it may also enhance security because previously exempt citizens who are threats to national security are now covered. Finally, eliminating the citizen/non-citizen distinction has the added benefit of compelling policymakers to confront the question of whether certain security measures, which will be applicable not only to a discrete and insular minority, are truly necessary.

674 National Commission on Terrorist Attacks Upon the United States, The 9/11 Commission Report 380 (2004).

675 Newton Report, *supra* note 165, para. 196. *See also* Fenwick & Phillipson, *supra* note 641, at 456.

PROLIFERATION SECURITY INITIATIVE: THE LEGACY OF *OPERACION SOCOTORA*

Walter Gary Sharp, Sr.[†]

Originally published in *Transnational Law and Contemporary Problems*, Vol. 16 (Spring 2007)

I. THE CHALLENGE OF COMBATING GLOBAL WMD TERRORISM

Terrorism in any form is pure evil. Terrorism that uses weapons of mass destruction[1] is an unconscionable evil that envisions human suffering and murder on potentially apocalyptic scales. WMD terrorism is one of the most devastating threats to humankind in the Twenty-first Century.[2] WMD terrorism is a transnational threat that

---

† Associate Deputy General Counsel for International Affairs, U.S. Department of Defense. Opinions, conclusions, and recommendations expressed or implied herein are solely those of the Author and do not necessarily represent the views of the U.S. Department of Defense or any governmental agency or civilian institution. While credit is conscientiously and faithfully provided throughout this Article for every thought not my own, it is nevertheless important to step back from specific citations to acknowledge that my framework of thought for this Article has been significantly shaped by daily interaction with my policy, military, law enforcement, and legal colleagues throughout the U.S. Government.

1 The Nuclear Threat Initiative (NTI) reports the "most widely used definition of 'weapons of mass destruction' (WMD) in official U.S. documents is 'nuclear, chemical, and biological weapons.'" Nuclear Threat Initiative, Definitions of WMD (Nov. 2006), http://www.nti.org/f_wmd411/f1a1.html. NTI reports, however, that "more recent U.S. laws [such as 50 U.S.C. § 2302(1)], official statements, and documents define WMD as including additional types of weapons, such as radiological weapons or conventional weapons causing mass casualties." *Id.* The U.S. Department of Defense defines WMD as

> weapons that are capable of a high order of destruction and/or of being used in such a manner as to destroy large numbers of people. Weapons of mass destruction can be high explosives or nuclear, biological, chemical, and radiological weapons, but exclude the means of transporting or propelling the weapon where such means is a separable and divisible part of the weapon.

U.S. Dep't of Def., Dictionary of Military and Associated Terms (Aug. 8, 2006), http://www.dtic.mil/doctrine/jel/doddict/index.html.

2 The United Nations (U.N.) Security Council has affirmed that the "proliferation of nuclear, chemical and biological weapons, as well as their means of delivery, constitutes a threat to international peace and security." S.C. Res. 1540, pmbl., U.N. Doc. S/RES/1540 (Apr. 28, 2004) (footnote omitted); *see also* S.C. Res. 1673, pmbl., U.N. Doc. S/RES/1673 (Apr. 27, 2006). The U.N. has also affirmed that "terrorism in all its forms and manifestations constitutes one of the most serious threats to peace and security." S.C. Res. 1735, pmbl., U.N. Doc. S/RES/1735 (Dec. 22, 2006). All U.N. Security Council resolutions are available online at

endangers every person in the world, and states must work together to construct an effective international approach to prevent it. However, the sheer volume and ubiquitous nature of global trade and commerce, the interdependence of states whose cooperative efforts to prevent WMD terrorism are strained by issues of national sovereignty and divergent regional agendas, and the eclectic collage of existing international and national laws and frameworks[3] intended to prohibit and prevent WMD proliferation and terrorism, make it extraordinarily difficult to prevent terrorists and rogue states from acquiring WMD technology and capabilities.

To add a real-world dimension to the extraordinary legal and operational complexities of combating global WMD proliferation,[4] imagine that shipping documents and contracts reveal an apparently lawful transfer of 120 ounces of the biological toxin BTx3$^{1:36}$ from a medical supplier in one state to an overseas medical research facility.[5] BTx3$^{1:36}$ is used for legitimate medical research, but is a perniciously deadly biological toxin. The port authorities of the transferring state report the shipment of this dangerous cargo to its domestic federal law enforcement agency. A third state, however, has classified scientific information indicating that the order contains twice the amount of the toxin the receiving research facility could use for legitimate research. A fourth state has sensitive law enforcement investigative information that the terrorist group FTO-33a,[6] a particularly vicious and active splinter group of al-Qa'ida, operates out of an authoritarian, military-dominated fifth state. A sixth state has classified intelligence intercepts that FTO-33a has been trying to obtain approximately sixty ounces of BTx3$^{1:36}$. The research facility refuses to justify its order, simply stating that it has the legal right to purchase BTx3$^{1:36}$ for legitimate medical research. University researchers of a seventh state have open source information indicating that just eighteen ounces of BTx3$^{1:36}$ evenly dispersed between Washington National, Baltimore-Washington, and Dulles International airports could likely kill over 90 percent of the population of the greater Washington, D.C. metropolitan area in six to ten days as well as tens, possibly hundreds, of millions of people around the world. An eighth state has highly classified human source

http://www.un.org/Docs/sc/. For more details concerning the lethality and effects of WMD, *see* U.S. Congress, Office of Technology Assessment, Proliferation of Weapons of Mass Destruction: Assessing the Risks, OTA-ISC-559 (Aug. 1993), *available at* http://www.wws.princeton.edu/ota/disk1/1993/9341/9341.PDF.

3 In contrast to legally binding international and national laws, frameworks are politically binding commitments agreed upon by states that set forth guidelines, criteria, or standards to meet common objectives or purposes. *See infra* Part IV.D, for a discussion of a number of international frameworks that apply to combating WMD terrorism.

4 Although these two scenarios may be tedious and challenging to think through, it is very important to recognize the contextual complexities of the environment in which the international community must shape an effective global WMD nonproliferation regime.

5 The biological toxin BTx3$^{1:36}$ and its properties are fictional and used for illustrative purposes only.

6 The terrorist group FTO-33a, its association with al-Qa'ida, and its intentions are fictional and used for illustrative purposes only.

intelligence that FTO-33a plans on attacking Washington, D.C. during its next annual National Cherry Blossom Festival, which is one of the most popular tourist events of the year in Washington.

Furthermore, imagine a second scenario: sensitive law enforcement investigative information becomes available to a state indicating that the medical supplier of $BTx3^{1:36}$ in another state is a known terrorist sympathizer and has reportedly offered sixty ounces of $BTx3^{1:36}$ to FTO-33a. Scientists of a third state have classified scientific information that $BTx3^{1:36}$ could be shipped in liquid, powder, solid, or vapor form, and that six ounces of $BTx3^{1:36}$ powder could be safely packaged in an airtight plastic cigar storage tube. A fourth state has information from classified intelligence intercepts that indicates that four ten-ounce vials of $BTx3^{1:36}$ have been secreted on board four different container vessels that are somewhere on the high seas bound for four different ports around the world. A fifth state has highly classified human source intelligence that two of the ten-ounce vials will be shipped to Washington, D.C. by air sometime in the next week.

Although these two scenarios are fictional and perhaps difficult to contemplate, they realistically demonstrate the devastating threat of WMD terrorism, as well as the legal and operational complexities in developing an effective mechanism for combating global WMD proliferation in a world dominated by global trade and commerce. In 2005, for example, there were 39,932 ships in the world merchant fleet (consisting of ships of 300 gross tons or more) with a capacity of carrying 880 million tons of cargo (deadweight tonnage) stored in upwards of 12,784 million cubic feet of containers.[7] World seaborne trade in 2005 reached 7.11 billion tons of goods loaded, and maritime activity reached 29,045 billion ton-miles (one ton of freight moved one mile).[8] In 2003, more than 48 million cargo containers moved between major seaports, and more than six million arrived in the United States.[9] Given this magnitude of global trade and commerce, how does a state, or group of states, even begin to search for four ten-ounce vials of $BTx3^{1:36}$ hidden on board four different container vessels that are somewhere on the high seas bound for four different ports around the world? Or, where and how does the United States begin to search for two ten-ounce vials that are being smuggled by one of over 550,000 passengers that arrive at one of the three major Washington, D.C. metropolitan

7 *See* Institute of Shipping Economics and Logistics (ISL) Market Analysis, *World Merchant Fleet: OECD Shipping and Shipbuilding*, 49 Shipping Statistics and Market Review 1 (Jan./Feb. 2005), *available at* http://www.isl.org/products_services/publications/pdf/comment_1-2-2005_short.pdf.

8 Press Release, United Nations Conference on Trade and Development, World Seaborne Trade Expanded in 2005—and Growth Continues in 2006, UNCTAD/PRESS/PR/2006/043 (Oct. 11, 2006), http://www.unctad.org/Templates/webflyer.asp?docid=7687&intItemID =1528&lang=1.

9 *See* Press Release, Department of Homeland Security, U.S. Customs and Border Protection, Singapore, the World's Busiest Seaport, Implements the Container Security Initiative and Begins to Target and Pre-Screen Cargo Destined for U.S. (Mar. 17, 2003), http://www.cbp.gov/xp/cgov/newsroom/news_releases/archives/cbp_press_releases/032003/03172003.xml.

airports every week?[10] Moreover, once on the ground in the United States, how do U.S. law enforcement authorities sort through more than 80,000 million ton-miles of domestic freight that move around the United States every week?[11] Clearly, multinational cooperation and information sharing are a critical foundation for coordinating cargo and passenger searches of this magnitude. However, multinational cooperation filtered through language barriers, time zones, national political agendas, and trade alliances is also a practical challenge. More than 93.5 percent of the total deadweight tonnage of the world merchant fleet was controlled in 2005 by approximately thirty states.[12] Moreover, in any given situation, any number of these states and jurisdictions around the world may be involved. These states and jurisdictions need to develop the legal basis and provide the necessary resources to interdict items of WMD proliferation concern. In the first scenario above, for example, the transfer of $BTx3^{1:36}$ is legitimate on it face. What international or national laws or frameworks are in place to scrutinize the legitimate transfers of goods that could be diverted for illegitimate purposes, i.e., dual-use[13] goods that could be used for peaceful purposes or terrorism? What prohibits the transfer of $BTx3^{1:36}$ to a legitimate medical research facility if the amount simply seems excessive? If it is not a prohibited transaction on its face, then what legal authority permits interdicting the shipment if it is suspected that the material may be misused or diverted to terrorists? Eight states are involved in the first scenario and up to nine states are involved in the second. When a suspect transaction occurs in one state, how do other states know when to share intelligence or non-government, open-source, or law enforcement information? What procedures and legal authorities are in place for states to request and share intelligence and law enforcement information? What international frameworks or laws support a global WMD nonproliferation[14] program? What national laws apply when multiple states are involved?

---

10 *See* U.S. Dep't of Transportation, Intermodal Transportation Database (figures utilized for the year ending Oct. 2005), http://www.transtats.bts.gov/airports.asp.

11 *See* U.S. Dep't of Transportation, Transportation Statistics Annual Report, ch. 2, sec. 1 (Nov. 2005), http://webbts.bts.gov/publications/transportation_statistics_annual_report/2005/html/chapter_02 /domestic_freight_ton_miles.html.

12 *See* Institute of Shipping Economics and Logistics (ISL) Market Analysis, Ownership Patterns of the World Merchant Fleet, Shipping Statistics and Market Review (SSMR) 1 (Apr. 2005), http://www.isl.org/products_services/publications/ pdf/COMM_4-2005-short.pdf. In 2005, the top twenty-five flags of registry by decreasing deadweight tonnage were Panama, Liberia, Greece, Hong Kong, Bahamas, the Marshall Islands, Singapore, Malta, Cyprus, China, Norway, Isle of Man, the United States, India, Germany, Italy, South Korea, Japan, Iran, the United Kingdom, Denmark, Saint Vincent & the Grenadines, Belgium, Bermuda, and Malaysia. *See* U.S. Department of Transportation Maritime Administration, World Merchant Fleet by Top Twenty-Five Flag and Type 2005, 3 (July 2006), http://www.marad.dot.gov/Marad_Statistics /2005%20STATISTICS/Flag-MFWYear-End%202005.xls.

13 Dual-use items, goods, or technology are those that could be used for legitimate and lawful purposes or diverted for illegal, military, or terrorist purposes.

14 Nonproliferation is defined by the U.S. Department of Defense as the "use of the full range of political, economic, informational, and military tools to PREVENT proliferation, reverse it

When a suspect shipment is on board a ship or aircraft, what national and international legal authorities permit a state to interdict, inspect, and possibly seize illegitimate cargo? And finally, though there are many more questions, when does a WMD terrorist threat invoke a state's inherent right of self-defense?

These illustrative scenarios and questions underscore the extraordinary importance of nation states working together to create an effective global WMD nonproliferation regime. This Article details one of the major international cooperative efforts to combat global WMD terrorism—the Proliferation Security Initiative (PSI). It first summarizes the genesis and tenets of PSI, and then describes how PSI activities are intended to coordinate states' WMD nonproliferation activities, as well as leverage existing international and national laws. This Article also provides an introduction to the existing legal regimes and frameworks relevant in the PSI context for intermodal (ground, maritime, and air) interdictions of WMD items of proliferation concern. However, since the applicable laws or frameworks for any potential interdiction are highly situation-specific, this Article does not attempt to detail every law or framework that may apply. Instead, it intends to provide a thorough understanding of the central tenets of PSI and the analytical framework needed to determine what set of laws or frameworks may apply. This Article concludes with an evaluation of the effectiveness of PSI and with recommendations that may help strengthen PSI and the global WMD nonproliferation regime.

II. THE GENESIS AND TENETS OF PSI

A. The *So San* Interdiction

Based upon intelligence the United States provided on December 5, 2002 that a suspicious vessel illegally trading in arms was operating nearby in the Indian Ocean, the Spanish frigate *Navarra* and support ship *Patino* identified the *So San*, a vessel operated

---

diplomatically, or protect U.S. interests against an opponent armed with nuclear, biological or chemical (NBC) weapons and the means to deliver them, should that prove necessary." U.S. DEP'T OF DEF., DEPARTMENT OF DEFENSE COUNTERPROLIFERATION (CP) IMPLEMENTATION, DoD DIR. 2060.2, ¶ 3.2 (July 9, 1996), *available at* http://www.dtic.mil/whs/directives/corres / pdf/206002_070996/206002p.pdf. The U.S. Department of Defense also defines nonproliferation tools to include "intelligence, global nonproliferation norms and agreements, diplomacy, export controls, security assurances, security assistance, defenses and the application of military force." *Id.* This directive defines counterproliferation as the "activities of the Department of Defense across the full range of U.S. Government efforts to COMBAT proliferation, including the application of military power to protect U.S. Forces and interests; intelligence collection and analysis; and support to diplomacy, arms control, and export controls." *Id.* ¶ 3.1. DoD Dir. 2060.2 is the current DoD issuance on counterproliferation policy. However, more recent documents define how nonproliferation and counterproliferation serve as components of the U.S. strategy to combat WMD. *See* WHITE HOUSE, NATIONAL STRATEGY TO COMBAT WEAPONS OF MASS DESTRUCTION (Dec. 2002), http://www.whitehouse.gov/news/releases/2002/12/WMDStrategy.pdf; U.S. DEP'T OF DEF., NATIONAL MILITARY STRATEGY TO COMBAT WEAPONS OF MASS DESTRUCTION (Feb. 2006), *available at* http://www.defenselink.mil/pdf/NMS-CWMD2006.pdf.

by the Democratic People's Republic of Korea (DPRK).[15] The *Navarra* and *Patino* were operating as part of an Operation Enduring Freedom maritime task force, and the United States requested that the ships interdict the *So San* and investigate the cargo it was carrying.[16] The Spanish called this maritime interdiction "*Operacion Socotora.*"[17]

The *So San* was navigating without a flag, but it was determined later to be carrying a Cambodian flag registered in Phnom Penh.[18] The *Navarra* hailed the *So San* at dawn on December 9, 2002, approximately 600 miles from Yemen. When asked, the DPRK captain of the *So San* responded that his ship was carrying cement.[19] The *So San* captain refused permission for anyone from the *Navarra* or *Patino* to board the *So San* and tried to speed off.[20] The *So San* failed to heed small arms warning shots, and Spanish Marines from the *Patino* fast roped by helicopter on board the *So San*.[21] These Marines and a second Spanish team, which subsequently boarded by inflatable boat, found a series of containers filled with weapons.[22] U.S. warships also operating in the area as a part of Operation Enduring Freedom then reached the boarding area, and a U.S. technical team assisted in identifying the cargo.[23] The boarding teams found fifteen medium-range Scud missiles, fifteen conventional-explosive warheads,[24]

---

15 *See Spanish Official Details High Seas Drama*, CNN.com World, Dec. 11, 2002, http://archives.cnn.com/2002/WORLD/europe/12/11/missile.ship.spain/index.html.

16 *Id.* For more background information on Operation Enduring Freedom, see, e.g., U.S. Dep't of Def., Into Afghanistan 2001–2005: Operation Enduring Freedom Marks Four Years, http://www.defenselink.mil/home/features/2005/Afghan_4 (last visited Feb. 15, 2007); U.S. Dep't of Def., Defend America: On the Ground Archive, Afghanistan, http://www.defendamerica.mil/otg/OTG-Afghanistan/AfghanistanOTG.html (last visited Feb. 15, 2007).

17 *Spanish Official Details High Seas Drama*, *supra* note 15. The operation likely was named after *Socotra*, a territorial island of Yemen located in the Indian Ocean approximately 220 miles south of Yemen and 160 miles off the Horn of Africa. *See* CIA World Factbook, Yemen, https://www.cia.gov/cia/publications/factbook/geos/ym.html (last visited Feb. 15, 2007).

18 *Spanish Official Details High Seas Drama*, *supra* note 15.

19 *Id.*

20 *Id.*

21 *Id.*; Al Goodman et al., *Shots Fired to Stop Scud Ship*, CNN.com World, Dec. 10, 2002, http://archives.cnn.com/2002/WORLD/asiapcf/east/12/10/ship.boarding. Official Spanish government photographs of this operation are published at *In Pictures: Missile Ship Seized*, BBC News World Edition Online, Dec. 11, 2002, http://news.bbc.co.uk/2/hi/middle_east/2566 493.stm.

22 *Spanish Official Details High Seas Drama*, *supra* note 15.

23 *Id.*

24 Photo Essay, *Spanish Warships Intercept a Shipload of Scuds: How North Korean Missiles were Seized in the Gulf of Aden*, Times Online, Dec. 12, 2002, http://www.time.com/time/photoessays/scudraid/index.html. DPRK "is thought to earn between $500m and $600m a year from exports of ballistic missile-related equipment and technology." Caroline Gluck, *South Korea Cautious over Missile Seizure*, BBC News World Edition Online, Dec. 11, 2002, http://news.bbc.co.uk/2/hi/asia-pacific/2566523.stm. For a concise analysis and history of the DPRK missile program, see, e.g., *North Korea's Missile Programme*, BBC News World Edition Online, July 5, 2006, http://news.bbc.co.uk/2/hi/asia-pacific/2564241.stm. For an overview of DPRK's nuclear, biological, chemical, and missile capabilities, see, e.g., Nuclear

twenty-three containers of nitric acid fuel,[25] and eighty-five barrels of unidentified chemical products hidden under thousands of bags of cement.[26] The Government of Spain handed over the *So San* to the United States on the same day, December 9.[27]

The United States had tracked the *So San* since leaving DPRK several days earlier and was 99 percent sure that the missiles on board the *So San* were bound for Yemen.[28] However, when the United States asked Yemen about the shipment prior to the interdiction of the *So San*, Yemen denied that the inbound shipment belonged to them.[29] The interdiction of the *So San* likely took place because Yemen denied that the suspected cargo of arms belong to it.[30] After the interdiction of the *So San*, Yemen acknowledged that the Scud missiles were destined for the Yemeni army to be used for defensive purposes and made a formal protest to the United States over the seizure of the *So San* and its cargo.[31] Yemeni President Ali Abdullah Saleh confirmed in August 2002 that it had previously bought Scud-C tactical ballistic missiles from the DPRK some time around 1999 and 2000. At that time he defended the purchase as a legitimate transfer since Yemen was not under any arms ban.[32] It is unclear whether the December 2002 transfer of Scud missiles on the *So San* were a part of this 1999/2000 purchase or a subsequent purchase. However, the United States imposed sanctions on the DPRK in response to its 1999/2000 sale of Scud missiles to Yemen.[33]

Threat Initiative, North Korea Profile (Dec. 2006), http://www.nti.org/e_research/profiles/NK/index.html. Scud is the NATO Reporting Name for a series of tactical ballistic surface-to-surface missiles developed by the former Soviet Union. *See* Andreas Parsch & Aleksey Martynov, Designations of Soviet and Russian Military Aircraft and Missiles (Nov. 2006), http://www.designation-systems.net/non-us/soviet.html#_System_NATO.

25 Robert Marquand & Peter Ford, *A New Doctrine and a Scud Bust*, The Christian Sci. Monitor, Dec. 12, 2002, *available at* http://www.csmonitor.com/2002/1212/p01s03-woap.html.

26 Al Goodman et al., *Scud Missiles are Ours, Says Yemen*, CNN.com World, Dec. 11, 2002, http://edition.cnn.com/2002/WORLD/asiapcf/east/12/11/scud.ship/index.html. U.S. military sources say "the North's chemical and biological weapons program is the 'most troubling' aspect of the regime." Marquand & Ford, *supra* note 25. DPRK "is estimated to have 5,000 tons of agents stockpiled—including VX nerve gas and sarin gas." *Id.*

27 Goodman, *Scud Missiles are Ours, Says Yemen*, *supra* note 26.

28 Al Goodman et al., *Scud Find 'Won't Change U.S. Policy,'* Cnn.com World, Dec. 11, 2002, http://archives.cnn.com/2002/WORLD/asiapcf/east/12/11/missile.ship/index.html.

29 Goodman, *Scud Missiles are Ours, says Yemen*, *supra* note 26.

30 Nick Childs, *Scud Affair Clouds US-Yemen Ties*, BBC News World Edition Online, Dec. 11, 2002, http://news.bbc.co.uk/2/hi/americas/2567637.stm.

31 Goodman, *Scud Missiles are Ours, says Yemen*, *supra* note 26.

32 Goodman, *Scud Find 'Won't Change U.S. Policy'*, *supra* note 28.

33 *Scud Affair Draws U.S. Apology*, BBC News World Edition Online, Dec. 12, 2002, http://news.bbc.co.uk/2/hi/middle_east/2569687.stm.

Since the *So San* failed to fly a flag, the United States announced that it appeared to be a stateless vessel, and Spain declared it a pirate ship operating illegally.[34] As a stateless vessel with weaponry aboard that was not on the ship's manifest, the United States defended the *So San* interdiction as lawful and reasonable.[35] The United States also defended the seizure of the missiles as consistent with its policy of interdicting transfers that could be used to make or deliver WMD, but conceded there was nothing in international law allowing for a seizure of conventional weapons not banned by treaty.[36] The International Institute for Strategic Studies (IISS) in London also observed that the transfer of missiles by the DPRK to Yemen was not illegal, since the DPRK "is not part of the international agreement limiting the spread of this technology, the Missile Technology Control Regime (MTCR)."[37] IISS also noted that several other Middle Eastern states had already bought Scud missiles from the DPRK.[38]

The United States released the *So San* and its crew after two days of high level discussions between the United States and Yemen, and the cargo proceeded to Yemen.[39] The U.S. White House announced that American concerns that the DPRK cargo was heading for a potential terrorist state proved unfounded, and that although there was "authority to stop and search [the *So San*], in this instance there is no clear authority to seize a shipment of Scud missiles from North Korea to Yemen."[40] The U.S. Deputy Secretary of Defense also congratulated the Spanish government on its successful interdiction operation but apologized for "how it all turned out."[41] The Yemeni Government said it had bought this shipment in 1999 and was puzzled why the Scuds were hidden under sacks of cement.[42] Yemen also assured the United States that it would not transfer the missiles to anyone else.[43]

---

34 Goodman, *Scud Find 'Won't Change U.S. Policy'*, *supra* note 28. The captain of the *So San* and its crew of twenty were all DPRK nationals. *Id.*

35 Childs, *supra* note 30.

36 Goodman, *Scud Missiles are Ours, says Yemen*, *supra* note 26.

37 Paul Reynolds, *North Korea Ratchets up a Crisis*, BBC News World Edition Online, Dec. 12, 2002, http://news.bbc.co.uk/2/hi/asia-pacific/2566277.stm. *See infra* Part IV, for a discussion of the MTCR and other international frameworks.

38 Reynolds, *supra*, note 37.

39 *U.S. Frees Missile-Carrying Ship*, BBC News World Edition Online, Dec. 11, 2002, http://news.bbc.co.uk/2/hi/middle_east/2567225.stm.

40 Press Release, U.S. White House, Daily Press Briefing by Ari Fleischer (Dec. 11, 2002), http://www.whitehouse.gov/news/releases/2002/12/20021211-5.html#2; *see also US Frees Missile-Carrying Ship*, *supra* note 39.

41 *Scud Affair Draws U.S. Apology*, *supra* note 33.

42 *Id.*

43 *Legal Maze Over Scud Seizure: Spain Acted on a Tip-off from US Intelligence*, BBC News World Edition Online, Dec. 11, 2002, http://news.bbc.co.uk/2/hi/middle_east/2565905.stm [hereinafter *Legal Maze*].

Despite some international criticism,[44] the *So San* interdiction was an example of successful multinational cooperation.[45] Those who criticized the legality of the *So San* boarding were uninformed. A warship of any state, including that of Spain or the United States, is justified as a matter of international law to stop and board a foreign ship, other than a ship entitled to "complete immunity," when there are reasonable grounds for suspecting it is without nationality, i.e., it is not flying or refusing to show its flag.[46] This unprecedented seizure dramatically underscored "Washington's new emphasis on using preemptive means to stop the spread of weapons of mass destruction" and was the first time a DPRK vessel was caught red-handed with shipboard documents that were clearly false.[47]

The *So San* interdiction was lawful, but the missiles and other items of concern were released. The release resulted after boarding officials found that the items of concern were intended for Yemen, which had the lawful authority to receive that cargo. However, this interdiction highlighted that had the cargo been bound for either a state or a non-state actor that sponsored terrorism; for example, it was unclear whether any international legal authority short of self-defense would authorize the seizure of the cargo. Thus, the *So San* interdiction underscored the shortcomings of international law as a unified legal framework for combating global WMD proliferation and emphasized the importance of national laws and multinational cooperation. Accordingly, the *So San* interdiction became the catalyst for the creation of the Proliferation Security Initiative.[48]

---

44 *See, e.g.*, Reynolds, *supra* note 37 (calling the *So San* interdiction a "tremendous blunder" that was "ludicrous. . . . You don't seize a ship, which is an act of war, unless you are prepared to stick to your guns—and they did not."). *Id.*; *Legal Maze*, *supra* note 43 (calling the *So San* interdiction "very much in a grey area" of international law).

45 Childs, *supra* note 30.

46 *See* United Nations Convention on the Law of the Sea art. 110, Dec. 10, 1982, 1833 U.N.T.S. 397 [hereinafter LOS Convention]. Thus, the boarding of the *So San* was neither an "act of war" nor a "grey area" of international law. For a searchable full text of the LOS Convention, see General Counsel of the National Oceanic and Atmospheric Administration, http://www.gc.no aa.gov/unclos.pdf (last visited Feb. 15, 2007). For further details, the full text of the LOS Convention, and a list of States that are parties to it, see Oceans and Law of the Sea, Division for Ocean Affairs and the Law of the Sea, http://www.un.org/Depts/los/index.htm. The United States is not a party to the LOS Convention; however, it takes the position that the LOS Convention "contains provisions with respect to traditional uses of the oceans which generally confirm existing maritime law and practice and fairly balance the interests of all states." Statement on United States Oceans Policy, 1 Pub. Papers 378–79, 379 (Mar. 10, 1983). Foreign warships, and ships owned or operated by a foreign state and used only on government non-commercial service are entitled to "complete immunity." LOS Convention, *supra* note 46, at arts. 95–96.

47 Marquand & Ford, *supra* note 25.

48 *See* David Munns, *Proliferation Security Initiative Seen as Start to Curbing Trade in Weapons of Mass Destruction*, 47 Sea Power (Nov. 2004), *available at* http://www.findarticles.com /p/articles/mi_qa3738/is_200411/ai_n9462526.

B. The Tenets of PSI

On May 31, 2003 in Krakow, Poland, less than six months after the *So San* interdiction, President Bush announced a new effort called the Proliferation Security Initiative (PSI). The PSI strengthens the means and authority of the international community to seize WMD and their components while in transit.[49] President Bush called upon America's G8 partners to help start this initiative, and he envisioned that it would be extended as broadly as possible over time.[50] On September 4, 2003, in Paris, France, eleven states adopted the PSI Statement of Interdiction Principles.[51] In announcing the adoption of these principles, the United States described PSI as a

> broad international partnership of countries which, using their own laws and resources, will coordinate their actions to halt shipments of dangerous technologies to and from states and non-state actors of proliferation concern—at sea, in the air, and on land. The PSI will reinforce, not replace, other nonproliferation mechanisms.[52]

The United States has also described PSI as a "part of a cooperative international counterproliferation effort intended to apply intelligence, diplomatic, law enforcement, military, and other tools at our disposal to prevent transfers of WMD-related items to states and non-state actors of proliferation concern."[53] On the first anniversary of PSI, more than sixty states had announced publicly their commitment to the

---

49 Press Release, White House, Remarks by the President to the People of Poland (May 31, 2003), http://www.whitehouse.gov/news/releases/2003/05/20030531-3.html [hereinafter Poland Press Release]. For more details concerning U.S. strategies to combat WMD proliferation and terrorism, see White House, National Strategy to Combat Weapons of Mass Destruction, *supra* note 14; White House, National Military Strategy to Combat Weapons of Mass Destruction, *supra* note 14; White House, National Strategy for Combating Terrorism (Sept. 2006), http://www.whitehouse.gov/nsc/nsct/ 2006/nsct2006.pdf; White House, National Strategy for Maritime Security (Sept. 2005), http://www.whitehouse.gov/homeland/4844-nsms.pdf.

50 Poland Press Release, *supra* note 49. The Group of Eight (G8) formed in 1975 to discuss economic problems of the day but has broadened its charter to include other important global issues such as climate change and HIV/AIDS. The G8 does not have a fixed structure or a permanent administration; it is organized and hosted by the G8 Member State that has the Presidency, which rotates annually. The G8 includes Canada, France, Italy, Japan, Germany, Russia, the United Kingdom, and the United States, as well as representation from the European Commission. *See* Germany 2007—Presidency of the European Union, http://www.eu2007.de/en/ (last visited Mar. 4, 2007).

51 Press Release, White House, Statement on Proliferation Security Initiative (Sept. 4, 2003), http://www.whitehouse.gov/news/releases/2003/09/20030904-10.html. These eleven founding PSI members are: Australia, France, Germany, Italy, Japan, The Netherlands, Poland, Portugal, Spain, the United Kingdom, and the United States. *Id.*

52 *Id.*

53 U.S. Dep't of State, Bureau of Nonproliferation, The Proliferation Security Initiative (May 2005), http://usinfo.state.gov/is/img/assets/4756/brochure1.pdf.

PSI Statement of Interdiction Principles,[54] and on its third anniversary, more than seventy states had announced their commitment.[55] As of November 2006, eighty states had committed to these principles.[56]

The PSI Statement of Interdiction Principles provides that PSI "is a response to the growing challenge posed by the proliferation of weapons of mass destruction (WMD), their delivery systems, and related materials worldwide."[57] PSI "seeks to involve in some capacity all states that have a stake in nonproliferation and the ability and willingness to take steps to stop the flow of such items at sea, in the air, or on land."[58] PSI also "seeks cooperation from any state whose vessels, flags, ports, territorial waters, airspace, or land might be used for proliferation purposes by states and non-state actors of proliferation concern."[59]

The PSI Statement of Interdiction Principles is provided verbatim at Annex A to this Article for easy reference. Careful study of these principles reveals how

---

54 Press Release, White House, Statement on First Anniversary Meeting of the Proliferation Security Initiative (June 1, 2004), http://www.whitehouse.gov/news/releases/ 2004/06/ 20040601-9.html.

55 Press Release, White House, President's Statement on Proliferation Security Initiative (June 23, 2006), http://www.whitehouse.gov/news/releases/2006/06/20060623.html.

56 United States Mission to the United Nations in Geneva, Daily Bulletin 3 (Nov. 16, 2006), *available at* http://www.usmission.ch/DailyBulletin/2006/November/1116.pdf. Other detailed introductions and discussions of PSI include, for example, Center for International Trade and Security, The Monitor, Vol. 10, No. 1 (2004) (an issue dedicated to PSI authored by U.S., Chinese, and Japanese academics and government employees that provides an excellent introduction and overview of PSI), http://www.uga.edu/cits/documents/pdf/monitor/ monitor_sp_2004.pdf; Herbert N. Warden IV, Overcoming Challenges to the Proliferation Security Initiative (Sept. 2004) (unpublished Masters dissertation, Naval Postgraduate School), http://www.fas.org/man/eprint/warden.pdf (analyzing the "serious legal, intelligence, and operational challenges to [the] sustained effectiveness" of PSI); Douglas Guilfoyle, *The Proliferation Security Initiative: Interdicting Vessels in International Waters to Prevent the Spread of Weapons of Mass Destruction?*, 29 Melb. U.L. Rev. 733 (2005), *available at* http://austlii.law. uts.edu.au/au/jour nals/MULR/2005/23.html#Heading13 ("[I]nsofar as the 'War on Terror' is a conflict with ascertained non-state actors, the law of belligerent contraband could allow high seas interdiction of weapons shipments bound for organizations such as al-Qa'eda.").

57 Proliferation Security Initiative, Statement of Interdiction Principles (Sept. 4, 2003), http:// www.proliferationsecurity.info/principles.html [hereinafter PSI Statement of Interdiction Principles]. This webpage is maintained by the government of Canada. The PSI Statement of Interdiction Principles, as well as additional detailed information about PSI, may also be found at U.S. Dep't of State, Proliferation Security Initiative, http://www.state.gov/t/isn/c10390.htm (last visited Mar. 4, 2007). The Government of Australia has two PSI websites: Australian Government, Department of Foreign Affairs and Trade, Proliferation Security Initiative, http://www.dfat.gov.au/globalissues/psi/ (last visited Mar. 4, 2007); and Department of Defence, Proliferation Security Initiative, http://www.defence.gov.au/PSI/default.htm (last visited Mar. 4, 2007).

58 PSI Statement of Interdiction Principles, *supra* note 57.

59 *Id.*

PSI works both to combat global WMD proliferation and to determine what international and national laws and frameworks may apply to any given situation.[60] For example, PSI is not an organization; it is an activity that facilitates cooperation and coordination among states.[61] PSI is not legally binding; it is a political commitment by like-minded states to work together. States may declare their commitment to the PSI Statement of Interdiction Principles either orally or in writing. PSI does not create any new law or legal authorities; all PSI activities must be "consistent with national legal authorities and relevant international law and frameworks."[62]

III. PSI ACTIVITIES: A FRAMEWORK FOR COORDINATING AND LEVERAGING

The greatest value of PSI is captured in the first sentence of the PSI Statement of Interdiction Principles: PSI participant states declare their commitment to build on existing efforts and to "*establish a more coordinated and effective basis* through which to impede and stop shipments of WMD, delivery systems, and related materials flowing to and from states and non-state actors of proliferation concern."[63] PSI activities bring states together in administrative and operational environments to learn how to harmonize and improve their national legal authorities and relevant international law and frameworks so that they work together more effectively to combat global WMD terrorism. States learn through PSI conferences, exercises, and real-world interdictions how to share information, communicate more effectively, and improve their national legal authorities and operational capabilities.

In very simple terms, the PSI Statement of Interdiction Principles encourages states to talk to each other, to develop processes and procedures that facilitate them working together efficiently and effectively, and to strengthen their own national laws to combat global WMD terrorism. Specifically, PSI participating states announce they are committed to four central principles.

First, PSI participant states commit to "undertake effective measures, either alone or in concert with other states, for interdicting the transfer or transport of WMD, their delivery systems, and related materials to and from states and non-state actors

60 Both the official PSI and U.S. Department of State websites have a series of "Frequently Asked Questions (FAQ)" that help clarify the nature of PSI. These FAQs may be found at Proliferation Security Initiative, Frequently Asked Questions, http://www.proliferationsecurity.info/faq.html (last visited Mar. 4, 2007); and U.S. Dep't of State, Proliferation Security Initiative Frequently Asked Questions (FAQ), http://www.state.gov/t/isn/rls/fs/46839.htm (last visited Mar. 4, 2007).

61 U.S. Dep't of State, Proliferation Security Initiative Frequently Asked Questions (FAQ), *supra* note 60.

62 PSI Statement of Interdiction Principles, *supra* note 57.

63 *Id.* (emphasis added).

of proliferation concern."[64] The PSI Statement of Interdiction Principles defines "states and non-state actors of proliferation concern" generally as

> those countries or entities that the PSI participants involved establish should be subject to interdiction activities because they are engaged in proliferation through: (a) efforts to develop or acquire chemical, biological, or nuclear weapons and associated delivery systems; or (b) transfers (either selling, receiving, or facilitating) of WMD, their delivery systems, or related materials.[65]

The PSI Statement of Interdiction Principles does not identify any state or non-state actor of proliferation concern. However, the U.S. Department of State has designated Cuba, Iran, DPRK, Sudan, and Syria as state sponsors of terrorism,[66] and it has designated forty-two foreign organizations as Foreign Terrorist Organizations (FTOs).[67] Additionally, Executive Order (EO) 13382 designated eight DPRK, Iranian, and Syrian entities that the United States believes to be contributing to WMD proliferation and authorizes the U.S. Department of Treasury to freeze any assets those entities and members of their support networks may have under U.S. jurisdiction.[68] Pursuant to its authority granted in EO 13382, the U.S. Department of Treasury has also designated twenty-five additional Iranian, DPRK, Syrian, and Chinese organizations suspected of contributing to WMD proliferation and subject to sanctions.[69] The U.N. Security Council has noted "with concern the close connection between international terrorism and . . . illegal arms-trafficking, and [the] illegal movement of nuclear, chemical, biological and other potentially deadly materials."[70] Accordingly, those state sponsors of terrorism, FTOs, and organizations suspected of contributing to WMD proliferation identified by the U.S. Departments of State and Treasury can certainly be considered as states and non-state actors of proliferation concern. The U.N. Security Council has also clearly identified DPRK as a state of proliferation concern[71] and declared that it is "[*c*]*oncerned* by the proliferation risks presented by the Iranian nuclear programme."[72]

---

64 *Id.*

65 *Id.*

66 U.S. Dep't of State, State Sponsors of Terrorism (2006), http://www.state.gov/s/ct/c14151.htm.

67 U.S. Dep't of State, Fact Sheet, Foreign Terrorist Organizations (Oct. 2005), http://www.state.gov/s/ct/rls/fs/37191.htm. This fact sheet lists the forty-two FTOs by name, details the legal ramifications and other effects of designation, and defines terrorism, terrorist organization, and terrorist activity. *Id.*

68 Exec. Ord. No. 13,382, 3 C.F.R. 170 (2005), *available at* http://www.access.gpo.gov/nara/cfr/waisidx_06/exec_06.html.

69 U.S. Dep't of Treasury, Nonproliferation: What You Need to Know About Treasury Restrictions (Jan. 9, 2007), http://www.ustreas.gov/offices/enforcement/ofac/programs/wmd/wmd.pdf.

70 S.C. Res. 1373, ¶ 4, U.N. Doc. S/RES/1373 (Sept. 28, 2001).

71 *See* S.C. Res. 1718, pmbl., U.N. Doc. S/RES/1718 (Oct. 14, 2006).

72 S.C. Res. 1737, pmbl., U.N. Doc. S/RES/1737 (Dec. 23, 2006).

Second, PSI participant states commit to "[a]dopt streamlined procedures for rapid exchange of relevant information concerning suspected proliferation activity . . ., dedicate appropriate resources and efforts to interdiction operations and capabilities, and maximize coordination among participants in interdiction efforts."[73] For example, the United States currently has bilateral ship boarding agreements with Belize, Croatia, Cyprus, Liberia, the Marshall Islands, and Panama.[74] These six agreements are "tangible examples of nonproliferation cooperation" that "facilitate bilateral cooperation . . . in international waters."[75] These agreements establish procedures for one party to request of the other confirmation of the "nationality of the ship in question and, if needed, authorize the boarding, search, and possible detention of the vessel and cargo."[76]

Third, PSI participant states commit to review and work to strengthen their relevant national legal authorities, as well as international laws and frameworks where necessary.[77] The participants accomplish this through many PSI activities, including those of the PSI Operational Experts Group (OEG), which is an "expanding network of military, law enforcement, intelligence, legal, and diplomatic expertise . . . [that meets] periodically to develop new operational concepts, organize an interdiction exercise program, share information about national legal authorities, and pursue cooperation with key industry sectors."[78] Sharing information about national legal authorities has been an extremely useful tool in facilitating intra-governmental and inter-governmental coordination. For example, through PSI information sharing and activities, agencies in a government are now working with other agencies in the same government when previously they had no reason to coordinate with them. The PSI OEG has met fourteen times between July 9, 2003 and December 5, 2006.[79] Currently, there are twenty PSI participant states that serve as members of the OEG.

Fourth, PSI participant states commit to take "specific actions in support of PSI interdiction efforts . . . to the extent their national legal authorities permit and consistent with their obligations under international law and frameworks."[80] By way of example, the PSI Statement of Interdiction Principles lists six such specific actions:

> a) Not to transport or assist in the transport of any such cargoes to or from states or non-state actors of proliferation concern, and not to allow any persons subject to their jurisdiction to do so.

---

73 PSI Statement of Interdiction Principles, *supra* note 57, ¶ 2.

74 U.S. Dep't of State, PSI Ship Boarding Agreements, http://www.state.gov/t/np/c12386.htm. Copies of these ship boarding agreements are also available at this website.

75 *Id.*

76 *Id.*

77 PSI Statement of Interdiction Principles, *supra* note 57.

78 The Proliferation Security Initiative, *supra* note 53.

79 U.S. Dep't of St., PSI Calendar of Events, http://www.state.gov/t/isn/c12684.htm (last visited Apr. 8, 2007).

80 PSI Statement of Interdiction Principles, *supra* note 57, ¶ 4.

b) At their own initiative, or at the request and good cause shown by another state, to take action to board and search any vessel flying their flag in their internal waters or territorial seas, or areas beyond the territorial seas of any other state that is reasonably suspected of transporting such cargoes to or from states or non-state actors of proliferation concerns, and to seize such cargoes that are identified.

c) To seriously consider providing consent under appropriate circumstances to the boarding and searching of its own flag vessels by other states and to the seizure of such WMD-related cargoes in such vessels that may be identified by such states.

d) To take appropriate actions to (1) stop and/or search in their internal waters, territorial seas, or contiguous zones (when declared) vessels that are reasonably suspected of carrying such cargoes to or from states or non-state actors of proliferation concern and to seize such cargoes that are identified; and (2) enforce conditions on vessels entering or leaving their ports, internal waters, or territorial seas that are reasonably suspected of carrying such cargoes, such as requiring that such vessels be subject to boarding, search, and seizure of such cargoes prior to entry.

e) At their own initiative or upon the request and good cause shown by another state, to (1) require aircraft that are reasonably suspected of carrying such cargoes to or from states or non-state actors of proliferation concern and that are transiting their airspace to land for inspection and seize any such cargoes that are identified; and/or (2) deny aircraft reasonably suspected of carrying such cargoes transit rights through their airspace in advance of such flights.

f) If their ports, airfields, or other facilities are used as transshipment points for shipment of such cargoes to or from states or non-state actors of proliferation concern, to inspect vessels, aircraft, or other modes of transport reasonably suspected of carrying such cargoes, and to seize such cargoes that are identified.[81]

PSI participant states also call upon all other states concerned with the threat of WMD terrorism to commit to these same principles.[82]

PSI participant states have been engaged actively in exercises to prepare for specific actions in support of PSI interdiction efforts. For example, PSI participant states completed twenty-five ground, maritime, and air exercises from September 10, 2003 through October 31, 2006.[83] These exercises were led by Australia, the United Kingdom, Spain, France, the United States, Italy, Germany, Poland, Japan, Portugal, the Czech Republic, Singapore, Norway, the Netherlands, and Turkey.[84] PSI participant states have also completed three major workshops that focused on shipping container security, the air cargo industry, and the maritime industry.[85] In 2007, New Zealand is planning to host an OEG meeting, the United Kingdom

81 *Id.*

82 *Id.*

83 PSI Calendar of Events, *supra* note 79.

84 *Id.*

85 *Id.*

is planning to lead a major exercise in the Mediterranean, and the United States is planning to host a proliferation finance workshop and a PSI gaming exercise.[86] New Zealand and Singapore are also planning a major PSI exercise in 2008 and 2009, respectively.[87] Operationally, PSI successes "cannot all speak for themselves, since the details often involve sensitive intelligence matters;" however, during the first nine months after the PSI Statement of Interdiction Principles was adopted, PSI participant states were involved in eleven successful efforts.[88]

U.N. Security Council Resolution 1540 does not mention PSI, but it is so similar to the PSI construct that it is frequently thought of as the Security Council's PSI resolution. In many respects, this resolution fundamentally adopts the PSI Statement of Interdiction Principles. However, in contrast to the voluntary nature of the political commitments of PSI, U.N. Security Council Resolution 1540, under Chapter VII authority, requires all U.N. Member States to refrain from providing support to non-state actors attempting to "develop, acquire, manufacture, possess, transport, transfer or use nuclear, chemical or biological weapons and their means of delivery."[89] All Member States are also required to prohibit such actions by non-state actors and to take and enforce effective measures to prevent such actions.[90] Security Council Resolution 1540 also calls upon all Member States "in accordance with their national legal authorities and legislation and consistent with international law, to take cooperative action to prevent illicit trafficking in nuclear, chemical or biological weapons, their means of delivery, and related materials."[91] PSI is a "positive way to take such cooperative action."[92]

IV. EXISTING LAW AND FRAMEWORKS: THE UNDERPINNINGS OF PSI

A. Peacetime Regime

A fundamental requirement for all PSI activities is that they must be conducted "consistent with national legal authorities and relevant international law and frameworks."[93] Indeed, PSI *exclusively relies upon* national legal authorities and international law for authority to conduct all of its activities. This section discusses national legal authorities, international law, and international frameworks applicable

86 *Id.*

87 *Id.*

88 The *Proliferation Security Initiative (PSI): A Record of Success*, Testimony of Stephen G. Rademaker, Assistant Sec'y of State for Arms Control, Before the H. Int'l Rel. Comm., Subcomm. On Int'l Terrorism and Nonproliferation, 109th Cong. (June 9, 2005), *available at* http://www.state.gov/t/ac/rls/rm/47715.htm.

89 S.C. Res. 1540, *supra* note 2.

90 *Id.*

91 *Id.*

92 The Proliferation Security Initiative, *supra* note 53.

93 PSI Statement of Interdiction Principles, *supra* note 57.

to the PSI context. It is also very important to note, however, that PSI is a peacetime construct. Accordingly, this article does not address those additional legal authorities available under the law of armed conflict or the law of neutrality that may authorize interdiction operations of belligerent and neutral ships and aircraft.

B. National Legal Authorities

National legal authorities such as domestic import and export laws, customs, anti-smuggling, counternarcotics, fiscal, safety, and environmental laws and regulations are legally binding on a state's citizens and those within its territory and jurisdiction who do not otherwise enjoy sovereign immunity. The jurisdiction of national legal authorities may also reach beyond a state's territory, and may authorize, for example, the search and seizure on the high seas of a ship flying its flag, or of that ship's cargo. States may also authorize another state to enforce their national legal authorities on their behalf. States may enact national legal authorities on their own initiative to address domestic concerns, or may enact these authorities in response to an international legal or political obligation. Additionally, the domestic law of a state may permit an international treaty to which it is a party to be self-executing.

C. International Law

International law consists of written agreements between states—referred to as treaties or conventions—and customary law as developed and recognized through state practice and acceptance. International agreements relevant in the PSI context, such as the 1968 Treaty on the Non-Proliferation of Nuclear Weapons (NPT),[94] the 1972 Biological and Toxin Weapons Convention (BWC),[95] the 1993 Chemical Weapons Convention (CWC),[96] the 1982 U.N. Convention on the Law of the Sea (LOS),[97] and the 1988 Convention for the Suppression of Unlawful Acts against the Safety of Maritime Navigation (SUA),[98] are legally binding on state parties.

The objectives of the NPT are to "prevent the spread of nuclear weapons and weapons technology, to foster the peaceful uses of nuclear energy, and to further the goal

94 Treaty on the Non-Proliferation of Nuclear Weapons, July 1, 1968, 21 U.S.T. 483, 729 U.N.T.S. 161.

95 Convention on the Prohibition of the Development, Production and Stockpiling of Bacteriological (Biological) and Toxin Weapons and on Their Destruction (BWC), Apr. 10, 1972, 26 U.S.T. 583, 1015 U.N.T.S. 163 [hereinafter BWC].

96 Convention on the Prohibition of the Development, Production, Stockpiling and Use of Chemical Weapons and on their Destruction (CWC), Jan. 13, 1993, 32 I.L.M. 800, 1974 U.N.T.S. 317.

97 LOS Convention, *supra* note 46.

98 Convention for the Suppression of Unlawful Acts against the Safety of Maritime Navigation (SUA), Mar. 10, 1988, 27 I.L.M. 668, 1678 U.N.T.S. 221.

of achieving general and complete disarmament."[99] The NPT has been "remarkably successful in achieving its main goals and—with nearly 190 parties—has become the most widely-adhered to arms control treaty in history" and serves as "an indispensable tool in preventing the spread of nuclear weapons."[100] NPT State Parties undertake a number of very specific obligations that impose political and legal barriers to the proliferation of nuclear weapons, and the International Atomic Energy Agency (IAEA) "is the primary mechanism for verifying that parties to the NPT are complying with its terms."[101] However, the NPT does not authorize any enforcement measures under international law for violations of its obligations.

The BWC "bans the development, production, stockpiling, acquisition and retention of microbial or other biological agents or toxins, in types and in quantities that have no justification for prophylactic, protective or other peaceful purposes."[102] The BWC also "bans weapons, equipment or means of delivery designed to use such agents or toxins for hostile purposes or in armed conflict."[103] There are currently 144 State Parties.[104] Article VI of the BWC provides that any "State Party to this Convention which finds that any other State Party is acting in breach of obligations deriving from the provisions of the Convention may lodge a complaint with the Security Council of the United Nations."[105] However, the BWC does not authorize any enforcement measures under international law for violations of its obligations.

The CWC "bans the development, production, stockpiling, transfer and use of chemical weapons, and also stipulates their timely destruction."[106] It also "mandated the Organisation for the Prohibition of Chemical Weapons (OPCW) to eliminate the scourge of chemical weapons forever and to verify the destruction of the declared chemical weapons stockpiles within stipulated deadlines."[107] All 181 CWC Member States are obligated to implement the provisions of the CWC at

99 International Atomic Energy Agency (IAEA), International Conventions and Agreements, http://www.iaea.org/Publications/Documents/Treaties/npt.html (last visited Feb. 13, 2007). For further details and the full text of the NPT, see *id.*

100 U.S. Dep't of State, Treaty on the Non-Proliferation of Nuclear Weapons, http://www.state.gov /t/isn/trty/16281.htm (last visited Feb. 13, 2007).

101 *Id.*

102 Biological and Toxin Weapons Convention, About the Biological and Toxin Weapons Convention, http://www.opbw.org/.

103 *Id.*

104 *Id.*

105 BWC, *supra* note 95, at art. VI(1).

106 Organisation for the Prohibition of Chemical Weapons, The Chemical Weapons Ban: Facts and Figures, http://www.opcw.org/factsandfigures/index.html (last visited Apr. 8, 2007).

107 *Id.*

the national level, and to criminalize prohibited activities.[108] However, the CWC does not authorize any enforcement measures under international law for violations of its obligations.

The purpose of the LOS Convention was to establish a comprehensive regime dealing with "all issues relating to the law of the sea."[109] The LOS Convention does provide states limited authority to exercise jurisdiction over foreign ships not entitled to sovereign immunity (this authority is discussed in Part V.B., *infra*). The LOS Convention is not, however, an exclusive set of authorities that governs maritime interdictions. The preamble of the LOS Convention specifically provides that "matters not regulated by this Convention continue to be governed by the rules and principles of general international law."[110]

The main purpose of SUA is to "ensure that appropriate action is taken against persons committing unlawful acts against ships . . . [that] include the seizure of ships by force; acts of violence against persons on board ships; and the placing of devices on board a ship which are likely to destroy or damage it."[111] SUA also obligates its 142 State Parties either to "extradite or prosecute alleged offenders."[112] However, SUA does not authorize any enforcement measures under international law for violations of its obligations.

Some international agreements also reflect or codify customary international law, and to the extent that they do so, are binding as such on all states. For example, the United States is not a party[113] to the LOS Convention; however, the United States takes the position that the LOS Convention "contains provisions with respect to traditional uses of the oceans which generally confirm existing maritime law and practice and fairly balance the interests of all states."[114] Under Article 110 of the LOS Convention and customary law, a state has the peacetime right of approach and visit for their warships to stop and board a commercial ship on the high seas when there are reasonable grounds for suspecting that it is engaged in piracy, the slave trade, unauthorized broadcasting, or that it is stateless or flying their flag. This right of approach and visit, however, only permits a warship to stop, board,

108 *Id.* For details of U.S. implementation of its obligations under the CWC, see the United States Chemical Weapons Convention Web Site, http://www.cwc.gov/ (last visited Mar. 4, 2007).

109 LOS Convention, *supra* note 46, pmbl.

110 *Id.*

111 International Maritime Organization (IMO), Convention for the Suppression of Unlawful Acts Against the Safety of Maritime Navigation, 1988, Convention Aims, http://www.imo.org /Conventions/mainframe.asp?topic_id=259&doc_id=686 (last visited Mar. 4, 2007).

112 *Id.*

113 United Nations, United Nations Convention on the Law of the Sea: Status (May 12, 2006), http://www.un.org/Depts/los/convention_agreements/convention_agreements.htm (follow the "Chronological list of ratifications/accessions/successions" hyperlink).

114 Statement on United States Oceans Policy, 1 Pub. Papers 378, 379 (Mar. 10, 1983).

and examine the documents of the ship. It does not authorize the warship to search for WMD, their delivery systems, or related materials.

Article 2(4) of the Charter of the United Nations provides that all "Members shall refrain in their international relations from the *threat or use of force* against the territorial integrity or political independence of any state, or in any other manner inconsistent with the Purposes of the United Nations."[115] Although Article 2(4) restricts a state's right to threaten or use force, Article 51 of the Charter recognizes the "inherent right of individual or collective self-defense" of all states found in customary international law, and specifically provides that nothing in the Charter shall impair that right.[116] For example, a state may stop, board, and inspect any ship or aircraft, and arrest or seize any persons or cargo (such as WMD, their delivery systems, and related materials) in the exercise of that state's inherent right of individual or collective self-defense. The Charter, however, does not define when a state may exercise its right of self-defense. Accordingly, a determination of when a situation involving WMD proliferation gives rise to a state's legitimate exercise of its inherent right of self-defense is a question of fact and law that must be subjectively analyzed in each and every case.

International law may give a state the right to inspect or search, but rarely any broad authority to seize items that may be otherwise condemned or prohibited by international law. Usually, international laws and U.N. Security Council resolutions that condemn or prohibit an activity, such as the proliferation of WMD, also incorporate an implicit or explicit corresponding political or legal obligation for states to prohibit or prevent that activity under national legal authorities. This can be seen in the above discussions of the NPT, BWC, CWC, and of the right of approach and visit consistent with the LOS Convention. Another example is provided by U.N. Security Council Resolution 1540, which requires all U.N. Member States to refrain from providing support to non-state actors attempting to "develop, acquire, manufacture, possess, transport, transfer or use nuclear, chemical or biological weapons and their means of delivery," but does not authorize any enforcement measures.[117] In Operative Paragraph 2, however, Resolution 1540 requires that all states "adopt and enforce appropriate effective laws" to implement its prohibitions.[118] Although it has not yet exercised its authority to do so, the Security Council clearly has the authority under Chapter VII of the Charter to authorize broadly the search

---

115 U.N. Charter art. 2(4) (emphasis added).

116 U.N. Charter art. 51, which provides "Nothing in the present Charter shall impair the inherent right of individual or collective self-defense if an armed attack occurs against a Member of the United Nations, until the Security Council has taken the measures necessary to maintain international peace and security." *See* JOHN NORTON MOORE & ROBERT F. TURNER, NATIONAL SECURITY LAW 72 (2d ed. 2005) (the Article 51 defensive right is "coextensive with the pre-Charter right of self-defense, that is, as an inherent or natural right of defense.").

117 S.C. Res. 1540, *supra* note 2, at pmbl.

118 *Id.* at para. 2.

and seizure of items prohibited under international law such as WMD, their delivery systems, and related materials.

D. International Frameworks

International frameworks relevant in the PSI context such as the 1978 Nuclear Suppliers Group (NSG),[119] the 1985 Australia Group (AG),[120] the 1987 Missile Technology Control Regime (MTCR),[121] and the 1995 Wassenaar Arrangement (WA),[122] are politically binding commitments agreed upon by states that set forth guidelines, criteria, or standards to meet common objectives or purposes. International frameworks offer no legal authority to search for or seize items otherwise prohibited by law. Similar to international law, however, frameworks may also incorporate an implicit or explicit corresponding political obligation for states to prohibit or prevent a prohibited activity under national legal authorities.

The NSG is a "group of [forty-five] nuclear supplier countries which seeks to contribute to the non-proliferation of nuclear weapons through the implementation of Guidelines for nuclear exports and nuclear related exports."[123] These guidelines are "implemented by each Participating Government in accordance with its national laws and practices" and decisions on "export applications are taken at the national level in accordance with national export licensing requirements."[124]

The AG is an "informal arrangement which aims to allow exporting or transshipping countries to minimise the risk of assisting chemical and biological weapon (CBW) proliferation."[125] AG participants have no legally binding obligations, and "the effectiveness of their cooperation depends solely on a shared commitment to CBW non-proliferation goals and the strength of their respective national measures."[126]

---

119 Int'l Atomic Energy Agency (IAEA), Information Circular: Communication of 29 April 1996 Received from Certain Member States Regarding Guidelines for the Export of Nuclear Material, Equipment or Technology, Document INFCIRC/254/Rev.2/Part 1/Add.1 (June 7, 1996), *available at* http://www.iaea.org/Publications/Documents/Infcircs/1996/inf254r2p1a1.shtml.

120 *See* The Australia Group, The Australia Group: An Introduction, http://www.australia group.net/en/intro.htm (last visited Mar. 4, 2007) [hereinafter The Australia Group: An Introduction].

121 *See* Missile Technology Control Regime (MTCR), Introduction, http://www.mtcr.info (last visited Feb. 13, 2007).

122 *See* Wassenaar Arrangement on Export Controls for Conventional Arms and Dual-Use Goods and Technologies (WA), http://www.wassenaar.org/introduction/index.html (last visited Feb. 13, 2007) [hereinafter Wassenaar Arrangement Website].

123 Nuclear Suppliers Group (NSG), http://www.nsg-online.org (last visited Feb. 13, 2007).

124 *Id.*

125 The Australia Group: An Introduction, *supra* note 120.

126 *Id.*

There are forty states, including the European Commission, participating in the AG, and they are all parties to the CWC and the BWC.[127]

The MTCR is an "informal and voluntary association of [thirty-four] countries which share the goals of non-proliferation of unmanned delivery systems capable of delivering weapons of mass destruction, and which seek to coordinate national export licensing efforts aimed at preventing their proliferation."[128] The success of the MTCR "rests on adherence to common export policy guidelines (the MTCR Guidelines) applied to an integral common list of controlled items (the MTCR Equipment, Software and Technology Annex)."[129] The MTCR Guidelines and Annex are available on the MTCR website.

The WA was "established in order to contribute to regional and international security and stability, by promoting transparency and greater responsibility in transfers of conventional arms and dual-use goods and technologies, thus preventing destabilising accumulations."[130] The forty Participating States utilize "their national policies, to ensure that transfers of these items do not contribute to the development or enhancement of military capabilities which undermine these goals, and are not diverted to support such capabilities."[131] Each Participating State has the "sole responsibility to transfer or deny [the] transfer of any item," and all implementing measures "are taken in accordance with national legislation and policies and are implemented on the basis of national discretion."[132]

PSI is itself an international framework, because it is a politically binding commitment agreed upon by states that sets forth guidelines, criteria, and standards in the form of principles to meet common objectives or purposes. It is not legally binding and provides no legal authority to achieve its purposes. The NSG, AG, MTCR, and WA provide independent but complementary international frameworks for concerned states to reduce the proliferation of nuclear weapons; chemical and biological weapons; unmanned delivery systems capable of delivering WMD; and conventional arms and dual-use goods and technologies, respectively. Similarly, the NPT, BWC, and CWC are also independent but complementary treaties that serve to prevent the spread of nuclear weapons and nuclear weapons technology, biological agents and toxins, and chemical weapons, respectively. PSI, however, is the integrating framework that provides the forum and activities that bring all relevant international frameworks, international laws, and national laws together in a concerted effort to combat global WMD proliferation.

---

127 The Australia Group, Australia Group Participants, http://www.australiagroup.net/en/ intro.htm (last visited Mar. 4, 2007).

128 Missile Technology Control Regime (MTCR), *supra* note 121.

129 *Id.*

130 Wassenaar Arrangement Website, *supra* note 122.

131 *Id.*

132 *Id.*

V. PSI: AN INTERMODAL ANALYSIS

PSI participant states declare their commitment in the PSI Statement of Interdiction Principles to "establish a more coordinated and effective basis through which to impede and stop shipments of WMD, delivery systems, and related materials flowing to and from states and non-state actors of proliferation concern."[133] The commitment is to "impede and stop shipments," and this can be done through diplomatic, law enforcement, or military interdictions. These shipments may be interdicted on the ground, at sea, or in the air, but all three modes pose practical challenges that may vary dramatically from territory to territory. Hong Kong, for example, has only thirty kilometers of land boundary,[134] but, in 2002, had a maritime container throughput of more than 25,418 million cubic feet[135] and handled more than 2.35 million tons of air cargo.[136] In contrast, the challenge of interdicting items of WMD proliferation concern is very different for the thirty-one Landlocked Developing Countries (LLDCs) whose volume of trade may be minimal in comparison.[137] However, the challenge of maritime interdiction may be just as daunting. In 2006, the average container ship could carry about 6,600 twenty-foot containers,[138] and the world's largest container ship could carry about 11,000 twenty-foot containers.[139] Because of the size of modern container vessels, interdictions that require an inspection at sea can be extraordinarily difficult, if not simply impossible, and interdictions of aircraft are equally problematic because of the speed of modern aircraft and the lack of available decision and response times.

Where the interdiction of a vessel (ship or aircraft) suspected of carrying an item of WMD proliferation concern will take place depends upon a range of factors such as the available legal authorities, where that item is in transit when information or intelligence becomes available that it may be an item of concern, the scheduled transshipment points and destination of the vessel, the flag state of the vessel, the

133 PSI Statement of Interdiction Principles, *supra* note 57.

134 *See* Central Intelligence Agency, The World Factbook: Hong Kong, *available at* https://www.cia.gov/cia/publications/factbook/geos/hk.html.

135 *See* Legislative Council of Hong Kong, Official Record of Proceedings, at 486 (Oct. 16, 2002), http://www.legco.gov.hk/yr02-03/english/counmtg/hansard/cm1016ti-translate-e.pdf. The reference provides the number 18.69 Twenty-foot Equivalent Units (TEUs), which is a container that is 20'x8'x8.5'. This was converted to cubic feet for ease of comparison.

136 *Id.* at 378.

137 *See* U.N. Office of the High Representative for the Least Developed Countries, Landlocked Developing Countries and Small Island Developing States, List of Landlocked Developing Countries, http://www.un.org/special-rep/ohrlls/lldc/list.htm (last visited Mar. 4, 2007).

138 George Raine, *A Sea Change in Shipping: 50 Years Ago, Container Ships Altered the World*, San Francisco Chron., Feb. 5, 2006, http://www.sfgate.com/cgi-bin/article.cgi?f=/c/a/2006 /02/05/BUGG4H2FIB1.DTL&hw=container&sn=001&sc=1000.

139 A.P. Moller-Maersk Group, Fact Sheet on Emma Maerck, http://www.maersk.com/NR/rdonlyres/53C3A206-24BD-4290-9FE9-417971C4A710/0/EmmaMærskL203 FactSheetUK.pdf (last visited Mar. 4, 2007).

behavior of the vessel and its crew, the threat that the item poses to the vessel or coastal and destination states, and the availability of resources for the interception.

The following discussion provides an overview of the available legal authorities for potential ground, maritime, and air interdictions without an accompanying analysis of practical or political concerns. A single domestic law may be available to authorize the search, seizure, and disposition of an item of WMD proliferation concern on board a vessel in port. More often than not, however, states may need to rely upon a combination of these domestic and international legal authorities to conduct a successful interdiction. For example, a state may need to rely upon international law to board and inspect a vessel on the high seas, as with the *So San*, but then must rely upon a national authority to seize and dispose of an item of WMD proliferation concern.

A. Ground Interdictions

Ground interdictions rely very heavily, if not exclusively, upon national legal authorities, which are discussed generally in Part IV.B. These national legal authorities include domestic import and export laws, customs, anti-smuggling, counternarcotics, fiscal, safety, and environmental laws and regulations that are legally binding on a state's citizens and those within its territory and jurisdiction who do not otherwise enjoy sovereign immunity. To detail those domestic authorities for any one state is beyond the scope of this Article. However, excellent sources, such as the country reports required under U.N. Security Council Resolutions 1540 and 1718, are readily available and provide details about these national authorities in the PSI context for a large number of states.

Operative Paragraph 4 of U.N. Security Council Resolution 1540 calls upon states to report to the 1540 Committee, established to oversee the implementation of the resolution, "on steps they have taken or intend to take to implement this resolution."[140] As of February 27, 2007, 135 states had submitted such a report.[141] The 1540 Report of the United States, for example, provides a sixty page "comprehensive review of United States laws, policies, projects, and initiatives to prevent illicit trafficking in weapons of mass destruction, their delivery systems, and related materials, and in particular to prevent terrorist acquisition of such items."[142] Because Security Council Resolution 1540 is so similar to the PSI construct and fundamentally adopts the PSI Statement of Interdiction Principles, an analysis of these 1540 Reports provides a revealing overview of how well states are prepared to fulfill

140 S.C. Res. 1540, *supra* note 2.

141 1540 Committee, List of Submitting Member States as of 27 February 2007, http://disarmament2.un.org/Committee1540/report.html.

142 Letter from the Deputy Permanent Representative of the United States of America to the United Nations Chairman of the Security Council Committee, S/AC.44/2004/(02)/5 (Oct. 14, 2004), *available at* http://daccessdds.un.org/doc/UNDOC/GEN/N04/561/49/PDF/N0456149.pdf? OpenElement.

PSI commitments. For those states that need to strengthen their national legal authorities, these 1540 Reports are excellent examples for modeling purposes.

Similarly, Operative Paragraph 11 of U.N. Security Council Resolution 1718 calls upon states to report to the Security Council "on the steps they have taken with a view to implementing effectively the provisions of paragraph 8."[143] Security Council Resolution 1718 was adopted in response to the "nuclear test proclaimed by the DPRK on 9 October 2006,"[144] and it imposed a number of political and legal obligations on all Member States of the United Nations in Operative Paragraph 8.[145] As of January 19, 2007, forty-four states had submitted such a report.[146] The 1718 Report of the United States, for example, provides a seven-page report that details the steps taken by the United States to implement the sanctions against the DPRK imposed by Resolution 1718.[147] Although there is certainly an overlap in the national legal authorities reported in the 1540 and 1718 Reports, an analysis of the 1718 reports will provide a clearer picture of how national legal authorities can be utilized to combat WMD proliferation.

B. Maritime Interdictions

The LOS Convention recognizes the breadth of the sovereignty of states and delineates a number of maritime zones that extend from the land territory of a state outward to the high seas. Article 2(1) provides that the "sovereignty of a coastal State extends, beyond its land territory and internal waters and, in the case of an archipelagic State, its archipelagic waters, to an adjacent belt of sea described as the territorial sea."[148] However, the sovereignty of a coastal state over its territorial sea is "exercised subject to this Convention [the LOS Convention] and to other rules of international law."[149] The territorial sea may extend up to a limit not exceeding twelve nautical miles, measured from baselines determined in accordance with the LOS Convention.[150] Beyond and adjacent to the territorial sea, a state may claim a contiguous zone up to a limit not exceeding twenty-four nautical miles, measured

143 S.C. Res. 1718, *supra* note 71, ¶ 11.

144 *Id.* ¶ 1.

145 *Id.* ¶ 8.

146 The U.N. Security Council does not have a S.C. Res. 1718 website created as of the writing of this article; however, these reports are available at United Nations, Official Document System of the United Nations, http://documents.un.org/default.asp (follow "Welcome" hyperlink; follow "Simple Search" Hyperlink; enter "S/AC.49/2006/*" in the "Symbol" field, and click on "Search").

147 Letter from the Permanent Representative of the United States of America to the United Nations Chairman of the Security Council Committee, S/AC.49/2006/11 (Nov. 30, 2006), *available at* http://documents-dds-ny.un.org/doc/UNDOC/GEN/N06/636/57/img/N0663657.pdf? OpenElement.

148 LOS Convention, *supra* note 46, at art. 2(1).

149 *Id.* at art. 2(3).

150 *Id.* at art. 3.

from the same baselines from which the territorial sea is measured.[151] Beyond and adjacent to the territorial sea, a state may also claim an exclusive economic zone up to a limit not exceeding 200 nautical miles, measured from the same baselines from which the territorial sea is measured.[152] Not all states claim the maximum breadth of these zones as permitted by the LOS Convention.[153]

As a foreign ship moves from portside through the territorial sea, the contiguous zone, and the exclusive economic zone onto the high seas, a coastal state's sovereignty—that is, its right to exercise jurisdiction—over that ship decreases. This regime balances the sovereign rights of a coastal state with the freedom of the high seas accorded to all states.[154] As an exercise of its sovereignty, a coastal state may place conditions (such as an inspection by the coastal state on the high seas of the ship or its cargo) upon ship entry into their ports or territory prior to arrival in port. A coastal state may also condition the provision of any or all services (such as bunkering, supply, and repairs) in its territorial sea upon prior inspection of the ship or its cargo by the coastal state. A state always retains jurisdiction over all ships flying its own flag, wherever located, and may grant consent to another state to inspect any ship flying its flag, or may grant consent to another state to exercise the law enforcement jurisdiction of any third state on board any ship flying its flag.[155]

Warships and other government ships that operate for non-commercial purposes have immunity from coastal state jurisdiction, but they must comply with the rules applicable to all ships during the conduct of innocent passage.[156] Compliance requires adherence to the laws and regulations that relate to innocent passage and those adopted by coastal states as permitted by the LOS Convention, Article 21.[157] However, if a "warship does not comply with the laws and regulations of the coastal State concerning passage through the territorial sea and disregards any request for compliance therewith which is made to it, the coastal State may require it to leave the territorial sea immediately."[158] Accordingly, warships and other government ships operated for non-commercial purposes may not be boarded or inspected by

151 *Id.* at art. 33.

152 *Id.* at arts. 55 & 57.

153 *See generally* U.S. Dep't of Def., Under Sec'y of Def. for Policy, Maritime Claims Reference Manual, DoD 2005.1-M (June 23, 2005), *available at* http://www.dtic.mil/whs/directives/corres/html/20051m.htm. This manual "provides a general reference concerning the maritime claims of all coastal nations. . . . Some of the claims are inconsistent with international law." Id. at Foreword.

154 *See* LOS Convention, *supra* note 46, at arts. 2, 87.

155 *See id.* at arts. 90, 94.

156 *Id.* at arts. 17–26. All ships other than warships and other government ships operated for non-commercial purposes that are not entitled to immunity are hereinafter referred to as foreign commercial ships.

157 *Id.* at art. 21.

158 *Id.* at art. 30.

a coastal state while in port or elsewhere. While on the high seas, a warship or other government ship operated for non-commercial purposes has complete immunity from jurisdiction of any state other than its flag state.[159]

While in port, in internal waters, within archipelagic waters, or in the territorial sea but not exercising the right of innocent passage, foreign commercial ships are subject to the complete exercise of coastal state jurisdiction over that ship. This includes the exercise of criminal and civil jurisdiction over any person on board.[160] Under these circumstances, a coastal state may board and inspect shipping documents and cargo to ensure compliance with national laws, question the master or crew concerning the ships journey or cargo, search for and seize any cargo that violates its national laws, and exercise flag or third state jurisdiction upon request.

However, when a foreign commercial ship is in the territorial sea exercising the right of innocent passage, the coastal state may only enforce laws and regulations with respect to eight general issues, including "the safety of navigation and the regulation of maritime traffic,"[161] "the conservation of the living resources of the sea,"[162] and "the prevention of infringement of the customs, fiscal, immigration or sanitary laws and regulations of the coastal State."[163] It may also conduct inspections within the territorial sea as necessary to enforce these laws and regulations, but may not do so in such a way that has "the practical effect of denying or impairing the right of innocent passage."[164] The coastal state also has limited authority to exercise criminal and civil jurisdiction on board a foreign commercial ship passing through the territorial sea.[165]

Within the contiguous zone, the coastal state may only exercise control (not sovereignty) necessary to "(a) prevent infringement of its customs, fiscal, immigration or sanitary laws and regulations within its territory or territorial sea; and (b) punish infringement of the above laws and regulations committed within its territory or territorial sea."[166] Within the exclusive economic zone, coastal states have "sovereign rights for the purpose of exploring and exploiting, conserving and managing the natural resources" of the zone, and limited jurisdiction over the "establishment and use of artificial islands, installations and structures; marine scientific research; [and] the protection and preservation of the marine environment."[167] Otherwise, ships

159 LOS Convention, *supra* note 46, at arts. 95-96.

160 *See id.* at art. 2.

161 *Id.* at art. 21(1)(a).

162 *Id.* at art. 21(1)(d).

163 *Id.* at art. 21(1)(h).

164 LOS Convention, *supra* note 46, at art. 24(1).

165 *Id.* at arts. 27–28.

166 *Id.* at art. 33.

167 *Id.* at art. 56.

within the exclusive economic zone generally enjoy the freedom of the high seas accorded all states.[168] Coastal state control and sovereignty within its contiguous zone or exclusive economic zone do not offer much authority for the conduct of PSI maritime interceptions.

When on the high seas, all ships remain subject to the jurisdiction of the flag state.[169] A flag state may, however, authorize another state to exercise its jurisdiction or the jurisdiction of the boarding or third state over its ships on the high seas. So, for example, a flag state may authorize the search and seizure on the high seas of a ship flying its flag and its cargo by a boarding state for violations of the customs laws of a third state. A warship also has the right to board a foreign commercial ship if there is a "reasonable ground for suspecting" that the ship is engaged in piracy, the slave trade, or unauthorized broadcasting; or that it is without nationality or is of the same nationality as the warship.[170]

C. Air Interdictions

With 189 Contracting States,[171] the 1944 Convention on International Civil Aviation (Chicago Convention)[172] is the principal body of international law that governs international civil aviation and international air transport services. Article 1 provides that the Contracting States "recognize that every State has complete and exclusive sovereignty over the airspace above its territory,"[173] and may promulgate regulations governing such overflight consistent with the Chicago Convention. The territory of a state is defined by Article 2 as the "land areas and territorial waters adjacent thereto under the sovereignty . . . of such State."[174]

The Chicago Convention only applies to civil aircraft.[175] State aircraft, defined as "[a]ircraft used in military, customs and police services," are not permitted to "fly over the territory of another State or land thereon without authorization by

168 *See id.* at arts. 2, 87.

169 *See* LOS Convention, *supra* note 46, at arts. 90, 94.

170 *Id.* at art. 110.

171 International Civil Aviation Organization Website, Contracting States, http://www.icao.int/cgi/goto_m.pl?cgi/statesDB4.pl?en (last visited Mar. 4, 2007).

172 Convention on International Civil Aviation, Dec. 7, 1944, 61 Stat. 1180, 15 U.N.T.S. 295, *available at* http://www.icao.int/icaonet/arch/doc/7300/7300_9ed.pdf [hereinafter Chicago Convention].

173 *Id.* at art. 1.

174 *Id.* at art. 2.

175 *Id.* at art. 3.

special agreement."[176] Civil aircraft, however, have the "right of non-scheduled flight."[177] This right provides that

> aircraft not engaged in scheduled international air services shall have the right, subject to the observance of the terms of this Convention, to make flights into or in transit non-stop across its territory and to make stops for non-traffic purposes without the necessity of obtaining prior permission, and *subject to the right of the State flown over to require landing.*[178]

In contrast, under the Chicago Convention, no "scheduled international air service may be operated over or into the territory of a contracting State, except with the special permission or other authorization of that State, and in accordance with the terms of such permission or authorization."[179] However, a transit agreement that was also signed at the same time as the Chicago Convention extends to scheduled international air services privileges to fly across the territory of Contracting States without landing and to land for non-traffic purposes, subject to the remaining provisions of the Chicago Convention.[180]

Contracting States also "have the right, without unreasonable delay, to search aircraft of the other contracting States on landing or departure, and to inspect the certificates and other documents prescribed by . . . [the Chicago] Convention."[181] Perhaps most importantly in the PSI context, Contracting States have the explicit right to implement cargo restrictions:

> (a) No munitions of war or implements of war may be carried in or above the territory of a State in aircraft engaged in international navigation, except by permission of such State. Each State shall determine by regulations what constitutes munitions of war or implements of war for the purposes of this Article. . . .
>
> (b) Each Contracting State reserves the right, for reasons of public order and safety, to regulate or prohibit the carriage in or above its territory of articles other than those enumerated in paragraph (a).[182]

Article 89 provides that in case of war or a declared national emergency, the "provisions of this Convention shall not affect the freedom of action of any of the Contracting States affected, whether as belligerents or as neutrals."[183]

---

176 *Id.*

177 Chicago Convention, *supra* note 172, at art. 5.

178 *Id.* (emphasis added).

179 *Id.* at art. 6.

180 International Air Services Transit Agreement (IASTA), Dec. 7, 1944, 59 Stat. 1693, 84 U.N.T.S. 389.

181 Chicago Convention, *supra* note 172, at art. 16.

182 *Id.* at art. 35.

183 *Id.* at art. 89.

Although Contracting States have a great deal of authority to promulgate regulations, with respect to air interceptions, Article 3*bis* of the Chicago Convention provides:

> (a) The Contracting States recognize that every State must refrain from resorting to the use of weapons against civil aircraft in flight and that, in case of interception, the lives of persons on board and the safety of aircraft must not be endangered. This provision shall not be interpreted as modifying in any way the rights and obligations of States set forth in the Charter of the United Nations.
>
> (b) The Contracting States recognize that every State, in the exercise of its sovereignty, is entitled to require the landing at some designated airport of civil aircraft flying above its territory without authority or if there are reasonable grounds to conclude that it is being used for any purpose inconsistent with the aims of this Convention[184]

The second sentence of Article 3*bis* above recognizes that Contracting States retain their inherent right of self-defense.[185] Article 3(d) of the Chicago Convention also requires Contracting States to "have due regard for the safety of navigation of civil aircraft" when issuing regulations for their state aircraft that may be enforcing the Contracting State regulations.[186]

The LOS Convention also has a number of provisions that address the rights of aircraft and the states they fly over. Article 2, for example, provides that the sovereignty of a coastal State "extends to the air space over the territorial sea."[187] Aircraft owned or operated by a State only on government non-commercial service are the only aircraft that enjoy sovereign immunity.[188] Military aircraft are also generally accorded the same rights as warships on the high seas; for example, military aircraft have the right to seize a pirate ship or aircraft on the high seas, and "arrest the persons and seize the property on board."[189] The LOS Convention also provides a right for all aircraft to over fly international straits and archipelagic sea lanes

---

184 Protocol Relating to an Amendment to the Convention on International Civil Aviation (Article 3*bis*), May 10, 1984, ICAO Doc. 9436, *available at* http://www.icao.int/icao/en/leb/3bis.pdf [hereinafter Article 3*bis*]. There are currently 136 parties to Article 3*bis;* however, the United States is not a party. *Id.* The U.N. Security Council and the United States have stated that Article 3*bis* is declaratory of customary international law. *See, e.g.*, S.C. Res. 1067, U.N. Doc. S/RES/1067 (July 26, 1996); U.S. Department of Justice, Memorandum for Jamie S. Gorelick, Deputy Attorney General, United States Assistance to Countries that Shoot Down Civil Aircraft Involved in Drug Trafficking (July 14, 1994), *available at* http://www.usdoj.gov/olc/shootdow.htm.

185 Article 3*bis*, *supra* note 184.

186 Chicago Convention, *supra* note 172, at art. 3(d).

187 LOS Convention, *supra* note 46, at art. 2(2).

188 *See id.* at arts. 42(5), 236.

189 *Id.* at arts. 105, 107.

without the consent of the coastal state.[190] Similar to LOS Convention provisions that balance the sovereign rights of a coastal state with the freedom of the high seas, the Chicago Convention balances the sovereign rights of over flown states with the right of international navigation.

Finally, the 1963 Convention on Offences and Certain Other Acts Committed on Board Aircraft (Tokyo Convention), provides that

> [a] Contracting State which is not the State of registration may not interfere with an aircraft in flight in order to exercise its criminal jurisdiction over an offence committed on board except in the following cases: (a) the offence has effect on the territory of such state; (b) the offence has been committed by or against a national or permanent resident of such State; (c) the offence is against the security of such State; (d) the offence consists of a breach of any rules or regulations relating to the flight or manoeuvre of aircraft in force in such State; (e) the exercise of jurisdiction is necessary to ensure the observance of any obligation of such State under a multilateral international agreement.[191]

Article 4 permits, however, an aircraft's flag state to waive these limitations.

The Chicago Convention, the transit agreement IASTA, Article 3*bis*, the LOS Convention, the Tokyo Convention, and the inherent right of self-defense constitute the primary body of international law that governs the conduct of air interdictions. This body of international law grants a very wide range of authorities and discretion for states to regulate aircraft overflight of their territory. The basic principle is that all states have complete and exclusive sovereignty over their airspace. In exercising their sovereignty, however, states must have due regard for the safety of navigation of civil aircraft. States also must refrain from resorting to the use of weapons against civil aircraft in flight, and in case of interception, the lives of passengers and the safety of civil aircraft must not be endangered. Over flown states retain their inherent right of self-defense.

By way of summary, all aircraft, civil and state, have the right to fly over international straits and archipelagic sea lanes without the consent of the coastal state. State aircraft, however, may not otherwise fly through another state's airspace or land on its territory without specific prior authorization of the over flown state. In contrast, civil aircraft have the right of non-scheduled and scheduled flights into or in transit non-stop across another state's territory and to make stops for non-traffic purposes without prior permission. However, a civil aircraft's right of overflight is subject to the right of the state flown over to: (a) require landing when there are reasonable grounds the aircraft is being used for a purpose inconsistent with the Chicago Convention; (b) inspect the documents of and search all aircraft on landing or departure (without unreasonable delay); (c) implement cargo restrictions based

190 *Id.* at arts. 38–39, 53–54.

191 Convention on Offences and Certain Other Acts Committed on Board Aircraft (Tokyo Convention) art. 4, Sep. 14, 1963, 20 U.S.T. 2941, 704 U.N.T.S. 219.

on public order and safety; and (d) exercise criminal jurisdiction under limited circumstances over an offense committed on board. Flag states may also grant additional authority to over flown states to require landing or otherwise exercise jurisdiction.

What is not clear in this body of law is the legal authority for states to intercept aircraft flying outside their territorial airspace. Analogies for state aircraft can be made to the authorities granted warships on the high seas under the LOS Convention, but the application of the law of the sea to aircraft in this context is not clear. Flag states always have jurisdiction over their aircraft, but given the speed of modern aircraft it may be difficult to obtain prior flag state permission for an interdiction.

VI. CONCLUSIONS: STRENGTHENING GLOBAL NONPROLIFERATION EFFORTS THROUGH PSI

No framework or approach to addressing the proliferation challenge is perfect, and the weakness in the legal underpinnings for PSI interdictions is the absence of explicit and broad international legal authority for intermodal interdictions and seizures of items of WMD proliferation concern. Currently, PSI must rely upon an eclectic array of international and national laws and frameworks. PSI has been and can continue to be moderately successful in this legal environment. However, an explicit grant of broad legal authority to interdict and seize items of WMD proliferation concern and an obligation to act, adopted by the U.N. Security Council under Chapter VII, would immediately establish much-needed legal authority. Under the existing framework, it can be very difficult, if not impossible, to identify a legal basis on which to search for and seize items of WMD proliferation concern, despite the fact they may be clearly identified or proscribed by international law or an applicable framework. For example, a U.N. Security Council Chapter VII resolution that authorizes the intermodal interdiction and seizure of any item identified or proscribed by the NSG, AG, MTCR, WA, NPT, BWC, or CWC, would be a significant step forward in developing a global ability to combat WMD proliferation.

An act of WMD terrorism could occur anywhere in the world, and its consequences could be devastating. The U.N. Security Council should take action before such a defining event, and it should not be forced into action by an unconscionable death toll that may have been prevented by unequivocal legal authority to interdict and seize items of WMD proliferation concern.

Absent U.N. Security Council action, the international community must continue to move forward in its PSI efforts to combat global WMD proliferation. Despite political will and good intentions, however, this is a slow process. States could cooperate broadly in an effort to develop legal authorities through a multilateral treaty. Such a treaty could grant in advance or at least facilitate the request for consent-based interdictions by working out the procedures for flag state consent, similar to the bilateral ship boarding agreements discussed in Part III. Although perhaps only a modest step, this approach would be helpful, at least among those states that have become parties to the agreement. There is a 2005 Protocol to SUA that "provides the first international treaty framework for combating and prosecuting individuals who use a ship as a weapon or means of committing a terrorist attack, or transport by ship terrorists or cargo intended for use in connection with weapons of mass destruction programs."[192] It also creates ship boarding arrangements "to facilitate the boarding in international waters of vessels suspected of engaging in these activities."[193] However, this 2005 SUA Protocol will only be effective among those states that become a party to it, and it does not go far enough in establishing a broad legal basis to search for and seize items of WMD proliferation concern.

PSI has been successful in many ways that are difficult to quantify and illustrate with publicly available information. Those who only measure the success of PSI by counting highly visible interdictions that uncover large illicit cargoes or conspiracies simply miss the point. The greatest value of PSI continues to be marked by the expanding group of PSI participant states that declare their commitment to PSI and then take affirmative actions to work together to combat global WMD proliferation. There have been tangible, specific successes as well. PSI cooperation, for example, among Germany, Italy, the United Kingdom, and the United States resulted in the diversion and seizure of the ship *BBC China* and its cargo of centrifuge parts bound for Libya.[194] This interdiction and additional cooperation from the United Arab Emirates, South Africa, Malaysia, Turkey, and several European states also led to the dismantling of the A.Q. Khan international nuclear proliferation network, and the imprisonment of many of its leading members.[195] PSI is also credited with encouraging Libya's "historic decision" to eliminate its WMD and longer-range missile programs.[196]

Given the extraordinary volume of global trade and commerce, PSI interdictions and operational activities are very heavily information driven. More often than not, dual-use technologies and goods, which require a high level of technical expertise in identifying items of proliferation concern, are involved. Each interdiction is unique, and participation in any given activity or interdiction is a national-level decision. Almost all PSI interdictions require the cooperation and coordination between two or more governments that also must coordinate internally among their

192 U.S. Dep't of State, Bureau of Int'l Security and Nonproliferation, Fact Sheet, Protocols to the United Nations Convention for the Suppression of Unlawful Acts Against the Safety of Maritime Navigation (SUA) (Oct. 21, 2005), http://www.state.gov/t/isn/rls/fs/58322.htm.

193 *Id.*

194 Robert Joseph, Under Sec'y of State for Arms Control and Int'l Security, Meeting the Challenges of Weapons of Mass Destruction Proliferation, Address at the University of Virginia Miller Center, Charlottesville, Virginia (Dec. 9, 2005), *available at* http://www.state.gov /t/us/rm/ 57874.htm.

195 *Id.*

196 *Id.*

respective domestic agencies. Accordingly, PSI can be strengthened through additional initiatives and activities that create and expand information and intelligence sharing arrangements; strengthen information and intelligence gathering capabilities; enhance global law enforcement coordination; develop technical expertise in boarding teams and reach back networks; exercise intra-governmental and inter-governmental coordination; establish a broader network of ship boarding agreements; and promote stronger networks of national laws.

Two additional approaches should be explored. The U.N. Security Council has condemned WMD proliferation and terrorism as threats to international peace and security and acted under its Chapter VII authority several times. Many of these resolutions also impose political and legal obligations on all Member States to prohibit and prevent WMD proliferation and terrorism. Greater commitment to action to fulfill these obligations is needed, however. First, focusing specifically on giving effect to U.N. Security Council resolutions, states could adopt domestic legislation or regulations that authorize the intermodal interdiction and seizure of any item identified or proscribed by the NSG, AG, MTCR, WA, NPT, BWC, or CWC. Second, all PSI states could agree upon and publicly announce the identity of all states and non-state actors of proliferation concern. Then the PSI participating States could implement legislation or regulations that require *all* cargo to undergo a thorough inspection prior to being loaded on board any ship or aircraft destined for declared states or non-state actors of proliferation concern. This would certainly increase the cost of being a known actor of proliferation concern, and encourage legitimate carriers to avoid doing business with them.

Operacion Socotora has been criticized because it failed to yield a seizure and destruction of a number of Scud missiles and other items initially thought to be heading to terrorists in the Middle East. However, *Operacion Socotora* was a great success in that it quickened the pace towards PSI, and that in itself has led to remarkable and promising progress in combating global WMD proliferation and terrorism.

ANNEX A

Interdiction Principles for the Proliferation Security Initiative[197]

PSI participants are committed to the following interdiction principles to establish a more coordinated and effective basis through which to impede and stop shipments of WMD, delivery systems, and related materials flowing to and from states and non-state actors of proliferation concern, consistent with national legal authorities and relevant international law and frameworks, including the United Nations Security Council. They call on all states concerned with this threat to international peace and security to join in similarly committing to:

1) Undertake effective measures, either alone or in concert with other states, for interdicting the transfer or transport of WMD, their delivery systems, and related materials to and from states and non-state actors of proliferation concern. "States or non-state actors of proliferation concern" generally refers to those countries or entities that the PSI participants involved establish should be subject to interdiction activities because they are engaged in proliferation through: (1) efforts to develop or acquire chemical, biological, or nuclear weapons and associated delivery systems; or (2) transfers (either selling, receiving, or facilitating) of WMD, their delivery systems, or related materials.

2) Adopt streamlined procedures for rapid exchange of relevant information concerning suspected proliferation activity, protecting the confidential character of classified information provided by other states as part of this initiative, dedicate appropriate resources and efforts to interdiction operations and capabilities, and maximize coordination among participants in interdiction efforts.

3) Review and work to strengthen their relevant national legal authorities where necessary to accomplish these objectives, and work to strengthen when necessary relevant international law and frameworks in appropriate ways to support these commitments.

4) Take specific actions in support of interdiction efforts regarding cargoes of WMD, their delivery systems, or related materials, to the extent their national legal authorities permit and consistent with their obligations under international law and frameworks, to include:

a) Not to transport or assist in the transport of any such cargoes to or from states or non-state actors of proliferation concern, and not to allow any persons subject to their jurisdiction to do so.

b) At their own initiative, or at the request and good cause shown by another state, to take action to board and search any vessel flying their flag in their internal waters or territorial seas, or areas beyond the territorial seas of any other state, that is reasonably suspected of transporting such cargoes to or from states or non-state actors of proliferation concerns, and to seize such cargoes that are identified.

197 PSI Statement of Interdiction Principles, *supra* note 57.

c) To seriously consider providing consent under the appropriate circumstances to the boarding and searching of its own flag vessels by other states, and to the seizure of such WMD-related cargoes in such vessels that may be identified by such states.

d) To take appropriate actions to (1) stop and/or search in their internal waters, territorial seas, or contiguous zones (when declared) vessels that are reasonably suspected of carrying such cargoes to or from states or non-state actors of proliferation concern and to seize such cargoes that are identified; and (2) to enforce conditions on vessels entering or leaving their ports, internal waters, or territorial seas that are reasonably suspected of carrying such cargoes, such as requiring that such vessels be subject to boarding, search, and seizure of such cargoes prior to entry.

e) At their own initiative or upon the request and good cause shown by another state, to (a) require aircraft that are reasonably suspected of carrying such cargoes to or from states or non-state actors of proliferation concern and that are transiting their airspace to land for inspection and seize any such cargoes that are identified; and/or (b) deny aircraft reasonably suspected of carrying such cargoes transit rights through their airspace in advance of such flights.

f) If their ports, airfields, or other facilities are used as transshipment points for shipment of such cargoes to or from states or non-state actors of proliferation concern, to inspect vessels, aircraft, or other modes of transport reasonably suspected of carrying such cargoes, and to seize such cargoes that are identified.

GETTING IT RIGHT: PROTECTING AMERICAN CRITICAL INFRASTRUCTURE IN CYBERSPACE

Sean M. Condron[†]

Originally published in *Harvard Journal of Law & Technology:* Vol. 20, No.2 (Spring 2007)

> The dogmas of the quiet past are inadequate to the stormy present. The occasion is piled high with difficulty, and we must rise to the occasion. As our case is new, so we must think anew and act anew.[1]

> Where once our opponents relied exclusively on bombs and bullets, hostile powers and terrorists can now turn a laptop computer into a potent weapon capable of doing enormous damage. If we are to continue to enjoy the benefits of the information age, preserve our security, and safeguard our economic well-being, we must protect our critical computer-controlled systems from attack.[2]

I. INTRODUCTION

The attacks of September 11, 2001 highlight the deadly intent of our adversaries and the nation's vulnerability to "different, unorthodox, and unimaginable" threats.[3] Due to the low cost and wide availability of computers, cyber attacks[4] are an attractive

† Judge Advocate, U.S. Army. Presently assigned as an Associate Professor, International and Operational Law Department, The Judge Advocate General's Legal Center and School, Charlottesville, Virginia. LL.M., 2006 (Commandant's List), The Judge Advocate General's Legal Center and School; J.D., 1998 (*cum laude*), Duke University School of Law; B.S., 1992 (Honor Graduate), United States Military Academy. The views expressed in this article are those of the author and do not reflect the views of the Department of Defense or the Department of the Army.

1 Letter from Abraham Lincoln, U.S. President, to U.S. Congress (Dec. 1, 1862), *available at* http://www.presidency.ucsb.edu/ws/print.php?pid=29503.

2 The White House, Defending America's Cyberspace: National Plan for Information Systems Protection, at ii (2000), *available at* http://chnm.gmu.edu/cip-digitalarchive/files/522_WhiteHouseNationalPlanInvitationtoDialogue.pdf.

3 James Kiras et al., Understanding "Asymmetric" Threats to the United States 15 (2002), *available at* http://www.nipp.org/Adobe/Asymmetry%20%20final%2002.pdf.

4 This Article uses the phrases "cyber attack," "cyber defense," "cyber warfare," "cyberspace," and other derivatives of the root word "cyber" to refer to activities centered on the use of a computer system or computer network. For example, a cyber attack would refer to an attack using a computer system or network or an attack against a computer system or network.

method of warfare.[5] Unlike traditional military weapons, an adversary can use a personal computer, which can be purchased almost anywhere for a few hundred dollars, to accomplish a military objective.[6] In 2003, the Computer Emergency Response Team Coordination Center received reports of 137,529 "incidents."[7] Attacks against network systems have become so common that, in 2004, the Computer Emergency Response Team stopped maintaining statistics showing the number of "incidents."[8] In 2004, the Congressional Research Service estimated that the economic impact of cyber attacks in the United States was $226 billion.[9]

Cyber attacks can originate from a number of sources. Michael Vatis, former head of the Institute for Security Technology Studies at Dartmouth College, has identified four categories of threats: terrorists, nation-states, terrorist sympathizers, and thrill seekers.[10] Of these threats, nation-states likely have the greatest capabilities and resources. For example, in the years ahead, the United States will probably face an evolving cyber threat from China. In particular, China is integrating "information warfare units" into its military operations that have the capabilities for "first strikes against enemy networks."[11] In August 1999, China launched several cyber attacks against Taiwan, initiating a "public hacking war" with the disputed island.[12] China may have attacked United States federal government computer systems in the past.[13] Nation-states, however, probably will not attempt major cyber attacks,

5 President's Comm'n on Critical Infrastructure Prot., Critical Foundations: Protecting America's Infrastructures 17 (1997), *available at* http://chnm.gmu.edu/cipdigitalarchive/files/5_CriticalFoundationsPCCIP.pdf.

6 *See id.* at 17–18.

7 Carnegie Mellon Software Engineering Institute, CERT/CC Statistics 1988–2005, http://www.cert.org/stats/cert_stats.html (last visited Apr. 14, 2007) ("An incident may involve one site or hundreds (or even thousands) of sites. Also, some incidents may involve ongoing activity for long periods of time."). The website does not further define the word "incident," but a discussion implies that it is some type of suspected attack on a computer system. *Id.*

8 *See id.* The Chief Information Officer and Assistant Secretary for Networks and Information Integration at the Department of Defense stated, "Our networks are under constant cyberattacks." Ian Martinez, *Cybersecurity at Center Stage for Advisory Committee*, Wash. Internet Daily, Dec. 20, 2006.

9 Eric Chabrow, *Homeland Security Tries to Get its Cybersecurity House in Order*, InformationWeek, Oct. 2, 2006, at 56, *available at* http://www.informationweek.com/story/showArticle.jhtml?articleID=193100332&cid = RSSfeed_IWK_All.

10 Michael A. Vatis, Inst. for Sec. and Tech. Studies at Dartmouth Coll., Cyber Attacks During the War on Terrorism: A Predictive Analysis 1 (2001), *available at* http://www.ists.dartmouth.edu/analysis/cyber_a1.pdf.

11 Dep't of Defense, Annual Report to Congress: Military Power of the People's Republic of China 35–36 (2006).

12 Peter Warren, *China Fires First Shots in Cyber War*, Scot. on Sunday, Aug. 22, 1999, at 8.

13 Bill Gertz, *Chinese Hackers Raid U.S. Computers*, Wash. Times, May 16, 1999 at C1. Following the errant bombing of the Chinese embassy in Belgrade, Chinese hackers launched cyber attacks on computers at the White House, State Department, and other federal agencies. *Id.*

unless it is a precursor to military action, because of the potential severity of the response. Nation-states have territory, property, and citizens to protect, all of which would be jeopardized if it were to conduct a major cyber attack.

Thrill seekers are a minor threat because they are generally driven by a desire to show off their skills, rather than a desire to destroy.[14] While they are certainly capable of causing some serious problems, both the media and self-promoters from this group have overstated their actual menace.[15]

Cyber terrorists may not have a robust ability to conduct large cyber attacks on critical infrastructure, but they are probably far more likely to try than other actors.[16] Cyber terrorists do not face the repercussions that nation-states would and probably have more destruction-oriented agendas than thrill seekers. Despite this concern, there have been no known attempts to stage such an attack by any major terrorist group.[17] According to Dorothy Denning, a professor of computer science at the Naval Postgraduate School, "[t]errorists have not yet integrated information technology into their strategy and tactics, and significant barriers between hackers and terrorists may prevent their integration into one group."[18] There are indications, however, that Al Qaeda and other terrorist groups are seeking to expand their capabilities in this area, perhaps by forging connections with hacker groups.[19] Michael Vatis argues that terrorist sympathizers are the most likely group to launch a cyber attack.[20] Unlike the other groups, these individuals do not necessarily lack the technological ability or incentives. As a demographic, they are hackers with not only the knowledge and ability to conduct a cyber attack, but also a cause shared by terrorist groups like Al Qaeda.[21]

The United States federal government has focused an unprecedented amount of attention, time, and financial resources on the threat from weapons of mass destruction[22] and terrorism.[23] The White House, recognizing the growing threat of cyber attacks

14 VATIS, *supra* note 10, at 14.

15 GABRIEL WEIMANN, TERROR ON THE INTERNET 158–59 (2006) (quoting Cyber *Terrorism and Critical Infrastructure Protection: Hearing Before the Subcomm. on Gov't Efficiency, Fin. Mgmt., and Intergov'tal Relations*, 107th Cong. (2002) (statement of Douglas Thomas, Professor, Univ. of S. Cal.)).

16 VATIS, *supra* note 10, at 12.

17 WEIMANN, *supra* note 15, at 165.

18 *Id.* at 167.

19 *Id.* at 169–70. "U.S. troops searching the caves in Afghanistan found plans by al Qaeda to attack computer systems after sending al Qaeda recruits to train in high tech systems." *Id.* at 170.

20 *See* VATIS, *supra* note 10, at 13–14.

21 *Id.* at 13.

22 *See* Robert Joseph, U.S. Under Sec'y for Arms Control and Int'l Sec., Dep't of State, Meeting the Challenges of Weapons of Mass Destruction Proliferation, Remarks at the University of Virginia Miller Center (Dec. 9, 2005), *available at* http://www.state.gov/t/us/rm/57874.htm.

23 *See* EXECUTIVE BRANCH OF THE U.S. GOV'T, NATIONAL STRATEGY FOR COMBATING TERRORISM 19 (2003), *available at* http://www.whitehouse.gov/news/releases/2003/02/counter_terrorism/counter_terrorism_strategy.pdf; *see also* THE PRESIDENT OF THE U.S., THE NATIONAL SECURITY

and the importance of protecting cyberspace,[24] has designated the Department of Homeland Security as the lead agency for addressing this threat.[25]

The government's approach to protecting cyberspace focuses on the concept of "critical infrastructure." The USA PATRIOT Act of 2001 defines critical infrastructure as the "systems and assets, whether physical or virtual, so vital to the United States that the incapacity or destruction of such systems and assets would have a debilitating impact on security, national economic security, national public health or safety, or any combination of those matters."[26] Critical infrastructure includes the following sectors: agriculture, food, water, public health, emergency services, government, defense industrial base, information and telecommunications, energy, transportation, banking and finance, chemical industry and hazardous materials, and postal and shipping.[27] Both government and private entities own and operate the critical infrastructure in the United States.[28]

Critical infrastructure is by definition essential for the survival of the nation.[29] Networked computer systems form the nerve center of the country's critical infrastructure.[30] The private sector is largely unable to adequately protect these computer systems and

---

Strategy of the United States of America 12 (2006), *available at* http://www.whitehouse.gov/nsc/nss/2006/nss2006.pdf.

24 Executive Branch of the U.S. Government, The National Strategy to Secure Cyberspace, at iv (2003) [hereinafter Secure Cyberspace], *available at* http://www.whitehouse.gov/pcipb/cyberspace_strategy.pdf.

25 *Id.* at 54.

26 USA PATRIOT Act of 2001 § 1016, 42 U.S.C. § 5195c (Supp. II 2002); *see also* U.S. Dep't of Homeland Security, National Infrastructure Protection Plan 103 (2006) [hereinafter NIPP], *available at* http://www.dhs.gov/xlibrary/assets/NIPP_Plan.pdf (defining critical infrastructure to include networks vital to the nation). There is a related but distinct concept of key resources, defined as "publicly or privately controlled resources essential to the minimal operations of the economy or government." Homeland Security Act of 2002 § 2(9), 6 U.S.C. § 101(9) (Supp. II 2002); *see also* NIPP, *supra*, at 104.

27 The President of the United States, National Strategy for Homeland Security 30 (2002) [hereinafter Homeland Security], *available at* http://www.whitehouse.gov/homeland/book/nat_strat_hls.pdf. Homeland Security Presidential Directive 7 suggests an expansion of critical infrastructure sectors when it assigns roles and responsibilities of sector-specific federal agencies. *See* President of the United States, Homeland Security Presidential Directive 7 (2003), *available at* http://www.whitehouse.gov/news/releases/2003/12/20031217-5.html.

28 *See* Executive Branch of the U.S. Gov't, The National Strategy for the Physical Protection of Critical Infrastructures and Key Assets 8 (2003) [hereinafter Physical Protection], *available at* http://www.whitehouse.gov/pcipb/physical_strategy.pdf. In 2003, the private sector owned and operated about eighty-five percent of the critical infrastructure in the United States. *Id.*

29 *See* 42 U.S.C. § 5195c (Supp. II 2002).

30 *See* Secure Cyberspace, *supra* note 24, at vii.

networks from major military and terrorist threats.[31] Civilian networks are often more vulnerable to attack than the Department of Defense network.[32] However, military networks are also vulnerable because they depend extensively on civilian networks for connectivity and transferability of information.[33] The well-being of the nation depends on a safe and secure cyber environment for its critical infrastructure.[34] Therefore, protection of the computer systems and networks supporting critical infrastructure in the United States should be the federal government's responsibility.[35]

Despite the magnitude of this threat, the United States currently operates under the presumption that a cyber attack constitutes a criminal activity, not a threat to national security.[36] Because law enforcement investigations that require the methodical collection of evidence are often protracted and resource-intensive, typically taking days, weeks, or even months, this presumption may result in a very slow response that may come too late to confront a cyber attack successfully.[37] A delayed response to a cyber attack on the nation's critical infrastructure may result in lives lost and massive damage.[38] For these reasons, the response should be nearly simultaneous with the attack itself.[39]

It may thus be preferable to approach cyber security as a threat to national security rather than as a criminal matter. This change would raise at least three issues. First, it may be necessary to revisit and clarify the government's current distinction between homeland security and homeland defense as applied to cyberspace. Second, this change requires consideration of the *jus ad bellum* paradigm that controls a state's self-defense response against a cyber attack. Finally, the delicate balance between national security interests and civil liberties should be considered in

---

31 *See generally* Physical Protection, *supra* note 28, at 8 (discussing the insufficiency of private sector protection of critical infrastructure).

32 *See* Arthur K. Cebrowski, *CNE and CNA in the Network-Centric Battlespace: Challenges for Operators and Lawyers*, 76 Int'l L. Stud. 1, 4 (2002).

33 *See id.; see also* Charles J. Dunlap, Jr., *Meeting the Challenge of Cyberterrorism: Defining the Military Role in Democracy*, 76 Int'l L. Stud. 353, 354 (2002).

34 *See* Secure Cyberspace, *supra* note 24, at vii.

35 *See* Chabrow, *supra* note 9, at 56.

36 *See* Dunlap, *supra* note 33, at 365; Kenneth A. Minihan, *Defending the Nation Against Cyber Attack: Information Assurance in the Global Environment*, U.S. Foreign Pol'y Agenda, Nov. 1998, at 5, 7; Walter Gary Sharp, Sr., *Balancing Our Civil Liberties with Our National Security Interests in Cyberspace*, 4 Tex. Rev. L. & Pol. 69, 70 (1999); *see also* Secure Cyberspace, *supra* note 24, at 28 (stating that "[l]aw enforcement plays the central role in attributing an attack through the exercise of criminal justice authorities").

37 *See* Sharp, *supra* note 36, at 71.

38 *See* Eric Talbot Jensen, *Computer Attacks on Computer National Infrastructure: A Use of Force Invoking the Right of Self-Defense*, 38 Stan. J. Int'l L. 207, 232 (2002).

39 *See* Sharp, *supra* note 36, at 71–72.

developing a strategy for responding to cyber attacks. This Article presents a framework for addressing these issues.

II. DEFENSE AND SECURITY: A BLURRED DISTINCTION

Following September 11, 2001, the executive branch made a policy decision to distinguish homeland security from homeland defense.[40] Homeland security has been defined as a "concerted national effort to prevent terrorist attacks within the United States, reduce America's vulnerability to terrorism, and minimize the damage and recover from attacks that do occur."[41] In contrast, "[h]omeland defense is the protection of US sovereignty, territory, domestic population, and critical defense infrastructure against external threats and aggression, or other threats as directed by the President."[42] The Department of Homeland Security is the federal agency in charge of homeland security while the Department of Defense is the lead federal agency for homeland defense.[43]

Such a distinction between defense and security poses several problems in the context of cyberspace. The first problem is that the distinction relies on a poor choice of words: defense and security are commonly understood to be synonymous.[44] Applying synonymous terms to two different concepts can lead to confusion. The Department of Homeland Security's National Response Plan exacerbates this confusion by creating categories that imply a distinction between cyber security of the United States and cyber defense of the United States without delineating the difference between the two.[45]

The second problem is that the executive branch has failed to clearly distinguish between defense and security. As previously defined, homeland security focuses on terrorist attacks within the United States, while homeland defense focuses on external threats and aggression towards the sovereignty, territory, domestic population, and critical defense infrastructure of the United States.[46] It is easy to envision threats that span both concepts. Consider, for example, a cyber terrorist attack perpetrated from outside the United States where the effects of the cyber attack are felt within the United States. Under the current definitions of security

40 *See* Homeland Security, *supra* note 27, at 13; U.S. Dep't of Def., Strategy for Homeland Defense and Civil Support 5 (2005) [hereinafter Homeland Defense], *available at* http://www.defenselink.mil/news/Jun2005/d20050630homeland.pdf.

41 6 U.S.C.A. § 111(b)(1)(A)–(C) (West 2002); *see also* Homeland Security, *supra* note 27, at 2.

42 Homeland Defense, *supra* note 40, at 5.

43 See Homeland Security, *supra* note 27, at 13; Homeland Defense, *supra* note 40, at 5.

44 Roget's II: The New Thesaurus 248 (3d ed. 1995).

45 *See* U.S. Dep't of Homeland Sec., National Response Plan, at CYB-6 (2004) [hereinafter NRP], *available at* http://www.dhs.gov/xlibrary/assets/NRP_FullText.pdf.

46 *See* Homeland Security, *supra* note 27, at 2; Homeland Defense, *supra* note 40, at 5.

and defense, it is not clear which agency would be responsible for preventing or responding to this threat.

The most serious problem with these definitions is their reliance on the concept of geographical borders. Geographical borders are almost meaningless in cyberspace[47] because cyberspace has no borders or boundaries in the traditional sense.[48] The Internet relies on "packet switching" by which packets travel the shortest electronic route to their destination.[49] However, the shortest electronic route does not necessarily correspond to the shortest geographical route.[50] Data transfer on the Internet "considers existing network traffic loads," and therefore "shortest" relates to time more than to geographic distance.[51] That route may cross physical borders during transmission, even when transmission is between domestically-situated entities.[52] This creates, in essence, a border-free space. Although the Department of Homeland Security has a definition for cyber security,[53] the definition does nothing to clarify this issue. Under the current formulation, differentiating between homeland security and homeland defense in cyberspace is essentially impossible.

Notwithstanding these definitional problems, government policy distinguishes between security and defense. With these distinctions, the government emphasizes security over defense with regard to cyberspace. The agency hierarchy is evidence of this priority. Under the National Strategy to Secure Cyberspace, the Department of Homeland Security assumes the lead role for cyber security,[54] with the Department of Defense relegated to a minor, supporting role.[55] Yet there is no comparable national strategy for cyber defense. This oversight has left a gaping hole in the protection of United States critical infrastructure because the Department of Homeland Security bases its concept of "security" on prevention and repair,[56] whereas the concept of defense has traditionally entailed a wider range of options. This section will outline some preliminary ideas about possible components that could be used to craft a cyber defense strategy.

---

47 *See* David R. Johnson & David Post, *Law and Borders—The Rise of Law in Cyberspace*, 48 Stan. L. Rev. 1367, 1370 (1996).

48 *Id.* at 1367.

49 David Tubbs et al., *Technology and Law: The Evolution of Digital Warfare*, 76 Int'l L. Stud. 7, 10 (2002).

50 *Id.*

51 *Id.*

52 *See* Johnson & Post, *supra* note 47, at 1372–73.

53 *See* NIPP, *supra* note 26, at 108 (defining cyber security as "[t]he prevention of damage to, unauthorized use of, exploitation of, and, if needed, the restoration of electronic information and communications systems and services (and the information contained therein) to ensure confidentiality, integrity, and availability").

54 Secure Cyberspace, *supra* note 24, at 54.

55 *See* NRP, *supra* note 45, at CYB-6.

56 *See* NIPP, *supra* note 26, at 108.

Generally, defensive military operations consist of two types: active measures and passive measures.[57] Computer network defense can also be classified using these categories. Computer network defense protects from both domestic and foreign threats.[58] Passive measures of computer network defense include encryption, firewalls, and automated detection.[59] Generally, active measures include some type of in-kind response,[60] in which "the entity attacked launches an offensive operation against the perpetrator using a method that is similar in nature to the one used against them."[61] For the most part, the federal government has classified the specifics of active measures of computer network defense.[62] A good example of an active defense is the counter-strike philosophy of an Internet security company, which offers counter measures including "flooding the attacking computers with data [and] rendering them Internet-blind."[63]

Computer network defense within the United States' Department of Defense "involves actions taken through the use of computer networks to protect, monitor, analyze, detect, and respond to unauthorized activity within DOD information systems and computer networks."[64] The Department of Defense does not have an organization dedicated to and focused on the cyber defense of critical infrastructure.[65]

---

57 *See generally* Carl von Clausewitz, Principles of War 16–17 (Hans W. Gatzke trans., 1942).

58 *See* Joint Chiefs of Staff, Joint Pub. 3-13, Information Operations, at II-5 (Feb. 13, 2006) [hereinafter Joint Pub. 3-13], *available at* http://www.fas.org/irp/dodder/ dod/jp3_13.pdf.

59 Jensen, *supra* note 38, at 230. Encryption is the process of producing ciphertext by scrambling the text in such a way that only individuals with the secret key can read and understand the text. Dorothy E. Denning, Information Warfare and Security 286 (1999). A firewall is "a network monitor or collection of monitors placed between an organization's internal network and the Internet or between two local area networks. The objective is to keep intruders, malicious code, and unwanted information out and proprietary or sensitive data in. A firewall is essentially a gateway between two networks." *Id.* at 353. Automated detection involves programs that "can scan computer records or on-line computer activity for patterns that indicate or suggest the presence of unauthorized activity." *Id.* at 361.

60 *Id.* ("[A]ctive responses may involve some in-kind rejoinder or 'hack-back' feature, either reflecting similar damage back to the sender or causing some other responsive action.").

61 Denning, *supra* note 59, at 392.

62 Jensen, *supra* note 38, at 231.

63 Matthew Fordahl, *Networks Lash Back at Cyber Hacks*, CBS News, June 18, 2004, http://www.cbsnews.com/stories/2004/06/18/tech/main624875.shtml (noting that customers for such active defense programs include government and military entities).

64 Joint Pub. 3-13, *supra* note 58, at II-5. The U.S. government defines the computer network defense mission as the coordination and direction of defense operations of "computer networks from unauthorized activity employing communications, law enforcement, counterintelligence and Intelligence Community (IC) capabilities in response to specific or potential threats." Joint Chiefs of Staff, Instr. 6510-01D, Information Assurance (IA) and Computer Network Defense (CND) at A-5 (June 15, 2004), *available at* http://www.dtic.mil/cjcs_directives/cdata/unlimit/6510_01.pdf.

65 *See* U.S. Strategic Command, Joint Task Force—Global Network Operations, http://www.stratcom.mil/fact_sheets/fact_jtf_gno.html (last visited Apr. 14, 2007). Joint Task

III. THE CYBERSPACE THREAT AND INTERNATIONAL LAW

The threats in cyberspace run the gamut from the teenager curious about what she can accomplish with her own personal computer[66] to a foreign military service separate and distinct from that nation's army, navy, and air force, devoted exclusively to information warfare.[67] That, indeed, is one of the challenges of this threat—a cyber attack could originate from any number of potential actors.[68] The attacker could be an isolated individual, a member of some organized group, or a state actor.[69] It is even possible that an attack could involve multiple actors, each with a slightly different intent.[70]

A. Use of Force in Cyber Self-Defense

The United Nations Charter and customary international law both govern the use of force by states and form the basis of the current *jus ad bellum* paradigm.[71] This paradigm prohibits the use or threat of force, except in limited circumstances.[72] The legal basis for the *jus ad bellum* paradigm is Article 2(4) of the United Nations Charter,[73] which states that "[a]ll members shall refrain in their international

Force—Global Network Operations protects the Global Information Grid. *Id.* The Global Information Grid is the network and computer systems supporting "warfighters, policymakers, and support personnel." JOINT CHIEFS OF STAFF, JOINT PUB. 1-02, DEPARTMENT OF DEFENSE DICTIONARY OF MILITARY AND ASSOCIATED TERMS 225 (Apr. 12, 2001 as amended through Mar. 1, 2007), *available at* http://www.dtic.mil/doctrine/jel/ new_pubs/jp1_02.pdf. This represents, at most, only a fraction of the nation's critical infrastructure.

66 In July 2005, a teenager in Germany "admitted creating the Sasser and Netsky internet worms which forced airlines to ground their fleets and the British coastguard to work with pen and paper." Hannah Cleaver, *Teenager Admits Virus Attacks*, DAILY TELEGRAPH, July 6, 2005, at 16. In a 2000 attack, a Canadian boy known only as Mafiaboy shut down several major websites including CNN.com, Amazon.com, and Yahoo.com. DeNeen L. Brown, *Teen Admits Attacking Web Sites*, WASH. POST, Jan. 19, 2001, at E1. In 1998, two California teenagers who wanted to test their computer skills "penetrated Pentagon computers and briefly disrupted the movement of troops participating in military exercises in the Persian Gulf." Chris Mondics, *Rep. Andrews Leads Charge for Cyber Security*, PHILA. INQUIRER, Dec. 26, 2002, at A25.

67 Bill Gertz, *U.S. Set to Take Warfare On-Line*, WASH. TIMES, Jan. 6, 2000, at A3.

68 *See* SECURE CYBERSPACE, *supra* note 24, at 6.

69 *See generally id.* at 6–7 (concluding that technology allows increasing numbers of actors to launch attacks on critical infrastructure in cyberspace).

70 *See* Barbara Demick, *Teenage Hacker Inspires Awe in Some Israeli Officials*, MIAMI HERALD, Mar. 26, 1998, at 2F (stating that teenage hackers in California joined with a teenager in Israel to attack Pentagon computer systems).

71 Yoram Dinstein, *Computer Network Attacks and Self-Defense*, 76 INT'L L. STUD. 99, 99 (2002).

72 *See* U.N. Charter art. 2, para. 4; *id.* art. 51; Dinstein, *supra* note 71, at 99.

73 Dinstein, *supra* note 71, at 99. Professor Dinstein and others argue that "there exists in international law today 'an absolute prohibition of the use or threat of force, subject only to the exceptions stated in the Charter itself.'" *Id.* (quoting Josef Mrazek, *Prohibition of the Use and Threat Force: Self-Defence and Self-Help in International Law*, 27 CANADIAN Y.B. INT'L L. 81, 90 (1989)).

relations from the threat or use of force against the territorial integrity or political independence of any state, or in any other manner inconsistent with the Purposes of the United Nations."[74] There are two exceptions to the prohibition on the use of force in the United Nations Charter: Security Council action pursuant to Article 42[75] and individual or collective self-defense under Article 51.[76]

Legal scholars disagree on the current state of customary international law as it relates to the use of force in self-defense and the proper interpretation of Article 51. Some scholars interpret Article 51 strictly, arguing that a state may not act in self-defense until that state has suffered an armed attack.[77] According to this school of thought, a state could not act in anticipation of an armed attack.[78] Other legal scholars argue that Article 51 incorporates customary international law as articulated by the *Caroline* standard, allowing anticipatory self-defense.[79]

It is important to note that the United Nations Charter was written before the Internet existed. There is no specific provision in the United Nations Charter that addresses cyber warfare, but the International Court of Justice has ruled that Article 2(4) and Article 51 apply to "any use of force, regardless of the weapons employed."[80] Although a question arises as to whether certain cyber attacks amount to a use of force under Article 2(4) or an armed attack under Article 51, many legal scholars would probably agree that a cyber attack *could* amount to a use of force or an armed attack.[81] More importantly, most legal scholars would probably agree that

74 U.N. Charter art. 2, para. 4.

75 *Id.* art. 42 (authorizing the Security Council to "take such action by air, sea, or land forces as may be necessary to maintain or restore international peace and security").

76 *Id.* art. 51 (stating that "[n]othing in the present Charter shall impair the inherent right of individual or collective self-defence if an armed attack occurs against a Member of the United Nations").

77 *See, e.g.*, Horace B. Robertson, *Self-Defense Against Computer Network Attack*, 76 INT'L L. STUD. 121, 123 (2002).

78 *Id.*

79 Jason Barkham, *International Warfare and International Law on the Use of Force*, 34 NY.U. J. INT'L L. & POL. 57, 75 (2002); Jensen, *supra* note 38, at 218–19. The *Caroline* case involved a British attack on a United States ship in 1837. 2 JOHN BASSET MOORE, A DIGEST OF INTERNATIONAL LAW § 217, 409–10 (1906). Several years after the attack, United States Secretary of State Daniel Webster accepted a British apology for the attack and concluded that a state may attack in self-defense when the "necessity of that self-defence is instant, overwhelming, and leaving no choice of means, and no moment for deliberation." *Id.* at 412 (quoting Letter from Daniel Webster, U.S. Sec'y of State, to Alexander Ashburton, Gr. Brit. Plenipotentiary (Aug. 6, 1842)). This quote is the *Caroline* standard of anticipatory self-defense.

80 Legality of the Threat or Use of Nuclear Weapons, Advisory Opinion, 1996 I.C.J. 226, 244 (July 8).

81 Jensen, *supra* note 38, at 222; Robertson, *supra* note 77, at 135–37; Michael N. Schmitt, *Computer Network Attack and the Use of Force in International Law: Thoughts on a Normative Framework*, 37 COLUM. J. TRANSNAT'L L. 885, 934–35 (1999); Daniel B. Silver, *Computer Network Attack as a Use of Force Under Article 2(4)*, 76 INT'L L. STUD. 73, 92–93 (2002).

the United Nations Charter system and customary international law bind state actions engaging in cyber warfare.[82]

B. Conditions for the Use of Force in Cyber Self-Defense

Under the *jus ad bellum* paradigm, a state response to an armed attack must meet three conditions to qualify as self-defense: necessity, proportionality, and immediacy.[83] To fulfill the principle of necessity generally, "non-forcible remedies must either prove futile *in limine* or have in fact been exhausted in an unsatisfactory manner."[84] Furthermore, the state must attribute the attack to a specific source, characterize the intent behind the attack, and conclude that the state must use force in response.[85] The principle of proportionality requires that the force used in the response be proportional to the original attack.[86] Lastly, immediacy prohibits the response from being "too tardy."[87] Under customary international law, the principle of immediacy is broad,[88] allowing a response days, weeks, or even months later.[89]

Attribution and characterization are especially important in the context of cyber warfare. A state must attribute an attack for two reasons. First, attribution helps to

---

82 *See* Dinstein, *supra* note 71, at 99, 102–03; Schmitt, *supra* note 81, at 929–30. *But see* Silver, *supra* note 81, at 93 ("The notion that the Charter represents the sole legal structure under which coercive force can be exerted by one State against another largely has been discredited."). An unusual problem arises when a state reacts in self-defense to a cyber attack; due to the nature of the Internet, a cyber attack and any cyber response to that attack may implicate the territorial integrity of a neutral nation. *See* George K. Walker, Neutrality and Information Warfare, 76 Int'l L. Stud. 233, 244–47 (2002); George K. Walker, Information Warfare and Neutrality, 33 Vand. J. Transnat'l L. 1079, 1175–76 (2000).

83 *See* Dinstein, *supra* note 71, at 109; *see also* Military and Paramilitary Activities (Nicar. v. U.S.), 1986 I.C.J. 14, 103 (June 27) (concluding that a self-defense response must fulfill the principles of necessity and proportionality under customary international law); Yoram Dinstein, War, Aggression and Self-Defence 183–84 (3d ed. 2001) (discussing a third principle of immediacy that must be fulfilled for a lawful self-defense response under customary international law). *But see* Oscar Schachter, *The Right of States to Use Armed Force*, 82 Mich. L. Rev. 1620, 1635, 1637 (1984) (arguing the anticipatory self-defense under customary international law requires necessity, proportionality, and imminency). Because this issue is not germane to the discussion, immediacy is used as the third condition to maintain consistency with the cited source.

84 Dinstein, *supra* note 71, at 109.

85 *Id.; see also* Jensen, *supra* note 38, at 231 (arguing that any active defense to a cyber attack must meet three longstanding limitations: attribution, characterization of the intent, and respect for the neutrality of other states).

86 Dinstein, *supra* note 71, at 109. There is some dispute about whether a state may aggregate many smaller attacks when determining the amount of counter-force authorized by law. *Id.* Professor Dinstein concludes that there is some support for the theory that suffering from many small attacks should permit a state to respond with one large counter-measure. *Id.*

87 *Id.* at 110.

88 Kevin C. Kenny, *Self-Defence*, 2 United Nations: Law, Policies and Practice 1162, 1167 (Rüdiger Wolfrum ed., 1995).

89 Dinstein, *supra* note 71, at 110.

ensure that a state does not target an innocent person or place.[90] Second, a state must attribute an attack because the laws governing a permissible response vary depending on whether the attacker is a state actor or a non-state actor.[91] A state actor includes state employees, such as members of the military, as well as independent contractors, such as hackers hired to launch a cyber attack. A non-state actor is someone acting individually or a member of a terrorist organization.[92] If the attacker is a state actor, the response must comply with the United Nations Charter[93] and customary international law.[94] On the other hand, if the attacker is a non-state actor, domestic criminal law will likely govern the response.[95] In addition, international law requires a state to characterize an attack to avoid using force against an entity that inadvertently launched a cyber attack.[96] A state may be able to use force against a hostile attack under its own laws, but international law prohibits the use of force against an inadvertent attack.[97]

When a state defends itself using an active defense measure, additional international law implications arise. The principles of necessity and proportionality forbid "retaliatory or punitive actions. . . . [I]n particular, the means employed for the defence have to be strictly necessary for repelling the attack."[98] Yet the principle of proportionality does not limit "a state, victim of an armed attack . . . to expelling the foreign troops from its territory in exercising its right to self-defence, but [also allows pursuit] across the border into their territory."[99]

The current *jus ad bellum* paradigm does not offer adequate safeguards from cyber attacks.[100] The problem with cyber warfare is that technology makes it nearly impossible to attribute the attack to a specific source or to characterize the intent

90 *See id.*

91 *See* Jensen, *supra* note 38, at 232–33.

92 Non-state actors also include international criminal organizations that specialize in areas such as drug trafficking, human trafficking, money laundering, fraud, computer crimes, and many other illegal activities. *Cf.* CarrieLyn Donigan Guymon, *International Legal Mechanisms for Combating Transnational Organized Crime: The Need for a Multilateral Convention*, 18 Berkeley J. Int'l L. 53, 94 (2000).

93 U.N. Charter art. 2, para. 4; *id.* art. 51.

94 Military and Paramilitary Activities (Nicar. v. U.S.), 1986 I.C.J. 14, 94 (June 27).

95 *See* Daniel M. Creekman, Note, *A Helpless America? An Examination of the Legal Options Available to the United States in Response to Varying Types of Cyber-Attacks from China*, 17 Am. U. Int'l L. Rev. 641, 661 (2002); Jensen, *supra* note 38, at 232–33.

96 Dinstein, *supra* note 71, at 109.

97 *See* Jensen, *supra* note 38, at 235; *see also supra* note 82 and accompanying text.

98 *See* The Charter of the United Nations: A Commentary 805 (Bruno Simma ed., 2d ed. 2002).

99 *Id.*

100 *See* Barkham, *supra* note 79, at 112; Creekman, *supra* note 95, at 680; Jensen, *supra* note 38, at 239; Schmitt, *supra* note 81, at 886. But *see* James P. Terry, *Responding to Attacks on Critical*

behind it. Moreover, a cyber attacker can launch her assault with the push of a key, completing the attack almost instantaneously.[101] A legal system that requires a determination of the attacker's identity and intent does not account for these features of the digital age.[102] The current international paradigm therefore ties a state's hands, making it difficult to effectively respond without risking a violation of international law.[103]

To address the unique nature of cyber warfare, international law should provide a safe harbor for states who initiate a good-faith response to an attack, thus acting in cyber self-defense, without first attributing and characterizing the attack.[104] State survival may depend on an immediate, robust, and aggressive response; therefore, international law should not always require a state to fully satisfy the traditional necessity requirements when acting in self-defense of critical infrastructure.[105] A preferable governing principle would be: when the attack targets the state's critical infrastructure, the state should be able to exercise active defense measures or launch a cyber attack in response without incurring liability.[106] In order to avoid an exception that swallows the rule, states should be required to maintain a publicly available list of critical infrastructure, which a state may protect with active defense measures and, if the identified critical infrastructure were subjected to a cyber attack, a state could respond in cyberspace without first attributing or characterizing the attack.[107] In these circumstances, such an exception would not fundamentally alter the *jus ad bellum* framework, but would instead allow the state to exercise its inherent right of self-defense.

IV. CYBER WARFARE AND CIVIL LIBERTIES

The anonymity of cyber attackers is not only a practical problem. It also raises civil liberties concerns. While cyber attacks by a foreign nation launched from abroad are unlikely to implicate constitutional liberties, the same cannot be said for cyber attacks originating on United States soil. The possibility of employing active defense measures against United States citizens may infringe certain civil liberties normally enjoyed by Americans. Although a cyber attack on critical infrastructure may threaten national security, the United States should take into account the civil

---

Computer Infrastructure: What Targets? What Rules of Engagement?, 46 Naval L. Rev. 170, 185 (1999).

101 *See* Jensen, *supra* note 38, at 232.

102 *See* Creekman, *supra* note 95, at 680; Jensen, *supra* note 38 at 239. *But see* Terry, *supra* note 100, at 185.

103 *See* Barkham, *supra* note 79, at 112; Creekman, *supra* note 95, at 680; Jensen, *supra* note 38, at 240; Schmitt, *supra* note 81, at 886.

104 *See* Creekman, *supra* note 95, at 681; Jensen, *supra* note 38, at 240; Schmitt, *supra* note 81, at 936.

105 Jensen, *supra* note 38, at 239–40.

106 *See id.*

107 *Cf.* Sharp, *supra* note 36, at 74.

liberties of the individual American citizen when determining the proper response. The law must therefore adjust traditional understandings of the right to privacy,[108] the right to protection against an unreasonable search,[109] and the right to due process,[110] given the practical necessity of responding to cyber attacks before determining the attacker's identity and intent. In considering this balance, policy-makers should keep in mind Justice Goldberg's statement: "[W]hile the Constitution protects against invasions of individual rights, it is not a suicide pact."[111]

In responding to those attacks originating on U.S. soil, passive defense measures like encryption and firewalls are not problematic. However, active defense measures and response actions may gather intelligence from information stored on a person's computer system, alter information on that computer system, or destroy the computer system. All of these actions could threaten the constitutional rights of that person. An additional complication is that cyber attacks often use the computers of unsuspecting users as vessels.[112] This makes attribution simultaneously more difficult and more important. While it may be possible to attribute an incident to a specific computer system, it may not be possible to attribute the incident to the specific person coordinating the attack. This raises the possibility of the government inadvertently infringing upon the civil liberties of innocent individuals.

The United States takes pride in the protection of civil liberties. The Constitution, and more specifically the Bill of Rights, was an attempt to protect the most fundamental civil liberties of a democratic society. Yet these liberties are not necessarily absolute. In times of armed conflict, the government may be forced to limit them in the interest of national security. As Chief Justice Rehnquist pointed out:

> [I]n any civilized society the most important task is achieving a proper balance between freedom and order. In wartime, reason and history both suggest that this balance shifts to some degree in favor of order—in favor of the government's ability to deal with conditions that threaten the national well-being.[113]

While Chief Justice Rehnquist was referring to declared wars, he referred in his argument to *Youngstown Sheet & Tube Co. v. Sawyer*,[114] which took place during the undeclared Korean War, and discusses the power of the President to restrict civil

108 *See, e.g.*, Griswold v. Connecticut, 381 U.S. 479, 484–86 (1965).

109 *See* U.S. Const. amend. IV.

110 *See* U.S. Const. amend. V.

111 Kennedy v. Mendoza-Martinez, 372 U.S. 144, 160 (1963); *see also* Terminello v. City of Chicago, 337 U.S. 1, 37 (1949) (Jackson, J., dissenting) ("There is danger that, if the Court does not temper its doctrinaire logic with a little practical wisdom, it will convert the constitutional Bill of Rights into a suicide pact.").

112 Fordahl, *supra* note 63.

113 William H. Rehnquist, All the Laws But One: Civil Liberties in Wartime 222 (1998).

114 Youngstown Sheet & Tube Co. v. Sawyer, 343 U.S. 579 (1952).

liberties outside a state of declared war.[115] It could also be argued that the formal declaration of war is obsolete, serving little or no purpose in international law.[116] "[I]t appears that no nation has declared war since the late 1940s," in spite of hundreds of armed conflicts during this same period.[117] The relevant paradigm is now "armed conflict";[118] its existence should be the relevant question in determining whether the balance should potentially shift. While a cyber attack may use different means than a traditional armed conflict, it is no less threatening to national security, and it thus requires policymakers to balance liberty and security as in a conventional armed attack.

A. Reversing the Presumption

The current U.S approach to cyber attacks can be understood to favor civil liberties at the expense of national security. The United States operates under the presumption that a cyber attack is a criminal act.[119] Pursuant to this presumption, law enforcement investigates a cyber attack in the same fashion and by following the same rules as any other criminal matter.[120] This process respects the civil liberties of a suspected cyber attacker.[121] Only if the perpetrator of a cyber attack has been determined to be a non-U.S. citizen operating outside United States territory may law enforcement pass the incident on to another agency for a responsive measure.

This presumption of a criminal act applies regardless of the cyber attacker's target.[122] A cyber attack on a computer system that is part of our critical infrastructure is subject to the same presumption as an attack on a local business.[123] The problem with this presumption should be clear from the previous discussion concerning the threats in cyberspace: it may take days or even months to investigate the attack.[124] Even if a law enforcement agency can attribute the source of the attack, which may not be possible, doing so days or months later makes it impossible to prevent the resulting damage.[125] In choosing whether to treat a cyber attack as a criminal matter

---

115 Rehnquist, *supra* note 113, at 218–19.

116 Curtis A. Bradley & Jack L. Goldsmith, *Congressional Authorization and the War on Terrorism*, 118 Harv. L. Rev. 2047, 2061 (2005).

117 *Id.* at 2061–62.

118 *Id.* at 2061.

119 *See* Dunlap, *supra* note 33, at 365; Minihan, *supra* note 36, at 7; Sharp, *supra* note 36, at 70; *see also* Secure Cyberspace, *supra* note 24, at 28 (stating that "[l]aw enforcement plays the central role in attributing an attack through the exercise of criminal justice authorities").

120 *See* Minihan, *supra* note 36, at 7; Sharp, *supra* note 36, at 71–72.

121 *See* Sharp, *supra* note 36, at 69.

122 *Id.* at 70.

123 *See id.*

124 *See id.* at 71.

125 *See id.*

rather than a national security matter, policymakers should balance the protection of civil liberties against the ability to immediately, robustly, and aggressively respond to a cyber attack against critical infrastructure.

One example of how our current presumption has led to unsatisfactory results occurred in February 1998, when three teenagers, two located in California and one in Israel, hacked into eleven unclassified computer systems of the Navy and Air Force.[126] The ensuing inter-agency law enforcement operation took nearly a month to identify and arrest the perpetrators.[127] Were it not for the presumption that a cyber attack is a criminal activity requiring a response in accordance with the criminal justice system, federal authorities could have immediately launched an aggressive defense that would have quickly ended the attack. Although this attack had a benign purpose and the time lag did not result in catastrophic consequences, it highlights the potential difficulties that might arise when attempting to respond to a more serious attack.

This Article argues that the only effective way to mount an immediate, robust, and aggressive response to a cyber attack on critical infrastructure is to reverse the current presumption.[128] The nation should initially presume any cyber attack on the critical infrastructure of the United States is a national security threat rather than a criminal activity, at least until federal authorities neutralize the threat and determine that the activity is actually criminal in nature. Such a new presumption would make room for the response necessary to protect critical infrastructure.[129]

B. Impact of the Posse Comitatus Act

Viewing cyber attacks as national security threats suggests that the Department of Defense should play a much greater role, if not the lead role, in the cyber protection of critical infrastructure. Department of Defense involvement in cyber protection within the domestic United States, however, may have Posse Comitatus Act implications that should be considered. The Posse Comitatus Act restricts federal military assets from performing traditional law enforcement functions absent separate authority.[130]

Congress passed the Posse Comitatus Act in 1878 in response to the alleged excesses of federal troops in the South during the Reconstruction Era.[131] The current

126 Lisa Hoffman, *Pentagon Confronts Challenge to Computer System Security*, Patriot Ledger, Apr. 8, 1998, at 16.

127 *See* Sharp, *supra* note 36, at 71.

128 *But see* Dunlap, *supra* note 33, at 366–67 (cautioning that the "the true threat is not what damage cyberterrorists can inflict upon our digital systems, but what freedoms they can force us to forfeit").

129 *See* Sharp, *supra* note 36, at 72.

130 *See* 18 U.S.C. § 1385 (2000).

131 *See* Brian L. Porto, Annotation, *Construction of Application of Posse Comitatus Act (18 U.S.C.A. § 1385), and Similar Predecessor Provisions, Restricting Use of United States Army and Air Force to Execute Laws*, 141 A.L.R. Fed. 271, 281 (1997).

version of the Posse Comitatus Act states that "[w]hoever, except in cases and under circumstances expressly authorized by the Constitution or Act of Congress, willfully uses any part of the Army or the Air Force as a posse comitatus or otherwise to execute the laws" will be punished pursuant to the Act.[132] There are two Constitutional exceptions to the Act:

> (i) The emergency authority. Authorizes prompt and vigorous Federal action, including use of military forces, to prevent loss of life or wanton destruction of property and to restore governmental functioning and public order when sudden and unexpected civil disturbances, disasters, or calamities seriously endanger life and property and disrupt normal governmental functions to such an extent that duly constituted local authorities are unable to control the situations.
>
> (ii) *Protection of Federal property and functions.* Authorizes Federal action, including the use of military forces, to protect Federal property and Federal governmental functions when the need for protection exists and duly constituted local authorities are unable or decline to provide adequate protection.[133]

While on its face the Posse Comitatus Act appears to preclude a major role for the Department of Defense in cyber protection, any response to an attack on the computer systems of United States critical infrastructure would fall under one of the two Constitutional exceptions to the Act. The exact exception would depend on the nature of the critical infrastructure being targeted. An attack on private, state or local critical infrastructure would fall under the emergency authority exception, while an attack on federal critical infrastructure would fall under the protection of the federal property and functions exception. By definition, critical infrastructures are national systems and assets.[134] If, as this Article advocates, a cyber attack against critical infrastructure is presumed to be a national security threat, it can be dealt with by federal rather than local authorities and trigger one of the two Constitutional exceptions to the Act.

If at some point during a cyber attack it became clear that local authorities were more capable of responding to the attack, the Department of Defense could hand the action over to them for a continued response. The military could also passively assist the local authorities without violating the Posse Comitatus Act regardless of the presumption applied.[135] For example, the military could continue to coordinate and exchange information with the local authorities, but could not participate in

132 18 U.S.C. § 1385.

133 32 C.F.R. § 215.4 (2006).

134 42 U.S.C. § 5195c (Supp. II 2002).

135 *See* Porto, *supra* note 131, at 283 (explaining that military personnel would only violate the Posse Comitatus Act if they "assisted in civilian law enforcement by making arrests, searching persons and/or property, seizing evidence, investigating crimes, interviewing witnesses, pursuing escaped civilian prisoners, and searching an area for suspects.").

the ensuing law enforcement functions.[136] Therefore, the Posse Comitatus Act should not exclude the Department of Defense from playing a major role in protecting cyberspace.

V. CONCLUSION

Each day the connectivity of the world increases. This increased connectivity in turn improves our standard of living, expands the speed and sophistication of our decision-making abilities, and fuels the global economy. However, these benefits come at a cost. The United States is more vulnerable now than it has ever been before. For the first time in history, an individual armed with nothing more than technical expertise, a computer system, and a network connection could theoretically bring our nation to its knees. At no more than the cost of an AK-47, a terrorist could cause large-scale death and destruction by launching a cyber attack on the critical infrastructure of our nation. We owe it to ourselves to avoid an attack of this magnitude in the future. The possibility of a substantial cyber attack requires policymakers to fundamentally rethink the way in which they approach protection of the networks and computer systems underlying the nation's critical infrastructure.

A cyber attack is not merely a criminal matter that the nation can effectively address under the rubric of the justice system, but rather is an issue of national security. As such, the federal government must resolve the blurred distinction between cyber security and cyber defense. In cyberspace we cannot distinguish between defense and security. In addition, international law must evolve to account for the nature of the cyber threat to critical infrastructure. The *jus ad bellum* paradigm must permit active self-defense of critical infrastructure and allow a self-defense response to an attack on critical infrastructure in cyberspace without first requiring attribution or characterization of the attack. However, *jus ad bellum* should only allow use of these measures in defense of critical infrastructure that a nation has pre-selected and publicly disseminated prior to the incident. Lastly, policymakers must strike the proper balance between civil liberties and national security interests as we confront this cyber threat. The nature of the threat requires a reversal of the presumption that a cyber attack on critical infrastructure is a criminal matter. The new presumption must be that a cyber attack on critical infrastructure is a national security threat.

The United States cannot afford to get this wrong. Failure to properly protect the computer systems and networks of the nation's critical infrastructure could result in catastrophic consequences for the United States.[137] As Leonardo da Vinci put it, "[i]t is easier to resist at the beginning than at the end."[138]

136 *See id.*

137 *See* Secure Cyberspace, *supra* note 24, at 6.

138 John Bartlett, Familiar Quotations 135 (Justin Kaplan ed., 16th ed. 1992).

SOFT POWER, STRATEGIC SECURITY, AND INTERNATIONAL PHILANTHROPY

Garry W. Jenkins†

Originally Published in *North Carolina Law Review*, Vol. 85 (March 2007)

INTRODUCTION

More than five years after the attacks of September 11, 2001, and three years after the release of *The 9/11 Commission Report*,[1] the United States is still engaged in a process of debating, considering, and now reconsidering strategies, approaches, and policies to effectively address the challenges of global terrorism. As we further understand the long-term nature of this struggle, we appreciate the constant need to develop new and strengthen existing relationships with allies, better utilize strategic advantages, and undertake sound policymaking to promote the short-term and long-term interests of U.S. citizens with respect to national security. Accordingly, current U.S. policy toward international grantmaking by private, independent charitable organizations warrants serious reconsideration.

The United States has long embraced a tradition of philanthropy.[2] American charitable organizations are responsible for a range of innovations that have improved

---

† Assistant Professor of Law, The Ohio State University Moritz College of Law. B.A., Haverford College; M.P.P., Harvard University; J.D., Harvard Law School. The author previously served as Chief Operating Officer and General Counsel of The Goldman Sachs Foundation, where he oversaw a $200 million international grantmaking program.

Many thanks to the people who read earlier drafts of this Article and provided helpful comments, especially Martha Chamallas, Amy Cohen, Lia Epperson, Arthur Greenbaum, Peter Shane, Marc Spindelman, Peter Swire, Donald Tobin, and the participants of the faculty colloquium series at the University of Cincinnati College of Law and The Ohio State University Moritz College of Law. I would also like to thank Phillip Eckenrode, Brian Smith, and Jennifer Storipan for their excellent research assistance.

1 *See* NAT'L COMM'N ON TERRORIST ATTACKS UPON THE U.S., THE 9/11 COMMISSION REPORT (W.W. Norton & Co. 2004) [hereinafter 9/11 COMMISSION REPORT].

2 Frenchman Alexis de Tocqueville on public associations in American civil life:

> Americans of all ages, conditions, and all dispositions constantly unite together. Not only do they have commercial and industrial associations to which all belong but also a thousand other kinds, religious, moral, serious, futile, very general and very specialized, large and small. . . . I have frequently admired the endless skill with which the inhabitants of the United States manage to set a common aim to the efforts of a great number of men and to persuade them to pursue it voluntarily.

humankind and aided people outside of the United States.[3] Although most of the activity of U.S.-based private foundations and public charities has been focused on domestic concerns, international affairs and cross-border initiatives play a pivotal role in America's philanthropic activities.[4] For example, generous Americans often respond to humanitarian crises all over the world,[5] and a range of U.S.-based organizations carry out programs and provide charitable support in all corners of

---

ALEXIS DE TOCQUEVILLE, DEMOCRACY IN AMERICA 596 (Gerald E. Bevan trans., Penguin Books 2003) (1835); *see* Peter D. Hall, *The Welfare State and the Careers of Public and Private Institutions Since 1945, in* CHARITY, PHILANTHROPY, AND CIVILITY IN AMERICAN HISTORY 363, 363–64 (Lawrence J. Friedman & Mark D. McGarvie eds., 2003) (noting the growth in the number of nonprofit organizations in the United States: 12,000 in 1940, 50,000 in 1950, 300,000 in 1960, 600,000 in the mid-1970s, and 1,500,000 by 2003). *See generally* CHARITY, PHILANTHROPY, AND CIVILITY IN AMERICAN HISTORY, *supra* (describing the history of American philanthropy and its importance in American society); Lester M. Salamon, *The United States, in* DEFINING THE NONPROFIT SECTOR: A CROSS-NATIONAL ANALYSIS 280, 280–88 (Lester M. Salamon & Helmut K. Anheier eds., 1997) (providing a general history of the development of the nonprofit sector in the United States).

3 For example, in the 1960s, the Ford Foundation and the Rockefeller Foundation were instrumental in creating research centers to develop improved production methods for wheat and rice. Two of the centers, the International Rice Research Institute in the Philippines and the International Maize and Wheat Improvement Center in Mexico, created new varieties of rice and wheat that greatly enhance crop yields, allowing developing populations to produce enough food to provide for their growing populations and prevent a world hunger crisis. *See* David S. Tilford, *Saving the Blueprints: The International Legal Regime for Plant Resources,* 30 CASE W. RES. J. INT'L L. 373, 389–92 (1998). Cures for several global diseases have been discovered due to the work of nonprofit organizations and the support of private foundations. *See, e.g.,* John G. Simon, *Charity and Dynasty Under the Federal Tax System, in* THE ECONOMICS OF NONPROFIT INSTITUTIONS: STUDIES IN STRUCTURE AND POLICY 246, 254 (Susan Rose-Ackerman ed., 1986) (attributing Jonas Salk's discovery of the polio vaccine to a $15,000 gift from the Sarah Scaife Foundation); Sabin Russell, *S.F. Nonprofit Helps Develop Low-Cost Cure for Black Fever,* S.F. CHRON., Nov. 9, 2004, at A6 (discussing the efforts of a nonprofit organization to provide a cure for black fever, which kills 200,000 people a year in poor countries, second only to malaria). Currently, U.S. funders are tackling equally vexing problems around the world, including the Bill and Melinda Gates Foundation's initiatives on infectious diseases and the Open Society Institute's extensive efforts to bring civil society to formerly authoritarian regimes. *See* BILL & MELINDA GATES FOUND., 2004 ANNUAL REPORT 6–10 (2005); Peter Baker, *Soros's Mission in Russia Ends, $1 Billion Later,* WASH. POST, June 10, 2003, at A14; David Holley, *Soros Invests in His Democratic Passion,* L.A. TIMES, July 5, 2004, at A6; Donald G. McNeil, Jr., *Millions of Lives on the Line in Malaria Battle,* N.Y. TIMES, Jan. 5, 2005, at F6; Ian Wilhelm, *A View Inside the Gates,* CHRON. OF PHILANTHROPY, Nov. 11, 2004, at 12.

4 *See* CTR. ON PHILANTHROPY AT IND. UNIV., GIVING USA: 2004, at 11, 44 (2004) (reporting that international affairs organizations, including U.S. intermediaries, received an estimated $5.3 billion in contributions in 2003, a growth of 14.8% from the previous year).

5 *See, e.g.,* Elizabeth Becker, *U.S. Nearly Triples Tsunami Aid Pledge, to $950 Million,* N.Y. TIMES, Feb. 10, 2005, at A3 ("Americans have given $700 million to charities for the relief effort."); Stevenson Swanson, *Tsunami Aid Pledges Turn into Cash,* CHI. TRIB., June 26, 2005, at C9 (reporting that Americans have donated an estimated $1.4 billion toward tsunami relief efforts).

the globe. For some nonprofit organizations, involvement in cross-border philanthropy is an integral component of their charitable and strategic mission.[6]

Although just a small portion of overall charitable activity,[7] international giving is critically important to both the nonprofit sector and U.S. security interests.[8] And for international giving by domestic U.S. private foundations, community foundations, and public charities, the past decade has presented the best and worst of times. On the one hand, both large and small U.S. funders, stimulated by globalization, an increasingly interconnected world, and global events, have a growing interest in supporting people and improving conditions outside the United States.[9] On the other hand, the federal government's responses to September 11 have made international giving more burdensome in what grantmakers perceive to be a hostile regulatory environment.[10] Furthermore, the U.S. policy approach on this issue has

6 *See, e.g.*, THE FORD FOUND., 2004 ANNUAL REPORT 5 (2005) ("The Ford Foundation is a resource for innovative people and institutions worldwide. Our goals are to: strengthen democratic values, reduce poverty and injustice, promote international cooperation and advance human achievement."); THE GOLDMAN SACHS FOUND., 2004 ANNUAL REPORT 48 (2005) ("The Foundation's mission is to promote excellence and innovation in education and to improve the academic performance and lifelong productivity of young people worldwide."); THE ROCKEFELLER FOUND., 2004 ANNUAL REPORT 22 (2005) ("The Rockefeller Foundation is a knowledge-based global foundation with a commitment to enrich and sustain the lives and livelihoods of poor and excluded people throughout the world."); W.K. KELLOGG FOUND., 2005 ANNUAL REPORT 24 (2006) (stating its mission "to help people [in the United States, Latin America and the Caribbean, and southern Africa] help themselves through the practical application of knowledge and resources to improve their quality of life and that of future generations"); *see also* Nina J. Crimm, *Through a Post-September 11 Looking Glass: Assessing the Roles of Federal Tax Laws and Tax Policies Applicable to Global Philanthropy by Private Foundations and Their Donors*, 23 VA. TAX REV. 1, 17 n.36 (2003) (describing historical connections between private foundations and international grantmaking).

7 *See* CTR. ON PHILANTHROPY AT IND. UNIV., GIVING USA: 2005, at 170 (2005) (estimating giving devoted to international affairs at 2% of total charitable activity).

8 *See infra* Part I.

9 This is perhaps best reflected by the ascendancy of the Bill and Melinda Gates Foundation, the nation's largest private foundation, which has emphasized international programming. According to an October 2006 Foundation Center study, "[i]f the Gates Foundation were excluded from the sample . . . international giving would have decreased 4 percent." LOREN RENZ & JOSIE ATIENZA, FOUND. CTR., INTERNATIONAL GRANTMAKING UPDATE: A SNAPSHOT OF U.S. FOUNDATION TRENDS 3 (2006), *available at* http://foundationcenter.org/gainknowledge/research/pdf/intl_update_2006.pdf. The June 2006 announcement that Warren Buffett would direct the majority of his personal fortune to be spent by the Gates Foundation on similar measures further highlights the prominence and positive trends of international giving. *See* Timothy L. O'Brien & Stephanie Saul, *Buffett To Give Bulk of Fortune to Gates Charity*, N.Y. TIMES, June 26, 2006, at A1.

10 *See* LOREN RENZ ET AL., FOUND. CTR., INTERNATIONAL GRANTMAKING III: AN UPDATE ON U.S. FOUNDATION TRENDS, at xiv (2004) (reporting that 78% of grantmakers believe international funding has become more difficult due to government regulatory initiatives since September 11); Jeff Jones, *Nonprofits Fear False Accusations of Terror Grants*, NONPROFIT TIMES, May 1, 2003, at 1.

not evolved to a state in which international philanthropy is treated as a valuable ally with the means to enhance and strengthen governmental strategic interests. The conventional justification for the government's policy responses is that the administrative costs imposed are necessary to enhance U.S. security and to protect citizens from terrorists.[11] However, this simple tradeoff fundamentally misperceives the debate. The full effect of the additional administrative costs placed on U.S. funders cannot be measured without considering the costs of the additional burdens for grantmakers, for their organizational effectiveness, and, significantly, for U.S. security interests. Not only is a robust cost-benefit analysis missing from this debate,[12] but, as a result, a full accounting of the security costs associated with the additional burdens remains unconsidered. The irony is that government efforts to make us more secure may actually leave us less safe. At the very least, the calculation used to determine the security benefits offered by greater regulation must be altered to ensure consideration for the corresponding security harms.

This Article details how international philanthropy advances U.S. security interests. Although the work undertaken by charitable organizations advantages its intended beneficiaries, it simultaneously generates several important byproducts that serve American interests. The United States as a whole also benefits from private overseas giving because philanthropy can be a powerful tool of public diplomacy: it enhances the U.S. image abroad, facilitates the sharing of ideas and values, and places U.S. institutions and people as partners in solving critical social ills. Scholars and policy analysts have increasingly recognized that it is in the United States's interest to see additional private resources brought to bear to assist developing countries build stable societies by addressing poverty, health crises, environmental degradation, economic development, educational challenges, and other global problems. In addition, it is through the support of private U.S. entities that foreign local nonprofit counterparts in the developing world can be sustained and strengthened so that they can contribute to the development of civil society. One central theme of this Article is that international philanthropy, although independent from government control, helps to generate "soft power"[13] for the U.S. government that is used to

---

11 *See Counterterror Initiatives in the Terror Finance Program: Hearing Before the S. Comm. on Banking, Housing, and Urban Affairs*, 108th Cong. 178 (2004) (statement of Samuel W. Bodman, Deputy Secretary, U.S. Department of the Treasury) (acknowledging government efforts to "enhanc[e] ongoing due diligence efforts, while balancing the demands on [private and charitable] institutions"); U.S. Dep't of the Treasury, Response to Comments Submitted on the U.S. Department of the Treasury Anti-Terrorist Financing Guidelines: Voluntary Best Practices for U.S.-Based Charities 7 (2006), *available at* http://www.treas.gov/press/releases/reports/0929%20responsetocomments.pdf ("We recognize that the information-collection practices are expansive . . . . This type of information-gathering is essential for the charity to . . . be assured that its assets will not be diverted to terrorist organizations or their support networks.").

12 *See* Daniel J. Mitchell, *Fighting Terror and Defending Freedom: The Role of Cost-Benefit Analysis*, 25 Pace L. Rev. 219, 231 (2005).

13 Joseph S. Nye, Jr., Soft Power: The Means of Success in World Politics (2004); *see infra* Part I.C.

influence others and garner cooperation in global affairs. I take the position that the U.S. government policy should support international philanthropy not only for altruistic purposes but also out of enlightened self-interest.

Despite the many benefits generated by international philanthropy, U.S. public charities and private foundations with active international programs bear significant burdens imposed by antiterrorism measures enacted following the launch of the federal government's "war on terrorism."[14] Significantly, a key element of the Bush administration's efforts to defeat terrorism has centered on attempting to stem the flow of funds to terrorist groups.[15] In addition to focusing on global money laundering and freezing assets of known (and suspected) criminals,[16] the federal government has also attempted to prevent nonprofit organizations from being used, even inadvertently, to support terrorist activities. This Article analyzes the battery of new legal tools that the federal government has adopted in order to protect charitable organizations and their funds from diversion, including Executive Order 13,224 ("Executive Order"),[17] the USA PATRIOT Act,[18] and the *U.S. Department of the Treasury Anti-Terrorist Financing Guidelines: Voluntary Best Practices for U.S.-Based Charities* ("Treasury ATF

---

14 *See* President's Address to the Nation on the Terrorist Attacks, 37 WEEKLY COMP. PRES. DOC. 1301 (Sept. 11, 2001), *available at* http://www.gpoaccess.gov/wcomp/v37no37.html; President's Address Before a Joint Session of the Congress on the United States Response to the Terrorist Attacks of September 11, 37 WEEKLY COMP. PRES. DOC. 1347 (Sept. 20, 2001), *available at* http://www.gpoaccess.gov/wcomp/v37no38.html; President's Address Before a Joint Session of the Congress on the State of the Union, 39 WEEKLY COMP. PRES. DOC. 109 (Jan. 28, 2003), *available at* http://www.gpoaccess.gov/wcomp/v39no5.html. For a critique of the Bush administration's "war" rhetoric to describe the effort to fight terrorism, see Bruce Ackerman, *This Is Not a War,* 113 YALE L.J. 1871, 1874–78 (2004); Mary Ellen O'Connell, *Enhancing the Status of Non-State Actors Through a Global War on Terror?,* 43 COLUM. J. TRANSNAT'L L. 435, 452–58 (2005).

15 "The war against terrorism is a new kind of war being fought on many fronts. Nowhere is this truer than in the fight against terrorist financing. The President has directed me to take all measures necessary to deprive terrorists of funds." *The State of the International Financial System and the International Monetary Fund: Hearing Before the H. Comm. on Financial Servs.,* 107th Cong. 54 (2002) (statement of Paul H. O'Neill, Secretary, U.S. Department of the Treasury); *see also* 18 U.S.C. § 2339C (Supp. IV 2004) (outlining the prohibitions against the financing of terrorism); James B. Johnston, *Implementing New Jersey's Anti-Terrorism Laws To Prevent Terrorist Financing: A Statutory Analysis of the "Material Support or Resources" Provisions of the September 11, 2001 Anti-Terrorism Act and the "Freezing Funds and Assets Related to Terrorism" Legislation in the New Jersey Criminal Code,* 29 SETON HALL LEGIS. J. 85, 86 (2004) (noting that terrorist financing investigations have become "an integral part of America's counterterrorism strategy"); John Crewdson & Cam Simpson, *U.S. Zeroing In on Terror's Money Trail,* CHI. TRIB., Sept. 5, 2002, at N20 (reporting the scope and progress of government efforts to stop terrorist financing).

16 *See* Matthew Levitt, *Stemming the Flow of Terrorist Financing: Practical and Conceptual Challenges,* 27 FLETCHER F. WORLD AFF. 59, 61–62 (2003). For more on money laundering and the U.S. effort to obstruct terrorist financing, see Eric J. Gouvin, *Bringing Out the Big Guns: The USA Patriot Act, Money Laundering, and the War on Terrorism,* 55 BAYLOR L. REV. 955 (2003).

17 Exec. Order No. 13,224, 66 Fed. Reg. 49,079 (Sept. 23, 2001).

18 Uniting and Strengthening America by Providing Appropriate Tools Required To Intercept and Obstruct Terrorism (USA PATRIOT) Act of 2001, Pub. L. No. 107-56, 115 Stat. 272 (codified in scattered sections of the U.S.C.).

Guidelines" or "Guidelines").[19] Undoubtedly, the chief goals of these laws, regulations, and guidelines are to protect U.S. citizens, ensure that charitable assets are not diverted to terrorists, and weaken support for terrorism. However, these policies may inadvertently cause more harm than benefit because they fail to account for the unintended security costs. This gap is particularly problematic because the security costs are significant and affect the core of our nonmilitary strategies addressing the threat of terrorism. These policies not only burden international giving but also implicate U.S. soft power and governmental effectiveness on the world stage.

This Article argues that the federal government's overall approach intended to protect charities from terrorism—particularly its emphasis on issuing guidelines constraining international giving—is undermining the efficacy of international philanthropic activities and thereby hindering the ability of private foundations and public charities to generate important security benefits for the United States. A barrage of criticism from the nonprofit sector since the Guidelines were issued in 2002 has prompted the Treasury Department to make modest changes to them.[20] Although the 2006 modifications to the Treasury ATF Guidelines have reduced some of the administrative burdens and addressed some of the specific objections from the nonprofit sector, the fundamental tensions remain. The government continues to pursue a policy approach that views international philanthropy through the prism of an exposed threat that requires containment rather than as a source of governmental power generating enhanced credibility and legitimacy.

As the government coerces nonprofits to collect and report data as if they were government agents, nonprofits are pressured into taking on investigatory responsibilities for which they are ill-equipped.[21] In addition, such actions begin to encroach on the charitable sector's independence from government and, accordingly, its claim to the high middle ground staked between the public and private sectors. These are not merely administrative costs or theoretical concerns; they also directly implicate organizational effectiveness and security interests. The government's approach affects nonprofit behavior[22] and adds levels of bureaucracy to international philanthropy, creating ripple effects that must be considered as part of an integrated counterterrorism strategy that embraces overseas development, seeks to combat negative perceptions of the United States in the world, and values international cooperation and influence.

This Article is less about what the federal government can and cannot do, and more about what deserves consideration when weighing the costs of the regulatory

---

19 U.S. Dep't of the Treasury, Anti-Terrorist Financing Guidelines: Voluntary Best Practices for U.S.-Based Charities (2006), *available at* http://www.ustreas.gov/offices/enforcement/key-issues/protecting/docs/guidelines_charities.pdf.

20 *Id.* at 2.

21 *See infra* Part II.

22 *See infra* Part III.

regime against speculative benefits. Although the government may regulate charitable giving abroad by U.S. entities, strategic policymaking in this area offers opportunities to advance U.S. and humanitarian interests. To begin our examination, Part I identifies several strategic advantages for the United States associated with international grantmaking activities by independent U.S.-based private foundations and public charities. Essentially, this Part details the ways in which philanthropy supports U.S. security interests, such as the promotion of civil society in developing countries through the nourishment of foreign nonprofit organizations and support for efforts to address the root causes of terrorism. This in turn creates a positive image of the United States among foreign audiences and generates the soft power necessary to lead and influence foreign governments. This Part explains and expands on the theoretical origins of soft power as they relate to nonprofit organizations and governmental power.

Part II provides a brief explanation of the relevant tax laws and regulations concerning overseas philanthropic activity in place prior to September 11 that provide ample due diligence mechanisms to guard against abuses. This Part also describes the new legal and policy restrictions on international philanthropy adopted after September 11 to protect U.S. organizations from being duped by foreign organizations. It also argues that the regulatory regime has misdirected its efforts by focusing on "indirect" charitable abuse, whereby legitimate U.S. charitable organizations purportedly are conned by foreign entities fronting terrorist operations.

Part III analyzes some specific problems with the policy approaches the federal government has followed. In particular, it explains how the seemingly modest suggestions put forward in the Treasury ATF Guidelines are not well-attuned to the realities and nuances of conducting philanthropy overseas and how they undermine the public perception of the nonprofit sector's independence from government and impede the sector's ability to generate the many aforementioned benefits of international philanthropy that can help enhance our long-term security.

Finally, Part IV concludes with a discussion of potential alternative policy prescriptions to balance the need to protect U.S. funders from unwittingly supporting terrorist activities while also supporting their efforts to engage in positive philanthropic endeavors across the globe that contribute to U.S. security. This Part argues for more expansive and formal cost-benefit analysis and the creation of safe harbors to protect U.S. charities engaged in international giving. It also explores reforms that might include altering new regulatory controls, such as the Treasury ATF Guidelines and the Executive Order, as well as revamping preexisting law governing procedures for international giving by private foundations.

In recent years, several commentators have criticized some of the government's post-September 11 policies and urged changes on a wide range of issues.[23] With respect

23 *See* David Cole, *Enemy Aliens*, 54 Stan. L. Rev. 953, 958, 989 (2002) (criticizing the government for acting "as if we are free to ignore international norms whenever it serves our interests"

to international grantmaking, our current regime has focused primarily on the potential benefits from increased regulation of charities in order to curtail the financing of terrorism, but there has been a systematic disregard of the costs—the security tradeoffs—associated with encumbering international philanthropy. Only by identifying the benefits generated by high levels of international philanthropy and the negative effects of additional regulation is it possible for our debate over appropriate policy choices to capture not just an understanding of the speculative security benefits from increased regulation but also a sense of some of the security costs. From that vantage point, a more accurate cost-benefit analysis can be developed, perhaps even leading to a more balanced and enlightened policy response that seeks to support, or even expand, opportunities for international engagement by American charities and grantmakers as a means of countering terrorism.

I. UNDERSTANDING THE CONTRIBUTIONS OF OVERSEAS GRANTMAKING

In today's complex world, U.S. security is bound up with global affairs and issues. In fact, in 2002, the Bush administration explicitly acknowledged foreign development aid as a key component of U.S. national security.[24] Of course, since World War II and throughout the Cold War, foreign aid has been an essential instrument of government policy.[25] After experiencing declines through the 1990s,[26] both military and nonmilitary development aid have increased significantly in the wake of September 11. Since those terrorist attacks of 2001, U.S. official development assistance ("ODA"), which represents nonmilitary support to developing countries for economic development and welfare, rose from approximately $10 billion in

---

as well as for "trading immigrants' rights for our own purported security"); Harold Hongju Koh, *On American Exceptionalism,* 55 STAN. L. REV. 1479, 1497–1500 (2003) (criticizing the Bush administration's largely unilateralist approach to combating terrorism and violating international law in the process); Winston P. Nagan & Craig Hammer, *The New Bush National Security Doctrine and the Rule of Law,* 22 BERKELEY J. INT'L L. 375, 402 (2004) (criticizing the influence of "isolationism and exceptionalism" on U.S. foreign relations policy); John S. Richbourg, *Liberty and Security: The Yin and Yang of Immigration Law,* 33 U. MEM. L. REV. 475, 477–80, 506–07 (2003) (criticizing the development of U.S. "immigration policies on the basis of fear" after September 11).

24 *See* THE WHITE HOUSE, THE NATIONAL SECURITY STRATEGY OF THE UNITED STATES OF AMERICA 21 (2002), *available at* http://www.whitehouse.gov/nsc/nss.pdf; Gail Russell Chaddock, *A Bush Vision of Pax Americana,* CHRISTIAN SCI. MONITOR, Sept. 23, 2002, at 1.

25 *See* Carol C. Adelman, *The Privatization of Foreign Aid: Reassessing National Largesse,* FOREIGN AFF., Nov.–Dec. 2003, at 9. Throughout the Cold War, however, development aid was often granted for geopolitical ends rather than strategic human development purposes. *See* Thomas Kleven, *Why International Law Favors Emigration over Immigration,* 33 U. MIAMI INTER-AM. L. REV. 69, 91 n.70 (2002); W. Michael Reisman, Commentary, *International Law After the Cold War,* 84 AM. J. INT'L L. 859, 863 (1990).

26 *See* Charles Babington & Thomas W. Lippman, *First Lady Joins Effort on Diplomacy Funds: Business, Other Groups Fighting GOP Budget Cuts,* WASH. POST, Apr. 14, 1999, at A25 (noting U.S. spending on foreign aid declined throughout the early and mid-1990s).

2000 to $19 billion in 2004.[27] Despite this dramatic increase in funding, which makes the U.S. government the world's leading donor in terms of overall volume, the United States ranks near the bottom (second to last) of the twenty-two major aid donor nations in terms of percentage of gross national income targeted to development assistance.[28] The U.S. ODA per capita contribution was more than forty percent lower than our continental counterparts in the European Union.[29]

Although foreign aid architecture is complex, involving multiple partners, when it comes to measuring contributions from the United States to developing countries, substantial foreign aid is delivered outside official government aid channels, primarily through nonprofit organizations. Although exact measures of foreign contributions by charitable U.S. organizations are difficult to obtain, estimates of private international philanthropy from U.S.-based public charities and private foundations would unquestionably greatly augment levels of overall aid to the developing world donated by the U.S. government. Economist Jeffrey Sachs writes that U.S. nongovernmental entities provide approximately $3 billion per year in development assistance.[30] The U.S. Department of State, however, estimated that U.S. private charitable sources donated nearly $7 billion to developing countries in 2004.[31] And recently, a private U.S. think tank—the Hudson Institute—issued a report compiling data on public and private engagement in the developing world.[32] While the overall report included several means of engagement with the developing world, it estimated that private charitable organizations based in the United States donated approximately $13.6 billion in 2004.[33]

27 *See* Larry Nowels, Cong. Research Serv., CRS Report for Congress: Foreign Aid: Understanding Data Used To Compare Donors 2 (2005), *available at* http://www.fas.org/sgp/crs/row/RS22032.pdf; Press Release, U.S. Dep't of State, The United States and International Development: Fostering Hope Through Growth 1 (May 31, 2005), *available at* http://www.state.gov/documents/organization/47055.pdf. Iraq's aid allotment accounted for approximately 16% and 37% of total U.S. development assistance in 2004 and 2005, respectively. *See* Press Release, U.S. Dep't of State, The United States and International Development: Partnering for Growth (May 10, 2006), [hereinafter Press Release, Partnering for Growth] *available at* http://www.state.gov/r/pa/prs/ps/2006/66060.htm.

28 *See* Nowels, *supra* note 27, at 5.

29 *See id.* at 6.

30 *See* Jeffrey D. Sachs, The End of Poverty: Economic Possibilities for Our Time 303 (2005) (citing figures from the Development Assistance Committee of the Organisation for Economic Co-operation and Development ("OECD")).

31 *See* Press Release, Partnering for Growth, *supra* note 27.

32 *See* Hudson Inst., The Index of Global Philanthropy (Karina Rollins ed., 2006), *available at* http://gpr.hudson.org/files/publications/globalphilanthropy.pdf.

33 According to the report, private foundations contributed $3.4 billion, public charities contributed $5.7 billion, and religious organizations donated $4.5 billion. *See id.* at 20–28. The report also measured corporate contributions, the monetary value of donated volunteer time, the value of university scholarships to American institutions, and private remittances. *See id.* at 22–34. However, I have excluded those amounts for the purposes of this analysis focused on international giving by charitable organizations.

Although the estimates of giving may vary, the significance of private aid is undisputed. Even taking the smallest estimate of $3 billion, the contributions of U.S. private foundations and public charities exceed the official development assistance aid of all but six of the twenty-two major government donors, including Sweden,[34] which is known as the "darling of the Third World"[35] because of the high amount of its foreign aid as a percentage of the country's overall gross national product ("GNP"). Obviously, the larger estimates simply magnify the effects. Moreover, as voices from the left call for even larger U.S. aid contributions commensurate with the GNP levels[36] of our counterparts and voices on the right claim that criticisms of U.S. aid levels are unfounded in part because they fail to account for contributions from private sources,[37] international philanthropy takes on an increasingly important position as part of the United States's international aid story. In many ways, even without a formal relationship, international philanthropy represents a form of a public-private partnership between government and charitable organizations through which the nonprofit sector is an ally in U.S. development assistance efforts. Accordingly, a strong public policy interest exists for encouraging international philanthropy.

Although these figures provide a sense of the monetary stakes, more than just money is at issue. As one commentator has noted, charitable organizations are "delivering more than just money to developing countries. They are delivering the values of freedom, democracy, entrepreneurship, and volunteerism."[38] In addition, charitable assistance contributes to increased security both abroad and here at home. International grantmaking facilitates the development of civil society in the developing world, contributing to greater global security and enhancing the public image and public diplomacy efforts of the United States. Perhaps more important, it serves as a means of engendering cooperation with allies through the buildup of soft power.

A. International Philanthropy as a Facilitator of Civil Society

International aid is a powerful weapon in promoting civil society and advancing social and economic development across the globe. To that end, development aid also advances U.S. security interests by alleviating some of the situational factors, such as poverty, political oppression, and social inequality, that may breed terrorists and produce weak states where terrorism thrives, and replacing them with conditions for economic growth, trade, and private investment.[39] As the United States seeks to

34 *See* Nowels, *supra* note 27, at 5.

35 *See* Jack Goldsmith, *Liberal Democracy and Cosmopolitan Duty,* 55 Stan. L. Rev. 1667, 1689 (2003) (noting Sweden's reputation in the developing world).

36 *See, e.g.,* Sachs, *supra* note 30, at 288–303.

37 *See, e.g.,* Adelman, *supra* note 25, at 9.

38 *Id.* at 14.

39 *See* Stuart Eizenstat et al., *Rebuilding Weak States,* Foreign Aff., Jan.–Feb. 2005, at 134, 135–36, 139–41; Kevin J. Fandl, *Terrorism, Development, and Trade: Winning the War on Terror Without the War,* 19 Am. U. Int'l L. Rev. 587, 599–600 (2004).

understand and respond to security threats as well as prevent further conflict, development aid emerges as a key element of foreign policy.[40]

The profound impact of the September 11 attacks and the resulting campaign against terrorism has led scholars and citizens alike to consider and debate the sources of anti-American terrorism and the proper responses to the challenges posed by such violence.[41] Although various arguments and theories have been put forward, several scholars and commentators have noted the ways in which economic desperation, disease, and global poverty, among other socioeconomic deficiencies, contribute to the foundational origins of terrorism.[42] Although there may not be

---

40 The case for foreign aid to developing countries has been put forward by a variety of economists, development experts, and political figures. *See, e.g.*, SACHS, *supra* note 30, at 244–65, 329–46 (arguing that countries beset by instability and poverty can, with adequate financial assistance, be transformed into emerging market economies); Colin L. Powell, *No Country Left Behind*, FOREIGN POL'Y, Jan.–Feb. 2005, at 28, 30 (former U.S. Secretary of State arguing that development assistance is an essential element of U.S. national security policy and acknowledging that the Bush administration recognizes a "link between terrorism and poverty"). Foreign aid, however, has been criticized for advancing multinational corporate interests at the expense of poor countries, *see, e.g.*, JAMES M. CYPHER & JAMES L. DIETZ, THE PROCESS OF ECONOMIC DEVELOPMENT 525–26 (2d ed. 2004); Michael Dobbs, *Aid Abroad Is Business Back Home*, WASH. POST, Jan. 26, 2001, at A1, and for extreme waste and corruption, *see, e.g.*, WILLIAM EASTERLY, THE ELUSIVE QUEST FOR GROWTH: ECONOMISTS' ADVENTURES AND MISADVENTURES IN THE TROPICS (2002); MICHAEL MAREN, THE ROAD TO HELL: THE RAVAGING EFFECTS OF FOREIGN AID AND INTERNATIONAL CHARITY (1997).

41 *See*, e.g., Graham E. Fuller, Terrorism: Sources and Cures, in A PRACTICAL GUIDE TO WINNING THE WAR ON TERRORISM 15 (Adam Garfinkle ed., 2004); Michael J. Kelly, *Understanding September 11th—An International Legal Perspective on the War in Afghanistan*, 35 CREIGHTON L. REV. 283 (2002); John Quigley, *Identifying the Origins of Anti-American Terrorism*, 56 FLA. L. Rev. 1003 (2004); Ruth Wedgwood, *Al Qaeda, Terrorism, and Military Commissions*, 96 AM. J. INT'L L. 328, 329 (2002).

42 *See, e.g.*, CORALIE BRYANT & CHRISTINA KAPPAZ, REDUCING POVERTY, BUILDING PEACE 26 (2005) (noting that al Qaeda and Osama Bin Laden's "support is strong among many poor who see him as working to fight the injustice they face in their lives"); PAUL R. PILLAR, TERRORISM AND U.S. FOREIGN POLICY 31 (2002) (discussing policy initiatives connected to root causes of terrorism); James Gomez, *September 11: Asian Perspectives*, 13 IND. INT'L & COMP. L. REV. 705, 712 (2003) ("Terrorism was seen as arising from surging global poverty and recommendations were made that this issue be dealt with effectively. In this respect, counter-terrorist strategies were urged to include the elimination of the root causes of poverty."); Lee H. Hamilton, *Fighting Terrorism*, 12 IND. J. GLOBAL LEGAL STUD. 379, 382 (2005) ("We need a comprehensive strategy that balances and integrates all elements of American power. . . . [including] helping to reverse the causes of terrorism by promoting social and political rights, and the rule of law in repressive societies; working to reduce the poverty and unemployment that create an opening for terrorist recruitment; [and] promoting education abroad, so young Muslims have alternatives to radical and hate-filled teachings . . . ."); Shashi Tharoor, *September 11, 2002: Understanding and Defeating Terrorism, One Year Later*, 27 FLETCHER F. WORLD AFF. 9, 11 (2003) (acknowledging the role of "the scourges of poverty, of famine, of illiteracy, of ill-health, of injustice, and of human insecurity"); Adam Garfinkle, *The Impossible Imperative? Conjuring Arab Democracy*, NAT'L INT., Fall 2002, at 156 (arguing that poverty and disinformation in Arab countries contribute to terrorism).

a direct causal link,[43] international development experts Coralie Bryant and Christina Kappaz persuasively argue that "poverty, inequality, and social exclusion create circumstances that lead to or abet violence."[44] Put slightly differently, poverty, poor health, environmental degradation, and other social ills provide fertile ground for terrorism to thrive. If we take these views seriously, as I think we should, the promotion of poverty reduction, self-determination, and human rights must be an integral part of a complete strategy to defeat terrorism.

In its final report, the 9/11 Commission indicated that a "comprehensive U.S. strategy to counter terrorism should include economic policies that encourage development, more open societies, and opportunities for people to improve the lives of their families and to enhance prospects for their children's future."[45] Addressing the socioeconomic roots of the discontent and inequity that lead to extremism is an important part of the strategy to enhance national security.[46] Accordingly, policymakers should be especially cautious when developing policies that directly and indirectly implicate strategic support for overseas development.

U.S. private foundations and public charities,[47] in control of substantial capital resources, are well equipped and positioned to provide financial and human resources to address those root-cause issues.[48] Unquestionably, philanthropic capital remains limited, and nonprofit organizations cannot solve global poverty and related problems alone. However, such private aid is particularly and uniquely valuable because of the sheer magnitude of resources nonprofits offer, the greater flexibility they possess as compared to the government in the allocation of funds, and the instrumental role independent nonprofits have in building coalitions across

---

43 *See* BRYANT & KAPPAZ, *supra* note 42, at 8; BRUCE W. JENTLESON, AMERICAN FOREIGN POLICY: THE DYNAMICS OF CHOICE IN THE 21ST CENTURY 407 (2004).

44 *See* BRYANT & KAPPAZ, *supra* note 42, at 159.

45 *See* 9/11 COMMISSION REPORT, *supra* note 1, at 379.

46 *See* JENTLESON, *supra* note 43, at 407; SACHS, *supra* note 30, at 330–31 ("Whether terrorists are rich or poor or middle class, their staging areas—their bases of operation— are unstable societies beset by poverty, unemployment, rapid population growth, hunger, and lack of hope. Without addressing the root causes of that instability, little will be accomplished in stanching terror.").

47 Both private foundations and public charities are tax-exempt organizations classified under the Internal Revenue Code. *See* I.R.C. § 501(c)(3) (2000). Private foundations are generally created, funded, and controlled by an individual, a family, or a corporation, and commonly engage in grantmaking as their primary activity. Public charities are nonprofits with financial support drawn from a broad base of donors, substantial government support, or some form of public control, and commonly operate their own charitable services or programs. *See* I.R.C. § 509; Susan N. Gary, *Regulating the Management of Charities: Trust Law, Corporate Law, and Tax Law*, 21 U. HAW. L. REV. 593, 631 (1999).

48 *See* Helmut Anheier & Adele Simmons, *The Role of Philanthropy in Globalization*, *in* RETHINKING PHILANTHROPIC EFFECTIVENESS: LESSONS FROM AN INTERNATIONAL NETWORK OF FOUNDATION EXPERTS 10, 23 (Dirk Eilinghoff ed., 2005); *see also* RENZ ET AL., *supra* note 10, at 19 (estimating that international giving by U.S. private foundations alone totaled $3.2 billion in 2002).

sectors and coordinating strategy among grassroots nonprofit organizations.[49] Even in terms of cash, nonprofit donations offer advantages because much of U.S. government assistance is delivered through "tied aid" that links contributions to the purchase of services and goods from the donating country.[50] Therefore, development aid through nonprofits is both more efficient and actually worth more to recipients than equivalent government dollars.[51]

Importantly, philanthropic activity, in the developing world in particular, helps foster democratic governance by supporting and nurturing independent voices, building social capital to support democracy, and developing natural allies with like-minded constituencies. For instance, in the Arab world, many local nonprofit organizations frequently provide alternatives to radical groups and ideas opposed to the United States.[52] Consistent with the charitable goals of their U.S. funders, foreign grant recipients often pursue goals associated with U.S. interests or mainstream American values or both, such as advancing education, youth development, microfinance, economic development, the environment, and women's rights.[53] The local foreign nongovernmental organizations ("NGOs"), which are frequently small with strong community ties, help alter political and social landscapes and provide critical building blocks for civil society.[54] Close working relationships with

---

49 *See* Anheier & Simmons, *supra* note 48, at 11.

50 *See* U.N. Dev. Programme, Human Development Report 2005, at 102 (Charlotte Denny ed., 2005), *available at* http://hdr.undp.org/reports/global/2005/pdf/HDR05_complete.pdf ("According to OECD reports on tied aid to least developed countries, the United States tops the tied aid list . . . ."); *see also* Curt Tarnoff & Larry Nowels, Cong. Research Serv., CRS Report for Congress: Foreign Aid: An Introductory Overview of U.S. Programs and Policy 18 (2004), *available at* http://www.usinfo.state.gov/usa/infousa/trade/files/98-916.pdf ("Most U.S. foreign aid is used for procurement of U.S. goods and services . . . .").

51 *See* U.N. Dev. Programme, *supra* note 50, at 102 (noting that tied aid reduces the value of assistance by 11% to 30%).

52 *See, e.g.*, Janine A. Clark, Islam, Charity, and Activism: Middle-Class Networks and Social Welfare in Egypt, Jordan, and Yemen (2003) (examining the structure and dynamics of moderate Islamic institutions, including the Islamic Center Charity Society in Jordan and the Islah Women's Charitable Society in Yemen, and the social and political impact of the organizations); Sabrina Tavernise, *Iraqi Charities Plant the Seed of Civil Society*, N. Y. Times, May 23, 2006, at A1; Holly Yettick, *Locals Fund Real Dream: A Pakistani Schoolhouse*, Rocky Mountain News (Denver), Feb. 11, 2002, at A12 (describing a Pakistani school modeled after U.S. schools intended to provide an alternative to religious madrassas).

53 *See generally* Renz et al., *supra* note 10, at 53–77 (describing the programmatic giving trends and habits of private funders engaged in international grantmaking).

54 *See* Robert D. Putnam, Bowling Alone: The Collapse and Revival of American Community 336–49 (2000); Miriam Galston, *Civic Renewal and the Regulation of Nonprofits*, 13 Cornell J.L. & Pub. Pol'y 289, 291 (2004) (stating that "participation in voluntary associations is one of the principal methods for assuring an active citizenry"); Dana Brakman Reiser, *Dismembering Civil Society: The Social Cost of Internally Undemocratic Nonprofits*, 82 Or. L. Rev. 829, 830–31 (2003) (describing the charitable sector's role in constructing and maintaining civil society).

experienced U.S. charitable organizations (something the U.S. government cannot offer) also can strengthen and educate a local foreign charity. Additionally, as explained above, private foundations in particular bring unique advantages in their ability to bring people together in ways that no formal U.S. government program is capable of doing.[55] In addition to providing altruistic benefit and helping address potential root causes of terrorism, international aid efforts to promote civil society and democratic governance advance U.S. security interests.[56]

Finally, active engagement by and support from U.S. funders working with foreign nonprofits advances U.S. policy interests by helping developing countries achieve economic growth, establish stable middle classes, and actively engage in the global economy,[57] all of which lead to more stable states and potential strategic allies.[58] Of course, grantmaking programs and giving priorities are diverse, but studies have revealed that international grant support increasingly has targeted grassroots "community improvement, microenterprise development, primary health care, primary and secondary education, refugee and migration issues, women's rights, resource conservation, and local media and communications."[59] Moreover, this presumably advances U.S. interests because successful economic and political development abroad opens new, stable markets to U.S. goods and generates new opportunities for investment.[60] Thus, philanthropy's increased support of development aid can provide the twin benefits of enhancing political stability and expanding markets

---

55 *See supra* text accompanying note 49.

56 *See* The White House, The National Security Strategy of the United States of America 33 (2006), *available at* http://www.whitehouse.gov/nsc/nss/2006/nss2006.pdf ("Development reinforces diplomacy and defense, reducing long-term threats to our national security by helping to build stable, prosperous, and peaceful societies. Improving the way we use foreign assistance will make it more effective in strengthening responsible governments, responding to suffering, and improving people's lives.").

57 *See* Karin Aggestam, *Conflict Prevention: Old Wine in New Bottles?, in* Mitigating Conflict: The Role of NGOs 12, 16–17 (Henry Carey & Oliver Richmond eds., 2003) ("NGOs have become significant actors in economic development [abroad], particularly in the last ten years . . . ."); *see also* Amy J. Cohen, *Debating the Globalization of U.S. Mediation: Politics, Power, and Practice in Nepal,* 11 Harv. Negot. L. Rev. 295, 323 (2006) (describing the "significantly enhance[d] . . . role of international donor agencies and NGOs in the regulation and negotiation of everyday life," particularly in weak states).

58 Research has found a positive relationship between aid and growth. *See* Henrik Hansen & Finn Tarp, *Aid Effectiveness Disputed, in* Foreign Aid and Development: Lessons Learnt and Directions for the Future 103 (Finn Tarp ed., 2000).

59 Renz et al., *supra* note 10, at 53.

60 *See* Jose E. Alvarez, *Political Protectionism and United States International Investment Obligations in Conflict: The Hazards of Exon-Florio,* 30 Va. J. Int'l L. 1, 12 (1989); Carl B. Kress, *The United States Government and Post-Conflict Economic Reconstruction,* 11 U.C. Davis J. Int'l L. & Pol'y 75, 94 (2004); *see also* Sachs, *supra* note 30, at 10–14 (discussing the success of nonprofit organizations in Bangladesh, including the Bangladeshi Rural Advancement Committee and Grameen Bank, at achieving economic growth and improvements in health and education and a place worthy of investment).

for U.S. products as well as reducing the potential pool of human capital recruits for terrorist groups.

B. International Philanthropy as an Agent of Public Diplomacy

Another important means by which international philanthropic activity supports U.S. security interests is through building a positive image of the United States and enhancing U.S. public diplomacy efforts. As America engages in its global effort to fight the growth and support of terrorist activities, it is critically important for the United States to secure the support of the peoples of the world. A successful campaign against terrorism will rely heavily on international intelligence, influence, and the cooperation of allies.[61] One important tool for acquiring the necessary influence and cooperation is public diplomacy.[62]

Public diplomacy captures a dimension of international relations beyond the official state-to-state diplomacy conducted through government officials. It seeks to inform and influence public attitudes of foreign citizens by generating understanding and goodwill, primarily through the delivery of information and communication outreach by government directly to the public, as well as through the promotion of direct dialogue between citizens (i.e., cultural and educational exchanges). Specifically targeted at a mass audience, public diplomacy is based on the recognition that public opinion abroad can exert influence on foreign governments and political systems.[63] Public diplomacy requires the effective communication of political messages and outreach aimed at generating goodwill.[64] As a result, the generosity of U.S. individuals and institutions helps develop positive reputational benefits and goodwill for all Americans and the country as a whole.

---

61 *See generally* PHILIP B. HEYMANN, TERRORISM, FREEDOM, AND SECURITY: WINNING WITHOUT WAR 114–18 (2003) (discussing the importance of relations with allies).

62 *See* PHILIP SEIB, BEYOND THE FRONT LINES: HOW THE NEWS MEDIA COVER A WORLD SHAPED BY WAR, at xvi (2004) (explaining the importance of public diplomacy after September 11); Henry H. Perritt, Jr., *Iraq and the Future of United States Foreign Policy: Failures of Legitimacy*, 31 SYRACUSE J. INT'L L. & COM. 149, 223 (2004) ("Public diplomacy is an essential—one might say the most essential—tool in the American foreign policy arsenal."). Certainly, I would acknowledge that public diplomacy is only part of the solution. While U.S. communications and image may not be the sole source of national security threats, they contribute to our ability to deal with the challenges arising from substantive policy disagreements, socioeconomic disparities, and political and religious extremism, especially in the developing world.

63 *See* SHAUN RIORDAN, THE NEW DIPLOMACY 123 (2003) ("[P]ublics matter more than before. . . . [because] governments, at whatever level, have to win support and legitimacy from domestic publics for their foreign-policy positions; they must also win over foreign publics if they want to secure the agreement to policy positions from their governments.").

64 *See id.*; Joseph A. Keeler, *Genocide: Prevention Through Nonmilitary Measures*, 171 MIL. L. REV. 135, 145–46 (2002).

With respect to the attitudes of foreign audiences, the United States faces mounting difficulties.[65] Several studies and public opinion polls taken worldwide reveal that America's image abroad has suffered in recent years. Attitudes toward the United States are especially negative in the Muslim world.[66] In a recent study, a majority of citizens in five of six predominantly Muslim countries surveyed (Indonesia, Jordan, Lebanon, Pakistan, and Turkey) expressed unfavorable opinions of the United States; Morocco was the lone exception.[67] Importantly, this phenomenon is equally pronounced among Western countries, as a 2005 survey in Australia indicates:

> [B]arely more than half the Australians polled had positive feelings about the United States, although 84 percent saw Japan positively, and 86 percent viewed the United Kingdom positively. Worse, 57 percent of Australians perceived America's foreign policies as a potential threat—equivalent to the percentage of Australians worried about the rise of Islamic fundamentalism.[68]

Further, Australia is hardly an outlier. Public opinion polls of the peoples of France, Germany, Great Britain, Russia, Spain, and Turkey, among other nations, have reported similar declines.[69] More troubling, another report reveals that, in addition to the United State's overall image problems, foreign views about the American

---

65 As recently as 2004, a U.S. Pentagon report declared U.S. public diplomacy to be in "a state of crisis." *See* U.S. Dep't of Defense, Report of the Defense Science Board Task Force on Strategic Communication 14 (2004), *available at* http://www.acq.osd.mil/dsb/reports/2004-09-Strategic_Communication.pdf; Robert Burns, *Panel: U.S. Actions Fuel Extremists,* Chi. Trib., Nov. 25, 2004, at 30.

66 *See* U.S. Gov't Accountability Office, GAO-06-535, U.S. Public Diplomacy: State Department Efforts To Engage Muslim Audiences Lack Certain Communication Elements and Face Significant Challenges 1 (2006), *available at* http://www.gao.gov/new.items/d06535.pdf.

67 Pew Global Attitudes Project, Islamic Extremism: Common Concern for Muslim and Western Publics 14 (2005), *available at* http://pewglobal.org/reports/pdf/248.pdf; *see also* 9/11 Commission Report, *supra* note 1, at 375 ("By 2003, polls showed that 'the bottom had fallen out of support for America in most of the Muslim world. Negative views of the U.S. among Muslims, which had been largely limited to countries in the Middle East, have spread.'" (quoting Press Release, Pew Global Attitudes Project, War with Iraq Further Divides Global Publics but World Embraces Democratic Values and Free Markets (June 3, 2003))); Farah Stockman, *US Image a Tough Sell in Mideast,* Boston Globe, Oct. 23, 2005, at A5 ("Opinion polls across the Muslim world suggest that favorability ratings of the United States have dropped into the single digits after the Iraq war, even in friendly countries like Egypt and Jordan.").

68 Joshua Kurlantzick, *The Decline of American Soft Power,* Current Hist., Dec. 2005, at 419, 419.

69 *See* Pew Global Attitudes Project, America's Image Further Erodes, Europeans Want Weaker Ties 1 (2003), *available at* http://peoplepress.org/reports/pdf/175.pdf; U.S. Gov't Accountability Office, GAO-05-323, U.S. Public Diplomacy: Interagency Coordination Efforts Hampered by the Lack of a National Communication Strategy 5 (2005) [hereinafter GAO Report, U.S. Public Diplomacy 2005], *available at* http://www.gao.gov/new.items/d05323.pdf (noting that opinion polling data from Western and Muslim countries "indicate that the United States faces a chronic and widespread image problem").

people have declined as well: "The favorability ratings of Americans have declined since 2002 in 9 of the 12 countries for which trend data exists . . . ."[70]

Negative foreign attitudes should be of concern to policymakers because, as a recent federal government report noted, weak images abroad can "increase foreign public support for terrorism directed at Americans, impact the cost and effectiveness of military operations, [and] weaken the United States' ability to align with other nations in pursuit of common policy objectives . . . ."[71] Thus, public diplomacy promotes U.S. national interests by informing, engaging, and influencing peoples around the world. Indeed, public diplomacy— with its long and rich history[72]— is becoming increasingly important in light of the limitations of government-to-government diplomacy produced by globalization and technological advances in communications.[73] There is now an even greater need for direct dialogue and communication, requiring government-to-foreign citizen communication through public diplomacy.

Although there are multiple tools of public diplomacy, philanthropic support from the United States for foreign nonprofit organizations is a vital one. Government need not be the only generator of public diplomacy; private channels, sources, and entities can help address U.S. "image" problems. For instance, "Americans' perceived lack of empathy toward the pain, hardship, and tragic plight of peoples throughout the developing world"[74] may be offset by charitable support abroad. Evidence demonstrates that aid and philanthropic activity make a difference in creating positive relations and goodwill. For example, research indicates that U.S. tsunami relief efforts in Asia have generated more favorable attitudes toward the United States.[75]

---

70 Pew Global Attitudes Project, U.S. Image Up Slightly, but Still Negative 20 (2005), *available at* http://pewglobal.org/reports/pdf/247.pdf.

71 GAO Report, U.S. Public Diplomacy 2005, *supra* note 69, at 1.

72 *See generally* Richard T. Arndt, The First Resort of Kings: American Cultural Diplomacy in the Twentieth Century (2005).

73 Saskia Sussen, Losing Control? Sovereignty in an Age of Globalization, at xi-xii (1996) (explaining that traditional governmental institutions and relationships have been transformed by globalization and technology); Victor A. Kremenyuk, *The Emerging System of International Negotiation, in* International Negotiation: Analysis, Approaches, Issues 22, 23–24, 26–27 (Victor A. Kremenyuk ed., 2002) (discussing the importance of actors other than nation-states in international relations in light of growing interdependence on environmental, economic, and security matters).

74 Peter G. Peterson, *Public Diplomacy and the War on Terrorism,* Foreign Aff., Sept.–Oct. 2002, at 74, 76.

75 *See* Craig Charney & Nicole Yakatan, Council on Foreign Relations, A New Beginning: Strategies for a More Fruitful Dialogue with the Muslim World 6 (2005), *available at* http://www.cfr.org/content/publications/attachments/Anti-American_CSR.pdf ("[F]ocus groups demonstrate that Muslims view the United States more favorably when they learn about American aid. . . . U.S. tsunami relief has improved attitudes toward America in Indonesia . . . ."); The Pew Global Attitudes Project, *supra* note 70, at 4 ("The U.S. tsunami relief effort led to more favorable views of the U.S. for most nations surveyed.").

Admittedly, because nonprofit organizations operate apart from and independent of the U.S. government, they are only partly responsive to its concerns. Nonprofits, like other private entities or persons acting outside the control of government, may even engage in activities or practices that can undercut a positive image.[76] On balance, however, it seems likely that the benefits of philanthropy for public diplomacy outweigh the risks of harm.

If public diplomacy is to be truly effective in communicating and educating the world about the United States, it must fully embrace the major components of American organizational life, including nonprofit entities. The United States is more than just government and business, and the critically important—and oft-overlooked—nonprofit sector reflects the very essence and values of the country and its citizens.[77] More than merely talking or theorizing about the United States and its values, international philanthropy places them on display. Philanthropy and charity are an important part of the American story[78] and, ultimately, a part of modern diplomacy.[79]

As globalization changes the world,[80] our approach to diplomacy must evolve to engage the benefits of both traditional government-to-government communication and public diplomacy, which demands sophisticated operations on both governmental and nongovernmental levels. Promoting linkages—a means of direct connection—between American institutions and foreign NGOs encourages the dialogue, sharing of ideas, and personal and institutional relationships that should be part of the new framework of our national diplomatic policy to support long-term security interests.

---

76 *See* Alastair Pennycook & Sophie Coutand-Marin, *Teaching English as a Missionary Language*, 24 Discourse: Stud. in Cultural Pol. of Educ. 337, 337–38 (2003) (raising concerns about Christian evangelicals using the false pretense of English language education to conduct missionary outreach in foreign countries).

77 *See* Garry W. Jenkins, *The Powerful Possibilities of Nonprofit Mergers: Supporting Strategic Consolidation Through Law and Public Policy*, 74 S. Cal. L. Rev. 1089, 1094–1102 (2001).

78 For a discussion of the role of philanthropy in U.S. history, see Charity, Philanthropy, and Civility in American History, *supra* note 2.

79 *See* Riordan, *supra* note 63, at 122.

80 *See, e.g.*, Anthony Giddens, Runaway World: How Globalization Is Reshaping Our Lives (2000); Saskia Sassen, Globalization and Its Discontents (1998); Antony Anghie, *Time Present and Time Past: Globalization, International Financial Institutions, and the Third World*, 32 N.Y.U.J. Int'l L. & Pol. 243, 246–47 (2000); Paul Schiff Berman, *From International Law to Law and Globalization*, 43 Colum. J. Transnat'l L. 485, 551–52 (2005); Laura Spitz, *The Gift of Enron: An Opportunity To Talk About Capitalism, Equality, Globalization, and the Promise of a North-American Charter of Fundamental Rights*, 66 Ohio St. L.J. 315, 338–41 (2005); Gary Minda, *Globalization of Culture*, 71 U. Colo. L. Rev. 589, 591 (2000) (reviewing Daniel Yergin & Joseph Stanislaw, The Commanding Heights: The Battle Between Government and the Marketplace That Is Remaking the Modern World (1998)).

C. International Philanthropy as a Source of Soft Power

International philanthropy can also provide a valuable source of power benefiting the United States. While related to, yet different from, public diplomacy, the concept of soft power both captures and broadens the benefits and effects associated with positive image abroad. Several experts and scholars have argued that an effective counterterrorism policy must rely on more than just strength. Political scientist Joseph Nye argues that to succeed in international politics, America must use both hard power (e.g., military and economic might) and soft power, which he defines as the ability to co-opt others to want the same outcomes as you through intangible attraction to shared values, thereby shaping the preferences of others.[81] Although hard power is well understood and often utilized on the world stage, soft power is less understood and, with respect to the United States, on the decline.[82] Professor Nye contends that the United States cannot defeat terrorism without attracting moderates around the world[83] and that the Bush administration may have "focused too heavily on hard power and not taken enough account of soft power."[84]

Although power has been defined many different ways, the definition typically includes an ability to influence or control others.[85] Rather than exercising power over others through military and economic strength, countries may also rely on indirect methods to achieve their goals, namely attracting and persuading other governments and publics to adopt the same goals.[86] Soft power reflects this indirect ability to elicit

81 *See* NYE, *supra* note 13, at 5.

82 *See* Joseph S. Nye, Jr., *The Decline of America's Soft Power*, FOREIGN AFF., May–June 2004, at 1; *see also* Robert Cooper, *The Goals of Diplomacy, Hard Power, and Soft Power*, *in* AMERICAN POWER IN THE TWENTY-FIRST CENTURY 167, 167 (David Held & Mathias Koenig-Archibugi eds., 2004) ("America seems to be hard power incarnate and Europe the embodiment of soft power."); Kurlantzick, *supra* note 68, at 420–21 (describing the decline of American soft power).

83 *See* NYE, *supra* note 13, at 131.

84 *See* Joseph S. Nye, Jr., *Hard Power, Soft Power, and "The War on Terrorism," in* AMERICAN POWER IN THE TWENTY-FIRST CENTURY, *supra* note 82, at 114, 124.

85 *See, e.g.*, JEFFREY PFEFFER, MANAGING WITH POWER 30 (1992) (defining power as "the potential ability to influence behavior, to change the course of events, to overcome resistance, and to get people to do things that they would not otherwise do"); Peter Blau, *Differentiation of Power*, *in* POLITICAL POWER: A READER IN THEORY AND RESEARCH 293, 293 (Roderick Bell et al. eds., 1969) ("[P]ower refers to all kinds of influence between persons or groups . . . ."); Jamison E. Colburn, *"Democratic Experimentalism": A Separation of Powers for Our Time?*, 37 SUFFOLK U. L. REV. 287, 304 n.48 (2004) (" '[P]ower' can take an infinite number of forms . . . . Many are best described as modes of influence."); Carrie Menkel-Meadow, *The Lawyer's Role(s) in Deliberative Democracy*, 5 NEV. L.J. 347, 354–55 n.40 (noting that "the definition of power involves the ability to control or influence other's behaviors"); Nye, *supra* note 84, at 117 ("[P]ower is the ability to get the outcomes you want, and to affect the behavior of others to make this happen."). *See generally* Daniel D. Barnhizer, *Inequality of Bargaining Power*, 76 U. COLO. L. REV. 139, 154–60 (2005) (discussing definitions of power).

86 ROBERT O. KEOHANE & JOSEPH S. NYE, POWER AND INTERDEPENDENCE 220 (3d ed. 2001) (defining soft power as "the ability to get desired outcomes because others want what you want" and "the ability to achieve desired outcomes through attraction rather than coercion").

cooperation through attraction to shared values, common aspirations, and the inspiration they ignite in others.[87] Drawn from a country's values, culture, and foreign policies,[88] soft power is built through a combination of government action and action by nonstate actors. Ultimately, nations with significant soft power "find that citizens of other countries aspire to share their values and institutions, and leaders of foreign countries view their policies as legitimate and want to follow their lead."[89]

Examining the level of transparency can help to differentiate soft power from public diplomacy. Efforts to influence foreign publics through public diplomacy are overt and focused on direct communication, whereas soft power, with its focus on attraction to values and ideals, exercises influence through more subtle, diffuse, and indirect means. To use an analogy to the corporate world, public diplomacy is more like public relations and soft power is more like brand image. Sophisticated corporations attempt to win customers through communication via the media and other sources using public relations, but they also devote substantial resources to developing a brand identity and image that commands awareness, meaning, and esteem. The best brand marketers ensure that all of their actions, communications, and other choices reinforce the brand image so that audiences understand and are attracted to the brand because of what it represents and because of its ability to tap into an individual's aspirations or self-image.[90]

Although governments certainly use soft power, it is not something that exclusively belongs to or is controlled by the province of government. To the contrary, both public and private sources can wield their own soft power, and Nye's interpretation of the concept recognizes that private, nongovernmental forces and institutions can enhance governmental soft power.[91] With respect to nonstate actors, Nye and others have focused largely on the influential role that culture[92] and commerce play

87 *See* Joseph S. Nye, Jr., The Paradox of American Power: Why the World's Only Superpower Can't Go It Alone 8–9 (2002).

88 *See* Nye, *supra* note 13, at 68 ("The image of the United States and its attractiveness to others is a composite of many different ideas and attitudes. It depends in part on culture, in part on domestic policies and values, and in part on the substance, tactics, and style of our foreign policies.").

89 Kurlantzick, *supra* note 68, at 420.

90 *See generally* David A. Aaker, Managing Brand Equity: Capitalizing on the Value of a Brand Name (1991); Douglas B. Holt, How Brands Become Icons: The Principles of Cultural Branding (2004); Kevin Lane Keller, Strategic Brand Management: Building, Measuring, and Managing Brand Equity (2d ed. 2003); Susan Fournier, *Consumers and Their Brands: Developing Relationship Theory in Consumer Research,* 24 J. Consumer Res. 343 (1998).

91 *See* Nye, *supra* note 13, at 10.

92 With respect to culture as a source of soft power, the United States's image and its attractiveness are shaped and expressed by mediums such as literature, art, education, and popular culture. *See* Nye, *supra* note 13, at 11; *see also* Josef Joffe, *Who's Afraid of Mr. Big?,* Nat'l Int., Summer 2001, at 43 ("U.S. culture, low-brow or high, radiates outward with an intensity last seen in the days of the Roman Empire—but with a novel twist. Rome's and Soviet Russia's

in "getting others to want the outcomes that you want."[93] For example, Nye notes that American soft power has been largely created by cultural forces transmitted through mediums such as popular films and television, multinational corporations, brand icons, and even celebrities and sports figures.[94] Since culture is crafted and deployed by a variety of forces—including those outside the control of government—it makes sense that cultural attractiveness is, in part, dependent on the products and efforts of private entities.

Nye's analysis of private interests contributing to a nation's soft power emphasizes contributions from corporations and Hollywood movie studios.[95] With respect to nonprofit organizations, he primarily stresses how charitable institutions exercise their own soft power to influence others on behalf of their own interests.[96] A more subtle point that Nye acknowledges, but one I wish to highlight and expand here, is the role that U.S. public charities and private foundations play in enhancing the interests—that is, the soft power—of the United States.[97]

Nye primarily views international nonprofit organizations as attracting their own followers, giving them clout to influence governments.[98] To the extent that Nye is principally conceiving of NGOs as large, multinational public charities, his

---

cultural sway stopped exactly at their military borders. America's soft power, though, rules over an empire on which the sun never sets."). These and other forms of U.S. cultural values are most obviously conveyed through mass entertainment but also through commerce, personal contacts, and citizen visits and exchanges. *See* NYE, *supra* note 13, at 44–55. The influential German foreign policy analyst and magazine editor Josef Joffe has argued that cultural attraction, ideology, and agenda-setting have become significant currencies of power in modern times compared to more traditional currencies tied to military strength. *See* Josef Joffe, *America the Inescapable,* N.Y. TIMES, June 8, 1997, § 6 (Magazine), at 38.

93 NYE, *supra* note 13, at 5; *see also* Josef Joffe, *How America Does It,* 7 FOREIGN AFF., Sept.–Oct. 1997, at 13, 24 (describing soft power as stemming from cultural and economic strength).

94 NYE, *supra* note 13, at 17 ("Much of American soft power has been produced by Hollywood, Harvard, Microsoft, and Michael Jordan."); *see also* KISHORE MAHBUBANI, BEYOND THE AGE OF INNOCENCE: REBUILDING TRUST BETWEEN AMERICA AND THE WORLD 3–5 (2005) (discussing the power of American culture, icons, and brands to influence and inspire foreign citizens); Josef Joffe, Editorial, *Looking Out for No. 1 by Looking Out for Others,* PALM BEACH POST, Sept. 28, 1997, at E1 ("[The United States] is definitely in a class of its own in the soft power game . . . . All [of Europe, Japan, China and Russia's] movie studios together could not break the hold of Hollywood. Nor could a consortium of their universities dethrone Harvard et al., which dominate academia while luring the best and the brightest from abroad.").

95 *See* NYE, *supra* note 13, at 12–13. Of course, actions by corporations and film and production studios may also work against government interests. For instance, "Hollywood movies that show scantily clad women with libertine attitudes . . . undercut government efforts to improve relations with Islamic nations." *Id.* at 15.

96 *See* NYE, *supra* note 87, at 11 ("[N]ongovernmental groups develop soft power of their own . . . .").

97 NYE, *supra* note 13, at 73 ("[N]onstate actors . . . also possess soft power that can be used to help or hinder the United States' achievement of its preferred outcomes.").

98 *See id.* at 90–91.

assessment is surely accurate. However, that perspective requires reformulation when thinking about the broader spectrum of private foundations and smaller public charities. A nonprofit organization that is able to generate its own soft power is the rare exception. Indeed, perhaps only a small handful of major "brand name" nonprofit organizations with substantial resources, such as Human Rights Watch, the Ford Foundation, the Bill and Melinda Gates Foundation, and a few others, can mobilize publics and attract their own followers, thereby accruing their own soft power. Most nonprofit organizations, however, especially smaller and less well-known funders acting abroad, directly contribute to the goodwill and attractiveness of their home governments based on the national affiliation of grantors. Simply put, when an American foundation gives money for a humanitarian project, beneficiaries are likely to associate the end product as produced by "American aid," rather than narrowly as generated by a specific foundation. For example, in the late 1970s when U.S.-based Rotary International embarked on a campaign to eradicate polio in the Philippines by immunizing six million Filipino children,[99] the philanthropic nature and reputation of the United States as a whole was enhanced. Today, Accion International's support for microfinance[100] and the Global Fund for Women's focus on educational opportunities for girls[101] in the world's least developed countries accrue reputational benefits to the United States.

In fact, many of the largest and most active international grantmakers are not particularly well-known and do not wield substantial independent soft power. For instance, the listing of the twenty largest international donors among U.S. private foundations includes such unfamiliar organizations as the Freeman Foundation, Lincy Foundation, and Harry and Jeanette Weinberg Foundation.[102] Moreover, the Foundation Center reports that the median grant dedicated to international affairs is \$50,000,[103] indicating that many grants are of such a small size that they are unlikely to generate enough attention and visibility to create a separate brand identity for the nonprofit donor. Accordingly, the collective efforts of little-known and smaller foundations are more likely to create cumulative soft power for the U.S. government rather than for those organizations individually.

Given this link, the United States, in order to fortify its soft power, should value international philanthropy and grantmaking by U.S. private foundations and public charities as a contributing source to its soft power. Recent foreign public opinion trends[104] and the lingering negative public relations effects associated with the

---

99 *See* Anheier & Simmons, *supra* note 48, at 15–16.

100 *See* Accion Int'l, 2004 Annual Report (2005), *available at* http://www.accion.org/pdf/2004_annual_report.pdf.

101 *See* Renz et al., *supra* note 10, at 4.

102 *See id.* at 35 (citing 2002 figures).

103 *See* Ctr. on Philanthropy at Ind. Univ., *supra* note 7, at 177 (citing 2003 figures).

104 *See supra* text accompanying notes 65–70.

"war on terrorism" have diminished U.S. attractiveness and standing, and limited its power to persuade on moral principle.[105] Thus, the United States should pursue a variety of means to attract others because that attraction is a form of power. Persuasion through soft power can yield more concession, cooperation, and enduring support for desired U.S. policy outcomes than coercion alone.[106]

As one commentator has noted, "in the old adage of catching flies, soft power is the honey and hard power is the vinegar."[107] Nye and others seem to have it right: hard power and soft power are both essential elements of sound U.S. policy on national security.[108] Our government policies, however, must be designed in a way that does not undercut our strategic interests, which requires taking international philanthropy into account as a valuable component in enhancing soft power.

Paradoxically, the contributions of nonprofit organizations to government soft power are, in part, a direct result of the sector's independence from government. As distinct from the state, the nonprofit sector can leverage altruistic values without being beholden to the government, its policies, or its geopolitical interests (which are often advanced through hard power). As a result, not only does the sector's independence enhance the effectiveness of its own philanthropic efforts[109] (and the attendant reputational contributions of the work), but this independence also allows nonprofits to contribute to governmental soft power. Put differently, international philanthropy—precisely because of its independence from the state—offers a direct, tangible, and genuine manifestation of culture, values, and people through action on the ground. This production of attractive cultural values, in turn, produces benefit—in the form of soft power—that inures to the state writ large.

II. GRANTMAKING ABROAD

Even prior to the September 11 attacks, making grants to institutions outside of the United States was considered extremely challenging.[110] Despite its long tradition, cross-border philanthropy was deemed to be among the most difficult, the most

105 For example, the "abuse of prisoners in Guantanamo Bay and Abu Ghraib . . . [has] devalued the attractiveness of American values." Kurlantzick, *supra* note 68, at 421; *see also* MAHBUBANI, *supra* note 94, at 130–34 (discussing the United State's decline in legitimacy and moral authority attributable to the detention of accused terrorists at Guantanamo and comparing that to the impact of the 1989 Tiananmen Square incident on China).

106 *See* NYE, *supra* note 13, at 129.

107 Louis Klarevas, *W Version 2.0: Foreign Policy in the Second Bush Term,* 29 FLETCHER F. WORLD AFF. 165, 168 (2005).

108 *See* NYE, *supra* note 87, at 141 ("Soft power is crucial, but alone not sufficient."); MAHBUBANI, *supra* note 94, at 196 (arguing that "[t]here must be an alignment between the impact of American 'hard power' and 'soft power'").

109 *See* Anheier & Simmons, *supra* note 48, at 23–24.

110 *See* JOHN A. EDIE & JANE C. NOBER, BEYOND OUR BORDERS: A GUIDE TO MAKING GRANTS OUTSIDE THE UNITED STATES 1 (2002).

time-consuming, and the most onerous forms of grantmaking for private foundations.[111] The set of tax laws and regulations governing such grants, in place long before September 11, provide detailed due diligence requirements to ensure that grantmakers are thoroughly familiar with non-U.S. recipient organizations and that grants are used for legitimate charitable purposes. To this end, private foundations, in particular, may choose one of two methods to facilitate cross-border giving. First, they may employ the process of "equivalency determination."[112] This entails a structured assessment of a foreign entity akin to the review conducted by the Internal Revenue Service ("IRS") for domestic organizations to determine whether the grantee is the equivalent of a U.S. public charity. Alternatively, they may opt to exercise "expenditure responsibility,"[113] which involves following a strict set of rules established by Congress requiring extra scrutiny and oversight management. Regardless of the selected methodology, the U.S. funder faces weighty procedural and recordkeeping requirements and detailed oversight by grantmakers and, frequently, legal counsel beyond the norm for traditional grants to U.S. entities.

Following September 11, the U.S. government altered the regulatory regime regarding international philanthropy.[114] Although the tax laws governing international grantmaking remained in force,[115] the executive branch adopted several important new measures, including an Executive Order permitting the indefinite freezing of assets of entities, including charitable organizations, deemed to have connections with terrorism.[116] In addition, the PATRIOT Act added penalties for providing material support to terrorists,[117] and the Treasury Department issued a set of voluntary guidelines outlining additional diligence measures and information U.S. funders should collect related to overseas giving.[118] Although designed as reasonable recommendations to provide added security for the United States and its citizens, these collective actions have created an inadvertent chill that impedes effective grantmaking in unforeseen ways and may paradoxically decrease our collective security. The heightened due diligence requirements in the Treasury ATF Guidelines, although voluntary, have a coercive effect when read in conjunction with the PATRIOT Act, the Executive Order, and other sources of antiterrorism authority from the U.S. government. As a result of the nonprofit sector's fear of severe penalties and its concerns about the high stakes associated with any potential

111 *See* Crimm, *supra* note 6, at 124.

112 *See infra* notes 132–40 and accompanying text.

113 *See infra* notes 141–46 and accompanying text.

114 *See infra* Part II.B.

115 *See infra* Part II.A.

116 *See* Exec. Order No. 13,224, 66 Fed. Reg. 49,079 (Sept. 23, 2001).

117 *See* 18 U.S.C. § 2339A(a) (Supp. IV 2004).

118 *See* U.S. Dep't of the Treasury, *supra* note 19.

misappropriation of charitable funds, the Treasury ATF Guidelines are beginning to acquire quasi-legal status.[119]

A. Legal Requirements for Cross-Border Grants

In order to understand the ways in which the U.S. government has followed an approach that undermines its strategic interests with regard to international grantmaking, it is first necessary to review the state and structure of current tax law regulating cross-border philanthropy. The specific legal rules governing overseas grantmaking vary depending on the legal classification of both the receiving charity and the grantmaking organization. The differing legal procedures to facilitate a grant to a foreign organization—each with administrative, recordkeeping, and due diligence requirements—depend on whether the foreign grant recipient is recognized by the IRS, as well as the legal status of the U.S. grantmaking entity as either a public charity or a private foundation under U.S. law.

1. Grants by Public Charities and Private Foundations to Foreign Organizations Recognized by the Internal Revenue Service

Procedurally, the least onerous method for a U.S. funder, either a public charity or a private foundation, to support a foreign entity requires the foreign charitable organization to apply to the IRS for recognition of exempt status under § 501(c)(3) of the Internal Revenue Code.[120] A foreign organization receiving such recognition from the IRS becomes eligible to receive grants from both U.S. public charities and private foundations on the same basis as U.S.-based recipient organizations with a determination letter from the IRS.[121]

While legally permitted to do so, most foreign charities in practice do not apply for IRS determination letters.[122] Although this procedure may ease burdens for the U.S. grantmaker, it places substantial burdens on the foreign grant recipient. The legal costs, administrative burdens, and language barriers associated with applying for 501(c)(3) recognition, as well as the fees connected with the continuing reporting requirements necessary to maintain exempt status, serve as significant deterrents,

119 *See* Press Release, Nat'l Comm. for Responsive Philanthropy, Philanthropic Grantmaking Institutions Must Refrain from Placing Inappropriate, Ineffective, and Unnecessary Responsibilities for Anti-Terrorism Enforcement onto the Shoulders of Nonprofit Grant Recipients (June 28, 2005), *available at* http://www.ncrp.org/anti-terrorism.asp (noting that some funders have "overreacted to the [Guidelines]" and treat them as "mandatory").

120 *See* Rev. Proc. 92-94, 1992-46 I.R.B. 34 ("Private foundations generally want their grants to foreign grantees to be treated as qualifying distributions for purposes of section 4942 of the Internal Revenue Code .... This treatment is assured if the foreign grantee has a[n IRS] ruling or determination letter ...."); Edie & Nober, *supra* note 110, at 8.

121 *See* Frances R. Hill & Douglas M. Mancino, Taxation of Exempt Organizations § 36.03[2] (2003).

122 *See* Edie & Nober, *supra* note 110, at 8.

especially for smaller foreign organizations.[123] As a result, for most overseas grant-making, both U.S. public charities and private foundations must rely on an alternative set of rules governing contributions to organizations that are not recognized by the IRS. I first examine the rules applicable to public charities giving abroad and then turn to private foundations making donations overseas.

2. Grants by Public Charities to Foreign Organizations

Public charities enjoy greater freedom to operate and make grants abroad than do private foundations. Public charities seeking to engage in foreign activities may choose either to establish and manage their own programs abroad or to make grants to foreign organizations.[124] In order to ensure that the public charity's donors maintain deductibility for any contributions directed to the foreign entity, a public charity's governing board must make certain that any funds it donates to a foreign organization are used for charitable purposes.[125] Generally, with any grant made to an organization with an IRS determination letter recognizing exempt status, a charitable purpose is presumed.[126] Otherwise, including instances when foreign charities not recognized by the IRS receive grant funds from a public charity, the grantor carries the burden of proving the grant was made in furtherance of an exempt purpose.[127] This requirement can be satisfied by demonstrating that the grant was made freely, without control either by the foreign beneficiary or by donors earmarking the distribution.[128] Accordingly, a U.S. public charity must be able to prove—upon IRS audit—that the charity maintained adequate discretion and control over the grant funds.[129]

3. Grants by Private Foundations to Foreign Organizations

Private foundations may choose to be involved in international philanthropy either by making direct cross-border grants to organizations overseas or through indirect support to U.S.-based organizations with operations abroad. Some foundations, seeking fewer administrative requirements, choose the indirect route—providing

123 *See id.*; Crimm, *supra* note 6, at 75.

124 *See* Rev. Rul. 71-460, 1971-2 C.B. 231.

125 *See* Edie & Nober, *supra* note 110, at 20.

126 *See* Hill & Mancino, *supra* note 121, § 36.03[2].

127 *Cf.* Rev. Rul. 68-489, 1968-2 C.B. 210 (finding that an organization will not jeopardize its 501 (c)(3) status by distributing funds to a nonexempt organization so long as it retains control over the funds and discretion over their use).

128 *See* Rev. Rul. 66-79, 1966-1 C.B. 48; Rev. Rul. 75-65, 1975-1 C.B. 79.

129 *See* Rev. Rul. 66-79, 1966-1 C.B. 48; Rev. Rul. 68-489, 1968-2 C.B. 210; Edie & Nober, *supra* note 110, at 20.

"international" support through gifts to a U.S.-recognized or U.S.-based organization with special expertise implementing programs outside of the United States.[130]

However, many foundations active in global philanthropy seek to offer direct support to projects and organizations of their own choosing that are not recognized by the IRS or organized under U.S. law. In such circumstances, to make direct grants to foreign organizations and avoid being subject to certain federal excise taxes, the foundations must elect to follow one of two procedural processes: (1) equivalency determination or (2) expenditure responsibility.[131]

Using the equivalency determination process permits a private foundation to make a grant to a foreign organization, without adverse tax consequences, after making a determination that the foreign charity is the "equivalent" of a U.S. public charity.[132] The test for equivalency demands strict adherence to the detailed standards applicable to § 501(c)(3) of the Internal Revenue Code and does not provide any flexibility to adjust to alternative cultural or legal structures. In other words, equivalency in this context does not mean "roughly comparable" based on the social organization or the national, local, or customary laws of the foreign country. Rather, the foreign organization must meet the rigid requirements of § 501(c)(3)[133] and be deemed a public charity under § 509(a),[134] including being organized and operated exclusively for purposes described in § 501(c)(3);[135] meet the prohibitions against private inurement, substantial legislative activities, and political campaign intervention;[136] and satisfy certain tests concerning the grantee's sources of support.[137]

130 For example, organizations such as Give2Asia, the Global Fund for Children, and the International Youth Foundation serve as financial intermediaries receiving gifts from individual donors, corporations, and foundations to regrant funds abroad. *See* Give2Asia, Solutions for Giving to Asia, *available at* http://www.give2asia.org/pdfs/brochure.pdf; Global Fund for Children, Annual Report and Resource Guide 2004–2005 (2005), *available at* http://www.globalfundforchildren.org/pdfs/GFC_Annual_Report04-05.pdf; Int'l Youth Found., 2004 Annual Report (2005), *available at* http://www.iyfnet.org/uploads/2004IYFar.pdf; *see also* Edie & Nober, *supra* note 110, at 4

131 *See* I.R.C. § 4945(d) (2000).

132 *See* Treas. Reg. § 53.4945-5(a)(5) (as amended in 1973).

133 *See* Treas. Reg. § 53.4945-6(c)(2)(ii) (as amended in 1972).

134 *See* Treas. Reg. § 53.4945-5(a)(5) (as amended in 1973).

135 *See* I.R.C. § 501(c)(3) (requiring that a charitable entity be "organized and operated exclusively for religious, charitable, scientific, testing for public safety, literary, or educational purposes").

136 *See id.* (stating that a corporation is exempt from taxation if "no part of the net earnings of [the corporation] inures to the benefit of any private shareholder or individual, no substantial part of the activities of [the corporation] is carrying on propaganda, or otherwise attempting, to influence legislation . . . and [the corporation] does not participate in, or intervene in (including the publishing or distributing of statements), any political campaign on behalf of (or in opposition to) any candidate for public office").

137 *See* I.R.C. § 509(a)(2).

Such a determination may be made by relying on a written opinion of legal counsel establishing that the foreign organization meets the relevant tests to be deemed a public charity equivalent, or the grantor may make its own determination without the assistance of counsel based on information provided by the foreign grantee in a written affidavit.[138] The process of determining that a foreign organization is equivalent to a public charity, however, is often time-consuming and expensive. Determining that a foreign charity is equivalent to either a U.S.-based public charity or a private foundation requires a detailed analysis of organizational documents, financial records, and applicable foreign law, which may often require translation into English.[139] Generally, whether an organization relies on an opinion of legal counsel or its own determination process, in practice, a detailed grantee affidavit is required.[140]

Alternatively, a U.S. private foundation seeking to grant funds abroad may elect to follow a specific set of oversight and monitoring procedures with regard to the grant known as expenditure responsibility.[141] The expenditure responsibility rules involve the following steps:

- the grantor must conduct a pre-grant inquiry to determine whether the proposed grantee is reasonably likely to use the grant for the specified purposes;[142]
- the grantor and grantee must sign a written grant agreement with specific terms;[143]

---

138 *See* Rev. Proc. 92-94, 1992-46 I.R.B. 34.

139 *See id.* For example, in order to establish public charity equivalency, many organizations must demonstrate that they would pass the mathematical public support test, which requires the analysis of at least four years of financial statements. *See* Treas. Reg. §§ 1.170A-9(e)(2), (e)(4)(i) (as amended in 2002).

140 A qualified affidavit, which must be written in English, *see* Rev. Proc. 92-94, 1992-46 I.R.B. 34, contains certain detailed information and representations similar to what a U.S. nonprofit would include on its application for recognition of exemption (Form 1023) and its annual information return (Form 990). *See* Edie & Nober, *supra* note 110, at 28. For instance, the affidavit requires a description of the organization's past and future activities, copies of its charter, bylaws, or other relevant documents, representations that the organization does not permit private inurement, substantial lobbying, or political intervention, information regarding distribution of assets upon dissolution, and detailed financial information for some types of organizations. Rev. Proc. 92-94, 1992-46 I.R.B. 34. Foreign organizations relying on the mathematical public support tests for public charity equivalency, which include most foreign grant recipients other than certain religious organizations, formal educational institutions, and certain medical institutions, must provide information regarding the sources and levels of their gifts, grants, and contributions from all sources, membership fees, and other income covering a period of four consecutive fiscal years so that the grantor or the legal counsel can determine that the grantee meets the tests detailed in I.R.C. § 509(a)(2). *Id.* In addition, the affidavit must be regularly updated. *Id.*

141 *See* I.R.C. § 4945(d)(4)(B).

142 *See* Treas. Reg. § 53.4945-5(b)(2) (as amended in 1973).

143 *See* Treas. Reg. §§ 53.4945-5(b)(3), (b)(5) (as amended in 1973). The agreement must specify the charitable purposes of the grant and commit the grant recipient to repay funds not used for

- the grantee must maintain the grant funds in a segregated bank account;[144]
- the grantee must submit a written progress report to the grantor at least once a year during the term of the grant indicating how funds are used, progress toward grant goals, and compliance with grant terms;[145] and
- the grantor must report each expenditure responsibility grant on its annual Form 990-PF filed with the IRS as long as grantee reports are required.[146]

B. The New Legal Environment After September 11

After the September 11 attacks, the federal government pursued a variety of policy responses intended to protect America and its allies from future attacks. A campaign to curtail the financing of terrorist groups, including funds channeled through charities, emerged as a top government priority.[147] As a result, several new tools were added to the government's arsenal to address terrorist financing, notably Executive Order 13,224, the USA PATRIOT Act, and the Treasury ATF Guidelines, all of which affect philanthropic organizations engaged in overseas giving. In addition, Congress has considered a variety of other proposals directly addressing terrorist financing or otherwise affecting the ability of certain U.S. funders to engage in overseas grantmaking.[148] These policies were surely implemented to create a regulatory

---

the grant's purpose, to submit annual reports, to maintain books and records available to the grantor, and not to use the funds for lobbying, political campaign activities, or other noncharitable purposes. *See id.*

144 *See* Treas. Reg. §§ 53.4945-5(c)(3)(ii), 53.4945-6(c)(2) (as amended in 1973).

145 *See* Treas. Reg. § 53.4945-5(c)(1) (as amended in 1973).

146 *See* Treas. Reg. § 53.4945-5(d) (as amended in 1973). The reports must contain the name and address of the grant recipient, the date and amount of the grant, a description of the purpose of the grant, the amount expended by the grantee, disclosures regarding any diversions of the funds, dates of reports received from the grant recipient, and the date and results of any verification of grantee reports. *See id.*

147 *See supra* note 15 and accompanying text; *see also* President's Radio Address, 37 Weekly Comp. Pres. Doc. 1397 (Sept. 29, 2001), *available at* http://www.gpo access.gov/ wcomp/v37no40.html ("We have also launched a strike against the financial foundation of the global terror network. Our goal is to deny terrorists the money they need to carry out their plans. We began by identifying 27 terrorist organizations, terrorist leaders, and foreign businesses and charities that support or front for terrorism.").

148 *See* H.R. 3162, 107th Cong. §§ 314(a)(1), (a)(2)(A) (2004) (granting the Secretary of Treasury authority to adopt regulations to create procedures for cooperation and information sharing among financial institutions focusing on "matters specifically related to the finances of terrorist groups . . . [that] transfer funds . . . through the use of charitable organizations, nonprofit organizations and nongovernmental organizations"). Also, as recently as 2005, the U.S. Senate passed a bill placing restrictions on donor-advised funds (a type of U.S. public charity) that would, among other things, limit such funds to providing grants to only those foreign nonprofit organizations approved by the IRS. *See* Tax Relief Act of 2005, S. 2020, 109th Cong. § 331 (2005). For more on donor-advised funds, see Malvin E. Bank, *Community Foundations: Are 'Donor-Directed' Funds New Vehicles for Utilizing Community Foundations?*, 7 Exempt Org. Tax Rev. 42 (1993); Evelyn Brody, *The Charity in Bankruptcy and Ghosts of Donors Past,*

regime that would enhance national security, but through their effects on U.S. public charities and private foundations that work closely with foreign organizations, they have changed the security calculus in unintended ways. Ironically, in the years following September 11, international philanthropy has become both more necessary and more difficult than ever before.

1. Executive Order 13,224

Within days of the September 11 attacks, President Bush signed Executive Order 13,224, which declared a national emergency and imposed economic sanctions under the International Emergency Economic Powers Act of 1977 ("IEEPA").[149] The Executive Order blocks property and property interests in the United States of persons and entities listed in the annex of the order.[150] These are foreign persons and entities the Secretary of State determines pose risks of committing acts of terrorism; persons and entities the Secretary of Treasury determines assist, sponsor, or provide support for acts of terrorism or for people on the annex list; or persons deemed to be owned or controlled by or who act on behalf of, or otherwise associate with, the aforementioned.[151] Furthermore, Executive Order 13,224 prohibits U.S. persons or entities from making contributions of funds, goods, or services for the benefit of those subject to the Executive Order or so designated as subject to the order at a later date.[152]

Present, and Future, 29 Seton Hall Legis. J. 471, 528 (2005). Specifically, the provision, which was included in the Senate-passed tax relief bill, prohibits grants from a donor-advised fund to any entity not described in § 170(b)(1)(A) of the Internal Revenue Code. S. 2020, 109th Cong. § 331(e)(1)(A)(i). Due to the fact that only a small number of foreign charitable organizations seek or receive an IRS determination of their status under § 170(b)(1)(A), *see* Edie & Nober, *supra* note 110, at 8, this provision, if passed, would substantially alter the ability and flexibility to use donor-advised assets to make grants to NGOs organized outside the United States. It seems unclear whether the donor-advised funds could use processes currently used by private foundations to determine that foreign NGOs are equivalent to § 170(b)(1)(A) organizations, but even if such an option were available it seems unlikely that the donor-advised funds or their clients would undertake the expense associated with doing so. My point here is that such a change would impact overseas grantmaking, and perhaps an assessment of the security tradeoffs would impact a determination regarding whether such a shift is warranted or beneficial, but currently such an analysis or debate does not appear to have occurred. In this case, neither the security costs nor the benefits connected with the policy proposal seem to be on the table.

149 Pub. L. No. 95-223, 91 Stat. 1625 (codified at 50 U.S.C. §§ 1701–06 (2000)); *see* Exec. Order No. 13,224, 66 Fed. Reg. 49,079 (Sept. 23, 2001). For a more detailed discussion of the presidential emergency powers and terrorism-support laws, see Robert M. Chesney, *The Sleeper Scenario: Terrorism-Support Laws and the Demands of Prevention,* 42 Harv. J. on Legis. 1, 4–21 (2005).

150 *See* Exec. Order No. 13,224, 66 Fed. Reg. 49,079 (Sept. 23, 2001).

151 *See id.*

152 *See id.*

The Executive Order authorizes the federal government to freeze the assets of anyone associated with terrorism, including charitable organizations that may have knowingly or unwittingly provided support to or associated with a terrorist organization.[153] The Executive Order does not require that a person or charitable organization that may be charged have any knowledge or intent in order to block their assets.[154] Therefore, assets can be frozen without any showing or allegation that the individual or entity violated any law. Professor David Cole has argued that this approach permits punishment based on guilt by association.[155] Perhaps intended to stop prohibited transfers, the laws in practice make it not just a crime to support terrorist activity, but also to support any group blacklisted as a terrorist group. Moreover, nonprofits are concerned that challenging a designation is extremely difficult because the federal government can deny blocked entities sufficient notice, an adversarial hearing on the underlying merits, and access to classified evidence used to justify the government's actions.[156]

2. The USA PATRIOT Act

Supported by an overwhelming majority in Congress and signed into law by President Bush in October 2001, the PATRIOT Act contains a variety of measures intended to strengthen the federal government's ability to obstruct terrorism. Most relevant to international grantmaking, the Act increases criminal sanctions and permits civil actions against U.S. organizations that knowingly or intentionally provide material support for terrorism or terrorist organizations.[157]

The Act defines material support broadly to include charitable grants, microfinance loans, and technical assistance.[158] Although the Act requires a knowing or intentional violation,[159] philanthropic organizations are concerned that, despite their best efforts to develop procedures to prevent inadvertently supporting a terrorist

---

153 *See id.*

154 For a more detailed history of the use of economic sanctions against terrorist organizations and Executive Order 13, 224, see Nina Crimm, *High Alert: The Government's War on the Financing of Terrorism and Its Implications for Donors, Domestic Charitable Organizations, and Global Philanthropy*, 45 WM. & MARY L. REV. 1341, 1354–73 (2004).

155 *See* DAVID COLE, ENEMY ALIENS: DOUBLE STANDARDS AND CONSTITUTIONAL FREEDOMS IN THE WAR ON TERRORISM 58–64 (2003); David Cole, *The New McCarthyism: Repeating History in the War on Terrorism*, 38 HARV. C.R.-C.L. L. REV. 1, 2 (2003). *See generally* David Cole, *Hanging with the Wrong Crowd: Of Gangs, Terrorists, and the Right of Association*, 1999 SUP. CT. REV. 203.

156 *See* Nicole Nice-Petersen, Note, *Justice for the "Designated": The Process That Is Due to Alleged U.S. Financiers of Terrorism*, 93 GEO. L.J. 1387 (2005) (arguing that the courts and Congress have permitted the executive branch to strip charities of due process protections under the guise of fighting terrorism).

157 *See* 18 U.S.C. § 2339A(a) (Supp. IV 2004).

158 *See id.* § 2339A(b) (defining material support).

159 *See id.* § 2339A(a).

organization, if their grants can be linked to such an organization or person, they may be found to have knowingly or intentionally provided material support.[160]

Such concerns may be reasonable for organizations operating in less-developed parts of the world. For example, organizations engaged in large-scale regranting may be especially vulnerable.[161] Suppose a U.S. private foundation makes a grant to a foreign organization working in Africa for the purpose of promoting community-based entrepreneurship and development through microfinance.[162] The foreign grant recipient receives a single large grant (perhaps of $500,000) and then redistributes funds to local individuals or community cooperatives (in small amounts of approximately $250 to $750) to assist them in starting their own small businesses. What if a handful of the several thousand small grants reach the wrong hands?

Or, suppose an organization providing humanitarian aid in a war-torn or politically unstable region finds it necessary to interact with or offer goods to a group with questionable ties (or even a U.S. government-designated terrorist organization) in order to ensure that aid trucks are not destroyed en route to the needy.[163] These are genuine areas of concern for U.S. funders active in the developing world where grantmaking is complex and precarious.

3. The Department of the Treasury Anti-Terrorist Financing Guidelines for Charities

Most regulations and guidelines concerning nonprofit organizations are issued by the IRS. However, in November 2002, the U.S. Department of the Treasury's Office

160 *See* Jones, *supra* note 10, at 1 (noting that nonprofits fear false accusations of making grants to support terrorism).

161 Foundations making grants in foreign countries sometimes work with local foreign grantmaking organizations because those groups often have better access to information about which projects are most likely to be helpful or effective, or they are better able to administer programs. Under this structure, a foundation makes a grant to a local entity (the initial grantee) that in turn regrants the funds to other smaller local organizations or individuals (the secondary grantees).

162 Frequently operated in developing countries, microfinance programs provide financial services to low-income people without access to traditional forms of capital and credit. Generally, microfinance programs combine small loans with business education/counseling to support entrepreneurial business enterprises and alleviate poverty. Examples could include small retail kiosks, sewing workshops, carpentry shops, and market stalls. For a more detailed discussion, see Michael S. Barr, *Microfinance and Financial Development,* 26 Mich. J. Int'l L. 271 (2004); Lucie E. White, *Feminist Microenterprise: Vindicating the Rights of Women in the New Global Order?,* 50 Me. L. Rev. 327 (1998).

163 For instance, in Sri Lanka, U.S. funders provide charitable support to people in geographic regions "controlled by the Tamil Tigers, a named terrorist organization. Trucks delivering [aid] cannot drive on roads controlled by the Tigers without at least their implicit permission." Barnett F. Baron, *Deterring Donors: Anti-Terrorist Financing Rules and American Philanthropy,* Int'l J. Not-For-Profit L., Jan. 2004, at 12, *available at* http://www.icnl.org/JOURNAL/vol6iss2/ar_baron.htm; *see also* Sally Buzbee, *Warlords Hold Unity at Gunpoint: Old Ways Pose New Dangers,* Richmond Times-Dispatch, Jan. 9, 2002, at A6 (noting the practice of regional Afghan warlords exacting bribes from foreign aid trucks for safe passage).

of Foreign Assets Control released the *U.S. Department of the Treasury Anti-Terrorist Financing Guidelines: Voluntary Best Practices for U.S.-Based Charities* to assist nonprofit organizations engaged in international philanthropy.[164] The Treasury ATF Guidelines outline procedures for governance, disclosure and transparency in governance and finances, financial practices and accountability, and antiterrorist financing procedures. The Treasury Department revised and updated the Guidelines in December 2005[165] and September 2006.[166]

The official name given by the Treasury Department seems to belie the status of the Guidelines. Commentators have noted that the Treasury ATF Guidelines are referred to as "best practices," but they actually represent a variety of new practices introduced by the Treasury Department that were never consistent with common practice in the nonprofit sector. As the Council on Foundations notes, "There is no consensus within the charitable sector as to what constitutes 'best practices'" regarding international grantmaking activity.[167] Practices in the field vary according to the type, size, and resources of the grantmaking organization. The Treasury ATF Guidelines fail to account for these differences, and, in many respects, the Guidelines recommend practices far more exhaustive than those previously employed by international funders.

Interestingly, the Treasury ATF Guidelines do not have the force of law and impose no penalties for failure to comply. Conversely, compliance with the Guidelines does not provide immunity from asset blocking under the Executive Order or prosecution under the PATRIOT Act. Despite their formal status as non-law, the Guidelines continue to receive significant deference in the field from nonprofit managers and their advisers. This is not because the sector views the Guidelines as likely to help prevent funds from being diverted to terrorists, but because it feels coerced.[168] The effect of the government's current regulatory approach—combining unclear voluntary rules with the uncertainty stemming from the possibility that the

---

164 U.S. DEP'T OF THE TREASURY, ANTI-TERRORIST FINANCING GUIDELINES: VOLUNTARY BEST PRACTICES FOR U.S.-BASED CHARITIES (2002) (on file with the North Carolina Law Review) [hereinafter ORIGINAL ANTI-TERRORIST FINANCING GUIDELINES].

165 U.S. DEP'T OF THE TREASURY, ANTI-TERRORIST FINANCING GUIDELINES: VOLUNTARY BEST PRACTICES FOR U.S.-BASED CHARITIES (2005) (on file with the North Carolina Law Review) [hereinafter 2005 REVISED ANTI-TERRORIST FINANCING GUIDELINES].

166 U.S. DEP'T OF THE TREASURY, *supra* note 19.

167 *See* Letter from Dorothy S. Ridings, President and Chief Executive Officer, Council on Founds., to David Aufhauser, Gen. Counsel, U.S. Dep't of the Treasury (June 20, 2003) [hereinafter Council on Foundations Letter], *available at* http://www.cof.org/files/documents/legal/treasury_comments_06.03.pdf. The Council on Foundations is a national membership organization of grantmakers promoting philanthropy.

168 Editorial, *Charity Screening: Post-9-11 Rules Could Stifle Legitimate Giving*, DETROIT FREE PRESS, Sept. 8, 2004, at A8 ("Though the [Treasury ATF G]uidelines are voluntary, foundations fear retribution from the government for not complying— especially since the executive order implies culpability for even unknowingly passing along funds that end up being used by an organization that aids terrorist causes.").

U.S. government may hold charitable organizations accountable for unknowingly funding terrorism[169]—has led to overcompliance by funders.[170] In part because they were issued by a government agency with the ability to freeze assets, the Treasury ATF Guidelines, despite their designation as "voluntary," are beginning to acquire quasi-legal status.[171] Even nonbinding guidelines can exercise a degree of constraint on certain activities when promulgated by a powerful government agency. Operating as they do against the backdrop of the PATRIOT Act and the Executive Order, the Treasury ATF Guidelines manage to conflate recommended practices with regulation. The quasi-legal status of these Guidelines has been bolstered by the fact that the Treasury Department has stated in the Federal Register that charities, at "a minimum, should follow the U.S. Department of the Treasury Anti-Terrorist Financing Guidelines: Voluntary Best Practices for U.S. Based Charities."[172]

This perception of the Guidelines as an integral part of the regulatory apparatus governing international philanthropy is a widely-held view. Even senior Treasury Department officials have acknowledged and informed Congress that the Treasury ATF Guidelines are being treated as more than just voluntary recommendations. In his 2004 Senate confirmation hearings, Juan C. Zarate, who was subsequently confirmed as Assistant Secretary for Terrorism Financing at the Treasury Department, stated that "the guidelines . . . frankly have been treated as regulatory guidance by the charities."[173]

Moreover, despite their title, the Treasury ATF Guidelines do not merely suggest procedures commonly employed by experienced foundations attempting to follow existing law regarding overseas giving.[174] Rather, they proffer several new administrative tasks that, to a great extent, pressure charitable organizations to engage in efforts to ferret out potential terrorist activity. Many of the recommendations are

---

169 *See* Tamara Audi, *Charities Do Detective Work in War on Terror: They Scour Watch Lists To See If Grant Recipients Turn Up*, DETROIT FREE PRESS, Sept. 6, 2004, at A1 ("Foundations fear that even an unintentional or indirect link to a terror group could ruin their reputations and cause the federal government to freeze assets.").

170 *See generally* John E. Calfee & Richard Craswell, *Some Effects of Uncertainty on Compliance with Legal Standards*, 70 VA. L. REV. 965, 966 (1984) (arguing that uncertain legal standards deter activities that may bestow social benefits).

171 *See* Press Release, Nat'l Comm. for Responsive Philanthropy, *supra* note 119 (noting that some funders have "overreacted to the [Guidelines]" and treat them as "mandatory"); Editorial, *supra* note 168.

172 Solicitation of Federal Civilian and Uniformed Service Personnel for Contributions to Private Voluntary Organizations—Sanctions Compliance Certification, 70 Fed. Reg. 67,339, 67,340 (Nov. 7, 2005) (to be codified at 5 C.F.R. pt. 950).

173 *Nominations of John O. Colvin, Stuart Levey, and Juan C. Zarate: Hearing Before the S. Comm. on Finance*, 108th Cong. 15 (2004) (statement of Juan C. Zarate, Deputy Assistant Secretary for Terrorist Financing and Financial Crimes, U.S. Department of the Treasury), *available at* http://www.finance.senate.gov/hearings/95478.pdf.

174 *See supra* note 167 and accompanying text.

burdensome and severely impact the independence, operations, and interactions of U.S.-based nonprofit organizations.[175] Although the government may certainly encourage citizens to remain vigilant and watchful to prevent terrorist activity, citizens (individuals or entities) should not be tasked with intelligence-gathering duties more appropriate for the U.S. government.[176] As one of the largest associations of nonprofits has written, "Almost without exception, the grantmaking community finds the Voluntary Guidelines unproductive, unrealistic and detached from the real-life experiences of the charitable sector."[177]

4. Cases of U.S. Charity-Terrorist Connections

Naturally, any effective prescription to resolve a problem requires a clear understanding and diagnosis of the actual abuses. An understanding of the facts and circumstances of the cases of alleged charitable abuses by terrorists provides significant guidance and a starting point for operating assumptions. Although policymakers always need to consider new risks and new abuses, a review of the available evidence regarding actual cases and patterns presented by past cases may inform decisionmaking on whether the current regulatory regime is working to protect security interests.

The government's approach, especially the Treasury ATF Guidelines, is clearly intended to provide mechanisms to prevent grants made by legitimate U.S. charitable organizations to foreign organizations from being inadvertently diverted to terrorist purposes, what I call "indirect charitable abuse." Significantly, however, neither the government nor the charitable sector itself has reported such cases of diversion.[178] Instead, the paradigmatic cases, if anything, suggest concerns about "direct charitable abuse," in which senior officers and directors of U.S. charities purposefully engage in deceptive fundraising, primarily from individuals, and then knowingly use the funds for noncharitable purposes.[179] Since September 11, the federal

---

175 *See infra* Part III.A.

176 *See infra* Part III.B.

177 *See* Grantmakers Without Borders, Post 9-11 Grantmaking: Anti-Terrorism Policies and International Grantmaking, http://www.gwob.net/advicegm/911.htm (last visited Feb. 17, 2007).

178 *See* Victoria B. Bjorklund et al., *Terrorism and Money Laundering: Illegal Purposes and Activities*, 25 Pace L. Rev. 233, 234 (2005) (noting that "if such diversions have been undertaken by U.S. donors or charities . . . the activities have been hidden and not well known to the charitable sector . . . . [Such diversion] is beyond the experience of almost all U.S. charities . . . .").

179 *See id.* at 239. Experts studying terrorist financing have determined that terrorists committed to laundering money through charities may attempt to use several different means, including the raising of funds through legitimate charities using formal fundraising, raising funds through informal cash collections, transferring funds through charities to terrorist groups, and establishing charities as direct covers for terrorist organizations. *See* Fin. Action Task Force, Report on Money Laundering & Terrorist Financing Typologies 2004–2005 (2005), *available at* http://www.fatf-gafi.org/dataoecd/16/8/35003256.pdf; *see also* 9/11 Commission

government has frozen the assets of five U.S.-based charities it suspected of funneling money to terrorists: the Global Relief Foundation, the Benevolence International Foundation, the Holy Land Foundation, the Islamic American Relief Agency, and KindHearts.[180] Each of these cases allegedly involves direct charitable abuse.

Furthermore, each of the five cases involves Muslim charities. All nonprofits, however, remain at risk. Two of the charities—the Global Relief Foundation[181] and the Benevolence International Foundation[182]—were alleged to have connections to

---

REPORT, *supra* note 1, at 170–71 (describing how al Qaeda used corrupt charities to provide financial support for its operations).

180 *See infra* notes 181–85 and accompanying text.

181 In December 2001, the Treasury Department froze and seized the assets of the Global Relief Foundation ("GRF") pending investigation into its ties to terrorism. *See* Global Relief Found., Inc. v. O'Neill, 207 F. Supp. 2d 779, 784–85 (N.D. Ill. 2002). Founded in 1992 as a U.S. public charity and headquartered in Illinois, GRF was organized to provide humanitarian relief to Muslims overseas, primarily in war-torn regions such as Bosnia, Kashmir, Afghanistan, Lebanon, and Chechnya. *See* JOHN ROTH ET AL., NAT'L COMM'N ON TERRORIST ATTACKS UPON THE U.S., MONOGRAPH ON TERRORIST FINANCING: STAFF REPORT TO THE COMMISSION 88–89 (2004), *available at* http://www.9-11commission.gov/staff_statements/911_TerrFin_Monograph.pdf.

The U.S. government alleged that the founders of GRF were formerly associated with Osama Bin Laden through an organization Bin Laden co-founded prior to al Qaeda for the recruitment and financial aid of mujahideen (resistance fighters) fighting the Soviets in Afghanistan throughout the 1980s. *See* Bjorklund et al., *supra* note 178, at 235. Although the FBI determined that GRF distributed substantial funds for humanitarian relief, the agency also believed that GRF supported terrorists by acquiring and shipping "large quantities of sophisticated communications equipment, [providing] humanitarian cover documentation to suspected terrorists and fund-raising for terrorist groups under the cover of humanitarian relief." ROTH ET AL., *supra*, at 91. In October 2002, GRF was designated a specially designated global terrorist ("SDGT") by the Office of Foreign Assets Control ("OFAC"), a division of the Department of the Treasury, pursuant to Executive Order 13,224. *See* Additional Designations of Terrorism-Related Blocked Persons, 68 Fed. Reg. 399, 400 (Jan. 3, 2003).

182 Founded in 1992, Benevolence International Foundation ("BIF"), a U.S. public charity, described its mission as "relieving the suffering of Muslims around the world." *See* ROTH ET AL., *supra* note 181, at 94–95. BIF's major programmatic activities included support for health initiatives, orphan sponsorship, and refugee aid to Muslims in Afghanistan, Bosnia, China, Pakistan, and Russia. *See* Matthew J. Piers, *Malevolent Destruction of a Muslim Charity: A Commentary on the Prosecution of Benevolence International Foundation,* 25 PACE L. REV. 339, 344 (2005).

BIF's founding board of directors included Sheikh Adel Abdul Jalil Batterjee. *See* ROTH ET AL., *supra* note 181, at 94–95. According to the U.S. government, Batterjee was also "affiliated with a group of wealthy donors from the Persian Gulf region" that provided support to resistance fighters in Afghanistan under the leadership of Bin Laden in the 1980s (an effort supported by the U.S. government). *Id.* at 94; *see also* Lisa Getter et al., *Islamic American Nonprofits Face Increased Scrutiny in U.S.,* L.A. TIMES, Nov. 4, 2001, at A1. In 1993, one year after its creation, the original directors were replaced by three new directors, and Enaam Arnaout became the new executive director. *See* ROTH ET AL., *supra* note 181, at 94–95. Although Batterjee was formally removed from the board, the U.S. government contended that Arnaout allowed Batterjee to dominate operations from behind the scenes. *Id.*

Osama Bin Laden. Three of the charities—Holy Land Foundation,[183] Islamic

---

In 2002, the FBI conducted a search of BIF's offices in Bosnia, where it reportedly uncovered evidence of "links" between BIF's leadership, Bin Laden, and al Qaeda. *See id.* at 102. The material seized included "minutes of al Qaeda meetings, the al Qaeda oath, al Qaeda organizational charts . . . and letters between Arnaout and Bin Laden." *Id.* at 102–03. *But see* Piers, *supra,* at 351 (explaining that Arnaout's connections to Bin Laden and al Qaeda were tenuous and dated back to the 1980s, when both men were involved in efforts to defeat the Soviet invasion of Afghanistan, a goal supported by the U.S. government). OFAC designated BIF as an SDGT pursuant to Executive Order 13,244. *See* Additional Designations of Terrorism-Related Blocked Persons, 68 Fed. Reg. 399, 399 (Jan. 3, 2003). Subsequently, in 2003, Arnaout was charged with criminal activity, but the indictment contained no claims that BIF provided any funds to al Qaeda. *See* ROTH ET AL., *supra* note 181, at 104.

Rather, the charges focused on BIF's support of Chechen and Bosnian fighters with "fraudulently solicited and obtained donations by falsely representing that the funds would be used solely for humanitarian purposes." *Id.* Arnaout pled guilty to one count of racketeering conspiracy for fraudulent diversion of $315,624 in charitable donations by providing tents, boots, medical supplies, and other similar resources to overseas combatants in Chechnya and troops in Bosnia. *See id.* at 108. While this constitutes a misuse of charitable funds, it did not amount to supporting terrorism because neither the Bosnian Army nor the Chechen separatists who benefited from the BIF supplies were considered terrorists by the U.S. government. *See Current Situation and Future of Chechnya: Hearing Before the U.S. Comm'n on Security and Cooperation in Europe,* 108th Cong. 5 (2003) (statement of Steven Pifer, Deputy Assistant Secretary, Bureau of European and Eurasian Affairs, U.S. Department of State) ("[W]e do not share the Russian assessment that the Chechen conflict is simply and solely a counterterrorism effort. We think it is a much more complex question. While there are terrorist elements fighting in Chechnya, we do not agree that all separatists can be equated as terrorists."); *Congress Funds Bosnia Mission,* ST. LOUIS POST-DISPATCH, Dec. 14, 1995, at A1; Elizabeth Sullivan, *Fears of New Danger Rise amid Hopes for Peace,* PLAIN DEALER (Cleveland, Ohio), Sept. 2, 1995, at A5.

Although Arnaout was sentenced to more than eleven years, the court rejected the government's request to apply sentencing enhancement for crimes of terrorism because "Arnaout does not stand convicted of a terrorism offense. Nor does the record reflect that he attempted, participated in, or conspired to commit any act of terrorism." United States v. Arnaout, 282 F. Supp. 2d 838, 843 (N.D. Ill. 2003).

183 Once one of the largest Muslim charities in the United States, the Holy Land Foundation for Relief and Development ("HLF"), a Texas-based public charity in operation for more than a decade, was established to provide aid to Palestinian Muslims in Israel and other parts of the Middle East. *See* Holy Land Found. for Relief & Dev. v. Ashcroft, 219 F. Supp. 2d 57, 64 (D.D.C. 2002). Pursuant to Executive Order 13,224, OFAC designated HLF as an SDGT based on its alleged "acts for or on behalf of" Hamas in December 2001. *See* Holy Land Found. for Relief & Dev. v. Ashcroft, 333 F.3d 156, 160 (D.C. Cir. 2003), *cert. denied,* 540 U.S. 1218 (2004). The U.S. government contends that HLF has funneled more than $12 million to Hamas-controlled entities and other Palestinian organizations that the United States considers sponsors of terrorism. *See* Toni Heinzl, *Indictment: Group Aided Terrorists; Holy Land Foundation Sent Millions to Hamas, Feds Say,* FORT WORTH STAR TELEGRAM, July 28, 2004, at A1.

However, Muslim advocates have challenged the government's characterization and argue that HLF's challenged donations, made to various local "zakat" committees throughout the West Bank and Gaza, were legitimate. *See* Laila Al-Marayati, *American Muslim Charities: Easy Targets in the War on Terror,* 25 PACE L. REV. 321, 324-25 (2005). HLF's defenders claim that the committees are local grassroots entities that include community leaders of various social and political affiliations, including the region's ruling political party (Hamas) and insist that

American Relief Agency,[184] and KindHearts[185]—allegedly maintained ties to Hamas.[186]

HLF's humanitarian grants were not directed to Hamas, even if some individuals associated with grantees may also have ties to Hamas. *Id.* None of the zakat committees were designated as terrorist groups by the United States. As a result of the designation, however, HLF ceased its operations in 2001. *See* Heinzl, *supra.*

184 In October 2004, the Treasury Department designated the Islamic American Relief Agency ("IARA"), based in Columbia, Missouri, an SDGT and blocked the organization's assets. *See* Islamic Am. Relief Agency v. Unidentified FBI Agents, 394 F. Supp. 2d 34, 40 (D.D.C. 2005). Recognized as an exempt organization by the IRS in 1985, IARA operated for more than nineteen years providing "charitable and humanitarian aid to refugees, orphans, victims of human and natural disasters, and other poor and needy persons and entities throughout the world, without regard to faith or political affiliation." *Id.* IARA was originally founded under the name Islamic African Relief Agency, but the organization changed its name when it began expanding its charitable activities beyond the continental borders of Africa. *Id.*

The Treasury Department has alleged that IARA and its senior officers maintained ties to both Hamas and the Islamic African Relief Agency of Sudan. *See* Press Release, U.S. Dep't of the Treasury, Treasury Designates Global Network, Senior Officials of IARA for Supporting bin Laden, Others (Oct. 13, 2004), *available at* http://www.ustreas.gov/press/releases/js2025.htm. IARA claimed that it did not support terrorism and had no connection to the Sudanese organization with the similar name. *See Islamic Am. Relief Agency*, 394 F. Supp. 2d at 40. Despite IARA's protestations, the U.S. district court upheld the Treasury Department's designation based upon its review of unclassified and classified information, much of which was not made available to IARA, determining that "the agency's decision to block the IARA-USA's assets was not arbitrary and capricious, but . . . supported by substantial evidence." *Id.* at 45. As a result of the government designation, IARA has ceased operations. *See* Peter Shinkle, *Case Shines Light on Columbia, Mo.*, St. Louis Post-Dispatch, Apr. 24, 2005, at B1.

185 On February 19, 2006, the U.S. Department of the Treasury froze the assets and blocked all property interests of KindHearts for Charitable Humanitarian Development, Inc. ("KindHearts"), a Toledo, Ohio-based nonprofit organization. *See* Cary Spivak & Dan Bice, *Questions Arise About Muslim Scholar*, Milwaukee J. Sentinel, May 19, 2006, at A2. Founded in 2002 after Treasury designated some of the nation's largest Muslim charities supporters of terrorism, KindHearts quickly became a prominent U.S. Muslim charity, raising more than $5 million by 2004 and distributing grants to Lebanon, Pakistan, and Gaza and the West Bank. *See* Amanda Garrett, *Muslim Charity Drawing Scrutiny; Group with Ohio Ties Denies Terror Connection*, Plain Dealer (Cleveland, Ohio), Dec. 6, 2005, at A1.

The Treasury Department has claimed that KindHearts contributed funds to Hamas, including more than $250,000 to the Lebanon-based SDGT Sanabil. *See* Press Release, U.S. Dep't of the Treasury, Treasury Freezes Assets of Organization Tied to Hamas (Feb. 19, 2006), *available at* http://www.ustreas.gov/press/releases/js4058.htm. Although KindHearts was not designated an SDGT as of the publication of this Article, pursuant to the Executive Order its assets have been blocked pending an investigation that has effectively closed the organization's operations and prevented the millions of dollars in contributions from reaching their intended recipients—humanitarian projects in the developing Muslim world.

186 Hamas is a Palestinian group—designated a terrorist organization by the U.S. government—accused of dozens of suicide bombing attacks in Israel. *See* Stephen Braun, *Texas Charity, Leaders Are Charged with Aiding Hamas*, L. A. Times, July 28, 2004, at A8; Press Release, U.S. Dep't of the Treasury, Shutting Down the Terrorist Financial Network (Dec. 4, 2001), *available at* http://www.ustreas.gov/press/releases/po841.htm. In 2006, it also became the majority

Assuming the facts of the five cases of alleged charitable abuse involving U.S.-based entities to be true, the story that emerges is unconnected to the injury the Guidelines have been designed to prevent: namely, an incident of a U.S. charity being duped by a foreign organization that heightened diligence would have prevented. Instead, these actual cases describe criminally motivated individuals directly using U.S. public charities (not foreign organizations) for noncharitable purposes in violation of law and the charities' own representations.[187] Perhaps the scarcity of incidents of indirect abuse indicates that the existing, rigorous diligence standards under federal tax law in place prior to September 11 have been and continue to be effective at rooting out illicit activity.[188] Or, perhaps the problem of indirect abuse is overstated.

As of the publication of this Article, none of these cases has resulted in any terrorism-related criminal conviction, although legal proceedings appear to have been concluded or do not appear forthcoming in four of the five matters.[189] All that can be said is that it is possible that some or all of the organizations may have been associated with terrorists groups, but it is also equally possible that they were not. Even more important for policy purposes, however, the facts of the cases do not suggest that additional diligence by the charitable sector would have prevented diversion of funds. Because all of these entities were organized under U.S. law, filed with and had all their paperwork approved by the IRS, and acquired an IRS determination letter, the government was best positioned to uncover these alleged charitable fronts. If the allegations are true, they all describe, in various forms, cases of direct charitable abuse in which illegitimate U.S. charities chose to purposefully deceive donors, an abuse not addressed by the Treasury ATF Guidelines. Again, the Guidelines would be relevant only to a case in which a legitimate U.S. grantmaker makes an imprudent grant to a foreign recipient organization engaged in illegal activities. Authors of a recent law review article, after reviewing cases involving U.S. charities and terrorist connections, concluded that their research revealed no incident "involv[ing] a diversion of funds granted by a U.S. grantmaker to a foreign recipient organization . . . where the diversion would have been uncovered but for the lack of appropriate due diligence and oversight procedures."[190]

While any allegations are troubling, notably the government has not substantiated claims that U.S.-based nonprofits are significant sources of terrorist financing.

---

ruling party of the Palestinian Authority. *See* Steven Erlanger, *Hamas Routs Ruling Faction, Casting Pall on Peace Process,* N.Y. Times, Jan. 27, 2006, at A1.

187 Even despite the reported links, investigations of GRF and BIF have not proven that either charity provided financial support to al Qaeda after the U.S. government designated it a terrorist organization in 1999. *See* Roth et al., *supra* note 181, at 111.

188 *See* Bjorklund et al., *supra* note 178, at 244.

189 Criminal charges were filed in the HLF case and a trial date is still pending. *See* Michelle Mittelstadt et al., *Muslim Charity, Leaders Indicted: U.S. Says Holy Land Foundation Funneled Money to Hamas,* Dallas Morning News, July 28, 2004, at A1.

190 Bjorklund et al., *supra* note 178, at 244.

The evidence to date does not demonstrate that charitable grants from legitimate U.S.-based public charities and private foundations provide a significant source of support for al Qaeda or terrorist activities.[191]

III. DEFICIENCIES OF THE CURRENT REGULATORY REGIME

At first glance, the post-September 11 reforms may seem benign, modest, or even eminently reasonable. However, the charitable sector has criticized the reforms primarily because they impose new administrative burdens, on top of an existing regulatory regime providing for substantial diligence, without a clear indication of how the additional reforms—particularly the Treasury ATF Guidelines—aid non-profits in distinguishing between legitimate foreign charities and illegitimate ones. Essentially, the nonprofit sector sees a disconnect between the new regulatory regime and its articulated purposes. The federal government, acting out of fear of further attacks and moral outrage that charitable funds might be diverted for terrorist uses, has pursued executive and legislative actions, including the Treasury ATF Guidelines, since September 11 to protect and aid U.S. charities.[192] What is lacking in the debate about administrative costs and the speculative nature of the security *benefits* from increased regulation is discussion of the security *costs* of the new regulatory environment.

In particular, many of the specific guideline terms increase burdens on what is already viewed as a cumbersome diligence process, thereby creating a marginal chill, at least for some funders, on international giving. Furthermore, the regulatory environment may impact the effectiveness of nonprofits in the field by changing relationships and perceptions between foreign grantees and U.S. grantors. Also, the government's approach has unintentionally created incentives that skew preferences in the form in which international aid is distributed in ways that undermine security. With the root causes of terrorism still at issue, U.S. public diplomacy suffering, and American soft power at stake,[193] the deleterious impacts of the various guideline requirements take on a new urgency once understood as security costs rather than merely as administrative burdens. So, although more diligence may or may not lead to information reducing the likelihood that charitable funds will inadvertently reach terrorists, the consequences of these added requirements must be measured as part of an overall calculus of whether the tradeoffs warrant the new regime.

---

191 *See* Roth et al., *supra* note 181, at 4.

192 *See* U.S. Dep't of The Treasury, *supra* note 19, at 2 ("[T]he Guidelines are intended to assist charities in developing . . . a risk-based approach to guard against the threat of diversion of charitable funds . . . by terrorists and their support networks."). *But see* Jon Frandsen, *The Right Takes Aim at NGOs*, 63 CQ Weekly 1417, 1417 (2005) (noting that groups associated with a conservative political agenda are mobilizing "to trim the powers of international aid, development and advocacy groups").

193 *See supra* Part I.

A. The Chilling Effects on Nonprofits

Since the release of the original version of the Treasury ATF Guidelines, several commentators and advocates for nonprofit organizations engaged in international grantmaking have criticized the Guidelines and questioned the likelihood that they will actually impact terrorist financing, especially when the end users of the information collected do not recognize it as valuable or useful.[194] As one commentator has noted, "Guidelines, reporting requirements, and other obligations imposed on large populations are unlikely to be effective. . . . [C]ollecting too much information means looking for a needle in a haystack. Making the haystack bigger may complicate the job . . . ."[195] Many grantmakers, even those with substantial resources, will have difficulty obtaining and analyzing much of the information outlined in the Guidelines.

For instance, the antiterrorist financing section of the Treasury ATF Guidelines suggests that, before any charitable funds are distributed to a foreign recipient organization, the U.S.-based funder should collect the names and addresses of any subcontracting organizations working with the foreign organization and background information about grantee board members and key staff.[196] The original version of the Guidelines also directed U.S. funders to collect information on banking affiliations of foreign grant recipients;[197] while this particular element has been removed from the modified version of the Guidelines, the overall thrust of the exercise remains. For U.S. charitable organizations that support a large number of overseas organizations, this level of detail could be extensive, especially considering that the information sought on subcontractors extends beyond those persons directly related to the proposed grant. Additionally, once collected, to be useful this information must be documented, stored, and presumably analyzed by someone within the organization. All of these activities require additional staff resources to manage and organize. At least one commentator has observed that the measures described in the Guidelines "would require a great expenditure of resources on the part of the charities, something that would be very difficult, especially for

194 *See* Crimm, *supra* note 154, at 1440; Piers, *supra* note 182, at 352–53 ("It is hard to see how the government's activities with regard to . . . charities have had any positive effect on targeting terrorism."); Council on Foundations Letter, *supra* note 167, at 8; *see also* Fred Stokeld, *Charitable Groups Draft Plan To Curb Terrorist Funding*, 46 Exempt Org. Tax Rev. 150, 150 (2004) ("Exempt organizations practitioners have . . . criticized the [Treasury ATF Guidelines] provisions they say would be burdensome . . . .").

195 Mitchell, *supra* note 12, at 231.

196 *See* U.S. Dep't of The Treasury, *supra* note 19, at 9–12.

197 The Treasury Department originally suggested that charities should "determine the identity of the financial institutions with which the foreign recipient organization maintains accounts [and] . . . seek bank references . . . ." *See* Original Anti-Terrorist Financing Guidelines, *supra* note 164, at 7. This provision was removed when the Guidelines were revised in 2005.

smaller organizations."[198] Also, as U.S. grantmakers pass along the burdens of heightened information requests to grantee recipients, groups in the developing world suffer the consequences.[199]

Additionally, the Guidelines are not attuned to the realities of the recordkeeping and information available abroad. As Barnett F. Baron, then the executive vice president of the Asia Foundation, observed, "The Guidelines erroneously assume that comprehensive and detailed information about prospective grantees is generally available and can be readily collected in the 'developing world,' just as in the United States."[200] For example, the Guidelines provide that funders should require copies of "official registry documents, annual reports, and annual filings with the pertinent government."[201] Unfortunately, all too frequently in the developing world this information either does not exist or may be considered confidential.[202] Moreover, in some regions of the world, communications systems make gathering and transmitting such information impractical. Some overseas charitable activities occur in places where access to copy machines, fax machines, the Internet, or even electricity is either intermittent or nonexistent, making compliance difficult.[203] In addition, some foreign nonprofit organizations operate without formal legal recognition because the benefits of official registration are minimal, registration does not exist, registration is denied to silence independent voices, or they prefer to remain outside the scope of corrupt government control.[204] For instance, the U.S. Department of State has acknowledged that some governments, such as Belarus and China, have denied registration or deregistered certain legitimate NGOs based on

---

198 Al-Marayati, *supra* note 183, at 330.

199 *See* Stephanie Strom, *Small Charities Abroad Feel Pinch of U.S. War on Terror*, N.Y. TIMES, Aug. 5, 2003, at A8 ("[G]roups in the developing world say that acquiring the data needed to allow their benefactors to meet the standards is too onerous a task . . . .").

200 *See* Baron, *supra* note 163, at 10.

201 *See* U.S. DEP'T OF THE TREASURY, *supra* note 19, at 10.

202 *See* Lester M. Salamon, *The Rise of the Nonprofit Sector*, FOREIGN AFF., Jul.–Aug. 1994, at 110; Adriana Ruiz-Restrepo, *Active Without Recognition: Obstacles to Development of the Colombian Third Sector*, INT'L J. NOT-FOR-PROFIT L., Feb. 2005, at 17, 20, *available at* http://www.icnl.org/JOURNAL/vol7iss2/IJNL%20vol%207%20no% 202.pdf.

203 *See* Paula D. Johnson et al., *Promoting Philanthropy: Global Challenges and Approaches, in* RETHINKING PHILANTHROPIC EFFECTIVENESS: LESSONS FROM AN INTERNATIONAL NETWORK OF FOUNDATION EXPERTS, *supra* note 48, at 25, 27 (noting that foreign nonprofits frequently face capacity impediments because of weaknesses in supporting infrastructure).

204 *See* Kimberly Bulkley, *Analysis of Nonprofit Organizations in Kazakhstan*, 3 OR. REV. INT'L L. 3, 5 (2001); Milton Cerny & Michael W. Dunham, *Tsunami: NGO Response: Now and the Future*, 47 EXEMPT ORG. TAX REV. 181, 184 (2005); Kareem Elbayar, *NGO Laws in Selected Arab States*, INT'L J. NOT-FOR-PROFIT L., Sept. 2005, at 3, 18–19, *available at* http://www.icnl.org/knowledge/ijnl/vol7iss4/ijnl_vol7iss4.pdf; Tatshat Stepanyan, *Armenian Governmental Commission Regulating Charitable Programs*, INT'L J. NOT-FOR-PROFIT L., Jan. 2006, at 23, 23, *available at* http://www.icnl.org/knowledge/ijnl/vol8iss2/ijnl_vol8iss2.pdf.

their willingness to discuss human rights abuses.[205] China uses the registration process to control nonprofits by imposing burdensome requirements and high fees on registration so that entities without adequate government ties and support cannot register.[206]

As another example, the list checking prescribed by the Guidelines[207] poses challenges and questions of efficacy. The original version of the Guidelines called upon U.S. charities to verify that potential foreign grantees and their affiliates, as well as the people associated with them, such as their board members and senior staff, were not on any of the various terrorist watch lists maintained by the U.S. government, the United Nations, or the European Union.[208] Although the revised version of the Guidelines no longer asks U.S. domestic nonprofits to consult as many lists, it still calls for checking against the U.S. lists.[209] Several problems remain with relying on such lists—even the OFAC master list of Specially Designated Nationals— for use by the general public. The watch lists are long and many of the names on them are so generic (equivalent to "John Smith" in certain foreign countries) that they fail to provide sufficient detailed assistance to narrow down the identity of individuals with whom to avoid dealings.[210] In addition, innocent persons frequently appear on such lists, either by error or because they share names with nefarious persons.[211] Because the watch lists continually change, some foundations have developed timely and costly procedures under which multiple

205 *See The Essential Role of Non-Governmental Organizations in the Development of Democracy: Hearing Before the S. Comm. on Foreign Relations*, 109th Cong. (June 8, 2006) (statement of Barry F. Lowenkron, Assistant Secretary for Democracy, Human Rights, and Labor, U.S. Department of State) [hereinafter Lowenkron, *Testimony Before S. Comm. on Foreign Relations*], *available at* http://www.state.gov/g/drl/rls/rm/2006/ 68658.htm.

206 *See id.*

207 *See* U.S. DEP'T OF THE TREASURY, *supra* note 19, at 11–12 ("With respect to key employees, members of the governing board, or other senior management at a [foreign] grantee's [organization] . . . [a U.S.] charity should assure itself that none of these individuals is subject to OFAC sanctions. . . . Charities should be aware that other nations may have their own lists of designated terrorist-related individuals, entities, or organizations . . . .").

208 *See* ORIGINAL ANTI-TERRORIST FINANCING GUIDELINES, *supra* note 164, at 6–7.

209 *Compare* U.S. DEP'T OF THE TREASURY, *supra* note 19, at 11–12, *with* ORIGINAL ANTI-TERRORIST FINANCING GUIDELINES, *supra* note 164, at 6–7.

210 *See* Strom, *supra* note 199.

211 *See* Peter M. Shane, *The Bureaucratic Due Process of Government Watch Lists,* 75 GEO. WASH. L. REV. (forthcoming 2007) (on file with the North Carolina Law Review) (criticizing the accuracy of secret watch lists and the availability of redress measures for individuals affected); Daniel J. Steinbock, *Data Matching, Data Mining, and Due Process,* 40 GA. L. REV. 1, 3-9, 21-23 (2005) (criticizing terrorist watch lists as overbroad and lacking a sufficient process by which those on them can review and appeal their status); Anthony D. Romero, Editorial, *You, Too, Could Be a Suspected Terrorist,* WASH. POST, Aug. 17, 2004, at A15.

lists are checked on a daily basis.[212] Of course, even if lists are checked regularly, clever terrorists intent on duping unknowing charities would likely attempt to thwart the watch list system by changing names or using assumed identities to avoid detection. Accordingly, the list checking carries significant financial and staffing burdens. By pushing U.S. charities and foundations to rely on these watch lists, "substantial cultural, political, and economic costs, in both the short and long term"[213] are levied against nonprofits to the extent false positives generated by such lists burden their charitable work.

U.S. public charities and private foundations are not the only American entities transferring funds across borders where risks of terrorist diversion exist. Nonetheless, the Treasury Department has not suggested that all financial institutions, for example, collect the names and home addresses of all board members and staff of every foreign corporation as well as those of any subcontracting business or organization working with the foreign corporation.[214] There are two plausible reasons for this disparate treatment. First, there may be a general reluctance to chill operations affecting corporate profits. Second, in the context of multinational corporations, it may seem intuitively obvious that the burdens of regulating all U.S. foreign transactions in the name of defeating terrorism so far exceed any conceivable benefits that such measures are impracticable, if not nonsensical.

Defenders of the Guidelines might argue that they are simply encouraging greater diligence to further reduce the chance that any monies will reach the hands of terrorists. However, no legitimate U.S. charity wants its charitable funds to be used for any noncharitable purposes, especially not for terrorism, and thus both government interests and the interests of U.S. public charities and private foundations are aligned on this point. It does not seem clear that the government needs to assert its authority to prevent legitimate charities from engaging in uninformed grantmaking. In this context, additional diligence is not purely good. Too much diligence and too many procedural requirements can hinder or chill charitable activity or use up resources otherwise available for philanthropy implicating security interests.

To be sure, cross-border giving will not dry up completely as a result of the Guidelines or the regulatory regime. However, the administrative burdens of the Guidelines, which reach beyond the preexisting detailed diligence requirements, encumber cross-border giving for all U.S.-based international grantmakers and may especially

---

212 *See* Audi, *supra* note 169 (noting that because of the Treasury ATF Guidelines the Ford Foundation, which funds more than 4,000 grantees worldwide, checks every charity against ten different watch lists each day).

213 Shane, *supra* note 211 (manuscript at 4).

214 However, the Bank Secrecy Act requires financial institutions to have comprehensive anti-money laundering programs to identify and report suspicious financial transactions to the Treasury Department. *See* 31 U.S.C. §§ 5311–30 (Supp. III 2003); *see also* Mitchell, *supra* note 12, at 222–24 (discussing anti-money laundering laws in the aftermath of September 11 and questioning the benefits in light of the private sector costs).

deter some funders, particularly smaller organizations, from pursuing direct foreign giving. In fact, initial evidence seems to indicate that direct cross-border giving has decreased as a result of the government's post-September 11 reforms.[215] Even though some funders, especially large, committed donors, can be expected to absorb the costs associated with heightened diligence, that does not justify the costs. Although a 2002 study of international grantmaking activity revealed that compliance cost estimates were not readily available,[216] the costs imposed on organizations by these measures are not insubstantial; this is especially true in light of the fact that international philanthropy has always been considered a costly endeavor for U.S. funders.[217] The Guidelines have also been criticized on other grounds.[218]

B. Impacts on Nonprofit Relationships and Effectiveness

Because of the Treasury ATF Guidelines, invasive background checks on foreign nonprofit board members, employees, and subcontractors, detailed information requests about banking relationships, and attempts to gather information and examine data on foreign recipient organizations' sources of income are becoming commonplace.[219] This has had the effect of turning U.S. charitable funders engaged in international activities into agents of the government, effectively conscripting grantmakers into service in the war against terrorism. Although the Guidelines do not require nonprofit organizations to pick up arms, they do enlist philanthropic entities to conduct intelligence gathering activities on the government's behalf.[220]

---

215 *See infra* Part III.C.

216 Crimm, *supra* note 6, at 124 ("Not one private foundation had maintained records from which it could discern its compliance costs . . . .").

217 *See id.* (reporting that foundations perceived international grantmaking to be "significantly more . . . financially costly than domestic grant-making").

218 For additional analysis of the original version of the Guidelines, see Crimm, *supra* note 154, at 1440–46; Joseph Younker, Note, *The "U.S. Department of the Treasury Anti-Terrorist Financing Guidelines: Voluntary Best-Practices for U.S. Based Charities": Sawing a Leg Off the Stool of Democracy*, 14 TRANSNAT'L L. & CONTEMP. PROBS. 865 (2004); Council on Foundations Letter, *supra* note 167, at 3 (noting the Guidelines contain provisions that are "internally inconsistent and/or contrary to federal and state laws"); Memorandum from Betsy Buchalter Adler & Thomas Silk, Silk, Adler & Colvin to an Unidentified Client 2 (Nov. 14, 2002), *available at* http://www.usig.org/PDFs/Treasury GuidelinesMemo.doc (criticizing the Guidelines for seeking to impose "a federal corporate governance standard, which conflicts with the laws of many states governing non-profit corporations").

219 *See* Jones, *supra* note 10, at 1.

220 In congressional testimony, the then-Deputy Secretary of the Treasury Department indicated that "[t]he private sector serves as the front-line in the campaign against terrorist financing. . . . [Treasury] will continue . . . working with . . . the charitable sector . . . to enhance their abilities to detect and report possible terrorist financing and money laundering activities." *Counterterror Initiatives in the Terror Finance Program: Hearing Before the S. Comm. on Banking, Housing, and Urban Affairs*, 108th Cong. 17–18 (2004) (statement of Samuel W. Bodman, Deputy Secretary, U.S. Department of the Treasury).

One of the key strengths of nonprofit institutions and a source of their effectiveness stems from their independence. Because they are neither government nor business, nonprofit organizations occupy a unique space between the public and private sectors, unfettered from both the constraints of the political system faced by government and those of market ownership faced by corporations.[221] Although the sector's activities may generate advantageous and even important byproducts for government or business,[222] and some charitable organizations frequently work directly with government or business, nonprofits remain independent and apart from their public and corporate sector brethren. Even the nomenclature encapsulates this fundamental feature, as the term "nongovernmental organization," emphasizing such organizations' unique role apart from government, has gained global acceptance.[223] Because of this independence, international funders are able to use their position to bring diverse coalitions together: foreign governments, the private sector, other funders, and citizen stakeholders who are normally excluded from decisionmaking processes.[224] Since U.S. security interests are linked to the development of civil societies and stable states abroad, policies exact security costs when they undermine—even marginally—the unique contributions that American nonprofits make in advancing overseas development. The Guidelines are contributing to the erosion of the vital independence and separateness from government that has been a hallmark of the nonprofit sector.

There are three principal problems with these efforts to conscript funders into carrying out these investigatory functions: (1) the process does not provide the transparency and fairness that typically accompanies government processes; (2) nonprofit organizations, especially smaller organizations, are not equipped to effectively carry out investigatory functions; and (3) the process diminishes the credibility of nonprofits operating abroad. The role thrust upon nonprofits by the Treasury ATF Guidelines is not comparable to those instances in which private entities choose to

---

221 *See* Peter Frumkin, On Being Nonprofit: A Conceptual and Policy Primer 1–5 (2002). Clearly nonprofits have their own set of stakeholders, but no one group can claim exclusive ownership the way voters and shareholders stake claims over government and business. *Id.* at 5.

222 For example, nonprofits aid government by providing social services that would otherwise be provided by government or by generating soft power, and the nonprofit sector may produce beneficial byproducts for the private sector by providing an educated workforce or a rich arts and cultural region to attract employees.

223 *See* Rubem Cesar Fernandes, *Threads of Planetary Citizenship*, *in* Citizens Strengthening Global Civil Society 319, 332 (Miguel Darcy de Oliveria & Rajesh Tandon eds., 1994) ("The expression nongovernmental organization comes originally from United Nations vocabulary to designate a special category of participants in the U.N. system . . . . The term is well known in the Western areas of Europe, as well as in Asia, Africa, and Latin America.").

224 *See* Anheier & Simmons, *supra* note 48, at 24.

conduct certain functions traditionally associated with the state;[225] here nonprofits are *coerced* into the role without corresponding benefit to themselves or society.

As previously noted, most nonprofit entities feel compelled to follow the Guidelines because of the catastrophic effects of having their assets frozen if the government were to deem the organization uncooperative.[226] This enlistment of private citizens (i.e., charitable organizations) to gather information—essentially to undertake an investigatory function—represents a partial shifting of traditional governmental functions and responsibilities. Significantly, the supplemental data that the Treasury ATF Guidelines ask nonprofits to collect are not necessary or helpful to improve the quality of grantmaking.[227] In practice, most funders find that they can gather enough information about the potential grantee, its leadership, its track record, and its uses of funds without the additional steps and information outlined in the Guidelines. As such, the information gathering in accordance with the Treasury ATF Guidelines appears to be for investigatory purposes on behalf of the government with the burdens and expenses placed on the nonprofit sector. Moreover, since the prescribed efforts generate no additional benefit for the nonprofit sector and speculative benefit, at best, for society, the government has not adequately justified the coercion of charitable organizations. Such coercion is troubling: transferring a public function to NGOs leads to a less transparent process, both to the public as a whole and to the constituency under investigation, and as a result potentially makes it more difficult to hold the government accountable. To the extent that potential grantee organizations investigated would like to challenge the results, criticize the manner of investigation, or even subject the process of the required investigation to public scrutiny or inquiry, the government has immunized itself from complaints regarding the ways such investigations are handled by shifting responsibilities to private charitable organizations doing work that more suitably falls under the government's direct purview.

Assigning investigatory tasks to nonprofits is ill-conceived because nonprofits are not likely to be well-equipped or effective investigatory agents. The Guidelines place nonprofits in the position of carrying out functions beyond those usually required to ensure the efficacy of charitable uses of grant funds. The suggested "data mining" tasks from the Guidelines fall outside the usual due diligence measures

225 For discussion of issues associated with voluntary public-private partnerships, see Martha Minow, Partners, Not Rivals: Privatization and the Public Good (2002); Jody Freeman, *Extending Public Law Norms Through Privatization,* 116 Harv. L. Rev. 1285 (2003); Paul R. Verkuil, *Public Law Limitations on Privatization of Government Functions,* 84 N.C. L. Rev. 397 (2006).

226 *See supra* notes 168–72 and accompanying text.

227 *See* Strom, *supra* note 199 (quoting a philanthropic executive as saying, " 'It's unclear how all this information [from the Treasury ATF Guidelines] would help us and what it has to do with our grant-making' ").

and expertise of charitable organizations.[228] Such organizations cannot be viewed as agents of the U.S. government if they are to effectively carry out their work. Several international philanthropists have expressed concern that the information collection activities will undermine the reputation of nonprofit organizations "for impartiality and operational independence from governments," which is a significant source of organizational strength that permits nongovernmental organizations to operate effectively in disaster areas and places of armed conflict.[229] Extensive government entanglement in ways that undermine independence may blur the lines between legitimate NGOs and less-respected government-organized NGOs ("GONGOs").[230]

The programmatic effectiveness of international funders depends, to a great extent, on relations with key stakeholders. Grantmakers often find that "[s]takeholder interactions improve the ability of foundations to achieve their missions in ways that help people and communities."[231] However, some recommendations of the Treasury ATF Guidelines seem to exacerbate tensions of cross-border philanthropy and underestimate the potentially delicate relationships at stake. For instance, the Guidelines direct grantors to generate lists containing background information (names, nicknames, nationality, citizenship, place and date of birth, residential information, etc.) on staff and board members at foreign recipient organizations.[232] Requesting the type of information recommended, however, could undermine relationships between grantors and prospective grantees.[233] In many parts of the world,

---

228 Although the Guidelines call for the collection of certain data and information on foreign grantees, *see* U.S. Dep't of the Treasury, *supra* note 19, at 9–12, they do not offer any direction or reveal how a grantmaking organization should analyze the data, once received. So, effectively the Guidelines have imposed a burden of collecting data on nonprofits without providing useful guidance on its uses.

229 *See* Grant Williams, *Safe and Sound? Charities That Work Abroad Caution That Antiterrorism Guidelines Could Hinder, Not Help, Their Efforts*, Chron. of Philanthropy, Aug. 7, 2003, at 8 (quoting a joint statement of InterAction and Independent Sector on the Treasury ATF Guidelines).

230 Certain human rights-violating governments have created "nonprofit organizations" that turn out to be GONGOs used to manipulate public opinion by advocating on their government's behalf or defending their government at the United Nations or other international conferences or events. *See* Lowenkron, *Testimony Before S. Comm. on Foreign Relations*, *supra* note 205 (noting Tunisian government intelligence members attending conferences and monitoring individuals and China's use of GONGOs at the United Nations); Melissa E. Crow, *From Dyad to Triad: Reconceptualizing the Lawyer-Client Relationship for Litigation in Regional Human Rights Commissions*, 26 Mich. J. Int'l L. 1097, 1132–33 (2005) (discussing GONGOs).

231 Thomas E. Backer et al., *Who Comes to the Table? Stakeholder Interactions in Philanthropy*, *in* Rethinking Philanthropic Effectiveness: Lessons from an International Network of Foundation Experts, *supra* note 48, at 111, 111.

232 U.S. Dep't of the Treasury, *supra* note 19, at 11.

233 *See* Strom, *supra* note 199 (quoting a nonprofit executive who explained that the Treasury ATF Guidelines place U.S. charitable organizations " 'in the position of seeming like police agents or spies' ").

"there appears to be a pervasive lack of trust and confidence in nonprofit organizations,"[234] which may lead some U.S. grantmakers to be viewed with greater suspicion; these invasive inquiries can support the perception that the nonprofit is working on behalf of foreign or domestic governments. And these fears may actually be warranted. In fact, in some countries, seeking the background information suggested may be misinterpreted as "intelligence-gathering" efforts on behalf of hostile local government officials, and may actually place organization staff at risk.[235] In addition to harm by insurgents, many foreign nonprofit employees around the world fear physical abuse at the hands of their government if their affiliation with certain humanitarian or pro-democracy NGOs were made public. For instance, in recent congressional testimony, a senior U.S. State Department official acknowledged unjust government harassment, beatings, and arrests of local NGO employees in Asia, Africa, and the Middle East.[236]

Further, because of the unequal power dynamics in the funding relationship and the perception of U.S. foundations as elitist, U.S. grantors have been seeking to develop symbiotic partnership relationships with their grant recipients.[237] When they follow these measures and request a written certification that the foreign organization does not deal with terrorists or "support terrorism,"[238] grantmakers may jeopardize the working relationship with their new partners before it even begins. This issue is particularly sensitive in dealings in certain parts of the world, such as the Middle East. Moreover, obtaining certification regarding terrorist support is a futile exercise because it is unlikely to deter a nefarious grantee seeking to dupe a U.S. charitable organization into donating funds that can be diverted to support terrorism.

Insofar as regulatory reforms interfere with grantor-grantee relationships between U.S. funders and foreign recipient organizations, charitable effectiveness may be undermined, thus lessening the ability of nonprofit organizations to contribute to America's soft power. Global nonprofits draw strength and influence from their ability to "represent[] broad public interests beyond the purview of

---

234 Johnson et al., *supra* note 203, at 26–27.

235 *See* Council on Foundations Letter, *supra* note 167, at 15; *see, e.g.*, Adrian Blomfield, *Aid Crisis as Charity Is Forced Out of Darfur*, Daily Telegraph (London), Dec. 22, 2004, at 10 (noting the murders of humanitarian aid workers from the British charity Save the Children in Sudan, the French charity Medecins Sans Frontieres (Doctors Without Borders) in Afghanistan, and the American charity Iraq for Care in Iraq).

236 *See* Lowenkron, *Testimony Before S. Comm. on Foreign Relations*, *supra* note 205 (noting that the government in Uzbekistan has "harassed, beaten and jailed" nonprofit workers and that "NGO employees have been convicted of criminal offenses for their work making it virtually impossible for them to find other jobs" and describing similar actions in Sudan and Syria).

237 *See* Backer et al., *supra* note 231, at 111 (noting that foundations are often perceived by stakeholders as "elitist institutions"); *id.* at 117 (addressing power differentials between grantor and grantee).

238 U.S. Dep't of the Treasury, *supra* note 19, at 10.

individual states."[239] The credibility and trustworthiness that nonprofits bring to communities are just as important, perhaps even more important, to the long-term success of funded projects as their funds and resources.[240] Much of that virtue is a function of their independence from national governments. If they become an extension of government or even perceived as such, nonprofits forsake the high middle ground between the public and private spheres.[241] Paradoxically, much of the benefit that nonprofits conferon government through the enhancement of soft power is dependent on the theoretical and actual separation between private nonprofit associations and official government entities. Security interests, it would appear, are thus tied into the effectiveness and the independence of charitable organizations.

C. Reducing and Skewing Direct Funding to Foreign Charities

Unfortunately, the federal government's current approach[242] has created incentives for U.S. philanthropic organizations to steer "international-related" grants toward U.S.-based intermediary organizations with operations abroad, instead of awarding grants directly to foreign nonprofit organizations. The initial evidence seems to indicate that shifts away from direct overseas giving are continuing, in part because of the regulatory environment. Data from the Foundation Center, which tracks trends in philanthropy, show that the proportion of international grant dollars awarded directly overseas versus given to U.S.-based intermediaries operating abroad declined by nearly five percentage points between 1994 and 2002.[243] Moreover, recent data covering the period between 2002 and 2004 revealed that total direct cross-border giving dollars by U.S. foundations to foreign charities declined an additional 3% with the actual raw number of such grants declining by 9% (compared to a 3% decline in the number of grants to U.S.-based recipients).[244] The downward trend data support findings from surveys of grantmakers suggesting that the Executive Order and the PATRIOT Act were partly responsible for the behavioral shifts causing funders to favor U.S.-based intermediaries.[245]

The creation of incentives to funnel grants through U.S. intermediaries is troubling because such a shift impacts not only the nature of philanthropy but also U.S. security interests. Security interests are implicated in two important ways. First, as

---

239 NYE, *supra* note 13, at 90.

240 *See* Crimm, *supra* note 6, at 119.

241 *See* Anheier & Simmons, *supra* note 48, at 23–24 ("Foundations tend to be viewed as 'apolitical' or more neutral organizations and can therefore engage local actors more easily. . . . Thanks to their independence, foundations can serve as catalysts and bring all types of groups together.").

242 *See supra* Part II.B.

243 *See* RENZ ET AL., *supra* note 10, at 43.

244 *See* RENZ & ATIENZA, *supra* note 9, at 4.

245 *See* RENZ ET AL., *supra* note 10, at 13, 15.

compared to indirect international grantmaking carried out by intermediaries or U.S entities, direct grants to local foreign nonprofits offer advantages with respect to institution-building and the development of civil society. For instance, local foreign recipient organizations offer a more sophisticated appreciation of local customs, a deep understanding of local problems and networks, and a permanent staff committed to the region. In addition, local foreign organizations may be better positioned to partner with local foreign governments to maximize resources and strategic responses. As a result, direct foreign grants help build the capacity of local, sustainable civil organizations abroad, and evidence indicates that such institutions are critical to the long-term success of development efforts.[246] While U.S. public charities conducting work abroad may serve local communities in valuable and significant ways, when the actual work is done by U.S. entities, rather than by a sustainable local organization, the nonprofit does not make the same contributions to the creation of social capital and civil society: teaching the skills of self-government, instilling the values of tolerance and civility, and mediating the space between the individual, government, and business.[247] This problem is magnified by the fact that, when it comes to individual giving, U.S. tax laws already offer strong incentives to U.S. citizens to favor U.S.-based charities over foreign organizations by limiting tax deductions to donations made to domestically organized charities.[248] Accordingly, because foreign NGOs have traditionally received much of their American financial support from philanthropic organizations, rather than from individuals, the new giving environment created by the federal government has the effect of redirecting the flow of institutional charitable funds away from foreign organizations, which can be especially crippling.

Second, private foundations face increased incentives to support international programs through U.S intermediaries (rather than giving directly to the foreign charity). Ironically, such incentives may actually lead to less due diligence with respect to foreign grant recipients, thus undermining security interests. Consider this hypothetical: A U.S. foundation seeks to donate $50,000 to combat HIV in a remote township in South Africa. The foundation identifies the sole nonprofit service provider working in the region as Ubuntu HIV Relief, an entity organized under South African law and run by native South African men and women. The foundation can choose to make the $50,000 grant either directly to Ubuntu or through the South African HIV/AIDS Fund, an intermediary organized under U.S. law as a public charity headquartered in New York City that raises funds in the United States and makes grants to deserving organizations in South Africa, and would make a $44,000 contribution to Ubuntu (using the remaining $6,000 to

246 *See* U.S. Agency for Int'l Dev., U.S. Foreign Aid: Meeting the Challenges of the Twenty-First Century 12 (2004), *available at* http://www.usaid.gov/policy/pdabz3221.pdf.

247 *See* Barbara K. Bucholtz, *Reflections on the Role of Nonprofit Associations in a Representative Democracy*, 7 Cornell J.L. & Pub. Pol'y 555, 571–78 (1998).

248 *See* I.R.C. § 170(c)(1), (c)(2)(A) (2000).

cover its general and administrative expenses). Under current law, if a private foundation makes grants directly to a foreign recipient organization, the foundation must follow a comprehensive set of laws and regulations requiring detailed due diligence, through the structured equivalency determination or the expenditure responsibility process.[249] However, if those same grant contributions are shifted to U.S. intermediaries, which are invariably public charities, the monies flowing overseas become subject to the less rigorous due diligence standards for U.S. public charities because the stricter foundation requirements do not apply.[250] To the extent that the foundation is concerned about the regulatory environment, it has incentives to resist direct giving to Ubuntu, with the effect that the amount of overall due diligence conducted on the foreign recipient might actually decrease (because the U.S. intermediaries receiving funds would be public charities), and fewer charitable dollars would actually reach the developing world, thus limiting the potential benefits.

D. Undermining American Values

If our national security interests rest, even in part, on "halt[ing] the creation of new terrorists by dealing, to the extent possible, with those grievances that are driving radicalization"[251] or on winning the struggle for the "hearts and minds" of peoples around the world through attraction to shared values, vision, and principles, or on both, we must consider the consequences of adopting policies that undermine our efforts to achieve those goals. The U.S. government's current approach to international philanthropy undermines long-term American interests, specifically its interests in enhancing public diplomacy and soft power, in several important ways.

The attraction that forms the basis for soft power is greatly influenced by a variety of factors, including the perception of the values for which the United States stands.[252] An image is shaped by more than just official press statements and media sound bites. Treatment of U.S. citizens, especially Arab-Americans, affects global perceptions of whether or not the United States lives up to the values it espouses. With respect to international philanthropy, all U.S. nonprofits are burdened by the new regulatory enforcement regime, but none more so than Muslim organizations.[253] This disparate impact raises deep concerns about civil liberties and abuses of power.

---

249 *See supra* Part II.B.3.

250 *See supra* Part II.B.2. However, public charities as a matter of best practice in the field maintain diligence procedures designed to ensure that funds are only used for legitimate and charitable purposes. *See* Edie & Nober, *supra* note 110, at 20–21.

251 Daniel Benjamin & Steven Simon, The Next Attack: The Failure of the War on Terror and a Strategy for Getting It Right 197 (2005).

252 *See* Nye, *supra* note 87, at 9 ("Soft power arises in large part from our values. These values are expressed . . . in the policies we follow inside our country. . . .").

253 *See supra* Part II.B.4.

More than just soured relations and public image are at stake; the government's approach also implicates the civil liberties of Muslim citizens and those who donate to charities committed to serving Islamic communities around the world. The changes in the law—especially the PATRIOT Act and the Executive Order—have permitted federal authorities to close large U.S.-based Muslim charities with minimal evidence and minimal attention to due process.[254] The evidence is not strong enough to support criminal convictions but suggests guilt by association. Additionally, the process is a secret one with limited court review,[255] and the accused nonprofit is denied access to much of the evidence used against it. As Professor Peter Shane notes, this type of governmental power, particularly when used against a specific targeted group, "strain[s] against the norms of openness and transparency on which democratic legitimacy is based."[256] This kind of governmental action reinforces the Muslim community's perception of ethnic profiling[257] and signals a willingness to saddle Arab-Americans and their supporters with the burdens of a "racial tax."[258] Thus, we have a variety of important values at stake worthy of consideration on their own merits. The negative impacts on public diplomacy and soft power also expand the costs beyond those borne solely by Muslim charities and their supporters to costs for U.S. security priorities.

IV. FROM COERCION TO COOPERATION: AVENUES FOR A NEW REGULATORY REGIME

Once we recognize and acknowledge the valuable contributions of international philanthropy to our security interests, we can begin to develop a more complete picture of the security costs (not just the administrative burdens) and tradeoffs associated with the current regulatory approach. Doing so could lead to a shift in how

254 *See supra* notes 181–86 and accompanying text.

255 Under the Administrative Procedure Act, the standard of review for the courts is quite limited. *See* 5 U.S.C. § 706(2)(A) (2000). Accordingly, the charities with their assets frozen have turned to the courts but have failed to prevail not because the courts have made determinations that these entities were terrorist fronts, but rather because the courts could not determine that the agency action was arbitrary and capricious. As such, the courts did not conduct their own factfinding. *See* Islamic Am. Relief Agency v. Unidentified FBI Agents, 394 F. Supp. 2d 34, 44–45 (D.D.C. 2005); Holy Land Found. for Relief and Dev. v. Ashcroft, 333 F.3d 156, 162 (D.C. Cir. 2003), *cert. denied,* 540 U.S. 1218 (2004).

256 Shane, *supra* note 211 (manuscript at 4) (referencing secret government programs).

257 *See, e.g.,* OMB Watch, Muslim Charities and the War on Terror 5 (2006), *available at* http://www.ombwatch.org/pdfs/muslim_charities.pdf; Al-Marayati, *supra* note 183, at 328–29.

258 *See* Randall Kennedy, Race, Crime, and the Law 138–63 (1997) (arguing that profiling imposes a "racial tax"); *see also* Jody David Armour, Negrophobia and Reasonable Racism: The Hidden Costs of Being Black in America 13–18 (1997) (describing a "Black tax" faced by African Americans due to racial stereotypes); Robert S. Chang, *Closing Essay: Developing a Collective Memory To Imagine a Better Future,* 49 UCLA L. Rev. 1601, 1609 (2002) (stating that the detention and questioning of thousands of men of Middle Eastern ancestry constitutes a "racial tax").

nonprofits are viewed in the global fight against terror. Instead of being seen as weak links in the security chain, they should be considered front line allies. In a complex world, the U.S. government should adopt policies that take account of the security costs associated with regulating international philanthropy and the importance of building soft power, encouraging public diplomacy, and reducing terrorism and its root causes. Terrorism remains a dangerous threat, but also a multifaceted one that must be addressed on multiple fronts. The Bush administration's focus on the prevention of further attacks is understandable, but foreign assistance is also part of the solution. As legal scholar and terrorism expert Professor Philip Heymann notes, "We have to maintain our foreign alliances, formal and informal."[259] International aid, through the U.S. government and through private institutions, contributes to those important relations.

A variety of potential avenues for reform might open if U.S. policy began to reflect the security-enhancing value that U.S. nonprofit organizations offer. Although the federal government and the nonprofit sector should certainly work in collaboration to prevent charitable funds from reaching terrorists, the response fashioned should be commensurate with the risks and reflect the new cost-benefit analysis advocated in this Article. Some potential policy changes might include the following.

A. Subjecting Policies to Cost-Benefit Analysis

Since the Reagan administration, the executive branch of the federal government has required a formal assessment of the costs and benefits of major regulation.[260] By issuing the Treasury ATF Guidelines as voluntary recommendations, these unofficial regulations have avoided the typical cost-benefit scrutiny required of significant regulatory action. Such avoidance is particularly ironic due to the fact that the George W. Bush administration has been a vocal proponent of using cost-benefit analysis to justify regulatory action.[261] At a minimum, given the impact

259 Heymann, *supra* note 61, at 14.

260 *See* Exec. Order No. 12,291, 3 C.F.R. 127 (1982); Exec. Order No. 12,866, 58 Fed. Reg. 51,735 (Sept. 30, 1993).

261 *See* John D. Graham, Adm'r, Office of Info. & Regulatory Affairs, Office of Mgmt. & Budget, Executive Office of the President, Remarks Delivered at the Brookings-AEI Conference on "Risk, Science, and Public Policy: Setting Social and Environmental Priorities" (Oct. 12, 2004), http://www.whitehouse.gov/omb/inforeg/speeches/101204_risk.html ("I believe President Bush's first term, when studied by historians, will be considered a period of refinement and reinforcement of the cost-benefit perspective. At OMB ... [we] have reaffirmed the important cost-benefit principles ...."); Cindy Skrzycki, *Future of Federal Rulemaking Caught Up in Election*, Wash. Post, Nov. 2, 2004, at E1 ("It is widely understood that the Bush administration thinks federal regulation should play a limited role in the economy and that costs and benefits of a rule are carefully considered. A chief proponent of that philosophy is John D. Graham .... [who] has instituted strict guidelines for reviewing the costs and benefits of proposed rules, has sent rules back to agencies for more justification, and has allowed third parties to challenge the data behind rules.").

the Guidelines have on behavior, it seems unjustified, if not hypocritical,[262] to avoid this important analysis when the charitable sector is affected rather than business. Since the entire thrust of the cost-benefit balancing process aims to minimize net social costs, the avoidance of such an analysis in this case seems to conflict with the dominant grain of administrative law governance.

Accordingly, private foundations and public charities should advocate for a formal cost-benefit review of the Guidelines. The introduction to the revised version of the Guidelines presents a thin veneer of consideration of costs and benefits by at least acknowledging "the vital importance of the charitable community in providing essential services around the world."[263] However, this approach is far too superficial and in many ways seems merely symbolic without any elaboration of the actual stakes. In particular, it fails to account for the critical role of nonprofit organizations in building alliances around the world and generating soft power and other benefits for the U.S. government. Specifically, it would be in the nonprofit sector's interests to insist upon a review that includes consideration of the security benefits, administrative costs borne by charitable organizations, and security costs of the Guidelines. The philanthropic community has gained some traction in its efforts to convince the federal government to make at least cosmetic revisions to the Guidelines addressing some administrative elements and including references to understanding the complexities of charitable work overseas. However, there has been no indication that a larger shift of the type I call for is underway to account for the security interests and social benefits implicated by the interplay between public diplomacy, soft power, and international philanthropy.

Clearly, such an analysis of the costs and benefits would require an assessment of more than just the quantified costs and the quantified benefits.[264] The intangible burdens and the broader social impacts also need to be adequately and seriously considered.[265] A formal and thorough cost-benefit review might be especially helpful in this instance because "[t]o the extent that people's emotions are getting

262 Critics charge that cost-benefit analysis has been primarily deployed as an anti-regulatory tool to advance business interests. *See, e.g.*, Robert Perks et al., Rewriting the Rules: The Bush Administration's Assault on the Environment 24 (2002); David M. Driesen, *Is Cost-Benefit Analysis Neutral?*, 77 U. Colo. L. Rev. 335, 335–36 (2006) (contending that cost-benefit analysis "has almost always proven anti-environmental in practice. . . . [Cost-benefit analysis] favors industry . . . ."); Barton H. Thompson, Jr., *What Good Is Economics?*, 37 U.C. Davis L. Rev. 175, 179 (2003) ("Opponents of environmental regulation have been the principal proponents of cost-benefit analysis . . . .").

263 U.S. Dep't of the Treasury, *supra* note 19, at 3.

264 When reviews are formally conducted by the Office of Management and Budget, agency analysts are instructed to at least consider "non-quantified benefits or costs . . . in the context of the overall analysis." *See* Office of Mgmt. & Budget, Regulatory Analysis, Circular A-4, at 2 (2003).

265 *See* Robert W. Hahn & Cass R. Sunstein, *A New Executive Order for Improving Federal Regulation? Deeper and Wider Cost-Benefit Analysis*, 150 U. Pa. L. Rev. 1489, 1498 (2002) ("[C]ost-benefit

the better of them, by producing massive concern about small risks, cost-benefit analysis should help put things in perspective, and at the same time might help to calm popular fears."[266]

B. Revisiting Post-September 11 Reforms

Although they were revised in December 2005 and again in September 2006 to address some of the concerns raised by the philanthropic community,[267] the Treasury ATF Guidelines continue to constrain and stifle international grantmaking activity. Consequently, as we weigh the speculative security benefits against the administrative and security costs, the Treasury Department might heed the nonprofit community's call for the retraction of the Guidelines.[268] Simply put, international philanthropy is just too important to be chilled by a set of measures based on untested assumptions.

Too many of the "best practices" suggested by the Guidelines are unworkable and unlikely to prevent the diversion of charitable contributions. In some cases, following the Guidelines may pose safety risks to international aid workers abroad[269] or undermine the effectiveness of nonprofits altogether. Although well-intentioned, the Treasury ATF Guidelines exact security costs while providing only speculative benefits. As I have argued, the nonprofit sector's independence from government, its ability to work and contribute effectively to global, social, and political development, and its contributions to U.S. soft power and public diplomacy are too important to be diluted without due cause. Further, the guideline approach in this area is too likely to become de facto compulsory in light of the regulatory environment.

---

analysis requires a full accounting of the consequences of an action, in both quantitative and qualitative terms.").

266 *Id.* at 1502.

267 *See* U.S. Dep't of the Treasury, *supra* note 19, at 2. For example, the 2005 revised version of the Guidelines suggested organizational records and minutes should be made available to any government authority upon request. *See* 2005 Revised Anti-Terrorist Financing Guidelines, *supra* note 165, at 4. Several commentators, including this author, have noted that in failing to at least acknowledge traditional due process safeguards designed to protect civil liberties (e.g., warrant requirements and subpoenas) the Guidelines might have been read as an attempt to ease the process burdens associated with procedural due process for the Treasury Department and law enforcement agencies seeking the information collected by the private funders. I have argued that this previous impression drawn from the language and the pressure nonprofits feel to comply with the Guidelines seemed to provide the government with information and cooperation through coercion under the guise of voluntary language and promoting "best practices," placing the perception of nonprofit independence from government at risk. The 2006 modification to the Guidelines calls for such cooperation with the government "[w]hen served with process or when other appropriate authorization exists." U.S. Dep't of the Treasury, *supra* note 19, at 5.

268 *See* Caroline Preston, *Charity Coalition Urges Government To Scrap Antiterrorism Guidelines*, Chron. of Philanthropy, Mar. 9, 2006, at 38.

269 *See supra* notes 234–36 and accompanying text.

In light of the subtle yet important security complexities at work, the Guidelines and their emphasis on indiscriminate data collection take on a different and costly character that may make them less relevant and worthwhile.

Additionally, the terms of the IEEPA and the Executive Order should be revisited to place limitations on the length of time assets may be frozen. Several million dollars of charitable assets earmarked for the Muslim world have been held by the government. Even if the government determines that freezing assets is required to prevent imminent transfer while an investigation is ongoing, such a freeze need not and should not be indefinite. In all five of the cases involving U.S. public charities accused of terrorist connections, the nonprofits received donations with the expectation that the funds contributed would be used to serve charitable purposes, primarily in the Islamic world.[270] The U.S. government should ensure that those funds ultimately are used for such purposes. After a reasonable period of investigation, perhaps three years, funds should be released so that they may reach the charitable stream as intended by the original donors.

C. Reconsidering the Restrictions of Equivalency Determination

Acknowledging the many benefits of international philanthropy and the ways in which it can enhance our national strategic interests may lead the U.S. government to do more than simply roll back regulation. Indeed, such a shift may lead to reconsideration of existing tax laws to affirmatively facilitate and encourage international philanthropy. Proactive changes to current tax laws governing philanthropy can promote overseas giving without placing our security at risk. Most notably, the requirements for equivalency determination should be liberalized to remove impediments affecting the ability of U.S. private foundations to support foreign organizations.

Many of the Internal Revenue Code rules that apply to the determination of a foreign NGO's equivalency status are both unnecessarily formalistic and fail to consider the effects of promoting charity abroad. For instance, nonprofit law scholar Nina Crimm has argued that the requirements constraining nonprofit lobbying reflect domestic concerns and considerations unrelated to foreign nonprofits, alternative political cultures, and contemporary policy goals.[271] To advance certain articulated U.S. government policy objectives such as the promotion of democratization efforts abroad, she calls for a liberalization of the lobbying restriction as applied to U.S. grantmakers supporting foreign organizations.[272]

270 For discussion of the cases, see *supra* notes 181–85 and accompanying text.

271 *See* Nina J. Crimm, *Democratization, Global Grant-Making, and the Internal Revenue Code Lobbying Restrictions,* 79 Tul. L. Rev. 587, 599 (2005) ("[E]xisting [Internal Revenue Code] lobbying restrictions . . . were developed with only domestic considerations in mind . . . .").

272 *Id.* at 655.

I support Professor Crimm's proposal and would further suggest additional reforms that broaden acceptable standards of equivalency to facilitate international grant-making. Ultimately, I would advocate overhauling the equivalency determination process to permit inclusion of foreign entities that are "comparable" to their public charity counterparts in the United States, rather than requiring that the foreign entity be an identical clone. While certain key aspects of what it means to be a public charity should be respected by all nonprofit organizations and equivalents, regardless of their country of origin (e.g., the nondistribution constraint[273] and the purpose requirement[274]), other elements of the test should be relaxed. If another country makes different policy choices regarding the ability of their charitable organizations to express political opinions or regarding the specific percentage cutoffs for different types of support to be generated from the public, those choices should be respected to permit a broader conceptualization of equivalency. For instance, in addition to removing the lobbying restrictions with respect to foreign organizations, I would also provide more flexibility with regard to the political campaign ban[275] and the public support test.[276] Although the limitations on political campaign intervention and the calculations of levels of public support may make sense for the regulation of domestic charities, they hardly seem to reach the core values defining nonprofit status, but rather reflect policy judgments used to define and police the parameters of the domestic nonprofit sector.

Importantly, liberalization in these areas would not seem to pose any risks that terrorists could more easily dupe U.S. funders into supporting their efforts. Even under my proposal, the level of due diligence and the process related to "getting to know the grantee" would not change even if some of the legal standards were relaxed, and it is through this process that U.S. funders become familiar with foreign grantee recipients and their activities to assess their legitimacy.

---

273 *See* Henry B. Hansmann, *The Role of Nonprofit Enterprise*, 89 YALE L.J. 835, 838–40 (1980) (noting that the "nondistribution constraint," which prohibits the distribution of net earnings and other forms of private benefit from nonprofit activity, is the defining characteristic of a nonprofit organization); James J. Fishman, *Improving Charitable Accountability*, 62 MD. L. REV. 218, 225 (2003) (stating that the nondistribution constraint is the fundamental distinction between a charitable nonprofit and a business corporation).

274 Section 501(c)(3) exempts only organizations "organized and operated exclusively for religious, charitable, scientific, testing for public safety, literary, or educational purposes, or to foster national or international amateur sports competition . . . or for the prevention of cruelty to children or animals." I.R.C. § 501(c)(3) (2000).

275 Section 501(c)(3) organizations are barred from "participat[ing] in, or interven[ing] in . . . any political campaign on behalf of (or in opposition to) any candidate for public office." *Id.*

276 A grantee other than a church, hospital, or educational institution must show that it meets the public support test, one or more of a series of tests to prove that an organization is entitled to public charity status (rather than private foundation status). *See* I.R.C. §§ 170(b)(1)(A), 509(a)(2). The tests are based on mathematical formulas combined with subjective factors requiring detailed analysis of financial information based on a rolling four-year formula. *See* Treas. Reg. § 1.509(a)-3 (as amended in 2002).

Accordingly, adjusting Internal Revenue Code restrictions could expand international philanthropy and magnify its positive effects. While a fuller analysis and the details of such a reform to the tax code and the equivalency determination rules are beyond the scope of this Article, the very idea of the reform reveals new possibilities and policy shifts that could flow from a more robust recognition of the benefits of international philanthropy and its contributions to soft power. Policy decisions motivated by an interest in using international philanthropy to produce soft power would provoke different reforms to federal law.

D. Adopting Safe Harbors and Mechanisms for Multinational Signaling of Legitimate NGOs

To the extent that the government's cost-benefit analysis determines a need to further regulate cross-border giving beyond existing tax law, it should pursue a different strategy reflecting recognition of the security benefits nonprofits and international grantmaking provide. The U.S. government's current approach, which coerces private funders into conducting their own investigations and relies on a "black list" of potential terrorists, neither enlists the cooperation of multinational partners nor leverages the benefits of collective research. Instead, the government could adopt a different approach creating safe harbors for private foundations and public charities funding activities abroad. The detailed basis for the safe harbor could take a variety of forms, but the real benefit would be to provide a formal mechanism offering incentives to funders to follow certain procedures and ensuring that assets would not be seized or frozen, nor individuals criminally prosecuted, if they followed the procedures.[277] Such an approach would treat nonprofits as allies and engender their cooperation.

A safe harbor could be either "funder-focused," dependent on the funder's grantmaking process meeting prescribed procedures, or "grant recipient-focused," dependent on the actual destination of the charitable funds. For instance, consider a system structured according to the first method. The safe harbor could be centered on a process-oriented set of standards to be followed by funders (e.g., a modified and more practical version of the Guidelines or some other set of explicit standards designed to regulate due diligence concerning foreign grants). Private funders choosing to follow the procedures established by the safe harbor would have the confidence and peace of mind that they could engage in international philanthropic activity without fear or risk of adverse government action against them. Such a system could achieve the purpose of preventing potential diversion of charitable funds while still encouraging international grantmaking, especially funding activity in the developing world, the Middle East, and other high-risk places where the aid may be most needed.

277 *See* Peter P. Swire, *Safe Harbors and a Proposal To Improve the Community Reinvestment Act*, 79 VA. L. REV. 349, 375 (1993) (stating that safe harbors may be particularly attractive under circumstances when entities encounter uncertain standards or are especially risk-adverse).

Alternatively, another option for structuring a safe harbor could focus on grant recipients themselves. Specifically, an authorized governmental body would spearhead an effort to create a pre-cleared list of NGOs (a "white list"), certified after review of a foreign recipient organization's compliance systems, financial controls and relations, and other pertinent practices sufficient to determine the legitimacy of the charitable entity.

The benefits of such a white list would be numerous. First, the investigatory work examining an organization's finances, leadership, and organizational links could be conducted by trained professionals with substantial expertise rather than by the untrained staff of U.S. nonprofits. Second, such a system would save each potential funder from incurring the costs in staff time and resources associated with conducting its own review, thereby providing shared cost savings across the sector. Similarly, this would minimize the burdens on foreign charities by requiring one review and all of its associated requests, as opposed to dealing with multiple equivalency determination and expenditure responsibility demands. Third, inclusion on such a white list would provide the foreign NGO a reputational benefit by offering a positive signal to potential grantmakers, as opposed to the current system that in effect encourages funders to treat all foreign nonprofits as terrorist fronts until proven otherwise.

Such an affirmative certification of charities would, of course, also pose risks. A primary concern would be that the system might be used for political purposes. One could imagine that a charitable organization might be denied certification unjustly because of its political stances or influence. Of course, the current use of a black list system is equally subject to political influences and similar abuses.[278]

More important, the use of a grant recipient-based safe harbor raises the question of which government authority would be responsible for creating and maintaining the white list. The U.S. government might well desire to maintain control of such a process. However, if the decisions were made in cooperation with other governments through a multilateral process, we might avoid the specter of politicized decisionmaking, as compared with the current system under which the U.S. Secretary of State makes such determinations.[279] If a multilateral approach were developed, through either the United Nations or some other collaboration, sufficient staff personnel and resources to efficiently administer such a system would need to be devoted to the project.[280] However, under the white list proposal, charitable

278 *See* Lowenkron, *Testimony Before S. Comm. on Foreign Relations*, *supra* note 205 (noting that some governments "resort to extralegal forms of intimidation or persecution [against nonprofits] . . . . justify[ing] their actions by accusations of . . . terrorism").

279 *See* Exec. Order No. 13,224, 66 Fed. Reg. 49,079 (Sept. 23, 2001).

280 However, it is worth noting that the U.N. already devotes resources to create and maintain its own terrorism watch list, which has received the endorsement of the U.S. government. *See* Memorandum from Mara T. Patermaster, Dir., Office of CFC Operations, to Local Fed. Coordinating Comms. et al. (Nov. 24, 2004), *available at* http://www.opm.gov/cfc/

organizations in multiple countries engaged in overseas giving, various U.N. and governmental agencies, and other multilateral funders could benefit from the collective vetting of organizations that would take place.

Finally, there is a concern that negative inferences might be drawn about entities that have not yet been vetted for inclusion on such a white list or that some small organizations would actually prefer not to be included on such a list, out of fear that inclusion may create a stigma or make them a target of their home government. In many respects, for a foreign organization to be on an approved U.N. or multilateral list may be less stigmatizing than to be on a list created solely by the United States. While an implicit black list may emerge, there are benefits associated with a shift toward a system with a positive legal consequence (i.e., a safe harbor for grantmakers) that still maintains the flexibility to make grants to those not on the list, after ample due diligence and a weighing of risks. If adopted, such a system could meet the U.S. government's goal of ensuring more aggressive reviews of foreign charitable organizations, but it could also permit U.S. funders to do what they do best—make grants to worthwhile organizations meeting their philanthropic goals, such as working to alleviate poverty, protect the environment, and provide relief.

Regardless of whether the safe harbor is funder-focused (emphasizing pre-grant due diligence) or grant recipient-focused (emphasizing a white list), a shift to a safe harbor approach would eliminate much of the uncertainty and angst grantmakers currently face and thereby encourage private foundations and public charities to actively engage in international philanthropic activity to the maximum level each funder seeks.

CONCLUSION

Writing about the legal and policy environments post-September 11, one legal scholar has eloquently noted that "[w]e live in a time of expanded possibilities and expanded fears."[281] More than five years after those devastating attacks, countering terrorism remains the nation's top national security concern. But, if time has taught us anything, it is that the threats posed by terrorism have challenged the United States to pursue a strategic, comprehensive, long-term campaign to protect our country and share our values with the world. With respect to international philanthropy, rather than meeting those challenges, our policies seem to be governed by fears. After September 11, government policymakers focused on measures they intuited would support the war on terrorism, yet the ramifications of the antiterrorist financing campaign for charities and the accompanying cost-benefit analysis may not support their intuitions.[282]

---

opmmemos/2004/2004–12.asp ("Although not required, OPM continues to encourage [charitable] organizations to consult the United Nations list.").

281 Sharon L. Davies, *Profiling Terror*, 1 Ohio St. J. Crim. L. 45, 101 (2003).

282 *Cf.* Mitchell, *supra* note 12, at 222–24 (making this point in the context of examining anti-money laundering laws post September 11).

Since September 11, U.S.-based international funders have become at best collateral damage and at worst targets in the government's campaign against terrorist financing. The terms of the debate and the thinking about nonprofits need to be revised. The perception that the regulation of international grantmaking pits security benefits against administrative costs misframes the stakes. Federal measures affecting international philanthropy entail security costs as well. U.S. public charities and private foundations working abroad should be viewed as essential, strategic allies in the effort to enhance the United States's global influence and strength and as such should be encouraged by both rhetoric and policy.

Although only a small fraction of foreign grants might be at risk of diversion to the support of terrorism,[283] the current federal government approach burdens all international grants. Undoubtedly, grantmakers and grant recipients active where U.S. charitable support is most needed—in the developing world of Africa, Asia, and the Middle East—are most affected. Philanthropy helps promote political and economic development and addresses the root causes of terrorism so that it can ultimately be defeated. Moreover, American NGOs are important and powerful actors and critical image influencers around the world, and initiatives that undermine their work and their independence exact security costs; policymakers must account for those costs as we consider the tradeoffs associated with greater regulation. The current regulatory treatment of U.S. funders discourages international giving, leading to a more isolationist philanthropic policy.

While the U.S. government has been focused on its hard power in recent years, its soft power has waned, and other countries are taking notice. In fact, the European Union, China, and even Islamic countries in the Middle East are seeking to attract converts to their values. For instance, the European Union has pooled its economic power to compete with the United States, and the EU's success in commerce, public diplomacy, and progressive social and political models is increasing its attractiveness.[284]

---

283 Again, the lack of documented evidence of U.S. entities making charitable contributions to terrorist fronts seems to indicate that legitimate U.S. funders using standard diligence practices have not been unwitting sources for terrorist funding. Although any diversion is to be avoided, due to the average size of grants and the level of resources potentially raised from diversion from unwitting donors, it seems that legitimate U.S. charitable grants would be unlikely to generate substantial resources for terrorist organizations because of the small scale and sustainability of financing. *See, e.g., Nominations of John O. Colvin, Stuart Levey, and Juan C. Zarate: Hearing Before the S. Comm. on Finance, supra* note 173, at 21 (statement of Sen. Bob Graham, Member, S. Comm. on Finance) ("[In discussing] terrorist financing, there is almost an inevitable gravitational pull to start talking about charities . . . but that is not where I see the real problem . . . . [T]he real problem is when governments . . . are providing the financial assistance."); U.S. Gen. Accounting Office, GAO-04-163, Terrorist Financing: U.S. Agencies Should Systematically Assess Terrorists' Use of Alternative Financing Mechanisms 9–12 (2003), *available at* http://www.gao.gov/new.items/ d04163.pdf (noting that other sources of terrorist funding include trading in illicit drugs, weapons, cigarettes, and diamonds).

284 *See* Marc Champion, *EU Tries Again on Foreign Policy: Reinvigorated Drive for Unified Action Draws Notice in Washington*, Wall St. J., Jan. 26, 2005, at A14.

In addition, China has achieved success in strengthening its own soft power, particularly in Asia, presenting its own political values and culture while investing in public diplomacy and development aid.[285] What does this mean for the United States? Europe and China will not push aside the United States, but their success underscores the point that soft power should not be ignored. A decline of soft power means the U.S. government loses persuasive powers, places itself in a weaker bargaining position with allies, and engenders less international cooperation.[286]

The 9/11 Commission highlighted the central role of U.S. foreign aid and public diplomacy in the long-term success of the fight against terrorism.[287] Accordingly, the federal government should adopt policies and develop an approach that marshal the expansive resources of the nonprofit sector to its side. International philanthropy is an important piece of the puzzle, and the United States should devote resources and develop policies to produce soft power. Public diplomacy, soft power, and concern for democratic institutions and human rights abroad are not peripheral, naïve, or insubstantial distractions. U.S. military strength is unsurpassed, and we have not been afraid to use it; our philanthropic strength is equally remarkable, and we should not be afraid to use it to even greater ends. We should not injure our own long-term security interests, or the interests of our friends, by overreacting to the fear of aiding our enemies.

---

285 *See* Kurlantzick, *supra* note 68, at 422–23 ("China has emerged as a potential rival to American soft power as . . . Beijing begins to enunciate its values and market its institutions and culture. To their Asian neighbors, Chinese officials . . . support[] a multipolar world in which nations do not aggressively interfere in other nations' affairs . . . . Public sentiment across Asia has become more favorable toward China . . . .").

286 Hard power alone does not always achieve desired results. Even a dictator must balance hard and soft power. Cooperation matters because, as Joseph Nye writes, "[o]ther countries' governments are quite often better placed to identify and arrest terrorists. Their cooperation is essential, and obtaining it will depend on both our hard and soft power." NYE, *supra* note 87, at 164.

287 *See* 9/11 COMMISSION REPORT, *supra* note 1, at 363–64 (finding that U.S. success against terrorism "demands the use of all elements of national power: diplomacy, intelligence, covert action, law enforcement, economic policy, foreign aid, public diplomacy, and homeland defense").

INDEX

B

C

E

F

G

L

O

P

Q

R

V

W

Y

Z